HUBERT

HUMPHREY

ALSO BY CARL SOLBERG

Riding High: America in the Cold War
Oil Power
Conquest of the Skies

HUBERT

HUMPHREY

A BIOGRAPHY

Carl Solberg

W·W·NORTON & COMPANY

New York · London

The text of this book is composed in 10/12 Janson, with display type set
in Granjon. Composition and manufacturing by The Maple-Vail Book
Manufacturing Group. Book design by Margaret Wagner.

First Edition

Library of Congress Cataloging in Publication Data
Solberg, Carl 1915–
Hubert Humphrey : a biography.

Bibliography: p.
Includes index.
1. Humphrey, Hubert H. (Hubert Horatio), 1911–1978. 2. Vice–Presidents—United States—Biography.   3. United States—Politics and government—1945–   . I. Title. E748.H945S65 1984   973.923′092′4
[B]   84–1641

ISBN 0-393-01806-7

W. W. Norton & Company, Inc.,
500 Fifth Avenue, New York, N. Y. 10110
W. W. Norton & Company Ltd.,
37 Great Russell Street, London WC1B 3NU

1 2 3 4 5 6 7 8 9 0

BT 19.95 / 11.95 - 7/84

B
Humphrey
So

To Bud and
Gratia

Contents

Prologue:

"The Sunshine of Human Rights"

I<small>T</small> W<small>AS</small> late on the final day of the 1948 Democratic Convention when Hubert Humphrey, mayor of Minneapolis, stepped to the rostrum. Under the glare of the klieg lights, he looked like anything but an arresting figure: a little more than average height, young (thirty-seven), pale, thin (he had lost fifteen pounds during the week's hectic meetings). Sweat matted his lank, black hair and dripped from his jutting forehead as he faced the packed Philadelphia hall.

The issue to be settled was civil rights, and Humphrey was speaking for a minority resolution that had been soundly defeated by the Platform Committee the night before. The string-tied Southern stentors had shouted their say; the regulars had raised their last roar for "unity"; and the leadership was pressing for a vote. In anticipation of President Truman's imminent arrival to accept renomination the Secret Service had shut all doors, and the temperature on the dais stood at ninety-three. Delegates were hot and restless—bored by the succession of droning speeches. Some could be seen lifting flasks to their lips—television cameramen had not yet been instructed to ignore such sights—as Humphrey, the afternoon's last speaker, began to talk.

He had never before addressed such a large assemblage, and many of the delegations hardly knew who he was. He spoke for only eight minutes. But by the time he had finished, delegates "were jumping on their chairs." In an astounding reversal, the convention voted to throw out the administration's standpat compromise and to support instead the daring course the young mayor proposed in his short but moving speech.

Suddenly, Humphrey was the man of the hour. He had carried a seemingly impossible fight to the party's conservative chiefs and won—with deep consequences for the Democratic party in that election year, and for America in years to come.

Fiery prairie Progressivism fused with an untrammeled gift of gab in the man who gained this fateful victory. Humphrey was a son of the Midwest who came on with a cyclonic speaking style the likes of which hadn't been heard at a political convention in a long time. Aroused, he could cut loose from a text, grab an audience, and, carrying his listeners with him, take off and sail before the wind. His best bursts shot out spontaneously—earthy, earnest, funny. Lyndon Johnson said of Humphrey's gift: "Hubert has the greatest coordination of mind and tongue of anybody I know."

What started Humphrey on his way to the rostrum in Philadelphia was his appearance only fifteen months before at a small political gathering in Chicago. It was the first Midwest conference held by the Americans for Democratic Action—a liberal group then being formed in Washington by New Dealers who were deeply concerned that the nation was losing its way after World War II and might lapse into blind reaction. Several leaders of the ADA traveled West to attend the meeting, at which Mayor Humphrey had been invited to speak.

In his old-fashioned black suit with a gold watch chain across the vest and his prairie-flat accent, the mayor looked and sounded to the Easterners like a figure out of another world. He began by telling a preposterous story about a talking cow—"We have them in Minnesota"—that took pity on its owner arriving back at the farm exhausted from a long political meeting. As the owner squatted down on the stool, Humphrey went on, the cow said: "You're too tired to milk me. Just put the milk pail between your legs and hang on, and I'll jump up and down." The crowd guffawed. The Easterners sniffed and looked at each other.

The mayor then proceeded to address the audience on, of all subjects for a cornfield midwesterner, civil rights. "Dazzled," Joseph L. Rauh, Jr., Harvard '32, former law clerk to Justice Frankfurter, graduate of a half-dozen Roosevelt alphabetical agencies, and card-carrying New Dealer, watched Humphrey bring the audience to its feet with an impassioned call for other communities to follow Minneapolis's lead and to pass a Fair Employment Practices ordinance. Afterward, in an uproarious evening of laughter and drinks, Rauh listened enthralled as the youthful heartlander told how he imported blacks to organize "self-surveys" of Protestants, Catholics, and Jews to rid the city of its name as "the capital of anti-Semitism" in America.

The Americans for Democratic Action included Eleanor Roosevelt, most revered of Democrats. They included famous New Deal administrators Leon Henderson and Chester Bowles displaced by Truman. But though Elmer

Davis, looking around at their founding meeting, could pronounce them "the government in exile," the fact was that none of them had ever held elective office, and few of them thought they could or would. So when Rauh and his friend James Loeb, the organization's secretary, brought Humphrey to Washington, the ADA took him to their hearts. They tagged him a comer. They elected him their vice-chairman, and as a proven vote-getter, one of their chief spokesmen.

Roosevelt's old lieutenants, looking to the 1948 elections, saw the party in disarray. It was no longer enough that the Democrats had triumphed over the Great Depression and led the nation through war to a peak of might. As much because of as in spite of their achievements, the Democrats by 1948 were in trouble. Having routed the destitution, hunger, and joblessness that originally drew them together, they had no cause that would bind together the forces of their coalition, and it was falling apart.

The most prominent of the old lieutenants, former Vice President Henry Wallace, had already declared a breakaway liberal candidacy on a third-party ticket. The ADA, which could not swallow Wallace's insistence that achieving peace required accepting Soviet-installed regimes in Eastern Europe, wanted to dump Truman but could not find another candidate. Still others, including important members of Truman's cabinet such as James Forrestal, thought the Democrats had simply run out their string and might as well let the Republicans, who had already captured Congress, take over the White House too. Even among seasoned professionals, measuring the Democratic party's chances in 1948 against the well-heeled candidacy of New York's Governor Thomas Dewey, the talk was defeatist. The Democrats who met to renominate President Truman in the steaming second week of July were a downcast and divided lot. If the party was going to make any kind of showing in 1948, it badly needed a new lease on life.

Mayor Humphrey, a candidate for the U. S. Senate in Minnesota, kept demanding national action on civil rights. When the administration seemed to be doing nothing about the findings of the 1946 President's Commission on Civil Rights, he wrote in *The Progressive:* "The Democratic party must lead the fight for every principle in the report. It is all or nothing." On the eve of the Philadelphia convention he got fifty Democratic notables to back his declared intent to write the report into the party platform. The report, entitled "To Secure These Rights," urged the federal government to act on four fronts: outlaw lynching; create a commission to curb discrimination in employment; ensure Southern blacks their rights including the right to vote; and open military service equally to all.

It may seem astonishing that regular Democrats trying to revamp their party were blind to the race issue that was to dominate U. S. politics for a generation. But when the commission's recommendations on civil rights reached President Truman's desk, he felt in no position to put them through. Not only did the Republicans control Congress, but renomination by his own party was uncertain. In the approaching convention the Southern white supremacists controlled such a large block of votes that Truman preferred to shelve the commission's proposals. As the Democrats met in Philadelphia the Platform Committee chairman, Senator Francis Myers of Pennsylvania, proposed a civil rights plank for the administration that merely repeated the pious affirmations adopted four years before by the last Roosevelt convention. It was a calculated move to mollify the Southerners and was to be followed a few days later by another—Truman's designation of the elderly border-states senator Alben Barkley as his running mate on a let's-all-hang-together ticket.

As author of the convention-eve manifesto backing the commission's report, Mayor Humphrey opened the fight in the committee for a stronger position. The Republicans, he warned, were fixing to write a forward-looking civil rights plank, and if the Democrats waffled, the party of Abraham Lincoln might reclaim leadership on this issue. At a session that lasted until four in the morning, Humphrey denounced the administration draft as "a bunch of generalities" and "a sellout to states rights." "Who does this pipsqueak think he is?" asked Senator Scott Lucas, a senior stalwart from Illinois. Of the hundred-odd members only ex-Representative Andrew Biemiller of Wisconsin and two or three others joined Humphrey's fight. Shifting tactics, Humphrey offered a substitute draft in general terms that left out the commission's four recommendations. It won the support of thirteen Northerners, and when the Southerners tossed in their states-rights resolutions and left for the night, the mayor grew bolder. Biemiller and Joe Rauh drew up a new, tougher draft that included the report's four specific points, and Humphrey took it back to the committee meeting on the top floor of the Bellevue-Stratford Hotel.

Fellow Minnesotans on the committee reported that Humphrey was working under terrific pressure. Orville Freeman, future governor of the state and the mayor's closest friend, sent notes urging him to keep up the fight. On the second evening his friends sent him food, concerned that because he had gone without sleep all week he might collapse. Lucas, who had had a few drinks, made a personal attack on Humphrey, accusing him of double dealing by offering a compromise the night before and then coming back with something stronger. The committee voted overwhelmingly for the administration's plank. But 30 of the 108 members cast their votes for Humphrey's version. Biemiller served notice that they would bring in a minority report when the platform went before the convention the next day.

Back at their rented University of Pennsylvania fraternity house two blocks from the convention hall, members of the ADA called for a caucus, and 125 aroused delegates showed up for it. On the first day, the leadership, exercising their discretion under convention rules, refused a rollcall on a credentials question, and Jack Shelley, a hulking Teamster from California, roared that he would charge the podium if the same tactic were used with civil rights. Biemiller declared that he would make sure his friend Speaker Sam Rayburn, taking over as permanent chairman, would, as he said, "protect my rights" and give them a hearing and a vote the next day. Rauh and others briefed all the young ADA volunteers berthed at the fraternity house to fan out and lobby hard in big-state delegations. Of the big states, only California was on their side. Minnesota's National Committeewoman Eugenie Anderson, writing home a few days later, said: "Practically everybody thought there was nothing to lose by carrying the fight further. But at the caucus the best count was about 150 sure and 100 probables for the Minority report, which we didn't think was too bad. We didn't have any idea we could really win."

Everybody at the caucus assumed that Humphrey would lead the next day's floor fight. He would make the key speech—technically a speech seconding Biemiller's motion—and Milton Stewart, the ADA's new rep in Manhattan and the young lawyer who had written most of the commission report, would draft it for him.

But would Humphrey speak? His fourth-floor room at the Bellevue-Stratford was a madhouse. The whole Minnesota delegation had piled in. Humphrey's brother Ralph had filled the bathtub with ice and beer bottles, but amid the wild wassailing a serious struggle was going on. The regulars had warned that Humphrey's battle stance would split the party and insure defeat in November. As a young candidate for the Senate from Minnesota, Mayor Humphrey had to consider what effect speaking out would have on his own race against the formidable incumbent, Senator Joseph Ball, and how it might color his standing in the party for years to come. Friends, pouring themselves beer from the bathtub supply, shouted conflicting advice. Labor chieftains said better not. Orville Freeman, "afraid we were going to lose and be laughed out of the hall," nevertheless counseled Humphrey to fight. Even the mayor's father, present as a delegate from South Dakota, was doubtful. "This may tear the party apart," he said. Finally, as Eugenie Anderson wrote, they "got Humphrey away from his room where he had been surrounded by people. Andy Biemiller, [Aide] Bill Simms and Orville Freeman came with him to my room where it was quiet. When Humphrey first got there he was so tired he was beginning to think it would be foolish to go ahead with it, that it would only split the party up. But he quickly regained his position after hearing from some of his friends that it was the right thing to do."

Humphrey got little sleep that night. In the morning people began milling around his room from the moment he got out of bed. Breakfast was held up while the mayor, trying to get dressed, hunted for his hernia truss. The room filled with smoke. Milton Stewart appeared. The speech writer wanted the mayor to sit down and dictate something that he could put into a draft speech. But first the text of the minority resolution itself had to be put in final form because the ADA had to mimeograph copies and distribute them to delegates before the Convention met. Mrs. Anderson wrote that "Humphrey thought the wording should be changed. He was trying to get some of these ideas he had through. It was a terribly tense moment. Everybody was sitting watching him and Shirley [Filiatrault] was trying to take dictation."

Eugenie Anderson, later the first woman to be U. S. ambassador, added a crucial nuance to the text. To precede the paragraph containing the Commission's four strong specifics she proposed the following sentence: "We highly commend President Harry Truman for his courageous stand on the issue of civil rights." With that deft interpolation, the anti-Truman sting was removed from the minority plank. "Okay," Humphrey shouted, and the next thing was to get ready for the speech.

He spent only ten or fifteen minutes with Milton Stewart and wrote most of the speech himself, in longhand. "The good phrases were his," Stewart said later. Biemiller, true to his word, had seen Rayburn early, ahead of the Southerners, so that the Southern reports would be offered as amendments to his and disposed of first. Rayburn had granted them an hour altogether. Thus Humphrey knew that Biemiller's resolution and his own speech, coming last, would have perhaps fifteen minutes at most before the vote. Humphrey called his wife in Minneapolis, who told him sixteen-month-old Dougie was fussing and added that she had the radio going full blast. Humphrey was tense, nervous—"more than I have ever seen him," Mrs. Anderson noted. He had started to put on a checkered suit, but since the Philadelphia convention was one of the first to be televised, Eugenie Anderson told him that it would not look good on television. Humphrey changed into a dark one.

Meanwhile delegates were lobbying intensively. Though no direct pressure was put on supporters of the minority plank by President Truman, the ADA assumed that the administration was not happy about their efforts. David K. Niles, Truman's assistant for minority affairs, told Rauh, "Joe, you won't get fifty votes on your minority plank, and all you'll do is ruin the chances of the No. 1 prospect for liberalism in the country." But the ADA's young lobbyists were at work, and as Rauh said later: "Our argument was: 'You want to build a Wallace movement? You want all these defections from the Democratic party? We've got to have a strong civil rights platform of our own.' " Operating out of the fraternity-house headquarters, Jon Bingham, future congressman from the Bronx, buttonholed Bronx Boss Ed Flynn, one of whose henchmen had just gone down to shattering byelection defeat at the hands of a Wallaceite. Richardson Dilworth and Joseph Clark, Jr., mayor-to-be of Philadelphia and future senator from Pennsylvania, visited their state leader, David Lawrence, and found him sympathetic. His support was particularly encouraging because he had the clout as chief of the Pennsylvania delegation to overrule Senator Myers, sponsor of the majority report. ADA Chairman Leon Henderson called on Illinois Chairman Jake Arvey, who said the minority report was "all right." George Weaver of the NAACP sent fellow black chieftains from Illinois and Pennsylvania to tell Senators Lucas and Myers that if they did not support the minority resolution, they would lose the black vote entirely. "In this fight," as Joe Rauh said later, "Henry Wallace was our secret weapon."

Biemiller walked on to the convention dais just before the session started. Rayburn told him at once: "Your rights are protected." The Southerners presented their case first, which gave the ADA more time to lobby delegates. As Humphrey and Biemiller awaited their turn, Boss Flynn came up and said to them: "Look, you kids are right. What you're trying to do is the only way we can wake up this country. We've got to stir up the interest of the minority groups in this election; otherwise we're dead." Then, as Biemiller recalled later, Flynn sent runners to fetch Arvey, Lawrence, and Boss Frank Hague of New Jersey, all of whom assured Flynn that their delegates would vote his way. Finally Senator Myers stepped up to Humphrey, congratulated him, and said he too would cast his vote for Humphrey's resolution.

Bill Simms brought this heady news to the Minnesota delegation, but they could hardly believe it. The speakers droned on; the crescendo built as Rayburn declared the Southern amendments defeated; and the climax came with Humphrey's speech. As he stepped to the podium, a big yellow Truman button in his lapel, the highly charged issue of civil rights hung in the balance. For once Humphrey read his speech. For once he spoke slowly, and his words rang out clearly.

He praised the "courtesy and forthrightness" of the Southerners, whose plank had been voted down and who now sat glaring under their states-rights banners. He saluted Senator Barkley's keynote mention of "equality," and the audience grew quiet, suddenly aware that someone they wanted to listen to was talking.

In a time of cold war, Humphrey said, when America was flying food into Berlin to hold Germany against the Soviet blockade, "we cannot use a double standard. Our demands for democratic practice in other lands will be no more effective than the guarantee of those practices in our own country." That stirred patriotic hearts, and when he evoked the "courageous trail blazing" of the "immortal" Franklin Roosevelt, the packed hall rocked with applause.

Then, thrusting out his chin and raising his fist, he shouted: "Harry Truman has had the courage to give the people of America the new emancipation proclamation." By this time the delegates were cheering every sentence he spoke.

There can be no hedging . . . no watering down. To those who say that we are rushing this issue of civil rights—I say to them, we are 172 years late.

To those who say this bill is an infringement on states rights, I say this—the time has arrived in America. The time has arrived for the Democratic party to get out of the shadow of states rights and walk forthrightly into the bright sunshine of human rights.

People—people—human beings—this is the issue of the 20th century.

In these times of world economic, political and spiritual—above all, spiritual—crisis, we cannot and we must not turn back from the path so plainly before us. That path has already led us through many valleys of the shadow of death. Now is the time to recall those who were left on that path of American freedom.

Our land is now, more than ever before, the last best hope on earth. I know that we can—know that we shall—begin here the fuller and richer realization of that hope—that promise—of a land where all men are truly free and equal, and each man uses his freedom and equality wisely and well.

My good friends, I ask my party—I ask the Democratic party—to march down the high road of progressive democracy. I ask this Convention to say in unmistakable terms that we proudly hail and we courageously support our President and leader, Harry Truman, in his great fight for civil rights in America.

Written or not, delivered in only eight minutes, it was a superb speech, resonating characteristically with Biblical and patriotic overtones that evoked the shared sense of a sacred past in summoning listeners to a future commitment. With his proclamation that America was addressing racial injustice 172 years late, Humphrey invited his listeners to think of the same dawn at Saratoga and Philadelphia to which Lincoln's "four score and seven years" referred in an earlier call for emancipatory advance. With his invocation of the path through the "valley of shadows" and the "many left on that path," Humphrey renewed for a later generation the emancipator's plea that the sacrifices of Antietam and Gettysburg should not have been in vain. And with the assertion that America was the Earth's last best hope, Humphrey called on that generation not only spared but raised to world leadership by a terrible war to set an appropriately worthy example.

At this level of advocacy, the speech became the man. Ambitious, shrewd, politician to the last nerve end of his fingertips, Mayor Humphrey was at the same time a most impulsive person. In this short oratorical burst he came out with—one might almost say he blurted—the leitmotif of his entire career: "People—People—human beings—this is the issue of the twentieth century." Humphrey was a man of the heart. He was what the Spanish call a *spontaneo*, excitingly capable of saying in a flash what was on the heart of multitudes. The metaphors shot out, rough and ready, often earthy. Never in his life did he utter a more memorable metaphor than when he called upon his fellows to "get out of the shadow of states rights and walk forthrightly in the bright sunshine of human rights." The phrase seems to have burst out in just this way. Milton Stewart said later it was not in the draft of the speech he prepared. It bears comparison with Bryan's "You shall not press down upon mankind this crown of thorns; you shall not crucify mankind upon a cross of gold," which capped the only convention speech that ever had a greater impact on the deliberation of the delegates and the fortunes of the orator. But Bryan was only declaiming a metaphor and indeed a speech that he had already practiced and perfected in many platform appearances around the country.

Humphrey's speech ushered in the second era of redressing racial injustice in America. Heard by an estimated 60 million on radio and by up to ten million on the primitive television network then existing, it made him famous. In the convention hall, as Humphrey stepped back from the podium, Eugenie Anderson noted that "whatever it is about his personality that attracts people came out at this time." A demonstration began. Down below the platform future-senator Paul Douglas shouted "Here goes" to Chicago Boss Ed Kelly, grabbed the Illinois standard, and swung into the aisle. Michigan, California, and Pennsylvania joined in. The demonstration lasted eight minutes before Rayburn restored order by dousing the lights.

Then came the vote. Orville Freeman held the tally sheet and recorded the score. With Alabama and Arizona, "nos" took the lead. The count ran close. Harry Truman's Missouri, Alben Barkley's Kentucky, Chairman Howard McGrath's Rhode Island, all voted "no." The "ayes" caught up as Humphrey's father rose to shout that South Dakota cast its eight votes for the minority plank. Not until Wisconsin cast all its votes for the minority plank was the outcome decided. A great shout went up as Rayburn announced the vote: 651½ to 582½, a victory all but unprecedented for a minority plank at a presidential convention. The Southerners started to leave, but Rayburn gaveled a recess; when the delegates reconvened a few hours later, they bolted. Delegates from four states went off to nominate Dixiecrat Strom Thurmond—the 1948 campaign's fourth candidate for president.

On her way out of the hall, Eugenie Anderson heard one newsman say to another: "Can you beat that, the ADA has licked the South." His companion replied: "They not only licked the South, they licked the administration too." Humphrey's speech and the vote that followed nailed civil rights to the masthead of the Democratic party and set the nation, as well as his party, on a new course. For even as the Dixiecrats bolted, Humphrey fired new life into the dejected Democratic party—and a fighting Harry Truman took it from there to win the biggest upset victory of the century in November. In that stunning outcome—and Humphrey won election too—Truman's slim plurality rested on the allegiance of both the Negro ghetto and those Northern liberals who would have voted for Wallace if the Democratic platform had not pledged action on civil rights.

The road to fulfillment of those campaign promises proved to be filled with obstacles. An aroused nation, chanting "We Shall Overcome," rallied to prevail over them, and Humphrey persevered to legislate in the Civil Rights Act of 1964 the "sunshine" of human rights to which he had so eloquently called the party in 1948. All told, he fathered more important legislation from origin to enactment than any other member of Congress in history. The issues he dramatized by his senate speeches, bills, and amendments were of such immediate concern to the country that he became a candidate for president not once but four times in his twenty-six years on the national scene. And yet this "No. 1 prospect for liberalism in the country" never attained the presidency.

It was the irony of Humphrey's career that for years he stood far ahead of public opinion, fighting to introduce all kinds of progressive ideas and educating the voters in the Senate forum that in our time produced the nation's leaders only to see Jack and Bobby Kennedy barge in from his right—a McCarthyite right. They preempted his place on the left until in 1968, Humphrey, surviving them both, met with defeat, having fallen *behind* American attitudes and opinions.

Bested by weight of wealth, provenance (a smalltown druggist in the topmost office?), personal traits such as the Kennedy cleverness, and geographical politics (an earlier example of which was the way Easterner Theodore Roosevelt snatched the Progressive party's nomination in 1912 from the prior Western leader, Robert LaFollette), Humphrey grew convinced that he could only become president by becoming vice president. His consequent submission to President Johnson was even more crucial to the fateful course of his career. "Nice guys finish last," is a tested American saying. If the life of Hubert Humphrey cannot be called tragic, its proportions were on a grand, operatic scale. Humphrey's destiny carried him so far beyond his obscure prairie origins to such high achievements and aspirations that it delivered him, as the drama of great and ambitious figures will, to destruction and untimely death. That is the story unfolded in the following pages.

PART ONE

The Prairie

1

Frontier Forebears

"Our branch has been preeminently agricultural. There have been in the family no artists, no musicians, no writers, no clergymen, no teachers, no scholars, no businessmen of truly outstanding merit. . . . We have been much addicted to hard work, have worried too much, have been thrifty, and have been too cautious in business matters to amass great material wealth. . . "

S UCH was the background of the Humphrey family according to a history composed by Hubert Humphrey's Uncle Harry. This scanty written record seems to support the observation that the farther west Americans go, the less they seem to know or care about where they came from. Hubert Humphrey, reared on the Dakota plains, was indifferently informed about his ancestral origins. To the end of his life he was content to rely on the account written by his elderly uncle, which traced the unremarkable family past to western Massachusetts around the time of the American Revolution. After that the line seemed to vanish. Uncle Harry, during a visit to some Eastern Humphreys, whose children all bore names such as Llewellyn, Gladys, and Goronwy, was convinced that his family stemmed originally from Wales. Even though he could not prove the connection, the old gentleman learned Welsh and painted a Welsh motto over his front door. Years later, Vice President Hubert Humphrey informed all who asked that "The Humphreys are of mixed Welsh and English and a little French Huguenot blood."

It would be satisfying to relate, if only to explain his loquacity, that Hubert Humphrey sprang from the same roots as did David Lloyd George and Dylan Thomas. But he was half Norwegian (his mother was born in Norway)— and no one ever called the Norwegians wordy. On the paternal side, the Humphrey roots trace back to England, not Wales. Hubert Humphrey was, in fact, an American of the eleventh generation, descended from the first person in America to bear the name—Jonas Humphrey, a black-hatted, silver-buckled Puritan who crossed from the town of Wendover, Buckinghamshire, and settled in Dorchester, Massachusetts, about 1637. The Humphreys of Dorchester were tanners, and godly folk. Jonas's son James was ruling elder of the town church for decades. The Humphreys of Dorchester married into such old, God-fearing New England families as the Capens, Basses, Newgates, Johnsons, and Wiswalls. Though he never knew it, Hubert Humphrey of the dust-blown West was distantly related to seven U.S. presidents, from John Adams to Franklin Roosevelt.

But if ever a family lived the life of the western frontiers, it was Hubert Humphrey's forebears. First to head west was the third Isaac Humphrey (1723–1793), who moved to a farm at Dudley in western Massachusetts. His son Elijah (1751–1817) fought three years in the Revolution and, Uncle Harry said, was "noted for his great physical strength." This was the first ancestor of his name who ever came to Hubert Humphrey's attention.

The second son of this Elijah, also named Elijah (1794–1846), married Hannah Bartholomew of an old New England family. About the time the Erie Canal opened up the Great Lakes region to trade and settlement, they moved west to a tract of land in the Western Reserve of Ohio, some twenty miles west of Cleveland. In due course their eldest son, Henry Mark Humphrey (1804–1880), married a neighbor named Electa Wadsworth, said to be a cousin of the poet Henry Wadsworth Longfellow, and took over the farm. By then, "westering" was in the Humphrey blood. In 1855, Henry and Electa sold the farm and with their five children pushed west, across Indiana and Illinois, to the banks of the Mississippi. There the railroad ended; the only way to their destination, which was the newly opened territory of Minnesota upriver, was by steamboat.

By that summer settlers were fast staking claims to the land of the new territory immediately adjoining the river. Men thronged the paddle-wheelers, slept as many as twenty-six per room at the riverside "hotels," and then set out in motley bands—"tramp, tramp, tramp," as Seth Humphrey comments—to scout for the best available tract. They trudged through stands of pine trees four feet through and a hundred feet up to the first limb; but the best land was already taken. At night they threw themselves down on buffalo robes in some Connecticut Yankee's cabin built of rough boards the previous week. Next day they stumbled into a patch of open prairie and in three days had spread out to stake out thousands of acres—160 acres per claim. At the river, 400 emigrant wagons crossed every week that summer. Numerous as were the families migrating from the Atlantic seaboard, they were few compared with the wave of those who, like the Humphreys, started from points in between.

Even in the parts not covered by vast, "Paul Bunyan" pinelands, Minnesota was not merely a prairie. Immediately to the south of the pine wilderness that blanketed most of the territory stretched a solid band of hardwood forest, and it was this that the settlers ran into first. They called it The Big Woods. Starting only a few miles west of the river, it extended northward past the infant town of Minneapolis as far as the older French settlement at St. Cloud. It occupied an area about one hundred miles long north and south and forty miles wide at the southern end. All of it, except the bottom lands of the Minnesota River and occasional marshes, was covered with thick forest, mainly oak. It was in the heart of the Big Woods, some fifty miles west of the Mississippi and in a settlement called Union Lakes, that the Humphrey family staked their claim in the summer of 1855.

Indian campfires burned nearby. Deer and elk were everywhere. Passenger pigeons flocked overhead, and prairie chickens darted on the ground, where children ran and caught them. And there was no want of fresh water, firewood, or construction timber. The first rude shanty rose quickly from logs chopped at the site. But clearing the land was slow, back-breaking work. The Humphreys discovered that even with three grown sons swinging the ax they could clear and plant only a few acres the first summer, and John, the youngest, was put to work at age five.

It was not long before the Indians, whose villages dotted the Big Woods, made trouble. In 1862 the Sioux rose in arms and massacred 350 whites; everybody had to flee. Not until 1864 were the Yankees of Union Lakes able to organize their first town government. That year Harry Mark Humphrey was elected one of the officers, his youngest son, John, was one of sixteen pupils who met with a teacher at the new Forest Township schoolhouse. By then the Humphrey family were housed on their forest farm in what Uncle Harry described as a "neat frame building." Also that year the two eldest sons, Louis and Horatio Hubert, enlisted in the 11th Minnesota regiment and fought in the Civil War.

John, the youngest, was destined to carry on the family's pioneering tradition. Skilled at hunting and woodcraft, fast on skates, and a strong swimmer, he was a frontiersman whose education, his son Harry wrote later, "was limited solely to a few months in winter and to such instruction as could be given by teachers who had never been schooled beyond the elementary grades." Having helped clear the last of the Union Lakes acres, he joined the next westward land rush—this time to the open prairies of western Minnesota.

As soon as he was twenty-one years old, John Humphrey staked a claim at Granite Falls on the banks of the Minnesota River—one hundred miles to the west of Union Lakes. A grist mill had opened to grind the settlers' first wheat for bread, and the young man took charge of the sawmill attached to it, sawing boards from the tree trunks floated downstream to the falls. In addition, whenever new settlers arrived, he manned the small ferry raft that floated them, one team and wagon at a time, across to the virgin prairie beyond.

On June 2, 1872, John Humphrey married Addie Regester, daughter of a settler who had arrived at Granite Falls from Union Lakes the previous year. Hubert Humphrey's paternal grandmother, she brought still another strain of old-stock American blood into the family—tracing back through nine generations of Quakers in America. First of this line to settle in the New World was George Smedley, who arrived from Derbyshire, England, in 1682, the year of William Penn's arrival. From Penn he bought 250 acres south of Philadelphia—land on which Swarthmore College now stands. In 1743 this devout Friend's granddaughter married Robert Regester of nearby Egmont, and it was their grandson, also named Robert, who first went West. That was in 1790, one year after the founding of the Republic, and his trek led over the Alleghenies to Columbiana County in eastern Ohio. He was a stonemason and a farmer. His fourth son, Aaron Regester, married Matilda Dwyer of the same Quaker settlement, and they took off across the Mississippi. After a brief pause in Iowa they crossed into Minnesota Territory in 1856, a year after the Humphreys, and carved out a farm in the rugged hills at Etna—a town that, like Union Lakes, has since disappeared from the map.

Always settling and never settled, this was the way of pioneers. The Regesters shortly pulled out to try farming at Union Lakes, where their daughter Addie first met young John Humphrey. In 1871 the Regesters hitched up their wagon again and pushed westward through prairie grass higher than their heads. At East Granite Falls, just across the Minnesota River from the sawmill where the young John Humphrey found work, they staked their claim. In due time Aaron Regester became notary public and postmaster in Granite Falls—Republican, of course. His daughter Addie was the town's first schoolmistress when she married John Humphrey in 1872.

The railroad came, and with it freightloads of lumber that put the little sawmill out of business. When grasshoppers then devoured his crops, John Humphrey retreated for a short time to Minneapolis and worked in his Uncle Horatio's butcher shop. Then it was westering again, first to Uncle Alfred Humphrey's farm in Oregon, then to the town of Albany, Oregon, where their third son, Hubert Horatio Humphrey (1882–1949), was born. Only a few months later John Humphrey took his young family back to Granite Falls and that fall bought a 200-acre farm at Elk River, thirty miles north of Minneapolis. Here on the banks of the Mississippi River, John and Addie Humphrey and their five children lived for the longest period of their restless lives. It was the time the children remembered most fondly. Harry, the eldest, wrote later: "I followed my mother in the flickering light of her home-made candle. I ate her home-baked bread and drank milk that she had with her own hands drawn from the family herd. I slept in a wee trundle bed that my father had ripped out of rough pine. Matches were too expensive to buy, so we used paper candle-lighters. We slept on straw bedticks. We ate fare drawn direct from the farm; we wore second-hand clothes, and made our first-best last for years. We seldom went to town, and when we did it was a thrill beyond price, unforgettable." Hubert, the next to youngest, carved his name in the barn timbers over the stall of his favorite horse, swam with the neighboring French-Canadian DuChese children in the Mississippi, and learned to climb on the piled-up logs that floated past on their way to the sawmills of Minneapolis.

The farm was in the heart of the section from which the National Grange movement had sprung a few years earlier, and John Humphrey regularly attended a Farmers Institute at Elk River. Here professors from the University of Minnesota would lecture on deep plowing, crop rotation, seed treatment, use of manure, and other advances in husbandry. His grandson later recalled that the soil of the farm, washed down from glacial deposits farther north, was sandy and its yields of small grain and potatoes below average. So John Humphrey turned to dairy farming, first in the vicinity to do so. He applied scientific methods of butter making and for years sold his butter for twelve and eighteen cents per pound more than its cost on the open market. He began taking the train to Minneapolis to deliver butter, cream, and garden produce to well-to-do city families.

Addie Humphrey frequently read aloud to her children and her husband. She had a musical vein and a taste for such writers as Scott, Dickens, Thackeray, and Hawthorne. It was largely her inspiration and keen interest, her son Harry said, that led her children to seek more schooling. He wrote later: "I believe I would have stopped short of completing my high school course but for her never-failing encouragement." Harry and his brother John went on to the University of Minnesota, and both later joined the Department of Agriculture. Hubert, the third of the four sons—Ford, the youngest, was crippled by a rheumatic heart and died early—attended the Hart College of Pharmacy in Minneapolis and became a druggist.

Dr. Harry Humphrey, eldest of the five, was the family intellectual. After graduating from the University of Minnesota he took his Ph.D. in plant sciences at Stanford in 1907 and joined the Department of Agriculture in Washington. Lifelong expert on rust and other wheat diseases, he edited a learned botanical journal *Phytopathology*, wrote countless articles, and traveled annually through the grain belt to observe crop conditions for the department. Four of his own children won their doctorates. By his visits and, even more, his correspondence he exerted an important influence on his brother Hubert's children. To the suburban town of Cabin John, Maryland, and his house—built with his own hands by a unique, "rammed-earth" method that rendered it snug in winter and uncommonly cool in summer—he invited his niece Frances Humphrey. He helped her enroll in George Washington University, bought her symphony tickets, and took her to the National Gallery to view the paintings of Mary Cassatt. Again and again he sent funds to his nephew Hubert in the West, enabling him to make his first visit to Washington in 1937, to remain at the university in 1931 when his funds ran out, to complete a year's graduate study in 1939 when again funds ran short. He read poetry in seven languages, including Welsh, became a Christian Science reader, and inevitably wrote the family history.

His heart was warm, his style ornate. When young Hubert wrote in 1941 affirming his faith that democracy would triumph over fascism, Uncle Harry wrote: "Your grand letter fortified my faith in the young—a veritable balm of Gilead in an atmosphere tinctured with the opiate of defeatism and a general miasma of ignorance as to the true nature of the disease now gnawing at the vitals of our dear democracy."

When Hubert Humphrey later abandoned higher learning for politics, Uncle Harry reminded him that opportunities to teach would be all the greater in public office. "Go to it," he wrote when his nephew filed for mayor. When the Metropolitan Opera paid a visit to Minneapolis—its first in several years— Uncle Harry sent a check to make sure that the young Mayor and Muriel should attend their first opera: *Don Giovanni*. Until his death in 1956 this sweet-natured old gentleman never ceased to send Hubert Humphrey long, beautifully handwritten letters urging him never to go back on his high ideals. Every time, the senator would reply: "I have read and re-read your letter. . . . " Uncle Harry, with his serene faith that education conquers all, left a strong imprint on Hubert Humphrey's life.

2

The Norwegian Connection

IN THE spring of 1889, a tiny caravan crept over a plain so wide that the sky met it at all points of horizon. Overhead there were only a few clouds. The sun poured down in a scalding shower of gold that spread to the curving limits of the earth. Now and then a gust of wind set the sea of grass in motion and sent waves of yellow and green and blue rippling across the plain. Once in a while a patch of blackness drifted across the pools and eddies of color— the shadow of a passing cloud.

The buffalo grass, already waist high in June, bent and flattened momentarily as the caravan pushed ahead. Then it sprang up again, leaving almost no trace of the party's advance. All the way to the horizon, not a tree was to be seen, only grass. There was no road, now that the caravan had lost track of an earlier party at the last slough. Anybody else's path was hard to follow in the sea of tall grass.

At the head of the caravan walked a wiry, sun-bronzed man in his middle years. Behind him a team of oxen ambled along; the oxen drew a battered, creaking wagon. Over the wagon box long willow saplings had been bent in supple arches, and on these arches, tied down to the body on each side, were blankets, sheepskins, and strips of old canvas that served for bed coverings at night. The rear of the wagon was stowed full of household items piled to the top. A large immigrant trunk took up much of the space; around and above it were piled utensils, tools, implements, and all the travelers' clothing.

A short distance behind the wagon followed four cows and a white mule. Every now and then the cows stopped to munch grass. Two girls carrying switches walked behind them prodding them onward. Keeping the animals on the track was quite a job for a pair of girls aged twelve and six, and the party moved very slowly.

Across the front of the box in the wagon lay a piece of plank. On the right side of this plank with a kerchief on her head sat a plump woman driving the oxen. Against her thigh rested the blonde head of a two-and-a-half-year-old girl fast asleep. Just behind her, in a tiny basket wedged against the pile of household belongings, lay a six-month-old baby girl, also asleep. Now and then the hand of the mother moved across the baby's face to chase away the mosquitoes, which had begun to gather as the sun lowered. On the left side of the plank, beyond the sleeping girl, sat a tousled blond boy four years old.

This was the caravan of Andrew Sannes, who with his family and all his possessions was trekking from Brandon in the newly settled part of Dakota territory to a homestead he had staked out on the virgin land 140 miles to the north. He had already walked this way alone in each of the three preceding summers—first to stake his claim and raise a sod shanty, required to confirm possession. Next he traveled there to build a four-room house fit to shelter his family through the bitter winters. Knowing the lakes, creeks, and hamlets along the way, Andrew Sannes walked ahead. Tomine, his wife, followed with the three youngest in the wagon; Anna, twelve, and Christine, six, tramped behind herding the animals.

The journey took nearly three weeks. Each night they stopped, unyoked the oxen to browse, built a fire of wood collected along the way, milked the cows, made a frugal supper of porridge, and slept on the ground beneath the wagon. At Brookings, the terminus of a newly built railroad, they got supplies to repair the wagon and stopped at the newly occupied homestead of Tomine Sannes's sister and brother-in-law.

Beyond Brookings there was not even a cowpath to follow, and as the land became more rolling, there were many marshes to skirt. It was slow going, but at last Andrew Sannes led his family to the little house on the prairie. Not a tree, not another building except for the old sod hut, was to be seen in any direction. But just over the ridge were other rude houses where the Hagens, the Sorensens, the Gimmestads—other Norwegian pioneers—had come to settle and till the plains of Highland Township, Day County, South Dakota.

Andrew Sannes, Hubert Humphrey's grandfather on his mother's side, had been a sea captain in Norway. Born Guttorm Andreas Sannaes in 1847 near the Norwegian seaport of Kristiansand, he was a younger son, hence unlikely to inherit the tidy little valley farm, where his family had lived for generations. So at fifteen he went to sea, first as a cabin boy, then as cook's helper, then as deckhand on the sailing ships that at that time still carried much of Norway's trade with the world. By the time he married Abel Tomine Larsen, daughter of a farmstead in the same little fjord-side valley, he had become master of his own ship and had voyaged as far as Cuba to bring back a cargo of sugar. On an even longer voyage, his bride and infant daughter, Anna, sailed with him to China and back.

But sailing vessels could not compete with steamers, and Captain Sannaes looked for an opportunity to try something else. In those years thousands of Europeans were leaving home to make new lives in America. The new world beckoned to the hardy seafarer. In the spring of 1884 a brother-in-law, Oliver Larsen, invited him to join in a river-boat business on the Missouri, taking Norwegians and other immigrants upstream to settle on the wide plains of the West. But as Hubert Humphrey said later, "He never was told that the Missouri was filled with sand bars." Arriving with his family at Sioux City, Iowa, "Andrew Sannes," as he spelled his name in America, found his barge-man brother-in-law had gone out of business.

So at thirty-eight the seafarer turned to the land. And what land! Broad, black prairies, incomparably richer than the flinty mountainsides of Norway, lay waiting for anyone to claim them and sink the first plowshare into the virgin turf. But first the captain had to set up a base for his growing family. Within a month or two after his arrival he bought a 160-acre tract in a settled part of Dakota Territory, some 80 miles north of Sioux City, and moved his wife and children into a neat, four-room farmhouse. This was near the village of Brandon, among Norwegian settlers. Through the farm, in fact, ran the same Split Rock Creek toward which the Norwegian hero of O. E. Rolvaag's pioneering epic *Giants In The Earth* had set his course.

By the time the Sannes family moved in, a railroad was in the process of obtaining rights to build a right of way across the farm. To Captain Sannes's mind, it made little sense to try raising crops on land divided by a railroad right of way as well as a good-sized stream. The real opportunity lay in the virgin lands opening up to the north and west—a challenge as compelling to him as the virgin prairie of Split Rock Creek had been to Rolvaag's Per Hansa. The very next spring Andrew Sannes walked north to stake the wilderness claim to which he was finally ready to lead his family three summers later.

In spite of his careful preparations, the Sannes family faced heavy privations on the northern plains. To begin with, there was no firewood. The sole tree to be found on the uplands was the cottonwood. In company with its relative the willow, it grew only in the deep gullies sliced by streams. The cottonwood's one merit was that it grew so fast. It seemed to take root anywhere. Like other settlers, Andrew Sannes planted cottonwoods for his first windbreaks. And when branches fell to the ground in a storm, they often took root. Later when the captain put up fences of green cottonwood posts, the same thing happened. The cottonwood was the Dakota settler's tree.

Meanwhile the Sannes children were sent out to cut the buffalo grass with sickles. They twisted the swatches into tight bundles, and these bundles, stacked like logs, were used as fuel. The first Sannes house was heated by a "straw burner"—something like an oil barrel. Into it were thrust the rolls of buffalo grass, which if rolled tightly enough, burned long enough to cook meals.

With the aid of straining oxen, Andrew Sannes broke the heavy sod and planted the first few acres. Until a well could be dug, Anna and Christine hauled water from a stream with the help of the white mule, Sam. Everybody had to work. Like all early settlers, the family lived in fear of prairie fire. When fire broke out, there being no water, they pounded it out. Once out of control, the fires could race miles in minutes. The only protection at each homestead was to plow out a firebreak—slow, hard work with the walking plow.

As it happened, almost all the first settlers in the area were Norwegians. With his large family—it grew to twelve in the next years—Andrew Sannes took a leading part in pressing for a school. Neighbors got together and raised a one-room schoolhouse four miles from the farm. They persuaded Fred Stone, an English-speaking neighbor, to teach classes for a few months during winter. At first he had a hard time making his pupils understand him, but except in the worst blizzards, the children insisted on attending. School was fun, the only means of meeting and playing with other children; and besides, if they stayed home, there was work to do.

In the summer, after a church was organized, the children attended a month-long session of parochial school. Instruction by the pastor, who farmed too, was in Norwegian. At home, grace was said in Norwegian. Andrew Sannes had two flagpoles, one for the American flag and one for the Norwegian. Every Norwegian holiday, the Norwegian flag went up. He and his wife spoke Norwegian—but the children, not excepting those born in Norway, spoke unaccented English.

A stern man, Andrew Sannes could curse eloquently in Norwegian; his children, or at least his daughters, were afraid of him. He had a pointed chin and piercing eyes. He kept a strongbox in his bedroom with a huge, bronze padlock on it. Years after the journey across the wilderness this frugal man took pride in using the same wagon, now well oiled and sprucely painted, that had carried his family to Day County. Always, when he cut his grain, he sent the small children out to glean the seeds that fell behind. For years he preferred first to collect the sheaves and pile them in tall stacks near his barn, rather than to thresh the crop directly in the field, because, extra work though it was, less grain was lost.

Tomine, or Minna, Sannes was ample and amiable. In the house, she knew how to produce almost everything the family needed, from soap to the clothes. With the spinning wheel she had brought from the old country she turned the wool into skeins for stockings and mittens. She could also climb on a machine and plow, cultivate, drag, disc, mow, and rake when necessary. She planted the garden and fed the chickens. Singing as she sewed, scrubbed, swept, cooked, and regularly baked twenty loaves a week, she was equal to all the rigors of frontier life that wore down so many women. She set her daughters to milking. One said later: "My earliest recollection was of milk being poured into wide earthen crocks and skimmed for cream after twelve hours." After the girls had churned the cream into butter, Minna Sannes would wash and salt the butter and put it in half-gallon crocks below the floor. "We never saw creamery butter until after we left home," the daughter said later.

As his fields bore fruit, it began to look as if Andrew Sannes's luck was improving. The Milwaukee railroad built a branch line through the wheat fields of Day County, and the magnates of Minneapolis constructed tall elevators at Lily to receive grain to be sold. Hard work paid off. Each Sunday Sannes hitched up a stylish, ornately painted surrey in which the family rode to Highland Church. One year he and Minna even traveled to their old home in Norway. And their eldest daughters—first Anna and then Christine—went off to study at the State College, which opened about this time at Brookings. Afterward Anna taught school in Minnesota, but Christine, after two years' training, came back and taught in one-room schools in Day County.

One evening at a church social she met a talkative, dark-haired young man who had just arrived at Lily and opened a drugstore near the Milwaukee depot. On Friday afternoons the children at the Wild Rose school west of town would see a livery rig coming and run inside to tell their teacher: "Humphrey is coming." A short time later, Hubert Horatio Humphrey called on Andrew Sannes to ask for his daughter Christine's hand in marriage. Andrew and Minna Sannes were pleased; it was a big honor to have a Yankee in the family. On April 16, 1906, the couple were married by Pastor Berven at the Highland church in one of the first services to be conducted in English. Like Andrew Sannes, Rev. Berven was a rock-ribbed Republican.

3

Pinky

In the early decades of the century, when Hubert Humphrey was growing up in Doland, South Dakota (population, 600), America had not yet become a mass society. The small town, at the settled heart of the agricultural hinterland, still exercised a profound influence on the nation's culture. Innocent of Old World walls, the Midwest small town stood serenely lawned, ivied, and tree-shaded at the point where Main Street met the railborne forces of the mysterious East. Though many later called it confining, its sheltering stability, its trading community, town hall, school, churches, lodges, and white, free-standing houses afforded some basic freedoms. There was a world of nature for a boy to explore no further away than the end of the street. Its range of humankind, though finite, was such that a boy got to know everybody, young and old. Altogether, the small town's dimensions of time and space were just about right to enable a child to satisfy his curiosity about his physical surroundings while learning to accommodate his unruly high spirits to the prescriptions enforced by the grownup world.

In Doland, the boy Hubert felt the wonder of the vast, bright sky, the song of the meadowlark, the slick of the snail on a stone, the cries of geese south-winging over a prairie slough. In this hamlet on the plains he spent all his school years, from first grade through high school graduation. He excelled in school and public speaking; he once informed Basketball Coach Irven Herther that he meant to be president of the United States but gave scarcely a glimmering hint that he would grow into one of the compelling liberal personalities of the age.

Although Hubert Horatio Humphrey, Junior, grew up in Doland, he was born in Wallace, an even tinier Dakota hamlet some seventy-five miles to the northeast. On May 27, 1911, he was born in a room over his father's drugstore and baptized in his mother's nearby country church three months later to the day.

He was a second son, his elder brother, Ralph, having been born four years earlier in Granite Falls, Minnesota, during the time that their father dropped out of the drugstore business and worked as a saleman peddling candy through the farming towns of the region. Two other children were born to the family, both girls. Frances was born at Wallace in 1914; Fern, the youngest, arrived in 1917, after the Humphreys had settled in Doland.

It is said that as a boy Humphrey never walked, he ran. The whole town of Doland, though two or three times the size of Wallace, contained only fifteen or sixteen blocks—and only one short main street. At one end of the street was the school; at the other, the railroad tracks. North from the depot and a cluster of grain elevators stretched the little row of storefronts: a pair of banks, a garage, a butcher stop, a general store, a furniture store, a hotel, two drugstores, and (over the furniture store) the Opera House. Hubert would run all the way from grade school, at the north end, to the Humphrey's large frame house, just off the main street's south end. Lunch would be waiting in the kitchen for Hubert, his elder brother, Ralph, and his tousled sister, Frances. Baby Fern took her meals in the high chair, her mother spooning in the pudding, and Happy, the hired girl, stood by to clear the table. Minutes later, pausing only to order his airedale Rex back to the house, Hubert was off to school—running.

To all of Doland's hundred or so families, Hubert was known as Pinky. So his mother called him from the time he was a baby—he looked so nice dressed in pink, she said. The name had nothing to do with his coloring, which was not especially pink. Dark-haired like his father and blue-eyed like his mother, Pinky had a distinctly clear complexion. His freckled, redhead sister Frances grumbled at his good fortune. He was a skinny boy, quick but sure in his movements. When the brothers tussled in the cottonwood tree by the house, it was Ralph, not Pinky, who lost his balance, fell, and broke a bone.

Pinky was all boy. Once he misbehaved and hid under the front porch. His father was sent to get him, and as he crept in, the eight-year-old called out: "Come on in. Is mother after you, too?" He was out of the house early and late, tunneling in the snowbanks after the winter blizzards, shooting marbles on the muddy schoolground in spring, and spinning tops with other third graders in the fall. In summer he ran barefooted. Sometimes he raced along the depot platform and caught big slivers in his feet. Other times he crossed the tracks, jumped on freight cars as they were being shunted on sidings, and hopped off as they rolled past the sandpit alongside the lumber yard. Still other times the game was baseball—"southenders" against "northenders." On these occasions Pinky, providing ball, bat, and gloves from his father's store, captained the southenders. On the first warm days the boys raced four or five miles northeast of town, past the cemetery, to skinny dip at a wide spot in a creek, a sport that had to be taken in season because the creek soon shrank to stagnation, and they couldn't stand the smell. Pinky, who provided ideas as well as equipment, thought up the games, but he would drive away his sister Frances, who adored him, saying: "We don't want you." Older boys, Ralph included, tried to scare him and sometimes succeeded. Finding the skull of a cow that had died in the pasture, they lowered it over the entrance to his lair with suitably eerie noises and gave Pinky a fright he remembered as long as he lived. The cave was an old gravel pit, and although the hill was only a slight rise, the boys marched up it as Napoleon's "army" in summer and slid down it on sleds in winter. At its foot was a tiny pond they used for skating, even though the clamps that fastened the skate runners on their shoes would come loose every time they tried to turn.

As a small boy, Pinky also had the run of a Dakota farm. It happened that Doland, unlike the towns the Humphreys had lived in before, had few Norwegians. Pinky's mother was almost the only one. In summer, therefore, especially in the first years, she liked to take her children back home for long visits. The children sat at the long tables with their country cousins, heard grace said in Norwegian, and ate platters of bread soaked in rich sour cream and sweetened with brown sugar. For a month at a time they attended the Lutheran parochial school, where they read lessons and sang hymns in Norwegian. Grandpa Sannes, stern taskmaster, set Pinky and the other children to gathering loose grain dropped in the field behind his reaper-binder. He even had them sweep up the straw outside the barn. Later he would go into the bedroom where he kept his strongbox. Emerging, he would open his long purse and from the side that held the coins hand each of them a bright silver dollar. Pinky followed him around, watched him milk the cows and slop the hogs, and saw the old wagon, kept in its shed, that had carried the Sannes family across the plains in 1889. When they left, Grandpa gave Pinky a few chickens, which the boy thenceforth kept in the shed behind the garage at Doland. He did not like to clean the chicken coop, but he liked the money he got by selling the eggs.

Pinky seems to have learned early about money. He said later that he started selling newspapers, the Chicago *Herald and Examiner*, at the age of six—"when I was too small to carry them and used a wagon. . . . My mother said she could always tell where I was by hearing me holler out the papers." That was during World War I, when sons had been drafted from almost every home, and people in small towns like Doland wanted all the news they could get. In 1918, war's end brought a sharp fall in world wheat prices that eventually shattered the placid prosperity of prairie towns. But what penetrated Spink County that year was the influenza epidemic raging across America. It laid Pinky low. "I was very sick and nearly died—old Doc Sherwood was at the house pulling me through."

Only a year or so later, while still in grade school, Pinky began helping out at the family drugstore. He was too short to reach the counter and wash dishes or make sodas. So his father built a little wooden platform on which he could stand to reach the fountain spigots. He also ran errands. Every evening, when the train pulled in at six, Pinky went down and mailed letters, slipping them into the little slot on the mail car. He got to know the men in the mail car by name. He would also pick up ice cream for the drugstore's soda fountain—big, wooden, ice-filled tubs shipped from a factory in Watertown, with the five-gallon containers of vanilla packed like capsules inside. Pinky hauled them to the store in a cart. His newspapers also came in on the train, but one day he stayed too long at a birthday party and failed to pick them up. His father announced: "Young man, I'm going to take you downstairs and give you a little trimming up so you won't forget to take care of this business." Afterward, though by then it was long after dark, he said: "Now you get out with those papers and see what you can do." The son said later:

> I was brought up to believe in work. I started writing checks when I was ten years old. I kept a ledger. The checking account was for newspapers. I was independent. I went across the street to Lovelace's restaurant for a ham sandwich and a glass of milk and wrote a check for it—15 cents. I could go to the state fair at Huron on my own money. I sneaked off to the Opera House for Saturday night movies too.
>
> I'd made up to $3 to $5 a week. I'd keep my money in one of those little ice cream cartons. Bought all my own clothes from the time I was twelve. I bought out my father's magazine business. Once I paid him $50 for his magazines. I proceeded to lose $100 on the magazines in three months because I was just too busy with too many activities—*Argosy, Bluebook, Redbook*—I didn't tear off the covers soon enough to get credit for those I didn't sell. Dad said, "That'll teach you a lesson."

The railroad, bringing in Main Street's goods and carrying out the farmers' wheat, was everything to Doland—and the early vehicle of Pinky's dreams. Sitting in school and listening to the morning train whistle eastward from Doland, the boy saw himself riding to the county seat twenty-two miles away, to the state capital, even to Washington, where his Uncle Harry lived and worked as a government scientist. When he stood on the slivered depot platform, he could look down the tracks nine miles without a curve to Raymond in the east. To Pinky, gazing off to where the tracks seemed to fade out of existence, this was not a branch that ran from somewhere in Minnesota to its terminus near the Missouri River one hundred miles to the west; it was the main line to the whole wide world.

The trains brought the smooth-talking drummers to his father's drugstore from Watertown and Minneapolis. In the fall they brought hunters from as far away as Chicago. They filled the town's hotel. Pinky earned up to three dollars per day in dusty cornfields, walking toward the hunters and flushing the pheasants out of the stubble for the slaughter. To Pinky and his friends the birds were as much a part of the world they grew up in as the cows in the pastures and the swallows in the eaves. Before he was twelve he went out with his own twenty-gauge shotgun and knocked off his daily limit of pheasants before class started. He shot rabbits and tossed them on the shed roof behind the house, where they froze solid until his mother was ready to cook a stew. That he was a pretty fair marksman never crossed his mind, it came natural to a Doland boy.

Two things were evident as Pinky grew up—he was a "good" boy and he was very bright. His Aunt Olga recalled later how older people liked him, kidded him, paid attention to him. "He would do things for them," she said, "little errands, always willing no matter what they'd ask—sure, he'd go." In a small town where everybody had a chance to be somebody, his older brother, Ralph, had performed creditably in class and in such outside activities as public speaking. But Pinky, as his mother had always said, was "special." He was into everything. In eighth grade he played Jack in *Jack and the Beanstalk* (and got a big laugh when his bloomers caught on a peg at the top). His teacher said he chattered all the time and ordered him to keep still. "He tried to, but he just bubbled," she said later.

In high school he played the lead in the junior and senior plays, wrote a "pep" column for the school paper, and played the baritone horn. He was on the basketball and track teams and played four years of football, two as a 120-pound starter at guard. In class he seemed to learn effortlessly: except for B pluses in Caesar and Plane Geometry, his grades were all A's. Girls were simply fun to him—though he "looked sideways at Helen Riddle," a teacher recalled later. He kept out of the pool hall.

In his later years of public life it was often remarked that Hubert Humphrey's speeches rang with the kind of fervor that could only be called evangelical. This traced to the religious environment in which the boy grew up in Doland. His mother was an intense and inward person who hoped more than anything that her son would grow up to be a minister. She made sure that he went to Sunday school without fail as a child, and after her husband joined the church both parents wished their children to be regular in attendance. Pinky went cheerfully. He often sat with his friend Julian Hartt, the minister's son. And when a visiting evangelist held revival services and called upon his hearers to "give their lives to Jesus," young Hubert went forward and knelt at the conversion rail. Later he said, "When I went out of church with my friends, I knew I'd done the right thing. I'd prayed, sung and listened with reasonable attention. And I was glad to get out and make some noise, talk with my friends, play with my dog. I liked church."

His favorite activity was debate. He made what appears to have been his public-speaking debut in 1926 at age fifteen, declaiming "Abraham Lincoln, Man of the Age" at a father-son banquet at the Methodist Church. Doland, even more than other small towns of the 1920s, took elocution seriously and rooted for its debaters the way other places backed basketball teams. In 1929 the Doland *Times-Record* observed that Pinky, paired with Julian Hartt and Earl Hanson, "showed great tact in discussing the McNary-Haugen [farm] bill." The paper proudly reported that this team won the district championship. Better yet, Doland's team twice won its way to the statewide tournament. In his senior year, Pinky's team, though outpointed in the finals, won compliments from the judge, Karl Mundt, speech instructor at Madison Normal School and future Senate colleague of Hubert Humphrey. Capping his forensic achievements, on May 29, 1929, Pinky stepped on to an Opera House platform bedecked with morning glories and, for Doland's sixteen graduating seniors, delivered the valedictorian's address: "I Am Responsible for My Own Life."

4

His Father

H E   W A S   a smalltown druggist to the end of his days. A broad-shouldered man, Hubert Humphrey's father was almost six feet tall with big, strong hands, a jutting chin, and the high forehead that was the most salient physical feature he bestowed upon his son. His rimless glasses gave him a professorial look. His waist bulged, and although he was certainly not athletic, he walked with a light step. Warm and friendly, a story swapper, he was, as befitted a former traveling salesman, extremely talkative. His customers said of him: "He never sells you a pill without selling you an idea." Solid family man and civic booster though he was, some thought him a bit too different. He was a shrewd enough merchant, but he was also a romantic. When people joshed him for his big talk about world affairs, the "good society," and learning, he would say: "Before the fact is the dream." This was Hubert Humphrey's father, who exercised far and away the strongest early influence on the mind and character of his son.

Hubert Horatio Humphrey, senior, was born in Oregon but grew up on his father's farm at Elk River, Minnesota. His generation of Humphreys finally broke away from the land-tilling traditions of their ancestors. And no doubt he wanted to follow his two older brothers to the University of Minnesota. But before he could do so, his parents sold the farm and retired to Granite Falls, the town where they had started out thirty-five years before. Hubert had to finish his last year of high school at St. James, Minnesota, where his eldest brother was teaching school. College seemed out of the question.

Times being hard, the young man went to work at a drugstore in Granite Falls, living for a time with his parents. Even as a young clerk he had his own ideas, rebel ideas. In the heart of the Bible belt, he bought a copy of Darwin's *Origin of Species*. He read Robert Ingersoll's *Why I Am an Agnostic* and became an agnostic. Amid the customarily Republican countryside of rural Minnesota, he heard William Jennings Bryan speak and became a Democrat. He talked a great deal about how he wanted to change the world, but he was so good-natured about it that others rather enjoyed disputing with him. For a time he worked as a printer in the nearby village of Dawson, where he made fast friends with another young man who liked to argue ideas—Theodore Christianson, future Republican governor of Minnesota who held the office for three terms. Not long after that he enrolled in the Drew College of Pharmacy, Minneapolis, and returned a qualified pharmacist. With a tiny stock advanced by a Minneapolis supply house, he opened the first drugstore in a corner of a general store at Lily, South Dakota. That was where he met and married Christine Sannes.

When the Lily venture proved unsuccessful, the young couple had to move back to Granite Falls and the prescription counter of B. F. Nelson's pharmacy. Their first child, Ralph, was born, and Christine sent her husband out one day for household supplies. He returned loaded down with books instead. She dumped the books in the Minnesota River. But "H. H.," as everybody called him, rebounded as always. With his gift of gab and his easy way with people, it seemed only natural for him to turn salesman, and for the next year or two he peddled candy to stores in the small towns of the region. Christine's sister Olga, who came to stay with her during that time, said later: "No brother could have been so wonderful to me as he was." Then in 1911 he got a second chance to open a drugstore, this time in Wallace, South Dakota, only a dozen miles from Lily and even closer to the farm that Christine's family owned. From Wallace, H. H. tried to help get the radical Non-Partisan League active in South Dakota. There they lived four years—and both Hubert and Frances were born. Then H. H. bought the drugstore in Doland and moved his family into one of the town's finest and biggest houses, acquired as part of the same transaction.

Dishing out ideas as well as pills at his drugstore counter, H. H. became one of Doland's leaders. Although he was one of about five Democrats in town, people liked and respected him. In 1923, when he was a town council member, most of Doland wanted to sell the municipally owned light plant to a private utility. H. H. fought the idea so hard that some seemed almost ready to take after him with clubs. On occasion, H. H. would take Pinky along to the drawn-out night sessions and put the boy in a chair by a corner window. Pinky would listen, doze off, then wake again when he heard his father's voice rising. Though H. H. lost that fight, his son never forgot his outspoken independence and principled stand. The boy remembered how these qualities never interfered with the mutual respect between H. H. and his neighbors. He later wrote about his father that "he was a rebel in a politically orthodox town, but they elected him mayor."

To build his business and provide for his family, H. H. worked at the store early and late. But he liked to have his family around him: "My best friends are my children, and then my books," he would say. Coming home late at night, he would rouse the children and read to them from his books—Raymond's life of Lincoln, stories about Jefferson, Elbert Hubbard's *Little Journeys to The Homes of the Great*. When Christine said he was keeping them up he said: "Mother, you go to bed for all of us." His son always loved to repeat his saying: "Never go to bed. Stay out of bed as long as you can. Ninety percent of all people die in bed."

Soon he had Pinky working at the soda fountain in the drugstore. "I had normal ideas to get outside," the son said later, "and Dad was very understanding about that. But I liked being there most of the time." At night, H. H. would sit down with a local lawyer named Zarneke, Doc Sherwood, the two bankers in town, Paul Brown and Fred Gross, and Al Payne, the postmaster. While the talk ranged all the way from Federal Reserve policy to the campaigns of Napoleon, Pinky back of the counter drank it all in. "I heard things that shaped my attitude toward people and ideas," he said later.

Once, set to mind the store while his father went to eat, the boy forgot to report that a woman had left a prescription to be filled. When H. H. later took him aside to say: "I place a lot of responsibility in you when you're alone here," the boy not only sensed that he had let his father down but also felt honored that his father treated him as if he were a grownup. And when he overheard H. H. saying to a salesman: "You know, my son Hubert, he knows every piece of merchandise in this store," Pinky glowed.

"Dad set high standards for me," he said. "The one fear I've had all my life was that I would disappoint him." There's no doubt that the son learned his prodigious work habits from the father, who opened the store at seven in the morning and never closed up until late at night. H. H. told him, "Son, you're not half as smart as you think you are. You're going to have to work twice as hard as you planned if you're going to succeed." When H. H. saw one of his sons momentarily idle he would say, pronouncing the word in a way they would mimic the rest of their lives: "Acti-vitty, boys, acti-vitty!" He was hardheaded about his bookkeeping and his inventory. More than once the boys missed out on a New Year's Eve party because they were still taking inventory of Lydia Pinkham's Compound, Tanalac, Peruna, and "Humphrey's Chest Oil" and calculating the value on hand for each item. H. H. believed that a businessman ought to keep records and know where he stood all the time.

H. H. never compromised his political principles but he could temper certain of his views when harmony at home seemed important. His wife,

Christine, came from a sternly Lutheran—and Republican—family. At the dinner table, where H. H. held forth upon the surpassing qualities of his idol Woodrow Wilson, it came out that she had voted for Warren Harding and Calvin Coolidge. Afterward, H. H. took Pinky and the others into the front parlor and said: "Now, you treat your mother with respect. Don't you argue with her and don't you ever speak harshly to her because she's my sweetheart." Then he added: "But remember, sometimes she's politically unreliable."

On the matter of religion, H. H. was prepared to give a lot more ground. She was a strict churchgoer, he had always been a free thinker. In the absence of a Lutheran church in town, Christine attended the Methodist church and insisted—while H. H. sat home reading Ingersoll and Tom Paine—upon taking the children to Sunday school every week. The situation was eased in 1924 when a new Methodist minister, the Rev. Albert Hartt, erudite, intellectual, trained at the Boston University School of Theology, arrived in Doland. Before long the Reverend Hartt was a regular participant in the late-night talkfests at Humphrey's Drug Store, where the radio sermons of Father Coughlin, Harry Emerson Fosdick, and the Rev. S. Parkes Cadman were frequent topics of conversation. H. H. and the Reverend Hartt became great friends.

The day came when H. H. was admitted to membership in the Methodist church upon confession of faith. Pinky was profoundly impressed. At the same time he and the other three children went forward to join too. Christine sat beaming in a front pew, but did not relinquish her formal membership in the Lutheran church back home, where she and the children had been baptized. Pinky and Julian Hartt, the minister's son who later became a Yale professor, grew to be close friends. Thenceforth, H. H. played a characteristically active role in church activities. He was especially concerned with the church's social ministry and talked of "the city of God on earth." He taught a Sunday school class, to which country folks came from miles around, and delighted in bringing a half-dozen at a time home for dinner.

Shantytown in Doland was where poor kids lived, and if it made Pinky's mother uneasy that he had friends there, it bothered H. H. not at all. One day Pinky took one of them into the store and told his father: "Dad, Jonathan here doesn't have any shoes, and his feet are so cold they're blue." H. H. took one look, pushed the No Sale key on the cash register, took out some money, and walked Jonathan down the street to buy him woolen socks and a pair of sturdy boots. Another time when a fellow townsman returned after serving a prison sentence for embezzlement, H. H. gave him a job at his store.

Once when a big road-building job on the edge of town brought Negroes to the Doland community, Pinky went out to sell them newspapers and was soon allowed to ride their mule teams and sit beside them on the steam shovel. When they came into town, people would stare at them. But the men would call Pinky by name as they went by, and Pinky would get on the wagon with them. This horrified his mother, but H. H. was pleased.

The dizzy boom that lifted Wall Street stocks to record heights in the 1920s never reached the Dakota farm country. Around Doland, several summers of good harvests postponed the slide, but wheat prices never recovered after the severe drop at the end of World War I. Many farmers had borrowed to enlarge their land holdings during the war years. Some, like Grandpa Sannes, cushioned the impact of depressed grain prices by diversifying into dairying. But as values shrank, the banks, overloaded with mortgage paper, found themselves at last unable even to meet depositors' withdrawals. Half the banks in South Dakota failed in the 1920s. In 1926 both of Doland's banks closed their doors. With that, local merchants like H. H. found their working capital wiped out, and bills coming due. It was a grim season—H. H.'s friend Paul Brown, of the State Bank, shot himself, the first dread signal of still darker times to come.

So it was that the Great Depression arrived years early in Dakota. Young Pinky, who lost his own $100 paperboy savings in the closing, told later how he learned the meaning of the Depression that day in 1927. "I was a junior in high school. I remember coming home from school late in the afternoon. I found my mother and father together under a big cottonwood tree on the front lawn. And there was another man there. And my mother was weeping and Dad, too, had tears in his eyes. I asked my father what had happened. He told me we simply had to sell the house. This was the only way he could cover and pay his bills."

What Pinky saw was that powerful forces outside one man's control could crush the heart of his little world. But the experience also showed, in a way that left an enduring mark on his own outlook, how his father overcame his worst defeat. "Through the years, I carried with me from that scene not just the picture of my father in tears, but the fact that after this terrible loss he carried not an ounce of bitterness, of apology, or defeatism. Right up to the time he died in November, 1949, he continued to do what he had always done—to plunge into life, the bitter and the sweet, with nothing held back, without protecting himself with suspicion, reserve or emotional caution."

He rented a smaller house on the edge of town. He enlarged his stock. "Listen, son," he told Pinky, "you can't make a living without merchandise. The customer that comes in here asking for something we don't have is a customer you won't see again." Humphrey's Drug Store sold paint in spring, rakes in summer, toys at Christmas, and chocolates for Mother's Day. H. H. even had his son run off circulars on a hand press and worked up a sizable mail-order business. He sold Edison phonographs ("The phonograph with a soul"), laid in a line of Victor Red Seal records, and brought artists to the Opera House upstairs from the furniture store for promotional recitals.

In his battle to keep the business going he took a little training and began selling vaccines and serums for farm animals. For an extra dime he went out to vaccinate the hogs, taking Pinky along. In 1928, ever the Populist and now Spink County Democratic chairman, H. H. traveled as a delegate to the Houston convention that nominated Al Smith for president. In his absence it was up to Pinky to visit the farms: "I put 25 cc of the serum just behind the front legs of all those little pigs, and then 2 cc into the muscle in the back. I'd take an old sow, put a piece of rope or wire around her snout, tighten it, and then with the farmer's help flip that old 200 pounder right over on her back and vaccinate her. It was hard, and I did hundreds."

Ralph, four years older, had gone to Dakota Wesleyan College, in Mitchell, but after H. H. lost the big house, he returned home to help at the store and make trips with the vaccinating needle. In 1929, Pinky graduated tops in his class from high school, and that fall H. H. and Christine agreed that he, too, must start college. It was an act of faith and courage, because few of the customers were paying cash at the store, and large, black storm clouds loomed ahead.

5

Wilderness
Years

In the fall of 1929, H. H. drove his son Hubert the 310 miles to Minneapolis in their new green Model A Ford, bought for eight hundred dollars. They went to the university and then to a rooming house they had heard about just off campus run by a Mrs. T. A. Zimmerman. Hubert was shown a room 10 feet by 12 feet at the rear of the ground floor. His Dad said, "From here on, it's on you," and drove off.

Hubert got in the long registration line, then wandered about until he could relocate his rooming house. As he told it later, his higher education commenced right then. Mrs. Zimmerman was one of those ample, knowing, immensely patient women who make a life of taking in boys from the country, feeding them heartily, getting them up for early classes, tolerating their japes and scrapes and generally helping them find their way in the big city. On her front porch the upperclassmen lounged in rockers, loudly admiring the passing coeds. Over the first dinner, Hubert, fresh from the wilds of Dakota, dropped the fact that he came from a town that knew nothing of junior or senior proms. Sizing up the new boy, Ma Zim, as they all called her, decided that before anything else he must learn to dance. She called in her daughter Grace to show Hubert the first steps. Then she said: "Now you go down to the Marigold Ballroom and get yourself a girl—and don't ever admit that you don't know how to dance." The Marigold was a popular Minneapolis spot for young people to meet, and the boy from Doland found it was fun. From there, Ma Zim steered him to the "sunlight dances" at the Student Union, where, his confidence growing, he acquired his first girl friend. "I was awfully sweet on Gloria Bock," he said later.

This was probably Hubert's most notable educational experience that first year. In class, Doland's whiz kid ran well back in the pack. He joined the freshman debate team but was turned down by the student newspaper. Often he hitchhiked home on weekends. And when he returned to Doland at Christmas his father, who had been sending him ten dollars a week to live on, said he could no longer afford the allowance. So Hubert, returning, got a job washing dishes at twenty cents per hour at Swoboda's campus drugstore, scrounging just enough food behind the counter to get by the rest of his freshman year. In the fall his father decreed it was the turn of his brother Ralph, who had stayed out in Hubert's favor the year before, to go to the university. "I can't have you and Ralph gone at the same time," he said. "I need one of you to help me in the store." So Ralph inherited Hubert's job at Swoboda's campus drugstore, and Hubert worked for his Dad until Christmas. Then Uncle Harry, who was the family's shining example and leading proponent of higher education, came to Hubert's rescue. A fifty-dollar check arrived from the plant scientist in Washington—"something to start you back in school," he wrote Hubert. On the strength of this slender sum, Hubert's father consented to his return for the university's winter quarter. Hitchhiking back to school, Hubert was able to pay his tuition bill with Uncle Harry's check. For the rest he eked out the term waiting tables for Ma Zim, swabbing floors at Swoboda's, and—after one quarter's study of the subject—tutoring in French.

For the Humphreys, 1931 offered the most desperate of winters—so desperate that H. H. decided to give up on Doland. Climbing into his Ford he took off for Minneapolis and hunted out Hubert at Swoboda's. "I've just got to get out," he said, and told Hubert of his plan to leave the failing business in Doland and make a new start in Huron. Fifty miles to the south, it was the fifth-largest town in South Dakota, with paved streets, traffic lights, a college, a courthouse—and five well-established drugstores. "But the town is growing, and I've found a place there to rent," he said.

The turmoil this news touched off in the son may well be imagined. But next day H. H. took Hubert along as he called on his wholesaler and got the financial help he had to have—an extension on his bills, a line of credit to start the new store. H. H. moved into a rented room in Huron, while back home in Doland Christine and his daughters stayed on so that Fern, the youngest, could finish school. In March 1931, the first ad appeared in the *Daily Huronite* for a new drugstore: "Humphrey's ADVANTAGES—3 candy bars for 10¢. Remember the slogan: 'Humphrey Wants to See You.' " When few came to see him, H. H. slashed prices ("candy bars 5 for 10¢; the world's thickest malted milk and your choice of 15¢ sandwiches for a quarter.") When his sons arrived home after winter-term exams, they dropped out of the university. They had to help if their father's business was to survive.

This touched off a painful and protracted conflict for Hubert Humphrey. He worshiped his father. He was as gregarious as his father, and he was ambitious. Within him, moreover, burned energies far more intense than those of H. H. Yet for the next five years, to help make a go of the business, Hubert repressed those drives and stayed in Huron. From age twenty to age twenty-six he vanished from college, from the city, from Ma Zim's, from the whole wide world of higher learning. It was something like that long spell in the early life of another son of the Missouri valley, Harry Truman, who stayed home and for a decade drove a four-mule gangplow on the family farm at Grandview.

What Hubert went through was a classic young-adult crisis of the kind that Erik Erikson described in writing about Luther and Gandhi. As identity crises go, Hubert's was unusually long and drawn out, with two symptoms: fainting spells and a nervous stomach. They plagued him through these years, during which he was thin, even emaciated; when he escaped from his father's store in 1937, they disappeared.

Like everybody in the family, Hubert threw himself into the initial fight to survive in the new town. Ralph checked the other stores' prices on Saturday night. Christine and the girls pitched in to cook the blue-plate specials and butter the sandwiches. The whole family ate lunch at the store. One day a man from the Chamber of Commerce came in to say that the other merchants were unhappy about their price-cutting. The usually mild-mannered H. H. lost his temper. Shouting that his family came first, he hauled down his Chamber membership sign, handed it to the man, and said, "Get the hell out of here."

Farmers, especially those whose bills H. H. had forgiven at Doland, were the most frequent patrons. In the absence of cash, the Humphreys bartered goods for potatoes, butter, eggs. They swapped drugs for chickens, which they duly killed, plucked, turned into salad, and sold in sandwiches. Down in the basement Hubert mixed big barrels of minerals into medicines for animal and man. That was when "Humphrey's Nose Drops" appeared on the counter alongside Vicks Vaporub. And out of the basement came also "Humphrey's BTV" (Body Tone Veterinary), an imitation of a radio-advertised concoction called Master Liquid Hogtone. H. H. bustled around the countryside peddling the stuff to farmers for worming their hogs, while his sons manned the store.

Though the town reacted coldly to the newcomers, the Humphreys were welcomed at church. The whole family transferred at once to Huron's Methodist church, which was much larger than Doland's. Hubert, lively, outgoing, fresh from the university, seemed an especially attractive new member. Dewey Van Dyke, one of the elders, approached him about taking over as scoutmaster of the church's Troop 6. Eager for acceptance by families in the community, Hubert was quick to agree. He started basketball games in the church basement. He brought the boys to the drugstore and gave them small tasks that could be done in a group. And although his scouts had no money for camp in 1931, Hubert found a way in the worst of the summer's dust-storm grit and grasshoppers to lead an overnight, cooking a great heap of inexpensive rice as the troop's only fare.

Everything that Hubert did had to be subordinate to making the store survive. This was hard on the effervescent youth in many ways—not only because of the long hours he had to work. Returning to Doland from his first college year, he had met Caroline Rich, a June graduate of the high school in nearby Waubay who had come to help her sister, Mrs. Margaret Hahn, run the town hotel. When they went out together, to a church social or to swim at Lake Kampeska Caroline had to provide the car. Hubert never had any money, and his father, Caroline said later, was "real strict, sharp, demand-ing." Hubert was "such a nervous person," so fidgety that Caroline's sister would say that when he came to visit she "had to put everything away—he never kept his feet or hands still." Hubert gave Caroline a ring—his grand-mother's—and they took it for granted they would marry. Hubert wrote her letters about how hard he worked, about having to become a pharmacist, never about political interests or ambitions. Finally, Caroline grew tired of waiting and married another. In Huron, Hubert then went out with one Ruth Guthmiller, known as Gutsy. She thought him a good dancer but not wanting the scouts, the church, the store, she dropped out of his life too.

Hubert seemed locked in. On Armistice Day 1932, the first dust storm hit Huron. "I didn't know what it was," he said later. "It looked like a terrible smoke cloud. It blacked out the sun. I thought it was the end of the world. Then a fine, terrible silt engulfed everything." In the harshest season of get-ting established in the new town, his father's interest in politics quickened. To the old Bryan Populist, it looked as if the hour had finally struck in South Dakota. Many farmers were dusted out and the rest were made radical by the wave of mortgage foreclosures, bank failures, and depressed grain prices, and when they marched through town to rallies, H. H. told his son, "Respect them. What they spend in our store keeps us going." The Democrats, having elected William Bulow their first senator in state history, came to life in Huron. In 1936, after the dust had darkened the skies for four straight years and Franklin Roosevelt toured the drouth-stricken plains, his train stopped at Huron. H. H. not only went aboard to shake his hand but brought along his son and introduced him to the president. Made chairman of the local party, H. H. met with state leaders and began to have thoughts of standing for Congress. His brother Harry wrote from Washington that "those who know you would like to have you represent them." But for the moment the word in the capital, Harry added, was that the new senator and his aides were barring the way.

In carrying out his political plans, H. H. determined to make a druggist of Hubert. He reasoned that if he were to run for office, someone else would have to fill prescriptions at the store while he was away. Of his two sons, only Hubert seemed up to qualifying as a registered pharmacist in the short time for which the father could afford schooling. Within the family there seems to have been no question about it. For Hubert, child of the Depression, uncontrollable economic forces were battering their lives, and only by utmost exertions could the family be saved. Summoning all his loyalty to his Dad, he agreed to go back to school, to the Capitol College of Pharmacy in Denver.

Organizing his days in a minute-by-minute schedule, setting his roommates to boning up on selected topics, Hubert more than met his father's highest expectations. By dint of memorizing the English and Latin names and prescribed dosages of all the drugs listed in the druggists' Pharmacopoeia, he completed a two-year course in six months. It was a prodigious achievement, a turning point—and a breaking point. His sister Frances believed that the effort profoundly changed him: "Some of the emotional and spiritual things he went through that year to physically and spiritually survive changed him. I remember his telling me that he became very faint right before the exam, and when he came to, a lot seemed very clear to him. He'd been working under such pressure, there were things that bothered him so much, and when he went in and took the exam he passed, I think, second highest. From then on he used to have what we call a nervous stomach."

Back in the piercing winds and blinding dust of Dakota, Hubert tried his gabby, cheery best to carry on at the prescription counter. But try as he would he could not always keep his strong drives bottled up. In the summer of 1933 the most exciting event in Middle America was Chicago's World's Fair, and Hubert, twenty-two, wanted to hitchhike to the opening. His father forbade him. A shouting match ensued. Hubert threatened to leave home for good—and took out his frustration by smashing glasses behind the lunch counter.

Still, Hubert continued to keep up with the scouts, sometimes took a girl dancing, and, after the Roosevelt visit, helped start the Young Democrats in Huron. But the hours at the store, now that his diploma hung alongside H. H.'s, grew longer than ever. He experienced stomach pains and fainting spells, but doctors could find nothing wrong with him.

One day Hubert met a Huron College sophomore, Muriel Buck. Although they may have seen each other earlier at a college dance, their important encounter took place when a friend of Muriel's took her into the drugstore to meet "this new boy in town." Hubert thought her "shapely, attractive, shyly charming and independent." To Muriel he seemed "so young, unbelievably skinny, 130 pounds at the most. And he had great big bony knees."

Muriel's father bought and sold produce—cream, eggs, chickens, turkeys. The family was Presbyterian and Andy Buck looked down on the Humphreys as pushy arrivists. But Hubert and Muriel began to date. She said later: "The store came first, always. Our dates came after the store closed.

Then his father would like to go for a ride. So we'd pile into the Model A Ford and drive out to the end of the cement highway—seven miles. And when we'd come back H. H. always wanted me to have a malt. Then after we'd got H. H. home, why then Hubert would take me home. So our dates would go into the early mornings, and Hubert's mother would have a fit."

Hubert's mother was problematic—and not only for Hubert's girl. Christine Humphrey was capable of inviting to the house a former girl friend of Hubert's, one for whom she could not have spoken a good word as long as Hubert dated her, simply to embarrass Hubert and spite Muriel. Hubert's mother, then and later, was often described as "nervous." She was as inward and withdrawn as her husband was outgoing. Her circle of friends seemed deliberately small and perhaps some buried inferiority complex kept her from extending herself to others. Yet she, too, was a strong personality, offsetting her husband not only by force of temperament but also by her stern religious upbringing. She joined her hail-fellow husband as a Methodist but remained rooted in an unsmiling Lutheran pietism. Long after her son had attained high office, she stubbornly wished that he had become, instead, a preacher. Moreover, it was an open joke in the family that she disapproved of Democrats, lamenting that her son had joined the other side. Thus if there was affection in this close knit family there were also tensions, tensions so deep and abiding that they left their mark on Hubert Humphrey.

While many forces at home conspired to keep Hubert a pharmacist in Huron, other people encouraged him to think of the future. His Uncle Harry in Washington, who had taken Frances into his home so that she could attend college there, wrote long letters urging him to get on with his education. His old high school principal at Doland reminded him that he had yet to tap his talent for public speaking. And his friends Dewey and Hazel Van Dyke— Hazel was watching over Muriel's dying mother—were like surrogate parents to the courting pair. In long talks at the Van Dyke kitchen table on Sundays, Dewey urged Hubert to *be somebody*. Muriel told Mrs. Van Dyke, "Hazel, there's too much family." All the time, H. H. laid his plans—which now included maybe opening branch drugstores in other Dakota towns—in the expectation that Hubert would go on working at the store.

Then in the summer of 1935 the Van Dykes, whose only son was a member of Hubert's troop, helped Hubert break away to lead his scouts to Washington. He stayed with his Uncle Harry, who took him to see what he most wanted to see: the Jefferson Memorial. They went on to the Senate gallery, where Hubert got to hear Huey Long deliver one of his fiery speeches. Then for once, so far from Huron, Hubert felt free enough to express what he could not bring himself to say back home. In its first innocent words, the letter he wrote Muriel reflected what Uncle Harry had been dinning into his ears: "This trip has impressed one thing on my mind, Muriel,—the need of an education, an alert mind, clean living, and a bit of culture."

But the tug of Huron was still strong as he went on to add: "I don't necessarily mean more college is necessary, but I need to do more reading, more writing, more thinking if I ever want to fulfil my dream of being someone in this world." Then, finally, he let his fantasy flow:

Maybe I seem foolish to have such vain hopes and plans but, Bucky, I can see how some day, if you and I just apply ourselves and make up our minds to work for bigger things, how we can someday live here in Washington and probably be . . . in Congress.

Don't laugh at me, Muriel. Maybe it does sound rather egotistical and beyond reason but Muriel, I do know others have succeeded. Why haven't I a chance? You'll help me, I know. . . .

Did Hubert feel liberated during that visit to Washington? His sister Frances, who gave up her room at Uncle Harry's and slept on the sofa, said later that she had never seen him so exhilarated, and he was free of stomach pains.

But back in Huron troubles returned, multiplied. Muriel's mother died, and her father lost his business. When he tried renting a few cabins at his Bigstone Lake retreat, Muriel went to help him, and the only way the young couple could meet was by Hubert hitchhiking the 150 miles to the lake after the drugstore closed Saturday nights. When both were in town they sometimes went out to Lampe's pavilion to dance on Wednesday nights. But H. H. still paid his son, age twenty-five, no salary, and Hubert was reluctant to take money from the till for their dates. When in September 1936 they were married, the wedding was held early in the morning—early, Hubert said later, so that his father could open the store on time. They honeymooned in his father's car (and paid expenses with her father's sixty-five-dollar wedding gift). At parental request his sister Frances tagged along in the back seat to catch a train at Watertown. At Minneapolis, the couple ate at the Forum cafeteria; at Duluth they went for a brief ride on a lake steamer. Then, twelve miles short of Huron on the way back, Hubert ran into a cow—and the battered car had to be pushed the rest of the way home from their honeymoon. Hubert had to pay the farmer twenty-five dollars for his cow.

In Huron they rented a tiny house from the Van Dycks. Muriel took a job as bookkeeper at a local power company, and for the first time in Hubert's life his father paid him a salary. The young pair had serious talks in the evening. As Muriel recalled later:

Hubert hated the wind, it really bothered him. And the dust! It would depress us terribly. You couldn't live in that country, you couldn't exist almost, if you didn't have some kind of imagination, and ideals that would keep you going.

We had a lot of serious talks. . . . We got a world map out, we lay on the floor and went over it. . . . But then we began talking about going to the University of Minnesota, and we talked with two other couples, and all made our plans to go back."

Muriel saved her seventy-five-dollar monthly pay ("It went right into Postal Savings, for fear of using a bank"). And as the young couple's intentions hardened, tension mounted at the Humphreys'. Having won election as state representative, H. H. went off to the legislative session at Pierre. Although Ralph could run the store capably enough, no one could fill prescriptions in H. H.'s absence but Hubert, who could also joke and jolly with the customers. But everybody remarked how thin he was, and his fainting spells continued. Hubert and Muriel went oftener for long talks at the Van Dyke kitchen table. Muriel finally said, "If we don't do something, we can't live together." The Van Dyke support for the youngsters' breakaway made the Humphreys very unhappy.

Hubert brought himself to speak his mind. One night as they worked late, his father suggested they go for a ride. Closing the store at midnight, they got into the car and drove down to the southeast edge of town. H. H. parked the car and, turning to his son, said: "Hubert, what's wrong with you?" Sympathetic, he expected to be told of some physical ailment. "Why, nothing," Hubert answered. "Well, what seems to be the matter?" the older man pressed. "I notice it in our business." Then Hubert gave him the answer, "Dad, I don't want to peddle pills."

H. H. sat for a long time silent. Then he said heavily: "If that's the case, we'll have to make other plans." He gave up the idea of running for reelection or standing for higher office.

It was from that moment that Hubert set his sights on finishing his studies at the University of Minnesota. By the fall of 1937, Muriel had amassed $675 in savings, and off they went. Hubert never again had fainting spells.

PART TWO

The City

6

Minneapolis, City on the Skids

T HE Minneapolis to which the young Humphreys moved in the fall of 1937 had been a city for some sixty years. The men who owned its industries and dominated its affairs were, most of them, the sons and grandsons of its founders. They had come west from New England and built a city in the wilderness. They had cut timber, laid railroads, and raised flour mills to grind the wheat of the Northern plains. They had built stately homes on Lowry Hill and around the city's seven lakes. They had established good schools for their children. They had laid out wide, elm-shaded streets and cool, green parks around the falls of Minnehaha and along the banks of the mighty Mississippi, Father of Waters. They had made Minneapolis a lusty, confident and beautiful city.

But in 1937 the city was torn by trouble and edgy with tension. It had been going downhill since the end of World War I. Its once-great lumber industry, having stripped the North Woods, had moved West; its flour-milling preeminence was fading; and the big iron mines to the north were operating at 10 percent of capacity.

The opening of the Panama Canal in 1920 made shipping goods from the West coast cheaper by sea than by land. Twin City railroad builders stopped dreaming of a rail-knit empire and commerce reaching to the Pacific coast and beyond. An Interstate Commerce Commission ruling in 1922 had put Minneapolis industries at a disadvantage in freight rates, compared with manufacturers who shipped from the big Eastern centers. Located as it was at the heart of a great farm region, Minneapolis had been hard hit by agriculture's failure to rally with the rest of the nation after the calamitous drop in farm prices at war's end. The city's farming hinterland had suffered hard times for years before the Wall Street crash of 1929 ushered in the Great Depression.

On the outskirts of Minneapolis were the bungalows and frame cottages of the city's middle class, of the white-collar workers and the small-town merchants who had retired when times were good and settled on the city's fringes. Many of them were Scandinavian. The ethnic character of Minneapolis was—and is—apparent in the faces of the men and women on the streets, appreciably blonder than most of the American population. They and their neighbors, who included many of German descent as well, worked for the gentry from New England on Lowry Hill.

In its heyday, Minneapolis had been a hard-driving Republican city, and its Yankee builders and their offspring managed to keep it an open-shop town. Led by Tom Lowry, the utilities magnate, they smashed a transit strike in 1916 and, thereafter, kept wages lower than in most other cities. As early as 1908 they formed the Citizens Alliance for the purpose of preventing their employees from organizing. With a huge pool of displaced lumberjacks and farmhands always available in the flophouses around Seven Corners and along the Washington Avenue riverfront, they were triumphantly successful. Throughout the 1920s only some twenty-five thousand Minneapolis workers belonged to unions, almost all in the conservative craft unions of the building trades.

For all the rockbound Republicanism of its biggest city, the state of Minnesota had experienced a good many political uprisings from the time that Jim Hill brought the Scandinavians to settle on farms along his railroad tracks. The Grange movement, the agrarian protest force largely responsible for the first railroad regulation enacted in the 1880s, sprang from the countryside sixty miles north of Minneapolis. The most picturesque of all Populists, Congressman Ignatius Donnelly penned his broadsides against the robber barons and his treatises on Shakespeare from a little town sixty miles to the south.

What stirred the farmers to fury was the unequal exchange between city and countryside. They felt themselves helplessly disadvantaged in having to sell at harvest time when the flood of grain drove the price to its lowest, and then being forced to buy city-made necessities at prices that seemed impervious to such ups and downs. The biggest and most combative cooperatives in America led by the Farmers Union, took root among the Minnesota growers who felt robbed by a system in which Minneapolis millers paid them little for grain but Minneapolis merchants shipped them machines, fuels, and processed feed at stiff prices. Demanding state ownership of flour mills, Charles A. Lindbergh, father of the aviator, ran for governor in 1920 as the candidate of two outfits known as the Farmers Non-Partisan League and the Working

People's Non-Partisan League. He lost, and, four years later, so did Minne-apolis's young county attorney Floyd Olson, who ran as candidate of a unified Farmer-Labor movement.

But Floyd Bjornstjerne Olson was an adroit politician with broad popular appeal. When banks failed across the state and farm prices plummeted, Olson swept into office in 1930 at the head of a militant Farmer-Labor party; and things began to change. So grim by then was the farmers' plight that the most desperate banded together in the Farm Holiday Association, demanded a moratorium on mortgage foreclosures, and smashed the trucks of those who did not join. In Minneapolis, where a quarter of all breadwinners were out of work, men lined up by the thousands on icy mornings for soup. Governor Olson, who had talked about establishing the Cooperative Commonwealth in Minnesota, was forced to seek resources at once to meet human needs. Spurning party lines in the 1932 elections, he organized Roosevelt-Olson campaign clubs and, as soon as the new President took office, rushed to Washington for emergency aid. Back in Minnesota, he rammed through an income tax, a mortgage moratorium, and relief for the hungry. If capitalism did not bring quick improvement, he told farmers on the Capitol steps, "I hope the present system of government goes right down to hell." To Farmer-Labor convention delegates he said: "I am not a liberal, I am . . . a radical. . . . I want a definite change in the system." The party platform led off: "We declare that capitalism has failed."

Violence was in the air. In St. Paul, where John Dillinger, Al Karpis, and Babyface Nelson were resident gunslingers, gangs kidnaped bankers and brewers and held them for ransom. In Minneapolis, where down-and-outers fought over bread crusts in riverside Hoovervilles, the Citizens Alliance mustered goons, spies, stool pigeons, Burns detectives, and grand-jury fixers to keep the unions down. Visiting the city in December 1933, Lorena Hickok, Eleanor Roosevelt's friend, wrote to Harry Hopkins: "The businessmen are organizing and preparing for a showdown with Labor. . . . The Citizens Alliance is getting into the show."

When the showdown came, it was practically civil war. On the employers' side stood Pillsburys, Washburns, Crosbys, Daytons, and such crusty old-sters as A. W. Strong, the Citizens Alliance president, who personally bossed his factory, paid his hands eighteen dollars per week, and sent turkeys at Christmas to those with perfect attendance records. Leading Labor's fight were a handful of activists schooled in the Puget Sound sawmill and Montana smelter strikes of the old Industrial Workers of the World. The most notable of these blooded veterans of Wobbly wars were the Dunne brothers.

Anything but outsiders, the six Dunne brothers had grown up in Little Falls, Minnesota, hometown also of Charles A. Lindbergh. Sons of an Irish immigrant laborer and French-Canadian mother, they attended parochial schools. The story goes that one day their priest caught the eldest, William F. (Bill) Dunne, reading a Victor Hugo novel to the others, tore the book to pieces, and banned them all from his confirmation classes. From that day, it is said, the boys became rebels.

Bill Dunne led a wartime strike in Butte, joined the Communists in 1919, worked for the Comintern in Moscow, and later edited the *Daily Worker*. His younger brothers—Vincent Raymond (Ray), Grant, and Miles—became Communists, too, but when the party split in the 1920s, they went with Trotsky instead of Stalin. Ray, who had also led strikes in the West, became their leader. But later he returned to Minneapolis and from 1921 to 1933 worked for the De Laittre Dixon Coal Company; he shoveled coal, drove a truck, and was a weighmaster, dispatcher, and even superintendent. His employers seem to have been fond of him, never objecting to his political ideas and even offering him stock in the company. Of the handful of Minneapolis Trotskyites, a few others worked in the coal yards, including his brothers, Carl Skoglund and Farrell Dobbs.

In 1933 a subsidiary of the Ford Motor Company took over the De Laittre coal yard and fired Ray Dunne for his political activity. Thereupon Dunne decided to organize the coal workers, choosing the International Brotherhood of Teamsters as his vehicle. The Teamsters had no more than 800 members in the city, scattered through separate locals of milk, ice, cartage, and others. The General Drivers Local 574 that he singled out had barely 90 members. But it had a usefully broad charter. The Dunne brothers, Skoglund, and Dobbs found a receptive ear in Bill Brown, president of Local 574 and head of the citywide Teamster joint council. The coal truckers were being paid 40 cents per hour—from twelve dollars to eighteen dollars per week for fifty-four to ninety hours' work—and had to wait in their trucks for hours without pay while the freight was loaded. Washington's first New Deal legislation had sparked some interest, and demand for coal was at its peak during the winter season.

As expected, the chief of the employers, a Citizens Alliance stalwart, would not even talk to Bill Brown. So on February 7, 1933, five hundred truck drivers and helpers struck for union recognition. Ray Dunne had planned it with military precision, mapping all 67 coal yards, setting up stationary and cruising picket squads, and handing their picked captains mimeographed instructions. Rather than picket every yard, the cruising teams centered on the big ones. When they caught a scab truck, they dumped its contents. After the first day, the Minneapolis *Journal* reported "not a wheel turning." The industry, the men said, was "shut tight as a bull's eye in fly time." On the third day, the employers capitulated and granted recognition to Local 574.

The coal strike was only a first scuffle. All of a sudden everybody else saw what Ray Dunne had seen: trucks were so essential to Minneapolis's function as a distribution center for the region that four thousand drivers held the life of the city in their hands.

On the union side, Dunne drove hard to line up members, staging big Sunday night forums capped by a huge Shubert Theatre rally to which Gov-

ernor Olson sent word that they should "organize and fight for their demands."
By early spring, three thousand men had signed up. On the employer front,
the Citizens Alliance stepped in to stiffen the backs of the trucking bosses.
In a strategy session at the West Hotel its leaders told representatives of the
eleven major trucking companies that the alliance had smashed the 1916 drivers strike at a cost of $25,000 and could do the job again inexpensively. As a
result, the Minneapolis Employers of Drivers and Helpers was formed; it
promptly rejected Local 574's demands for the closed shop, shorter hours,
and weekly pay of $27.50. On May 15, only three months after the coal
drivers' strike, the membership of 574 voted overwhelmingly to strike the
city's trucking industry.

Again, Ray Dunne laid plans like a commanding general. The union rented
an old garage at Eighteenth and Chicago Avenue for field headquarters. Picket
captains stationed around the city sent in messages of truck movements. In
the office, aides at four telephones wrote down the reports and passed them
to Farrell Dobbs, the dispatcher. Over a loudspeaker, Dobbs or Dunne then
ordered cars out by number and assigned men to them from a pool of hundreds
of strikers standing by in the garage. When police tapped the wires, messages
were transmitted in code. A scouting force of five motorcyclists roamed the
streets nonstop looking for trouble spots. Pickets posted on some fifty roads
stopped every truck entering the city and turned back all without union
clearance papers. Guards prowled the garage for stool pigeons. On the roof,
four sentries armed with tommy guns watched for intruders.

Inside the garage, where mass rallies took place nightly, members of the
cooks' union with the help of 120 women served meals around the clock to
as many as ten thousand strikers and their families; a pair of doctors manned
a first-aid post; and fifteen mechanics kept the one hundred trucks and squad
cars in repair.

With all but unionized ice, milk, and coal wagons stopped, the employers
mobilized for action. Mayor A. G. Bainbridge and Police Chief Mike Johannes lent their aid. On the morning of May 21, a Citizens Army—businessmen deputized as auxiliary law officers for the day—marched into Minneapolis's
Central Market. One member was Alfred Lindley, a socially prominent young
man back from Yale, who wore jodhpurs and a polo helmet. At strike headquarters, the dispatchers flashed their orders, and from flanking sides two
columns of pickets converged on the market. At the sight of the first column
of six hundred, marching into the market in military formation, four abreast,
each armed with a club, the Citizens Army fell back. Then when the police
drew their guns at approach of the second column, the strike leaders ordered
"Picket's Charge." A truck loaded with twenty-five unionists drove into the
police ranks at high speed. The cops scattered right and left and thereby, as
Dunne foresaw, lost any chance of using their guns without endangering
their own forces. The pickets then took on the cops hand to hand and carried
the day by force of numbers. Some thirty policemen and three or four pickets
were injured—but nobody was shot. By what their strike newspaper exult-

antly called the Battle of Deputies Run, the Teamsters held the market.

But Chief Johannes was determined to clear the streets, and the battle resumed next morning. Both sides took up positions in the market. A merchant moved a few tomato crates before his shop. Seizing one of the boxes, a picket heaved it through the plate-glass window. Vicious hand-to-hand fighting broke out. The police did not use firearms. More numerous and better armed with baseball bats and lead pipes, the pickets won control of the market place within an hour. Pickets chased the police and remnants of the Citizens Army through the streets. But in this second day of the Battle of Deputies Run, two members of the Citizens Alliance had been killed, including C. Arthur Lyman, vice president of the Citizens Alliance. Some fifty were wounded.

After the shock of such bloodshed, Governor Olson won a truce by threatening to call out the National Guard. Collective bargaining started up, but neither side would talk to the other. Mediators sent in by Washington spent their time running back and forth between the two headquarters with proposals and counter-proposals. On May 25, the Regional Labor Board announced an "agreement"—a Board "order" in language so ambiguous it settled nothing. Truck operations resumed in Minneapolis—and both sides prepared for the next round of warfare. The Citizens Alliance raised a lot of money; Local 574 laid in a lot of food, including meat and potatoes brought in by the Farm Holiday Association. The union newspaper advertised: "FOR SALE: one half bushel of special deputy badges—very slightly used."

On July 17, the May "agreement" having fallen apart, the union struck again. The federal mediators proposed a new settlement, which the strikers accepted. Again the employers rejected the deal. Their plan now, with police complicity, was to stage a riot that would force Governor Olson to call out the National Guard—and break the strike. There is reason to believe that Dunne and Dobbs at their dispatcher's telephones understood what was up but, as class warriors, took the bait anyway. At 2 P.M. on "Bloody Friday," July 20, when the thermometer stood at 102 degrees Fahrenheit, fifty heavily armed police escorted a truck to the market area, where a few boxes were loaded. Then, closely followed by a police convoy, the truck moved off into the next street. On orders from strike headquarters, a vehicle carrying pickets cut across the truck's path.

The police fired. Two men toppled back into their truck. Other pickets rushed in. The police fired again. As the pickets ran to pick up their wounded, the police peppered them with buckshot. Another line of union skirmishers came in. The police kept firing. It was over in a few minutes. Sixty-seven persons were wounded, two fatally. One policeman was hurt. That night at the city hospital nurses showed the strikers' wounds—almost all in the back of the head and legs—to the Minneapolis *Star*'s Eric Sevareid. He wrote: "They had been shot while trying to run out of the ambush." Sevareid also said: "Suddenly I knew . . . what Fascism was."

The union now had slain martyrs. Henry Ness, a picket, war veteran, father of four, received thirty-seven slugs in his body. A throng numbering between twenty thousand and one hundred thousand marched with his body from strike headquarters to the cemetery.

By now, Minneapolis was in chaos, and on July 25 the federal mediators proposed a vote on union recognition and minimum wages of fifty-two and a half cents per hour for drivers and forty-two and a half cents for helpers. Local 574 voted 1,866 to 147 to accept. The employers refused. Governor Olson thereupon proclaimed martial law. Though the governor's sympathies were with the strikers, the military, as the employers had anticipated, granted permits freely. In a few days truck traffic was two-thirds of normal. At a huge protest meeting, Bill Brown, president of Local 574, denounced the "strikebreaking" state government, and it looked as if the employer strategy of provoking martial law would pay off. Faced with union defiance, Governor Olson had to assert the sovereignty of the state by the use of force. At 4 P.M. on August 1, guardsmen with machine guns surrounded the garage at Eighteenth and Chicago and arrested Ray and Miles Dunne along with Bill Brown. The strikers were disarmed; the three captured leaders were imprisoned in a stockade at the fair grounds; and warrants were issued for those at large.

But Olson was not done. On August 3, rumbling that "the Citizens Alliance dominates and controls the Employers' Advisory Committee," he sent the National Guard to raid the Citizens Alliance building. Then he cracked down on the truck owners, drastically limiting permits for most unless they agreed to the mediators' peace plan. At this, forty-seven smaller companies caved in and signed up. But the more important employers not only resisted but went to court in a move to break the governor's power. They sought an injunction against his martial law as a deprivation of property under the fourteenth Amendment. Accepting the challenge, Olson said he would argue the case in person. But first he secured a two-day delay.

This was to allow him time to visit a friend in Rochester. The friend was President Roosevelt, who had stopped off in southern Minnesota to pay tribute to the Mayo brothers at their clinic on his way home from a Pacific tour. A delegation of Minneapolis labor leaders, none of them from Local 574, had already tried to see the president in Rochester and left a statement with his secretary that the Citizens Alliance was blocking "collective bargaining" of the kind his administration upheld. Behind the alliance, they wrote, stood "appointees of the federal government who through the control of credit are presenting a settlement of the strike." Three Minneapolis officials of the Reconstruction Finance Corporation, all bankers and "all reactionary Republicans held over from the Hoover regime," their memorandum charged, were compelling "employers to join [the Citizens Alliance] . . . in the war on trade unions, or find their credit ruined."

Unlike the unionists, Olson had a private audience with the president. Nothing is known of what was said, or whether he told Roosevelt the bankers were using their financial power to enforce employer resistance. But that

same day, Jesse Jones, head of the Reconstruction Finance Corporation, telephoned the federal mediator in Minneapolis, who later said that Jones "suggested getting in touch at once" with the bankers. Despite two more phone
calls from Jones, the bankers stalled until Olson, arguing that his martial law
was necessary to preserve property and life in Minneapolis, induced the court
to turn down the employers' request for an injunction. The mediators then
submitted a new plan. Once again, the union accepted and the employers
rejected it. Once more, presumably at White House prodding and evidently
with some force, Jesse Jones intervened with the bankers. At last, resistance
among the trucking employers collapsed, and on August 21 agreement to the
mediators' deal was announced, ending the strike.

With that, Minneapolis ceased to be an open-shop town. The dictatorship
of the Citizens Alliance was smashed. In two years' time, Local 574 signed
contracts with five hundred Minneapolis employers and became the state's
biggest union. Operating as militant unionists, its Trotskyite* leaders—the
Dunnes, Skoglund, Dobbs—emerged victorious not only over the Lowry
Hill nobs but also, for the moment, over Dan Tobin, the crotchety old craft-
unionist boss of the International Teamsters Union who had tried repeatedly
to oust the Trotskyites as proponents of the mass-union heresy. While Tobin
sought unavailingly to draw the members of 574 to a more docile local, the
nimble-witted Dobbs went on to rouse the Teamsters in Chicago. There he
invented the "leapfrog" tactics of organizing over-the-road drivers in the Upper
Midwest, by which the Teamsters grew into America's biggest and most
powerful labor combine—a mass union on a semi-industrial basis of course.
Jimmy Hoffa, rising through the Central States Council started by Dobbs
before he abandoned union work for revolutionary politics, always remembered Farrell Dobbs as "a very far-sighted individual . . . draftsman and
architect of our road operations."

After the big truck strike, Minneapolis lived through some tense years.
Unemployment still ran high. A few first-family members talked hysterically
of fleeing the city, and small businessmen feared for the security of their
shops. Violent crimes occurred. President Bill Brown was murdered, as well
as another high Teamster official. Truck owners growled about union "dictatorship." Newspapers inveighed against "Communist control," and indeed
after Moscow's party-line switch to favoring alliance with non-Communist
elements in 1935, the Trotskyites faced rivals on the left. Communists of the
Stalinist stripe moved into Minnesota in significant numbers, infiltrating
Olson's Farm-Labor party and local units of the newly formed CIO.

In the flush of its success, labor elected a mayor of Minneapolis. But a
peculiarity of Minnesota politics was that for many offices candidates stood

---

*Trotskyites made up a small but extremely articulate group of Communists who sided with
Leon Trotsky against Stalin in the struggle to lead the movement after Lenin. When the exiled
hero of the Revolution formed his Fourth International, they took up his program of world
revolution and the establishment of pure revolution. Pronounced guilty of deviating from Moscow's "line," American Trotskyites were expelled by the Communist party in 1928.

without party designation—and this was true of the new mayor. In the poisoned air of fear and hate left by the big strike, he quarreled both with his backers and with his police. Underworld elements moved into the city's night spots, while fundamentalist clergy and evangelists, influential in a city of fervent Protestants, roared from their pulpits against Communists, labor "racketeers," and, in thinly veiled attacks, against Jews. The most striking feature of anti-Semitism in Minneapolis had always been the lack of Jewish participation in the leading economic activities of the city. Governor Olson, who had grown up among Jews on Minneapolis's north side—and could deliver stump speeches in Yiddish as well as Swedish or Norwegian—appointed the first significant number of Jews to state office. Following pulpit and other manifestations of prejudice, the fascist Silver Shirts became active in Minnesota, and it came out that George K. Belden, president of the Citizens Alliance, had attended one of its secret meetings. At this the Trotskyites organized a Union Defense Guard, consisting of two hundred members who drilled, engaged in target practice, and carried out a test mobilization.

In the midst of all the bitterness, Floyd Olson died of cancer, and that brought about a big shift in the balance of local forces. His unruly followers immediately fell to quarreling, and as the 1938 elections approached, the Farmer-Labor party split down the middle. In the outpouring of personal rancor and factional recriminations, prejudice against Jewish party and state officials who had been close to Olson played an ugly part. Capitalizing on the Farmer-Labor disarray, the Republican opposition easily recaptured the statehouse. At once labor found itself on the defensive, and the Trotskyist victors of the 1934 truck strike were subjected to daily harassment by state and local officials.

By 1941 the impact of the nation's preparing for war brought the federal government back into Minneapolis's civil strife—this time on the side of old Dan Tobin and the employers. Wanting to bring the Teamsters into line with President Roosevelt's rearmament program, Tobin decided he could tolerate Trotskyist control of Minnesota transport no longer. Appointing a receiver for the maverick local, he got a court order with the help of state officials and sent in hundreds of strong-arm types to seize its headquarters. Just two days later, Justice Department agents swooped down on the dispossessed Trotskyite leaders, arresting them under the newly enacted Smith Act. Two weeks before Pearl Harbor, Ray Dunne and seventeen others were convicted in Minneapolis federal court of conspiring to overthrow the U. S. government and sentenced to two years in prison. Attorney General Francis Biddle always denied that the prosecutions, the only ones ever carried out under the Smith Act, had anything to do with Dan Tobin's important help, financial and otherwise, to Roosevelt's third-term campaign the previous year. For Minneapolis, the crushing of the Dunnes ended an era of labor militancy but left a legacy of civic problems that were to provide an opportunity for a totally different political leader, such as Hubert Humphrey.

7

Return to the Campus

WHEN Hubert Humphrey came back to the city in the fall of 1937, the University of Minnesota was the third-largest institution of higher education in the land—only Berkeley and New York University were larger. As the state's sole land-grant school, located moreover in the state's largest city, its practice was to admit anybody in Minnesota with a high-school diploma. Along with the nominal tuition fees (slightly higher for out-of-staters like Humphrey), this practice responded to the powerful drive toward equal opportunity that Toqueville identified long ago as uniquely American. The equality thus assured to all comers lasted until the end of the first term, at which point the faculty asserted its own standards. Then a third of all entrants, having failed their exams, disappeared from the classes.

Those who survived to upper-class years found the campus was not quite so crowded. Humphrey, returning after six years' absence, entered this smaller, more serious world of learning. He was an upperclassman and he was married, which was not nearly so common on campus then as later. He was married, furthermore, to a young woman who had dedicated all her prior earnings to pay for his return to college. Hubert Humphrey had good reasons to apply himself.

According to his wife, re-entry was difficult. Humphrey said later: "I hadn't made up my mind what I really wanted to do. I just wanted to get away from the tension, the gloom back home. I wanted to strike out on my own." He signed up for every course he could get into. When the dean of students, crusty old Edward Nicholson, called him in to point out he had signed up for twenty-one hours when fifteen was the usual load, Humphrey replied that he was twenty-six years old and in a hurry to get through. Humphrey took a special course right away in how to study, and it helped. "He'd been away for so long," Muriel said later.

The atmosphere on campus reflected all the tensions that afflicted the surrounding city in the 1930s. When the Minneapolis truckers struck in 1934, boys from the Greek fraternities lined up with the police and the Citizens Alliance. Others marched with the strikers. In the depths of the Depression, students began to call for establishment of the Farmer-Labor cooperative commonwealth. The Jacobin club, sparked by Richard Scammon, strapping son of the medical school dean, wrested student offices away from the fraternity conformists. They assailed President Lotus Coffman and Dean Nicholson for serving a failing economic system rather than the cause of truth.

Of all the instruments designed to uphold the existing order, the rebels raged loudest against the military establishment. Phil Potter, a leading Jacobin and editor of the university daily, wrote fiery attacks on the military training that was compulsory for all students at land-grant institutions. Coffman and Nicholson replied by imposing censorship. When that failed, they tried intimidating the writers. Defiantly, Scammon assembled three hundred students in the recreation building one day to repeat the Oxford Oath: "I will not bear arms for flag and country." As a grim jest, they joined the "Veterans of Future Wars." Led by a University Peace Council, they staged a series of peace strikes. Then, when President Coffman refused them the auditorium for one such meeting in 1935, Governor Olson himself arrived to address the protesters from the steps of the forbidden hall. Denouncing the munitions makers then being grilled by Senator Nye's committee in Washington, Olson told the students that the profit motive lay at the root of much war propaganda and urged that steps be taken to eliminate it. In a mock convention in 1936, the students nominated Olson for president. With the governor plainly on the students' side, President Coffman bowed and halted compulsory military training. The change took effect not long before Humphrey arrived back at the university.

"I didn't have much time to join a protest movement," Humphrey said later. "I was concerned about being able to earn enough to eat." The young couple moved into a one-room apartment on the third floor of an old frame house facing Prospect Park. Another college pair, who had the other garret, shared the bath and kitchen. When Muriel's father dropped in for a visit, the first thing he noticed was the absence of any fire escape. He went out and bought a rope and laid it coiled by the window. By then the Humphreys could already see that Muriel's $675 savings would never see them through the year. Despite his heavy class load, Humphrey took a job as part-time pharmacist at Brown's campus drugstore. Muriel took off her wedding ring (with so many breadwinners out of work in Minneapolis, married women were not being hired) and went looking for a job too. Finally she found one as a bookkeeper at fifty cents per hour. When she was promoted to full-time work at $65 per month, she put her wedding ring back on.

Exhilarating as it was to be out from his Dakota bondage, Humphrey was not intellectually stimulated until after Christmas, when he enrolled in a class in American Constitutional Government, taught by a young instructor named Evron Kirkpatrick. For the returning student, the introduction to political science was his moment of takeoff. That was when the university became what he later called it—one of the three formative influences of his life (along with the Dakota dust bowl and his Dad). Sandy-haired, broad-faced, fun-loving, richly read in the art of government, and intensely interested in how to apply it, Kirkpatrick was an Indianan who had just taken his Ph.D. at Yale. He was also new at Minnesota, and younger by a year than Humphrey. His course, as he described it later, was "a review of the basic political arrangements we live under."

It was as if Humphrey had been living for this moment. As fast as Kirkpatrick opened topics, all the old ideas that Humphrey's father had put forth at the drugstore and supper table flooded to the surface of his consciousness. All the information that his father and friends had tossed around in those endless conversations by the soda fountain now gushed out of the storehouse of the young Humphrey's memory—and much of it spilled out in the machine-gun delivery of the Huron soda-slinger. He was forever bobbing up to speak; then after the bell rang he stood around at the front of the room talking further with the instructor. It was the same in Professor Benjamin Lippincott's class in political theory. Lippincott, somewhat older, was known around the campus as a philosophical radical, a Yale man trained in London by the socialist Harold Laski. He delighted in pushing students against the wall, puncturing their preconceptions with uncomfortable facts, making them justify their stands. Humphrey not only defended his positions but launched into speeches that Lippincott had to cut short to give others their chance. "You sit down," the professor barked. Humphrey sat down, grinning. Others took offense at the Socratic treatment, but not Humphrey. At term's end, Lippincott gave Humphrey a B and wrote beside his name: "Too glib." It was the only B Humphrey ever got in his straight-A record in Political Science at Minnesota.

Like Lippincott's, Kirkpatrick's class was small. One day another member, a football player named Orville Freeman sounded off during a discussion of European immigration movements into America. Freeman took the conventionally conservative line that northern Europeans were more stable and had contributed more to U. S. development than those from Mediterranean countries. To Humphrey this was an affront to the egalitarian spirit of America and an insult to the Greek and Roman origins of democracy. He burst into a round of citations from Jefferson and Bryan and Woodrow Wilson that turned the discussion into a debate that, Freeman said later, "Humphrey won." After class the two walked out together, and Humphrey swung the talk to football. "More than anything else," Freeman said, "he would have liked to play football. But he was just a spindly little guy—legs no bigger than a toothpick." Humphrey talked the quarterback into going out for debate, and the two became fast friends.

It was just a step from Burton Hall, where the class met, to the Humphrey garret, and sometimes the three of them, Humphrey, Freeman, and "Kirk," adjourned for sandwiches and several hours more talk at the Humphrey third-floor table. Other days the talk simply spilled out the classroom door and onto the Burton Hall steps, where Humphrey's bubbling discourse attracted not only other class members but also passing students. The topic might be the League of Nations, bankers, trade unions, the peace movement. Mostly, it was Humphrey talking. Every now and then there was a burst of laughter because his sallies had humor, his retorts had wit.

William Anderson, chairman of the department and eventually Humphrey's faculty adviser, had yet to meet the new boy. One day he called Kirkpatrick to a window and said: "Come here, look. I want to know who that fellow is. I see him every day on the steps with a big crowd around him." Kirkpatrick, looking down at his pupil carrying on amid fifteen or so grinning students, said: "That's Hubert Humphrey. I have him in my class."

The Humphreys, moving a half dozen times in two years, found a place where Humphrey acted as janitor in return for reduced rent. When fellow students dropped in for popcorn and talk late at night, they sometimes ran into their friend carrying a load of ashes out to the curb. Humphrey said later: "I swabbed toilets, I repaired the roof, fixed the plumbing, cleaned the sewers, shoveled the snow, and besides that, worked six hours a day in the drugstore for 20 cents an hour." Somehow, perhaps because he never seemed to go to bed, that did not keep Humphrey from these talkfests. Freeman and Humphrey's debate partner, P. Kenneth Peterson, who was Republican and conservative (and later ran against Humphrey for the Senate), cordially disliked each other and contrived never to drop in at the same time. On occasion the Humphreys went along on their friends' dates. With Freeman and his girl friend Jane and another couple, they rode off to a football weekend at Iowa City. Freeman was one of the few non-Dakotans permitted to call Humphrey, "Pinky."

The novelist Feike Feikema, visiting a Dakota friend at a campus rooming house, ran into "a slim, dark-haired fellow with high forehead and quick, dark-blue eyes" and heard him greeted as Pinky. Within minutes, he recalled later, Humphrey drew from him that he came from an Iowa farm, loved chess, was engaged, and already wrote for the newspapers. Dropping in at the drugstore to josh with his new friend, Feikema was "taken aback by the way he could be overly polite with a customer one moment and then the next argue intensely with me. I had always looked askance at store clerks with ass-licking manners." Dick Scammon, the Jacobin, also got to know Humphrey through stopping in at Browns and getting an argument about the peace movement along with his purchase of cigarettes.

By the time Humphrey landed on campus, Floyd Olson was dead, and his Farmer-Labor party already starting to break up. People were talking about a rising young Republican named Harold Stassen, who had designs on the statehouse. Humphrey, who had cast his vote twice for Roosevelt back in South Dakota, found himself practically unaligned in Minnesota, where Democrats had never amounted to much in state affairs. Even then, at a time when Roosevelt was denouncing "malefactors of great wealth" and releasing the names of all taxpayers with incomes of twenty-five thousand dollars or more, Humphrey was not exactly raising the roof over the inequitable distribution of property. In class he declared it was wrong and favored a much more widespread distribution of wealth. But as Lippincott recalled their sessions later, he was not dogmatic about it, even in comparison with other classroom Democrats. To Lippincott, "he was a liberal Democrat willing to find the middle every time." Yet he was strongly outspoken in defense of the poor. In class and out, he argued for giving the poor the justice they were denied in the courts of the day. In these discussions there was little talk about the black poor—simply, the poor.

Making his way through nineteen political science courses on the way to graduation, Humphrey read the basic writings of political thought: Plato, Aristotle, Locke, Hume, Montesquieu. He read Tocqueville and Bryce on America. He read the legal philosophers—Blackstone, Powicke, Sir Henry Maine. He read Laski's *Grammar of Politics*. He did not read all of these works, and there is no record that he owned a single one of them. But there is no question that he considered earning his living as a teacher of political science and was preparing himself accordingly.

On a Labor Day weekend, Humphrey and Freeman teamed up to organize what Lippincott recalled as a "socialist" conference. Typically, they invited conservative Professor Arthur Marget to speak the same evening as his radical colleague Professor Hans Lange. Those present thought Lange, who became Poland's foreign minister after the war, got much the better of it. But Humphrey insisted they had not planned it that way. Similarly, at the height of Farmer-Labor Governor Elmer Benson's 1938 reelection campaign, Humphrey and another of his debate teammates, C. Donald Peterson, addressed a youth rally at Minneapolis's Eagles Hall. As Peterson, later senior Republican member of the Minnesota Supreme Court, remembered it, they were only practicing their skills.

Touring Big Ten campuses as an intercollegiate debater, Humphrey was already developing a fairly pugnacious platform style—perhaps too much so for a prospective college professor. In November of that year he appeared at Madison to argue the negative on the question: "Resolved, the U. S. should form an alliance with Great Britain." A University of Wisconsin freshman noted that though Humphrey "had the poorest physical appearance and demeanor," used "questionable" grammar, and "talked out of the corner of his mouth like a Chicago gunman," he excelled in "ability to make contact with his audience." He won laughs and even applause with "satire and caustic humor." Another device he used was "to ask the audience a question and then go right on answering it: 'Do you want a war? Of course not!' " He also had "a clever way of belittling his opponent: 'Listen to Mr. Short, The fascists are coming, the fascists are coming? Believe me, professor, not on your life.' " Professor A. D. Huston of Urbana, on the judge's stand, awarded the decision to the negative. Humphrey, the judge held, "gave the impression of knowing more," and his team's rebuttals were more dextrous—evidence that Humphrey was already adept at ad-libbing.

On the other hand, a critique by the woman who taught Humphrey's Speech 98 course in his senior year has been preserved, and it is not flattering. She disliked the harsh intonations he had carried away from the wide open Dakotas and faulted him for sloppy enunciation. She noted that he had a "hard" voice, nasal to a degree. "He jammed the epiglottis down so the air could hardly get out the larynx. He humped his tongue densely in the back of his mouth. He pushed hard with the muscles of his throat instead of depending on his abdominal muscles to do the work. Consequently, he rasped and quacked."

These vocal habits "worked against him . . . setting off muscle tensions of resistance and escape in his audience," which "found him tiring to listen to for more than a few minutes." The instructor wrote he was "so concerned with his subject that he seldom worried about skids in grammar or slips in pronunciation ('AD-dress' for 'ad-DRESS,' 'kep' for 'kept,' dropping his g's). Although she awarded him an A and recorded that "his logical outlines were quite the best in the class," she deplored his inclination to "believe that attention to tone was a frill." She concluded: "If he does not change his habits of vocalization while he's a student, he will probably persist all his life in the unsatisfactory tension patterns, and will arouse an unnecessary amount of antagonism to his points of view, which will make him a less effective public servant."

There is perhaps a wry significance in this early comment about a speaker later acclaimed one of the best public speakers of his generation. Then and later, Humphrey's persuasiveness rested on the content of his speeches and the impassioned quality of his concern. He was something like the baseball pitcher who had an overpowering fast ball: with such a blazing pitch, he didn't need a curve. Yet Humphrey was not a natural such as William Jennings Bryan, whose marvelous voice rose from abdominal depths and carried effortlessly to the back of the biggest hall. Humphrey, in the words of his teacher, was "fighting the larynx" all his life.

At the time, the kind of "public servant" he was aiming to be was a teacher. Certainly he was not talking about running for office in his college years.

"How could we?" his wife said later. "We had no money." But even in the study of political science, what interested him most was its practical application. That is what brought him so close to the one teacher, Evron Kirkpatrick, who shared his intense interest in the practice of politics. A second, and older, member of the department accompanied Kirkpatrick several times to Humphrey's apartment during the student's last college year. This was Asher Christensen. More than any of his colleagues, Christensen, serving on committees and mediating in industrial disputes, had been drawn into local community affairs. Well and favorably known among labor leaders, he had been approached several times to run for mayor of Minneapolis, where the political situation had deteriorated after the bitter Teamster strike. Once he almost allowed his name to be entered, but at the last minute drew back from the primary contest. Kirkpatrick and Humphrey heard the arguments for and against his race. Acutely aware that Democrats ran a poor third for elective offices in Minnesota, they saw that a Democrat stood a much better chance contesting for mayor of Minneapolis because party labels were banned in contests for this office.

But Humphrey seemed destined for the academic track. That spring he was elected to Phi Beta Kappa. His adviser, William Anderson, urged him to go to graduate school. Years later Humphrey said he might have preferred attending Princeton, Woodrow Wilson's school. His wife added that "The press orientation would have been entirely different—I think he would have been president if he'd gone there." But he had no money, and that spring Muriel gave birth to their first child, Nancy. Kirkpatrick helped him get a $450 teaching fellowship at Louisiana State University, and so Humphrey started on the road to the Ph.D. that would lead to a life of college teaching.

8

In Huey Long Country

Life for the young couple was if anything even more straitened at Baton Rouge. Humphrey found rooms in a poor-white district of the city. After Muriel and her baby arrived, she buttered jelly sandwiches every day for her husband to sell to his fellow students at lunchtime. Work had to be found for her so that the little family could stay on. She typed papers for students and instructors, but after she had paid for the babysitter and carfare, not much was left of the ten dollars she made in a week. It became necessary to sell their refrigerator to pay the rent. His department head, Professor Hyneman, came to the rescue by passing along to Humphrey a chance to address a New Orleans women's club on state taxes. The fifty-dollar fee enabled the Humphreys to hang on until Christmas, and the club president phoned Hyneman to say it was the best speech they had ever heard.

The memory of Huey Long was still fresh in Louisiana when the Humphreys arrived. Humphrey himself vividly recalled the sight of the great Kingfish on his one visit to the Senate in 1935—"sweep[ing] into the chamber, a sudden, compelling presence in white shoes, cream-colored suit and orange tie." Dominating his state as a "people's governor" against the bitter opposition of all the vested interests—the banks, the utilities, and above all the oil companies that had never paid their share of taxes—he had built a powerful machine, installed a henchman as governor, and continued to run Louisiana from his Senate seat until his assassination in 1935. In Baton Rouge all the fancy new buildings Long had had built on the campus of Louisiana State University stood as a kind of monument to his ascendancy. But after his death his rivals gained the statehouse amid political combat more virulent and vitriolic than anything Humphrey had ever seen. Right before his eyes as he entered the building where the political science department was housed were gaping holes where the plaques memorializing the late Kingfish had been ripped from the marble façade by his successors. One day the victorious anti-Long forces dragged a cage through town with several apelike figures dangling on ropes inside. One easily recognizable face was that of Huey's university president, James M. Smith, by then in jail for embezzling funds.

Humphrey got to know Huey's son Russell, a student at the law school and later elected to the Senate the same year as Humphrey. Campus politics were a microcosm of state politics, so when Russell Long stood for student body president, the state's "Long organization" financed his campaign. He won, as Humphrey never tired of telling later, with a pledge of five-cent laundry for all undergraduates.

Humphrey was a favorite with his teachers and fellow students. When feuding broke out among the graduate students, Humphrey was the one member of the political science department on good enough terms with both sides to make peace. As a teaching assistant, Humphrey ran a small class in American government I—next door to Professor Robert Harris's office. All doors and windows being wide open most of the time in Louisiana, Harris could not help hearing his lectures. "They were well organized, lucid, persuasive and crowded with statistics," Harris said later. "His class was a public performance." When visiting debaters from Oxford University came to the campus, Humphrey volunteered along with a member of the speech department to take them on. He tried to stick to the issues, but of course the visitors treated the occasion as a joke and simply poked fun at Humphrey and his confederate.

Before the year was half over, Muriel left for home to help her financially hard-pressed father, and Humphrey was lonely. The younger professors invited him to dinner and evenings of bridge. But Humphrey proved to be an indifferent bridge player and always wanted to talk politics. A couple of campus Troskyites tried to win him to their views but found that he already held firm convictions. He told Harris that meeting Franklin Roosevelt had been "the greatest thrill of my life." It was early decided that the subject of Humphrey's master's thesis would be the political philosophy of the New Deal. His first draft was so overwhelmingly pro-Roosevelt that his supervisor, himself sympathetic to the New Deal, made Humphrey rewrite it. Published forty years later by the Louisiana University Press, it still reads like a document of personal commitment.

The paper fused Humphrey's first-hand experience and his intensive reading into a statement of core beliefs and values that endured all through his political life. From the Great Depression he learned two lessons. The first was that individuals, far from being masters of their own fate, could become powerless victims of catastrophes—drought, dust storms, bankruptcy, foreclosures. The second was that government could help people—specifically, the Humphrey family in their drugstore, through federal farm relief and other emergency funds assisting their customers—survive the buffets of such forces.

Poring over books as he never did again, Humphrey capped his five years of political science study by an analysis of the New Deal in the light of the classic texts. Aristotle, Locke, Jefferson, Wilson, Beard, Dewey—he read them all as he deepened his view of a social democracy so ordered that the individual could fulfill his own talents and destiny in America. A strong case can be made that John Dewey was both the most influential and the most representative American mind of the first half of the twentieth century. Humphrey drew upon Dewey to give coherence to the prairie pragmatism he had already learned in Doland. He latched on to the "experimentalism" of Dewey's thought. He said: "The main characteristic of the pragmatist is action." The political pragmatist—and of course Roosevelt was a great one—proceeded "by trial-and-error." He was bold, he took risks, and above all he avoided the "doctrinaire and dogmatic." Such a policy maker always knew that he would find no perfect solutions, no certain answers, no flawless implementations, only approximations. The pragmatic method, Humphrey wrote, "is scientific in temper, everlastingly desirous of going forward, and of doing something about an unsatisfactory situation, even if one experiment must be abandoned and a new one tried."

Humphrey wrote at the time of economic breakdown everywhere. Uppermost in his mind were the alternative courses being chosen in other countries of the world. He scoffed at conservatives who equated the New Deal's program with the fascism of Italy, the nazism of Germany, the sovietism of Russia. He began his essay by noting that the day after Franklin Roosevelt took office and inaugurated the New Deal, Adolf Hitler's National Socialism took absolute power in Germany. That was one alternative of the 1930s, and Humphrey had read Lawrence Dennis's *The Coming American Fascism*. But in liquidating the German republic at a stroke, Humphrey said, fascism "sacrificed" freedom for some sort of security, and security bought at such a price was abhorrent. Nor did the Marxist alternative exert any appeal for the young Humphrey.

There were, for Humphrey, "rigid" limits within which subjective, pragmatic trial-and-error should proceed. The limits he had in mind were set by the Constitution and by "the essential features of the capitalistic economy." There was no question that both must be accepted, but the former took commanding precedence.

As Humphrey saw it, the founding fathers "wrote one of the great compromises of history—a compromise between centralized power and individualized liberty." By virtue of this fruitful balance between order and freedom,

citizens could pursue their well-being with a due regard for private property
as an important element for every man in the control of his own life. But the
rise of great industries brought "ever increasing concentration of wealth and
property in the hands of a minority." The rugged individualism and unbri-
dled capitalism of the years before the New Deal upset the founding balance
and led to a crackup. Such manifestations of "negative liberty" were simply
not suited for a modern industrial society.

Not "negative" but "positive" liberty was the rightful goal. For Humphrey this meant that in a state existing to promote "the good life" for all
citizens as Aristotle defined it, the government should do for the individual
what he could not do for himself.

Those who stood in such a relationship to the state, however, were more
than an aggregation of individuals. They were a community, and seeking the
greatest good for the greatest number fostered their sense of community. In
a state where such ethical norms prevail, the measure of fulfilling the Aris-
totelian purpose "lies in the extent that the government is willing to apply
social values in place of pecuniary values."

To this emphasis on the community and on the ethical content of social
life, Humphrey added a third specification: in modern industrial society, the
state accepts "responsibility for keeping the economic machinery in operation." Such considerations prompted Humphrey to ask further whether
socialism might not stand as a kind of economic parallel to political democracy. "Democracy and socialism," he said, "are alike motivated by the desire
to free the individual from oppression and to guarantee to each an opportunity for personal happiness, for self-realization, for practical liberty and spiritual freedom."

There is more than a hint in these reflections that Humphrey, naming
"social democracy" his goal, might have been verging toward an espousal of
socialism. Later in life he found the company of West European socialists
personally congenial and attended, the only other American invited besides
Walter Reuther, the select conversations of Socialist statemen organized each
summer by Sweden's Social Democratic Premier Tage Erlander. Not only
that, Norman Thomas, whom Humphrey often visited, said: "Hubert was
what in Europe would be called a Socialist."

But as Jeane Kirkpatrick wrote: "This son of a small-town druggist also
valued private property and understood the importance of property to control of one's own life." So it was that here, as often in his later life, Humphrey shied away from political polarities. He called instead for both protection
of private ownership and a planned economy. Democrat rather than Socialist, he took his stand in favor of both freedom and equality, private property
and social security, big government and individual responsibilities.

Humphrey wrote his essay while the sounds of Roosevelt's battles to right
the imbalance caused by the gross inequality of economic power still rang in
the air. Arguing for his "positive liberty" over "the unfettered exploitation

. . . of the public," he drew up "a series of new rights" for Americans that contained the central principles of New Deal policy, and considerably more. The six "new rights" that Humphrey drew up in 1940 contained the philosophical basis for all the legislation he worked for down to the Humphrey-Hawkins Full Employment Act of 1978. They were

> the right to profitable and creative employment, profitable not only to the individual but to the community;
>
> the right to an adequate standard of living;
>
> the right . . . through collective bargaining . . . to a substantial share in the management of industry;
>
> the right to security against the hazards of unemployment, accident, illness and old age;
>
> the right to the maintenance of health; and
>
> the right of leisure and its effective use.

Though only a few of these rights had been enacted or even proclaimed up to that time, all sprang from the New Deal's central philosophy that rights guaranteed by government were required to protect modern man against the devastation to which industrial society left him vulnerable. All, Humphrey insisted, stemmed from the New Deal. As he interpreted them, they amounted to a charter not only for that day but for the future—"logical developments of a people experienced in democratic government attempting to review and remold political doctrine" to suit changing times. The great compromise of the founders, in short, must be brought up to date. Out of this bill of modern rights flowed Humphrey's postwar demands for equal rights for the labor movement, for Jews, for blacks, for equal opportunity for all Americans.

To formulate this philosophy, founded four-square he said "in the American tradition," Humphrey had to recognize and surmount certain contradictions in his own political inheritance. A good many of his predispositions could be traced to the ancestral Populists, to the Bull Moosers, to his father's revered New Freedom. But the pragmatic and "scientific" approach of the New Deal's flexible planning, he acknowledged, could never have been accepted by the "much more idealistic" Woodrow Wilson. Yet the single most important error of the New Deal, Humphrey also stated, was "the blunder of isolationism—the early insistence upon independent national economic recovery." Far from trying to go it alone, American democracy must see that, as Wilson had said, the world was "bound" together: "There can be no peace, no prosperity, no security in a world forming a total economic unity unless all the people in the world become benefactors of the common heritage. The task of democratic statesmanship is not only to evolve programs looking to national security but to gear their thinking in terms of a world."

Thus the young Humphrey's progressivism, rooted in the frontier egalitarianism of the prairie as it was, carried no taint of the isolationism that had always prevailed in the Upper Midwest. In this early affirmation of internationalism too, the young Humphrey spoke in the same voice that was to be heard from him to the end of his life.

There is a famous story about the oral examination conducted after Humphrey had submitted his thesis. From the outset it had been understood between Humphrey and his professors at Minnesota and Louisiana State that the year in Baton Rouge was to be a stepping stone to his return to finish his doctorate at Minneapolis and teach. In fact, the elders at Minnesota had already set aside a place for him by the time, in midsummer, that he had his thesis rewritten, "stripped bare of exaggeration" and acceptably "objective." But some of those with whom he had played bridge and argued late about Roosevelt's court-packing plan knew him well enough to have formed some other ideas about the Humphrey personality. Although his classwork and thesis had been highly regarded, one of his examiners could not resist opening the session by saying: "Humphrey, we're going to fail you on your thesis. We want to get you out of this servile profession, and get you into politics where you belong." Grinning nervously, Humphrey took this for the kidding that it was. But as Harris, another examiner, said later, the remark carried a further meaning: "Politics needs men like that."

Other signals of life-changing importance reached Humphrey during his year at Louisiana. Scarcely had the year begun when, eating breakfast with Muriel in their tiny kitchen, he heard on the radio that World War II had exploded in Poland. "Terribly upset," the young couple collected their dimes and rushed to a newsreel to goggle at the blitzkrieg and to hear Hitler rant. Humphrey bought and read *Mein Kampf*. The Louisiana year, plunging Humphrey into the Deep South, also showed him for the first time the dark facts of race. He became physically aware of the poverty and oppression of Southern blacks. He saw with dismay the segregation of whites in pillared houses and blacks in paintless shanties. He saw the manicured green lawns of Baton Rouge's white neighborhoods, the open sewer ditches running through the town's black quarter. For the first time in his life he saw WHITE and COLORED signs over toilets (and exclaimed naïvely: "Why, it's uneconomic."). He said later: "The shock and outrage . . . at what I saw there [gave] flesh and blood to my abstract commitment to civil rights." Like the young Lincoln rafting down to New Orleans to witness a slave auction in 1825, the young Humphrey saw inhumanity and injustice that he, too, resolved to right if he ever got the chance.

9

Working for the W. P. A.

WHEN the Humphreys returned to Minnesota, they settled once again on the edge of the University of Minnesota campus and resumed all their old friendships. It was understood that Hubert was going to work for his Ph.D. in political science, but now as never before his talk returned to political affairs. The long evening sessions with such close companions as Evron Kirkpatrick, whom Humphrey saw two or three times a week, and Orville Freeman, whom he saw even oftener, touched on the most intimate concerns and ambitions. The summer of 1940 was a time when it was hard *not* to talk about politics.

In stunning succession, Norway, Denmark, Holland, Belgium, and then France fell before the might of Hitler's invading armies, and Britain stood alone before the onrushing Germans. If Britain went down, nothing would remain between America and the conquering Nazis.

Congress passed a peacetime draft law, voted aid to Britain and China, and moved to scrap the Neutrality Act. Both political parties, reacting to the world crisis in a presidential election year, took drastic action. The Democrats named President Roosevelt to continue in office for an unprecedented third term. The Republicans, equally perceiving an emergency, nominated Wendell Willkie, a rank outsider who believed that America must rise to meet the threat of spreading Nazism.

As his master's thesis attested, Humphrey believed that summer that

Americans must arm to resist the threat. So he argued over beer and crackers
to his friends. But there was another young man who had already emerged
in Minnesota in a far better position to summon Minnesotans to turn against
their long-asserted isolationism and to recognize that danger so dire had to
be met well beyond the water's edge. This was Harold Stassen, then completing his first term as governor of the state.

The dominating presence of Stassen on the Minnesota scene had everything to do with the circumstances under which Hubert Humphrey embarked
on a political career.

"Humphrey thought of himself as a Democrat," Evron Kirkpatrick recalled
later. Orville Freeman said the same. But Democrats were mere also-rans in
Minnesota politics. Up to this time the two parties that contended for power
in the state were the Farmer-Laborites and the Republicans. So long as Floyd
Olson lived, the Farmer-Laborites had ruled. Invariably, Olson formed "all-
party" committees to make it easy for Democrats and Republicans to give
him their votes. Even before Franklin Roosevelt was elected in 1932, Olson
entered into an unofficial alliance by which his Farmer-Laborites cast their
votes for the Democratic presidential candidate and the Roosevelt forces made
no great effort to aid Democrats contesting for state office. In the Olson years
the state vote fell into a fairly regular pattern of 5–3–1: Farmer Laborites on
top, Democrats on the bottom, Republicans in between.

The Farmer Laborites may have been the most militantly extreme political party ever to hold statewide power in America. Olson himself was a rebel
at heart. He told his followers; "I am frank to say I am what I want to be—a
radical." In 1934 the party's platform, written by an old socialist, said in so
many words: the capitalist system is doomed. It called for public ownership
of mines, utilities, transportation, banks, and factories. The party was also
pacifistic, and certainly neutralist, forever passing resolutions condemning
du Pont and other munitions makers as the fomenters of America's wars.
Olson himself, like his Republican opponents in a state with huge Scandinavian, German, and Irish constituencies, was violently opposed to any
embroilment in Europe's affairs.

But on the eve of the 1936 election campaign, Olson, stricken with
abdominal cancer, died abruptly—at the age of forty-four. The successor
chosen by the governor's aides was Elmer Benson, a smalltown banker. Benson had been Olson's commissioner of banking. He had never run for elective
office before. Swept to victory on a wave of mourning for the lost governor,
Benson turned out to be less than another Floyd Olson. For one thing he had
a very short fuse. Where Olson had been easy and disarming, loaded with
charm, hail fellow with workers and bosses alike, Benson was grim, stubborn, strained, impatient.

To make matters worse, there was a resurgence of the Communist issue.
Even when they organized mass demonstrations and led marches on the capital, Olson had been able to handle Communists—Stalinist or Trotskyite.

But in Benson's time, as Hitler's threat to Russia mounted, the Moscow party line shifted. Communists everywhere began calling for a Popular Front alliance of anti-fascist and pro-democratic elements. In the United States they began cultivating the New Deal, the CIO, and outfits like the Farmer-Labor party. In Minnesota, Communists and Communist sympathizers found places in the Benson administration.

When some aides pointed out the danger to midwestern progressivism in the new Communist tactics, Benson brushed them aside. To him such warnings were the irresponsible smears of business interests trying to cloud the more important issues of unemployment and social justice. But all the time, investigations by conservative legislators kept turning up irregularities in state agencies that led critics to challenge the competence of his administration.

When Benson survived a bitter 1938 primary assault by a scant sixteen thousand votes, it was already apparent that public sentiment, stirred by the charges of the governor's incompetence and indifference to Communist infiltration, had swung away from the left. And this was where Stassen, ready to exploit the opportunity after having defeated an old-style Republican standpatter in the primary, came in.

Blond, gangling, with a head as big as a cabbage, Stassen was a truckfarmer's son from south of St. Paul. He had earned an imposing record at the University of Minnesota well before Humphrey appeared on the campus, taking top prizes in law, winning election as all-university student president, captaining a championship rifle team. He had supported himself through law school working as a sleeping-car conductor on the overnight run to Chicago. Elected county attorney in South St. Paul at twenty-four, he formed and led the Young Republican League against the party mossbacks and, at thirty-one, won the right to oppose Benson.

Presenting himself as a proponent of "enlightened capitalism," Stassen said he favored such "New Deal" goals as aid for the needy, the aged, and dependent children. Like Olson, he invited all-party support. But he hammered hardest on the Communist issue, and in the atmosphere of fear and hate that enveloped the 1938 contest, it was sometimes hard to tell where the Red-baiting left off and outright appeals to racial prejudice set in. For this time, the anti-Semitic hate was directed not against Jews in clubs and corporations but against Jews holding office in a left-wing state government. Well-heeled Republican rightists put out a scurrilous pamphlet *Are They Communists or Catspaws?*, which lumped Elmer Benson with four aides, Jewish every one of them, and listed their alleged Communist activities. Pulpit-thumping Minneapolis evangelists called on all Christians to defeat Benson and his "Jewish Communist" auxiliaries. The Silver Shirts, fascists led by William Dudley Pelley of North Carolina, spread their racist poison. Stassen headquarters issued its own Red-baiting pamphlet *Here is the Proof*—featuring a photograph of Governor Benson riding in a New York parade with a youth flaunting a Young Communist League banner in front of him.

But it was Benson himself who dug his own grave. A fortnight before the voting, as he finished a speech at Red Lake Falls, a member of the audience rose to ask him whether he had Communist sympathies. Benson lost his temper. "Who is this man?" he shouted. When the questioner identified himself as the Rev. Paul H. Bergdorf, the local Lutheran pastor, Benson exploded: "If you really believed in Christian principles, you wouldn't come to a meeting like this and attempt to disrupt it. You preachers aren't going to get away with this sort of thing in this campaign."

The sole reporter who happened to be present at this meeting in the North Woods hamlet was Joseph H. Ball, political writer for the St. Paul *Pioneer Press*. His story, headlined all over the state, was later called by Stassen "the turning point of the campaign." As Ball wrote: "Gloom in the Benson caravan afterward was so thick you could see it. If Governor Benson can be re-elected after the show he put on in Red Lake Falls last Thursday night, then all the rules by which political candidates and parties have guided themselves in the past to do not mean a thing today." Stassen won by a landslide.

As Minnesota's "boy governor," Stassen attracted national attention. Under his leadership the state legislature adopted a civil service system, increased social security benefits, extended Olson's mortgage moratorium, and passed an anti-loan shark measure that Olson had sought without success. But what caught the public eye was the way the new governor cooled off labor militancy in Minnestoa. Under his Labor Peace Act, unions and employers had to give ten days' notice of any work stoppage to a state labor conciliator, after which the governor could delay a further thirty days awaiting a report from a fact-finding commission. This, along with the crushing of the Minneapolis Teamsters' Trotskyite leadership accomplished under the Smith Act in 1941, effectively curtailed strikes in the state. The cooling-off concept for damping labor strife was adopted nationally with enactment of the Taft-Hartley law in 1949. Minnesotans liked it. A Gallup poll showed 81 percent approval for Stassen, re-affirmed by large majorities in 1940 and 1942.

The Stassen ascendancy was all the more significant for a young man of Humphrey's views and ambitions because foreign policy came to loom large in Minnesota when war broke out in Europe. Isolationism, stridently voiced in the midwestern tradition by Republicans and Farmer-Laborites alike, had seemed unassailably strong as late as 1939, when the entire Minnesota delegation voted for the Neutrality Act. The Scandinavians of the Farmer-Labor party were dead set against European involvement, the Irish and the Germans of the Democratic party even more so.

But 1940 saw the beginning of a tremendous change. Stassen said in his keynote address: "Lights are going out in Europe. The blackouts of the dictators take the place of the lighthouses of free men. Our interests lie with the encouragement of freedom." After delivering these words at the Republican National Convention, Stassen took over as floor manager for the successful candidacy of Wendell Willkie, who proclaimed 'One World.' And when the isolationist Farmer-Laborite Senator Ernest Lundeen died that year in a plane crash, Governor Stassen appointed Joe Ball to his place. The St. Paul newsman had aided immeasurably in Stassen's first campaign triumph. But he was a confirmed internationalist too, and Stassen, having taken such a strong foreign-policy stand, wanted a like-minded man to keep the Senate place warm until he should run for the seat himself—a notion discarded when Pearl Harbor swept the United States into war and Stassen joined the navy instead. Roosevelt was grateful, and not only eased Ball's way to reelection in 1942 but brought Stassen to San Francisco in 1945 as a participant in the founding conference of the United Nations.

Stassen and Ball are to be credited for their bold leadership in transforming the world outlook of Minnesotans. But a change of such proportions in the views of two million middle Westerners was not to be accomplished overnight. The Scandinavians of the state began to shed their isolationism in the shock of Hitler's invasion of Norway and Denmark in 1940. The Irish and Germans within the traditional Democratic party took much longer to overcome their ingrained aversion to overseas involvements that seemed always to bring the United States in on the side of the English. The switch took so long to complete—requiring the impact not only of World War II but, after 1945, of the cold war against Russia—that Hubert Humphrey arrived after all in time to help engineer it. In retrospect we can say that it was Stassen first and Humphrey later, with the help of the Cowles newspapers in Minneapolis and the Ridder publications in St. Paul and Duluth, who swung majority opinion in Minnesota over to the international side.

HUBERT HUMPHREY may have been born, as his friend Kirkpatrick believed, to go into politics, but it was sheer poverty that led him to leave the campus for his first government job. The plight of the Humphreys was well known to all their friends. His professors in Louisiana pleaded with the university's financial aid officer in vain to get them just a few more dollars for living expenses. In Minneapolis, Kirkpatrick went to great lengths to find Humphrey a month's summer work to fetch the little family a precious two hundred dollars. The job was training adult-education teachers at Duluth State Teachers college under the Depression-born Works Progress Administration. To save as much of this sum as possible, Muriel and the eighteen-month-old Nancy stayed in South Dakota. As a WPA teacher, Humphrey, enacting Lincoln-Douglas debates for a roomful of cast-off school teachers, was in his element, and "they seemed to like me."

That fall, as Humphrey started his Ph.D. work and part-time campus teaching, his family income for the school year consisted solely of the university's $600 stipend. Humphrey had not yet returned to clerking in a drugstore. But for Muriel, with the baby, there was no longer any possibility of outside employment. At this uncertain point in their lives an opportunity came along that Humphrey, "broke, married, with a daughter," simply could not pass up. As a result of his impressive summer's teaching, the WPA invited him back as director of the Twin City Workers Education program at a salary of $150 per month. Professor Anderson of the political science department rushed in with a promise of $300 worth of extra university teaching after the first of the year if he would stay on, and Orville Freeman urged him to take it and get the Ph.D. But Humphrey told him: "It's just too much of a hardship for my family to go on like this." Thereupon, Freeman, a 1940 graduate who had saved up $350 working as a tourist guide in Minneapolis that summer, lent Humphrey $250 to buy the car he needed to take the job.

At the time it may not have seemed such a momentous change. After all, the job involved teaching, and teaching was to have been Humphrey's life-long career. He still lived in off-campus quarters and spent his spare time with graduate-school companions. But Humphrey found more to do than teach. The Workers Education operation looked slack to him. Taking vigorous charge, he ordered staff teachers to fill their schedules. Some, mostly feuding Stalinists and Trotskyites as he later told it, were not even meeting their classes. He gave them until Thanksgiving to shape up, and when some did not, he fired them. Impressed, his boss said: "I never thought I'd find a man with guts enough to fire someone on WPA for not working." He made Humphrey district and then state director of the program.

Up to this time, Humphrey had thought of himself not only as a prospective college professor but as a South Dakotan. Now he hustled after the president of the South Dakota federation of labor, a friend of his father's, to help him gain entry with high union officials in Minnesota. He wrote offering to start classes for Minnesota farm cooperatives, for trade unions in the northern part of the state. Soon he was writing his Louisiana professor Charles Hyneman: "I've contacted hundreds of union groups—invaluable experience." As was his wont, he made lifetime friends at first encounters. He was invited to explain his program before both the AFL and the CIO state conventions. And not for a moment did he neglect his campus ties. Soon the night-school courses at his downtown Minneapolis "Labor College" were being taught by eight university professors. By the summer of 1941 he could brag to Hyneman that his classes were "reaching 18 to 20 thousand people a month." Directing his staff to work more material on the war into the curriculum, he went off to teach his teachers at another two-month workshop in Duluth. "We missed his jabber, jabber, jabber," an aide in the office wrote.

Humphrey was getting around. After joining a Congregational church in southeast Minneapolis, he met a young minister named Russell Nye, who invited him to teach every Sunday morning in the "University of Life" at the city's leading Methodist church. One week he reported: "I was out on speaking engagements every night." At first the talks were mostly labor-oriented. He told unionists in Duluth: "The majority of Americans do not own property; their only property is their job. Courts have upheld the contention that a job is the property of a wage earner—and the right to life, liberty and property must be protected."

Then on May 16, 1941, six months before Pearl Harbor, Humphrey wrote to the newly organized Minneapolis chapter of William Allen White's Committee to Defend America by Aiding the Allies that "At any time you need my assistance, I shall be at your service. I have had considerable speaking experience." "This is our war" was his topic addressing the Duluth junior chamber of commerce that fall; after war was declared, he used the same speech to labor groups. He told Hyneman: "I've been doing a lot of speaking around the state, raising particular hell with the Minnesota isolationists."

Herbert McClosky arrived that year from Princeton to study for a doctorate in the Minnesota political science department. Pinch-hitting for one of his professors at a Minneapolis forum soon after the Nazi invasion of Russia, he discovered that Humphrey was moderating the debate. The first speaker, a Soviet partisan who had flipflopped the moment the Soviet Union was attacked, led off with a pro-war speech. In reply, McClosky, in the student-radical fashion of the 1930s, dismissed the war in Europe as nothing but a row between competing capitalisms. Then, as McClosky recounted later, Humphrey began to talk:

> He demolished me. He understood much better than I did what democracy meant, not only in war but in the threat posed to democracy and civilization if the Nazi armies overran all Europe. The force of his arguments, the rhetoric, the power with which he organized his thoughts to disclose the absurdity of my standard radical clinches, overwhelmed me. He wasn't being pro-Soviet. He was just teaching me a lesson—that I had finally met someone who could handle me.
>
> It was all very sweetly done. Instead of being angry, I went up to him afterwards and thanked him. I knew in my heart he was right but I hadn't made the transition from my student rhetoric to full appreciation of what was involved.
>
> That experience is seared in my mind as a crucial turning point in my life. We became very close friends.

If Humphrey spoke so often and forcefully for the war, why did he not volunteer for military service? The question dogged him all his life, but the answer was never very clear for the young family man. After the nation went to war he acknowledged that WPA work seemed "dull and inconsequential." He had registered for the draft in southeast Minneapolis in 1940 and been deferred as a father. By the time the war broke out he knew that Muriel was pregnant again: "We are in the baby business—shipment due July 1942."

While continuing to talk politics at night with his university friends, he cast about for some sort of war work. His sister Frances having landed a job in Washington helping Mrs. Roosevelt organize the Office of Civilian Defense, Humphrey thought for a time he might have an opportunity there. Through his friend Hyneman he put in for a place at the Bureau of the Budget but wondered whether he could afford to move his family to wartime Washington. Next he applied for a place as a field examiner for the National Labor Relations Board and, because of his work with trade unions, expected to get it. But all his applications were turned down. In the end he stayed on in Minneapolis with the WPA, finally becoming divisional director for training and re-employment of the War Manpower Commission. The assignment was, in effect, to liquidate the WPA. His method was to set up vocational training units throughout the state, mostly in high schools, and send on the re-treaded "leaf rakers" to jobs as riveters, shipfitters, and the like in labor-scarce war plants. Every one of his eight thousand "graduates" received elaborate diplomas signed by Humphrey—some are said still to be hanging on the walls of homes in Minnesota.

To friends such as Kirkpatrick these diplomas were the budding politician's advertisements for himself; and Humphrey writing Hyneman in early 1942 said: "I've found this work splendid training in public relations." By then Humphrey had "gained the confidence" of enough Minnesota labor officials and addressed enough church and civic groups for him to admit to friends he was thinking of running for public office.

But where should he make his entry? And where could he find support? Clearly, Stassen dominated the state's Republican party, and the Democrats were weak sisters. Prospects were also not attractive in the Farmer-Labor party, where the influence was still wielded, as the two friends analyzed the situation in their off-campus bull sessions, by the likes of Meridel LeSueur, John Jacobsen, and Roger Rutchick. The first of these was a Communist party member, or close to it, who wrote for the *New Masses;* the second, regional director of the CIO's Political Action Committee and very open about his party membership in his talks with Kirkpatrick; and the third, who had been Benson's secretary, they wrote off as a fellow traveler. With such people in charge, and Benson likely to head the election ticket once again, they agreed the Farmer-Labor party could not hope to command a popular majority Kirkpatrick said later: "I thought Hubert ought to be in politics— like everybody else did who knew him. He had wit. He had humor. He had intelligence. He had knowledge. His father had spent a lot of time talking to him. And what he heard, he retained. Give him any kind of a chance to talk, even to just one person, and he had them."

Their first serious talk about a Humphrey election plunge came in early 1942. It concerned running for Congress in Minnesota's Third District. At the time, the Third was a horse-shoe-shaped district that centered on the working-class north side of Minneapolis and took in the outlying parts of Hennepin and Washington counties—the rest of Minneapolis lay in the Fifth, or bluestocking, district, which was firmly held by the Republicans. Until the 1938 Benson debacle, Farmer-Laborite Henry Teigan a union official, had represented the Third District. At the moment, an upstanding Republican of forward-looking views and impeccable first-family standing named Richard Pillsbury Gale held the seat. Humphrey and his campus friends took the idea of trying for the Third District seat fairly seriously; in June his friend Professor Robert Harris wrote from Baton Rouge, "All of us here are wishing you best luck in your race for Congress." But Humphrey never took the plunge. The Republican Gale, he said later, "looked unbeatable." More precisely, as Kirkpatrick explained later, Minnesota's three-party pattern made it hopeless to try. Election figures showed that the combined votes of Farmer-Laborites and Democrats surpassed those of the Republicans in the Third District. But when all three parties entered candidates, the Farmer-Laborites had small chance to win; the Democrats none at all.

That summer, having shelved the idea of making a race in 1942, Humphrey told his sister he was thinking of applying for a navy commission. The trouble was that Muriel's ailing father was now a member of the household. "With him and the baby, it's not a simple matter to move all over the country," he wrote. So Humphrey put that idea aside too. To Local Draft Board Number Two he sent this word the following week: "I am reporting a change in dependency status due to birth of a son, Hubert H. Humphrey III, June 26, 1942."

That spring, Governor Stassen announced that he was enlisting in the Naval Reserve. The stage was set for Humphrey when Stassen left for the navy, set for Humphrey to play the internationalist role in Minnesota. The question remained where to make his entry.

10

Dashing Out of Nowhere

E v e n after Humphrey shied away from the Third Congressional District contest, Kirkpatrick never ceased urging his friend to get into politics. They met almost nightly for beer and pretzels, sometimes in the Kirkpatrick apartment, less often in the crowded Humphrey rooms at the rear of a fourplex. After the McCloskys joined the sessions, the evenings often started with gin rummy. Then when Humphrey breezed in late from a meeting, the game would break up. "Just listen to what I told 'em tonight," he would chortle, and at once the men began talking politics. The subject might be anything that caught Humphrey's fancy—the latest Minneapolis underworld killings, the hungry dustbowlers, the city's new war-spawned industries. Whatever the topic, Humphrey held forth "fresh, funny, striking off country-hick metaphors" with a spontaneity and force that, the Easterner McClosky said, "without his meaning to, could make you want to rise off the ground and say, 'We'll follow you.' " It was not all politics. The friends went fishing— Humphrey "loved" to fish. In a jalopy loaded with beer and sandwiches they would drive to some chilly northern lake and float around in rented rowboats: "Hubert always in very good humor, very down to earth, cracking off wry, marvelously funny remarks all day, and not catching a damn fish, not a sunfish or crappie among us." The friends could not help seeing how poor Humphrey was, buying McClosky's discarded refrigerator for $85, hauling ashes and swabbing toilets to knock $10 off his $30 month's rent, speaking to any little neighborhood group for the $5 fee.

One outfit that Humphrey addressed that summer was the Saturday lunch club, a group of old Farmer-Laborites, and Judge Vince Day happened to be present. Day was the nearest thing to a boss in Minneapolis courthouse politics. He had been Floyd Olson's chief aide and, even after Olson named him to the bench, his most intimate adviser. Day had seen the party through some extremely lean years and was looking, he said, for "new blood." A few days later he invited Humphrey to his courthouse office and suggested that he run for mayor in 1943.

That was when Kirkpatrick decided it was time to introduce Humphrey to Arthur Naftalin. Naftalin was another of Kirkpatrick's talented graduate students. A native of Fargo, North Dakota, he had graduated from the university the same year as Humphrey but had known him scarcely at all. Thereafter, Naftalin had worked as a reporter for the Minneapolis *Tribune* before returning full time to the campus in 1941 to get his Ph.D. degree. If Humphrey were to run for mayor, Kirkpatrick reasoned, somebody with public relations experience and skills and access to the city newspapers would be essential for the effort. Naftalin was the man.

An important consideration in standing for mayor was that votes in the city election were cast on nonpartisan ballots. As yet, Humphrey had not declared himself any sort of public candidate and was keeping his own counsel. Over in Minneapolis's Fifth District, Dr. Walter Judd, a medical missionary recently returned from China, had brought off the election coup of 1942 by ousting an isolationist in the Republican primary. Judd thought about world affairs as Humphrey did, and Humphrey had said so publicly at the Saturday lunch club. After Judd won, Humphrey visited the doctor in his consulting room, and in the course of asking how he might repeat Judd's success in the Third District, gave Judd to understand that he agreed with him on domestic issues too. According to Judd, he said: "My father was a total Populist—he wanted to break up everything. But I've been studying political science over at the University and down at Louisiana State, and I know you can't do that sort of thing." And as Judd recounted later, Humphrey said he had voted for Stassen and Willkie in 1940. Humphrey himself later said he voted for Ball in 1942.

The next congressional elections being two years off, Judd asked Humphrey if he had thought about running for mayor. Humphrey replied: "I might do that, I might run for mayor." Thereupon, Judd picked up the phone and arranged for Humphrey to meet the five young men who had organized and managed his campaign just ended. Two days later, Humphrey was discussing a race for mayor over lunch at Freddy's café with a tableful of Republicans—a young advertising executive, a lawyer, several insurance men, and Gideon Seymour, executive editor of the Minneapolis *Star Journal*. Highly impressed, Ronald Welch of General Mills pulled out his checkbook and announced: "It takes $10 to file for office. I'm writing my check for $15. If each of us gives $15, that will cover your filing fee—and leave you $65 for your campaign expenses." Afterward, Welch telephoned Judd and said, "We're going to take on another campaign like the one we just finished for you." And Humphrey, without saying whom he had seen, told Naftalin, "Gee, they're really hot for me to run for mayor. Do you think I should?"

A short time later, Judge Day called top Minneapolis Farmer-Laborites, mostly union men, to his home and suggested Humphrey's name for the 1943 race. The name of George Murk, head of the musicians' union, was proposed. But Murk was not young. He was not, Day said, "new blood." And the judge asked the seniors present to listen to a young aide, Frank Adams, former president of the University Farmer-Labor club. Invited by Day expressly for the purpose, Adams proceeded to describe for his elders the stunning impact Humphrey had made on other students when he addressed a peace rally staged by Adams back in 1938.

Lacking money, Humphrey hesitated. He dined several times with Judge Day. But the enthusiasm of Judd's young Republican evaporated when they heard that Humphrey consorted with CIO "leftists." Humphrey also professed himself uneasy about Minneapolis's unsavory reputation as a haven for racketeers and criminals. The city had a string of unsolved murders involving gangster types, and there was evidence that City Hall was riddled with corruption. Naftalin, who knew something of the underworld influences from his days as a reporter, told Humphrey his concern about the crime problem was justified.

Humphrey was eager to run. But as an unknown, strapped for funds, he had to have support first. The Republicans had backed away, but labor was still to be heard from. Finally in April 1943 the AFL's Central Labor Union approached him about running with labor endorsement. That offer, which came from two union leaders he ran into on a Sunday morning stroll past the Nicollet Hotel, was all he needed. Rushing to check again with Kirkpatrick and Naftalin, he seized the bid. Only nineteen days before the May 10 primary, Humphrey quit his government job and filed for mayor.

In the nonpartisan contest he was one of eight candidates. Mayor Marvin Kline enjoyed the backing of Stassen's Republicans and had some labor support. Other candidates were also better known. But Humphrey raced around the city addressing every neighborhood club that would listen to him. Naftalin, put on the Central Labor Union's payroll as a publicity writer, produced an *Election News* broadside headlined: "A New Star Is Born." With Central Labor Union funds, Humphrey got on the air for four brief appeals— the first in support of the newly proclaimed United Nations, the next an invitation to think about "postwar Minneapolis." Seeking CIO support, he pledged an open door to members' grievances, and when a Communist said, "Yes, but what about the international situation?" Humphrey retorted: "I don't think the mayor of Minneapolis will be concerned with any international relationship with Russia," and picked up more union backing. Kirkpatrick worked the telephone scheduling his speeches, McClosky drove the car. When the votes were counted in the primary, Humphrey came in a respectable second to Mayor Kline: 29,752 to 16,148.

At this, the Minneapolis *Star Journal* said: "A new leader, literally unknown to the general public a month ago, has come dashing out of nowhere to stage a colorful fighting campaign to win this high honor." But the press had not gone over to Humphrey. His dynamism only impelled the Stassen organization to throw its strength behind Kline, and the newspapers fell in line.

Since the runoff was not until June 14, there was now a little more time to mount a campaign. The Central Labor Union set up a skeleton ward organization, but it was a handful of Humphrey's university friends who provided most of the volunteer effort. Naftalin wrote press releases, worked up issues, kept the checkbook, and occasionally raised money to pay for the radio shows so important for getting the candidate known. Kirkpatrick handled strategy and schedules and prodded CIO unions to lend a hand. Some of the campus friends rang doorbells and handed out lawn signs. The legend "Make Minneapolis Hum—Humphrey" was printed in orange because that was the color Dr. Bill Kubicek's med-school research in optics had shown was most arresting to the eye.

In this campaign, if there had ever been any doubt, Humphrey discovered his "capacity to move audiences." McClosky, who drove him around, insisted later that a totally impromptu Humphrey discourse in a Plymouth Avenue garage on his yen for office and the art of motorcar repair, which had grease-stained mechanics and loafers alternately pounding their hands and slapping their thighs, was the greatest speech that Humphrey ever made. Sometimes as they raced from church basement to lodge hall, the grad-student chauffeur would pour out his best thoughts on what Humphrey should say—and at the next stop listen dumbfounded as "I'd hear the kind of things I'd suggested, plus what he'd had in mind, woven into the most elaborate tapestry—and elevated far beyond what I'd been able to tell him." It might seem ridiculous, McClosky recalled as a Berkeley professor long afterward, to write speeches for such an incandescent improviser. But some speeches had to be shaped to fit radio time, and McClosky wrote these, with assistance from Humphrey's six-foot-eight-inch novelist friend Feike Feikema. Having stayed up late the night before writing them, McClosky fought to extricate Humphrey from a parents-teachers meeting ("He was so powerful that people would hang on him and ask questions, and you couldn't get him out of there"). Then, rushing him with minutes left to the radio station, he had to listen to Humphrey's chaffing him for exceeding the speed limit. In one speech, Humphrey offered a ten-point program for turning Minneapolis around through new industry, better labor-management relations, expanded air and river transport, retrained war workers, and expanded housing. How much of this could have been attempted was problematic—but the candidate proposed establishing a postwar development council to plan for it. Afterward, as the others sank exhausted at headquarters, Humphrey strode in and spotted a pile of literature lying on the table. "What are these doing here?" he shouted and led a midnight outing to stuff leaflets under apartment-house doors. Next he dragged the others to an all-night restaurant. "What do we do tomorrow?" he barked. "It *is* tomorrow," growled Naftalin, and Humphrey reluctantly agreed to go home.

It was a good try. By June 14 a good many voters knew that the candidate was a trained political scientist, a registered pharmacist, and a family man who taught Sunday school twice every Sunday. Naftalin's final brochure, in an open bid for Republican votes, pictured Humphrey reading Wendell Willkie's new best-seller *One World*. And when Mayor Kline tried to make capital of former Teamster Boss Ray Dunne's endorsement of Humphrey, the candidate, trailed by reporters, walked into the startled mayor's office to insist that the Mayor acknowledge that he had repudiated the Trotskyite endorsement.

But the Humphrey brashness and dynamism could not make up for the lack of organization. He raised about $12,000 for the race, the bulk of it from fifty-five union locals. "We were desperately short of money," he told his uncle. And while "we were bucking a well-heeled [Republican] machine properly oiled with money and ward-heelers," the kind of report that came in to Humphrey headquarters was all too often like this: "The Fourth Ward fell down—the chairman backed out and never contacted any of the workers." On June 14, Hubert Humphrey met defeat in his first campaign for office. The vote: Kline, 60,075; Humphrey, 54,350.

11

Fusion on
the Left

Not long after Humphrey's losing race for mayor, Herb McClosky drove him home one night. As the two friends sat parked in front of the fourplex, Humphrey unburdened himself to McClosky about a conversation he had had earlier in the day. The conversation was with Gideon Seymour, editor of the Minneapolis *Star Journal,* right-hand man of publisher John Cowles. Seymour had been one of the five young Republicans who briefly wanted to support Humphrey's race, only to back out because Humphrey accepted CIO help. In a nonpartisan contest, of course, Humphrey had bid for Republican votes, and the *Journal* afterward had called his campaign "spectacular." Complimenting Humphrey on his run, Seymour invited him to become a Republican. As McClosky heard it, Seymour told Humphrey: "Look, we'll make you governor, we'll make you senator. We have the power in the state to make a man of your capacities anything he wants politically. But we'll only do this if you become a Republican. If you won't, we'll break you; we'll break you."

Humphrey's talk of the Seymour proposition overflowed until four in the morning. As McClosky recalled, it was "almost a Faustian struggle." Humphrey was tempted, no question about it, torn between his upbringing and the "lifetime career" dangled before him. Then he went in and told his wife some other details. As she recalled it later, "Hubert was offered this beautiful lake home—I think it was valued at something like thirty-five to thirty-nine thousand dollars, in those days a fortune."

A day or two later, Humphrey went back and told Seymour, "I can't do it—I am a Democrat." According to his wife, "It would have been the end of us—it almost was anyway." Having ended the campaign $1,300 in debt to the printer, Humphrey was rushing to neighborhood picnics, Kiwanis suppers, Lutheran men's clubs, anywhere he could earn a small fee—"and in those two years," Muriel recalled, "we had another baby and another baby and I lost my Dad, and Hubert became very much involved in pulling together the Democratic and Farmer-Labor parties."

M a n y years later, Humphrey told a reporter, "I'm going to be immodest. I think my greatest contribution to Minnesota politics was as the catalyst for the amalgamation of the Democrats and Farmer-Laborites." It is not necessary to insist that he singlehandedly accomplished the fusion of the two Minnesota parties. No doubt President Roosevelt wanted it to happen and gave the Democratic National Committee a nudge, and no doubt Elmer Kelm, the Democratic state chairman, realized after the 1942 election drubbing that he must take the initiative if the state were not to become a closed Republican preserve. And on the Farmer-Labor side, Humphrey's friend Kirkpatrick said later, the real impetus came when Moscow—to win maximum wartime support—scrapped the Comintern, its official agency for the fomenting of revolution in other lands, and U. S. Communist Leader Earl Browder called for all-out backing of President Roosevelt. After that, said Kirkpatrick, the leftists in the fading Farmer-Labor organization began pressing for merger with the Democrats, and Elmer Benson, after first grumpily resisting, decided to put himself at the head of the movement.

Yet it must be said that Hubert Humphrey stepped into the picture at the critical moment, and success followed swiftly.

The transformation of Minnesota politics to which the merger led, however, was by no means inevitable either for the party or for Humphrey. It would be a decade before the united party gained the Minnesota statehouse. For Humphrey, the significance of his role in the merger was its opening access to Democratic national politics—even before he won his first election as mayor. In this way, grasping the lead for fusion became for the man so recently tempted by the Republicans one of the shaping experiences of his political life.

Lesser men, of course, had seen the impossibility of winning statewide or even congressional elections so long as the Farmer-Labor and Democratic parties kept dividing the non-Republican vote. It was the force of this arithmetic that had led Humphrey to pull back from the Third District race in 1942. If he expected to win the seat in 1944, as he and Kirkpatrick and Freeman hoped, he would have to have a unified party behind him.

Such thoughts prompted him to write a twelve-page letter in July 1943 to Postmaster General Frank Walker, the Democratic national chairman. Setting forth the numbers he had gone over with Kirkpatrick, he termed Minnesota's Republicans "a plurality party" and yet a party holding the state in fief simply because the Democrats and Farmer-Laborites never got together. When Walker gave the appeal no attention, Humphrey decided to take the family's seventy-seven-dollar nestegg and go to Washington to present his arguments in person. Arriving by bus, he was fobbed off by Walker underlings and after four days was ready to go home when he remembered that his father had told him to call a family friend from South Dakota, former Assistant Postmaster General W. W. Howes. Humphrey called Howes from the Willard Hotel and after conveying greetings from his dad explained his unfulfilled mission. Howes told him to wait there and he would be right over.

Humphrey spent his last fifty cents on a scotch-and-soda in the hotel bar, then hastily chewed some mints to cover the smell of liquor on his breath. Howes arrived in half an hour and after hearing Humphrey's tale of frustration called Walker and urged him to see Humphrey. As Humphrey recalled later: "By God, inside of five minutes a limousine that made my eyes pop out parked right in front of the Willard, picked me up and took me to the postmaster-general's office. I had never seen an office so big in my life and I was scared to death. But I went in and told him my story and he said, 'All right, this is a good idea. I'll send a man out to work with you.' "

At this same time, Humphrey landed what he badly needed: a job. Macalester College in St. Paul, its junior faculty gone off to war, needed someone to teach introductory political science classes for a year. David Winton, a Minneapolis lumberman on Macalester's board had been impressed by Humphrey's campaign and suggested his name. As a result, that summer Humphrey began teaching a course in political philosophy for both regular undergraduates and air force cadets training on the campus. One of the first classes, taking off from a discussion of John Roy Carlson's book *Undercover* (about his personal infiltration and exposure of the American Nazi party) lasted five and one-half hours and ended with Humphrey's admonition: "Get into politics—don't just be cheering from the bleachers." By popular vote three successive classes of air force "ninety-day wonders" chose Humphrey to give their commencement addresses. As usual he made lifelong friends among faculty and students. Walter Mondale was one of his students.

In August, Walker and Oscar Ewing, the man he had designated to represent the national party, arrived for talks with Minnesota leaders. Humphrey was already reporting, after talks with Minneapolis AFL and CIO officials, that unity was "entirely possible." Up to this time local Democrats had thought only in terms of absorbing the Farmer-Laborites. Humphrey now urged: "Let's call it the Democratic-Farmer-Labor party. I say this because the Farmer-Labor name means 175,000 to 200,000 votes."

After that, things went faster. In September the Farmer-Laborites publicly acknowledged they were discussing merger. Lawyers for both sides began wrestling with the intricacies of matching constitutions and executing name

changes. In November negotiators for the two sides met formally, Kirkpat-
rick and Naftalin present as aides to the six Democrats, leftists such as Viena
Johnson, Marian LeSueuer, and John Jacobsen among the equal number of
Farmer-Laborites, Humphrey acting as liaison between the two groups. By
early 1944 they had advanced so far with Ewing's help that Humphrey organized a unity dinner and invited Vice President Henry Wallace as speaker.
When Wallace arrived to address nearly ten thousand from the two parties,
Humphrey introduced him, stayed at his elbow throughout, and afterward
wrote him: "Progressive forces look to you for inspiration and leadership."

In the midst of the negotiations, Muriel Humphrey's father died. At pre-
cisely that moment the two parties met in simultaneous conventions. Last-
minute talks hit a snag, and unity almost went on the rocks. Humphrey, as
Democratic convention chairman, decided to stay and work for merger while
Muriel, alone, took her father's body to South Dakota for burial. Some of
the Farmer-Laborites "got so cockeyed mad" at the constitution voted by the
Democrats that Humphrey appointed a committee that met with Farmer-
Labor leaders until agreement was achieved at 6:30 A.M.

It was not difficult, Humphrey wrote his friend Hyneman, to get the
Farmer-Labor convention's approval of these revisions,

> since the Fusion Committee report included all the demands they had
> made. In the Democratic convention it became my task to see to it that
> the Fusion Committee report was driven through and accepted. Kirkpat-
> rick was very instrumental in gaining the Report's approval, and at 11
> Saturday morning the two parties were one.
>
> On Saturday afternoon, April 15, the Farmer-Laborites and the Dem-
> ocrats met together in joined convention to endorse candidates and to pro-
> pose resolutions and platform. There was no difficulty as to resolutions
> and platform, but when it came to candidates, that's where the trouble
> began.
>
> Early in April I said that I was not a candidate for any office. It was
> my intention to go into the Armed Services—I cannot help but believe
> that if a fellow is going to have any political future, he had better be in
> the Armed Services.
>
> I made this decision plain to the nominating committee. Again and
> again leaders of the Party came to me and asked me to run, and as many
> times I refused. Finally, at about 8 A.M., with over 800 delegates present,
> someone took the floor and in a rousing speech nominated me for the office
> of Governor. Then all hell broke loose. There was one seconding speech
> after another, with the entire delegation standing on their feet cheering
> like wild men. They stomped their feet and shouted: "We want Hum-
> phrey!" until I felt it necessary to leave the hall. The demonstration lasted
> for over an hour. Finally, I was informed that the delegates had drafted
> me for the office.

. . . Thinking Uncle Sam was going to take me into the Navy, and also realizing that no one of us had a chance to beat the incumbent [Governor Ed Thye], I rejected the endorsement . . . and we finally came up with my friend Barney Allen. . . . That was the time I should have filed for Congress. I knew this, and had it not been for a very confused personal life—I sure as the devil expected to be in the Army or Navy—I might have. . . .

But that was not the end. After the convention, Humphrey was notified he had flunked the physical exam for a navy commission. He was colorblind, and had a calcification of the lungs and a double hernia. And although his draft number was coming up, it seemed doubtful that the army would take him either. At this point, Elmer Kelm, chairman of the unified party, stepped in and named Humphrey to run its first election campaign. At Kelm's request, Humphrey's draft board then deferred his army callup.

When amidst all this Humphrey's landlord, complaining that he was neglecting his janitorial duties, served notice that he was raising the rent to $54.50 per month, Humphrey raised a howl of protest. A month later the Humphreys put down a few dollars and took title to a seven-room brick house on the northern fringe of the University campus. Life was changing, horizons were expanding.

That summer, Humpharey attended the Democratic National Convention in Chicago. Like his father, on hand as a delegate from South Dakota, he took Henry Wallace's side when President Roosevelt decided to drop Wallace in favor of Harry Truman as his running mate. Not only did he join the Farmer-Laborites in holding Kelm and other oldline Democrats to their Wallace pledge but when Wallace's name was placed in nomination Humphrey seized the Minnesota standard and led a wild Wallace parade around the floor. As he wrote years later: "No man seemed more closely aligned with the Midwest, with the Populist liberals, Farmer-Laborites, Non-Partisan Leaguers and ardent New Dealers than Wallace."

In the campaign, Humphrey wrote Hyneman, "I was busier than a cat on a tin roof filled up with castor oil. I spent my time tearing around the state, meeting with county committees, seeing to it that our candidates were scheduled at meetings." After one foray into Republican country, a local newspaper denounced him as "weak, polluted, devoid of principle." But when he wheeled into Mankato for a radio speech at the teachers college, Tom Hughes, his local contact, took him around to meet Clifford Russell, editor of the staunchly Republican *Free Press*. Dazzled by the Humphrey eloquence, Russell informed his readers next day: "We have not seen his like since Floyd Olson." Crusty Elmer Benson, however, called Humphrey a "fascist" even while serving on his state campaign committee.

As campaign chairman, Humphrey met the party stars. He welcomed the new party chairman, Robert Hannegan. He hit it off so well with Georgia's

Governor Ellis Arnall that after a rally and a convivial night together, Arnall commenced calling him Pinky, the only such personage ever to do so. Humphrey's favorite visitor was Wallace. When Truman came through, Humphrey thought he spoke "without force." At the end, Humphrey could take satisfaction that the Roosevelt-Truman ticket carried Minnesota by a comfortable eighty-two thousand votes. The Democratic-Farmer-Labor party also elected its first two congressmen. Frank Starkey took the Fourth District in St. Paul, and in Minneapolis William Gallagher, sixty-six, won the Third District seat, which Humphrey had wanted. But the Republicans swept all state offices, and Humphrey, sensing a retreat from the brave internationalism of the first war years, wrote Wallace:

> I am deeply concerned at what is going on in Washington, particularly in the State department. For three and four years I have devoted my time to building a public attitude sympathetic to international organization for peace, and now [I] see the old 19th century power politics [returning in] Britain and Russia and even America, [weakening] public confidence in the soundness and effectiveness of a postwar United Nations.
>
> The progressives didn't win this election for men like [Will] Clayton and [Jesse] Jones. . . . It's about time that those persons with real power and influence in labor, farm groups and other progressive organizations rise up and demand recognition. . . .
>
> Some of us had hoped that you would be Secretary of State. . . . We are looking forward to having you as our presidential standard bearer in 1948.
>
> I am young at the game and surely inexperienced, but I do believe in putting up a fight, and I am looking for no favors. I intend to make my opportunities by hard work and by devotion to the principles I believe in.

Wallace replied: "You typify in my mind more than almost anyone I know the hope of an effective constructive liberal party in a position of national responsibility."

Meanwhile, Humphrey and Naftalin formed a small public relations firm that was mainly a front for their preparation for the next mayor's race.

12

"I'm Mayor!"

"MY LIFE is in a kind of uproar," Humphrey wrote Mrs. Barney Allen early in 1945. While standing for mayor of Minneapolis, he was classified I-A in the draft. He took a pre-induction physical exam and passed it. "I am to report for induction on February 12," he wrote Evelyn Petersen, "and unless the gods are on my side I will be one of Uncle Sam's GI Joes." "If the doctors pronounce me alive and warm Monday, there may not be a municipal campaign as far as I am concerned," he told Mrs. Allen.

From Huron, his mother wrote Muriel: "He has made such plans, he has worked so ungodly hard, it would be terribly hard for him to give them up." His father, equally sympathetic, saw further: "I surely feel sorry for you, but who knows? If you join the forces now, your chances politically when you return will be much better than had you not been in the army or navy."

The issue that was to dog Humphrey in his later campaigns was resolved, as it seemed to him then, in his favor. When the candidate, trailed by reporters, appeared at the Fort Snelling induction center, he failed his medical test. A doctor announced that a defect, a right scrotal hernia, had been found that had escaped notice in the earlier exam. "I am a lousy IV-F," Humphrey wrote his fighter-pilot friend, Bob Gannon.

Without question, Humphrey stood a far stronger chance of winning the election this time. Combined at last in a United Labor committee, AFL, CIO, and the railway unions had already endorsed him. And despite the fact that his leading role in the party merger and the 1944 statewide campaign had clearly defined him as a Democratic-Farmer-Laborite, Humphrey looked as though he might swing the city's business leaders to his side too.

Backed by both labor and capital? By liberals and conservatives? Unlikely as this may seem, it was of course possible because the contest for mayor was nonpartisan, and no Republican need feel he was deserting his party to cast a vote for Humphrey. It was possible also because the issues that Humphrey raised stirred voters on both sides.

Only his greenness, Humphrey told friends, had kept him from winning over the businessmen on the first try. Now he knew who the real leaders were, and he sought them out, offering them a city hall administration that would end the disgracefully lax law enforcement and the neglect of good community relations that were starting to drive industry and people out of the city. A key figure was John Cowles, the Iowan who had bought the Minneapolis *Star, Journal*, and *Tribune* and had a big stake in seeing the city go forward after its years of strife and decay. In 1943, Humphrey had talked only to Cowles's assistants. This time the two met for lunch. "I intend to be community-minded," he told Cowles. "While I am most appreciative of the endorsement given me by organized labor, I have made it clear to them that I am not, if elected, labor's mayor or special representative." Cowles, "very much impressed," opened doors. The men Cowles arranged for Humphrey to call on were not the young strivers Humphrey had met in 1943 but the principals—men such as John Pillsbury of Pillsbury Mills, F. Peavey Heffelfinger the grain merchant, President Lucian Sprague of the Minneapolis and St. Louis Railroad.

"Law and order"—the same issue that would play such a big part in defeating Humphrey's campaign for president a quarter-century later—was what propelled him toward his first successful race. To the businessmen he said: "The gangsters of Chicago are out to take over the city and are on their way to doing so unless they are stopped. We are starting to see business move out of the city—and people are going, too, to the suburbs. This must be halted if Minneapolis is to go on as a city."

Coincidentally, in early 1945 one Arthur Kasherman, publisher of a scandal sheet called *The Public Press*, was gunned down in the street, murdered, as the newspapers reported, "in a manner reminiscent of gangland executions during the prohibition days." In its last issue, Kasherman's paper had charged that Mayor Kline's regime was "the most corrupt within memory—racketeers in complete control." Moreover, on the morning of his death Kasherman had walked into the sheriff's office and told deputies that a Nicollet Avenue crap game was taking in $75,000 per month for a Chicago syndicate. The murder went unsolved, and when the Nicollet Avenue joint was closed, federal officers, not the police, carried out the raid.

Humphrey told businessmen, as he had told Cowles, "I am no blue nose. I do not intend to campaign on this issue alone. [But] one is not worthy of

respect and confidence of the community if he becomes a pawn or stooge for
. . . some outside influences, some invisible government. I have no intention
of letting some outside influence select the Superintendent of Police."

That was also the message Humphrey carried to churchgoers, a potent
constituency in middle-class Minneapolis. Often it was hard to tell, as the
candidate expounded the civic virtues, where a stump speech ended and a
sermon began. Three years of evangelizing addresses in church basements
had already established him a following, and he was favorably known for his
Sunday evening "University of Life" classes at the city's biggest Methodist
church. Of course Norwegian ancestry and Lutheran origins were prime
assets in Minneapolis voting, and Humphrey claimed both. At the outset of
his campaign he successfully appealed to the Rev. Tenner Thompson, an
influential Norwegian Lutheran pastor, for aid in lining up "a sizable portion
of the Minneapolis clergy." He wrote Thompson:

> I was born in a little Norwegian settlement at Wallace, South Dakota.
> My grandparents were natives of Norway. I was baptized in the Highland
> Lutheran church in a rural section just north of Lily, South Dakota. It
> just so happened when we moved to Doland, South Dakota, that there
> was no Lutheran church and our family affiliated with the Methodist church.
>
> I give you this information only that you may know that I have long
> been interested in community work. . . .

Before long, Humphrey was denouncing "the leeches of crime, vice and corruption" before Reverend Thompson's cheering parishioners.

Even as Humphrey reached out to other elements of the community, he
never doubted that "the militancy of labor in political affairs" would be decisive in his campaign. Although his university friends worked for him as hard
as ever, it was the unions that turned out the great bulk of his three or four
thousand volunteer workers. The leftist-led CIO Political Action Committee, which had shown its clout in Roosevelt's 1944 victory, mobilized support
for Humphrey. When Bob Wishart, the Communist chairman of the Hennepin County CIO, handed over names of all CIO unionists in the Eighth
and Thirteenth wards, much of the south side of Minneapolis sprouted
Humphrey-for-Mayor lawn signs. On the grimier north side, the oldline
unionists of the AFL rallied working-class neighborhoods for Humphrey.

The United Labor Committee raised fifteen thousand dollars for the campaign, almost all of which went into the Humphrey effort. The Democratic
National Committee, breaking a rule against municipal involvement, chipped
in too. The largest individual contribution reported, however, was two hundred
dollars from Hubert H. Humphrey, Sr., of Huron. The "Businessmen for
Humphrey" willing to list their names in newspaper ads were young or little
known. One small-businessman who joined Humphrey before his 1945 election and became lifelong keeper of his campaign funds was Fred Gates,

Lebanese owner of a penny arcade offering five-minute movies on hand-cranked machines in a Hennepin Avenue doorway.

The most notable Minneapolis business leader to speak out for Humphrey was Bradshaw Mintener, general counsel for Pillsbury. Dedicated to obtaining law enforcement for Minneapolis, Mintener was a trustee of Macalester College and a member of the church where Humphrey taught adult Sunday school classes. Convinced that Humphrey was a "sound fellow" and would "choose a police chief who [would] clean up the city and drive out the racketeers," Mintener addressed Rotary lunches and high school assemblies. When his Lowry Hill friends pointed out that Humphrey was a Farmer-Laborite and a Democrat, he asked: "Do you want the gangsters in here or do you want a decent administration?" The Daytons, Yankee Republican owners of the city's biggest department store, were slow to respond. But Pat Carr, a lesser Nicollect Avenue merchant, wrote Humphrey: "Businessmen are coming to the conclusion that a level-headed, sincere and earnest person that has the confidence of labor would have a distinctly good influence upon labor in the city." And George K. Belden himself, the old Citizens Alliance strike-breaker, agreed to meet with Humphrey to discuss his idea of a labor-management committee for promoting industrial peace.

Even before the primary vote, the Stassen organization knew that Mayor Kline was in trouble. When the *Tribune* reported that "14" and "Hooligan," two forms of gambling with dice, were going strong in downtown taverns, Kline rashly charged that the newspaper had printed the story to aid his opponent. "A boner—it don't pay to get on the outs with the press," Humphrey Senior wrote his son, and he proved right. After Humphrey swept the primary 2-to-1, the Cowles newspapers endorsed him, Democrat or not. After that the Republican state committee washed its hands of Kline. Humphrey wrote Freeman: "Every gambling joint in the city is doing business. Apparently [Kline] needs campaign funds, and the price of the contribution is the permission to have full sway during the election." On June 11, 1945, Humphrey was elected mayor by 86,377 votes to 55,263, the biggest majority in the city's history.

When Humphrey took office as mayor on July 2, his first two appointments acknowledged labor's role in his victory. He named George Phillips, president of the United Labor Committee and an AFL stalwart, to the Civil Service Commission, and he appointed Bob Wishart, his strongest CIO backer and head of the United Electrical Workers' big Honeywell local, to the Board of Public Welfare.

But the all-important appointment was chief of police. In Minneapolis's weak-mayor system, the police department was the one for which the mayor and not the city council was explicitly responsible. Humphrey's union backers would have liked to pick the chief because of their bitter memories of the vicious anti-labor police actions in the bloody 1934 truckers' strike. But Humphrey sided with the businessmen who saw the need for an incorruptible professional to enforce the law. He made Mintener of Pillsbury Mills chairman of the advisory committee of business, labor, and public representatives to recommend a candidate. Mintener's candidate was Ed Ryan, the one member of the force who had undergone training at J. Edgar Hoover's FBI academy in Washington and was certifiably free of corruption. A six-foot-four, 220-pound Irish neighbor of Humphrey's with whom he had often talked city crime on his front porch, Ryan was also Humphrey's choice from the start.

Wishart, the CIO representative on the committee, held out even when the vote was 12-to-1 for Ryan. A sturdy organizer who had built his Local 1145 at Minneapolis Honeywell's main war plant into the state's biggest union, Wishart had risen to prominence in the fast-growing CIO. For the Communists he played the part of the friendly, cooperative front man who could somehow always bring his followers around to a pro-Soviet position. As long as the war went on, cooperation between Wishart and Humphrey posed no big problems, either in the statewide election campaign Humphrey managed in 1944 or when he campaigned for mayor in 1945. But after the death of Roosevelt on April 12, 1945, and even more after VJ Day ended the wartime Soviet alliance in September, it became awkward for Wishart to play both sides. When Wishart resisted the Ryan nomination, Humphrey led his friend into the corridor to tell him, "Bob, I know what's bothering you. You figure Ryan worked too closely with the FBI and that bothers some of your friends. But I tell you Ed Ryan is not a witch hunter, not anti-labor. He's honest— and I need him." Though Wishart finally went along, his vote nearly cost him his place at the head of the Hennepin County CIO Council, and Humphrey himself had to go on the radio and mobilize public pressure to get the city council, after two weeks' delay, to accept Ryan, 21 to 4.

Even before Humphrey moved into city hall he was tested. Chickie Berman of the Syndicate, hearing a rumor that Humphrey had a price but a high one, asked to see the mayor-elect. When Bill Simms, Humphrey's aide, pointed out that he'd campaigned trumpeting that his door would be open to anybody, Humphrey agreed but said, "I want you to sit in." As Simms later recalled, Berman began by asking straight off: "What do you want?"

"What do you mean, 'what do I want?' " asked Humphrey.

Berman said: "Well, what do you want so we can operate like we used to? I don't mean absolutely—we don't mind getting knocked off once in a while so you can keep your record clear. But you're going to ruin our business."

Humphrey replied, "Well, what's your proposition, Berman?"

Berman said, "Twenty-five percent of the take."

Humphrey answered: "I don't think that's a good deal for me. Let's make it 75–25, my 75 and your 25."

Berman was shocked and cried: "My God, that would break us."

Jumping to his feet, Humphrey announced: "That's exactly right—and that's what's going to happen to you."

Action followed at once. Mayor Humphrey issued an order, which Chief Ryan simply posted where all cops could see it: "We will enforce the law." As Humphrey said later: "Our job of closing down the town and keeping it closed was facilitated by the very fact that illegal operations had been so well organized. In the past the single order of the racket bosses put the gambling devices 'down' whenever the heat was on. When the heat was off, up would come the boards, the dice, the after-hour spots, the one-armed bandits, again by the single and mysterious order from the top. The stern words from our Police Department put them down, and they stayed down as long as our administration [was] in office."

At the same time, when an officer sent a youth under age twenty-one into a Hennepin Avenue restaurant to buy a drink and then arrested the owner, Humphrey would chide the officer, saying there would be no more "entrapment." Later he called all tavern owners and their wives to city hall and told them he wanted them to go before the city council and ask for pay increases for the police, the funds to come out of the increased amount they would pay for their tavern license. "I know," he told them, "you are paying off policemen now—this must stop. Don't you wives want your husbands to be involved in a legitimate business that doesn't bribe policemen?" He pointed out that he had put an end to entrapment. "Miracle of miracles," said a friend of Humphrey's who happened to drop in during the session, "they voted to cooperate."

It wasn't easy. No sooner was Humphrey in office than another underworld shooting took place. Late at night at the Casablanca, one of the downtown clubs controlled by the mob, a Teamster official was shot dead by the owner, Rubin Shetsky, also known in Chicago as "Big Wayne Saunders." "The gangsters are out to embarrass you—more power to you, boy," wrote Mintener. Ryan's police rounded up witnesses. But on the day the jury convicted him, Shetsky fled. With the FBI's help, Ryan finally caught up with Shetksy in California and brought him back to serve his term of life imprisonment. After that the gang killings ceased, but Mintener received telephoned threats. One chilling night as Muriel unlocked the door for Humphrey, arriving home from a meeting, a shot rang out in the driveway. Sure that it was an attempt to scare, not kill, him, Humphrey went out in the dark and searched the bushes for the intruder. Obviously his administration had gained the upper hand. But the city council never got around to reforming liquor licensing, and racketeers Kid Cann and Tommy Banks unlawfully holding multiple licenses under false names, survived Humphrey's term in office.

Of equal importance was how Humphrey's police arm handled labor disputes. Again, following talks with union chieftains, Humphrey gave Ryan plain orders: "The Police department will respect a picket line and shall not escort workers through such lines. If police are present, their presence shall be for the express purpose of maintaining order and upholding the law as pertains to property and the rights of workers to picket."

Not once while Humphrey held office did the police intervene in a labor dispute. To an important extent this was because Humphrey, ever sure that "true collective bargaining" could settle all differences, threw himself again and again between the disputing parties and got them together, often in his office, where he chivvied and cajoled the contending sides until they broke down and settled. Three months after he became mayor he stepped into a dispute at Minneapolis Honeywell's main plant, where the union was on the point of striking for lost war-work overtime pay, and helped negotiate a trend-setting peacetime "necessary wage adjustment." "In this testing time of reconversion," he wrote his friend Julian Hartt, "we have had no serious strikes. We are well on our way to a healthy readjustment into peacetime production." Later there were plenty of strikes, including one by city hospital workers and another by teachers.

But none was too hot for Humphrey to handle, not even the 1947 telephone strike in which unionists broke the law against mass picketing. When Bell system supervisors tried sleeping in the offices to avoid the picket lines, Humphrey ruled, "If you want to run a hotel, you will have to apply for a license." He confessed in so many words to not enforcing the [anti-picketing] law, and when the Minneapolis *Star* castigated him for it, Humphrey, furious at the reproof, wrote Cowles, "I didn't send in police because it would have precipitated a police battle."

From the start, Humphrey was determined to do something about improving the dismal state of community relations in Minneapolis. "Members of the Jewish faith," campaign aide Henry Piper wrote pointedly, had been "among those who contributed most liberally" to his election drive. In office, he wrote to Nell Russell of the Minneapolis *Spokesman*, a black newspaper: "I fully recognize that the Negro people of our city have not been given the opportunity for a private business nor have they been the recipients of fair treatment in our housing."

Within a week after being sworn in, Humphrey headed for Chicago with Elmer Kelm to find out from Mayor Kelley about that city's proposed Fair Employment Practices ordinance. On his return he met with liberal aldermen to push a stronger measure for Minneapolis. Soon he was writing Grace Langley in chagrin, "I have already learned that it takes a lot of patience to accomplish anything." As mayor he could, and did, shame a leading hotelkeeper into admitting a prominent black visitor to whom he had refused a room. But after brief hearings, a council subcommittee voted down the mayor's bill 3-to-2.

As with law enforcement and all other matters on which he had to fight for community support, Humphrey's strategy was to form a citizens' committee. Race, he wrote a friend, was the most "ticklish" matter of all. For a starter he set up a huge advisory panel that numbered practically all the top names in business, labor, and the professions. Then he created a smaller group called the Mayor's Committee on Human Relations. And here he made an inspired nomination. To head the inner group he named the Rev. Reuben K. Youngdahl. If anybody carried enough prestige and power of persuasion to sway civic and moral opinion in the Minneapolis emerging from World War II it was this young, Swedish Lutheran pastor. He had built his neighborhood church in less than a decade into one of the largest Protestant congregations in the country. He was attractive, eloquent, forward-looking. He happened also to be the brother of Judge Luther W. Youngdahl, elected Republican governor of Minnesota in 1946.

The committee set about its assigned task of "reordering the pattern of social relationships" in Minneapolis. It was high time. A slashing polemic by Publicist Carey McWilliams in a 1946 magazine article labeled Minneapolis "the capital of anti-Semitism in America." To attack the festering problem the committee launched a "self-survey" of the city's racial attitudes. The survey, organized by Dr. Charles S. Johnson and five other Fisk University sociologists on funds raised privately in the city, enlisted no fewer than six hundred volunteer data-collectors. Blacks and Jews walked side by side with Yankee housewives and Scandinavian farmers' sons to check out discriminatory practices in specific areas—offices, factories, schools, churches. Confrontations occurred daily; consciousness was raised fast. On the publicity front, Humphrey, Youngdahl, and Mintener kept up a cannonade. One year after the first setback, the city council passed Humphrey's Fair Employment Practices ordinance. The big banks and department stores began hiring young blacks in increasing numbers. Though the Minneapolis ordinance had sharper teeth than Chicago's, the Mayor's committee dealt out few fines. Instead, when restaurant owners and others resisted, Humphrey simply brought them together in private with Reverend Youngdahl, who pressured them into line. Progress was made, but the battle was not won. As late as 1961, when Art Naftalin was elected mayor, the Minneapolis Club, bastion of the old order, delayed sending him the mayor's usual honorary card of admission. After a reporter from the *Tribune*, asked about it, the card arrived, with a formal and polite but not especially warm letter, and Mayor Naftalin became the first Jewish member. The Minnekahda club, where the same people played golf, barred Jews until at least a decade later.

"An office or position can be one of importance or strength," Humphrey had told Cowles, "if the occupant has the enthusiasm, the initiative and the capacity to so make it." Who could doubt the enthusiasm and initiative of a mayor who raced around town to union picnics, teachers meetings, and housing sessions with veterans' wives, who rushed off to Washington to testify for a Missouri Valley Authority five hundred miles away ("We have a very large trade territory")—or who complained when the local Civic and Commerce Association met to discuss bridging the city's railroad tracks without him? Apologetic but dazed, the Association's president replied: "We are not used to a mayor who wants to get involved." When Humphrey met the president of Cargill, world's largest grain firm, his first question was why had the company shifted the site of a fuel depot from the city to a suburb?

The mayor's capacity for making the most of his limited powers was shown in the handling of a matter vital to the city's commercial future. Hearing that Northwest Airlines was on the point of moving its headquarters to Seattle, Humphrey rushed to tell its president, Croil Hunter, that the city needed him. Hunter said the airline wanted to stay at its Wold Chamberlain airport base, but members of the Metropolitan Airports Commission had told him there was no room for expansion. Checking, Humphrey discovered that the army was about to turn over Fort Snelling, the post adjoining the airfield, to the Veterans Administration. Humphrey flew to Washington to see General Omar Bradley, the European war commander who had come home to head the Veterans Administration. "I cannot tell you how pleased I was with this conference," Humphrey wrote a friend. Not only was Bradley agreeable to ceding much of the army's land to enlarge the airfield. He also informed the Mayor that a huge Veterans hospital would be built on the remaining portion of the site. Said Humphrey: "It means that the city will be one of the great national centers for veterans' affairs and also have one of the finest airports in the country. A tenstrike!"

The mayor did not do everything himself—but he tried. He often said later it was the best job he ever had. He rode with the cops on their night patrols. He raced to fires. He read the comics over the radio to kids kept home during the polio epidemic. He took a swing in a park department hole-in-one tourney ("What a bum player you are," wrote a friend who happened by). He saw all visitors. When his friend Ellis Arnall of Georgia came to town to address a Jackson Day dinner, he rushed out to the airport to meet him. In doing so he upstaged General Mills Chairman Harry Bullis, who had arranged a welcoming luncheon. Somewhat testily Bullis wrote: "Thanks for attending the luncheon I thought I was giving in honor of Governor Arnall. Thanks for taking the time to go out to the airport to meet Governor Arnall and bringing him to the Minneapolis Club so he could meet the group which I had invited."

He was not so good at delegating. He had a way of coming into the office after late-night meetings and going through people's desks to see if they had done their jobs. Then he would go through his mail, and next morning his two aides, Art Naftalin and Bill Simms, would find it all in their baskets, every item marked RUSH! He never kept to schedules, not only because he liked to talk but equally because others liked to listen to him. Naftalin and Simms marveled at how a scrap of information in a memo, mysteriously mated with items from the capacious mayoral memory, blossomed, for example, into a flowery garland for the city's textile industry or a full-blown appeal for youth employment. On a weekend dash to Huron he was pressed into the pulpit, after which his father wrote: "Harry Carlson told me that more money was taken in the loose collection Sunday morning than in memory—

some sixty-nine dollars. You surely know how to shake them down."

After Humphrey failed to arrive for an appointment, his university colleague Frank Rarig wrote: "You are getting a reputation. If you continue on your present course, you will run down your health and end up by pleasing nobody in your effort to please all." Visitors who noted the young mayor's "jet-black hair" were already adding "what there is left of it."

Republicans or DFLers, they came to see the mayor. Republican Bob Naegele, the outdoor advertising man, dropped in to complain that the city clerk had said he could not lease a city-owned vacant lot for one of his billboards. Humphrey called in the city clerk, who repeated that it was illegal. "Are you the city attorney?" barked Humphrey, who then summoned the city attorney. Asked his opinion, the city attorney said that leasing the lot for a signboard was lawful. He turned and left, the city clerk huffed out, and Naegele shook the mayor's hand and departed whistling.

Working late one night, Humphrey heard a din outside and went to the window. On the street below was a knot of noisy college boys. Teetering atop the parapet along the street was Doug Kelm, son of DFL Chairman Elmer Kelm in town from St. Johns University on a jape with classmates. "What the hell are you doing, Kelm?" shouted the mayor. Young Kelm said he was broke and hungry. Humphrey said: "I'll send you down twenty dollars if you'll get the hell off that wall and get your ass back to St. Johns." In a moment Bill Simms appeared and handed Kelm a twenty-dollar bill, and the boys went off and had a party.

One day a letter landed on Mayor Humphrey's desk from his old professor in faraway Louisiana inviting him to apply for a teaching vacancy. Humphrey gleefully dictated his reply. "Dear Doc Harris: I'm delighted at the offer but for one little immediate problem—I'm mayor!" He told Harris: "I haven't been home for supper five times in three months." On the first New Year's Eve of his term he found time for a "hilarious house party," he wrote a South Dakota friend, but on the way home he "had to learn out the window and give forth of that wonderful bourbon." In his first term in office, Humphrey delivered one thousand speeches. His wife, following a practice that was to continue for years, went off alone with the children to a rented lake cottage for the summer; Humphrey joined them on occasional Saturday nights. To Gideon Seymour, who had run a complimentary editorial in the *Tribune* on his first anniversary in office, Humphrey wrote: "I literally live for the job." When his sister Frances took him to task for saying he "could not afford to get involved in Humphrey 'family emotions,' " he replied that it was only "Humphrey style" to "put my work ahead of my family." But then he added: "I know that is inexcusable. Letters like yours make me realize what a jerk I am."

That was rare self-reproach. Humphrey had indeed "grown in stature," as Frances wrote, and was busily adding cubits. He had already been mentioned for cabinet office. He had been designated Minneapolis Man of the

Year (in a vote that named Stassen *Minnesota* Man of the Year). And as the next mayoral election in 1947 drew near, it appeared that he had more than met his supporters' expectations. Only one big item remained unfulfilled—reform of the city charter—and this became his talking point for a second term as he stood for reelection in 1947. By that time he rated so high with the voters that the opposition had a hard time finding a candidate to oppose him. For his second race, in addition to the backing of organized labor, the president of the Chamber of Commerce, the vice presidents of General Mills, Pillsbury, and Honeywell, and David Winton of Winton Lumber served on his campaign committee, and all the city newspapers backed him. Even the diehard Daytons contributed to his campaign. And in the June runoff election, he rolled over his opponent, Frank F. Collins, by 102,696 votes to 52,358. The fifty-thousand-vote margin set a new record in Minneapolis city elections.

But Humphrey never accomplished the promised charter reform. The blue-ribbon committee he had named to draw up a restructured government for Minneapolis held more meetings than any other. But labor had misgivings from the first. The council members, many of whom had union ties, figuring their friend would not always be mayor, drew back from enlarging the powers of the mayor's office. When Humphrey first pledged it in 1945, the business community was all for charter reform as a way of tightening city finances and reducing taxes. But after Humphrey's 1947 sweep, some of these people also began to fear that their friend might not remain at City Hall—and turned cool to charter reform. This was because they were Republicans and feared that the mayor would use a charter triumph to grab for the Republican-held Senate seat in the following year's elections. Their attitude, signaling an end to Humphrey's bipartisan honeymoon as the time for his decision about 1948 drew near, led him to protest to Mintener:

> I hope you feel that I have kept the faith—but I am very disturbed about the continuous political maneuvering that is going on in certain quarters. Some of our Republican friends have stated quite frankly that they are not going to cooperate in charter reform because if such reform takes place it will be a feather in Humphrey's cap.
>
> Are we going to sacrifice the charter on the altar of partisanship? I have had the courage to resist and oppose my political friends on this issue, and I think it is about time that some of the bigwigs of the Republican party realize that the writing of a city charter is not a Republican or Democratic program.

For once, Humphrey was not enthusiastic about being the man in the middle. Siding with those who charged that the city was headed for insolvency under the old hand-to-mouth system, the mayor took the lead in forcing a showdown. The board of education, strapped for funds, announced it would have to shorten the school year by a month. Thereupon, as expected, the teachers struck against the pay cut.

So it was that the referendum on the new charter came up as voters fumed over their closed schools. That too was expected, and it infuriated the council members fighting the new charter. It also prompted Wishart to warn Humphrey, "The relationship between you and the CIO and AFL is to say the least considerably strained." At the last minute the state supreme court ruled that the proposed change that the charter commission had so laboriously prepared was improperly posed as a substitute instead of an amendment. With the referendum off, Humphrey, obliged to find funds to settle the teachers' strike, was forced to back an unpopular 1 percent emergency levy on all ratepayers.

In the end the mayor's commission recast its proposal to comply with the court's ruling, and when put to a vote in the fall of 1948 the revised version was soundly defeated. Humphrey called the court's decision "a hard blow," but it scarcely hurt him. By the time his charter lost, he was locked in a bigger battle. The Republicans' suspicions were confirmed: Mintener, who had seconded Humphrey through all his tough mayoral bouts, had to tell him that as a Republican he could no longer sit in his corner. For Humphrey, seizing the most telling themes of his mayorship and fusing them dramatically with issues of national urgency, was now fighting for a partisan prize: the Republicans' Senate seat.

13

Fission on the Left

WORLD WAR II never came close to winning the peace and freedom and plenty that Humphrey had proclaimed so often and so ardently as its goals. When it ended, President Truman cut off lend-lease to all allies and withheld further economic aid to the Soviet Union. If these moves were meant to induce Russian cooperation in postwar arrangements for conquered Europe, that hope was soon dashed. Instead the Russians insisted on Moscow-dominated regimes in all lands their troops occupied. Thereupon statesmanship failed; the so-called United Nations turned into a cockpit of confrontation—and the alliance dissolved into cold war.

This abrupt development, as we now know, set the framework for the rest of our lives. It did so especially for Humphrey. The Communists to his left, having survived the successive flipflops of the Moscow line, could hang on for one more hairpin turn. The great bulk of Americans to his right, whose dominant sentiment toward world affairs was an attachment to their own nationality, hardly felt the force of the split with the Soviets at all. But for Humphrey and all progressives like him who thought World War II not only a just war but a war fought because peace had at last become indivisible, the break with the Communist ally was so wrenching that drastic personal readjustment became necessary.

In Minnesota, though he never said so, Humphrey had been a Popular Front man. He had worked quite comfortably with the Communists and their sympathizers to unify the Left in the 1944 Democratic-Farmer-Labor party merger. He continued to work with them as he stood for mayor. In January 1945 he wrote his friend Freeman, in the marines: "As far as I'm concerned, Orv, people can be so damned far to the left that they're on the other side of the world. I have no intention of interfering with anyone's politics. You know that I have always considered myself to have a few friends who have been classed as so-called radicals and that's never bothered me. . . . I hate to be put in the class of a person who does 'red baiting' and I refuse to be lined up with those persons and forces who are hanging on every little detail of a mistake and dissension that may exist on the part of Britain, Russia and the U.S."

For the young Humphrey, imbued with a Wilsonian vision of world order, Henry Wallace was the national leader to look to in 1945, Wallace too was a midwesterner who saw the world as one. Just as Humphrey had preached internationalism in the union halls and church basements of Minnesota, Wallace as Roosevelt's vice president had proclaimed postwar abundance for America and unified government for the world. He promised sixty million jobs and an enduring peace in the "century of the common man." For the renomination of this most visionary of New Dealers as vice president, Humphrey fought to the end of the 1944 Democratic convention. When Truman won out and Roosevelt then made Wallace secretary of commerce, Humphrey wrote: "Minnesota is expecting you to be our presidential candidate in 1948." On the day of Roosevelt's death in 1945, he wrote Wallace: "I simply can't conceal my emotions. How I wish you were at the helm. I know Mr. Truman will rise to the heights of statesmanship. But we need you as you have never been needed before."

Elected mayor shortly thereafter, Humphrey was at once caught up in city affairs. He had less to say about developments abroad. He was even too busy to attend to Minnesota affairs, sending Naftalin or Freeman to represent him at DFL committee meetings. At the end of 1945, writing Democratic National Chairman Robert Hannegan about DFL Chairman Kelm's plan to step down before the following year's campaigning, he commented that "there will be an attempt made by the old Farmer-Labor section of the party to force through one of their own choosing." Confidently he added: "This attempt will not be successful." When Elaine Cox reminded him thereafter that "leftwingers" in the CIO Political Action Committee might "get control" of the party, he replied simply that he wished "not to become publicly identified with any faction." Not a radical, he was still talking like a Popular Fronter.

The left wing struck first in the party's spring 1946 caucuses. Assigning key leftists responsibility for each city district, they picked up no fewer than 120 of the 160 delegates in Humphrey's own Hennepin County. In his own Second Ward, Tony DeMaio, organizer for the United Electrical Workers and a Communist, packed the precinct caucuses and sent both Humphrey and Naftalin down to defeat. Popular as he was, Humphrey got to the state convention in St. Paul in June only because the Hennepin County convention subsequently sent him as a delegate at large.

Although both Naftalin and Eugenie Anderson, delegate from Red Wing, warned of trouble, neither Humphrey nor his other friends were prepared for what happened next. As the party's most prominent officeholder, Humphrey was expected to deliver the keynote address. But when he arrived he was jeered at and spat upon. His wife was refused admission until Humphrey got his police driver to escort her in. His supporters had to muscle their way in. As Humphrey rose to speak, there were cries of "fascist" and "warmonger." A beefy sergeant at arms shouted at him, "Sit down, you son of a bitch, or I'll knock you down." He was not allowed to finish his speech.

It was an outright coup. The totally organized left wing took command of the DFL convention, its rules, its procedures. They passed resolutions excoriating Winston Churchill for his "iron curtain" speech, Truman for "betrayal" of Roosevelt's war aims and peace plans. They put through their platform, their party nominees, their election slate. They picked Harold Barker, a smalltown legislator from northern Minnesota, as party chairman and named him, a captive figurehead, as their candidate for governor.

The Humphreyites were flattened. Freeman, as he said later, was "just mad." Humphrey, resolved to salvage something from the rout, went late that night to his Communist friend Bob Wishart and said that for unity's sake the party had better give his people a couple of places. Wishart consulted with Bill Mauseth, the Communist director of the state CIO Political Action Committee, and grudgingly the victors agreed to take Eugenie Anderson, Humphrey's supporter from Red Wing, as second vice chairman and Orville Freeman, the newly returned veteran, as treasurer. Next day, as the list was read off, Bob Sharon, a law student who was later to be chief justice of Minnesota's supreme court, leaped to his feet and in an impassioned speech persuaded the delegates to make Freeman party secretary instead of treasurer.

It was a small enough concession. The Humphrey forces knew they had been whipped. Humphrey confided to Dudley Parsons that he was tempted to challenge the winners then and there by entering the party primary as candidate for Congress in Minneapolis's Third District. He did nothing of the kind. Instead he continued to work with Wishart and other leftists in city affairs as if nothing had happened and told Freeman and others who wanted to fight back that nothing could be done until after the November elections.

But greater forces were at work that could not be stayed. Abroad, the cold war loomed as Communists were forced out of government in France and Italy, and democratic leaders were excluded from office in Poland, Rumania, and Bulgaria. At home, strikes and scarcities spawned discontent with Truman's rule. While militant young liberals such as Walter Reuther and James Carey fought to wrest control of the big CIO unions, conservatives around the country caught the changing national mood and called for a crackdown on labor. At this point, James Loeb, a Washington liberal in touch with Mrs. Roosevelt and prominent New Dealers, wrote in the *New Republic* of May 13, 1946, that progressives opposed to Communism had to mobilize or the American Left would be lost to the Communists.

On her Mississippi River bluff at Red Wing, Eugenie Anderson read Loeb's call to action and invited him to discuss it with Minnesotans "struggling with the same problem." It happened that Loeb vacationed that summer in nearby Wisconsin. One day he came to lunch with Humphrey, Naftalin, Kirkpatrick, and Mrs. Anderson. Loeb made his pitch that liberals would have to split away and drive the Communists and their friends out of the progressive movement if the country was not to lapse into blind reaction. Afterward, Mrs. Anderson was jubilant. Humphrey, she wrote Loeb, had accepted "the position we had been pleading with [him] to take since the week after the DFL convention." Echoing Loeb, he had told an AFL gathering, "Not only must we say what we're for but what we're against." Two days later, speaking to U.N. supporters, the mayor said the Popular Front was washed up and urged liberals to compare their allegiance to Roosevelt's Four Freedoms with the actual status of these freedoms in Russian-occupied Europe.

At this awkward moment, Humphrey's old idol Secretary Wallace delivered an extremely important speech on September 12, 1946, to a mass rally of liberals and radicals at New York's Madison Square Garden. To win peace in a world that seemed rapidly to be losing it, Wallace declared, the United States should accept Russia's arrangements for Eastern Europe. This was music to the ears of Communists and their sympathizers. And to liberals such as Humphrey's friend and benefactor President Charles Turck of Macalester College, who believed that peace was paramount, the Wallace message had powerful appeal. But Wallace's argument completely undercut Secretary of State James Byrnes's efforts to negotiate peace treaties in Paris and brought Wallace's instant ouster.

For Humphrey, the speech forced a parting of the ways. Dismayed that "a very personal friend, courageous, progressive . . . is out of the cabinet," Humphrey said at first, "I just happened to disagree with one small paragraph." But of course that was the paragraph for which Wallace had been fired. "Mr. Wallace says there are spheres of influence—I say this is one world," Humphrey told a gathering of workers and farmers in Minneapolis. To L. M. Allen he wrote: "Whatever happens in any part of the world finally concerns us. . . . I cannot accept the philosophy that Eastern Europe and Asia should be left to the Russians, and Western Europe and Latin America should be left to the U.S. That is the philosophy that motivated Chamberlain at Munich. That is what brought on the World War."

When Wallace came to Minneapolis soon afterward, Humphrey met with him in private, explained how Communists and their sympathizers had captured the Minnesota party, and pleaded with Wallace to say in his speech next day that his sympathy with the Soviet position was not to be construed as an endorsement of the American Communists. But Wallace never said it.

Even after his break with Wallace, Humphrey was so loath to cut loose that, as Eugenie Anderson said later, "we seemed to be fighting for his soul." His friends by now were calling on the FBI and writing to people as far away as New York for evidence of Communists in the new DFL leadership. Orville Freeman actually charged Douglas Hall, the party's candidate for Congress in the Fifth District, with being an unacknowledged party member. Angrily protesting, Bob Wishart reminded Humphrey that Hall had been his "staunch supporter." Humphrey, while withholding outright endorsement, took a position sufficiently ambivalent for Hall to send thanks after the campaign for "your encouragement."

But after the Republicans swept the 1946 elections, Wishart himself came under pressure to repudiate his Communist past. At the national CIO convention in November, President Phil Murray suddenly offered a policy resolution stating that "this organization is not and must not be Communist controlled and inspired"; he followed this up with another requiring local CIO councils to conform to national policy. In Minnesota, Communist Bill Mauseth had to resign as director of the CIO's state Political Action Committee, and as a first step toward divesting himself of such ties Wishart, head of the Minneapolis CIO council, withdrew from the national board of the Communist-controlled United Electrical Workers.

It was in 1947 that Humphrey finally tore loose from his last remaining Popular Front links and openly seized the leadership of the fight to recapture Minnesota's DFL party from the leftwingers. On January 4, 1947, the mayor and his friends took part at Jim Loeb's invitation in the founding meeting of Americans for Democratic Action in Washington. The aim of this small but potent group was to establish a political and trade union leadership on the left that was not Communist. Reinhold Niebuhr, the most influential American theologian since Jonathan Edwards, was the founding spirit. Mrs. Roosevelt was very much present. Walter Reuther, David Dubinsky, and Emil Rieve represented labor. The Easterners, meeting Humphrey for the first time, could hardly credit their senses. Here was a recruit so youthful, so eloquent, so expressive of precisely their sentiments, and yet so midwestern. To old New Dealers such as Leon Henderson and Chester Bowles, here was a liberal with a future. They elected him vice chairman.

Humphrey, standing for reelection in the spring of 1947 in yet another nonpartisan race, still did what he could to keep his support on the left. When Loeb sent a visiting British Labour party leader to Minneapolis for an enormously enthusiastic session with prospective ADA members, Humphrey absented himself from the meeting. He also sought the endorsement of the Democratic-Farmer-Labor Association, stronghold of the leftists, and got it by signing a pledge of unity. But again large events supervened. On March 12, 1947, President Truman went before Congress to proclaim the cold war. Asking military aid for Greece and Turkey, he vowed that the United States would aid these or any other countries threatened by international Communism. This was the Truman Doctrine, and its polarizing effects were felt everywhere, including Minnesota. Isolationist ex-Governor Elmer Benson went on the radio to denounce the President as "imperialist." The Farmer-Labor Association leftists, with whom Humphrey had tried to compromise, demanded that Truman take back what he had said. Thereupon Humphrey, whose reelection campaign was just getting under way, called together his ADA supporters and in a rousing, two-and-one-half-hour speech attacked the Communists and their sympathizers within the DFL as "totalitarians of the Left." He said: "We're not going to let the political philosophy of the DFL be dictated from the Kremlin. You can be a liberal without being a Communist, and you can be a progressive without being a Communist sympathizer, and we're a liberal progressive party out here. We're not going to let this left-wing Communist ideology be the prevailing force because the people of this state won't accept it, and what's more, it's wrong."

At last, Humphrey was out in the open. From that time on it was outright war between Humphrey and the ruling leftwingers for control of the DFL—"them or us," he said. Despite the enmity of the left, Humphrey won reelection in Minneapolis with as big a labor vote as ever. But he already saw overthrow of the leftist state leadership as "a life and death matter" for "my own political future." For he was now looking beyond the mayoralty to a higher personal goal, to standing in the 1948 elections for state office, either the governorship or the U. S. Senate. There could be no chance of winning so long as the leftwingers ran the party and kept adopting resolutions and issuing statements that were critical of U. S. foreign policy and often downright pro-Soviet. "So long as this leadership is in control there would be no possibility of electing anybody in Minnesota," he informed Gael Sullivan at Democratic national headquarters. When leftists denounced the Marshall plan for European recovery, he told DFLer Clarence Madsen: "A political party that has to go around apologizing for the foolish and irrational resolutions of a militant minority is a party that is doomed politically." He wrote Dudley Parsons: "Unfortunately for the success of the DFL party, it finds itself made the tool of a militant minority which delights in resolutions that follow dictates from sources other than the DFL philosophy. People in Minnesota just won't take this. This is a state made up of wholesome people, people who are Catholics, Lutherans, Methodists, Baptists, etc. They are confused by the twists and turns of what appears to be the official position of the DFL party."

In the war that Humphrey now waged he sought more outside help. In an "exhilarating" five-and-one-half-hour session with CIO President Murray in Pittsburgh, he obtained the full-time assistance of a veteran coal-field organizer to help swing members of the Steelworkers union on the Iron Range to his side. Walter Reuther, victorious in his scrap to oust Reds from United

Auto Workers leadership, agreed to pay for a skillful CIO full-timer from Washington to work among union members in the Twin Cities. Jim Carey, CIO secretary-treasurer, lent one of his best men part time to help line up members of Minneapolis's black community.

For the Humphreyite fight to win back party control, Orville Freeman's role was of key importance. His election as party secretary at the 1946 convention was a concession extracted from the leftwing victors as the price of immediate peace. Long before the mayor himself declared open war, Freeman had been preparing the Humphreyites' comeback drive to recapture the DFL when the party met again at the June 1948 showdown convention.

In this drive the Minnesota ADA formed the nucleus. Though it never numbered more than one hundred in all, the group functioned as a kind of continuing caucus in which the leaders, with Humphrey at the center, talked out their battle plans. Throughout the state the party's seventy-odd county chairmen also came to play a pivotal part. Most were old Democrats—Irish Catholics or Germans. A few were linked up with the ADA. But regardless of their past allegiances, they were brought into the Humphreyite combat formations by that decorated (Legion of Merit, Purple Heart) Marine field commander (Bougainville), Orville Freeman. "They were begging for leadership," Freeman recalled later. As soon as they realized that the party secretary who sought them out in their homes was bent on a fight to the finish, "they became fiercely loyal to me." Thus Freeman during 1947 and early 1948 created a base for his own as well as for Humphrey's subsequent career in Minnesota politics.

An important early battle of the Humphreyite drive to recapture party control took place at the first Young Democrat-Farmer-Labor statewide convention in November. This meeting, called because the Democratic National Committee wanted to start a Young Democrat chapter in the state, turned into the first successful party uprising against the ruling leftists. Freeman said later: "I recruited five young men right after the war—students. They were Don Fraser, son of the university law school dean and later congressman and mayor; Fritz Mondale, later senator and vice president; Doug Kelm, son of the Democratic National Committeeman and Fraser's roommate; Tom Hughes, later director of the U.S. overseas agricultural service; and Dale McIver, later assistant U.S. attorney general. Fraser and Kelm were then at the University, Mondale and McIver at Macalester, Hughes at Hamline."

Like Freeman himself, certain of these young men got their first experience of combat against Communism in the American Veterans Committee. In the summer of 1946, Fraser and Kelm formed a Minnesota AVC chapter and at once tangled with party activists. Going on to the national AVC convention at Milwaukee the following year they linked up with such leaders as Franklin D. Roosevelt, Jr., and Michigan's Soapy Williams to defeat a Communist bid for control. Housing in Minneapolis was almost unobtainable then. But when Fraser and Kelm were offered rooms by a landlord who refused to rent to a Nisei veteran, they raised a stink. With Mayor Humphrey on their side, they got the city council to pass an ordinance outlawing restrictive covenants in real estate.

Starting a Young Democratic-Farmer-Labor club at the university, these activists applied other lessons learned in the AVC. Only about eight turned out for their first meeting, at which Naftalin was the "older person" invited to speak. He suggested each man bring ten to the next meeting. They did, and when eighty students appeared the next time to hear Freeman, who was at twenty-nine another "older person," Fraser called on all present to bring five apiece to the third meeting. This time a crowd of 600 showed up at the Teamster hall, addressed by Humphrey himself, and the meeting ended with Fraser urging all present to bring *one* person to the organizing convention of the Minnesota YDFL at the Minneapolis Labor Temple two weeks later.

The Democratic National Committee and the state DFL party both sent representatives to organize the convention, but the Humphreyites had all the momentum. Kelm said later: "We had created such a steamroller that we couldn't control it. We were successful beyond our fondest dreams." The boisterous Humphreyites shouted through their motions and resolutions. DFL Chairman Harold Barker, when he finally got the floor, accused them of being "Goebbels types." Leftist Paul Martin, nominal co-chairman, was swept aside. The victors escorted Bill Kubicek, picked because at 32 he had "stature," to the platform as their chairman. From this fight the young Humphreyites went on to the national Young Democratic Clubs convention at Cleveland, where they fought so uproariously for civil rights that one Southern regular said, "If these are right-wingers, God save us from their left-wingers."

Shortly afterward, on December 29, 1947, Henry Wallace announced his third-party presidential candidacy. Dining with Freeman that night, Gus Tyler, another old AVC graduate and David Dubinsky's right-hand strategist in the garment workers' union, exclaimed: "It's all over—we've won." It was a prescient comment, as things turned out, anticipating that voters would turn away from a Communist-backed insurgency. But that was certainly not how prospects looked to other anti-Communists on the left as 1948 began. Nationally, President Truman scraped bottom in the polls. In Minnesota, Elmer Benson announced for the left-wingers that when the DFL convention met, it would undoubtedly name electors for Wallace—and Truman would be left to run as an independent in Minnesota if at all.

If 1948 was the year of decision in Minnesota, the cold war helped decide the winners. Bread-and-butter issues may have bulked larger as election time neared, but when the Russians sent troops into Prague and blockaded Berlin, and then the United States struck back by airlifting food to Berlin and moving A-bombers into Britain, the Humphreyites leaped on their foes as Soviet apologists. They forced bitter personal confrontations within families, between union brothers, among faculty colleagues. Humphrey did not hesitate to address identical letters to five DFL chieftains who had allowed their names to be used by the Wallaceite Independent Voters of Minnesota: "May I suggest as one friend to another that you resign. . . ." Rather than be pilloried as a pinko, a former lieutenant governor caved in and replied that he would quit. The mayor, now upbraided daily for the red-baiting he once shrank from, wrote Henry Olson: "The only ones I have ever called Communists are those who are Communists." But in Humphrey's "life or death" fight, partisans drew few distinctions. The left-wingers railed at Humphrey as a "fascist." It was impossible to call crusty old Elmer Benson a Communist— he was a millionaire landowner. But the Humphreyites' idea of holding back on name-calling was to say of an opponent: "If he's not one, he's gypping the party out of its dues." For the greater number who simply insisted as lifelong Farmer-Laborites on siding with the Left, Humphrey's contemptuous appellation was "mushhead."

Hectoring, pressuring, plotting, planning, the Humphreyites reached the point that winter where they were ready to pull a coup of their own. The left-wingers had been ruling through a small committee within the Executive Committee that effectively excluded even Freeman and Eugenie Anderson from participation. The ultimate party authority between conventions, the large and unwieldy Central Committee of more than a hundred members, had not met at all. But the party constitution provided that if a group could get the signature of twenty members, they could call a full Central Committee meeting. Having won over so many of the county chairmen who were ex officio members of that body, Freeman thought the Humphreyites could muster a majority and, therefore, forced a session on February 20 at the St. Paul Hotel. For most of the night before, the Humphreyites "practiced" in a room upstairs, simulating opposition tricks and maneuvers, agreeing on motions and seconders, even deciding how often and long to let the opposition speak. Next morning they went down and, winning every vote, set the call, the date (June 15, 1948), the place, and the rules for the decisive state convention.

Outraged at this unexpected turn of events, the left-wingers unloaded on Humphrey. Busy trying to settle a strike of telephone workers in Minneapolis, the mayor had not even been present. But by this time the Minneapolis newspapers were pitting him in opinion polls against incumbent Senator Joe Ball, and it was perfectly apparent that the mayor was only waiting for his partisans to carry the state convention to enter the lists as the DFL candidate in the November elections. Labeling Humphrey "the DFL Stassen," the left-wingers' newspaper, the *Minnesota Leader*, informed him that "your associations with the unsavory Americans for Democratic Action, created nationally to serve as liberal window dressing for the Wall Streeters and militarists behind Truman and created in Minnesota as a haven for reactionary elements in the Democratic and Farmer-Labor parties, is another indication of the character of your associations."

The new "steering committee" appointed by the Humphrey-controlled St. Paul meeting set the caucuses for April 30. In the past no more than four to six voters had turned out in most precincts; in some cases, nobody showed up. As the Humphreyites had learned at their own expense in 1946, the precinct caucus presented the ideal opportunity for infiltration by a small, disciplined group. This time, taking no chances, Humphrey's supporters were more than ready. They had long since drawn up voter lists for every one of the state's four thousand precincts, singled out and trained captains for each, and in city wards staged small living-room meetings at which their partisans were told just what to do. In Minneapolis their instructions came with the printed warning that the Communist party—"with only three hundred members"—would dispatch one card-holder to each precinct with orders to carry that caucus for Wallace. On April 18, the Humphreyite command moved boldly to head off any such stroke. The steering committee announced that third-party supporters—"like Republicans"—were disqualified from taking part in the regular DFL caucuses and conventions. Freeman, for the committee, called on all county chairmen who identified themselves with Wallace to hand over their credentials to the next-ranking DFL leader. The state chairman for Wallace dismissed this as "talk," and told two thousand followers at a St. Paul auditorium rally that they were "legally entitled to participate in all DFL caucuses and should do so en masse."

But by that time the Humphrey forces had gained the upper hand. The state AFL had already endorsed Humphrey for senator, and under stiff orders from national headquarters most CIO locals were swinging to his side. Among the farmers of Minnesota no chieftain was heard with greater respect than M. W. (Bill) Thatcher, of the potent Farmers Union Grain Terminal Association in St. Paul. An elated Humphrey wrote Barney Allen: "Bill said he told Henry [Wallace] he had followed him blindly for years, but this was the one point where he got off the train." Furthermore, in return for Humphrey's recognition of DFL Chairman Barker as state patronage dispenser, the supposed captive of the left not only stopped protesting the St. Paul coup but began upholding all of the new steering committee's rulings.

Even so, Humphrey, asserting that his foes had twenty-five full-time organizers at work in the Twin Cities alone, told Gael Sullivan of the Democratic National Committee, "We may lose." There was always the chance that the left-wingers would pull some shenanigans. In Hennepin County, which sent by far the largest number of delegates to the convention, the Wallaceite chairman, a barbecued and fricasseed "mushhead" in the Humphrey lexicon, refused to turn over credentials to the next-ranking officer, and as a result the two sides prepared to hold rival caucuses in Minneapolis.

The law provided that precinct meetings be held at polling places, but the custom was to adjourn somewhere else more comfortable. Keeping to their battle plan, the Humphreyite telephone committees alerted their supporters to appear at seven P.M. sharp "because the left wing is planning to act immediately at seven in hopes that our people haven't arrived." At the same time they warned all to "set aside the whole evening—to midnight or later, because *delay* is a typical Communist tactic and we must be prepared to outlast them." Boiling out of their homes, the Humphreyites took over almost every caucus around the state. In Minneapolis, where the mayor's partisans had to caucus separately, members of the core ADA group were the captains of almost every ward and precinct, and it was noted that those who trooped in came mostly from the ranks of labor. In St. Paul and Duluth, where fierce contests had been anticipated, the Humphreyites rolled up margins of six to one. Gene McCarthy, the young St. Thomas College sociology professor Humphrey had placed in charge of the action in St. Paul, reported that the left-wing county chairman had gone down to defeat in his own precinct. On the Iron Range their margin was smaller, but substantial.

Charging that the Humphreyites had waged "one of the most vicious campaigns of fraud, intimidation and treachery ever put on in Minnesota," left-wingers claimed unconvincingly that the Wallace candidacy had "won a clear majority of delegates to the state convention." At first they announced that they were sending their delegates to the state DFL convention set by the new steering committee for June 15 at Brainerd. But after the county conventions went against them, they abandoned that plan. Protesting that Chairman Barker had named a Humphreyite Credentials Committee, headed by "an illegal delegate from an illegal [county] convention characterized by the most flagrant violations of democracy," they called on "all Progressive DFL delegates" to meet in "a Progressive state convention" in Minneapolis on the same date.

On the appointed day, four hundred DFL delegates met for a convention at Brainerd. Humphrey had to take a seat in the gallery until the Credentials Committee upheld the victory of his faction in Minneapolis. Thereupon he hustled to the platform to deliver the keynote address, interrupted this time only by cheers.

His forces took complete control of the party. By overwhelming majorities the delegates voted to replace the left-wing officers with the officers of the state ADA—Eugenie Anderson, ADA chairman, became National Committeewoman; Orville Freeman, ADA vice chairman, became DFL state chairman; and so on. Delegates shouted through resolutions condemning the Soviet invasion of Czechoslovakia and demanding support for pro-Western candidates in the crucial Italian elections.

Well before the convention voted to endorse Hubert Humphrey for senator, the left-wingers "rumped." Five of their stalwarts marched from the hall, stood in a circle on the sidewalk, and, declaring the proceedings inside unlawful, voted to adjourn to the Nicollet Hotel ballroom in Minneapolis. There they joined five hundred other left-wingers pledged to back Henry Wallace's Progressive party candidacy and James A. Shields, Freeman's father-in-law, as their candidate to oppose Humphrey in the DFL senatorial primary. Stopping off at the secretary of state's office in St. Paul, the five rumpers duly pulled off their shenanigans. While the Humphreyites celebrated victory two hundred miles to the north, they filed the list of Wallace-pledged electors as the DFL slate for the November elections. It was a neat trick because the Republican secretary of state accepted the list. It kept President Truman off the ballot until the state supreme court ruled in September that the Humphreyites were the rightful DFL electors. Coming so late in the year, that should have put the President at a heavy disadvantage. But 1948, by any standard, was a most extraordinary campaign year, and the voters were yet to be heard from.

The Humphreyites had won back the party from the left-wingers. They had earned their triumph by tremendous exertions. Eugenie Anderson, taking telephoned field reports and pencilling her charts at ADA headquarters, all but abandoned her Red Wing home. Ione Hunt, rustling volunteers in Elmer Benson's own western Minnesota pastures, ran up the biggest telephone bills ever recorded in the town of Montevideo. Art Naftalin mobilized a good share of the faculty and students of the nation's third-largest university for his boss. Orville Freeman was on top of everything—"If Hubert Humphrey had had Oville Freeman's organizing abilities, he would have been president of the United States hands down," one volunteer said later. Gerry Heaney, who "gave a third of my time—eight hours a day" to carry the fight for Duluth, explained how Humphrey led the total effort: "We were the organizers, he was the candidate. We lined up volunteers, we reactivated those who had fallen away after 1938. Humphrey was not much for detail of that kind. His life was not taken up with nuts and bolts. But don't get me wrong. Humphrey was engaged and involved. When you needed him, he was there. He would arrive, a little late, and he would give that battle speech—exciting, charismatic, inspiring, whether before an audience or in a pep talk before our workers."

Overwhelmingly, the mayor's workers were new people—and young. A whole new generation fought the good fight to capture the party in 1948, and a good many of them never stopped working for the DFL party as long as Hubert Humphrey lived. On the strength of this virtual crusade, leaders such as Freeman and Gene McCarthy rode forward to outstanding careers as DFL leaders. And out of the younger ranks stepped a whole group of able comers such as Walter Mondale and Don Fraser who would follow in Humphrey's steps.

From this fight the Humphreyites emerged invulnerable to the charge that being liberals they must be soft on communism. Their credentials were proved. They were militants who succeeded in institutionalizing their militancy. Having learned to fight at Minnesota's grass roots, they kept the habit of fighting from the precinct level up. They took up the neighborhood caucus, turned out for meetings the year around, and built an organization that did not have to be created from scratch again before each campaign. After recapturing the party, as Heaney said, "we forgot about the ADA; it had served its purpose." The Farmer Labor Association, the base from which the left-wingers had seized command in 1946, perished too. But the Humphreyites had started something that did not stop for decades. They had founded a broad movement, embracing students and young professionals as well as workers and farmers. Led by the prairie Progressive from Doland, the Democratic-Farmer-Labor party was on its way to becoming the dominant political force in Minnesota.

14

Victory over Ball

W A S Hubert Humphrey ambitious? Yes, and more than a little naïve. Even before he left Minneapolis's City Hall, he was measuring himself against Franklin Roosevelt.

He had already rejected the conventional stepping stone of his state's governorship. Sizing up the incumbent, Republican Luther Youngdahl, he confided to a friend: "His views are too much like mine. And I lack his down-to-earthness." Instead, airily informing Gael Sullivan of the Democratic National Committee that "I don't think anybody else could do it other than myself," he aimed straightaway at winning the U. S. Senate seat held by Republican Joseph Ball.

But was Humphrey also thinking already about following in Roosevelt's footsteps? Indeed he was.

Even while waging his local battle to recapture party control from the left-wingers so he could run for the Senate, Humphrey embroiled himself in national election-year politics. As winter waned and polls showed President Truman's popularity plummeting, Humphrey told his new ADA friends that the Democrats were going to lose the White House in 1948. He wrote Jim Loeb: "We not only face defeat in November, we face the possible disintegration of the whole social democratic bloc in this country." He told Chester Bowles: "The reelection of the President is a political impossibility." As Humphrey saw it, liberal Democrats might well have to accept banishment to the political wilderness for a time, driven from power after the Roosevelt years just as they had been after Woodrow Wilson. And that gloomy prospect posed a suddenly hopeful question in the ambitious mayor's mind: Should he, ADA efforts to dump Truman for another candidate failing, skip his Senate race and, following in the young Franklin Roosevelt's footsteps, go on the losing ticket in 1948 with Truman?

At the time Humphrey got this inspiration he was in frequent touch and on good terms with members of the Roosevelt family—Mrs. Roosevelt, James, Elliott, and young Franklin (he had spent a particularly memorable weekend with Junior at the latter's Long Island home draining bottles of vodka presented to his father by Stalin). Now, watching efforts to find an alternative to Truman falter, Humphrey felt he needed to sound out Mrs. Roosevelt on whether it had hurt her husband's career or helped it to run with James Cox in 1920 on a losing ticket. He persuaded three of his ADA friends—Loeb, Joe Rauh, and Eugenie Anderson—to journey to Hyde Park and ask her whether it would be wise for him to run as vice president even if he got shellacked. The three dutifully made the trip and said, as they later recalled: "Mayor Humphrey asks your advice. In view of Franklin's experience in 1920, should Hubert accept the vice-presidential nomination with Truman if he can get it?"

"Of course," Mrs. Roosevelt replied. "You're going to get better known."

As late as nine days before the convention in Philadelphia, Humphrey hoped that ADA's stop-Truman drive, even if it did not stop the president, might at least get him on the ticket with Truman. On July 2 his father, who had been chosen a delegate from South Dakota, wrote him from the Humphrey drugstore in Huron, "Bill Simms informed me over the phone the other night that you contemplated having your name presented to the Convention as a candidate for vice president, that Mrs. Roosevelt would nominate you, and that you wanted me to give one of the seconding speeches."

Of course, nothing of the kind ever happened. The ADA's drive to draft General Eisenhower for president, led by James Roosevelt, fizzled out totally two days later when the general announced he would have nothing to do with it. The ADA board, meeting on convention eve, gave up the fight and decided instead to go all-out for a strong civil rights plank. That was Humphrey's opportunity, for a Humphrey vice-presidential nomination was never in the cards at Philadelphia. But civil rights was truly Humphrey's issue, and the mayor's headlong courage in the fight that followed and his electrifying speech preceding the decisive convention vote probably did more for the Truman campaign, and brought Truman more votes in his November upset victory, than anything the president's actual nominee for vice president, Kentucky's Alben Barkley, was able to add.

His convention triumph also put Humphrey on the victory trail in his Minnesota race. No other Democrat had ever won popular election to the Senate from Minnesota. But the mayor, arriving back in Minneapolis, was greeted as a hero. Waving homemade signs, unionists, Farmers Union members, Jewish leaders, and party workers organized by his friend Freddie Gates jammed the railroad station, hoisted him on their shoulders, and marched two blocks to a caravan of eighty cars that escorted him the rest of the way to City Hall. In terms of Minnesota's tiny black vote, Humphrey's convention success was of no great moment. But Humphrey's civil rights leadership at Philadelphia so decisively took the liberal play away from the Wallaceites that it spelled the doom of the third-party candidacy in Minnesota.

In the ensuing primary, Humphrey rolled over his Progressive opponent James Shields by eight-to-one, causing Wallaceites to abandon all thoughts of opposing him in the November elections and leading Wallace himself, in a decision virtually forced by liberal opinion, to endorse Humphrey's Senate candidacy.

In the final race with the Republican Ball, Humphrey had all the advantages except money. Harold Stassen, who had dominated Minnesota politics for a decade, pulled out of the state in midsummer to head the University of Pennsylvania after losing his bid for the Republican presidential nomination to Tom Dewey. In August, Stassen made only the most tepid endorsement of Ball, whom he had originally appointed to office: "I disagreed with him in his position on the Marshall plan and in his early stand on labor legislation. . . . I was keenly disappointed in his not supporting the Republican nominee for President in 1944." As if that were not wounding enough, Stassen, presenting the Republican party's 1948 farm program at Detroit, charged the Democrats with trying to prop up food prices. That gave Humphrey his chance to slash into what had been the areas of greatest Republican strength in the state—the rural districts. Already frightened by falling prices, farmers listened gravely that fall as Humphrey, later joined by Truman in his whistle-stopping tours, warned that they would lose their farms unless they voted Democratic in November.

The Republicans, moreover, proposed to tax cooperatives, which were especially strong among Minnesota's farmers. None swung heftier clout than the Farmers Union Grain Terminal Association of St. Paul and its redoubtable manager Bill Thatcher. Starting back in his Non-Partisan League days, Thatcher had built his grain-marketing cooperative into one of the biggest and most prosperous in the nation. Thatcher ran his outfit like a political organization; the fires of his prairie evangelism burned brightest when he assembled his cohorts for their annual conventions. He had been a supporter of Henry Wallace from earliest New Deal days and had quarreled publicly with Humphrey in the fall of 1946 after Wallace's foreign-policy split with the Democrats. But Thatcher refused to join Wallace's third-party adventure and early in 1948 came out for Humphrey's Senate candidacy. Humphrey addressed his annual convention on the iniquity of the proposed levy on cooperatives, and Thatcher mobilized his elevator managers and fuel distributors around the state for Humphrey.

For Humphrey, Ball was in many respects a perfect opponent. He had not served—a sensitive point for Humphrey in all his campaigns—in World War II either. His voting record was vulnerably erratic. Once a militant Newspaper Guildsman, he introduced the most punitive of the union curbs enacted in the Taft-Hartley law. So fervently internationalist in 1944 that he bolted his party to support President Roosevelt, by 1948 he had swung so far the other way that he voted against the Marshall Plan for European recovery. Humphrey, ever the internationalist, charged that "if American policy had been decided by the vote of the senior senator from Minnesota, we might be negotiating with the Russians now in London instead of Berlin."

Ball and Humphrey met only once, for a radio debate staged by the League of Women Voters. It was not much of a contest. By actual count, Humphrey could talk three times as fast as the craggy, slow-moving Ball. "He could talk a bird off a tree," Ball said later. Ball thought to make socialism an issue. Humphrey judged correctly that he had laid that specter to rest by driving the left-wing extremists out of the DFL party and could now bid boldly for mainstream voters. As Orville Freeman explained to an aide at the time: "We have tried to slant this campaign so that the so-called middle class will be led to recognize where their interests lie. Humphrey is especially effective at reaching this kind of folks." And indeed Humphrey never left a smalltown audience without telling them that he had clerked five years in a Dakota drugstore and if elected would do his utmost to get "effective assistance" for small business, the true rampart of "individual liberty" against the onslaughts of monopoly. "I want to break up these monopolies," he would say, "because monopoly is the socialism of the big corporations."

But where did issues leave off and personalities begin when the campaigner was as effervescent and hyper-energized as this ambitious young mayor? Clearly, the candidate was his own best asset. In the language of baseball, he could run, he could field, and he could hit. So the candidate was on the road day and night. First a loudspeaker-equipped jeep wheeled into a town, alerting the citizenry that Humphrey was about to arrive. Next a flatbed truck pulled up at the best spot on Main Street, and a collegian, Tom Hughes, got out and placed a microphone on the tailgate. Next the candidate himself rode up in a Buick driven by his friend Freddie Gates, hopped on to the truck, and started speaking.

"In his speeches he lets the corn grow high," the *New Republic* reported. "But Humphrey is not shallow. He has a well-knit liberal philosophy and a powerful urge to right wrongs." "What did I say of the Republicans' tax bill?" he asked at New Ulm. "I said, it is a horse and rabbit tax law—it gives the little man a rabbit-size income tax reduction and the big-income man a horse-sized cut." Wolfing a brown-bag cheese sandwich as he drove, Humphrey would visit eight or ten towns a day (a doctor might be asked to stand by at the next town to spray his throat), ending at some bigger town such as Willmar or Mankato or Rochester, where he would address a larger crowd in the high school auditorium and then hoist a beer with the local folks at somebody's house before racing back at midnight to Minneapolis. "He wore us twenty-five-year-olds all out," said Doug Kelm. Freeman's logs attest that Humphrey visited every one of Minnesota's eighty-seven counties at least twice, attended almost every county fair, and handshook and babykissed his way through the Sauerkraut Festival at Springfield, Watermelon Day at Sanborn, Turkey Day at Worthington, the Bohemian Dance at Owatonna, and the Finnish Society at Duluth. He ate twenty-five ears of corn at Ortonville's Corn Feed and downed fifteen cups of coffee at Willmar's Kaffeeklatsch. When the Kolacky Day platform began to sag at Montgomery, he said: "This reminds me of the Republican platform." When a fire alarm went off at Goodhue, he said, "This is the first time a speech of mine rang the bell." By Freeman's estimate, he made seven hundred speeches and traveled 31,000 miles, and he quite visibly enjoyed it.

The big city newspapers backed Ball, and so did all the fatcats who had contributed when Humphrey ran for his second term in the no-party mayor's election the previous year. Bradshaw Mintener, Humphrey's strong ally in the Minneapolis law-enforcement drive, informed him that as a Republican he would have to oppose his DFL candidacy. But the cities were also where the trade union strength lay, and organized labor joined ranks behind Humphrey in a grim determination to drive Ball, the man who thought the Taft-Hartley law was not tough enough, out of public life. Dropping their earlier flirtation with the Wallaceites, CIO elements got behind Humphrey's ex-Communist friend Bob Wishart, named honorary chairman of his Minneapolis campaign. Virtually every major U. S. union sent money and manpower into Minnesota to help Humphrey beat Ball. On the Iron Range, Phil Murray's personal representative Smaile Chatek went from mill to mine whipping rambunctious United Steelworker locals into line. In the Twin Cities, President Emil Rieve of the Textile Workers personally led stomp-out-Ball strategy sessions. The UAW's Walter Reuther paid the salary of Darrell Smith, perhaps Humphrey's most effective campaign aide. The Minneapolis Central Labor Union put in six telephone lines and hired sixteen operators to call members to register so that on election eve registration in the city stood at an all-time high. Wishart arranged for four hundred electrical workers to leave their jobs on election day and go door to door getting out the vote in working-class districts. At labor's climactic rally, AFL President William Green appeared as featured guest and threw an arm around Humphrey, after which six thousand unionists, the Minneapolis *Tribune* reported, heard one of the candidate's "virtuoso performances."

On election day, Humphrey bowled over Ball by 243,000 votes, carrying eighty-five of eighty-seven counties. At the top of the ticket, President Truman scraped through in the political upset of the century; the 11 electoral votes of Minnesota helped make the difference. Labor's League for Political Action's $5,500 topped the list of contributors that Humphrey submitted to

Minnesota's secretary of state. The list, totaling only $39,373, was obviously incomplete, yet by any later standards, including Humphrey's, he had won with astonishingly little financial help. Heaviest backing came from members of the Jewish community, who were to be Humphrey's most loyal and generous givers to the end of his days. On the list also was the name of Dwayne Andreas, identified as an official of Cargill Inc., the giant Minneapolis grain company. It was a name that would figure even more importantly in Humphrey's financial life.

The fundamental origins of Humphrey's victory were not to be obscured by its triumphantly personal nature. To challenge the historic Republican preeminence in the state it had been necessary first to fuse the disparate Democrats and Farmer-Laborites on the left into one party. Next Humphrey had to beat the better-disciplined, closely knit, but numerically small elements of the party's extreme left at their own organizational game. To that end he brought together able and devoted young lieutenants who conquered the party precinct by precinct, caucus by caucus. Installing them in the leadership offices of the reorganized party, he moved out in his campaign to preempt the left-of-center ground from which it became possible to command majority support in Minnesota. His election, and that of two additional members of the state's congressional delegation, represented a first payoff. Others would climb the ladder from the broad base he marked out, men who were also political educators as well as organizers, men such as Orville Freeman and Eugene McCarthy, Don Fraser and Fritz Mondale. For in winning the way he did, Humphrey had put his party in a position where, by reaching out to and identifying with a rising generation of middle-income voters, it could push the Republicans aside and itself become the enduringly dominant political force in the state. Freeman said later: "Gene McCarthy or any of the rest of us could never have gotten anywhere in politics without Humphrey. The guy who put it all together, the symbol, the figurehead, the guy with the charisma, was Humphrey. He couldn't have done it alone, but certainly until some of us could fly alone, he was the leader."

Humphrey's victory attracted national attention. Signaling the depth of sectional feeling that seethed against him in the South, the Dothan, Alabama, *Register* commented: "His name is anathema. It will remain for history to tag him as the demagogue he is." The Louisville *Courier Journal* concluded that Humphrey's "defiance of the entrenched political order" at Philadelphia more than anything helped to elect President Truman, and his ability to tie CIO and AFL into his campaign and to attract farm and city worker votes alike showed "a certain genius." Even the barbs about his loquacity had to be tempered by the evidence that it persuaded. The St. Louis *Post Dispatch's* reporter, noting that Humphrey had spent more time behind the drug counter than he had in public office, explained that "druggists are the finest talkers in the world, better than bartenders or barbers."

On December 1, Humphrey, wrapped in a new, fur-collared coat, resigned his mayor's office. A few days later a group of Minneapolis businessmen organized a five dollar-per-plate dinner and presented Muriel Humphrey with a new Plymouth stationwagon. With the aid of Morris Ebin, vice president of Minneapolis's biggest wholesale liquor company, Humphrey found a house big enough for his family in a suburban tract in Chevy Chase on Washington's western fringe. He had arrived at the place where, as a young tourist in 1936, he said one day he would.

To get there he had fought to possess the flag of Progressivism in his state, and won. He had led the fight for the soul of the national Democratic party, and won. "You have given expression to my innermost desires and longings," wrote his father. "You are a great liberal fighter for the right. Keep it up, Hubert, speak the voice of the people, and some day you will find yourself chief of this nation."

PART THREE

The Senate

15

The Unhappy Warrior

WHEN Humphrey, aged thirty-seven, arrived in Washington, *Time* magazine put him on its cover—as a whirlwind spiraling into town from the West. Although hardly the one to call the newcomer brash, *Time* characterized him as a "glib, jaunty spellbinder with a 'listen-you-guys' approach who talks and looks like a high school teacher who coaches basketball on the side." The new senator, *Time* warned, "has the cyclonic attack of an ad salesman."

In a freshman class that included Lyndon Johnson, Estes Kefauver, and Paul Douglas, *Time* was singling out Humphrey because of what he had already done and what he was expected to do. He certainly looked like a comer. This was the "No. 1 prospect for liberalism in this country" who had grabbed the lead at last summer's Democratic convention when the party faced defeat. He it was who by nailing civil rights to the mast had pushed the party onto a course that took the wind right out of the Wallaceite sails on the left and turned a blind eye to the sight of Southerners leaping over the side to starboard. Far from sinking the Democrats, this seemingly reckless course had righted the party's foundering ship, propelled it forward past the startled Republicans, and steered it triumphantly back to Washington in control of Congress as well as the White House. More than any other Democrat, except the president dancing gleefully on his quarterdeck, this young fellow had made possible the Truman triumph he himself, just six months before, had thought out of the question.

There was still another reason to pay attention to the newcomer at this moment. Shortly after being elected, Humphrey accepted the chairmanship of Americans for Democratic Action. Formed only a year or two earlier by impatient New Dealers such as Leon Henderson and Chester Bowles who thought the party needed a thorough overhaul, that gadfly group, was already looked on by the regulars with a distaste that bordered on loathing. Small as it was, the ADA had shown an unexpected potency by helping to swing the civil rights vote at the Philadelphia convention and then electing members to high office in Connecticut, New York, and Michigan as well as Minnesota. Humphrey's decision to head up the outfit thrust him to prominence as spokesman for a national constituency. That constituency, made up so far of amateurs and academics of a rampantly New Deal persuasion, would bulk far larger if, as Humphrey anticipated, the rest of organized labor's leadership followed the UAW's Walter Reuther into its ranks.

If the Philadelphia triumph and the ADA connection made the new senator a marked man at once, they also put him on the spot. In Minneapolis, Humphrey had thrived on public attention. There he had been the big fish in a local pond. He had been the mayor—a hyperactive one. He had taken a job that did not have much power and with a strong flair for publicity dramatized his social and economic projects, pulled in people to run them, and then mobilized public opinion to put them over. Shamelessly showboating, he was out in front all the time, preaching and exhorting, wheedling and cajoling. City halls, city streets, city churches, city lunch clubs—all were his pulpit. But in Washington he stepped into a different kind of forum. In the Senate he was only one of many—and as a freshman he was not supposed to pop off at all.

The Senate proceeded to cut him down. In 1949 Washington was still pretty much a Southern town, and the Senate was a citadel of Southern seniority and power. States such as Georgia and Mississippi, all with single-party, lily-white electorates, had been sending Democratic senators to Capitol Hill for years and years. These Southern elders, undisturbed by the electoral storms that rocked the urban North, held most of the Senate committee chairmanships.

The Senate moreover was very much a club in those years—a Southern-dominated club. A member of that club, for example, was Strom Thurmond of South Carolina. Far from excluding Thurmond for bolting the party after Humphrey's Philadelphia coup and standing against the Democratic president in the November elections, senior Southerners closed ranks around him and other Dixiecrats. The truant Thurmond was welcomed back in. But Humphrey, to the Southern clubmen, was an irregular, a political "sport" thrust into sudden prominence by the momentary outburst of 1948, product of a passing aberration in the voting habits of Minnesotans. Was he not the first Democrat that state had ever sent to Senate? And the sole member of his party elected to the Senate from his section of the country? Such men came and went. Yet here was this callow upstart, noisily elbowing his way into their company and already calling for changes that threatened their power at home and in the Senate itself. He deserved to be put down.

For Humphrey, by his civil rights resolution, had committed the Democratic party to topple the white supremacy upon which the Southern senators' preeminence rested. Even before he set foot in the Senate, Humphrey called a Washington press conference and with righteous disdain informed thirty reporters that "there are enough votes in Congress [to enact civil rights reform] if [members] are honest and sincere—and I warn them that if they are not honest and sincere they may have trouble in the future." To senators such as Richard Russell, these were wild and arrant words, uttered by someone who knew not what he was talking about—and, indeed, he did not.

If the press conference was not enough to guarantee Humphrey a frosty welcome, the new senator threw another challenge at the Southern bourbons. Bigtime industrial expansion was just getting started in the South, and if there was one thing the Southern chieftains wanted for their long downtrodden section it was to get factories going in its towns and cities. After the war they saw their chance. What the South had to offer big business was plenty of cheap labor, untrammeled by union pressures for better wages and working conditions that kept lifting manufacturing costs ever higher in the North.

The most important cement that bound the conservative Republican-Southern Democratic alliance in Congress together in the postwar years was the identity of interest between corporations eager to move their plants away from union strongholds, and Southern communities avid to receive them. In almost all legislative matters the practical effect of this reactionary lashup was negative: to block civil rights and other social reform. But the alliance produced one decisively shaping piece of domestic legislation: the Taft-Hartley Act.* It deprived labor of important bargaining advantages bestowed by years of New Deal enactments and rulings and effectively put an end to trade union growth in the United States. The measure was written and passed in 1947, when Republicans controlled Congress. It became law over President Truman's veto by the votes of Southern Democratic legislators determined to keep their section union-free and thus attractive to corporations looking to shift operations where labor would cost less.

Humphrey had gained his Senate seat by defeating a principal architect of Taft-Hartley, and President Truman had campaigned across the country demanding the law's repeal, winning his astonishing reelection victory with the help of a flood of labor votes. In December, before he arrived in Wash-

---

*The Taft-Hartley law stiffened federal control of labor disputes, outlawed the closed shop, and reintroduced the use of injunctions by the government to delay for eighty days any strike it deemed a peril to national health or safety. A further proviso specified that to qualify for collective bargaining a union had to submit affidavits that its officers were not Communists, a requirement that split the CIO, until then the fastest-growing sector of organized labor.

ington, Humphrey addressed a meeting of the United Textile Workers, a union that already feared it might not survive the flight of factories to the open-shop South. The labor movement, Humphrey warned, was "no longer content with winning on election day and letting the other fellow win all the rest of the year." He proclaimed that his election and that of President Truman constituted a mandate for repeal of the Taft-Hartley "slave" Act.

As soon as the Senate organized for business, the battle commenced. When the Southerners caucused the day before under Russell's command to discuss anti-civil rights strategy, Humphrey, noting that his fellow freshmen Estes Kefauver of Tennessee and Lyndon Johnson of Texas stayed away, wrote Kefauver his satisfaction "that you and Lyndon are not permanently lined up with that crowd." But the next day, Southern votes elected as new Majority Leader Illinois's Scott Lucas, who had fought Humphrey's civil rights resolution at Philadelphia. As befitted an utter freshman, Humphrey was put on the Post Office committee and the Government Operations Committee. In addition, he took the juniormost seat on the Labor and Welfare Committee, whose ranking Republican member was none other than the formidable Robert A. Taft of Ohio, author of the law that Humphrey was committed to repeal.

What followed, Humphrey said later, were "dark days—I despaired." One day as Humphrey walked past a knot of senators, he heard Dick Russell turn and ask the others, "How in hell could the people of Minnesota elect a damn fool like that to the Senate of the United States?" As politicians went, Humphrey was an open fellow, and such deliberate slights hurt. Driving home in his old Buick, Humphrey wept.

Yet Humphrey's troubles were not all of Southern making. Brassy and strident, he did not go down well with Easterners either. Joe Rauh, the Washington lawyer who "fell in love" with Humphrey the first time he saw and heard him in Chicago, acknowledged that the Humphrey manner was "different." Carl Auerbach, a Brooklynite who later became dean of the University of Minnesota law school, remembered Humphrey at the early ADA meetings: "He was this brash and bouncy young man from Minneapolis who was going to be the liberal hope for president." Auerbach could see that Humphrey felt uncomfortable in these Eastern circles. "Once when he was in the Senate I helped arrange for him to speak at a Harvard law review banquet. It was a bust." Rauh said: "Hubert never felt at home with Eastern intellectuals, with people like Arthur Schlesinger."

A union lobbyist introduced him to James H. Rowe, a Montana-born Washington lawyer who had been one of President Roosevelt's six young "anonymous assistants" and was to become another lifelong friend of Humphrey's. Lunching at a nearby table was Arthur Krock, bureau chief of the *New York Times* and an arch-Southerner who often used his influential column to air the anti–civil rights views of his Southern friends in the Senate. Pausing in his chatter as Rowe pointed out Krock to him, Humphrey said:

"I'll knock his block off." He fired off a belligerent letter to the *Times* attacking Krock by name. That brought warm praise from Chester Bowles, now governor of Connecticut and a letter from the editor of the Milwaukee *Journal*, stating that "I think you are a man of destiny." A few days later, Humphrey hustled into the Senate dining room with Cyril King, a black member of his new staff and future government secretary of the Virgin Islands. Loudly insisting that King be served, he integrated the club that had snubbed him.

While President Truman's aides sparred with the Southerners over the administration's long list of proposed measures, Humphrey traveled to New York and Chicago to address meetings on civil rights and Taft-Hartley repeal. When Truman outlined his Fair Deal program in his victor's state of the union message and put both issues at the top of the list, Humphrey again pointed to the November mandate for action. For a little more than a month he stayed quiet on the Senate floor, as freshmen members are supposed to. Then Senator James Murray of Montana brought in a bill to create a Missouri Valley Authority that would do for the dust bowl what the Tennessee Valley Authority had done for the hillbilly hollows of the South. Humphrey, who had gone with Murray to the White House and found President Truman "enthusiastically supporting" the proposal, broke his silence.

> Mr. President, I rise today to address the Senate for the first time. This is a fitting issue and an appropriate moment for my first address on the floor of the Senate of the United States. . . . The Missouri Valley Authority is vital to the Midwest. It is vital to my birthplace, South Dakota. It is essential for the progress of my present home, Minneapolis. It is a carefully planned program for the prosperity of the nation.
>
> Our people have been looking at the miracle of the Tennessee Valley. They have seen cheap electric power created from the river's flow; they have seen industries grow up near the cheap power; and they have seen the great atom plant working in the Tennessee Valley for the progress and peace of the world. They have seen irrigation and soil conservation, flood control and navigation improve constantly in the Tennessee Valley basin. . . .
>
> Politically, the Missouri Valley Authority is a symbol, symbol of liberalism to the large majority of Americans who voted liberal last November and in other Novembers. . . .

But Congress shelved the MVA.

One day later, the administration made its first moves to carry out the party's new pledge to act on civil rights. Senator Russell promptly swung his Southern forces into the reactionary tactic that was to become familiar in the following years. Taking advantage of the upper house's tradition of unlimited debate, the Southerners set out to talk the proposed action to death. To keep the filibustering minority from prevailing, the administration had a plan.

Vice President Barkley handed down a ruling. He stated that each newly convened Senate had power to make its own rules. Therefore the present Senate, if it so chose, could by a simple majority vote of its membership cut short debate. It need not feel bound by Rule XXII, originally adopted in 1917, which ordained that a two-thirds vote of the membership was required to close off debate.

But Richard Russell had an understanding with Robert Taft. The Southern Democratic alliance with the Republicans held fast. Senators unwilling to surrender their prerogative of unlimited debate voted forty-five to forty-one to disregard Vice President Barkley's ruling. Majority Leader Lucas, who had little appetite for a scrap, called Senate Democrats to a caucus to discuss a compromise settlement. The Southerners marched in in solid formation, Strom Thurmond shoulder-to-shoulder with Dick Russell. Only the young Humphrey rose in the caucus to insist that the regular party fight it out with the filibusterers to the end. The Southerners had won. Just five months after the election, civil rights was dead in Congress.

Defeated on one front, Humphrey fought the alliance on a second. "I am going to remember every commitment I made to you folks," he wrote Minneapolis labor editor Robley Cramer. "We are going to work on the Taft-Hartley Act. It will be repealed." Hearings in the Labor and Welfare Committee got under way at once. Chairman Elbert Thomas of Utah and Senator Murray, who should have carried the ball, were elderly and indecisive. Humphrey elbowed forward.

Boisterously assertive, he charged into the hearings, took on the formidable Taft—and ran into trouble. It was Taft's style to draw from the parade of witnesses approving words for one specific proviso or another of his law, thereby building up a body of assent to a measure that none might have accepted individually. Humphrey, arriving late one day, broke in to cry foul. "That's not the right way to go at it," he said. To this, Taft retorted, "Do I understand that if you do seven just things, each one right in its field, then as a result all of them may not be just?" As pencils scribbled furiously at the press table, Humphrey spluttered: "Wait a minute. I don't think we should permit inferences such as this to be drawn." Then when Humphrey defended union practices that had been outlawed by Taft-Hartley, Taft caught him up on his facts. Stung, Humphrey began to ask why, if Taft-Hartley required union officials to sign affidavits that they were not Communists, corporation officers should not be asked to do the same. As reporters, startled at the notion of capitalists swearing they were not Communists, looked up from their notes, Humphrey exclaimed: "I don't want to make this look absurd" and, reddening, let his question drop.

Another day, AFL President William Green was answering reports that his organization was considering supplementing the salaries of union members elected to legislatures. Humphrey broke in, and Senator William Langer of North Dakota thought the ensuing exchange so inane that he put it all into the *Congressional Record* next day:

SEN. HUMPHREY: Have you ever heard of any legislators representing any corporations that were ever elected to office?

MR. GREEN: Well, I cannot name any at the moment.

SEN. HUMPHREY: Well, I can. (Laughter) I mean who have as their clients. . . .

MR. GREEN: It has been my impression that there have been a good many representatives of corporations in Congress, in the Congress of the U.S.

SEN. HUMPHREY: Well, all of us have to have a means of income. I think that is perfectly true.

MR. GREEN: Yes, it is true.

SEN. HUMPHREY: Do you think there would be any difference, for example, if the American Federation of Labor put a man on their payroll, let us say as an organizer, after he was elected to the legislature, as compared to a man—I am talking about the legislature now: we are not talking about the honorable body of the U.S. Congress—you think there would be any difference between that and having a man who was elected to the legislature who, let us say, was an attorney for a public utility?

After that bit of silliness, pounced on by Langer before it could find its way into the *New Yorker* magazine's "Wind on Capitol Hill" department, the Minneapolis *Tribune*, reprinting it, commented that Humphrey had been "royally trimmed" by Taft. And Bill Henry of the Los Angeles *Times* wrote that Humphrey, making an unfavorable impression with his conduct at the labor hearings, was wearing out his welcome faster than any new senator. In March the *Nation*, which had hailed Humphrey's courage in opposing compromise with the Southern filibusters, said that the senator "who first loomed as a dominant figure in the civil rights group, appeared after three weeks as a moderate-sized man with an unfortunately self-righteous style of speaking."

Already wounded by the Senate snubs, Humphrey felt betrayed by the press. He complained to the editor of the Minneapolis *Tribune* that they were trying to pillory him. To this, his old nemesis Gideon Seymour replied:

You are simply a fellow with a great gift for publicity. Almost no day fails to bring complaints from some of our readers about the amount of publicity we give you. You have been mentioned 50 times on the *Tribune*'s editorial page since November 4, 18 times favorably, 12 times unfavorably, and 20 times simply in matters of fact or news.

We attempt in your case to present a reasonable cross-section. When the *Nation* says you are a disappointment, I think we ought to reproduce it. As for the dialog which Langer put in the *Record*, maybe it was not Humphrey at his best (which is pretty magnificent) but it was certainly a fair sample of the free-wheeling Humphrey who now and then turns his conversation on and goes away and leaves it running.

Humphrey was wordy. Humphrey was corny. And what few in the capital yet knew, he was also immensely likeable. In Minneapolis, where he went everywhere and sat up late gabbing with all comers after his speeches, lots of people knew and liked the young mayor's warmth, openness, and spontaneity. After a bit even sophisticated Washington began to find out about these traits: spontaneity, for instance.

Shortly after Humphrey was formally elected chairman of ADA, Republican Senator Albert Jenner of Indiana rushed out on the Senate floor waving a paper. "Senators, listen to this," he cried. With the air of a man who had just encountered the devil himself, Jenner held up a leaflet that had been handed that morning to a teen-age Senate page—an ADA leaflet urging such youths to join a summer study trip to Britain. "Americans for Democratic Action has a deep and sympathetic interest in the program of Britain's Labour government," he read and exclaimed: "The word 'democratic' has been subverted." Humphrey interrupted. Defending the outfit he headed, he asked some pointed questions about what Jenner thought was "democratic." "What are you trying to do, young man, put me on the political spot?" roared Jenner.

Republicans eager to pin the radical tag on ADA flocked to the floor to bait its chairman. Kem of Missouri began to read off a list of ADA directors. Donnell of Missouri got Humphrey to identify ADA's London secretary as a Labour member of parliament. But when Humphrey said studying British democracy seemed worthwhile, Styles Bridges of New Hampshire, a much bigger Republican gun, opened up. He fired a series of questions about rights— free speech, free press, free assembly, free political participation—asking after each: "We have all these freedoms in this country have we not?" "Indeed we have," answered Humphrey. Then Bridges asked: "What have the British got that we haven't got?" "Westminster Abbey," Humphrey shot back. The galleries roared with laughter. The gavel pounded, Bridges blushed and gave up.

"I've never worked so hard," Humphrey wrote his friend Orville Freeman. In between Senate hearings and debates, he charged around the country delivering speeches for fees to pay his income taxes—he had had to ask for an extension. He spoke often and long, too often and too long. Before a black audience at Howard University he denounced the Southern filibuster as "purely and simply an undemocratic technique to permit rule by a minority. They will fail because history is against them, the people are against them, the times are against them, the president of the United States is against them." He denounced the "rotten political bargain" by which Republicans and Southern Democratic "monopolists and reactionaries" blocked human rights and economic reform. He told a tenants' group bluntly that rent control should not be turned over to local governments "because it then becomes a political ploy." At an ADA rally he came out for more federal aid to housing, education, and social security, and for "public ownership and development of all stages beyond [uranium] mining in the field of atomic power." In Wheeling, West Virginia, he charged "reactionaries" with traducing "an honorable word in American history" by wrongly linking "welfare" with "aid to the poor and the helpless—charity." Said Humphrey: "Progressive social legislation, if wisely drawn, is the only hope we have of preserving [our] system—and I am in dead earnest about that."

When the Southern filibuster ended in April, the freshman senator began pouring bills into the hopper. He offered resolutions to carry out each of the four civil rights reforms demanded in his plank at the 1948 convention. He wrote an article for the *American Political Science Review* demanding overhaul of the Senate's seniority system. He offered a bill to abolish the electoral college. He cosponsored the health insurance bill that—sixteen years later— became Medicare. He proposed establishing an accident prevention bureau in the Department of Labor. He introduced a bill for $500 million federal aid to school construction. He put in a bill to extend Social Security to cover federal and state employees. In all, he offered 57 bills and joint resolutions in his first year in the Senate, inserted 180 items in the Congressional *Record*, from blue babies to river parkways, and spoke on 450 topics.

Of course he was spreading himself too thin. Yet the rude reverses he suffered in the Taft Hartley hearings drove him at the same time to tackle issues of the law's repeal in depth. "I am battling my heart out for the labor movement," he wrote grandly to the Minneapolis Central Labor Union chief at this time. He held lengthy strategy sessions with both President Phil Murray of the CIO and President Bill Green of the AFL. He spoke so often on the radio for Taft-Hartley repeal that he said: "I have been the administration's radio spokesman on that act." And when the bill for repeal finally reached the floor in June, Humphrey delivered by far the most comprehensive speech of the debate.

By that time it was already fairly clear that Taft had the votes to win. As Taft pointed out, the same election that gave Truman his victory also returned 221 representatives and 52 senators who had cast votes for his law. The Republican-Southern Democratic alliance that Humphrey called a "rotten political bargain" still prevailed. Having taken his lumps from Taft in the earlier skirmishing, Humphrey came armed with a speech so painstakingly prepared and so thickly studded with legal citations that Taft at one point expressed polite surprise that the speaker was not a lawyer. The address took four and a half hours to deliver and put organized labor's case so well that afterward unions printed it up as a handbook. But so few senators bothered to listen that old Senator Thomas, the bill's manager, had to ask for several quorum calls. Almost the only interruption came from Humphrey's fellow freshman and Chevy Chase neighbor, Russell Long of Louisiana. Long, in accents reminiscent of his populist father, asked friendly questions about strikebreakers and "poolhall loafers" who testified as employer stooges in "right-to-work" hearings under the law Humphrey was challenging.

Taft-Hartley, Humphrey said, was a law put over by giant corporations that wanted to go back to the union-busting injunctions, yellow-dog contracts, spies, Pinkertons, and machine-gunning goons of the bad old days. Pointing to profits that rose tenfold between 1940 and 1946 while "American workers were on the job producing" for war, Humphrey argued: "Big business said, 'We have done quite well, perhaps we can have a showdown.' " So at war's end the corporations "got price controls lifted" for yet more profits— and "set off a raging inflation" in 1946 and 1947 that drove union members to strike. Thereupon, Humphrey said, by a terrific propaganda campaign on which the National Association of Manufacturers and others may have spent $100 million, the notion was planted in the public mind that strikes were inundating the country. This, Humphrey cried, was "a cruel hoax." Pointing to graphs on flip charts that he had set up on the floor beside him, he insisted that there had been more strikes after the first world war than the second.

Unfortunately for America, he went on, the free bargaining between labor and management that had proved essential to good industrial relations since the New Deal was now disrupted by the repressive Taft-Hartley law. Labor injunctions were back. Banning the closed shop cost unions their bargaining status in some places and all but barred them from winning such status in many more. The law brought the government into the union-management bargaining process, as unwelcome, Humprey said, as a mother-in-law at the kitchen-table tiffs of newlyweds. This brought Taft to his feet:

SEN. TAFT: Does the senator think we should have an act?

SEN. HUMPHREY: I think the Wagner act [of 1935] was far superior.

SEN. TAFT: Let me ask whether he believes that once the government enters the field of labor-management relations it should at least cover the field so as to prevent abuses?

SEN. HUMPHREY: I say there is a basic minimum of restraints.

SEN. TAFT: Apparently it comes down to a question of what is an abuse and what is not.

SEN. HUMPHREY: It comes down to a question of how far to go. In other words I am in favor of traffic lights, but I would not have them located every two feet.

Humphrey's metaphors were telling, but the "rotten alliance" brushed them aside. The bill to repeal Taft-Hartley, already loaded with amendments, went down to defeat. The freshman from Minnesota lost out not only on Taft-Hartley but on civil rights and indeed on every one of the fifty-seven measures he proposed.

"We have taken quite a beating," Humphrey told a friend. "The concentrated monopolistic corporate business interests of this country have done their level best to fight off every piece of progressive legislation. And Humphrey continued to be a marked man. In August he confided to Cormac Suel, "The Republicans and Dixiecrats have apparently decided to do a job on me. A local Minnesota committee representing Senator Harry Byrd's Committee on Non-Essential Expenditures—a phony if there ever was one—has listed all the bills of which I am a sponsor. They have seen fit to estimate the total appropriations for each bill. Following this they have totaled the several bills and come up with some fantastic figure around $30 billion." The first blow, Humphrey wrote, was struck by a former Minnesota country editor with a well-deserved reputation as a Republican hatchet man: Rudolph Lee. After Rudy Lee swung his ax, Humphrey said, the Minneapolis *Star and Journal* "took up the smear job" by publishing Lee's figures. Next the right-wing radio commentator Fulton Lewis, Jr., aired the charge in Washington, but put the price of Humphrey's proposals at only $23 billion. Either way, the numbers so loosely totaled by his opponents added up to charges that could seriously damage Humphrey's political prospects. Within days, Humphrey had to defend himself on the Senate floor.

Opposition Republicans had introduced an amendment in Congress that would have required President Truman to slash federal spending by a flat 10 percent in every department. Humphrey, as member of a Government Operations subcommittee, filed a dissenting report. Thereupon, Minority Leader Kenneth Wherry, the ex-funeral director from Nebraska, rose and, "to show the inconsistency of the senator from Minnesota," asked unanimous consent to place the Lee list in the record. Senator Wherry said: "He has introduced or endorsed pieces of legislation which, if figured up, would authorize the expenditure of more than $30 billion. That is how he believes in economy."

"I object," cried Humphrey, and he launched into a point-by-point rebuttal of the charge that his proposals would cost anything like a fraction of $30 billion, followed by an analysis of the president's proposed $41 billion budget that left only about $17 or $18 billion non-defense expenditures where cuts could be made. His conclusion: "I want to sum up my argument by saying that I see no reason or justification for representative government if we are going to abdicate the greatest power that representative government has, namely, the power of taxation, and say we are unwilling to use it. This amendment will give more power to a President in peacetime than any President ever possessed."

Humphrey won that round. (He wrote his friend Philip Duff, "I don't want to brag, Phil, but I think I took his britches off."), but defeat of Wherry's amendment was not the end of the affair. There was still the score to settle with the Joint Committee on Reduction of Non-Essential Federal Expenditures; for its staff had provided Rudy Lee with his numbers. Humphrey thought that committee should be abolished, as it appeared to duplicate the work of the subcommittee on expenditures in the executive department of which he was a member. But this committee happened to be the personal fief of one of the Senate's biggest poohbahs, Senator Harry F. Byrd of Virginia. It had been created back in the Roosevelt years for the old aristocrat to air his indignation at New Deal spending. After the outlays of World War II made the New Deal's extravagances seem picayune by comparison, the Byrd committee continued to put out its occasional releases of highly selective statistics. Such was Byrd's lofty status in the Senate club however that the committee not only survived the wholesale Congressional Reorganization Act of 1946 but was left under the Virginia Democrat's chairmanship throughout the Republican Eightieth Congress.

The slightest hint from a new boy that the committee might be redundant would have been enough to set up a mighty clamor among Byrd's clubmates. But on February 24, 1950, the junior senator from Minnesota rose and said: "This committee's very existence is a wanton waste and extravagance. The money"—some $127,000—"appropriated for this committee's staff and printing costs stands as the Number One waste of the taxpayers' dollars." And Humphrey, shouting as if he were going after thieving aldermen in Minneapolis, went on to assert that the Byrd committee "violates the purpose for which it was created," "is merely used as a publicity medium," and "issues undocumented reports" couched "only in generalities." Humphrey ended by introducing a resolution to abolish the committee.

It happened that only two or three of Byrd's friends were on the floor to hear the attack. It also happened that Byrd himself was away from Washington visiting his ailing mother. The fundamental discourtesy of mounting a personal attack in Byrd's absence instantly became the focus of senatorial outrage. Six days later the chamber was ominously full when Byrd rose and, in his softest accents, began to "correct" what he called the "misstatements" of the senator from Minnesota. Just before attacking the Byrd committee's expenditure of $127,000, for example, Humphrey had sought twice that sum for a study of the coal industry. And for Humphrey of all people to lay the charge of publicity-mongering was ludicrous. Byrd finished his speech by saying: "I have mentioned nine misstatements in 2000 words. This is on average one misstatement in every 250 words—and the Senator speaks like the wind." The Senate, he concluded, could abolish the committee—which had not even met since 1947—if it wished, "but I do not want it done as the result of misinformation such as that which has been presented to the Senate."

Georgia's Walter George, most respected of Senate elders, rose and said Byrd was "doing a magnificent job." There followed an anti-Humphrey demonstration that went on for nearly four hours. One by one, Byrd's allies, including nearly all the patriarchs of both parties, got up to defend Byrd and condemn Humphrey, who sat slumped in his chair after vainly trying to win recognition from the presiding officer. When Humphrey finally got the floor,

Byrd and his supporters turned their backs on him and walked out.

Even after this hazing, Humphrey continued to attack. He wrote a long letter to the *New York Times* calling Byrd's committee "a violation of the intent and purpose of the Legislative Reorganization Act and . . . a brazen example of the continuance of overlapping functions and duplication of activities in the legislative branch." He accepted a liberal group's invitation to speak in Richmond and when Byrd declined to appear got a letter from Truman saying that "The senator from Virginia wouldn't have dared to debate with you." And even years later Humphrey sounded anything but contrite: "Harry Byrd was a phoney on this issue," he told a friend in 1970.

Defiant still in the face of Southern senatorial disapproval, Humphrey staged a second incursion into his adversaries' territory in June. Responding to a cry from his friend Emil Rieve, president of the United Textile Workers, he flew to Morristown, Tennessee, where he took on-the-spot testimony from union organizers and members beaten up by deputies and National Guardsmen sent in by the governor to crush a strike. Back in Washington he issued a subcommittee report blasting the use of the Taft-Hartley injunctions to keep unions out of the new textile plants springing up in the South. But Humphrey, the textile union, and the labor movement had to accept defeat in the effort to organize Southern factories.

In the midst of these scuffles the attention of the nation suddenly shifted abroad. The heightening tensions of the cold war in Europe and Asia exploded in the Communist invasion of South Korea. President Truman and the United Nations rallied to repel the first armed aggression against collective security since World War II. Humphrey, ever the dedicated cold warrior, praised the president's decision to act, contrasting it with the democracies' passivity when fourteen years earlier Hitler "marched his legions into the Rhineland." In his Senate speech he said: "This may be the biggest blow for peace in the twentieth century."

To further collective action against the spread of Communist aggression, Humphrey was more than willing to back the gigantic rearmament program that Truman sent to Congress. But when the bills to raise the necessary billions moved to the Senate floor, he took it upon himself to see them thoroughly debated, to see that all citizens should pay their fair share of the new taxes.

For when Humphrey entered the Senate, he had noticed that the leadership put all the liberals in the Labor committee. Not a single progressive-minded senator had been admitted to the Finance committee, which had the hold, through taxes, on the nation's economy. Furthermore, his friend Walter Heller, the University of Minnesota professor who had been a Treasury aide, had told him how the Finance committee in 1943 put through a wartime tax bill with so many exceptions for the rich that President Roosevelt vetoed it for providing "relief not for the needy but for the greedy."

Humphrey saw the huge new tax bill, worked out by some of the same

Senate hardshells (Harry Byrd was one), rolling toward passage virtually unchallenged. The committee's ranking members, Chairman Walter George of Georgia and Republican Eugene Millikin of Colorado, were sharp minds, long versed in the intricacies of the tax code, and their fellow club members deferred to them almost without question. As Humphrey saw it, with young men already falling in Korea, profiteering at home must be held to a minimum. It would be unconscionable, he felt, to send the tax bill through without debating its merits. So one day after getting an earful about what needed scrutiny from the clerk of the House committee that had sent the bill to the Senate, Humphrey returned to his office saying: "I've got to learn about taxes."

With Walter Heller's help he brought together a team of expert advisers, men such as Joseph Pechman and Al Oberdorfer from the Treasury and Justice Departments. At first they were skeptical, warning that he was tackling the most complicated subject in Congress and that George and Millikin were very smart old hands and would make a monkey out of him. Taken aback, Humphrey called in Paul Douglas, who was not only a senator but a card-carrying economist, former president of the American Economic Association. Douglas encouraged him to go ahead. But, severely wounded in World War II combat, he warned that he lacked the stamina to do more than help. Humphrey would have to make the floor fight.

For ten days, Humphrey sat up until two and three in the morning with the experts boning up on the arcana of the oil depletion allowance, in-oil payments, intangible drilling, collapsible corporations, family partnerships, gift taxes, capital gains preferences—all loopholes by which the rich escaped their share of taxes. "He was the quickest study I ever met," said Pechman later. "We would be trying to explain how the family partnership device could be used to split income and thereby cut down to lower brackets, and Hubert would break in: 'You mean to say that one-year-old Charlie could be taken into the firm and made a full partner of this accounting firm and get all these emoluments and therefore deserve the tax reduction?' "

When the debate took place, Humphrey spoke from a prepared paper. Millikin and George interrupted, dripping with sarcasm. But they were nit-picking, and in the long-drawn-out colloquies Humphrey's good humor and good nature came out. One-year-old Charlie was mentioned, and there were others. Humphrey could dramatize a loophole in language that made everybody laugh, including George and Millikin. Walter Heller, looking down with Pechman from the gallery, could see that other senators were enjoying the show and secretly, he thought, wishing that they had the guts to do what Humphrey was doing.

Humphrey held the floor for two full days. From time to time, Paul Douglas would get up and ask some such question as: "Is it true that this provision is designed to help taxpayers in the top bracket, which consists of one-tenth of 1 percent of all taxpayers?" He would go on for five minutes, giving Humphrey a rest. To no one's surprise, the Dixiecrat-Republican alliance held firm, and all of the twenty-seven amendments that Humphrey and Douglas offered were batted down—all, that is, but one that kept the minimum time for capital gains from being shortened by three months. But at the end, Millikin and George walked over to Humphrey, put their arms around him, and embraced him. They chaffed and joked with him. They admitted him to their friendship.

That performance *made* Humphrey in the Senate. It earned him the respect that was shown him from that time on. Moreover, from that day just about every taxpayer in the land knew what tax loopholes were—and that there were some big ones. Humphrey had the text of his remarks printed as a forty-eight-page book, of which unions bought and distributed half a million copies. Although Humphrey repeated his performance the following year, his amendments again went down to defeat. But he never gave up. Finally, in 1975, Senator Humphrey had the satisfaction of seeing Congress join him in a vote to abolish the most notorious of all tax loopholes—the big oil companies' depletion allowance.

The first year in Washington was a bad time for the Humphreys. To start with, the senator had to borrow from his father to pay the movers' hefty bill, which had to be settled before they would unload the household goods hauled from Minneapolis. The young couple unpacked their belongings amid crying children: Nancy, aged ten; Skipper, seven; Robert, five; and Dougie just twenty-two months. After the last diapers were changed, Hubert and Muriel worked far into the night to put things in some semblance of order.

Like innumerable other young families in the years after World War II, they had bought a brand-new tract house in a suburb. The suburb was Chevy Chase, and they had bought the house for twenty-six thousand dollars and a big mortgage. Humphrey's aide Bill Simms moved into a similar place down the street. The Humphrey house stood in a sea of mud approximately 100 by 200 feet, with an attached garage and carport for the 1946 Buick and the new Plymouth stationwagon given Muriel at a farewell dinner by Minneapolis businessmen. In the basement was a recreation room, for the family television set. On the second floor were four bedrooms—the big one for the parents, another for Skip's and Bob's bunk beds, and the smaller rooms for Nancy and Dougie. There was an extra bed in Dougie's for a guest. On the main floor were a big kitchen, living and dining rooms, and a den, where Humphrey installed his record collection and such prized books as the biographies of Lincoln, Jackson, and Jefferson. There was a finished attic where the children could play when the weather was bad. The boys had their electric train there, and that was where Humphrey kept his fishing and hunting gear.

Humphrey kept the checkbook. "We have a big grocery bill and seem to spend a lot of money on clothes," he informed a constituent. But it was Muriel Humphrey who enrolled Skip and Nancy in the Rosemary public school. It was she who took Nancy to the hospital for the sudden appendectomy. It was she who took on the job of seeding grass in the muddy yard and clothing the flanks of the naked house with a decent cover of shrubbery. It was she who decided there ought to be a sandbox, swing, and climbing bars at the back of the house for the kids. Not that Humphrey was unequal to changing diapers and administering discipline; he had often done so. But even more than in Minneapolis he was seldom home. Although he probably exaggerated, as usual, Humphrey told a friend that he did not have dinner at home eight times in his first three years in Washington. Mornings, he said, were "our fun times," but he frequently hurried away in his Buick to breakfast meetings downtown. On Sundays, about the only day he was likely to be home, he was faithful to his father's example. He packed the family into the car and drove them to Sunday school and church services at the Chevy Chase Methodist church. The Humphreys attended regularly for years but kept their membership at First Congregational church in Minneapolis. "All the way home in the car, Dad would comment on the sermon," Robert said later.

That first winter in Washington was filled with tensions. Adjusting to life in the East was a strain for every member of the family, none more so than Muriel Humphrey. The discouragements that her husband faced in the Senate were more than matched by the miseries at home. When Humphrey had a terrible time at work, he could not help bringing some of his frustrations and disappointments home at night. He would get angry. Voices were raised. Once after coming home from a party, his wife said, "You have to make a choice between the social whirl and the real Humphrey." At the end of the first six months, Muriel Humphrey felt so worn down that she went into the U. S. Hospital at Baltimore for tests. They showed no sign of disease. The doctor told her: "Your difficulty is purely on the basis of fatigue associated with some emotional tension." A few days later, as soon as school was out, she drove the four children to Minnesota. It was a punishing, twelve-hundred-mile trip, but it brought the relief she needed. That summer she stayed with the children in a rented cottage at Shady Knoll on Leech Lake, two hundred miles north of Minneapolis. Always a lover of the outdoors, she had spent a lot of time with her father at his South Dakota lake place and even helped him rent out boats when he had to sell his produce business in Huron and move to Bigstone Lake. In that summer of 1949 she taught Skip to swim by tossing him in the water with a rope tied around his middle. As soon as the Senate adjourned, Humphrey joined them, but it was only for a few days. Afteward he flew back to Washington, and Muriel Humphrey and the children followed in the stationwagon.

She dreaded the return. That fall a woman came in daily to help her around the house. And in November, with funds from the $8,933 in fees that Humphrey charged for his outside speaking engagements in 1949, the Humphreys set out for a European vacation. Just as they were boarding the train to New York, Humphrey was called to the telephone at Union Station: his father had suffered a stroke while delivering a sermon on layman's Sunday at a South Dakota church. They cancelled their European trip. A few days later, Hubert H. Humphrey, Sr., sixty-seven, suffered a second and fatal cerebral hemorrhage. Humphrey flew to his father's funeral mourning, as he said, "my best friend."

16

Cold War Caper

AFTER his election to the Senate in 1948, Humphrey had said at a sendoff dinner given by the merchants of Minneapolis, "I don't care if you were for me or against me, I'm going to serve all the people of Minnesota."

He was already running for reelection.

Even as he asserted leadership in Washington on national issues like Negro rights, for which there was no great constituency in Minnesota, Humphrey took good care to guard his home base. He told his aide Bill Simms that every Minnesota letter should be answered the day it was opened, that every Minnesota request should be treated as a command. To fulfill these impossible orders, Humphrey drove himself hardest of all. In between Senate sessions and speaking engagements he was constantly on the telephone browbeating federal bureaucrats for favors and then, late at night, dictating quick letters reporting what he had won. He blustered for labor. He wangled for small business. And he hustled for businesses that were not so small. Minnesota bankers and grain merchants soon found that they could get faster and better service through Humphrey than through his Republican colleague Ed Thye, who was neither so well connected in the Administration nor half so industrious.

Humphrey had good reason to cultivate Republicans. Although his party had gained successes on the national ticket, the Republican grip on Minnesota state offices remained unshaken. Harold Stassen, who had established the Republican dominance when he won the governorship in 1938, remained a potent presence even though he had just assumed the presidency of the University of Pennsylvania. His supporters controlled all state offices and both houses of the legislature. In Governor Luther Youngdahl, who ran an even more forward-looking administration than Stassen's, the Republicans had the state's best vote-getter. Humphrey, looking to higher office in 1948, chose to try for senator rather than contest against the popular and progressive Youngdahl. Big, blond, impressive, the governor came from a remarkable Swedish family in Minneapolis. An elder brother had served in Congress and a second, the Rev. Reuben Youngdahl, had built his Minneapolis parish into one of the country's largest Protestant congregations. He himself had twice served with distinction as a judge. In winning reelection in 1948, Luther Youngdahl rolled up a bigger majority than Humphrey.

But one cannot be governor indefinitely, and Humphrey and his friend DFL Chairman Orville Freeman were already concerned about their party's prospects for the 1950 race for governor. They considered how the DFL might move ahead in Minnesota with Youngdahl blocking the way.

It happened that Youngdahl had an intimate friend who had also become friendly with Humphrey—Ray Ewald. With his brothers, Ewald ran a substantial Minneapolis dairy business founded by their father, an immigrant milkman from Schleswig-Holstein. The Ewald boys grew up next door to the Youngdahls in south Minneapolis, and when Luther Youngdahl ran for governor Ray Ewald headed his finance committee. As a Republican member of the Minneapolis city planning commission when Humphrey took office as mayor, Ewald, as he later recalled, "thought at first he was just a young blabbermouth. But I changed my mind in a hurry. We'd get in a hot wrangle over something. Humphrey would come in, straighten things out in a hurry, and send everybody away happy. He had a way about him." Ewald, though a good Republican, contributed money to Humphrey's campaigns. When Humphrey flew back to Minneapolis during his first winter in the Senate, it was Ewald's Cadillac that usually picked him up at the airport. In 1953, Ewald rented his Waverly Lake cottage to the Humphreys for the summer, and the Humphreys felt so at home that they bought adjoining lakeshore lots from Ewald and subsequently built their permanent residence there.

Youngdahl, contemplating another reelection race in 1950, confided to his old friend Ewald that he would prefer to go back to the bench—the federal bench. His problem, however, was that the Democrats controlled federal judiciary appointments. Some time early in 1949, Ewald communicated this information to Humphrey. Although Humphrey had long since told Freeman that the first available judgeship in Minnesota must go to a deserving Democrat, he was interested. He liked and had always got on well with Youngdahl. And if Youngdahl went on the bench, not only would the DFL path to the statehouse be opened, but the strongest candidate the Republicans could put up to oppose Humphrey's own reelection in 1954 would be taken out of the play. He asked Ewald to arrange a meeting.

Humphrey and Youngdahl met at dinner at the Lake Minnetonka home of Republican Robert Naegele. Naegele said later:

> Ewald opened the subject, and then handed over to Humphrey. Humphrey said: "I'm doing this because Ray Ewald asked me to, and Ray has been so good to me." And Humphrey proceeded to open up the possibility that he, a Democratic senator, was prepared to go to bat, if Youngdahl was interested, to see if he could get him a federal judgeship.
>
> Interested? Youngdahl went after it like a muskie taking a bullfrog. He said: "Absolutely, yes."

Time passed. Youngdahl ran for an unprecedented third term in 1950 and won. Then, almost two years to the day after the Minnetonka meeting, Humphrey opened his newspaper in Washington and read that Judge T. Alan Goldsborough of the District of Columbia federal court had died of a heart attack. He threw down the newspaper and rushed to the office. There his aide Max Kampelman was waiting with the same newspaper story in hand. The date was July 1. On July 2, Humphrey saw President Truman and proposed Minnesota's Republican governor for the D. C. vacancy. To Humphrey's delight, Truman responded that Youngdahl was the only governor who had written to commend him when he fired General MacArthur. He told Humphrey: "Get him down here." On July 5, Ewald and Youngdahl arrived in Washington. The meeting in Truman's office was brief. The President didn't even bother to check with the Justice Department. He told Humphrey: "Don't even tell Matt Connelly [his appointments secretary] on the way out." The Minnesotans went straight to the White House press room, where Humphrey announced that the president was appointing Luther Youngdahl, Republican governor of Minnesota, as federal judge in the District of Columbia.

The surprise was complete. Minnesota's Republicans reeled in disarray. Stassen, who had a date to discuss campaign plans that day with Youngdahl in St. Paul, bellowed like a stuck steer. Truman sent Humphrey a note: "Looks as if our judgeship appointment was a ten-strike."

"It has surely been of help to me," Humphrey wrote back. It was the kind of stroke that gained him real respect in the Senate, and *Time* magazine commented: "Hubert Humphrey now has professional standing in the big leagues."

The 1954 election, however, was still a couple of years away, and as a Truman Democrat Humphrey was caught up in the rising political disquiet over the stalemated Korean war. As an outspoken liberal, he was an especially obvious target for the anti-Communist smear attacks by which Republican Senator Joseph McCarthy was in these years terrorizing bureaucrats, newsmen, and fellow members of the U. S. Senate. Just about the time that McCarthy was opening up on his colleagues, William Benton entered the Senate from Connecticut and was quickly drawn into the fight. In the ensuing melee over McCarthyism, another one of Humphrey's lifelong friendships was formed.

Benton, a high-powered merchandiser from Madison Avenue, was born in Minneapolis. Son of a University of Minnesota geology professor, he spent his formative years around the same campus from which Humphrey leaped into politics. He was a dozen years older than Humphrey and had taken his degree at Yale. But he prided himself on his Minnesota ties, served on the board both of Minnesota's Carleton college and of Shattuck military academy, in Minnesota. In his expansive way, he liked to refer to himself at times as Minnesota's third senator.

A multimillionaire liberal with access to corporate boardrooms and Eastern salons, Benton could introduce Humphrey to aspects of life he had not yet seen. With his Yale classmate Chester Bowles, Benton had built the firm of Benton & Bowles into one of the country's leading ad agencies. Even before Bowles left to become Roosevelt's wartime price administrator, the restless Benton took off to join another Yale classmate, Robert Hutchins, as vice president of the University of Chicago. Shortly afterward, he bought up the old Encyclopedia Britannica property that had been bequeathed to the university and, with his gift for the promotional hard-sell, made more millions hawking the aging ornament of British learning door to door, like magazines and bibles. In World War II he was called to push propaganda at the State Department and left it with an unrequited desire to head that department or at least represent it at the Court of St. James. Had either Adlai Stevenson or Hubert Humphrey become president, one or both ambitions might have been fulfilled, but he was only named ambassador to UNESCO. He contributed substantially to Democratic party coffers, and the numerous yearbooks and other publications of Encyclopedia Britannica blossomed with lavishly paid articles by Democratic influentials. Then quite unexpectedly in early 1950 a Senate seat fell vacant in Connecticut, and Governor Bowles, faced with a difficult choice among competing contenders, named his old partner to fill the seat until the fall elections.

At once Benton joined the efforts led by Senator Millard Tydings to answer McCarthy's charges that the State Department was riddled with Reds. That fall the supposedly unbeatable Tydings was defeated when McCarthy led a smear campaign against him in Maryland, but Benton won reelection in Connecticut for the remaining two years of his term. Back in Washington, Benton conducted a thorough inquiry into the methods used by McCarthy to defeat Tydings, such as faking a photograph to show Tydings in apparent conversation with ex-Communist party chief Earl Browder. On August 6, 1951, Benton called on the Senate to censure and expel McCarthy in a closely documented speech much admired by Humphrey. Although Humphrey had not hesitated to charge McCarthy with using Hitler's Big Lie techniques, the older man now took his friend in hand saying: "Don't worry, we'll get him soon enough. You stay out of it."

The two grew close. After a session, Benton would write, "I am an old

hand, Hubert, at judging skills with words—you were superb yesterday."
When Humphrey was less successful on radio, Benton, the practiced pitch-
man, instructed him how to be blunter on the air. When Humphrey complained of his treatment by the Minneapolis newspapers, Benton intervened
with publisher John Cowles. They talked about their fathers, and after
Humphrey told about his Depression days in the dust bowl, Benton wrote
DeWitt Wallace of the *Readers Digest*, another Minnesotan: " . . . The kind
of story you like—Hubert moving into Huron because they were being starved
out of the smaller town in which they were trying to operate a drug store,
and fourteen years later they had knocked out the other competing drug
stores in Huron . . . prosperous . . . still owned by the Humphrey family."
After Humphrey confided that he wished for an honorary degree (he later
collected forty), Benton wrote: "I'm working on one for you." When Humphrey looked drawn and in need of a vacation, Benton packed him off for a
week to his Arizona spread. And when Benton joined a congressional junket
to Europe in December, he insisted that Humphrey be asked along too.

It was Humphrey's first venture abroad—"a thrilling and exciting experience," he wrote home from his first night at Claridge's in London. In Britannica's chauffeured car, Humphrey took in the sights. And with the help of
the Ediphone dictating machine that Benton showed him how to use, Humphrey reported every detail of his month-long jaunt to the newspapers of
Minnesota. Everywhere he went he took notes ("made myself a terrific bore").
He pained Benton by asking for a hamburger in a three-star Paris restaurant.
Benton took over the ordering, and Humphrey reported: "The French are
truly artists in the kitchen." But he still complained: "Water, plain, good,
old, sparkling drinking water [is] the one thing most difficult to obtain anywhere in Europe." He goggled at Soviet troops in Vienna, found Germany
still dominated by cartels, and pronounced France "the weak pillar of NATO."
At the interparliamentary conference in Strasbourg, he came down with the
flu and had to confine his remarks to the Ediphone: "I say the German question is a question of bygone days. The question now is the Russian question.
. . . ." Parting company at last with Benton, Humphrey visited Minnesota's
Eugenie Anderson, whom President Truman had sent to Denmark as the
country's first female ambassador, and then went to Norway for a day in
Kristiansand, his mother's birthplace. He drank coffee and sang songs with
cousins in the ancestral coastal valley farmhouse. That night in Oslo, after
reporting this experience for his numerous Scandinavian constituents back
home, he summed up: "Brother, if you ever appreciate the U. S. with all its
faults, you really do appreciate it after you have visited Europe."

Humphrey was Minnesota's favorite-son nominee for the Democratic
presidential nomination in 1952 and might have received consideration after
Truman's announcement that he would not run again threw the race wide
open. Senator Brien McMahon of Connecticut, forced to withdraw when
stricken with cancer, urged him to try. But Estes Kefauver had already

preempted Humphrey by winning primaries in Midwest states, where Humphrey might have established a base. Humphrey's big chance ought to have come as convention keynoter—Truman was reported to favor him for that role. But Dixiecrat hatred was so strong that Humphrey got no chance to cap his 1948 performance. Instead, bouncing from hotel to hotel trying to get liberal unity in platform and seating scraps, he was caught out of position when the move to draft Governor Adlai Stevenson of Illinois swept the convention. On the final ballot he threw half his state's votes to Kefauver, half to Stevenson. He never addressed the convention at all.

Humphrey drove his family to Yellowstone Park for a camping vacation. At forty-one he could wait. But 1952 was not a Democratic year. Humphrey wrote Benton an incisive critique of the Stevenson effort:

> Politics is a strange admixture of mind and body, of ideas and guts. The people know that Stevenson can think their thinking for them. The question is, does he "feel" for them?
>
> Adlai has been giving remarkable speeches. They are masterpieces. But don't forget, Bill, that politics is not a fulltime activity with the majority of citizens. Politics absorbs but little of their time. There are so many activities and events crowding in on people today that unless the political story is told in the most dramatic way—in bold strokes, even in exaggerated terms—it will not command attention. I'm one of those who believes it's just as easy to get people aroused over a good cause, a positive program, as it is to excite them over the negative abuses such as corruption, etc. We Democrats have got to challenge our people. We have to make them feel that they are an integral part of a great crusade for human freedom. Mr. American Citizen must realize that he is one of the privileged people of the world—privileged to lead, privileged to give, and privileged to help save his fellow men. Perhaps even want to save themselves or save someone else. There is a quality of heroism and pathos in every soul.
>
> Keep fighting, Bill. Keep telling people of the opportunities that lie ahead as well as the problems. We're a young nation and we have a wonderful people. This country is too good and its people too fine to be debauched and misled by meanness, guilty by associations, frustration and despair.

Benton, going down to defeat before McCarthy's mudslinging, called Humphrey's letter "thrilling." He wrote, "I do not see how you are ever going to be defeated for the Senate when you can write letters like this one." Humphrey wrote back he was "heartbroken" at the outcome in Connecticut.

Humphrey was already beginning to get a name around Washington as a senator who could come up with a lot of ideas—not all of them good ones. With the air of a young fellow who had stumbled on the solution to the world's problems, he dashed off a letter to President Truman urging creation of a Department of Peace—and got back this testy answer, "The Department of Peace is located in the State Department, where it belongs." After Truman's Korean decision, Humphrey got the idea that the president should emulate Woodrow Wilson's fourteen points for the Europe of 1917 by proclaiming an even more inspirational program for Asia. He dispatched a fifteen-point program to the White House, and Truman shot back one of his longhand letters: "Your proposed 15-point program is a good one for an educated, well-conditioned, middle-class-controlled country, but for poor [lands] the foundation has to be laid with a Point Four program [of technical aid]."

After leaving it to other Democratic senators to rebut Joe McCarthy's wild charges, Humphrey also came up with a scheme for joining the anti-Communist crusade. The vehicle for his involvement was his subcommittee on labor-management relations. This was the subcommittee he had used earlier in his unsuccessful effort to draw attention to the use of force to keep unions out of the South. Now he thought to aid his anti-Communist labor friends in their drive to cleanse the CIO of Communists. In 1949, President Phil Murray's own CIO inquiry had found nine of its member unions to be Communist-dominated and expelled them. But some leaders, notably CIO Treasurer Jim Carey, struggling to build up a rival union against the ousted United Electrical Workers, felt the cleanup was far from complete.

Another who thought the job was unfinished was Humphrey's aide and political strategist Max Kampelman. A young New York-born lawyer, Kampelman was well connected in the labor movement. He first came into Humphrey's life when as a conscientious objector in World War II he chose to do his alternative service as a human guinea pig in starvation experiments at the University of Minnesota medical school. Upon his release he took up graduate study in political science at the university just as Humphrey launched his political career from that department. After the war, Kampelman shed his pacifism, joined ADA, and underwent the same cold war conversion to anti-Communism as other Humphrey adherents. After taking part in the Humphreyite drive against Minnesota's left-wingers, he wrote his doctoral dissertation on "The Communists and the CIO"—an analysis of Phil Murray's Red purge.

By the time Humphrey reached the Senate, Kampelman had gone off to teach at Bennington College in Vermont. Invited to Washington to help Humphrey recruit a staff, Kampelman wound up as Humphrey's legislative counsel. It was a connection that was to last a lifetime. In 1956, Kampelman left Humphrey's payroll to take up his own lucrative law practice in the capital. He never ceased to be Humphrey's close adviser and, indeed, his personal lawyer. As Humphrey rose, so did Kampelman, whose clientele reached into Humphrey's labor and liberal constituencies. It was a typical Washington political law practice that found Kampelman often doubling as a Humphrey fund raiser. He was sometimes called the "Jewish Tommy Corcoran." But Kampelman, unlike FDR's braintruster-turned-lobbyist, returned to government in later life and served as unsalaried chief of the U. S. delegation to the Madrid conference on European security under Carter and Reagan.

Counseled by Kampelman, Humphrey set out to hold hearings where the CIO inquiry left off. But in the meantime, its top leaders having been tried and imprisoned, the Communist party of the United States had gone underground. Humphrey could show that the United Electrical Workers, biggest of the unions expelled by the CIO, still had the same officers whose Red ties had been the ground for the union's expulsion. These officers had simply signed affidavits, as required by the Taft-Hartley Act, that they were non-Communists. But the only evidence Humphrey could adduce that they were Reds was the old-hat CIO trial testimony that they had followed the Communist line on international affairs. Humphrey's fellow senators seldom bothered to attend the hearings. Humphrey himself did not press his final recommendation that the National Labor Relations Board be empowered to crack down on false affidavits. In 1953 the Republicans came to power, and Republican senators led by McCarthy took over all investigating committees. Humphrey's subcommittee went out of existence.

But Humphrey still thought there was a problem and continued on and off to discuss the unfinished business of Communists in the ousted unions with Kampelman. The summer of 1954 arrived, when Humphrey was up for reelection. The cold war hit its peak frenzy—the McCarthy-Army television hearings, the disgrace of Robert Oppenheimer, the suicide of Wyoming's Senator Lester Hunt under the most intimidating McCarthyite innuendos. On Capitol Hill it was said that McCarthy, who had been drinking hard, would be taken off the bottle and sent forth to smear other Senate Democrats besides Hunt who were up for reelection—and thereby build up the Republicans' razor-thin 48-to-47 edge in the November voting.

At this point, as the miasma of fear and hatred spread over Washington, Senator John Marshall Butler, Republican of Maryland, brought in a bill addressed to the very problem that had vexed Humphrey. With administration support, Butler proposed that the attorney general be empowered to bring any organization adjudged to be "Communist-infiltrated" before the Subversive Activities Control Board, which might then deny the "organization" any right to engage in collective bargaining.

Tossed in at the peak of the Communist-hunting spree, the proposal really frightened organized labor. In the hands of an anti-labor attorney-general—"and we have one," cried Wayne Morse, Independent of Oregon—the bill would open the door to union busting. If the scheme frightened some, it angered Humphrey, who saw Republicans cynically exploiting the problem he had identified as one more phoney move to sway voters against liberal Democrats. He decided to give the Republicans a dose of their own anti-Communist poison. On August 12, shouting, "I am tired of having people play the Communist issue," he offered as a substitute amendment something far more extreme: an outright ban on the Communist party.

As a political act to dish the Republicans, Joseph and Stewart Alsop wrote, Humphrey's move was "cleverly conceived, ruthlessly executed and politically adroit." Every single liberal senator, given the chance to record his anti-Communism before the November balloting, leaped to side with Humphrey. And the Republicans, unwilling to appear less anti-Communist, backed the proposal unanimously as it was tacked on to Butler's bill and whooped through, 85-to-0. Next day of course it came out that the Republican Administration wanted nothing so strong. So in return for rephrasing that took the anti-union sting out of Butler's part of the package, the Humphrey ban on the party was rendered meaningless by removing the penalties for belonging. So modified, this piece of political claptrap became the Communist Control Act of 1954.

The motives of a public man like Humphrey are complex. Basically there were two, one political and the other ideological. Gerald Siegel of the Senate legal staff later called the amendment "unconstitutional and unconscionable—but the only way to keep out a vicious anti-labor bill." By his bill, Humphrey was insuring his own reelection. However, he already led comfortably in the polls and knew that Val Bjornson, the moderate Republican running against him, had no intention of inviting McCarthy into his campaign. At this very time, Humphrey wrote a constituent, Joseph Stiepan that "On McCarthy, my opponent seems to agree with me." On another political level, Humphrey said in the closing debate: "I'm tired of hearing this talk of twenty years of treason" and, as if to underline this motive, said later that his actions had saved a couple of Democratic seats in 1954. In fact, far from losing seats in November, the Democrats picked up enough to recapture control of both House and Senate.

At the time, Humphrey said over and over he was dead serious in proposing to make Communist membership a crime. "The Communist party isn't really a political party, it's an international conspiracy," he said. He had no trouble getting Wayne Morse, a former law school dean, to cosponsor the measure. In the preamble to his amendment, Humphrey cited Learned Hand, the most respected constitutional authority of the day. To wait for "clear and present danger" before acting, Judge Hand held, was no longer good enough when "the violent capture [of all governments] is a commonplace among [Communist party] initiates. . . . The gravity of the evil, discounted by its improbability, is greater than the mischief of its repression."

Humphrey argued, following Kampelman, that his action would enlarge, rather than curtail, civil liberties. McCarthy, he said, was tarring and feathering innocent people who had no proper place to defend themselves and clear their names. But if the Communist party were outlawed and membership in it made a crime, then each individual, once named, would have his day in court where under the rules of evidence he could ascertain the charges against him, confront hostile witnesses, and present his defense. Kampelman went further and said that once party membership were defined as a crime, McCarthy could be sued for criminal libel.

Humphrey's "superpolitical ploy," as Joe Rauh called it, infuriated his ADA friends, but mostly they looked upon it as a momentary aberration and forgave him. After voicing "grave doubts," Arthur Schlesinger wound up: "Anyway, good luck in the campaign." Humphrey's old friend Marvin Rosenberg was more severe, sending his campaign contribution with the explanation that it was not for Humphrey "personally," but to insure election of a Democratic Senate. In later years, Humphrey was heard to say: "It's not one of the things I'm proudest of."

But he *was* anti-Communist, and that was basic. He had fought Communists in the Electrical Workers union as his deadliest Minnesota foes in 1947 and 1948; he went after the same bunch in his 1952 hearings; and he returned to the attack in the hysterical summer of 1954. With every allowance for his weakness for oratorical excess, it is a fact that Humphrey said before casting his vote for the Communist Control Act: "These rats will not get out of the trap."

Humphrey's initiative is, therefore, not to be seen as an isolated or impulsive action. He was a defender of civil liberties before the nightmare summer of 1954, and he would further distinguish himself in the battle for civil liberties in years to come. But he was also a cold warrior whose most important decision on his way to political power in Minnesota was waging war on leftists he identified as Communists. And when at the height of the McCarthy fever the Republicans moved to preempt his anti-Communist cause, Humphrey listened to Kampelman rather than Joe Rauh and carried his anti-Communism to a length never proposed by Joe McCarthy. Humphrey's move, which seemed at the time such a devastating thrust, appeared to be tactical, temporary. It wasn't. Stemming from ideological depths, his action prefigured his later embroilment over Vietnam. It led an elderly professor at the University of South Dakota to observe at the time that Humphrey's espousal of this measure revealed a flaw in his political character that would keep him eventually from becoming president of the United States. Sooner or later, the old man said, he would trip on some other issue. George McGovern, a young Dakota Wesleyan instructor who "adored" Humphrey, bridled at hearing the remark but recalled it much later. It was a prophecy that would come true.

17

Learning the Hard Way

BEFORE he went to the Senate, Humphrey, vehemently convinced that the Democratic party must stand as a "liberal and progressive force," held that it would have to undergo a "rearrangement in structure." "The Southern Democrats ought to be over in the Republican party—in other words, let's get where we belong," he wrote his friend Dudley Parsons. For a moment after the 1948 convention, when the Democratic party adopted his ringing civil rights plank and the Dixiecrats bolted, Humphrey looked like getting his wish. As usual, however, Humphrey was ahead of his time.

For when Congress met, it did not work out that way at all. Try as he would, Humphrey could not stir up action on civil rights or any of the other progressive items in the Fair Deal program President Truman laid before the legislators. The old lineup returned unchanged: the Southern Democrats dominated both Senate and House and continued to vote like Republicans. Humphrey's attack on Senator Byrd, which can be seen as an attempt to read the old boy out of the party, backfired badly, and Humphrey was isolated.

Senate seniors shunned him. But a couple of other members of the class of 1948 did not. One was Russell Long of Louisiana, who had known him slightly as a fellow student at Baton Rouge before the war and was now Humphrey's neighbor in suburban Chevy Chase. The other was Lyndon Johnson of Texas, tall and lanky, to whom Long introduced Humphrey at the Senate's first Democratic caucus. Johnson, already an old hand in Washington who had served six years in the House of Representatives, was on intimate terms with Speaker Sam Rayburn, the most powerful figure on Capitol Hill. "Landslide Lyndon" they called him: he had scraped in by a margin of eighty-seven votes including the contents of a ballot box found after the polls closed in Duval county on the Mexican border. Johnson, even though he joined the Southern bloc and assiduously cultivated its leader, Richard Russell, found time for an occasional friendly word with the outcast Humphrey. Humphrey said later: "He knew the senators, I didn't. He got along with Russell and Byrd and George, and understood the pieces, the personal relationships. Johnson joined the Southern bloc, but unlike the others he didn't treat me like a pariah."

Humphrey got into a shoving match with Republican Homer Capehart following a hot radio debate over the president's dismissal of General MacArthur, and was only kept from punching the fat Indianan when aide Bill Simms grabbed his arm. Senate elders, offended at this undignified display, repeated Vice President Barkley's crack: "Minnesota is a great state— first they send us their Ball, then they send us their Thye, and now they've sent us their goddam ass."* But Johnson was different. Even after the other senators scourged Humphrey for his attack on Byrd, Johnson sought him out and made a joke of it. Humphrey said later: "He said he wanted to crossbreed me with Byrd. If he could get two pints of Byrd's blood into me to cool me off, and a little of Russell's restraint, I'd be great."

Johnson tutored Humphrey in the Senate's unwritten rules, urged him to become a liberal doer and not just a liberal talker. Made Democratic whip in 1951, he studied the little knot of Northern liberals and saw in Humphrey, brashest of the "bomb throwers," the likeliest bridge to that group. Humphrey had first-class liberal credentials, yet welcomed Johnson's advances. Humphrey said later: "He didn't enjoy talking to that group. He didn't think they had any sense of humor. . . . Our little group was very suspicious of him."

Rather than coming at Humphrey head-on, Johnson used flattery. It was a very slow process of calling Humphrey in and saying, "Do you think you can help me among your liberal friends on this?" They had some things in common: they had entered the Senate together, they had both been teachers, both were country boys from west of the Mississippi in the alien East; both were ambitious, extroverted, on the make.

Did they, even in these earliest sessions, give voice to their ambitions? They certainly saw eye to eye on the cold war. The first letter to pass between them, in September 1951, shows Humphrey complimenting Johnson on his first report as chairman of the armed services subcommittee on preparedness. It was a position in which, had the Korean conflict spread worldwide as

*Joseph Ball, senator, 1940–49; Edward Thye, senator, 1946–59.

many expected, Johnson would have played an attention-getting role similar to that Senator Harry Truman held as head of the War Investigations Committee after Pearl Harbor. The second letter, again from Humphrey, followed immediately after the heroic Humphrey tax-bill effort that won him the Senate's esteem; it conveyed his thanks to Johnson "for your support on some of our amendments."

The Texan and Minnesotan were beginning to help each other. Johnson began to invite Humphrey to his office for talk and drinks. So far had Humphrey's stock risen after the tax-bill fight that sometimes Richard Russell, the Southern chieftain, was also present. The day came when Russell Long took Humphrey to the senators' inner dining room where no outsiders were permitted. There, Democrats sat at one big table and Republicans at another; senators relaxed, told stories, and took their lunch in an atmosphere of camaraderie. In this informal setting, where everybody was equal, Humphrey's conviviality and good humor won friends.

In 1952, Senate Democratic Leader Ernest McFarland of Arizona lost his seat to Barry Goldwater, and the Southerners backed Lyndon Johnson to take his place. At that point, Johnson, voting South on civil rights and Southwest on oil and gas, personified just about everything that Northern liberals detested. Yet if Johnson were to be leader, he would need a line to these liberals. He turned to Humphrey to ask his support. Humphrey put him off. Johnson indicated he had expected a friendlier response, particularly since he had in mind making Humphrey whip.

Humphrey later called that hint, with all it implied about his admission to the club, "exhilarating." But to have accepted would have been a liberal sellout. He met with other liberals. They insisted on nominating their dean, James Murray of Montana, who was seventy-seven years old, to oppose Johnson. But they also wanted better committee assignments and places in the Democratic policy-setting hierarchy. Humphrey led a delegation—Senators Lehman, Douglas, and Lester Hunt of Wyoming—to bargain with Johnson. He told them he had the votes and sent them packing. But he called Humphrey back, saying, "Let me tell you something, Hubert. You're depending on votes you don't have. Senator Hunt, who was just in here, is going to vote for me. You ought to quit fooling around with people you can't depend on."

Sure enough, when the senators cast their secret ballot, Murray had only a handful of votes. Humphrey went back to Johnson's office; this time the Texan asked: "Now what do you liberals want?" Humphrey requested that Murray be put on the policy committee. Johnson agreed and added Humphrey to the steering committee, which made him Johnson's go-between to the liberal camp. A few days later he gave Humphrey the seat on the Foreign Relations Committee that Humphrey had longed for.

Much has been made of Lyndon Johnson's taming of the independent Senate to his will—and Humphrey ("the others felt I was being used by

Johnson") was part of the act. Around 7:30 at night Johnson would telephone and say: "Hubert, come over. There's something I want to talk to you about." If Humphrey said his family was waiting, Johnson answered: "Damn it, Hubert, you've got to make up your mind whether you're going to be a good father or a good senator." Over and over Johnson made his pitch: "Your speeches are accomplishing nothing. Support me and deliver your liberal friends. Otherwise you'll suffer the fate of those crazies, those bomb-thrower types like Paul Douglas, Wayne Morse, Herbert Lehman. You'll be ignored, and get nothing accomplished you want."

Humphrey was drawn into the Johnson "system"—the incessant quorum calls, the night sessions, the crafty requests for unanimous agreement by which the Leader drove through the measures he wanted and held up those he did not. He felt the force of the Johnson "treatment"—the flattering notes, the hectoring phone calls, the whispered confidences imparted so intimately in cloakroom and office that Leader and led bumped eyeglasses. The Johnson "network," captained by twenty-six-year-old, ex-Senate page Bobby Baker, kept track of senators night and day, winkled out their most private hopes and fears, shepherded them to rollcalls. Humphrey said later: "Johnson had his own private FBI. If you'd had a drink, if you'd been out on a date, if you'd attended a meeting, danced with a girl at a night club—he knew it."

Senator Earle Clements of Kentucky, a bald and gregarious border stater who got on well with most factions, operated as Johnson's whip. But Johnson also had intricate understandings with senior Republican Styles Bridges of New Hampshire that enabled him often on the floor to toy with the official Majority leader, the elephantine William Knowland of California. As for Humphrey, he was not really a member of Johnson's circle of trust until much later. He still disagreed with Johnson on many matters, but could now barge into the Leader's lair, meeting Johnson's queries on how the "bomb throwers" would vote with a bantering demand for help from "you and your fascists" for a liberal proposal in his pocket.

> By this time [Humphrey said later] we were hitting it off. . . . I told him he was a lot more liberal than he thought he was, and he insisted I was a lot more conservative than I realized. . . .
>
> He was a marvelous conversationalist. He told a lot of stories. He'd been close to Roosevelt, my hero. He knew the operations of the House. He knew all the personalities. He knew all the little things they did. He was a great mimicker. He lived and breathed and walked and talked politics. Totally immersed—I found him fascinating right from the beginning.
>
> He was really different, not a Southerner. When he went home it was to the ranch, not to the plantation. He was a cattleman, he identified with the economy of the West.
>
> And my kind of politics met with Johnson's in this sense that while I

was a man of liberal persuasion, I often knew that you couldn't get as much as you wanted. I was willing to settle for less. That was heresy among the liberals. . . .

And that was when Humphrey told a *Time* reporter: "I've stopped kicking the wall."

After talking with Johnson, he persuaded the other liberals at the start of the 1955 session that fighting to change Senate rules to stop another Senate filibuster against their civil rights package would be futile. Then he proceeded to introduce each item in the package one by one. Lyndon Johnson buried them one-by-one in Southern-led committees.

Being on the Foreign Relations Committee gave Humphrey new standing and a chance to open important initiatives. U. S. world leadership peaked during these years, and the committee provided the best possible forum for senators with national ambitions—such as Humphrey and John Kennedy, who came on two years after Humphrey. As a member, Humphrey could develop issues on which he had already taken strong positions. He had been the first senator to champion India. As early as 1946, Kampelman recalled, he had been "the foremost Zionist" at an evening with Jewish friends in Minneapolis, and from his first day in Washington addressing United Jewish Appeal and Israeli bond drives became a regular part of his life. Already a committed supporter of the Truman Doctrine and Marshall Plan, he backed the NATO pact in June 1949 with a speech that was a model of cogency— even brevity. And when Taft initiated the "great debate" of 1951 over stationing troops in Europe, Humphrey got in some good licks for the U. S. commitment.

Johnson's innovations as leader provided that Senate Democrats, even the most junior, would receive one major committee assignment. In return for his place on Foreign Relations, Humphrey had to relinquish the membership in the Agriculture committee he had recently obtained. Though Johnson promised him the first Democratic vacancy available on Agriculture, none opened until more than a year later. This did not keep Humphrey from finding a way to make farm issues paramount in his 1954 reelection strategy. He did so by important and creative use of his perch on the Foreign Relations Committee.

He had begun to study up on agriculture the way he had on labor law and tax loopholes. He brought into his staff Herbert Waters, a moon-faced Californian who had been secretary of agriculture Charles Brannan's assistant. And when Ezra Taft Benson, taking office as Brannan's Republican successor, called price supports "disaster insurance" in a St. Paul speech, Humphrey seized on the words as proof for Minnesota farmers that the Eisenhower administration was already undermining the life-support system created for them by Democratic subsidies.

That summer, with his 1954 reelection contest still eighteen months away,

Humphrey left his family at Ewald's lake cabin and raced around the state shaking hands and talking to farmers. "Had fun pitching bundles of wheat to an old-fashioned, steam-powered threshing rig at the threshing bee in New Ulm," reported the sometime pharmacist and political science professor. "Watched the state corn-picking contest at Delevan." Waters was one of a succession of Humphrey aides to remark on the senator's way of working out new ideas as he talked. In the summer of 1953, Waters said later, he watched Humphrey evolve from speech to speech a new concept in farm policy.

In the postwar period of huge, yearly crop carryovers, Washington had set up the Commodity Credit Corp to buy wheat, corn, and cotton and thereby to keep farm prices from plunging. It was Humphrey's idea to take some of these surplus farm stocks, whose size also kept farm prices from rising, and as part of the U. S. foreign aid program let needy nations buy them with local currencies rather than scarce dollars. That would be good for hungry nations and, because it unloaded some of the U. S. stocks that kept domestic prices down, good for Minnesota farmers too. This was the seed of what was to become a major U. S. foreign trade policy.

When Humphrey first offered it as an amendment to the Foreign Assistance Act of 1953, the idea caught on so fast the Republican majority insisted on substituting their own identically worded version. Then Humphrey climbed down from the high missionary principle of aid to needy foreigners and laid before his Southern colleagues the value to cotton growers of unloading their government-held surplus in markets they could not otherwise penetrate. With Southern help, Humphrey saw his expanded program enacted as the Agricultural Trade Development and Assistance Act of 1954, better known as Public Law 480.

Cloaked in the guise of international assistance and administered by the State Department, the measure escaped the opprobrious "dumping" label that might have been hung on it had it originated in the Agriculture Committee. But it was precisely the promise of unloading surplus crops outside domestic markets that commended the program to farm-bloc conservatives who regularly voted against "foreign aid." Walter George of Georgia, the same Walter George who had led the hazing of Humphrey after his attack on Bryd but who now sat as Humphrey's colleague on Foreign Relations, wrote, "You are certainly entitled to great credit for initiating this program."

Led by Bill Thatcher and his huge Farmers Union grain cooperative, Minnesota's farmers showed a lively desire to get in on Humphrey's scheme for international agrarian action. But it was among the bigtime Republicans in the Minneapolis commodity exchanges that Humphrey's program had the biggest impact.

Minneapolis, the "flour city," was the headquarters not only of Pillsbury and General Mills but of some of the great commodity-trading enterprises of the world. Starting with small country elevators that bought the grain the farmers hauled into town, these companies had grown huge and rich by exploiting the economics of the national market in league with the railroads. Populists such as Humphrey's father denounced them for being oppressors as wicked as Rockefeller and the other robber barons.

The younger Humphrey, bursting on the scene as mayor and senator, discovered that the oppressors of the grain trade had become his potential allies. Helped by federal dredging along the upper Mississippi, they floated their product downriver to New Orleans and Houston, and looked on the whole world as their market. Humphrey, militantly remolding the Democratic-Farmer Labor party to lead Minnesota out of its isolationism, called for U. S. participation in all world affairs—including trade.

Other changes were afoot in this farm region so long in decline. The farmers—and the grain merchants of Minneapolis—had discovered a new product, the soybean. Before Pearl Harbor, it was an exotic import from China. During World War II, industrial uses were found for soybean oil. In 1946, intent on mixing soybeans and oil into livestock feed on a big scale, Cargill, largest of all Minneapolis grain merchants, bought a couple of Iowa processing plants. The company hired one of the brothers who ran them, Dwayne Andreas, twenty-eight, as vice president for soybeans.

Raised in a devout Mennonite family in Iowa and sent to the evangelical Wheaton College in Illinois, Andreas was a midwesterner of proverbial provinciality. Traveling the continents for Cargill in the next years, the boy from the cornfields mastered the sophisticated intricacies of the international market. Like Humphrey, he saw the world as one—as one vast market, that is. By terms of the Cargill deal, Andreas and his brothers emerged as agribusiness capitalists in their own right. They hung on to the Minnesota unit of their Honeymead soybean-processing operation. With Lowell, the younger brother, in nominal charge, the Andreas brothers expanded their stake in the booming soybean market.

In 1948, Ray Ewald introduced Dwayne Andreas to Humphrey, and Andreas contributed to Humphrey's campaign. Four years later, Dwayne Andreas entertained the Humphreys and Simmses at a Miami Beach hotel he had acquired. By this time, Andreas had cut loose from Cargill and with Honeymead as his base was trading on an ever-bolder scale. Early in 1954 he made news when he struck a deal to sell the Soviet Union 40 million pounds of surplus butter and 14 million pounds of surplus cottonseed oil, only to have the State Department withhold approval. Andreas was at Humphrey's elbow as Humphrey introduced his bill for overseas sale of surplus products, including soybeans. When the Agriculture Department backed down on its plan to lower cottonseed-oil support, Humphrey crowed: "We kept after them right to the finish." "You bet we're pleased," Andreas wrote back, since the price of competing soybeans would rise by 25 cents per bushel as a result.

That was the kind of concrete accomplishment Humphrey counted on to carry the farmers with him in the 1954 campaign. There had been an unsettling moment in the fall of 1953 when Republican National Committeeman George Etzell's country newspaper printed a story that Joe McCarthy's investigating committee might look into a resolution that Humphrey had sponsored for a company in some financial trouble. But nothing more was heard of it, and the Cowles papers, while opposing Humphrey, did the Republican cause no good by reporting the successive notables, from Walter Judd to Dr. Charles Mayo, who turned down the chance to run against him.

In February 1954, Secretary Benson announced his decision to lower dairy price supports to 75 percent of parity with the price of articles the farmer had to buy.* Finally, in May the Eisenhower administration won its struggle for legislation authorizing "flexible," that is, lower, price supports; from then on, Humphrey had the Republicans of Minnesota on the run. State Treasurer Val Bjornson, chosen to oppose him, said later that one Republican congressman told him, "If you so much as say a decent word about Ezra Benson, we won't campaign with you in our district." "The plight of the farmer," Bjornson said, became the theme of the race.

Even then, rather than risk being pulled down by the rest of the DFL ticket, Humphrey took care to set up a separate headquarters and run a separate campaign. Although Waters was his manager, Humphrey himself ran the show—*was* the show. He was not nearly so well organized as his old friend Orville Freeman, the party's candidate for governor. But unlike Freeman, he loved to get out and meet the people. The problem with Humphrey was not to get him out on the campaign trail but to get him to go on to the next scheduled event. "Orv was the ornery Marine," said Bill Kubicek, chairman of Freeman's volunteer committee. "Hubert was the Rembrandt with words." Gerald Heaney, the national committeeman, said: "If Humphrey had had Orville Freeman's organizational abilities, he would have been president of the United States hands down. If Orville Freeman had had Humphrey's charisma, he could have been president just as well."

It was the custom for each party's senatorial campaign committee to send senators of their party into other states to help defeat colleagues of the opposite party. Milton Young, a conservative senator from North Dakota, was asked to go into Minnesota to help knock off Humphrey. He refused. He said he would go into any other state to campaign against a Democrat. Asked why, he said: "He's the only one who sometimes comes to my desk to ask me how I'm feeling. He's the only man here who knows that on many days I suffer migraine headaches and feel just terrible." On the other hand, Lyndon Johnson broke off his own reelection campaign to fly to Minneapolis to address businessmen at a Humphrey fundraiser. "I disagree with most of

---

*Parity has been defined as "the price calculated to give the farmer a fair return in relation to the things he must buy." New Deal legislation first established an equivalence between farmers' current purchasing power and their purchasing power at a selected base period, originally 1910–14. Thereafter Congress would require the federal government to support agricultural commodity prices at designated ratios—85 percent, 90 percent, 100 percent—of this equivalence.

what your senator stands for," he said, "but I earnestly urge you to return him to Washington—he is one of the ablest men in the U. S. Senate." It took hardly any persuasion from Johnson to get Walter George, now a Humphrey friend and admirer, to write a letter to the Minneapolis *Star* urging its readers to return his Minnesota colleague to the Senate.

In the end, Humphrey managed somehow to show up at all the county fairs. When not blistering Ezra Benson, he was to be seen working his way slowly through the grandstands, shaking the calloused hands, slapping the overalled backs, kissing the blushing farmgirls, and astonishing not a few by calling out their names. At each fair he got the names of all prize-winning exhibitors and from Minneapolis sent each one a note of congratulations. Decrying low grain prices at a Farmers Union meeting in Waseca he said, "Any country that can explode the hydrogen bomb can solve the farm problem." He joined in the laughter when his aide Gene Foley reminded him that six years earlier he had proclaimed at the Watermelon Festival in Kellogg that "Any country that can explode the atom bomb can solve the farm problem."

He debated his opponent four times and shared the platform on numerous occasions. When they spoke at a Farmers Union stronghold in Montevideo, Bjornson said later, Humphrey supporters howled the Republican down, "and Humphrey did nothing to stop them." But when they met for Flax Day at Windom in Republican country, "Hubert was throwing his arms around me." Bjornson, state treasurer before and after that contest for eighteen years and an accomplished and ingratiating campaigner himself, said later, "Humphrey had that human warmth that is recognized by anyone. Made it easy to disagree without being disagreeable."

Humphrey won by 162,000 votes: "An earthquake," the Republicans called it. Orville Freeman was swept into office as the first DFL governor; the party took all but one of the other statewide races, and its members made big gains in both houses of the legislature. His home base apparently secure, Humphrey now turned all his energies to the national scene.

18

Compromise Is Not a Dirty Word

"Y ES, Bob, I've mellowed a bit. My convictions are much the same, but I've come to appreciate they're not necessarily infallible." So Humphrey, aged forty-three, wrote his cousin Robert Humphrey as the Eighty-third Congress opened in January 1955.

Although he returned from Minnesota with the prestige of an impressive reelection victory, it was not a completely favorable season for Humphrey. He could draw headlines at Foreign Relations Committee hearings by challenging some of John Foster Dulles's more imperious assertions. But it had been Lyndon Johnson who had put him on that committee, and now Johnson was demanding something substantial in return: "harmony" from Humphrey and the liberals as the Leader maneuvered between the Eisenhower White House and his restive colleagues in the Senate majority. Humphrey was torn. The opening of a new Congress was the moment to make the fight for changing the cloture rule that permitted Southerners to filibuster civil rights legislation to death. But Humphrey, as he later said, "knew from my own private polls that we would be lucky to get fourteen votes, possibly only nine or ten—less than the eighteen or twenty we got the time before. It would be foolish to cut [our] strength in half—you've got to progress." So, for better or worse, Humphrey deferred to Johnson and persuaded the liberal group not to make the fight.

At this retreat, Walter White of the NAACP shouted "Abject surrender," and the Southerners openly jeered. When by agreement with Johnson, Humphrey and others then introduced their individual rights bills (to certain defeat), Allen Ellender of Louisiana charged that they did so "as political sops to pressure groups and for no other reason." Angered at this public show of contempt for his restraint, Humphrey came as close to calling down the Leader as he could bring himself to: "You have always talked straight from the shoulder to me, so I am going to reciprocate. . . . You and I know that this does not add up to strength for the Democratic party."

This was followed by another long talk over drinks in Johnson's sanctum, but there ensued no change. If anything, Southern resistance hardened in the year after the Supreme Court's decision that segregation in schools must end. The first stirrings of Southern black militancy manifested about this time. One day in Montgomery, Alabama, Mrs. Rosa Parks refused to move to the rear of the bus, and blacks led by the young Rev. Martin Luther King, Jr., boycotted the buses until they were opened to all without discrimination. It was also the period when trainloads of blacks, pushed off Southern land by mechanization of agriculture, were departing daily for Northern cities. Humphrey tried to impress upon Johnson and other Southern Democrats why Bronx Boss Ed Flynn had backed his civil rights stand at the 1948 convention—namely, because black votes were beginning to count heavily in Northern cities. After the Court's school segregation ruling, Humphrey warned his Southern colleagues that "if we are to have a majority here in Congress, we must have representation from cities like Philadelphia—over 400,000 Negroes now—Detroit, Cleveland, New York, as well as California." He added that failure to act could "lead to diminishing strength in some of the Southern areas as well." In May, urging his bill to establish a Civil Rights Commission on Senator Tom Hennings of Missouri, he reminded his colleague: "You and I know that the Democrats are losing support in the Negro community in Missouri." He stressed the moderation of his bill, noting that his proposed commission would not even carry enforcement powers. When Johnson balked at a liberal amendment to deny funds in a proposed school construction bill to districts defying the 1954 Supreme Court decision, Humphrey proposed a compromise: let all districts receive funds except those not in compliance with a specific court order. Johnson, invariably siding with the Southerners on race issues, stalled. Humphrey told Party Chairman Paul Butler: "I needle him at every opportunity."

It is hard to see what Humphrey was getting in legislation in return for his cooperation with Johnson. Not a single one of his measures went through in these years. The best the Democrats seemed able to do was to use their thin majority to turn back fitful Republican efforts to dismantle the enactments of the New Deal. The Eisenhower administration, for its part, seemed loath to extend anything except highways and found it easy to stifle the occasional Democratic try at enlarging a housing, school, or farm program. As the liberal go-between, Humphrey was reduced to acclaiming as feats of

Lyndon Johnson's leadership such items as extension of the reciprocal trade act, upping of minimum wage from seventy-five cents to a dollar, and passage of Eisenhower's interstate highway program. "In the light of the political temper of the country," he told a Minnesota audience, that was "as much in terms of a liberal program as the country can expect."

When Johnson was knocked out in July by a heart attack, the pace of legislation lagged still further. Humphrey sent the Leader a note: "I miss having you get after me." In October he paid his first visit to the ranch to consult with the convalescent. Johnson, recovering, issued a thirteen-point program for the next session, billed as a "Program with a Heart." Joe Rauh, Humphrey's ADA friend, dismissed it as "mere slogans and promises." Top item on the list was a bill to end regulation of natural gas. In Washington, Humphrey told a press conference he would fight the bill. Johnson, obviously his old self again, telephoned Humphrey to demand what he meant by splitting away even before the Senate re-convened. Humphrey's reply can only be described as abject.

> I really hope, Lyndon, what I said did not upset you. I praised Lyndon Johnson, I praised the program. A very fine batting average, 12 hits in 13 times at bat. But you've got to leave me a little room on the gas bill.
>
> I'm learning a great deal from you. You're the one teacher who makes a fellow like what he's being taught. Hurry up and get back to Washington. I'm lonesome.

The reported split made headlines in Minnesota newspapers, prompting Humphrey's old Farmer-Labor friend Jim Markham to write: "Don't you cut, shuffle or deal with that son of a bitch, he's owned lock, stock and barrel by Texas oil and gas interests." Servile as he sounded, Humphrey still sensed a coming opportunity in working with Johnson. He told Markham that "Lyndon is no battling liberal . . . but he is about as liberal as you will find in the South. . . . Don't you worry about the fat boys ever getting to me. I am not in their lodge. They know it and I know it, and I may add, I like it that way."

Nothing much came of the rest of Johnson's proposals, but the gas bill giveaway went through both houses amid lobbying so blatant that when Francis Case of South Dakota announced in the Senate that an oil man had offered money for his vote, President Eisenhower vetoed it. Meanwhile, Humphrey's civil rights bills died again in committee. Again Humphrey fought long hours for farm, atomic energy, school, and housing legislation; when Johnson stepped in to stave off an amendment that all but cut off remaining funds for federal housing aid, Humphrey rose in the Senate to praise his leadership "in behalf of an effective Democratic party liberal program."

In this season of conservative ascendancy, the country approached another presidential election. Last time around, Humphrey had been a favorite-son candidate, only to be swept right out of the picture by the draft-Stevenson wave. Following a solid reelection triumph that carried his friend Orville Freeman to the Minnesota statehouse along with him in 1954, Humphrey was determined not to be left out again. By all the signs, Adlai Stevenson appeared the party's certain nominee for 1956. Eager to get on the wave early this time, Humphrey and Freeman invited Stevenson to visit Minnesota just before the campaign got under way. Their plan: to offer Stevenson endorsement if he would enter the state's early (March 20) primary and try to get Humphrey on the 1956 ticket with him. It was a neat plan, but it backfired because they could not deliver their state for the candidate.

On October 27, 1955, Stevenson flew to Minnesota. In his typically spontaneous way, Humphrey insisted on taking the governor on a spur-of-the-moment detour to watch the University of Minnesota–University of Southern California football game. An unprogrammed snowstorm blew up, and the party skidded over icy roads from Minneapolis to a late arrival at the big rally in Duluth. There Orville Freeman took command, and events became if anything too well ordered. All the notables of the 1954 victory shared the evening's platform in tribute after tribute to the distinguished guest. When Stevenson thanked the Freemans and Humphreys for their hospitality, Muriel Humphrey made the reply, assuring him that their support was based on esteem, though some might interpret it as wanting to get aboard the bandwagon. Immediately afterward, the DFL state central committee met in extraordinary session and voted an unprecedented early endorsement of Stevenson for president in 1956. As if on cue, two weeks later Stevenson announced his candidacy, adding: "I propose to enter the Minnesota primary."

Minnesota's Democratic-Farmer-Labor party set great store by its self-starting independence, an independence so warily respected by Humphrey that he had never before endorsed anybody, even his friend Freeman, before the state convention had made its decision. But as Democratic National Committeeman Gerald Heaney said later: "Orville Freeman ran a mighty taut ship. There were times when he got some people angry." Those who grumbled at "bossism" found a willing ear in Senator Estes Kefauver, a practiced grass-roots campaigner who had entered more primaries than any candidate up to this time. Kefauver paid a visit to Humphrey, who tried to persuade him to enter Wisconsin's primary instead, where he would be unopposed. The plea was in vain. Suddenly Stevenson found himself with a fight on his hands.

While the governor delivered high-minded addresses to roughneck audiences on the Iron Range and refused absolutely to endorse the Farmers Union program of high price-supports, Kefauver ambled from hamlet to hamlet, shaking hands across snowbanks and saying simply: "I'm Estes Kefauver. I'd like your vote." As early as February, Humphrey was writing home from Washington: "The situation is all fouled up. I suppose I should have taken a firmer hand." He had always been the glue that held the party together, but in the final campaign weeks he was twelve hundred miles away fighting around the clock in the Senate to put over a bill backed by the Farmers Union.

Even so, Freeman's DFL "machine" would have delivered Minnesota to Stevenson but for the nature of the state's preferential primary. So open were Minnesota contests that in 1952 an independent committee had been able to organize a last-minute write-in for General Eisenhower that brought 108,692 votes in the Republican contest and nearly wiped out Harold Stassen in his home state. Under such wide-open procedures, members of one party were perfectly free to cross over into another party's primary—and this the Republicans proceeded to do. In the final week, while Humphrey was waging his futile fight for the farm bill (Eisenhower vetoed it), Stassen came into the state, and the word went out to Republicans: give the Democrats a knock by casting ballots for Kefauver.

Thirty years later there is little doubt that Stassen gained his revenge. Richard Scammon, the Washington election expert who had grown up in Minneapolis, saw the pattern at once. It was not only that Edina, the most rock-ribbed of Minneapolis's Republican suburbs, went heavily for Kefauver. The state's four top Republican counties, all of which had cast more than 75 percent of their vote for Eisenhower in 1952, now cast more DFL ballots than Republican—and in each case Kefauver got the lion's share. Not only that, the voters of these top four GOP counties went right back to their customary ways and voted for Republican Ike in November.

In the March count, Kefauver's slate of unknowns defeated Humphrey, Freeman, and the other party stars by 245,885 to 186,723. "Heartsick," Humphrey wrote Eugenie Anderson: "Those Republicans really slipped one over on us." When Stevenson brought himself to mention the Minnesota "disaster," Humphrey, having failed to deliver for his friend, replied: "I'm walking around in ashes and sackcloth." By June, Stevenson had come back and knocked out Kefauver in primary victories in Indiana and California and could look forward to assured renomination at the Chicago convention. But for Humphrey, trying to re-glue the shattered pieces in Minnesota, no such swift recovery was possible. As he later told Wisconsin's Senator Gaylord Nelson: "Old Humphrey had to go around that state for a whole year kissing asses."

But that was not all. His friend Bill Benton might try to assure him that the Minnesota setback was "already forgotten," that even the masterful Lyndon Johnson experienced like troubles in Texas, where the liberal Ralph Yarborough was mounting a successful insurgency. But Humphrey's careful strategy to advance his ambitions nationally had been knocked awry. To overcome the widely held belief among regulars that he was not one of their own, he had addressed sixty Democratic dinners in two years and voiced the aspirations of the faithful so convincingly that after the one in Charleston in January, West Virginia's veteran Senator Matthew Neely pronounced it "the greatest political speech I ever heard." It was Humphrey's hope and expectation that as an orator of incendiary appeal he would be called on to rouse the delegates to fighting pitch by delivering the keynote at the 1956 convention. In December, Benton had relayed word that Stevenson thought he would be "wonderful" for this role.

But after Minnesota, Stevenson and Chairman Paul Butler suddenly seemed to think it important to placate the South. Southerners had not forgotten the dramatic 1948 speech by which Humphrey turned the convention against them. Liberals such as Chester Bowles did their best to hold the national committee to the early intention of picking Humphrey, but neither Stevenson nor Lyndon Johnson put in a word for Humphrey. Butler accepted Governor Frank Clement of Tennessee as a border-state compromise, and Humphrey lost out for keynoter by one vote. "I expected it," he wrote bitterly.

In July, Humphrey's hopes revived. Johnson, who had been disclaiming his own interest in second place on the national ticket, made a significant gesture. He arranged a big pre-convention "unity" feast under the chairmanship of the senior Southern senator, Walter George, and had Humphrey give the principal address. All the top people of the party attended, and Stevenson sent word that he wanted to meet with Humphrey afterward in his suite in Washington's Mayflower Hotel.

Arriving with his adviser Max Kampelman, Humphrey told Stevenson of his frustration at losing out for keynoter—"the one thing I had in my craw." Stevenson told him not to worry and turned to the subject of the vice presidency. Assuming he was being asked his views about the others, Humphrey ran through the list—Albert Gore, Robert Wagner, Mennen Williams, John Kennedy, Averell Harriman, Stuart Symington—offering his comments on one after the other. Then Stevenson leaned forward and asked: "Well, Hubert, why don't you think about yourself?" To his surprise and delight, Humphrey then heard himself warmly praised by the man who would be making the choice. Stevenson said he wanted a vice president qualified to step in as president, and a man who could help him politically.

All people hear what they want to hear—and Humphrey said later that was his mistake. As he heard it that night, Stevenson stated that Hubert H. Humphrey of Minnesota was his man for the vice presidency. But Stevenson's aides heard otherwise. They heard something like this: 'Hubert, if you are acceptable to the leaders of the South, I could support you. But if you want the nomination, you had better go out and work for it.' Stevenson himself said later he never made a commitment.

Sure that he had the candidate's nod, and that he had only to arrange for some of the Southerners to tell Stevenson that he, Humphrey, was acceptable, the senator as Kampelman said later, "left the hotel with stars in [his] eyes." On the strength of what he had heard, Humphrey did what nobody had done before: he openly announced his candidacy for vice president. Walter George, dean of Southern senators, had already told him he favored him. Lyndon Johnson had offered to help. So had Sam Rayburn, Lister Hill and John Sparkman of Alabama, and Brooks Hays of Arkansas. Humphrey dispatched Congressman Gene McCarthy across the country to stir up support. And as Fred Gates arrived in Chicago to set up Humphrey-for-Vice President headquarters at the Blackstone Hotel, Humphrey settled into his suite and began sketching an acceptance speech.

Then came the bombshell. Kefauver had begun to show interest in second place. Stevenson had read a memo on behalf of John Kennedy, the young senator from Massachusetts, that argued Catholic voters were essential to a Democratic victory and could best be gained by placing a Catholic on the ticket for the vice presidency. Impressed, Stevenson asked Kennedy to nominate him. With his own nomination cinched, Stevenson cast about for ways to enliven convention proceedings. He decided, instead of naming the vice-presidential candidate himself, to throw the convention open and let the delegates pick the man.

Humphrey was devastated. His Minnesota friend Eric Sevareid, bumping into him directly after Stevenson's announcement, said: "I've never seen him so upset." Caught off guard, he was also caught in the middle. In the wild melee that broke out, Kefauver, with four hundred delegates pledged in primaries, seemed to have the best chance. But young John Kennedy, who had arrived in Chicago saying "Hubert, I'm for you," made a strong impression with his speech nominating Stevenson and with still another appearance as narrator for a film. With Stevenson's abrupt announcement, Kennedy moved in fast. Working from a firm New England regional base, he picked up surprising strength in Southern delegations hostile to the "renegade" Southern liberal Kefauver.

Had Humphrey got his chance to keynote, or to organize disciplined support like Kefauver's, he might have profited by a standoff between these two front-runners. At a breakfast caucus, Lyndon Johnson made an effort to swing the Texas delegation to Humphrey, but it was not successful. Congressman Jim Wright of Dallas said: "We told him the delegates didn't know Hubert and didn't want to take him."

With that, Humphrey's last-ditch hope that the convention might yet turn to him faded. At the end of the first ballot he stood eighth in a field of nine, totally out of the running. Then Kennedy took the lead in the second ballot and states began to shift their votes. As Humphrey sat watching the television screen in Chairman Sam Rayburn's little office behind the dais, a horrifying realization dawned on him: he, the man who had arrived in Chicago thinking himself the vice-presidential nominee, would have to decide which of the two who had beaten him out was going to get it. His few votes were pivotal. To make his position not only painful but ignominious, however, the Kefauverite chairman of the Minnesota delegation, Robert Short, had contrived to convey, in announcing the state's first-ballot vote for Humphrey, that it was merely a gesture of courtesy, and that next time Minnesota would switch to Kefauver. In other words, Humphrey might not even command his own state.

At this ghastly moment, as Humphrey sat watching his chances go down the drain and feeling miserable about the whole fiasco, a young man ran up to him and, as if offering an audience with royalty, announced that Senator Kennedy would like Senator Humphrey to come to his hotel room and see him. Before Humphrey had time to explode at this affront, Orville Freeman bolted into the room and said melodramatically: "It's all over." It wasn't quite; there was no way out of the trap for Humphrey. Estes Kefauver burst in. "Hubert," he pleaded, "you've got to help me, you've GOT to help me." Kefauver was crying, Humphrey was crying. Everybody crowded around him. Eugenie Anderson said: "Leave Hubert alone. . . . He's got to make his own decision. Leave him alone."

The rollcall neared Minnesota. Humphrey could not escape Kefauver's plea. He had come without delegate's credentials; he had lost his chance to deliver the keynote; and he may have forfeited his chance to be Stevenson's running mate—all because Kefauver had gone into his state, snatched his primary, split his party, and threatened destruction of his state DFL rule at the November election. And now the Tennesseean was demanding the second place he had earlier spurned. Subjected to all that, Humphrey might well have preferred to give Kennedy the prize. But he had to think of all those Kefauverites in the Minnesota delegation. Above all, he had to think of getting his sundered DFL party back together again in time to save its candidates from defeat in the fall.

He could not bring himself to say the word to the Tennesseean. He turned and gave the message to Senator Fulbright, who had nominated him, "I'm for Kefauver." He raced out of the room to tell the Minnesotans. Unable to get through the mob, he climbed on a chair and signaled to them. Minnesota's switch stopped the slide to Kennedy. The nomination went to Kefauver.

Hubert Humphrey suffered heavier defeats in his life, but his wife said later, "That was the worst, that was the bitterest defeat. He felt he had been made a fool of. He never would talk about it." John Sharon of Stevenson's staff met him leaving the hall and said later, "I've never seen a guy so white. He looked as if he'd just heard his mother had died. He was in shock, trembling."

Afterward, Humphrey wrote to Kennedy, "I dreamed about you two or three nights in a row—and not very pleasant dreams either. My guilty conscience plaguing me through the night, I guess." Replying, Kennedy said it was nothing. He took his loss gracefully, as well he might. He was young; he had come so close; his prospects were bright. From that time on, he figured high in the polls both of the public and of party leaders—which was, of course, exactly the position Humphrey had hoped to be in after keynoting the convention and running for vice president with Stevenson. Johnson wrote:

"In my mind you would have been the best choice." And when Humphrey admitted he felt "very low" and wondered "how in the world I ever got involved in the whole affair," Johnson replied:

> You certainly have had a rough year, and my heart goes out to you. There is only one consolation. I long ago realized that you were one of those bold spirits that is tempered rather than weakened by adversity.
>
> As a liberal, you have breasted the current and clung fast to the position that there is nothing incompatible with liberalism and achievement. I know what this has cost you in terms of some of your personal relationships with others. But it has also given you a unique status in the life of our country—a status which means that you will be on the scene as a national leader long after the others are forgotten. . . . I am proud to call you "friend," and nothing will ever affect your standing in my eyes.

Humphrey did bounce back, as he always did, and soon was telling others that he had learned certain lessons from the disappointments of 1956. "They build character, as my daddy used to say to me," he wrote his friend Clara Sarvala. One lesson learned, he said, was that "politics is a cold, tough, hard-headed business and personal feelings sometimes can't enter into decisions." Thus his friend Estes Kefauver could barge right into his backyard for votes just as his protégés Gene McCarthy and George McGovern would do later. Old friends in the New York delegation, he noted, looked him straight in the eye and said they were for Kefauver. A second lesson was that to mount a serious campaign it was necessary to have not just his state but a solid regional block of Midwest support behind him. More than anything it became evident that to press a national candidacy, thorough and detailed organization would be needed.

It was by no means clear, however, that Humphrey had learned that lesson.

Gamely Humphrey leaped into the struggle against Eisenhower and the Republicans. In an effort to bridge the North-South gap in the party, Lyndon Johnson had named George Smathers of Florida chairman of the Senate Democratic campaign committee and appointed Humphrey vice chairman. When Northern liberals protested and demanded a new party alignment, Humphrey scolded them as "defeatists." He campaigned in ten states, including South Dakota, where, he told his friend Frank Rarig, "a young friend named George McGovern, teacher at Dakota Wesleyan University, was elected to Congress. He is tops, a liberal, intelligent, articulate and plenty of personality. I campaigned extensively, and in fact got McGovern to run." In the final two weeks in Minnesota, Humphrey traveled five thousand miles, addressing five meetings a day. He described the period later, saying, "I put everything I had into this campaign. I did my level best to get people working together. There has been some bad leadership at home, or should I say inept. Too much of this power politics, and not enough common sense with a little forbearance and understanding."

In the November balloting, Freeman scraped through to another two-year term in Minnesota, and the Democrats hung on to their majorities in Congress. But Eisenhower buried Stevenson in a landslide. In the aftermath of this rout the ADA called on the Senate to replace Lyndon Johnson as leader. Although Humphrey had no part in this action, when Party Chairman Paul Butler formed a Democratic Advisory Council of prominent members outside Congress to prepare a more aggressive opposition program, Humphrey accepted membership. Johnson and Rayburn refused to join in, considering it meddling in Congress's business. Actually, Congress had done so little business that it was precisely to prod the leadership into some kind of constructive effort that the committee came into being. Johnson resented Humphrey's taking part. He passed word to other members of the Senate club that Humphrey was no longer in good standing. He was to get the cold shoulder.

As Congress met in January, Humphrey telephoned Johnson to discuss a routine matter. Johnson's response was brusque. "You broke faith with me," he said. Humphrey, stroking Johnson with his voice, said: "Now Lyndon, you know I wouldn't do that. You can get more votes out of this body than anybody can get. You are a great, great leader, Lyndon. I was simply trying to make you an even better leader." It was another of what Humphrey's friends called their "love spats." Again, it was Johnson who flew off the handle. Afterward, Kampelman got in touch with Bobby Baker of Johnson's staff. In a few days it was patched up, and Humphrey informed his old Farmer-Labor friend Markham that he was dealing again for the liberal group with the Majority Leader.

It would not be correct to picture these two strong men as simply the Leader and the led. Clearly Johnson had the upper hand. Even leaving Johnson's power of office out of it, Humphrey was less determined. If he felt he was hitting his head against a stone wall, he would desist. But Humphrey had some chips. He never controlled votes, but he could influence some liberal votes that Johnson could not ignore. Their support was essential to Johnson's leadership. In a sense, Johnson and Humphrey worked as a pair of faction leaders who were not very far apart politically. On social policy, for instance, Humphrey and the populist Johnson saw eye to eye. The sticking point, and a big one, was civil rights, but that too was about to change.

When Humphrey read the November election returns, he served notice that there would be no holding back this time from the fight to head off filibusters. "We've got to change Rule 22," he announced. Eisenhower had scored significant gains in black neighborhoods in Northern cities. Philadelphia's liberal Mayor Joseph Clark, Jr., a militant proponent of rights reform, won election narrowly as senator from Pennsylvania with the help of black votes. The meaning of these signs was clear to Republicans and Democrats alike. When the session opened, Humphrey found Republican Minority Leader William Knowland interested as never before in rules change. And as manager for the liberals, Humphrey was able to recruit an effective new partner in Clinton Anderson, a moderate Democrat from New Mexico. "We wanted someone in between. Anderson was that man," he said later. "I did not always get myself out in front of the debate." And though Humphrey's forces lost the rules fight, this time the group wound up with thirty-eight votes for change—a "wonderful omen," his friend Markham wrote from Minnesota.

At this point, Lyndon Johnson made the move of his political life. For the Republican administration, Attorney General Herbert Brownell had already offered a civil rights bill. Earlier, when Johnson's aide Gerald Siegel had asked whether he was going to move for consideration of the bill, Johnson had snapped: "What do you want me to do, just move it and resign from the Senate next day?" A Texan who had never cast anything but a segregationist vote in his twenty years in Congress, Johnson now detached himself from the Southern bloc.

With the argument that the rules vote shift showed that the Republican-Dixiecrat bloc was crumbling, he persuaded Senator Russell to head off a Southern filibuster for once. And, bringing in the bill he had said he never would, Johnson proceeded in cloakroom and committee to attend to its defanging. When Russell said of the provision for a fair employment practices commission: "That comes out, by God, or the blood flows," Johnson dropped it; Paul Douglas responded, crying: "You've gutted the bill." That was only the beginning. Out went any suggestion that the Congress of the United States upheld the Supreme Court's order for desegregating the schools. Eisenhower, like Humphrey, thought that the right to vote was a civil rights area less sensitive than schools, jobs, or housing—and a good first place to make the necessary moves against discrimination. Since the provisions for a civil rights division in the Justice Department and creation of a permanent Civil Rights Commission seemed relatively innocuous, they became the heart of the bill.

Even so, the modest provisions proposed for enforcement were too strong for the Southerners. The bill specified that anyone who violated a federal court order enforcing voting rights could be prosecuted for criminal contempt. Southern senators demanded that the person accused be guaranteed a jury trial. The administration's lawyers balked, and everything came to a stop. Thereupon, Humphrey called in his friend, Wisconsin Law Professor Carl Auerbach, whose suggestion that the offense be defined as a civil rather than criminal contempt, broke the impasse. For civil contempt, only petty fines could be levied, and jury trial would be inappropriate.

It was one more concession to the Southerners, and it made such difficulties with his liberal group for Humphrey that he called these days "the most exhausting and at times frustrating period of my life." But the compromise won passage of the Civil Rights Act of 1957, the first civil rights legislation enacted in nearly a century. Joe Clark called it "a pallid little measure." Humphrey wrote his classmate friend Anton Thompson: "Not as good a bill as I would like, but it does represent a singular advance. I grow more mellow with the years, and find myself willing to accept less than I had hoped for. After all, that is the essence of the legislative process." He defended himself to Eugenie Anderson, his old ADA ally: "I did not yield on principle. I fought the good fight, and in fact I am sure we made some impression on our colleagues."

Humphrey's note carried an allusion to one he had received from John Stennis, the highly respected conservative senator from Mississippi:

> Last night during the closing part of the debate on the jury trial amendment, I was presiding when you were recognized for five minutes. Even though we are on opposite poles on this question, I want to tell you that I believe you made the best and most powerful five-minute speech by way of summary and challenge that I have ever heard. I did not agree, but I know a good speech when I hear it. The way you posed the question: "Now what are you going to do about it?" was powerful, and pinpointed the issue in a marvelous way. You are one of the most accomplished debaters that I have ever heard.
>
> I am glad that your energies will continue to flow into other fields. Your word on many of the policies—including some of our major economic problems—certainly has proven that your contributions bring forth fruit.

Yes, Humphrey had "mellowed." On the greatest national issue left unsettled by the Constitution, and indeed by four years of bloody civil war, Humphrey was willing, and rightly, to settle for "a singular advance." That the bill became law was more important than what the bill contained. Of course it was Johnson's switch that opened the way, and in truth the key to its passage was the coalition of more moderate members that Johnson put together. But Humphrey and the votes he influenced were essential to Johnson's leadership, and the outcome represented a far greater concession by Johnson than by Humphrey. Yet not even Humphrey said so, or perhaps even thought so, at the time. It was all pragmatic give and take. In a speech at the time, Humphrey proclaimed: "Compromise is not a dirty word. The Constitution itself represents the first great national compromise."

In personal terms, Humphrey gained at last what he had long sought. From this time, as Gerald Siegel said, Humphrey was accepted into the circle of Johnson's trust and friendship. John Stennis's personal tribute to the erstwhile wild man from Minnesota testified to how Humphrey had gained the respect and, indeed, the affection of his fellow members of the Senate: he could disagree with them without being disagreeable. That could be said of few others.

19

Lifted Out
of the Pack

T HERE had never been any question that Humphrey was passionately interested in international affairs. Long before he won office in Minnesota, he was traveling about the state to impress upon women's clubs and high school audiences the importance of the League of Nations, collective security, and a strong stand for democracy against fascism. But all through his first term in Washington his uncertainties were so great that, even after gaining a seat on the Foreign Relations Committee he permitted himself only one three-week trip abroad. As one aide put it, he was "defensive" about foreign travel, fearing that his Minnesota constituents might turn on him for overseas "junketing." Indeed, the aide, Max Kampelman, thought that in these earliest Senate years, Humphrey exhibited a sense of inferiority in the field of foreign affairs.

All this changed after his election to a second term. In this period, when President Eisenhower was saying the cold war might last forty years, Humphrey made himself a leading opposition spokesman on a wide range of international issues. He laced his bread-and-butter domestic speeches with foreign-policy themes. He wove foreign-aid data into his newsletters to farmers back home. Named a U. S. delegate to the United Nations, he made friends with all kinds of foreign personages. Alert and inventive, athirst for knowledge and involvement, he took up the tattered and supposedly sterile issue of disarmament—and by well-planned, thoroughly researched effort, found a way to bridle the arms race. Searching endlessly for solutions, he traveled abroad. Consequently, by the time of his 1958 meeting with Soviet Chief Nikita Khrushchev in 1958, he had turned himself into something of a "national" senator and even a world figure.

Not until years later, when U. S. opinion split sharply over whether the national interest was served by sending American troops to fight on the Asian mainland, were politicians tagged either "hawks" or "doves." At no time should the feather merchants of Washington have tried to tag Hubert Humphrey simply one or the other. He first came on the scene as a cold warrior. He spoke out for the Truman Doctrine, the Marshall Plan. He voted for NATO. He understood the nature and threat of Stalinism. He always voted for military appropriations. In fact, he prided himself that he never voted for a cut in a military budget.

But a duality could be discerned in Humphrey's approach to foreign affairs. Wanting to fight Hitler, he nonetheless accepted the deferments open to a young father rather than seek a place in the fighting forces. When he did try—unsuccessfully—for a navy commission, it was only after he had stood for public office. As a senator, he was torn and used to talk about it at length with Kampelman, who was also a strong anti-Communist but had been a pacifist in World War II. Committed to the struggle of the cold war, Humphrey was yet a religious man who believed strongly in peace and the brotherhood of man. Important to his support of Truman's decision to fight in Korea was the commitment to act through the United Nations.

Truman and Rayburn had urged Johnson to name Humphrey to Foreign Relations, believing that the Democrats needed a tough, skillful debater on the committee as the party went into opposition in 1953. In the peak years of cold war that followed, when John Foster Dulles was threatening the Soviets with "massive retaliation," the allies with "agonizing reappraisal," and the neutrals with everlasting damnation, Humphrey acted as a kind of Democratic point man. He attacked effectively when the Republican right, which claimed Roosevelt had sold out to the Russians at the Yalta summit, called on Dulles to release the 1945 conference papers. He pointed out that Eisenhower, as European commander when Germany was divided, had been responsible for carrying out key Yalta decisions. When Dulles, under pressure, leaked the Yalta documents to the press, Humphrey accused him of disloyalty to his boss, of cowardice in "caving in" to the rightwingers, and of hypocrisy for slipping papers to outsiders while "going around like Fearless Fosdick" hunting spies in his department. Then, readily getting the conservatives Knowland and Bridges to say they "repudiated" the agreements that Ike had executed, he wound up the debate jeering that the Republicans were "split wide as the Grand Canyon." Regaling Eugenie Anderson next day with his account of how "we really took Mr. Knowland and Mr. Bridges to town," Humphrey wrote: "I hesitate to say it as egocentric, but several of the Senators present told many others that my reply to Knowland was the best speech they had ever heard in the Senate."

Rejoicing in his front-line role, Humphrey took advantage of opportune targets. In January 1956 he tangled bare-knuckled with Dulles. In an interview with *Life* magazine, Dulles had seemed to boast of brandishing the bomb, of skirting the "brink of war" three times to win victories for the United States—in Korea, Vietnam, and Taiwan. Humphrey, charging that Dulles was distorting history and harming U. S. prestige with his "brinkmanship" claims, won big headlines. Such one-on-one confrontation with Dulles made Humphrey visible and dramatic. Next month, Humphrey tore a bulletin off a newsticker about the United States sending eighteen tanks to Saudi Arabia. Humphrey publicly protested, and Eisenhower stopped the shipment. Humphrey also criticized Dulles for trying to fence Communism out of the Middle East with paper pacts, and when Dulles, meeting resistance in some capitals, stated that "neutrals are immoral," Humphrey ran with that for days. It was a time of favorable publicity for him. He was informed and alert, faster and brighter on foreign affairs than other senators, and people listened to him.

Being Humphrey, of course, he covered a huge swath. He sounded many inconsistent themes—but his reach was brilliant. One could find in the same *Congressional Record* a resolution he inserted for Ukrainian independence and an appeal for détente. The range of his substantive interests was breathtaking, including at one and the same time pushing for a foreign-aid agreement with Sri Lanka, fostering social democrats in Latin America, blasting Dulles on Middle East policy, and championing the émigré politicians of Eastern Europe. There was nothing pacifist about his fiery speeches for Wilsonian self-determination among the "captive nations" behind the Iron Curtain. In 1953 when the West watched impassively as tanks put down the East Berlin revolt, he was greatly upset. He felt even worse at U. S. inability to cope when the Hungarians rose in 1956.

Interest groups were identified, of course, with Humphrey's varied concerns, and the causes they favored could not be easily reconciled. Several powerful political constituencies, for instance, dealt with Humphrey through his aide Max Kampelman—Jewish elements, labor people, as well as ADA and Eastern campus liberals. But Humphrey was also the Democratic senator who spoke most strongly for the agricultural interests of the Middle West; these forces, along with the party chiefs of the upper Midwest, tended to make their views known to Humphrey through his aide Herb Waters.

All these elements looked to, and influenced, Humphrey in foreign affairs. His close associations with such labor leaders as Walter Reuther and David Dubinsky from early ADA times helped Humphrey form friendships with European Social Democrats. The love affair between Humphrey and the Jewish community began early: he was making speeches at United Jewish Appeal and Israeli bond rallies from the time he arrived in the Senate in 1949. He developed warm personal relationships with such ambassadors as Avram Harman and Abba Eban.

In the Middle East, Humphrey stood for a firm, undeviating commitment to Israel, though he was always looking for solutions. Soon after the Anglo-French invasion of Suez, he visited Cairo and raised Jewish hackles by reporting Nasser less belligerent than other Arab leaders. On this trip he took along Waters and the Minneapolis agribusinessman Dwayne Andreas because his main goal at the time was marrying Midwestern agriculture to foreign policy. In one capital after another, while Humphrey made his pitch to prime ministers to expand Public Law 480 spending, Andreas went around urging merchants and bankers to get busy and import American farm commodities. In Cairo they found a sore need for hot school lunches; in Palestine refugee camps, a shortage of rations; in Madrid, a threat of breadlines—all of which could be met from the bursting granaries of Minnesota. Humphrey reported that "The stocks of food and other agricultural commodities which the U.S. is fortunate to possess are an asset, not a liability. We have cheapened the spirit behind our humanitarian food contributions abroad and weakened our own bargaining power in negotiating trade agreements for food and fiber, by continually proclaiming our food reserves are something for which we have no use, and want to get rid of at any cost."

This message went out to Humphrey's agricultural network, at the center of which was Bill Thatcher and his Farmers Union—powerful in Minnesota but packing plenty of heft in a half-dozen neighboring states as well. Transmitted by Andreas, it also went to the big grain merchants and flour millers of Minneapolis who were making common cause with the giant cooperatives in marketing surpluses abroad. These forces were all for grain sales to India, to Egypt, to Spain and, for that matter, to Soviet Russia. They sought, as a practical matter, soybean and other markets to develop in the Middle East and were quite non-Zionist in their international outlook.

Just as remarkable as the breadth of Humphrey's affiliations was his success in keeping them despite their obviously disparate interests. Partly this was because of the attractiveness of the Humphrey personality. Enormously likeable, he was also accessible, and his circle of friends often included people who themselves were not on speaking terms. He managed to stand as a champion for such wide-ranging constituencies as garment workers and grain brokers, Zionists and Arabists, supporters of Eastern European liberation and advocates of nuclear disarmament. In this way he broadened into much more than a regional senator—though, of course, his attention to émigré politics, for example, responded to the desires of Slav voters on Minnesota's Iron Range quite as much as to those of the Hungarians and Rumanians in Scranton and Pittsburgh. Speaking out on such a wide spectrum of issues, he grew in this one six-year term to be known and heard well beyond his home state and the nation's capital.

Yet no more in Foreign Relations than in his other Senate committees did Humphrey ever attain anything like senior standing. At the time, the long-lived Theodore Green of Rhode Island seemed an all-but-perpetual chairman. Even among the committee's young members, Fulbright of Arkansas outranked Humphrey. At first outraged and disillusioned by Fulbright's joining filibusters against civil rights, Humphrey drew closer when the Arkansan took a strong part in Stevenson's 1952 campaign. When Fulbright then urged creation of a liberal caucus in the Senate, they became quite good friends. Mike Mansfield of Montana joined the committee at the same time as Humphrey. For the effervescent Humphrey, the relationship with the glum and uncommunicative Mansfield was always difficult. Mansfield especially resented, after his elevation to Majority Whip, that Humphrey continued to be on close terms with Lyndon Johnson and to perform legislative tasks for the Leader when Mansfield was Johnson's deputy. Mansfield also could not forgive Humphrey for failing to back his resolution for withdrawing U. S. troops from Europe. A third committee colleague, John F. Kennedy, had been put on Foreign Relations after his father made an urgent personal plea to Majority Leader Johnson. Humphrey was uncomfortably aware of Kennedy as a presidential candidate, and even before the 1956 vice-presidential set-to was vexed that Kennedy could assemble the best staff that money could buy, whereas he scrounged to offer aides half as much pay. It further annoyed Humphrey that after he had clearly moved out front in foreign affairs in 1956, Jack Kennedy, not half so diligent, could step forward the following year and with a single speech command national attention—a Senate address on the Algerian question, which he rightly suspected had been crafted for Kennedy at Harvard.

The one committee opportunity that came Humphrey's way he created for himself. This was to assume the chairmanship of a Foreign Relations subcommittee formed in 1955 at his insistence. Its task was to study an issue that, in that cold war year, interested no other senator: disarmament. Because the obvious subject for study was arms—nuclear arms—Majority Leader Johnson insisted that the subcommittee be a composite one. It meant that Humphrey had to accept colleagues from the Pentagon-minded Armed Services and Atomic Energy committees as well as a couple from Foreign Relations.

Under such constraints, the Disarmament subcommittee got under way slowly. But outside Washington's world of military-industrial procurement, a clamor was already growing. Other nations, led by Nehru of India, were demanding an end to bomb tests like the 1954 explosion at Bikini atoll, which rained radioactive death on a Japanese fishing boat two hundred miles away. When Humphrey held his first hearings in January 1956, they attracted wide attention. Harold Stassen, Eisenhower's newly named Disarmament adviser, Dulles and Lewis Strauss, chief of the Atomic Energy Commission, took the stand. Stassen offered the administration's "open skies" proposal for aerial inspection of atomic sites—a bold ploy, as it turned out, for legitimating the U-2 spy planes that Washington was preparing to send over Russia. But it was the testimony of Thomas Murray, another AEC member, that the U. S. had bombs enough and should stop testing large weapons, that won big headlines. Within a week, Adlai Stevenson, preparing to run again for president, called for suspension of all H-bomb tests in the atmosphere.

Administration spokesmen from the president down treated the idea as all but treasonous. Editorialists derided it, saying that superior technology had given America its primacy, and to quit testing was to hand over its big advantage to the Communists. At the time, there was not the slightest doubt that America *did* hold a big advantage. It was said that the Russians, bent on catching up, would cheat and test on the sly. The American public overwhelmingly agreed. At the November elections, the voters by a huge majority again entrusted the nation's security to General Eisenhower.

But Humphrey was not satisfied. Had not the aged Churchill thrown up his hands at the "balance of terror"? In the face of mutual extinction, he felt, the arms race must be brought under some degree of control. Continuing to search, he met with many visitors—such as Leo Szilard, one of the fathers of the A-bomb, who had come to the conclusion that it was technically feasible to monitor an agreement on arms control. He began holding regional hearings—in Boston, Minneapolis, St. Louis. And he succeeded in installing his own nominee at last as staff director: Betty Goetz, League of Women Voters foreign policy specialist, University of Minnesota graduate, and first of her sex to join a Senate committee staff. Humphrey authorized her to start a new study of "Technical Problems of Disarmament." Foreign Relations seniors wanted such studies to be bland. Humphrey, bursting to *do* something, demanded forthright reports. With such conservatives as Knowland, Hickenlooper, and Byrd on his subcommittee, there was no chance for that. A compromise was struck: Humphrey could say his say in a preface—but the studies themselves must remain academic, noncontroversial.

Having been named a member of the U.S. delegation to the United Nations in 1956, Humphrey chanced to be in New York just as Secretary Dulles announced that East-West talks on the latest U. S. general disarmament "package" had broken down. But Chief Negotiator Stassen and Ambassador Henry Cabot Lodge had a private word with Humphrey, who rushed back to Washington to tell Betty Goetz: "They think the Soviet Union would be interested, notwithstanding the breakdown, in a test ban." Once again, as he had years before on Taft-Hartley repeal and on tax loopholes, Humphrey set to work to master all the details of a big subject and pack them into one, long Senate speech.

Even as Humphrey applied himself, however, the political environment changed around him—not to his advantage. The technological imperative that Americans revered turned suddenly against them. At the climax of World War II it had placed unspeakably destructive weapons in their hands. As the Russians gained the same terrible weapon, the hurtling thrust of technology delivered to both sides the means to unload destruction within minutes on each other.

But the Russians got theirs first. In September 1957, they announced successful testing of the first intercontinental ballistic missile. And a few weeks later they orbited their Sputnik, proof to all the world, and most devastatingly to Americans, that the Soviet Union had led the way to the new weaponry. When the U. S. spacecraft intended to display matching prowess sputtered out ignominiously on its Florida launching pad, a spasm of pain shot through the American body politic, only partially allayed by the subsequent orbiting of substitute craft rushed by the military to what was then named Cape Canaveral. Could General Eisenhower have permitted the Soviet Union to go ahead in the technological competition? Led by Lyndon Johnson in the Armed Services Committee and John Kennedy in Foreign Relations, Senate Democrats began asking questions about a lost primacy and a "missile gap" that presaged a further escalation of the arms race.

Not until two months after the Florida fiasco was Humphrey ready to take the floor. His text was so long that his office gave out a table of contents with each copy. The night before, in characteristic fashion, Humphrey got some new ideas and drastically recast it. Before he rose to speak he posted Betty Goetz at the back of the chamber, "Sit on the couch, in case I need you." His friend Lyndon Johnson had agreed to make the speech an important event, and Democratic senators, even if they disagreed with Humphrey, were present in supporting numbers.

Humphrey began by acknowledging the impact of Sputnik and by insisting, as he always did, that the kind of disarmament he espoused was anything but unilateral—far from weakening the United States, it would be accompanied by safeguards that insured security while delivering strength, balance, and enduring peace to the nation and the world. It was the first major speech in the Senate on the subject since World War II. He called on the administration to break up the comprehensive disarmament "package" it had always insisted upon and to try for a ban on nuclear weapons tests. But in the seventy-page speech, he ranged over the entire spectrum of U. S. weaponry, bases, and alliances. He urged separate talks for stopping further output of fissionable materials. He called for an agreement to outlaw surprise attacks. He said that the United States should enter into negotiations with the Russians for thinning out troops in Europe and for the establishment of a nuclear-free zone on both sides of the Iron Curtain. He also proposed such zones for the Middle East, for Asia, and for Latin America.

Humphrey was on his feet four hours. A dozen other senators, primed by Johnson, kept popping up. But though they made sympathetic noises, they shied away from any commitment to disarmament. The next day's *New York Times* took exception to almost every one of Humphrey's proposals. From Bonn, Chancellor Adenauer sent a private message to Dulles urging him to beware of Humphrey's ideas for any kind of pullback, whether of troops or nuclear weapons, in Central Europe.

But again, Humphrey did not give up. Incensed at the administration's lack of response to the Soviet's announcement of unilateral test suspension, in the week of March 31, Easter week, he delivered five-minute speeches in the Senate each day. Letters poured in, nearly all supporting him. Scientists volunteered information. In a move to placate world fears about radioactive fallout, the United States had tried out its first underground nuclear explosions some months before—the so-called Rainier tests in Nevada.

The Atomic Energy Commission announced that the explosions had been detected in Los Angeles. Los Angeles was only 250 miles from the test site, and the public, including Humphrey, took this announcement as proof that it would be impossible to verify compliance with any treaty banning tests from outside a country the size of Russia. Humphrey had never supposed that the Russians—or the United States—would agree to having inspectors posted at arms factories, test sites, airfields, ports, and depots inside their borders.

At this point, when hope of finding a workable way to police tests seemed to have vanished, Betty Goetz got a telephone call from Washington journalist I. F. Stone: why not try talking to the United States Geodetic Survey agency in the Department of Commerce, which had many seismographic stations scattered around the country? Betty Goetz called the agency and, without saying why, asked for a list of stations that had detected the tests. At the other end of the phone a voice read off the list—including "Fairbanks, Alaska, distance 2,150 miles." So excited that she forgot to give Izzy Stone his scoop, Betty Goetz rushed to Humphrey. Reading off the information in the Senate, Humphrey pointedly commented that the remarkable discrepancy with the AEC's original announcement "gives the impression that scientific facts are being used by someone to prove a political point."

After that, new technical leads followed fast. The head of the Executive Branch committee on evaluating Soviet tests was Hans Bethe, the Nobel laureate at Cornell. Unlike Edward Teller and other bomb-builders, Bethe testified that monitoring underground weapons tests was probably feasible. Thus, against every kind of official foot-dragging and delay, Humphrey seemed to be gaining authoritative confirmation that he was on the right track in seeking this kind of disarmament.

Sure enough, President Eisenhower within a month invited the Russians to send scientists to discuss with U. S. experts whether technical grounds existed for negotiating a test ban treaty; Premier Khrushchev accepted for the Soviets. The outcome was sufficiently promising for the convening of an eighteen-nation Disarmament Conference at Geneva on October 31, 1958, to discuss not only a possible test ban but a treaty to prevent surprise attacks and another to halt production of fissionable weapons materials. Humphrey, who had arranged to travel to European capitals in connection with his proposed legislation for international health research, enlisted Lyndon Johnson's help to sit in briefly with the Geneva negotiators.

I T I S customary to treat Humphrey's famous eight-hour gabfest with Nikita Khrushchev as a fortuitous event that took place when Humphrey, in Moscow on other business and getting little attention from lesser officials, was suddenly haled into the Soviet chieftain's presence. That is true as far as it goes. But it is evident from the account of Humphrey's part in getting East-West arms talks back on track that there is more to the story.

In the waning years of the Eisenhower administration, Khrushchev was looking for "peaceful coexistence," or what later came to be called détente, with the United States. His country had not only acquired the H-bomb but by firing the Sputnik into orbit had shown that it had the means to launch ICBMs at any target in North America. From the Soviet standpoint, some sort of accommodation with the powerful Americans might now be advantageous. Shortly before Humphrey's trip, the Soviet chieftain, considering that his side had made the first conciliatory move by pulling out Russian forces from Vienna, was impatiently demanding the same kind of troop withdrawal by the three Western powers from Berlin. Every U. S. public figure, Humphrey not the least, viewed this new Soviet pressure with hostile suspicion. But Humphrey in one important respect was far in advance of hardened American cold war opinion. He was in favor of negotiating with the Russians a carefully hedged ban on nuclear-bomb tests. And when Humphrey stopped by the Soviet embassy to pick up his visa, he mentioned to "Smiling Mike" Menshikov, the Soviet ambassador of the day, that he hoped to see his boss in Moscow.

Officially, Humphrey's trip was to look into how the United States might obtain international cooperation in health programs and medical research. In certain health programs, a single politician could do more than the ablest physician. All the doctors treating malaria, for example, could not match the impact of what Humphrey could accomplish by obtaining a big appropriation to fight the disease. On an even bigger scale, Humphrey's unceasing struggle to expand Public Law 480 to the Food for Peace program was a contribution to better world health. This was "healing" in broad strokes.

Julius Cahn, who had been a Foreign Relations staffer, helped Humphrey plan his trip. These were the years when biologists were unraveling the fundamentals of life with their discoveries about DNA, and in Paris, Humphrey climbed the stairs of the cluttered old Pasteur Institute to hear first hand from Jacques Monod and André Lvov about the work that was to win them Nobel prizes in 1965. In Germany, he quizzed cancer specialists; in Sweden heart specialists. In Denmark and Belgium he visited children's hospitals. Putting on his other hat, he stopped in at the East-West arms talks in Geneva long enough to tell Vassily Kuznetsov, the chief Soviet delegate, that he was heading for Moscow and wanted a word with the boss. But in Berlin the Russians were putting on the heat. "Now of all times," he wrote home, "a U. S. senator should show up in Berlin." Visiting his friend Mayor Willy Brandt, he proclaimed: "We cannot and must not back down."

In Helsinki, Humphrey almost refused to go on when the Soviets held up a visa for Dr. Michael Shimkin, the Russian-speaking Baltimore cancer specialist he wanted to bring along as an interpreter. At the Moscow airport no one was on hand from the U. S. embassy to meet him—only an Intourist car, as for any other tourist visitor. Humphrey took exception to that too. With his wife and aide he put up at the old National Hotel, and for days, Cahn said later, "it was total iron curtain." They met some health officials and got to meet the minister of agriculture. But Humphrey did not think much of that. At a cocktail party he bumped into Frol Kozlov, of the ruling praesidium, and was unimpressed. Whiling away the days visiting the symphony and Bolshoi Ballet, he sensed a runaround.

That was Monday morning. After luncheon came the telephone call. The message required him to call back. It was in this way that Humphrey learned, a little more than a half hour beforehand, that the chairman of the Council of Ministers would see him at three. And all at once it became evident that the Russians had programmed the event with some care. America's opposition party, of which Humphrey was a member, had just swept the elections for Congress, and the United States was being stubborn at Berlin. To the Russians, the chairman of the Senate disarmament subcommittee was an important visitor after all. It was anything but a Khrushchev improvisation.

Thus, only Humphrey was to appear. That enabled Khrushchev to have his interpreter present while Humphrey would have nobody to corroborate—and later, when Humphrey related Khrushchev's criticisms of China's communes, Khrushchev would call him a Baron Munchausen purveying "fairy tales." With no chance to prepare, Humphrey was ushered into the big office at three minutes to three and, with only one other person present, Interpreter Oleg Troyanovsky, the two men fell into a conversation that lasted eight hours and twenty-five minutes.

It is true that Adlai Stevenson, Walter Lippmann, and Eric Johnston all had paid visits to the new Soviet chief. Visitors had also had sharp brushes with him at embassy cocktail parties. And President Eisenhower had met him for the Vienna summit exchange in 1955. But at the time Premier Nikolai Bulganin still shared the leadership, and it was hard to tell who was in charge. Nobody from the United States had ever had such a chance to size up Stalin's successor.

Humphrey began formally—"I had no small talk because I knew nothing of his family"—by asking for Soviet cooperation on the health programs that were the official purpose of his visit. "Da, da, da," said Khrushchev, "uninterested as if I were talking to a fence post," Humphrey said later. And when an hour or so had passed, Humphrey said: "It looks like I've taken more of your time than I should," Khrushchev, who had been taking the measure of his visitor, declared: "No, let's talk."

Thereupon, Humphrey raised the subjects of Berlin and the test ban, and soon all the big issues of the cold war were on the table. Observing how Troyanovsky by taking notes could translate even after Khrushchev had been holding forth for five minutes, Humphrey asked if he could take notes too. Khrushchev told the interpreter to give him paper. Humphrey asked what the Russians would like to buy from the United States. Maybe petrochemical equipment, Khrushchev said: "But I must thank the Americans for compelling us to depend on our own resources. The U.S. blockade [the cold war ban on virtually all exports] has led us to develop our internal resources so that we're relatively self-sufficient."

Humphrey replied that Soviet aggressiveness in the late 1940s and in Korea compelled the United States to re-arm quite as much as the U. S. refusal to trade had forced Russia to develop its internal resources. Khrushchev retorted that the Russians had more than matched Western re-armament, and began to josh Humphrey about Soviet arms superiority: "You know, we are having trouble testing our ICBMs—they shoot too far. Now you Americans have lots of space and bases everywhere to shoot your rockets."

Humphrey replied: "If you are having all this trouble, we will be glad to test your rockets for you."

Nothing doing, said Khrushchev. But he went on: "I will tell you something you do not know and your government does not know. We have a new one with a range of 14,000 kilometers [8,700 miles].

That *was* a disclosure, but Humphrey replied stoutly that the West was fully satisfied with its missiles too.

Khrushchev said he had been informed of Humphrey's visit with Kuznetsov. And he scoffed at the American proposal at Geneva for a year's trial test ban: "Who are you trying to fool? You know it takes almost a year to set up a new series of tests. Your proposal is no proposal at all." But he intimated he was serious about a treaty to outlaw tests because Russia now had all the bombs it needed. "I'll tell you a secret," he said, and told Humphrey that the Soviets had exploded an H-bomb equal to five million tons of TNT, using but a tenth of the fissionable material previously needed.

On Berlin, Khrushchev was most vehement of all. The Western presence was a thorn, a cancer, "a bone in my throat." Why, "unless you want to make war," should the three countries want to maintain twenty-five thousand troops in a city surrounded by the East German Republic? He had proposed making Berlin a free city and guaranteeing Western access, but the West was stubborn. Worse, Western generals had said the United States would break through with tanks if the East Germans barred the way. "Don't threaten me," he said, raising his voice. The Soviet Union suspected that the United States was arming West Germany with nuclear arms to make war, he said and added, "I know that you do not decide, but you will play a part. You are a member of the Democratic majority, and a member of the Senate Foreign Relations committee."

He led Humphrey to a map on the wall and pointed out Moscow, Sverdlovsk, and other targets he said Western generals talked of striking. "If you just keep talking about bombing us," he said, "why, by God, we'll bomb you." The next moment, Khrushchev asked where his visitor came from. Humphrey pointed to Minneapolis. "We will never bomb Minneapolis,"

Khrushchev said. Humphrey took this for defensive talk—"defensive in an offensive way, insecure in a superconfident way." Indeed, the Russian told Humphrey at one point: "We will never make war while I am first minister."

Humphrey heard more about the sources of the Soviet chieftain's defensiveness. He learned that Khrushchev's son had been killed in the war, and that, unlike Stalin, Khrushchev refused to live in the Kremlin. In earlier years, when Stalin had asked him to move there, he had declined, saying there were too many police around and he wanted "to have some friends." Now, he said, there were "no political prisoners" in Russia. He told Humphrey that Molotov had been for "the old order." But teaming up with Bulganin as premier ("incompetent but a good fellow"), he had arranged to meet with President Eisenhower for the first East-West summit since the war. There he found Ike "weak, poorly prepared, [with] Dulles over his shoulder. . . . everything written for him." Britain's Eden seemed "smart but weak," and the French representative was not much either.

By this time, Khrushchev was addressing Humphrey almost as one politician to another. As Humphrey recorded it, Molotov and the others had opposed his ambitious plan for decentralizing the Soviet economy. At a meeting of the ruling Praesidium the vote had gone against Khrushchev seven-to-four. "They thought seven was bigger than four. They knew arithmetic but not politics." And he told gleefully how he went to the larger Central Committee, obtained majority support—and won. "Even the seven votes" came over to his side, Khrushchev said.

Finally Khrushchev got up to go to the toilet. They had been talking four hours, and Humphrey had taken twenty-three pages of notes. Khrushchev suggested they have something to eat. As aides and waiters scurried about, Humphrey said he was reminded of a story about Winston Churchill. Once, the story went, Churchill and Opposition Leader Clement Attlee had had an unusually vituperative debate about nationalizing British industries; at the end, Attlee went to the men's room. Churchill followed, but instead of taking the urinal alongside went all the way to the end of the row, appearing most uncordial. Angered, Attlee said: "I thought as English gentlemen we leave our arguments behind once we're outside the House. Why do you go all the way to the other end of the room?" Churchill removed his cigar and said: "Look, Clem, you socialists are all alike. Whenever you see something that is big and functioning smoothly, you always want to nationalize it."

Khrushchev roared. He had Humphrey repeat the story for the interpreter to take down and said he would have it sent to Russian ambassadors around the world. From that point on, there was no more notetaking and the talk flowed freely.

When Humphrey said it was hard to get into the Kremlin, Khrushchev replied: "People should come in here. I'm going to get rid of these secret police and military police." Humphrey asked Khrushchev point blank about the Hungarian uprising and got this answer: "Oh, that was started by American agents—that $100 million spent for subversion in these Eastern countries." ("I gave him the cold fishy eye," Humphrey said later.) Khrushchev went on: "We had elections in Hungary, November 16—you didn't expect that, did you, senator?"

"Only one party—what kind of election is that?" asked Humphrey, who, glass in hand, proceeded to tell another story. This was about the Kentucky congressman who got mixed up in a tax on hunting squirrels. Half his friends were for the tax, half his friends were against it. Forced to declare himself, the congressman announced: "I stand with my friends." That was the nearest to a Communist-style unanimous vote Humphrey could think of in America. And when Khrushchev, "jabbing and poking like a boxer," kept saying the two camps should have economic competition, Humphrey replied: "Wait till the Democrats get in. We've got a lot of young people coming up. When we get in power, we are going to run you right out of Gorky Park."

Khrushchev smiled and said: "I welcome it."

Humphrey countered that Minnesotans—"born on skates"—would give the Russian ice hockey team a tussle in the Olympics.

"Yes, let's compete," Khrushchev came back.

After the snacks, on linen laid across the conference table, the two were served dinner—caviar, pheasant, chicken, beef, fish, fruit. Khrushchev offered mineral water from Georgia, which he said helped his kidney trouble. Humphrey asked what the label said; when Khrushchev read it off, Humphrey-the-pharmacist identified the salts in the bottle for him.

Toward the end of dinner the talk turned again to foreign trade. Khrushchev said: "I don't know much about that. I'll call up my Armenian rug peddler." Within fifteen minutes, Deputy Premier Anastas Mikoyan arrived, and the three men talked for another two and a half hours. Mikoyan picked up a brandy bottle to fill Humphrey's glass.

Humphrey stopped him, saying: "No, I've already had my brandy with the Chairman." Mikoyan insisted.

Khrushchev interrupted with: "You drink the brandy. My friend from Minnesota and I have already had our brandy. You drink three brandies."

Humphrey reported later: "By golly, Mikoyan belted down three brandies, one after the other."

Finally, at about 11:25, after Humphrey had been asked to tell his Churchill story again for Mikoyan, and after Khrushchev had said he wanted to travel to America as Mikoyan once had, Mikoyan stood up and said: "I am tired. It's time to go home." Preparing to go, Humphrey told Khrushchev he had not asked him all the questions he had wanted to. He had not brought up China. Khrushchev, eyes narrowing, said: "You are a subtle man, you are trying to trap me into talking about China."

Humphrey answered: "Let me ask you a question."

Khrushchev replied: "No, no, they're our ally."

Humphrey persisted: "Can I ask you about agriculture? I don't want to get you into the ally business."

Khrushchev's response was perhaps the long day's most revealing disclosure: "About the communes, they are old-fashioned. They are reactionary. We tried that right after the revolution. It just doesn't work, not nearly as good as the state farms and the collective farms. You know, senator, these communes are based on the principle—from each according to his ability, to each according to his need. Well, you know that won't work. There is no incentive. You can't get production without incentive."

Startled, Humphrey said: "That's rather capitalist."

Khrushchev replied: "Call it what you will, it works."

When Humphrey got back to the U.S. Embassy residence, it was midnight. He was very high—partly vodka and brandy, partly the exhilaration of the experience. Straightway he dictated an account for transmission to the State Department and Eisenhower. It says much about how fundamentally little-known Humphrey still was that the New York *Herald-Tribune* headlined news of the meeting: "Khrushchev Meets Senator." Julius Cahn, listening to Humphrey dictate his midnight cable, urged him to hold back much of his story so as to gain a wider audience on his return. But Humphrey, always more prone to talk than calculate what might do him most good, shed all the secrets in what Arthur Krock called "an itinerant press conference, a sort of publicity strip-tease" that continued at airport stops from the Kremlin to the White House. It made little difference. Humphrey's marathon interview made world headlines for weeks. When he returned to Washington he told two hundred waiting reporters that he had a special message to deliver to the President—that the Soviet chieftain would welcome an invitation to visit the United States. Then, as if the home fences were still the only ones to mend, Humphrey flew to St. Paul to deliver the address at the annual Farmers Union convention.

Even the "Humphrey in 1960" banners on the wall behind him as he spoke carried a certain ambiguity. It was the year he would be up for reelection to the Senate too. And when *Life* magazine put him on its cover, he was at pains to make sure that the long article inside gave the Republicans back home no slightest chance to turn what he said into charges that he was soft on Communism. But all that was behind him. Humphrey returned from Moscow never to be perceived the same way again. Brewing in the national consciousness was a realization that in Hubert Humphrey the country had a man who could hold his own in eye-to-eye give-and-take with its chief international adversary.

"Mr. Humphrey will now be studied more carefully," wrote James Reston. The interview, the *Economist* reported, "has lifted him out of the pack of aspirants for the Democratic presidential nomination." But there was a domestic as well as an international dimension to Humphrey's suddenly altered prospects—a dimension added by the November election returns, of which the Russians also seemed to have been aware. Doris Fleeson wrote: "Circumstances have suddenly meshed to give Humphrey the kind of attention which fixes his presidential capabilities in the mind of the public." For the big swing to the Democrats after six years of Republican rule seemed to signal a change at the White House in the presidential voting due in 1960. And Humphrey, identified with the party's progressive wing, had improved his standing in the November elections with the victory of his protégé Eugene McCarthy in the Minnesota senate race while his two closest rivals on the left, Governor Harriman of New York and Governor Mennen Williams of Michigan, had, respectively, lost and won narrow reelection. Asked by a panel of college students about prospective presidential candidates for 1960, Eleanor Roosevelt said Hubert Humphrey came closest to having "the spark of greatness."

On December 29, Muriel Humphrey wrote to Eugenie Anderson:

> As it worked out it was best that we went to Russia at this time. It would have been better for Hubert to have been better prepared—but in his own way he is always far better prepared than others. Now the important thing is that, whether we seek it or not, we are in the race for 1960. I am no longer pulling back—it would be just too naïve and coy.
>
> On Ira Polley's Christmas card there was a very urgent and very wise piece of advice—"Humphrey, you need a pro!" I think and think about this—maybe some day we'll meet or think of just the right person. Pretty soon the blocks have to fall into position.

For a long time, Muriel Humphrey had followed her husband's fortunes from a certain distance. It was true that his earliest office-seeking plans had been hatched at her kitchen table, and when he campaigned for mayor and senator, as she recalled later, "I'd say something while taking care of my babies and later it would be part of his speech." But in his great moments at the Philadelphia convention she had been back in Minneapolis taking her small charges swimming by day and keeping her ear glued by night to the radio: "the voices all fuzzy, and then you came on clear and concise and just really good. . . . I'm so proud of you and love you very dearly." And for those first years in Washington she had to hold the young family together while Humphrey scrambled to survive amid Senate hostilities. She ironed his shirts the way he liked them. She made drapes for all the windows. She grew tomatoes in the yard. She took the children to the army and navy club grounds, where senators had privileges. She got Nancy started on the piano and took lessons from the teacher herself. After that third Washington winter, Humphrey wrote Eugenie Anderson (by then U. S. ambassador to Denmark): "Muriel is a great homemaker. She loves her garden, flowers, children and even her husband. She has been a great help to me. I find myself being more in love with that woman every day." In that summer of 1951, while Humphrey battled in the Senate to plug the tax-law loopholes, she took the children to a rented lakeside cottage at Alexandria, Minnesota. But before long, Humphrey began to draw his wife into his public life too. Overseas trips were something the couple had dreamed and talked of in their Model A

courting rides in Huron. And when Humphrey was invited to an interparliamentary conference at Strasbourg in the fall of 1951, Muriel left the children
with a woman brought from Minnesota and flew to Europe with him. In the
preliminaries to Humphrey's reelection run in 1954, the whole family trailed
along to county fairs. In the actual campaigning his wife took an active part
for the first time, working through an outfit called Minnesota Women for
Humphrey. Afterward, Humphrey told his friend Doris Kirkpatrick: "Muriel
helped out a lot, visiting dozens of coffee parties, even making some short
speeches, and she did very well. Over 2,000 paidup membership—kind of
nice to have better than 2,000 Minnesota Women for Humphrey."

Of course any senator as frenetically busy as Humphrey was a sometime
father. His secretaries might mark his calendar in block letters: "FEBRUARY
3—DOUGIE'S BIRTHDAY DINNER," but Humphrey was all too apt to miss the
party. After their mother set Skip to playing the cello and Robert the clari-
net, Humphrey turned up, a little late, to hear them play in the school
orchestra. When Skip graduated from junior high, his father appeared and
presented him with a watch. Sometimes the boys got to go along on his
trips—once Skip went with him to the Army-Navy football game, another
time to Gettysburg when his father had to give a speech, and Robert later
got a chance to go with him to a missile launch at Cape Kennedy. When their
parents began to take brief vacations in Florida and Arizona, the kids went
along. After one outing to Bill Benton's spread at Phoenix, Humphrey wrote:
"The boys and their Dad had a wonderful time together. They missed a few
days of school but we went up to the Grand Canyon, we swam in the pool,
we played tennis, we played croquet, we went hiking and in general just had
a first-class good time, father and sons together with Mom sort of overseeing."

But these occasions were rare. Humphrey exaggerated when he wrote a
friend: "I have not had supper with my family ten times in eight years." But
Sunday was about the only day he would be home. He followed his father's
sabbath example in churchgoing and was proud that his daughter Nancy
sang in the choir. He himself was quite unmusical, joining loudly in the
hymn-singing but dropping his voice every time he came to the high notes.
Sometimes on Sundays he led an outing to the zoo and afterward stopped at
the Lake Pharmacy, almost as if he were in Huron, to treat everybody to a
cherry smash or a cherry coke. He loved to take moving pictures and about
once a year would say: "Let's take out the old movies and have popcorn."
The boys would shout: "Let's see the baby pictures." He liked to watch
"Gunsmoke," Sid Caesar and Imogene Coca, the "Ed Sullivan Show."

He could get down on the ground and fix bicycles, having learned by
repairing other boys' bikes for pin money back in Doland. Sometimes he
called on the children to help clean out the attic or tidy up the garage. "It
had to be perfect—or we were in hot water," Skip later recalled. Humphrey
was a notorious cleaner-upper, going about all his life obsessively whisking

dust specks off desktops, emptying ashtrays in hotel rooms—a quirk that some thought traceable to early training at the prescription counter. At one point, years later, his children presented him with a gold-handled broom.

Humphrey was a "firm" disciplinarian. Again and again, echoing his father's old prescript, he warned: "Be good to your Mom, take care of your Mom." "To your room" was the penalty for lesser slips and the little belt that he kept in the broom closet came out only when someone mistreated Mother. He was not free with allowances—"you could count mine in quarters in one hand," Robert said later. Having smoked until he was forty-five, he confined his counsel against cigarettes to telling of his own experience. He told Robert: "I quit as soon as I heard about the link between cigarettes and lung cancer. A doctor had already told me to quit. Well, I just quit." On performance in class, Humphrey was as gentle with his children as he was forgiving with all the people who crossed him in politics. He could say, writing to Eugenie Anderson: "We have a loyal family, Eugenie, and are justly proud of our children. There isn't a genius among them, but they have good normal instincts and wholesome attitudes. To me that is most important."

The best times were after the Senate adjourned in late summer. Following the 1952 Democratic Convention, Humphrey piled the whole family into the car and led a camping trip to Yellowstone, where he showed the boys how to catch trout. A couple of summers later he reported enthusiastically to Lyndon Johnson on swimming, boating, and fishing with the family in Minnesota's Lake Minnetonka. "I have seen more of my family these past three weeks than I have in the past three years. I am a lucky man."

In 1952, Ray Ewald, the Minneapolis dairyman who had helped get Governor Youngdahl appointed judge in Washington, began renting his summer cottage to the Humphreys. It was on Lake Waverly, forty miles west of Minneapolis. After a second summer, the Humphreys decided to build a cottage there. Humphrey had thought it desirable that he own property in the state he represented, and the children loved the place.

With little cash to spare in the Humphrey bank account, it was not until the fall of 1956 that Humphrey closed the deal. The price paid for the six lots acquired from Ewald on the short shore of Lake Waverly could not have been much more than twelve hundred dollars. But the fact that the price was never made public left Humphrey open to Republican charges that the property came to him as a gift for political favors rendered.

By the time it was theirs, the Humphreys had decided to build not a summer cabin but a substantial year-round home. To pay for it, Humphrey had to take outside speaking engagements. In addition he had to get a $5,000 mortgage at the Waverly bank, a $15,000 loan from Morris Ebin, the Minneapolis businessman who had lent money to help him buy his home when he first moved to Washington, and $3,500 more in personal loans to meet the cost of furnishings. In October 1957 the place was ready, and Humphrey described it in a letter to his brother-in-law Gordon Buck: "A lovely place

. . . a four-bedroom, completely winterized modern home, well-constructed of paneled wood, each room with a different kind—oak, cherry, walnut, butternut. A fireplace divides the living room from the kitchen, which is completely modern. There's an upstairs dormitory-type room. In the living room, a beamed ceiling. A little over two acres of ground, and a wonderful lake." There was also a boat for water-skiing—a fourteen-footer with 35-hp motor. To pay for it, for two and a half years the children performed daily chores, their father meanwhile depositing in the Chevy Chase bank the equivalent of what the help would have received.

By the time the Humphreys moved in at Waverly, the older children were starting to leave home. Nancy, after a freshman year at the University of Maryland, transferred to a nurse's training program at Northwestern Hospital in Minneapolis. And one day Humphrey mentioned to his friend Benton that Skip was making indifferent progress in tenth grade at his crowded suburban high school in Kensington. Benton, in his customary take-charge fashion, declared that Shattuck—a military academy at the time and now a private boys school in Faribault, Minnesota, was the place for Skipper. Benton had prepped at Shattuck, served ten years on its board of directors, and established a scholarship there that Skip should surely have. He had been a scholarship boy at Shattuck himself, he said. It was quickly arranged, and Skip entered Shattuck the year the Humphreys moved in at Waverly.

In 1960, Benton took a hand again in the education of the Humphrey sons. Through the years 1957, 1958, and 1959 Humphrey's income from fees for speaking rose from $27,647 to $36,499 the highest for any senator. But in 1960, the year he ran for the presidency and the Senate, his outside income necessarily fell to no more than a third of its former level, and he had to meet his rising obligations pretty much out of his Senate pay. In evident embarrassment he wrote the Shattuck headmaster: "I am a man of modest means. I am going to send a little something along to the Fathers' Club, but this has been a rather rough year on the Humphrey treasury."

At this point, Benton arranged that when Skip graduated in June, the Benton scholarship at Shattuck be transferred to Douglas, the youngest of the Humphrey boys. And when Humphrey's agribusinessman friend Dwayne Andreas expressed a desire to help, Benton instructed him in how he could do the same for Humphrey's second son, Robert. With Benton paving the way, Andreas's educational foundation duly made a $3,000 grant that fall to Shattuck. At word from Benton, the school awarded a scholarship of that amount to Robert. The switch was as successful for Bob as for his brothers, and he too continued as a scholarship boy until his graduation, three years later.

20

Flattened by the Kennedys

PEOPLE began to talk about Humphrey as a future president when he was still mayor. His father forecast it when he went to the Senate. Brien McMahon, one of the most senior Democrats, urged it upon him only four years later. And three years after that, following his reelection to a second Senate term, the Minneapolis Central Labor Union began circulating petitions for his nomination as president in 1956.

The senator himself looked a bit further ahead—to 1960 in fact. For Humphrey the 1956 convention and campaign were to have been the powder and shell that would blast him toward the presidency four years later. That, he told Max Kampelman later, was why he was so disappointed at losing the second spot at Chicago in 1956. "I didn't think that we could win the [1956] election," he confessed. But to have made the 1956 race "would have meant [gaining] a position of influence in the party. Stevenson would have been twice up and twice down. And if you were an active, good campaigner for vice president, . . . you would make an imprint upon the country." In short, Humphrey would have had a powerful head start toward the prize in 1960.

Veiling his disappointment, Humphrey called, after the Stevenson rout, for a renewed "liberalism" to replace the "centrist" philosophy that he said had characterized the Democratic congressional leadership. He said: "I don't think a party should run on 'trouble,' on economic difficulty. We must design a new liberal program" and, joining the new Democratic Advisory Committee, he helped draw up a sixteen-point plan for action on civil rights and other progressive legislation.

Looking ahead to 1960, it was plain that Kennedy had gained the place Humphrey had hoped for as front runner. But all the hopefuls had handicaps, Kennedy included. Humphrey had his strengths, and one was surely his two-term record as the Upper Midwest's spokesman on its biggest issue: a fair deal for its farmers. If he could only line up a solid block of regional support behind his leadership, he could yet arrive at the 1960 convention as a real contender.

To gain such support would require topnotch political organizing, and nuts-and-bolts management was not a Humphrey skill. After Orville Freeman graduated to the governorship Humphrey did not land such a manager until Larry O'Brien, who had organized for Kennedy and Johnson, agreed too late to manage for him in 1968. The problem for a Midwest-based candidacy was the region's primaries. Open to all comers, they invited outside incursions. In Minnesota, where Kefauver had barged in and upset Stevenson to Humphrey's everlasting embarrassment, Freeman knew how to handle the problem. Making common cause with Republican regulars who still remembered the devastating Eisenhower write-in vote that smashed the presidential hopes of Harold Stassen in 1952, his DFL forces simply abolished Minnesota's presidential preferential primary outright.

But there was no getting around Wisconsin's primary, notorious for having extinguished the supposedly sure-thing candidacy of Wendell Willkie in 1944. It commanded extra attention because it fell early in the year—the first week of April. And it carried special risks because voters were free to "cross over" and vote on whichever ticket they preferred. Humphrey's championship of the farmer, above all his efforts in behalf of milk-price supports, had won him many friends in a state whose license plates bore the legend "America's Dairyland." People sometimes spoke of him as Wisconsin's third senator. On a swing through the state in mid-1953, Humphrey made a valiant attempt to clinch a prior endorsement from his friend Governor Gaylord Nelson that might dissuade any other candidate—John Kennedy above all—from entering. Although Nelson had stumped for office arm in arm with Humphrey, he now saw the political risks as simply too great, and Humphrey had to go back to Washington without a commitment.

After this setback, Humphrey's candidacy began to get some breaks. His marathon interview with Khrushchev later that year loosed torrents of publicity, lifting him for the first time into serious consideration for 1960. At the same time, the leftward swing in the 1958 elections, suggesting that the nation might be ready for a liberal Democrat after Eisenhower, further sharpened the focus on Humphrey. For while his Minnesota DFL rolled up big gains, electing McCarthy to the Senate, Averell Harriman, as already noted lost the governorship of New York to Nelson Rockefeller, and in Michigan Mennen Williams gained reelection by a margin so narrow that he chances were snuffed out.

When fifteen hundred invitations to speak poured in on him in two months and he toyed with the idea of seeking a follow-up interview with China's Mao Tse-Tung, a serious Humphrey campaign began to take shape. The "pro" he so badly needed—his old friend James Rowe, Jr.—joined his camp. Portly, witty, Harvard-trained, Rowe was an Irish Catholic from Montana who had worked for Franklin Roosevelt in the White House and then formed a Washington political law practice with his fellow braintruster Thomas Corcoran. Rowe was such a close friend of Lyndon Johnson from his White House days thet he felt obliged to ask Johnson first whether he intended to run. When Johnson said no, Rowe offered his services to Humphrey. Exhilarated, Humphrey's millionaire friend Benton wrote: "The decision of Jim Rowe will help offset the image that the Senator's only support was from the more radical left."

After a couple of scouting trips through the West, Rowe laid down a twenty-six-page memorandum entitled "The Strategy of Hubert Humphrey." The memorandum charted the outlines of Humphrey's 1960 campaign so trenchantly that they guided Humphrey's actions for the rest of his life. Primaries, the very contests that Humphrey had sought to avoid, were pivotal to the plan. Rowe agreed that they defeated many candidates and had never, by themselves, insured the winner of nomination. Primaries were physically exhausting. They had worn out Stevenson and Kefauver and "ruined them for intelligent, post-Convention campaigning." Primaries were unrepresentative. They were expensive. They were uncontrollable. They were terribly risky. But, Rowe said, this particular candidate had to face tough realities: Humphrey, not a household name, lacking in funds and organization, coming from a small state, had only an outside chance of winning the nomination. Yet, Rowe prophesied, "if he does not take this stern and bloody path," he has *no* chance whatsoever.

Only by going the primary route could Humphrey gain what he needed—prolonged exposure and the indispensable aura of a winner. Only by competing in primaries could Humphrey hope to compel the attention of the power brokers—the small group of "organizational professionals" controlling the key states such as New York, New Jersey, Pennsylvania, Ohio, Michigan, Illinois, and Texas. These were the men, said Rowe, who would gather privately at the convention and decide on the nominee. Above all, they wanted a winner. They were generally more conservative than the voters—and unfriendly to Humphrey, whom they saw as a divisive candidate and unacceptable to the South. But "these men do not operate as individuals. They are essentially catalysts—catalysts who remain in power by reflecting accurately the moods and desires of their constituents. The constituents happen to be minor organization politicians but these in turn often reflect accurately the mood of the voters. These men are, in turn, affected by the action of the candidates. So the 'professionals'—like other politicians—are subject to political pressures from below."

By entering carefully selected primaries and winning them, Rowe said,

Humphrey might hope to arrive at Los Angeles in July with from 150 to 200 votes—enough to give him a base for bargaining with the power brokers, a major voice at the convention, and possibly a shot at the nomination itself.

But what primaries should Humphrey select? Rowe advised him to choose small states—states with a liberal-labor base like Minnesota's, states where hard-driving personal effort could make up for lack of money, states where Humphrey could unleash what Rowe called his "secret weapon" (his bubbling, take-it-to-the-people style of campaigning). The two places Rowe singled out for their social and political likeness to Minnesota were Wisconsin and Oregon. South Dakota and Nebraska might be good too, if funds could stretch so far. The District of Columbia was small, but a good place to show Northern bosses how Humphrey could turn out their increasingly important black inner-city vote. Rowe added West Virginia as the state where Humphrey might best show that his was a national appeal.

Humphrey accepted Rowe's plan, and he also accepted another piece of Rowe advice: "The first foot forward in a quest for the presidency should always come from and by the candidate's home state, [and the candidate should] make no reply . . . other than to say he's flattered." On cue, after a big meeting with Humphrey and Rowe at Minneapolis's Leamington Hotel, Orville Freeman and Eugene McCarthy announced the formation of a Humphrey for President committee. All Humphrey said, in a letter to his friend Berwyn James, was: "My position is third or fourth or fifth. I have to work myself up the hard way."

Just how hard the way would be Humphrey found out at once. Even with Rowe at his side he could not get Montana's commitment. In California the Democrats gave him standing ovations, then told him they still preferred Adlai Stevenson. And at breakfast at Lyndon Johnson's ranch, Johnson dropped a bombshell: "Hubert, you are going to do me out of the nomination." This was the first Humphrey knew that Johnson was in the race too: the Johnson strategy envisioned a solid Southern bloc plus a scattering of Western support adding up to three hundred votes, enough to force a convention deal for the top spot.

But the front-runner only ran faster. John Kennedy's publicity, Humphrey sighed, was "unbelievably good." By this time his prize-winning bestseller *Profiles in Courage*, ghosted by Theodore Sorensen and a Washington professor, was being studied in schools. *Life* and *Time* splashed cover stories; *McCalls* invited him to write on "Three Women of Courage"; and his articles appeared in foreign affairs, education, business, and labor journals—"all the good spots," Humphrey noted enviously. The most famous article on Kennedy, a discussion of his views on religion and politics, appeared in *Look* in late 1958. Absenting himself freely from the Senate, Kennedy flew in and out of Wisconsin, West Virginia, Oregon—the very states Humphrey had to win. After a visit to Milwaukee, Humphrey reported to McCarthy in dismay: "The Kennedy people moved in pretty hard. Our people [are] in somewhat of a state of shock." It seemed that the state Democratic chairman,

Pat Lucey, had already gone over to Kennedy. In December, Lou Harris, Kennedy's own pollster, published findings that Kennedy had snatched the lead from the fading Kefauver and stood No. 1 nationally. Humphrey was far back at 5 percent, just ahead of Governor Meyner of New Jersey.

Already people such as George Ball and Averell Harriman were saying the Humphrey campaign had not "gotten off the ground." In September he finally told Rowe he was appointing him campaign manager. But he never brought himself to announce it. He told Rowe he wanted action on "details, a P. R. program, and some money—I am running a poor man's campaign." That was the trouble. Humphrey kept trying to run the show himself. His weakness for impromptu management was already apparent. Orville Freeman, organizer of his early victories, had asked in vain for "marching orders." Humphrey thought that Lt. Governor Karl Rolvaag had more time, and asked him to organize the Midwest for him. But Rolvaag lacked the breadth and drive for the assignment, and in Wisconsin he was simply out of his depth. The plan, suggested by Rowe, was that an army of DFL volunteers, who had performed so dynamically in Minnesota's last election, should fan out across the border in a people-to-people movement, Minnesota county committees making contact with Wisconsin county committees, to turn out the voters for Humphrey. In December, Humphrey finally and most uncharacteristically relieved Rolvaag and sent in Minnesota's National Committeeman Gerald Heaney to try and get the Wisconsin effort moving.

There was no turning back, though Humphrey might tell friends that his chances were no better than one in ten. In mid-December he met with Rowe and Kampelman, with Loeb and Rauh of the ADA, and with his staff operatives Herb Waters and Bill Connell and a few others; all agreed he should go. On December 30, beating Kennedy to the takeoff by three days, Humphrey formally announced his candidacy before eighty Washington reporters. He was forty-seven. He had been fifteen years in public life, eleven on Capitol Hill. "Of one thing I am sure," he said. "If victory is to come to the Democratic party, the plain people must find in the Democratic standard-bearer a man they sense to be their true friend, their spokesman."

It was Humphrey's unique claim. All the other Democratic contenders were millionaires. Identifying himself as a "victim of the Depression," Humphrey asserted that he would speak for people "who like myself are of modest origin and limited financial means—who lack the power or the influence to fully control their own destiny."

"Old Bob LaFollette and William Jennings Bryan would have loved it," wrote James Reston in the *New York Times*, and Reston could have added the name of Humphrey's populist father, who could never bring himself to trust banks. Here was another son of the Middle West standing forth embattled, eloquent, gifted with the common touch, ready to rescue the disinherited. "I have no illusions," he said, "it will be an uphill fight."

IN THE last analysis, after every allowance was made for the slim funds Humphrey could command, his campaign depended not on money but on the ideas and emotions he could arouse in the hearts of the electorate, on the extent to which he could put across his reforming enthusiasm to the people directly. If he showed himself in tune with public sentiment, if his own gut feeling about what should be done met responsive emotion on the part of the voters, if his alliance of labor, intellectuals, and farmers that clicked in Minnesota could be somehow multiplied across the land—then he could win. Wisconsin, next neighbor to Minnesota, was to be the testing place.

At once, problems loomed. The strategy of pouring troops across the border from Minnesota, while fine for a low-budget operation, placed a terrific strain on Humphrey's DFL party and its vaunted cadre of volunteers. The burden was simply too great, and before the year was out it split Humphrey from his friend Governor Freeman, who faced his own 1960 campaign and harbored national ambitions of his own besides. And Gerry Heaney, taking over in Wisconsin, reported that Humphrey was not nearly so well known in the eastern cities, where two-thirds of the state's voters lived. Most disconcerting of all perhaps, the national labor picture had suddenly altered with subtle but significant impact on the Humphrey campaign. After a Senate investigation sparked by young Robert Kennedy had exposed racketeering and corruption in some of the biggest unions, John Kennedy, as a Labor committee senator, had intervened to help tone down the worst excesses of the anti-labor Landrum-Griffin Law, passed late in 1959. Humphrey, who had been the great union favorite but no longer served on that committee, was not going to get labor's endorsement in Wisconsin, Heaney reported. Even Walter Reuther, Humphrey's old comrade in ADA, was said to be leaning to Kennedy.

Kennedy delayed entering a few days, but Rowe had correctly predicted that he would "go for broke." Easterner though he was, Kennedy knew that Wisconsin's 32 percent Catholic population was the largest in the west, and his pollster Lou Harris told him that he held a sixty-to-forty lead over Humphrey.

On what grounds would Humphrey attack him? Kennedy's biggest handicap was precisely his Catholic affiliation, the others being his youth and presumed inexperience, and his father's reputation, in that order. Still, even if Humphrey was a past master at the old stump trick of bellowing: "I'm not going to talk about my opponent's Catholicism . . ." ("It's not the Pope but the Pop," was how he put it in Wausau), he was far too much of a fighter for civil rights to let bigotry seep into his campaign. And as a personal matter, he was inclined to accept Rowe's counsel that it was bad politics to talk about the other fellow's money except to say how poor he was himself. Under these rather narrow constraints, Humphrey was reduced, on the rare occasions when his cool-headed adversary gave him the opportunity, to sputtering against Kennedy's "acting like a spoiled juvenile."

Humphrey would have liked to fight the campaign on issues. Kennedy, leading in the popularity polls and extravagantly favored in all the publicity, refused to debate Humphrey and said there were really no issues between them. Humphrey said: "I hate to do this, but I'm tired of hearing 'there's no difference between the two candidates. We're in politics, we're not making love. If it's true there's no difference, then I ought to win because I'm older and have more experience." Kennedy replied blandly that the only question was who could best beat Richard Nixon, and the self-evident answer was himself. This exasperated Humphrey, who saw Kennedy as a candidate who had nothing particularly liberal in his past but had simply decided that the way to win was to vote for anything that labor favored. Arthur Schlesinger, Humphrey's former ADA ally, explained that Kennedy's recent liberalization had been arrived at by a process of rational thought, whereas Humphrey received his liberalism "spontaneously" at an early age, and had since had to contrive his intellectual justification for it. Fuming, Humphrey shot off a memo to his Washington staff: "We ought to get Herblock to do a cartoon showing Humphrey walking down the road with a healthy stride—on his coat, the words 'THE ISSUES'—and Jack Kennedy tagging along, hanging on his coattails, saying: 'Me too.' "

It was only partly because he was poor that Humphrey lacked flacks capable of going to town with such ideas. If Kennedy outspent him, he outmanaged and outorganized him too. Kennedy's Ivy League classmate volunteers, all working full time, fanned out to open offices in every corner of the state. The candidate, and all members of the family except his father, flew in and out on the *Caroline*, the Kennedy private plane. His glamorous wife and sisters appeared at well-publicized coffee parties and four R. S. V. P. receptions. His brother Robert coordinated the rough stuff, spreading the word early that Jimmy Hoffa, chief target of the rackets investigations, was pouring $1.2 million into the state for Humphrey. At Milwaukee headquarters, Larry O'Brien's boiler-room operation fed the candidate up-to-the-minute information on what to say where and when. A last-minute telephone drive passed the word to the Polish households of south Milwaukee that public housing—a code word for blacks—might spread from the north to the south part of their city if they failed to turn out for Kennedy. "I feel like an independent merchant competing against a chain store," groaned Humphrey.

Even as a corner-store venture, Humphrey's campaign lacked coherence. Disorder was a bigger Humphrey handicap than was his thin purse. Aides at his national headquarters split into conservatives around Rowe and liberals around Joe Rauh. Humphrey's Minnesota friends detested his chief Washington staffer, Californian Herb Waters. There was even a want of confidence between Governor Freeman and Lt. Governor Rolvaag, whom Humphrey had put in charge of his Midwest delegate drive. On the Wisconsin battlefront, Heaney rushed in his fellow Irish Catholic from Minnesota, Eugene Foley, to try to stem the big slide among eastern Wisconsin's Poles,

Germans, and Irish to Kennedy. At the same time, he proposed to Humphrey that they concentrate on six of the state's ten congressional districts
where he thought they stood a better chance to win.

Humphrey agreed, but insisted that they try to carry the statewide popular poll as well. Humphrey was thus forever pulling away from Heaney's
schedule in answer to the importunities of his friends in the hardshell conservative districts of the northeast, where he never really had a chance. He
would deliver his usual fiery speech; the friendly audience would climb on
their chairs and cheer; and Humphrey would leave, exclaiming he simply
had to come back for more. Driving along the highways he would see a radio
station's aerial tower and say, "Let's stop," and if someone in the party had
a few dollars, Humphrey would buy an instant half-hour's time. Impromptu
would have been too strong a word for the disorganized nature of these
adventures. People would call in, not about presidential topics like Berlin or
foreign aid but with the kind of question they might ask their congressman.
Out of his unrivaled knowledge as a member of Congress, the candidate for
president would field questions about pensions or schoolteachers' pay, and
once in a while there would be exclamations of "God bless you, Hubert."
Obviously, Humphrey loved campaigning, but he admitted that Kennedy
was getting better political mileage from smiling studio dialogues with senior
citizens on statewide TV.

All the same, Humphrey was gaining ground in the last couple of weeks.
With his wife and eighteen-year-old son Skip at his side, he offered himself
as a Midwesterner, a man of the people, "one of us" as contrasted to the
moneyed Kennedys, outsiders from the East. By car and bus the Minnesota
helpers swarmed through western Wisconsin staging joint rallies with local
Democrats. Minnesota sent $75,000 into the state, $27,000 of it raised in a
barnyard drive by two Minnesota dirt farmers. Jim Loeb, the practiced ADA
fuse lighter, moved into Madison to fire up one of the nation's most liberal
university towns for Humphrey. The candidate himself, speaking at the rate
of 250 words per minute, worked hardest of all. Though forced out once by
a touch of the flu, he managed to put in twenty-eight days of campaigning to
Kennedy's twenty, and had pulled up to within four or five points in the
Roper poll when a bombshell broke.

Up to this time neither Humphrey nor Kennedy had spoken of the big
underlying issue of the race: whether the voters were prepared to choose a
Catholic for president. If the candidates kept silent, hardly anyone else did.
The national press played it up. When television cameras panned over Kennedy's crowds, they always picked out the nuns. The state's leading newspaper, the Milwaukee *Journal*, even while inveighing editorially against bias
and prejudice, recorded in its news columns that twenty-two of twenty-three
hostesses at a Kennedy coffee party were Catholic. Of course the Humphreyites looked for votes in the Protestant West just as the Kennedy camp
did in the Catholic East. But Humphrey felt strongly that Kennedy had first

sought advantage in the religious matter; near the end of the campaign he told Arthur Schlesinger that intolerance had been used as a weapon against him. He was not bitter against Kennedy, he said, but was "bitter at the use of religion against me in this campaign." His friend Eugenie Anderson went further. "Unconscionable appeals to bigotry" by "the hidden Kennedy forces in Wisconsin," she said, had so angered Humphrey that win or lose Humphrey would go on to fight the West Virginia primary rather than "concede anything that might help Kennedy."

In this charged atmosphere, an ad signed "Square Deal for Humphrey Committee" appeared on the Thursday before the voting in every country weekly newspaper in the state: "Protestants: a leading pollster reports five out of six Catholics interviewed favor Kennedy over Humphrey, many of them normally Republican voters who say they would back Nixon against any Democrat but Kennedy. Should these Republican voters determine who the Democratic nominee should be? Let's give Humphrey a square deal."

The lid was off. Milwaukee and Chicago newspapers headlined: "Prejudice Rears Its Head in Wisconsin." Both sides rushed to find out who had blown the religious issue wide open. But the damage had been done. Heaney, "devastated," and suspecting a dastardly Kennedy trick, repudiated the ad. The Kennedys supposed desperation had led the Humphreyites to take leave of their senses, and Kennedy chairman Pat Lucey demanded an investigation. Governor Gaylord Nelson, who had feared such warfare could cost the Democrats the state in the fall, called for a report. In the last hours, newspapers found out only enough to suggest that the ads might have been placed by a sometime Democratic party worker named Charlie Greene, who had insinuated himself briefly into Humphrey's Milwaukee office and later decamped to Florida. After the campaign the state attorney general's office established that a dubious character involved in Teamster pension funds had given Greene the twenty-five hundred dollars to pay for the ads. So, though it could not be proved, it seemed all too likely that Teamster Boss Hoffa, his mishandling of Teamster funds exposed by the Senate investigating committee of which John Kennedy was a member and his brother the crusading counsel, had reached in and struck his avenging blow at the Kennedys, cost what it might to Humphrey.

No one can say what effect the ad had on the April 5 election, in which Kennedy carried the state by a 56 percent majority, rolling up 474,024 votes to Humphrey's 366,753. Kennedy also carried six of the ten congressional districts, thereby assuring himself of twenty delegate votes to Humphrey's ten.

But the religious issue had been thrust into the open to a degree Humphrey did not realize. When the votes were analyzed, the result was almost to turn a numerical victory for Kennedy into a defeat. There had been a huge crossover vote, all right, but it appeared to have benefited the two candidates almost equally. If Catholic Republicans in the conservative Northeast had entered the Democratic primary in large numbers to vote for John Kennedy, Lutheran Republican farmers around Madison and further west had crossed in strength to cast ballots for Hubert Humphrey. Indeed, if one looked at returns from non-Catholic areas, John Kennedy did not appear to be such an impressive vote-getter at all.

In these circumstances, Humphrey acted almost as if he had gained a moral victory. Far from sounding discouraged, he trumpeted that if the campaign had lasted a little longer and given him time to turn a few votes in central Wisconsin, then he and not Kennedy would have won six of the ten congressional districts. Even before the votes were in, he had made up his mind to go on to West Virginia. When Schlesinger suggested that if Humphrey withdrew after Wisconsin he would be the "natural" for vice president with Kennedy, Humphrey replied "with some vigor": "I have talked this over with Muriel, and I have no interest at all in the vice presidency." Later that same day, Humphrey bumped into Kennedy at a United Auto Workers rally at Kenosha. Humphrey told Kennedy: "I talked to Arthur about West Virginia. It's no use—I'm going to have to go through with it."

Humphrey's advisers tried to talk him out of it. Rowe pointed out that his long-shot presidential strategy had always been premised on winning Wisconsin for a starter. His finance people reminded him that he had thrown all his money into the Wisconsin gamble, overspending by at least $17,000. Still, he told the friends gathered in his Milwaukee hotel room on primary night: "I've paid a $1,000 filing fee in West Virginia, and I'm going on." He borrowed $2,000 from his New York friend Marvin Rosenberg and flew to Charleston.

Just because Humphrey was such a forgiving fellow did not mean that he never got angry. And just because Kennedy campaigning was as cold-eyed and calculating as Humphrey's was warm and impulsive did not mean that emotion was lacking on the Kennedy side. Bitterness at what he believed was Kennedy's undercover exploitation of his Catholic affiliation in Wisconsin played a big part in Humphrey's decision to fight on in West Virginia, and outrage at what he saw as Humphrey's perverse refusal to give up after losing his next-door state in Wisconsin fueled Kennedy's brutal attack on Humphrey in the campaign that followed.

Humphrey thought his chances were good in West Virginia, one of the few states that had backed him in his losing race for vice president four years before. He had talked with Democratic chieftains, who were close to Lyndon Johnson, and had reason to expect their support. That West Virginia was more countrified than urban seemed to invite Humphrey's folksy stump style. The state, moreover, was a citadel of labor. It was depressed; unemployment had hit hard; and coal miners' families were hungry. Humphrey felt he could talk to such people, who were 95 percent Protestant and deep-dyed Bible-belters besides.

His first five-day swing through the coalfields was "very gratifying," he reported. Polls showed him well ahead in the state. Having spent all his money in Wisconsin, he depended entirely on hand-shaking and riproaring roadside speeches. But at Morgantown he also offered a ten-point program for West Virginia economic revival—including food stamps for the impoverished counties, health care for senior citizens, a Youth Conservation Corps for the idle young, a higher minimum wage for workers, research for new markets and uses for the state's coal. A staff of four handed out press releases describing how his vote differed from Kennedy's on raising personal income-tax exemptions.

Kennedy went after Humphrey with a vengeance. Boldly casting himself as the underdog, he brought his Catholic connection into the open as if Humphrey's wilfulness in fighting West Virginia left him no choice. At his opening appearance in Fairmont, Kennedy demanded, "Is anyone going to tell me I lost the primary before I was born?" And before any questions could be asked, he vowed his recommitment to the separation of church and state. Recalling the Purple Heart he had won in the Pacific war, he cried, "No one can tell me that I am not as prepared as any man to meet my obligations to the Constitution of the United States."

The reporters who had sniffed for religious prejudice in Wisconsin had no trouble finding West Virginia mountaineers who said such things as: "My preacher's been preachin' for years that when a Catholic gets President, the end of time is come." As if his opponent stood for such attitudes, Kennedy called for an end to religious prejudice, shaming West Virginians to vote his way, saying in effect: "If you don't vote for me, you're a bigot." Humphrey, the lifelong champion of tolerance and equality, found himself forced to be defensive over an issue on which there was no conceivable retort, either in his heart or in practical politics.

At his father's prompting, Kennedy also brought Franklin Roosevelt, Jr., into his campaign. It was said that the young Roosevelt, who had been Humphrey's good friend in earlier days, was in need of money. He appeared repeatedly at Kennedy's side in West Virginia, where his father was revered as a hero. Kennedy used the younger Roosevelt to strike Humphrey at his politically most vulnerable spot, his lack of a war record. Saying "I don't know where he was in World War II," Roosevelt handed out papers provided by Robert Kennedy charging that Humphrey was a draft dodger. Much later, Roosevelt gave Humphrey a written apology and retraction, but the damage was done.

Humphrey's hip-pocket operation was no match for the Kennedy onslaught. Kennedy volunteers poured in to open offices in thirty counties. Kennedy pamphlets and bumper stickers deluged the state; Kennedy ads saturated the newspapers. At the same place where Humphrey addressed 250, Kennedy's advance men turned out 2,500 the next day. Kennedy forces made lavish use of TV and radio; one of the few times Humphrey got on television was when Kennedy, playing the underdog, consented to debate him as he would not in

Wisconsin. Kennedy won the toss, let Humphrey speak first, then said that only he had a chance to gain the nomination and bring West Virginians the aid Humphrey had called for.

Since it would have been ridiculous to deny it, Kennedy made light of his heavy spending. At a dinner in New York he said, "I got a wire from my father" and then read: "Dear Jack, don't buy one vote more than necessary. I'll be damned if I'll pay for a landslide." This was the season when the older Kennedy was confiding to James Landis: "What's a hundred million if it will help Jack?" West Virginia's rules were different from Wisconisn's. County organizations needed money for sheriff and other local contests, especially for cars, whiskey, and "walk-around money" to get out the vote on election day. It was customary that candidates for governor, and possible that candidates for president, be "slated" (i.e., listed with the locals on the slips of paper handed voters) by these county machines. But, as a Humphrey aide advised, this cost money: "One thousand dollars to get on a slate in a populated area." Since there were fifty-five counties and heaven knew how many "populated areas," it was not a game Humphrey could play. When one Humphrey worker rashly handed a county boss twenty-five hundred dollars, it was returned with the explanation that Larry O'Brien had already presented five thousand dollars for the Kennedy cause. Ecumenical forces were also at work. Boston's Cardinal Cushing smilingly told Humphrey some years later how he had personally helped the elder Kennedy overcome possible antipathy to Kennedy and Catholicism by contributing to Protestant churches in West Virginia, particularly in black communities: "We decided which church and preacher should get $200 or $100 or $500. What better way to spend campaign money than to help a preacher and his flock? It's good for the Lord, for the church, for the preacher—and for the candidate."

Rowe said afterward that the election was bought, and assuredly the Kennedys spent far more than the $100,000 officially reported—Joe Kennedy's biographer thought more like $1.5 million. The Kennedys also ruthlessly cut off Humphrey's flow of support by threatening the New York Stevensonians who had given him early funds that if they sent Humphrey more, Stevenson would never be Kennedy's secretary of state. As a result, Humphrey, forced to use much of his time calling friends to raise money, spent something like $23,000 in all.

Toward the end, when it looked as if Kennedy was going to pull it out, Lyndon Johnson, who had not dared enter the primary himself, tried to throw Humphrey a financial lifeline. A few Johnson friends sent one-thousand-dollar contributions from New York, and Johnson's Senate whip Earle Clements appeared in West Virginia to check on convention delegates to be chosen by the state Democratic committee. But late cash from Johnson sources could not compete with what Larry O'Brien disposed of, and Clements found such supposed neutrals as the candidate for governor, Wallace Barron, already bespoken.

Against the brute force of massed dollars, Humphrey scurried around the state in his bus with the banner: "Over the Hump with Humphrey." To his campaign aide Bob Barrie he sent cries for help: "I need people, not miles. I have traveled so many miles in these twisting West Virginia roads I feel like a corkscrew. But I am not getting to enough people [and] this is do or die for me." Barrie replied that a handful of volunteers had arrived from Minnesota and would go out where they could, but "most of the staff is on the bus."

Meanwhile, Kennedy was cannonading the mass audience on television (his telecasts alone cost more than Humphrey's total outlays) with nightly barrages against Humphrey as a "hatchet man" used by Lyndon Johnson and Stuart Symington in a "stop Kennedy" gangup. Yet there were lots of Protestants along those West Virginia highways, and five days before the election Humphrey was telling his brother Ralph: "I think I can win this one."

Ambition, drive, courage, conviction, a demonstrated capacity to speak the dreams and desires of his fellow citizens—these qualities had carried Hubert Humphrey a long way from the prescription counter in South Dakota. They had lifted him to mayor, sent him to Washington, and thrust him into the contest for the ultimate prize in American affairs. Putting misgivings aside, grasping the long-shot gamble, he had fought the good fight before the nation's eyes in Wisconsin. He had not won, but he had glimpsed the top; it was that peak that he kept in mind as he battled to the end in West Virginia.

On the Saturday before the voting, Humphrey was eating breakfast in Charleston, and preparing one more foray into the hills north of the capital. His aide Herb Waters appeared and informed him that the television station that had booked him for one last Sunday-night half hour was threatening to cancel unless paid cash in advance that day. "Pay it," roared Humphrey. But there was no money. Humphrey rolled his eyes expectantly toward Jim Rowe, sitting across the table. But Rowe, who had spent so much of his own money in the campaign that he was broke, said nothing. There was nowhere else to turn. "All right, I'll pay it myself," Humphrey snarled and pulled out his checkbook. He scribbled a check for $750. Muriel watched him sadly, for it was family money that had been earmarked for their daughter Nancy's wedding the following Saturday. With this, and another $750 somehow found later in the day, the last thirty minutes of the television campaign were bought.

It was the climactic moment not only in the 1960 presidential drive but in setting the course of his life. He had reached for the family money. From such an action there was no turning back. Humphrey had been bitten by the presidential bug, an infection, as Senator George Aiken once said, that only embalming fluid can cure.

The election was a rout. Humphrey had thought his empty-pocket sincerity would be more appealing to the impoverished miners and hungry farmers than the sleek, obvious wealth of John Kennedy. Far from it, the voters of West Virginia preferred the rich man for president. Kennedy won by 236,510 votes to Humphrey's 152,187, taking 60.8 percent of the ballots, a bigger margin than in Wisconsin. Humphrey was crushed.

As the returns flooded in, there was a knock at the door of Humphrey's Charleston hotel suite. In the rainy night, Robert Kennedy, author of the hardest blows in the campaign, had come to shake hands. The crowd parted like the Red Sea before Moses as Kennedy advanced toward the Humphreys, who stood transfixed at the other end of the room. He leaned over and kissed Muriel Humphrey. Her eyes flashed, and she trembled. Joe Rauh recalled later: "I swear to God she was going to hit him." But Humphrey, very serious and quiet, listened as Bobby said he wanted Humphrey to come over to Kennedy headquarters. Humphrey agreed. Still shaking, Mrs. Humphrey turned to Geri Joseph, the Democratic National Committeewoman. Geri Joseph said later: "We were three in the car, Muriel and Hubert and I. Muriel said, "I can't, I can't, I can't." Humphrey was very quiet with her. "All right," he said, "you go back with Geri." And we went back. It was the only time I ever saw her unable to do something for him. She was unable to pretend that all was well between Humphrey and the Kennedys at that point."

Humphrey offered no excuses but he simply announced, "I am no longer a candidate for the Democratic presdential nomination." He flew straight back to Washington, where his aide Jack Flynn informed him that Senate Leader Johnson had called up for action that very day a tax bill that Humphrey was supposed to manage. Taking the floor, Humphrey promptly lost himself in a four-hour running fight with Senator Mundt of South Dakota. Over lunch he told Geri Joseph: "I'm going to do whatever I can to make Jack Kennedy a good president." "You're unbelievable," she told him.

After West Virginia, Humphrey acknowledged to Eugenie Anderson: "It was foolish to go on." He was a candidate only for reelection to the Senate. At the altar of a Lutheran church in Minneapolis he gave away Nancy in marriage to Bruce Solomonson, whom they had met at Lake Waverly, the driver of Humphrey's car in much of his Wisconsin campaigning.

Arthur Goldberg and other labor men wanted to see Humphrey on the ticket with Kennedy. On June 9, Kennedy told Joe Rauh, "It will be Hubert or another midwestern liberal." In late June, Kennedy visited Humphrey's office and brought up the subject. "You might be the strongest person I could add for second place on the ticket—I'm weak with the Jews, and you're strong; I'm weak with labor, and you're strong; I'm weak with the farmers, and you're strong. What would you think?" It was not an offer, but Humphrey did what he had done in 1948. He sought Mrs. Roosevelt's advice. He sent his ADA friend Marvin Rosenberg, who returned with word that he would have to make up his own mind. Humphrey said later, "I never could see why Kennedy, after having defeated me on the issues in which I was involved— and he was running as a liberal by then—why he really needed another Northern liberal." Publicly he said at the time that he could not risk another defeat offering himself for vice president after Wisconsin and West Virginia. He said: "I do not want it. I wouldn't run for it—I did that once. I would not reject it. My candidate is Orville Freeman." The Kennedys had already begun to court Freeman in hopes of picking up the 67½ delegates pledged to Humphrey.

When Humphrey went to Los Angeles, it was still not quite certain that Kennedy had the votes to win. Lyndon Johnson had amassed some four hundred delegates from the South and West, and Californians especially were avid for Adlai Stevenson to stand again. Tempted by the vice presidency, Freeman was ready to swing to Kennedy. Of others around Humphrey, Joe Rauh had already switched to Kennedy and was working feverishly to head off any chance that Lyndon Johnson might get the second spot. It was Rowe, seconded by the Minneapolis corporation lawyer Pat O'Connor, who brought Humphrey together with Johnson as the convention met. The upshot was that Humphrey came out for Adlai Stevenson, thereby joining the "stop Kennedy" movement. Asked to make the nomination speech, Humphrey declined. Instead he suggested that Eugene McCarthy be asked. Delivering the most eloquent speech of the convention, McCarthy gained his first recognition as a political figure who could compel national attention. Meanwhile, as Humphrey continued to hold back Minnesota's votes, Kennedy not only asked Freeman to place his name in nomination but sent word that he was the midwestern liberal he wanted most for a running mate.

As things turned out, Kennedy took the nomination on the first ballot. No one knows whether Kennedy really expected that Lyndon Johnson, the runnerup, would then reject his tender of second place on the ticket. To the general surprise, Johnson accepted—and by that sudden turn, Freeman missed his chance to become president of the United States. Humphrey had already rejected the chance but even in defeat had given Minnesota's governor and its junior senator a chance at the national stage.

Back in the home state the Republicans put up the mayor of Minneapolis, a lawyer named P. Kenneth Peterson, against Humphrey. As an old debating partner from University of Minnesota times, Peterson was able to recall how a visiting Australian opponent once silenced Humphrey by saying: "If you'd put less fire in your speech and more speech on the fire, we'd be able to resolve our argument." Chasing the resilient campaigner from Kolacky day in Springfield to Paul Bunyan day in Bemidji to Sauerkraut day in New Ulm, Peterson finally caught up with him for a debate at Rochester. Primed with Humphrey's hottest primary blasts at Kennedy, his old partner demanded to know how the senator could now sing Kennedy's praises. Humphrey was not to be silenced again. "Well, that's politics," he huffed. "Politics is the art of the possible." Humphrey, whose sense of the possible seemed infallible when talking to the home folks, trounced Peterson by 230,000 votes and flew to Washington to help Kennedy organise the administration he had hoped to lead.

21

Master
Legislator

Humphrey's smashing reelection by a quarter of a million votes lifted him out of the ashes and into the most satisfying and productive period of his life. In his first twelve years in Washington, he had been a pioneer, proposing and promising. Now, as he saw it, the liberal hour had struck, and he had risen to the station from which he could seize the chance to put across his ideas. Compelled by his failure in the 1960 primary to accept the role of senator, he showed himself to be the most creative of legislators, enacting into law measures he had first put forward years before. He was zesty, jolly, driving, ranging into almost every field of human activity. To many around him he seemed a figure larger than life. He could discern and discuss the nation's needs on the grandest scale—and at the same time throw himself into the minutest details and cloakroom swaps to inch his bills toward passage. Denied the presidency, he proved himself the premier lawmaker of his generation.

The new Washington scene gave Humphrey a chance to work with the first Democratic president since Truman. Kennedy sought his advice on major appointments: on Orville Freeman as secretary of agriculture, on Walter Heller of Minnesota as the new chairman of the council of economic advisers, on George McGovern as Food for Peace administrator. It was Humphrey's insistence that McGovern's be a White House appointment that gave him

White House stationery and every chance to make a name so that he could run and win a Senate seat in 1962. In December, Humphrey was in New York urging Adlai Stevenson to accept Kennedy's offer of the ambassadorship to the United Nations when Vice President-elect Johnson telephoned him. "They want me to be majority whip," he reported. Stevenson counseled against it, arguing that Humphrey would have more independence for his political future if he were not locked into wheelhorse chores. Humphrey replied: "I can't tell you one thing and tell myself another." Accepting, he told a reporter: "I have made mudpies and dreamhouses long enough—now I want to do something." Rowe sent him mocking congratulations: "I am sad when I think how disciplined the senior senator from Minnesota must be. Sitting all day on the floor, knowing the ins and outs of all those bills, indulging in no brilliant oratorical flights because he is spending all his time trying to get other Senators to be brief—is this a way of life for Hubert Humphrey? Still, he is a young man. If my counting is correct, he will be 57 in '68. . . ."

Taking the job, Humphrey got Mike Mansfield, the new majority leader, to put him on the influential Appropriations Committee and proceeded to make himself indispensable to the new administration. Humphrey liked to say that his losing primary battles in Wisconsin and West Virginia had at least committed John Kennedy to positions that guaranteed a liberal presidency. Actually, the Kennedy administration came into office by only the narrowest electoral margin, and even though the Democrats held a big edge in Congress, the president felt he had to tread warily.

This was where Humphrey came in. He was willing to work hard for the limited measures Kennedy felt constrained to put forward—expansions of existing programs for minimum wage, housing subsidies and unemployment benefits, the kind of marginal stuff Congress had occupied itself with in the unproductive Eisenhower years. Operating out of a small whip's office on the third floor of the Capitol, just above the Senate chamber, Humphrey outhustled, outtalked, and outworked all other presidential helpers, including his chief, Majority Leader Mansfield. He wrote his brother Ralph: "I am in the thick of things. Every Tuesday morning at 8:45 I am over at the White House for a good breakfast—about eight of us [congressional leaders]. I find the President wants to consult with me." Since Humphrey was notorious for his open, outgoing ways, however, both Rayburn and Johnson as old hands at these affairs felt compelled to warn him about "tattling." They could have saved their breath. Humphrey proved so intent on buttonholing the president after the sessions to talk further about some matter he was pushing that he never went near the press room. Somewhat later, Kennedy actually requested him to go out and brief the newsmen "because you can explain things better than the others."

Humphrey was effective because he was patient, good-humored, and—important clue to the man—ready to work day and night at the job. He showed real flair for the tactical details of floor leadership—the nose-counting, the resorts to procedure, the stalling for time, the switching of votes, the timing of amendments—and of course he was nimble in debate. With his ability to be pleasant despite differences, it was the rare senator who did not count him as a friend. He knew these men better than he knew the members of his own family, he said later. Like Johnson before him he studied their idiosyncrasies, but unlike Johnson he twisted no arms. Southern or Northern, he carried their requests to the president. With his ringing laugh, his sports-page chatter, his cheery questions about wives and grandchildren, there could be no lash in Humphrey's whip. It was impossible not to like Hubert. Such were his powers of persuasion that once, when the president gave him a list of a dozen doubtful senators whose votes he wanted on a pending bill, Humphrey won eleven of the twelve votes the following day. He was flexible. When his friend Paul Douglas balked at a compromise way of financing the Area Development bill he was managing, Humphrey said: "I'll bargain for you—I'm not so pure," and made concessions that won conservative assent to the measure. "I don't have to prove I'm a liberal. I don't have to tell people I didn't sell out," he said when some of his ADA friends grumbled at his help in getting some right-wing Kennedy appointees cleared through the Senate.

As things turned out, it was Humphrey who provided the best ideas for what became the administration's New Frontier program. These were legislative proposals that he had pioneered during his earlier years. Many of them had once been condemned as visionary and even radical. Now, because they fit the philosophy that had gained the president his majority over Nixon, Humphrey—using his entree at the White House to lobby for them and then employing his key position on Capitol Hill to push them through the Senate—built an imposing record of achievement in his years as whip.

A good example was the Peace Corps. Humphrey first proposed the idea in 1957, at which time it was dismissed as silly and unworkable. But the young president, seizing this measure to dramatize his inaugural proclamation that "a new generation" had come to power in Washington, put all the prestige of the White House behind it, and with Humphrey wielding his feathery whip, it won swift enactment. Before the year was out, he had the satisfaction of seeing thousands of eager volunteers go out to help push Third World projects in villages all around the globe.

Having proposed a Youth Conservation Corps during the Eisenhower years, Humphrey saw the program he had conceived incorporated into an anti-poverty measure as the Job Corps for training the unprivileged young to make the difficult transition from ghetto streetcorners to a place in the world of work. In the Kennedy years, Humphrey's program for using farm surpluses as foreign aid—entitled "Food for Peace" and placed in the White House under his protégé George McGovern—became a leading part of American policy in the Third World. One of the fundamental advances in safeguarding the American workplace, first proposed by Humphrey in 1951, was made law as the Occupational Safety and Health Act at this time. A Humphrey bill, introduced as S–1 in January 1961, first outlined the mobilizing of resources for what Kennedy and Johnson came to call the War on Poverty. The Medicare bill he introduced in 1949 now stood high on administration priority lists.

The Kennedy years carried the cold war to new ground, and here too Humphrey's trailblazing work of the 1950s paid off. After the Cuban invasion fiasco, the Soviets stepped up pressure on Berlin. As a top Foreign Relations Committee member, Humphrey made a quick trip to Europe; his thirty-two-page memorandum, couriered to the president at Hyannis Port, contained two major recommendations. Kennedy accepted the first, which was to go on television and assure his fellow citizens, the Europeans, and the Russians that America would never go back on its commitments in Berlin. In a speech from the White House the president called for an arms buildup to counter the Communist threat. Kennedy then invited Humphrey to the White House to discuss his second recommendation.

The two men stripped and swam in the White House pool—"skinny-dipped" was how the senator described it. Afterward as they lunched at a little table set up in the Rose Garden, Humphrey put his case: It was essential to prepare, "at this very hour when we build our armed strength," for East-West disarmament. Humphrey had a bill ready to drop into the hopper: to set up within the government a separate Disarmament agency to develop plans for curbing the arms race. But, he said, it stood not a prayer of success without the president's all-out support. Go ahead, the president replied; no doubt the Defense Department would weigh in with qualifications, but the administration would back Humphrey's bill. Out of this pool-and-garden conference came the Arms Control and Disarmament Agency, an independent agency housed in the State Department, after a hot fight and a close vote, to carry out the tasks defined over the years by Humphrey's Disarmament subcommittee. William C. Foster, a Republican investment banker was named chief, and Humphrey's former staffer, Betty Goetz, became a principal aide. The search for agreement with Russians went forward with new vigor and authority.

In 1962 the Cuban missile crisis cleared the air. And as the Humphrey subcommittee had shown, a ban on nuclear tests was the place to begin. American opinion had come a long way since 1955, when the subcommittee held its first hearings and a Gallup poll showed no more than 20 percent of the public in favor of a test ban. Most recently, as part of a $100 million expenditure on seismic research, the agency had verified the subcommittee's finding that underground bomb tests could be monitored.

Humphrey took the lead in the Senate. When Richard Russell of the Armed Services Committee called the agency's work a giveaway to the Russians, Humphrey abandoned his Senate post to fly to Geneva and get from the negotiators first-hand information countering the charge. Back in his whip's office he persuaded Thomas Dodd of Connecticut, another Armed Services Committee member, to co-sponsor a resolution affirming readiness to accept a pact banning tests in the atmosphere and oceans. Thirty-four senators joined them. With this kind of support, President Kennedy called in a speech at the American University for a test ban. A few days later, Premier Khrushchev offered to settle for the limited ban described in Humphrey's resolution. Kennedy dispatched a high-powered negotiating team to Moscow, and the deal was struck.

"Limited" was the word for the agreement—some even said it was just a warrant for more and bigger underground testing. Be that as it may, the Treaty of Moscow was the first disarmament pact between the United States and Russia since World War II, and the consequences were enormous. First of all, the Chinese Communist party promptly, fiercely, and openly denounced the treaty as a Soviet sellout. The Russians snarled back in kind, and the split between Peking and Moscow became official and irrevocable. All at once the West realized that it no longer confronted a monolithic East. Thus, abruptly and unexpectedly, the treaty for which Humphrey had labored so long ended the cold war. The age of détente began.

At Humphrey's suggestion the senatorial delegation to the Moscow ceremonies of which he was a member was bipartisan—a coalition of Republicans and Democrats that, under his whip, ratified the agreement, 80-to-17. In a final ceremony in Washington on October 7, 1963, President Kennedy signed for the United States, saying: "Hubert, this is yours. I hope it works." It did, and it didn't. Afterward the two superpowers signed nonproliferation, outer-space, and strategic-arms limitation treaties, and moved out of the bipolar confrontation in which they had been frozen since Truman-Stalin times. But once the United States understood that the East was split, it was emboldened to do what it might not otherwise have hazarded after the Korean War; it involved itself in outright war on China's other flank. For Southeast Asia, for America, and for Hubert Humphrey himself, Vietnam was a tragic, unintended consequence of the Treaty of Moscow.

NOT all of Humphrey's creative ideas found acceptance in these years. As a senior member of the Senate Foreign Relations committee he was consulted, but never drawn into, the international crises that overtook the Kennedy administration. After the Bay of Pigs disaster ("Oh, how we botched it—and for no reason," he wrote a friend), Humphrey took off on a trip around Latin America. Not content with official visits, he sought out opposition leaders and took copious notes wherever he went. He returned convinced that only infusions of economic aid could counter Castro's appeal to the rising expectations of the masses; perceiving the Export Import Bank's loans as chiefly a crutch for U. S. entrepreneurs, he recommended instead that aid granted directly to the *latinos* receive Washington's highest priority. To vitalize the administration's Alliance for Progress he urged that the region's food and fiber producers band together in farm cooperatives similar to the Farmers Union groups in his own Middle West. As Humphrey saw it, agriculture was one of the world's two or three greatest problems—a poser for every nation capitalist or Communist and for those of the Third World most of all. His idea of marketing cooperatives especially appealed to the small growers allied with the Social Democrats and Christian Democrats in places like Venezuela and Chile. But the owners of the vast ranches and plantations that dominated the socially polarized continent scorned such notions, and when President Johnson came to power the consensus he immediately sought at home forced a reorientation of goals. The result was ever greater assistance to U. S. corporations staking out markets in Latin America and virtual abandonment of Alliance for Progress programs.

In June 1963, Humphrey's old friend Walter Reuther invited him to join a meeting of European socialist leaders. The Humphrey-Reuther relationship was a curious one. Each time Humphrey ran for president, Reuther seemed to back somebody else. Yet the two men were rather close. Reuther often asked Humphrey to sit in on UAW executive board meetings. Son of an immigrant German Social Democrat, Reuther in his youth had worked for a year in a Soviet automobile plant; in the Detroit of the 1930s he led bloody strikes; and later he won the presidency of his union by turning on its Communists about the same time Humphrey was purging the DFL party of its far-leftists in Minnesota. Together they had helped found the ADA as a non-Communist outpost on the left, and on a wider front they had fought, Humphrey in the Senate and Reuther in the international labor movement, for a democratic left as a cold war alternative to Communism.

The meeting—held on a July weekend in 1963 at Harpsund, the summer residence of the Swedish prime minister—was nothing less than a Socialist summit. Present were the prime ministers of Britain, Sweden, Denmark, and Norway—and Willy Brandt, the future chancellor of Germany. "You and I will be the only U. S. representatives," wrote Reuther. Humphrey brought along his Minneapolis friend Dwayne Andreas, who was acceptable to the socialists as a top official of one of America's biggest farm cooperatives. Strictly private, the meeting was simply for the informal exchange of ideas— but what ideas! Here were the top statesmen of Europe, social planners by conviction and experience, men who could rear back and sight grand designs in public affairs. In this company, Humphrey, who had never governed anything bigger than Minneapolis, was surprisingly at home. No Socialist, he was nevertheless a big-picture man.

Humphrey's own scribbled notes indicate that both he and the Europeans settled on unemployment, agriculture, and the international balance of payments as the main problems. Invited to respond as the senior legislator present, Humphrey remarked offhandedly that technology had so transformed agriculture that "we stand on the eve of the possibility of eliminating hunger from the world. But our economic and fiscal people are so puzzled by this development that efforts to make the miracle available to the world are endangered." Unfortunately, he went on, the cultural consensus lags far behind the technology, and the paradox—"Empty stomach, full head; full stomach, empty head"—was often true for American voters. It had been Eisenhower's style, he said, to call in the representatives of the well-off nine-tenths and say: "What are you complaining about?" while ignoring the unemployed one-tenth and thereby avoiding progressive action. And Humphrey went on to state that it would be necessary to create eighty-thousand new jobs every week for the next ten years in America—in other words, adding an enterprise as big as General Motors every five weeks—just to absorb the additions to the labor force.

Impressed, Brandt responded that to deal with unemployment it would probably be necessary to keep the young in school for a year or two more training, and at the same time channel pensions to the elderly so that their purchasing power would not be lost when they stepped aside to make room for all the thousands joing the work force. Even with such programs, Humphrey agreed, a massive investment would be required just to stay even.

Britain's Harold Wilson arrived the second day, and Andreas noted that "though Wilson had nothing like the political instincts of Hubert, they got on to an easy conversational basis almost instantly." By this time, Humphrey had drunk, stayed up late, and bathed in the Baltic with the other ministers, and it was hard to tell Democrat from Socialist. According to Andreas, the group had agreed that the grand strategy called for using the idle people and plant capacity in the developed economies of Europe and America to produce for the unmet needs of the less-developed lands elsewhere. If that could be programmed, peace and prosperity could be kept in sight for the rest of the century. Onetime Oxford don in economics, Harold Wilson spun out the solution: a new international institution, set up of course in London, which all the strong nations would support and which would generate funds, utterly without gold backing or, as the dazzled Andreas reported, "out of thin air." Andreas wrote: "It could create an international deficit, so to speak, in which we would all owe ourselves and which would therefore just become a large international journal-entry system. It would create large quantities of credit without creating advertised, conspicuous national deficits, and therefore could be used to create enormous demand from the underdeveloped countries which could be channeled in such a way as to employ the unemployed in the devel-oped countries." Humphrey listened, entranced. Unemployment, agricul-ture, the international balance-of-payments—all the great problems of the twentieth-century economies—seemed on that summit afternoon in Sweden to be within grasp. "Humphrey was like a sponge," Andreas said. "He was always learning more—and weeks later he could tell you in detail what Har-old Wilson said at Harpsund." The following year, Humphrey was asked again, and wanted to go. But that was an election year, and Lyndon Johnson was thinking of running him for vice president in the fall. Humphrey thought he had better mention the invitation to Johnson. A socialist summit? "My God, no," roared Johnson, appalled to hear that Humphrey had gone the year before.

OF COURSE when Humphrey got to be whip, he thought his chance had come at last to put through the civil rights reform he had sought for so long. But John Kennedy felt his freedom of action was limited because he had been elected by such a slim margin. He was reluctant to move on an issue so explosive. At least twice at his leadership breakfasts he rebuked Humphrey, for whose efforts on most matters he was so grateful, for pressing him toward action on the civil rights front. At one point, Humphrey told him: "The leadership for civil rights either has to take place in the White House or it is going to take place in the streets."

Neither the president nor the Congress could long ignore the turmoil of the 1960s. Claiming a birthright long denied, the blacks of America thronged out of the Southern backlands into Northern cities and, throughout the South, staged lunch-counter sit-ins and freedom marches. These events, culminating in the confrontations led by Martin Luther King, Jr., at Birmingham in 1963, when police dogs, cattle prods, and firehoses were turned on black protesters before the eyes of millions watching on television, roused the conscience of America. Shortly afterward, President Kennedy proclaimed in a nationwide broadcast: "We are confronted primarily with a moral issue—as old as the scriptures and as clear as the American Constitution. . . . The time has come for this nation to fulfill its promises . . . for Negroes."

That summer white students from northern colleges and seminaries went South to help rebuild black churches and houses that had been burned by segregationists. Schoolteachers and university professors organized and trained civil rights workers. In an outpouring such as had never been seen before in the nation's history, two hundred thousand Americans—blacks and whites together—marched to Washington's Lincoln Memorial to hear Martin Luther King, Jr.,'s lyric refrain: "I Have a Dream . . ."

The legislation Kennedy sent to Congress on June 19 was a comprehensive bill to remove legal barriers, principally in the South, that were either unconstitutional or contrary to the majority views of the country. First and foremost were the rights of equal access to buses, restaurants, and other facilities. But the bill in the House also called for the removal of discrimination in employment, in schooling, and in access to federal funds, and it empowered the attorney general to aid citizens denied their right to vote.

The measure was before the House when Kennedy was assassinated. But Lyndon Johnson, the Texan who now moved up to the leadership of the nation, proclaimed that his mission was to continue the work that Kennedy had begun. With Johnson's support the House passed the bill in early 1964, and the issue was put squarely to the Senate, up to this time the citadel of Southern white supremacists. Johnson and majority leader Mansfield assigned the job of pushing the bill through to Humphrey, who, as Mansfield explained, had "been one of the nation's leading advocates of federal action in the field of civil rights since the 1948 convention." Johnson said: "This is your test. But I predict it will not go through." Humphrey accepted the challenge.

Despite his vaunted prowess, Johnson had never in all his years of Senate leadership put through legislation remotely so consequential. Controversial as it was, moreover, the bill could not pass unless Humphrey mustered the two-thirds majority necessary to impose cloture beforehand. And since 18 of the 59 Democrats were bitter-end Southern segregationists, he could not hope to put together the 67 votes needed unless he could co-opt the Republican opposition, most of whom had never before voted for cloture. Nor, as he knew from personal experience, could he expect to assemble that many votes in the showdown unless he could hold the notoriously fractious liberal Democrats together longer than the drawn-out filibusters the Southerners would assuredly mount.

The task called for minute organization, patience, courage—and tact. Humphrey said later: "I realized it would test me in every way. I had to make up my mind as to my mental attitude and how I would conduct myself. I can recall literally talking to myself, conditioning myself to the long ordeal. I truly did think through what I wanted to do and how I wanted to act." Cancelling his out-of-town engagements, Humphrey met first with Thomas Kuchel of California, assigned by Minority Leader Everett Dirksen as the Republican go-between for the bill. He then appointed seven "title captains," one for each of the bill's seven titles; they included Warren Magnuson of Washington, who managed the all-important public accommodations section, and Joseph Clark of Pennsylvania, who took responsibility for the extremely touchy Title Seven governing equal opportunity in employment. Later, Humphrey added other captains, several of them Republicans. Other senators were assigned to be on the floor watching for Southern tricks when Humphrey was off holding meetings in his office. Since the filibusterers kept demanding quorum calls, Humphrey set up a duty roster that required thirty-five Democrats and fifteen Republicans to be in Washington ready to rush to the floor at any time. Before every day's session, Humphrey held "skull-practice" meetings, and his staff got out a newsletter capsuling and analyzing each day's doings.

Russell of Georgia led the filibuster, deploying his eighteen Southern debaters on the floor six at a time in his battle-tested three-platoon system. Russell figured that he had only to keep the talk going until the civil-rights liberals fell to fighting, as they always did, among themselves; and that their backers, organized into the so-called Leadership Conference (of civil-rights proponents), could be counted on to pressure senators, especially the pivotal Republican Leader Dirksen, to the point of alienation. And with his eighteen Southern Democrats plus the Republican newcomer John Tower of Texas, Russell needed only twelve more votes from the ranks of the conservative

Republicans and border-state Democrats to thwart Humphrey's drive.

President Johnson pointedly announced: "I am in favor of [the bill] passing the Senate in its present form." But Humphrey was in no hurry to bring the issue to a test because his count showed at least thirteen senators "reasonably against the bill." So he encouraged his forces to debate the Southerners section by section, and kept on friendly personal terms with everybody. One afternoon Willis Robertson of Virginia walked up to Humphrey at his front-row desk and proffered a small Confederate flag for his lapel. Humphrey accepted it. Compliments were exchanged on the floor, then they retired to the whip's office for some early-evening refreshment.

From the start, Humphrey cultivated Dirksen, praising him on television, predicting he would place country above party and support a good rights bill. Dirksen began by saying he was opposed to compulsory enforcement for access to public accommodations and wanted no part of equal opportunity in employment. Humphrey, ignoring Johnson's advice, did not discourage Dirksen's plans for amendments. He said later: "I'd ask him, 'Well, Dirk, when do you think we ought to meet and talk over some of your amendments?' And he'd say, 'Well, give us a couple of more days. It isn't time yet.' " Midway through the second month, Dirksen, counseling: "If you don't get a whole loaf of bread, you get what you want," dropped in a bunch of amendments. The most important seemed to gut the equal employment opportunity part of the bill. Joe Rauh and his Leadership Conference people hit the roof. But Humphrey counseled patience. Wait, he said, to see the full complement of Dirksen's demands, not only on equal opportunity in employment but on public accommodation and the rest of the bill.

Russell, waiting for the liberals to crack, figured he could reject compromise. Toward the end of April he threw his forces behind an amendment that would have extended the right of trial by jury to persons brought to federal court for failure to enforce the proposed regulations and accused of criminal contempt. Humphrey, his eye on Republican votes, brought out a substitute amendment containing a limited jury-trial formula—and got Mansfield and Dirksen to sponsor it. But after the Southern amendment lost narrowly, Russell disdained a vote on the Mansfield-Dirksen substitute. From that moment, Humphrey's fortunes gained. First of all, Russell's stalling angered Mansfield, who thought he had Russell's agreement for a vote and was thenceforth almost as eager as Humphrey to throttle the filibuster. Secondly, Dirksen, also showing impatience at the lack of floor action, let Humphrey know that he was ready to negotiate for a civil rights bill. That brought into sight the chance of twenty-six Republican votes—enough to lift the bill's backing to the necessary two-thirds

Angelic choirs could not have sounded sweeter than Humphrey as he sang the praises of the senator from Illinois. To the press it was "statesman," "patriot," "moral idealist." To Dirksen it was: "What would you like?" and "How can I help?" His newsletter saluted Dirksen as the shining leader marching with the forces for civil rights. "I would have kissed Dirksen's ass on the Capitol steps," Humphrey remarked later.

At Humphrey's insistence the negotiations took place in Dirksen's office. With half a dozen senators and Attorney General Robert Kennedy hanging on his every word, the Republican chieftain began by proposing to shift the burden of enforcing equal employment opportunity from the proposed federal commission to the individual complainant. He also said that state employment agencies should, if they wanted, take over jurisdiction. Though shocked, Humphrey thought that the wily Illinoisan was still probing, and left it to his Republican captains Kuchel, Javits, and Case to tone him down. But to add to the liberal dismay, Bourke Hickenlooper of Iowa, supposedly one of Dirksen's Republican votes, listened for a while and then stalked out. When the Leadership Conference heard what had been said, they were appalled. Eyes flashing, Clarence Mitchell of the NAACP called for a full-scale attack on Dirksen. Humphrey broke the tension with: "Clarence, you are three feet off your chair."

Day after day the talks went on in Dirksen's office, not so much between the senators, who dashed in and out on their way to the floor, as between their aides and Attorney General Kennedy's men, Nick Katzenbach and Burke Marshall. Dirksen gave ground, and in return Humphrey and the others agreed to treat the package under negotiation as a substitute for the House-passed bill. Outside in the corridor, Rauh and his group sent in anxious messages. On the tenth day of palaver it was one of Dirksen's aides who finally found the middle ground: the federal government should have authority to initiate action against discrimination only where there existed "a pattern or practice of massive resistance in any geographical area." The "pattern or practice" formula broke the impasse. Humphrey saw that he had a strong bill, because under such terms the federal sanction would apply in the South, where they were most needed. And he could concede jurisdiction to state employment agencies in places like Illinois, which turned out to be Dirksen's concern.

At this point, with things still very much up in the air, Humphrey went before his old supporters at the 17th convention banquet of the ADA and said: "Not too many Americans walked with us in 1948, but year after year the marching throng has grown. In the next few weeks the strongest civil rights bill ever enacted in our history will become the law of the land. It is not saying too much, I believe, to say that it will amount to a second Emancipation Proclamation. As it is enforced, it will free our Negro fellow-citizens of the shackles that have bound them for generations. As it is enforced, it will free us of the white majority of shackles of our own—for no man can be fully free while his fellow man lies in chains."

The very next day, Humphrey and others met in Dirksen's office for the conclusive negotiations. Humphrey opened by saying that agreement hinged on Dirksen's willingness to accept cloture on the whole package and not just on its individual parts. By the end of the day's haggling, Dirksen conceded

Humphrey's main point. But during the bargaining over the equal opportunity section, Joe Clark, manager for that part of the bill, walked out—a signal to Dirksen that the civil rights activists would bolt if he asked too high a price. By mid-afternoon with most points resolved, Humphrey emerged to say that the bill was on its way: "I feel like someone going off a ski jump the first time and landing on his feet."

In the briefing that followed, Humphrey made the most of the "patterns or practice" breakthrough and hailed Dirksen's leadership in moving the bill toward passage. When Katzenbach expressed concern to his chief Robert Kennedy that Humphrey might be talking too much, Kennedy grinned and said: "Don't knock his talking like that. After all, that's what made Jack president." Some Democrats grumbled to Humphrey that he was giving Dirksen too much credit. On his side, Dirksen kept getting complaints from his restive midwest Republicans that his amendments did not go far enough "to meet the real evils of the bill." Humphrey, his nosecount changing almost daily, decided to make all possible marginal accommodations that individual senators asked for.

On March 26, sixty-one days after the Senate began debate, Dirksen introduced his omnibus amendment incorporating all the changes threshed out in his office. Humphrey praised the package as "stronger than the House bill." Russell denounced it as aimed only at the South. "It puts Charles Sumner, Thad Stevens, and Ben Wade to shame."

By Humphrey's count he still needed twelve more firm votes for cloture. To win, his forces would have to bring the rebellious Hickenlooper and several other holdout members of Dirksen's midwestern bloc to their side. Since these senators were accounted invulnerable to labor pressure, the Leadership Conference activists mobilized their constituent religious forces. Home-state bishops showered the midwesterners with telegrams, ministerial groups placed conference calls to their Capitol Hill offices, and thousands of churchgoers sent them letters. The Commission on Religion and Race of the National Council of Churches held daily vigils in a church a block from the Capitol, and seminarians prayed night and day at the Lincoln Memorial. Humphrey, who met a hundred times with churchmen during the fight, brought some right on to the Senate floor in the last days.

Finally, at the end of May, Mansfield rose to say he thought the Senate had talked long enough. Then he and Dirksen jointly announced that they would petition for cloture two days hence, the vote to follow three days later. Both Russell and Hickenlooper now said they wanted to bring forward amendments. Mansfield replied with a grin: "Beginning tomorrow a number of senators have indicated their desire to speak on the Dirksen substitute." In other words, the pro-civil rights forces were mounting their own filibuster to prevent any votes before the cloture showdown.

Hickenlooper, always jealous of Dirksen's leadership, had been sniping at the Humphrey-Dirksen package. With Mansfield's deadline impending, Hickenlooper pressed for unanimous consent for a vote on three Republican amendments. This was the opening for Humphrey. He had learned from one of Hickenlooper's fellow-holdouts that if their amendments came to a vote, most of the group would vote for cloture whether the amendments carried or not. On cue, Mansfield agreed to the votes; Humphrey, going further, pledged that any amendment adopted could be accepted by the leadership. When Russell complained that he had been accorded no such concession, Humphrey cracked: "Well, Dick, you haven't any votes to give us for cloture, and these fellows do." Outmaneuvered, Russell had to leave the field to the Hickenlooper group, which had privately assured Humphrey: "All we want is the chance to show that Dirksen wasn't the only Republican on the floor."

In the final hours one of the rebel Republicans' three amendments carried, a proviso that gave anyone charged with federal contempt under the bill the right to a jury trial. With that, the way was cleared for the vote. Humphrey had not felt it necessary to ask President Johnson's personal intervention with any senator. But they were in close touch. On the last night, with a strong assist from the Leadership Conference activists, Humphrey worked hard to nail down the votes of three teetering Democrats. Then he telephoned Johnson that he thought he had the votes for cloture. The president was still doubtful.

On June 9, the seventy-fifth day of the fight, the Senate assembled in theatrical solemnity. Consistent to the end, Humphrey left it to Dirksen to deliver the closing oration. The words of Victor Hugo rang forth in the organ tones of the Republican chieftain: "Stronger than an army is an idea whose time has come." Then in almost total silence the clerk called the roll. A full hundred responded. California's Clair Engle, sick of cancer and wheeled in on a stretcher, cast his vote by pointing to his eye. Hickenlooper's holdouts, and the three last Democratic waverers all crashed through for Humphrey. The President Pro Tem, old Carl Hayden of Arizona, cooperated by staying in the cloakroom until the two-thirds were cast; only then did he vote against the resolution. Lee Metcalf of Montana, presiding in his place, announced the result, 71-to-29—four votes to spare.

After the cloture triumph, Humphrey had to get the bill itself to passage. As he fought off the Southerners' last assaults, he received dread news: his son Robert, seventeen, faced surgery at the Mayo Clinic for cancer of the lymph glands. Humphrey stayed at his post. After the operation, Bob called his father. He said: "Dad, I guess I've had it." Humphrey protested: "Don't be silly, I've talked to the doctors and everything is going to be all right." Then he hung up the phone and cried. After the final vote on June 19, he flew to the bedside in Minnesota. Bob made a complete recovery.

In his memoirs, Humphrey called passage of the Civil Rights Act by the Senate "my greatest achievement." He had every right to make the claim. It capped all his other legislative accomplishments. He led his liberals with exemplary firmness. Against Lyndon Johnson's counsel, he accepted amendments. He outplayed the formidable Richard Russell at his own waiting game. To Dirksen he traded away glory for substance and then, by astute trading and persuasiveness, won over those Republicans Dirksen could not command. It was a superb performance.

Shortly after passage of the act, Humphrey wrote Walter Lippmann: "The Civil Rights Act is without doubt the most significant piece of legislation of this century." Humphrey's natural exuberance often inflated his sense of history. But he was right again. The act was the high-water maker of the Second Reconstruction, the most substantial measure addressed in our time to problems so profound that civil war itself could not resolve them.

If the real test of a law is its acceptance, the Civil Rights Act of 1964 did its job: it changed American behavior. Less than two decades later its prescriptions were taken for granted, the new patterns it set were woven into the mores of the country. So thoroughly were the sanctions against unequal access to public accommodations—the main point of the law—accepted, in the South and elsewhere, that children who had grown to junior high school age in the second decade thereafter found it hard to believe that once things were different.

As much could not be said for equal opportunity in employment, though there, too, important progress had been made. As for the cutoff of federal funds to contractors and any institutions receiving Washington's grants, this sanction became the accepted law and worked mightily to equalize opportunity. By the Civil Rights Act of 1965, the voting rights to which the 1964 law gave only incomplete protection gained conclusive acceptance throughout the South. Thereafter the fight for rights spread to such fields as schooling and housing, where defeats continued to outnumber victories. But Jim Crow was dead, slain by the Civil Rights Act of 1964. Not even the child labor amendment, perhaps not the Social Security Act itself, wrought greater change in the conduct of American social life.

22

Private Moments of a Public Man

Humphrey's legislative success called attention to his personal qualities. He was at once so buoyant, so open, and so naïvely and even guilelessly amiable that others were charmed. He couldn't be stopped from joining every lodge, sending out fifteen thousand Christmas cards every year, and pausing to talk with any adult or child who came up to him. Warm and caring, he genuinely liked people. "He never crossed anybody," said his aide and successor as mayor, Arthur Naftalin. And it is almost impossible to exaggerate the number of people who considered him their friend.

Among those drawn into his many campaigns he built up a large and affectionate following. His friend Judge Miles Lord said later: "Being around him was to be touched like the guy in the Bible who climbed the tree to see Jesus: their eyes met and his life was changed." Yet few of those who left what they were doing and followed Humphrey drew really close to him. The intimate friends of this most gregarious man were few, and perhaps only his wife was privy to his inmost thoughts. Max Kampelman, his legislative counsel in his first Senate years, later shared confidences as Humphrey's lawyer. Of all the senator's staff, David Gartner, who joined his office to help with constituents' letters in 1961 and later performed every sort of personal chore, alone remained at his side to the very end. There can be no pretending that all Humphrey's relationships rested solely or even largely on the affection and loyalty he inspired. He was too trusting. As he rose in power and prominence there were those who used him.

One who did not was Fred Gates, the Lebanese penny-arcade operator whom Humphrey asked to hold the Bible when he was sworn in as vice president. Gates, who could scarcely write a grammatical sentence, would drop everything to run Humphrey's Minnesota errands, straighten out his insurance, drive him to meetings, watch over his children, lend him small sums. For years, Humphrey talked to Gates once and sometimes twice a day. Gates could and did walk in on the senator at any time, often to warn in blistering terms against phonies and sharpies taking advantage of the senator's friendly ways. In time, Gates's enterprise expanded into a prosperous vending machine business, and Humphrey helped him get some small concessions at the Minneapolis airport. He also tried without success to land Gates a lucrative beer distributorship in the Twin Cities.

Some spoke of Fred Gates as Humphrey's "bagman." This was true, but only to the extent that Gates knew how to wrestle up contributions for the always underfunded candidate—and watched over their subsequent expenditure with fierce vigilance. If Humphrey learned how to use the telephone like few other officeholders, it was Gates who taught him. Working side by side in a Minneapolis hotel room, each at a telephone, they were a marvel to behold. In front of Gates was his list of prospective donors. He would start the calling, and as fast as the party came on the line he would slip Humphrey a note with the man's first name and perhaps those of his wife and children, hand the telephone to the candidate, and start working the next prospect on the list. While Gates was holding a succession of donors in conversation, the candidate was saying: "This is Hubert. Fred is sitting right here with me. I want you to know. . . . I saw your wife Geraldine . . . and how are my friends in Kansas City, Joe and Jerry?" In an hour, without ever dialing, Humphrey could contact perhaps thirty important givers.

Another close friend was Miles Lord, who hailed from northern Minnesota, rose through the ranks of the state DFL party, and was probably the senator's favorite companion on fishing trips, all the more so because they had sons of about the same age who went along on their outings. It would be off the mark to describe the senior judge of the U. S. District Court in Minnesota as Humphrey's "jester." But there was no getting away from the fact that Lord was a wag, and Humphrey relished his companionship in fun.

Once, headed in a minibus for the canoe wilderness near the Canadian border, they were snailing along a narrow trail to the jumping-off point when a bus full of out-of-state tourists stopped ahead of them. Humphrey and Lord got out and walked forward. A wire across the road had somehow gotten tangled around one of the bus's rear wheels. Humphrey bent over to look at the wheel, but Lord went to the front, hopped into the bus, and introduced himself as follows: "I'm the mayor of this jurisdiction, and I want to welcome you. I can tell you that we have wonderfully clean water here, and we have tall trees and good living, and our roads are well-engineered. We do have a few mosquitoes, and we have our local color. We have a fellow here who looks like Senator Humphrey, and in fact says he is Senator Humphrey. He'll spear a drink off you, but he's perfectly harmless. Leave him alone, folks, but don't believe him. . . ."

With this, Lord hollered: "Hey, Humphrey, come here. These people want to meet you." Humphrey came with a bound, climbed to the front of the bus, and rubbing his hands said: "How do you do, folks? I'm Senator Humphrey, and I'm glad to see you." At this the passengers all laughed and looked at each other. Somebody called out: "And I'm Soapy Williams." Another hooted: "And I'm Pat Brown." And they laughed and laughed until Humphrey turned and glared at Lord: "Miles, God damn you, what have you done?" Then Humphrey laughed too. The following summer they returned to Basswood Lake. Lord got there first, and when Humphrey descended in a floatplane, Lord was out on the dock made up as a bronzed and blanketed Chippewa brave. Humphrey addressed him with senatorial solemnity, then recognizing the way Lord rolled the cigar in his mouth, he stopped short. The senator threw the judge in the lake.

Humphrey initiated his share of practical joking. About the time he sent in Lord's name for U. S. attorney in Minneapolis, Lord got a telephone call from an Italian-accented party in New York who said: "My people want to help you. You've been very cooperative with my people. We want to write an endorsement for you to be the U. S. attorney and enforce the laws in Minnesota." Lord, pleased to get an endorsement, answered: "Tell me more about yourself." The heavily accented voice replied: "Well, I'm the head of a group that thinks a lot of you, and you've never caused us any trouble." Lord queried: "What's the name of your group?" The voice said: "We're called the Mafia." "Well," Lord came back, "there's no Mafia around Minnesota." Then the accent switched from Sicilian to South Dakotan: "There will be if you get to be U. S. attorney." With a triumphant cackle, Humphrey hung up.

Installed as prosecutor, Lord obtained the conviction of one Ben Dranow, a Minneapolis department store official who was in cahoots with the Teamsters' Jimmy Hoffa. But the man disappeared, and months went by. Lord's boss, Attorney General Robert Kennedy, badly wanted the man to further his prosecution of Hoffa. Lord's phone rang at home late one night and a monotone voice announced: "We know where Dranow is." "Where?" Lord asked. "He's at this lake across the border in Canada. Get out your book and look—Lake de Mille Lacs." Anxious to get on the good side of the boss he had denounced only the year before stumping Wisconsin for Humphrey against John Kennedy, Lord got out his atlas and was told to look for a town on the lake's northern shore. Then, as if suspicious at the delay, the voice on the telephone said: "You're double-crossing me." "No," Lord protested. "You'll squeal." "No," Lord promised. "You may be tapping my call." "No, on my honor," Lord said. Then the line went dead. Lord went to tell his wife. "Sure it wasn't Humphrey?" she asked; "He called me first."

Lord got his own back when he went to Washington to testify at a Humphrey session on the proposed Boundary Waters Canoe Area. He found a large crowd, mainly young people, waiting at the door of the Senate caucus room. "Inside, everybody, inside," he said firmly. After all had taken their seats, Lord stepped to the microphone and began issuing instructions: "He's going to be late, he's always late, as many of you know. Now, he should be punished. I'll tell you how. He'll hurry in like this—[Lord imitated Humphrey's quick step]—and he'll start talking right away. He'll give a greeting, expecting a big hand. Now don't clap. Don't clap until you hear the words 'Miles Lord.' Then jump on your seats and applaud until I say the word 'autograph' " In due course, Humphrey arrived, late, and, sure enough, started right out: "My young friends—." He paused, but there was no applause. So he continued to speak until suddenly he caught sight of his friend in the corner and shouted: "Miles Lord!" At this the audience clapped and clapped and clapped. Finally Lord said: "Don't applaud me. If you don't sit down, I won't give you my autograph." At the word "autograph" they stopped. Humphrey was "pretty ticked off," but, Lord said later, soon joined in the laughter.

A third friend who drew close to Humphrey in these years was Dwayne Andreas. "We were family friends," Andreas explained later. The Humphreys often joined the Andreases and their children as guests for brief winter vacations at the Sea View Hotel in Miami Beach, which Andreas owned. And it seemed natural that the Humphrey family would live in the Andreas Lake Minnetonka guest cottage the summer they were building their own place at nearby Lake Waverly. Humphrey was the godfather of Mick Andreas. It was, as noted earlier, Andreas's foundation that put Bob Humphrey through the Shattuck military academy in Faribault, Minnesota.

If their families brought Humphrey and Andreas together, so did their respective ambitions. Andreas knew people who could help the senator. When Humphrey tried for the presidency in 1960, Andreas not only contributed four thousand dollars but took the candidate to lunch at the Minneapolis Club to meet other well-to-do givers. Humphrey, for his part, knew people it was useful for Andreas to know. When the Kennedy administration was forming in 1961, Andreas was at Humphrey's side the day they found Bobby Kennedy on hands and knees over a huge chart of federal jobs on the floor of a Mayflower Hotel suite. With Humphrey he helped fill in some empty squares, and together they helped get George McGovern appointed director of the Food for Peace program. Later, Humphrey got Andreas placed on the president's Food for Peace Council advising McGovern. In 1963 the pair made a quick trip to Bonn to protest the tariff imposed to keep U. S. chicken exports out of West Germany. "My farmers vote too," Chancellor Ludwig Erhard told them, and the tariff stayed up. But the West German chieftain agreed to open the market to chicken *feed*—and U. S. commodity firms began selling the Germans feed grain and soybean meal as never before. Every time

Humphrey traveled overseas, Andreas went along. After one tour of the Middle East and Europe, Andreas wrote Humphrey: "how much I appreciate your inviting Inez and me on the fabulous trip—I wouldn't trade the experience for a million dollars or a college education."

Andreas's formal education had stopped after the first year of college, but he already had his million and more, having built one soybean business after another during the years when that commodity grew into one of the principal products of U. S. agriculture. The first time he sold out it was to become a vice president of the giant Cargill trading company—it was then that he first met Humphrey, who was running for reelection as mayor. After that he built an even bigger business and sold it to the huge Farmers Union grain cooperative, which was probably the strongest farm-belt backer of Humphrey's political fortunes. But even while maximizing profits for the soybean growers of an outfit with a long history of agrarian radicalism, Andreas pursued other interests. Through his own holding company, the Interoceanic Corporation, he invested in real estate, founded Minneapolis's first new downtown bank in forty years, and kept his ties with the tight little circle of bigtime capitalists who dominated international commodity trading. Such men tended to be Republicans, like his lawyer Thomas Dewey, twice candidate for president and frequent visitor at the Sea View, where he sometimes joined Andreas and Humphrey for golf.

Through the 1960s both the senator and the soybean trader were on the rise. Before Humphrey, loomed the vice presidency, and with the possible exception of Jim Rowe no man outside the staff spent more time than Andreas counseling with Humphrey about this prospect. It was apparent that Humphrey-the-Progressive had to broaden his base to convince Lyndon Johnson that he would make a good running mate. Andreas saw to that by introducing Humphrey to big business leaders at his forty-second-floor apartment in New York City's Waldorf Towers.

Nominated at Humphrey's behest to the advisory committee on foreign aid, Andreas plugged hard for expanding U. S. farm exports. From his first years as a senator, Humphrey had favored bigger farm exports. But Andreas's unrelenting emphasis on lifting controls for greater sales abroad ran up against opposition from Agriculture Secretary Orville Freeman, who had to balance export gains against the need to keep U. S. consumers provided with food at reasonable prices. Freeman was never a man to trifle with, and in a 1965 report to President Johnson he denounced Andreas by name as "someone who has benefited from the actions of this administration and then turns on the administration [with] a vicious attack" on its production-control policies. This put Humphrey squarely in the middle. On farm policy, as on everything else, he was loyal to the administration, but he was "worried," he wrote Freeman, "to see two of my good friends hurling brickbats at each other." He added: "Andreas, right or wrong, has been too helpful to too many of us to deserve a dressing-down in a memo to the President. He has helped substantially such senators as McGovern, Gaylord Nelson, Bill Proxmire, Gale McGee, Lee Metcalf, Ted Moss—all good Administration votes."

When Humphrey moved up to vice president, he followed the president's example and placed all his stocks and bonds (a ragbag collection worth about $85,000) in a blind trust to avoid conflict of interest in office. To no one's surprise, he chose Andreas to manage the trust. Then later that year, Humphrey's friend took a significant step up in the world. A business opportunity presented itself in Minneapolis. Archer-Daniels-Midland, one of the city's oldline commodity companies, felt the hot breath of competition and found itself falling behind such giants as Cargill and Pillsbury, which knew how to operate in markets on the opposite side of the world from Minnesota and were fast converting themselves into that form of international capitalism known as agribusiness. Family owned, A-D-M needed the range and experience of just such a globe-trotting enterpriser as Andreas. In the fall of 1965, when A-D-M could not cover its dividend, a member of the Archer family invited Andreas in by offering to sell him one hundred thousand shares of stock. Over the next months, Andreas acquired a controlling ten percent of the company. In February 1966, resigning from the Farmers Union office, he joined the board and executive committee of A-D-M. His cooperative connection, always important to Humphrey, was severed. Thenceforward the friend who had helped Humphrey, and whom Humphrey delighted to help, was an out and out enterpriser, building A-D-M into one of the giants of agribusiness, though he did not assume the title of chief executive until 1971.

No doubt it was the complexity of such relationships that kept the intimate circle of this open, outgoing politician as small as it was. There were always friends ready to help a man in high office so agreeable, so instantly ready to help others as was Hubert Humphrey. He was used, and on rare occasions he acknowledged it. Once, showing Gene McCarthy around his new house at Waverly, he led the way proudly from room to paneled room, showing his colleague every feature—the thermopane windows, the refrigerator, the microwave stove. Suddenly he stopped and said: "You know, I've got a problem. I've got too many damn friends who can get it for me wholesale." It was a problem, and it would grow.

Family life was changing for the Humphreys. The children were growing up, and the time had passed when Dad could lead a family camping trip, or leave the children in the safekeeping of his Aunt Olga while he and his wife flew to Europe. He could no longer even fuss because his eldest, Nancy, "a teenager, likes to drive cars, likes to have more clothes than anyone should have—the house is like Grand Central station when everyone's trying to get home at Christmas. . . ." For Nancy had married and begun raising her own family in Minneapolis. Skip, finishing boarding school, had enrolled in Washington's American University. And by the fall of 1962 both Bob and Doug, the two youngest, were away at Shattuck military academy. That same year, Humphrey's mother, aged eighty-one, gave up the house where she had lived alone since her husband's death in 1949 and moved into a Huron nursing home.

The life in which Humphrey was caught up left little time for family. How could there be in a year in which he stood for president, ran for reelection, then took on the Majority Whip job in the new Kennedy administration? "My Whip duties have practically whipped me," he wrote happily to his friend Tony Thompson. And his boasted busy-ness continued even when he arrived at his home on Christmas Eve from checking on the Alliance for Progress in Central America: "You should have seen me doing housework, . . . I still swing a wicked vacuum cleaner." Confessing himself a workaholic, he wrote his brother Ralph: "I feel guilty about taking a vacation. I guess we were taught early in life never to relax. Vacations were a sort of man-made sin." But power brought perquisites, and amidst the whirl of work, comforts were creeping up on the prairie populist. As assistant majority leader, he now rushed to meetings in a chauffeured limosine. As a senior Foreign Relations committee member, he now buzzed in and out of distant continents in VIP style. He took his brief rest in the best hotels, bolted his food in the fanciest restaurants, and wherever he touched down, in Washington, in New York, in foreign capitals, he was seldom called to pick up the tab. It was while keeping this high-flying schedule, on a dash from Puerto Rico to St. Thomas to Bermuda on legislative business, that he discovered the Virgin Islands. Caneel Bay Plantation on the Island of St. John's was one corner of the United States where it made no sense even to Humphrey to think about work. The broad beach, the palm-thatched cabanas, the sumptuous cottages, the flowing rum punches and exquisite meals served by discreet, white-coated attendants—it was all pretty plush, laid out by Laurence Rockefeller to a Rockefeller's taste. But it was, Humphrey declared, the perfect place to relax. "I want to go right back," he said, and for the rest of his life he tried to get away regularly to Caneel Bay—late in the year as a rule, after Congress adjourned, after election day, almost always at Thanksgiving.

With a Dad so busy, a son might make his own plans. In the summer of 1963, when Humphrey flew in and out of Berlin reporting to Kennedy on the East-West crisis, Hubert Humphrey III was also traveling to Europe. His father noted sketchily: "Skip is over in Switzerland working on a construction crew. On weekends he travels to other parts of Europe." It seemed that on those weekends, Skip was visiting another young tourist, daughter of a Navy captain, whom he had met as a fellow student at American University. In August, Humphrey wrote his son's old headmaster: "Skip has returned from Europe and believe it or not, he has married a very lovely young lady here in Virginia—Nancy Lee Jeffrey. They were married in Europe so they could enjoy a little honeymoon there. We are very happy at the whole situation. The young people will continue their schooling."

The following year, Lyndon Johnson was president and Humphrey was working day and night to push through a civil rights bill before a convention that, he wrote Eugenie Anderson, "may very well determine my future." He added: "Our sons were home with us for Easter vacation—everyone seems to be doing very well." Then on June 17, 1964, in the critical hour of his fight to break the Southern filibuster against his civil rights bill, came the shattering word from Minnesota that his second son, Bob, by that time a 19-year-old student at Mankato State College, faced surgery for cancer. Miraculously, Bob made a quick and total recovery.

In the summer of 1966, Bob was engaged to be married to Donna Erickson, from Minneapolis, and the vice president decided that nothing was too good for the son who, he wrote, had "taken all this trouble in stride." "He has a lovely girl, pretty, bright, sensible, and she finished her college training this past year. She will be a teacher. Bob has a year to go and is studying business administration. The wedding is going to be the highlight of the social season in Minnesota. We will hold the reception out at our lake home and expect anywhere from 600 to 700 guests."

Humphrey had a swimming pool built for the occasion, and for a honeymoon his first thought, in consultation with Dwayne Andreas and Dave Gartner, was "to work out a trip to the Virgin Islands right after the reception." Gartner subsequently reported that arrangements had been made for Bob and Donna to honeymoon instead at the Hilton Hawaiian Village in Honolulu, "compliments of the vice president of the Hilton hotels." On August 27, 1966, in a ceremony covered by television, the young couple were married at St. Olaf's Roman Catholic church in downtown Minneapolis. Luci Johnson arrived out of the sky by helicopter. The reception afterward, at the Waverly estate, was also a television event, with music provided by the TiJuana Brass—a group flown in from California at the vice president's special request.

In the midst of the nominating hurlyburly at Chicago in 1968, Humphrey broke off his meetings with delegates to lead a party at his headquarters celebrating Bob and Donna's second anniversary. And that fall, Bob and Donna, like Skip and Lee, criscrossed the country in a Dodge Camper, stopping in small towns, visiting small colleges, speaking and answering questions for Dad. Bob said later:

> I had my own schedule and advance man. I traveled 100,000 miles and occasionally our paths would meet. Dad chided me—in California I got twice the publicity he did, 1,000 articles. We'd call each other. I'd say, "Dad, you're in Los Angeles today—how'd it go?" And he'd ask: "How'd you go?"
>
> It was scary, because our age-group was the one worked up about Vietnam, and it was grueling—up at 5 and going until 1 and 2 the next morning. My wife got sick. I think it hurt our marriage.

Bob and Donna were divorced seven years later.

Bob never had to answer the question why the Humphrey sons, all three of them graduates of a military academy, were not in Vietnam. But the vice president did—and his answer, which invariably silenced the questioners, was to tell the story of Bob's harrowing brush with cancer. Later, when he ran again for senator, Humphrey explained to questioners that his son-in-law Bruce Solomonson was father of four children, his son Skip father of three, and Bob IV–F. His youngest son, Doug, also married, had his draft number but was never called up.

PART
FOUR

The Vice
Presidency

23

"You Can Rely on Me, Mr. President"

Every American of sufficient age remembers where he was and what he did and thought on at least two occasions in his life—the day Franklin Roosevelt died and the day John Kennedy was killed. When Hubert Humphrey, campaigning for mayor of Minneapolis, heard of Roosevelt's death in 1945, he was just finishing a letter to Henry Wallace, for whose nomination as vice president he had worked hard but unsuccessfully the previous year. The thought that Wallace had missed becoming president by a hundred days haunted Humphrey as he scribbled a postscript: "I simply can't conceal my emotions. How I wish you were at the helm."

The day after President Kennedy's assasination on November 22, 1963, an older and considerably more guarded Senator Humphrey dictated an eighteen-page, single-spaced memorandum on how he had received the news, which far more than Roosevelt's death affected him personally: "I was at the Chilean embassy attending a luncheon for about forty persons, including Ralph Dungan of the White House staff. . . . Ed Morgan of ABC News whispered in my ear that the President had been shot. . . . We excused ourselves from the table for the moment. I listened to the radio out in my car. . . . I stood by myself for several minutes in the library room. A great wave of emotion spread through my mind and body. . . . I tried to regain my composure and then, when I thought I had, I walked into the luncheon room where I announced that the President had died."

In his recital, Humphrey told how he went to the White House (where Pat Moynihan recalled his bursting in, throwing his arms around Dungan, and crying: "What have they done to us!"). He told how he went to Andrews Air base (where Theodore White noticed his eyes were "red with weeping") to meet the plane bearing the fallen president and his successor from Texas. And in further passages he recounted his trip to the Capitol for the Rotunda rites, on foot behind the gun carriage to St. Matthews cathedral, and finally across the Potomac to the burial at Arlington. Not once in his recital did he suggest that the thought crossed his mind that he, not Lyndon Johnson, might have been the successor. Not once did he hint at the thought that flashed like lightning through his friends' minds—that the death in Dallas put Humphrey right back in presidential contention.

Excessive caution rather than excessive altruism seems to have governed his thoughts as he tried to absorb and record his reactions to his shattering event. Within hours of Kennedy's death, in fact, people telephoned Humphrey asking about his plans for 1964. On the day of the funeral he discussed the possibility with Chester Bowles that he might run for vice president on Lyndon Johnson's ticket. He talked about his chances with Adlai Stevenson and Bill Benton. And he called his friend Marvin Rosenberg in New York to say: "Come down on Thursday. It's very important." Rosenberg walked into the Whip's office to find Humphrey with Max Kampelman, Joe Rauh, and Bill Connell. Humphrey told them: "You fellows are my closest advisers. I want to become president, and the only way I can is to become vice president."

The announcement, however, met opposition. As Rosenberg recalled later: "All four of us argued against it. We said he'd lose his freedom. We said Johnson would cut his balls off." But Humphrey insisted: "Look, I'm a poor man. I don't have rich friends. I come from a small state. I just can't do it on my own. The only way I can become president is first to become vice president, and I want you to help me."

They agreed, and began to hold quiet weekly strategy sessions at Kampelman's home.

From the start, Humphrey figured Johnson would pick his running mate late. And he was sure it would not be Robert Kennedy. Johnson could never forget that Bobby Kennedy had fought his nomination as vice president in 1960 and during his brother's presidency had treated Johnson with dismissive contempt. He kept him on as attorney general, and was well aware that Robert Kennedy wanted the vice-presidency. But if there was anything Johnson did not want, if he could possibly avoid it, it was a Kennedy name alongside his on the ticket. He was bent on winning reelection in his own right. The sympathy accorded Johnson taking over from the assassinated President seemed to Johnson's outsized ego only a challenge to show what he could do—and what he could do, using his power and skills on Capitol Hill, was to ram through all the legislation Kennedy had been unable to. More, if he could triumph in Congress and throughout the country, the bills would be seen as his measures. In such schemes, there was a place for Hubert Humphrey—but not for Bobby Kennedy.

With other congressional leaders, Humphrey had already gone to Johnson within hours of his return to pledge his support, and when Humphrey lingered Johnson threw his arounund him and said he needed him desperately. It happened that Humphrey's last business with President Kennedy, discussed with him on the morning of his departure for Dallas, was the first matter he took up right after the funeral with the new President. It was Senator Karl Mundt's bill to bar any government credits for sales behind the iron curtain, and Kennedy had wanted it defeated. When Johnson called Humphrey at home to discuss his plans for a commission to investigate the assassination, Humphrey told him Mundt's bill was due on the floor the day after the funeral. Johnson asked: "How many votes do you have?" Humphrey said he was not sure. Johnson said: "Well, that's the trouble with the place up there, you fellows don't have the votes counted." As Humphrey's recital continued:

> I told him I'd give him a good tabulation. So on Monday, even before the President's funeral, we checked every Democrat. I told the President that evening I thought we'd carry the vote by about 56 to 37. Next night I called the President around 9:15. I said: "Mr. President, I want to report your first victory—and I'm sorry I misinformed you last night. We have defeated the Mundt bill by 57 to 35.
>
> He laughed, congratulated me and asked: "What are you doing for dinner?" I said: "Well, I have eaten a bite." He said: "Come over and have something to eat anyway."
>
> At The Elms [Johnson's private residence] the President was at the table with Abe Fortas and Jack Valenti, Mrs. Johnson and their daughter Lynda Bird. . . . The President asked for drafts of his speech. We went over two or three of them. I was frank. I said the speech ought to be short, and somewhere he ought to make it crystal clear that he intended to follow through on the policies and programs of the late President. After considerable discussion the President said: "Hubert, you and Abe Fortas go ahead and redraft these speeches."
>
> I was able to add in references to Roosevelt and the Youth Employment program, a special paragraph on strengthening the U.N. and the Alliance for Progress. I also developed the line: "Let us continue," and a paragraph pledging that we will keep our commitments of alliance and world leadership. We concluded our work at 2 in the morning.

"Let us continue." That was the theme of the president's first speech, delivered not as Secretary Rusk and others urged at a White House desk but, on Humphrey's advice, "in his natural environment"—before a joint session of Congress. A great tide of sympathy welled up for the new president, who kept Kennedy's men close around him and proceeded with his practiced skill in handling Congress to push through all the measures, both domestic and foreign, that had been bottled up in Kennedy's time. The single exception was in the Latin American area, where Johnson named a new top team and, rejecting Humphrey's advice, began dismantling the ten-year program of the Alliance for Progress. It was the first signal that the new president, whose wealthy Texas friends thought private enterprise could fuel Latin America development, would work much more closely with business. Swallowing his disappointment, Humphrey worked doggedly to get Johnson's Latin American nominee, Tom Mann of Texas, confirmed by the Senate. At Johnson's request, he shot him memos on education, jobs for youth, foreign aid, and other subjects that later emerged in Johnson's Great Society program.

One night, Johnson summoned Humphrey to fetch his old Senate nemesis Harry Byrd to the White House, where together they plied the elderly chairman of the Finance Committee with drinks and stories until Johnson extorted Byrd's promise not to oppose—i.e., not to bottle up—the former president's tax-reduction bill. Then Johnson turned to Humphrey and said: "Hubert, you tell him every day that the President is waiting for action. You just keep at him to make sure that bill comes out." Byrd eventually appeared in the Senate with the bill in hand, made a brief, inaudible speech, and then leaned over Humphrey's desk: "Now, you tell the President that I kept my word— that I've reported out the bill, that I've made my speech, and now I'm leaving." Wonder of wonders, the tax bill went through. So did a fistful of foreign aid and other appropriation bills that Mansfield and Dirksen had said would never make it. Johnson pushed and Humphrey delivered.

Humphrey was at the peak of his powers. He was more of a leader than the retiring Mansfield. He worked hard, was well liked, and got things done. Early in January 1964, Eugenie Anderson wrote to congratulate Humphrey on an Associated Press poll of Democratic county chairmen that showed him well in the lead for the vice-presidential nomination. Humphrey replied: "The president calls on me a great deal. . . . The political pot is really boiling and I'm in the middle of it." Later that month, Johnson began to send Humphrey political signals through their mutual lawyer friend Jim Rowe, who had kept himself clear of the strategy meetings at Kampelman's house so that he could talk freely with the president. The first message: Humphrey could take confidential soundings and scout for support for the vice presidency. For Humphrey could give the needed Northern balance to the ticket, he carried impeccable credentials, and he was a Johnson man.

He was quick to react. In three weeks, between efforts to pass a touchy farm bill as well as the tax and appropriation measures, Humphrey managed to work in visits to New York, New Jersey, Florida, and the West Coast. In California his charm and liberal eloquence captivated State Democratic Chairman Eugene Wyman, who from that moment became a strong supporter and fundraiser for Humphrey. Instead of taking a four-day midwinter break in Bermuda, at Kampelman's urging he flew to Jamaica, where Tom Loughery, former postal union chief and close friend of George Meany, was ambassador. Loughery arranged for Humphrey to stop off in Miami where Meany was holding the AFL-CIO Executive Council's annual meeting. After breakfasting with Humphrey, Meany led him upstairs, the first politician ever so honored, to address the assembled union presidents of America.

Humphrey had wanted to be president in 1960. Instead, he was crushed and his hopes extinguished. Now the president dangled the vice presidency before him, and, as Gene McCarthy remarked later, "it was like giving him life." He was totally in his element. What had been denied as he thought, so conclusively was now, improbably, held out before him. The 1956 vice-presidential rout, the harsh defeat at the hands of Kennedy in 1960, these were the prior events that helped create Humphrey's subsequent loyalty to Lyndon Johnson. Offered a chance he had thought lost, he would feel obligated for the rest of his life.

With such glittering prospects, Humphrey threw himself into the Senate fight to put over the civil rights bill he had sought so long. Teamed with Johnson, he saw all the other liberal measures he had introduced over the years in line for enactment. He needed no leadership breakfast commands as he worked. In smaller matters as in big, he flogged for the Johnson program. A White House aide sent the president this memo: "In the week ending April 18 we had 16 [pro-Johnson] editorials placed in the *Congressional Record*—15 by Senator Humphrey. Planning 20 next week."

In all, Rowe said later, Johnson sent him seven times to talk to Humphrey about the vice presidency: "Johnson always had these saving phrases: 'Everything being equal, you're the candidate.' And I always softened the comments a little bit, no doubt because I remembered Humphrey's 1956 vice-presidential disappointment. I was more cautious than Johnson. I'd say, 'This is what he said—and I think he means you. . . .' "

In the spring of 1964, while Humphrey was battling against the Southern civil rights filibuster, Johnson, taken with the efficiency and force of his defense secretary, started talking about Robert McNamara for his No. 2. When he brought up the name at a meeting with his political aides, Rowe blurted: "Mr. President, the party won't take him. He's not a Democrat; he's a Republican." The comment cooled off Johnson, and by the time it was established that McNamara had cast Democratic votes he had been discarded as part of Johnson's solution to the "Bobby problem."

Johnson, detesting his attorney general and determined to win reelection without the help of the Kennedy name, asked his political strategists Abe Fortas and Clark Clifford to find a way to exclude Robert Kennedy from vice-presidential consideration. The device they hit upon was for the president to announce that his cabinet members were too busy carrying out his programs to campaign with him as running mate. Johnson gave the bad news to Kennedy in a vituperative exchange, and then announced it on television.

Humphrey was not informed of the announcement and when told of it by a reporter remarked to an aide that the reporter must be having hallucinations. The cabinet ban knocked out McNamara as well, of course, along with Orville Freeman, and because it also specified "those sitting with the cabinet," it eliminated U. N. Ambassador Adlai Stevenson too. "Disappointed," Stevenson said at once: "This means Humphrey."

Not necessarily so. At Johnson's direction, however, Rowe had already invited Humphrey over to his house, seated him on the front porch, and subjected him to what he called "the horse shedding." As he said later:

> I asked him every question in the world: how much money does your family owe? where are the mortgages? are there other women in your life? and so forth.
>
> Finally Hubert blew up at me saying: "My God, I've been in public life twenty years. Everybody must know everything about me. Why do you ask these things?" I said: "Hubert, you're in the big leagues now. Every question I ask, the Republicans are going to be asking also."

Every poll, especially after Barry Goldwater emerged as the Republican candidate, indicated that Johnson could win no matter who occupied the second spot on his ticket. "President Johnson right now has universal acceptance—he occupies the center," Humphrey wrote Eugenie Anderson. A poll taken for Humphrey showed that a Johnson-Humphrey ticket would defeat a Republican slate pairing Goldwater with Pennsylvania Governor William Scranton by more than 70 percent—and of those who identified themselves as Republican, no fewer than 41.3 percent said they would vote for a Johnson-Humphrey ticket in November.

As the convention neared, Johnson kept dropping other names: one day, Mayor Robert Wagner of New York; another day, Governor Edmund Brown of California. He toyed with the name of Sargent Shriver, husband of Eunice Kennedy and director of the anti-poverty program; but the Kennedys let it be known in no uncertain terms that the family would accept only blood kin on the ticket. Concerned about the Catholic vote, when Johnson visited Minneapolis in July he said he liked both of Minnesota's senators—a reference to Gene McCarthy, who was indeed Catholic. McCarthy was also favored by Texas's Governor John Connally, who told his old chief that the prospect of Humphrey was unappealing, not only for its effect on Texas voting but also for the leftward tilt it would give the national ticket. The Kennedy politicos who still surrounded the president preferred Humphrey, both because they thought he deserved the chance and because they had taken his measure in 1960 and thought him more beatable in a possible contest with Bobby later on. When Johnson assembled his top political advisers, who were Catholic almost to a man, Larry O'Brien, Kenny O'Donnell, and the others all said no, the president did not need McCarthy on his ticket—not even after the Republicans nominated representative William Miller, a Catholic, for the office. Only presidential aide Walter Jenkins spoke up for McCarthy as a Catholic candidate and he did so, Rowe remarked later, only because Johnson had told him to.

Humphrey was on tenterhooks. One day Stevenson talked about the vice presidency with him at lunch. Humphrey threw his hands in the air and said Johnson probably would not give him the job, just two more clerks and a larger office as whip. But Johnson sent Rowe to Humphrey again, this time with specific questions about his understanding of a vice president's relation to the president. Rowe then said: "I am going to call the President, and I want you to tell him that you and I have talked. I want you to tell him that you understand completely the concerns I have expressed on behalf of the President."

Rowe placed the call and handed Humphrey the telephone, and Humphrey proceeded to make a fateful pledge: "Mr. President, Jim Rowe has been here to visit for the past hour. I understand your concern about relationships between the President and Vice President. You can rely on me. I will be loyal." Still, the president made no comment in reply, and when on convention eve Humphrey and McCarthy appeared together on "Meet the Press," he had a good word to say for both men.

As if these games did not make Humphrey nervous enough, an ominous cloud hung over his vice-presidential hopes as the convention neared: the black Mississippi Freedom Democratic party was preparing a challenge for the convention seats of the state's regular Democratic organization. The last thing President Johnson wanted was a divisive black versus white credentials fight at the convention. He told Humphrey that it was his job to get the matter headed off without a bruising convention fight. Humphrey telephoned his friend Joe Rauh, who was representing the challengers: "Joe, the President is very concerned about this, and I've got to tell him something."

At this last face-to-face meeting before the convention, Johnson told Humphrey he favored a compromise plan for seating the regular Democrats while admitting the black Mississippians as honored guests without votes. But the Freedom party took their case to Atlantic City. Aaron Henry and Fannie Lou Hamer of the challengers went before the Credentials Committee and told how the whites beat them up when they sought to organize a party pledged to the new Civil Rights Act. As Rauh said later: "Johnson saw it on TV and went right up the wall. He told Humphrey bluntly that he was doing a rotten job."

The president sent in Walter Reuther to twist liberal arms, and Humphrey worked with both camps to settle the conflict before it got to the floor. Rauh said: "Each night before I went to bed I would go to Humphrey's suite and try to extract some further concession for the Freedom Party. We would be alone at four in the morning negotiating. Never once, even with his vice presidency at stake, did he say: 'Joe, please, for all the years we've worked together, accept this settlement to help me.' To me, that . . . represented the highest standard of political ethics that I have witnessed in my lifetime."

Finally, as the convention got under way the Credentials Committee, with Humphrey's prodding, voted to give the Freedom party two at-large seats along with the regulars, and to recast party rules by 1968 to forbid racial discrimination in the seating of delegates. Although the Freedom party rejected the committee's action, Rauh himself saluted it as a civil rights victory. The full fruits of that victory were to be seen four years later when Aaron Henry and Fanny Lou Hamer walked on the convention floor as leaders of the duly accredited Mississippi delegation.

As the convention opened, both Humphrey and McCarthy had set up headquarters as "candidates" at Atlantic City. Humphrey was still uncertain of his fate. McCarthy sat waiting at his hotel, too, though he said later: "I was playing a game. Hubert was serious, very serious." Johnson, as Rowe later said, was still "horsing around." Out of the blue he asked Rowe to sound out his fellow Montanan and Catholic, Senator Mike Mansfield, about accepting nomination as vice president. As Rowe expected, Mansfield knew better than to take Johnson seriously, snorted "Nonsense," and told the president he wanted nothing to do with it.

On August 20, Rowe had presented Johnson with a forthright memorandum. "Like you, I have had a serious heart attack," he wrote, and went on to say that Johnson ought to bear the mortality of twentieth-century presidents in mind. Since the president held such a commanding position that he could choose anybody, he ought to pick the man most competent to succeed him—Humphrey. Three days later, still dragging out the suspense over the only unsettled matter left in a cut-and-dried convention, Johnson gave an interview outlining the qualities he sought in a vice president. Competence he called "paramount," but loyalty stood high as ever on the detailed list of qualifications.

Only on the day before his own nomination was Johnson ready to give the word, and even then he left Humphrey half-paralyzed with uncertainty. From the White House he called his man Jenkins in Atlantic City and said: "Get Humphrey and tell him." Then he said: "No, let Jim do it, and this is what I want to tell him. Tell Jim to find a copy of the interview in today's *Star*. That says it."

Try as he would, Rowe could not locate a copy of the Washington *Star* in Atlantic City. But he found a copy of the Washington *Post*, which contained much the same write-up, and took notes. Then, as Rowe said later:

> I had to find Humphrey. I found him in a meeting with Walter Reuther about his assignment to settle the dispute over the seating of the Mississippi delegation. I had to knock on 7 or 8 doors before I got all the way in to find him. It took me 45 minutes. They had guards.

It has been said that Humphrey was not to get the nod until and unless

Christine Sannes Humphrey and Hubert Horatio Humphrey, Sr., ca. 1910. CREDIT: HUBERT H. HUMPHREY COLLECTION/MINNESOTA HISTORICAL SOCIETY.

Mayor Humphrey at a war bond drive in Minneapolis, ca. 1945, with Charles Johnson, left, and Jack Dempsey. CREDIT: HUBERT H. HUMPHREY COLLECTION/ MINNESOTA HISTORICAL SOCIETY

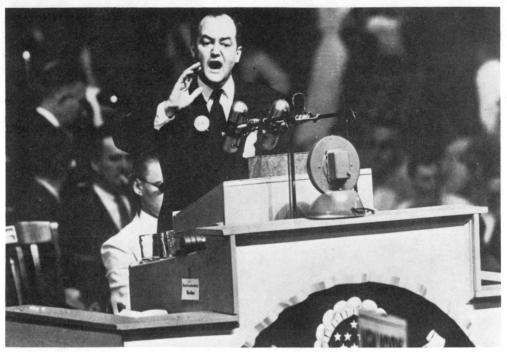

Humphrey delivers his pivotal speech on the civil rights plank at the 1948 Democratic National Convention.

Ralph, Fern, Hubert Jr., and Mr. and Mrs. Hubert H. Humphrey, Sr., November 1948.

At the Waldorf Astoria in 1959, a dinner in honor of Eleanor Roosevelt. CREDIT: HUBERT H. HUMPHREY COLLECTION/ MINNESOTA HISTORICAL SOCIETY.

1960, the West Virginia primary campaign. CREDIT: HUBERT H. HUMPHREY COLLECTION/MINNESOTA HISTORICAL SOCIETY.

John F. Kennedy and Hubert H. Humphrey in 1960. CREDIT: HUBERT H. HUMPHREY COLLECTION/MINNESOTA HISTORICAL SOCIETY.

Humphrey in 1964 as Vice-President, with President Lyndon Johnson. CREDIT: USIS.

Hubert Humphrey campaigning in Texas during the 1968 campaign. CREDIT: HUBERT H. HUMPHREY COLLECTION/ MINNESOTA HISTORICAL SOCIETY.

Hubert Humphrey addresses the U.S. House of Representatives, November 3, 1977. CREDIT: HUBERT H. HUMPHREY COLLECTION/MINNESOTA HISTORICAL SOCIETY.

he cleared up the Mississippi trouble first. This was not so. Johnson gave him the word while he was still at work on the problem.

I finally got to Hubert and said: "You're it." I paraphrased that write-up as I talked—all the stipulations against disloyalty. One of the stipulations was: "You can be against me in our conferences until as President I make up my mind; then I want you to follow my policies."

And I said: "You're supposed to fly down tonight and meet with him in the morning. Be at my room and we'll wait together for the word."

But the ordeal was not over. Humphrey and his wife, and Kampelman and Connell went to Rowe's room to await the call. After they had ordered something to eat, Walter Jenkins telephoned and said: "You can't land a plane in Washington; there's too much fog." Nerves were fraying. Rowe, following orders, had sworn Humphrey to secrecy: "You can't even tell Muriel." Humphrey fumed: "This is ridiculous; a man can't even tell his own wife." Finally Rowe relented and said he could talk about it.

Then Jenkins called again: "You can't go until tomorrow." At this, Rowe later recalled: "Humphrey just blew his top—the only time so long as I've known him. Just raised hell. Swore. Said this was ridiculous. I said: 'Hubert, tonight you're just a senator from Minnesota but this time tomorrow night you'll be a candidate for vice president and then we can both tell Johnson he's a shit.' " That calmed him down, and Humphrey went back to his hotel. Yet doubt still lingered. At one A.M., Rowe telephoned Humphrey to warn that the nomination was gone if what he had told him leaked out.

Signals had changed, not because of fog but because Johnson had got the notion to fly both Humphrey and McCarthy to the White House. But through all the hugger-mugger, Gene McCarthy had read the signs—and concluded that he was being used. During the night he drafted a telegram to Johnson withdrawing from contention; he sent it before Johnson could get Jenkins to stop him. This untrammeled exercise of personal power cost President Johnson dear. It ended his friendship with McCarthy, who was deeply hurt; four years later, it was this same Gene McCarthy who took it upon himself to oppose the President's bid for another term and, by his strong showing in the first 1968 primaries, forced Johnson to stand down.

Humphrey heard the news at breakfast that McCarthy had withdrawn his name. He asked his son Dougie: "How would you like your Dad to be vice president?" Douglas, sixteen, answered: "Swell." Humphrey said: "Well, he's going to be." But then Humphrey learned there would be another passenger on the flight to Washington—Senator Thomas Dodd of Connecticut. "What, is Tom Dodd being considered too?" Humphrey exploded. Rowe said: "No, this is just a cover. It will keep the press off balance and continue the speculation. That's what the president wants."

Exhausted, Humphrey slept for most of the short flight. Dodd, totally in the dark about his invitation to see the president, said little. At Washington,

Jack Valenti met them, but the limousine circled aimlessly through the streets for fifteen minutes—to ensure that Lady Bird's arrival at Atlantic City would command undivided television attention. When the "finalists" pulled up before the massed cameras at the White House, Dodd was led in to the president's office first. Humphrey napped in the car until a voice awakened him: "Senator, the president wants to see you." The president met him and said: "Let's go into the cabinet room." It was five P.M.

Did the two men understand each other? Humphrey was often called the most "open" politician of his generation, and Johnson said later he could never have told Humphrey any sooner because Humphrey would never have been able to keep it to himself. At the time, the president said: "If you didn't know you were going to be vice president a month ago, you're too damn dumb to have the office."

According to Humphrey's memoirs, Johnson asked: "Hubert, do you want to be vice president?" and Humphrey answered: "Yes" and went on to state that he fully expected Johnson to win in November and to run for reelection in 1968. But those who worked close to Humphrey for the longest time said that one never knew his innermost thoughts. Later that week he did say to his brother that he wished their father, who always predicted Hubert would be president some day, were alive. That was the closest he came to saying what was on everybody else's mind: that he was not only advancing to an office a heartbeat away from the presidency but to four years as second man to a president whose heart had already once nearly stopped beating.

But if Humphrey knew he had won far more than the consolation prize that the vice presidency usually is, Johnson did not even at this moment allow him to forget the price he meant to exact. That is clear from Humphrey's own account of the interview in the cabinet room.

Johnson said: "This is like a marriage with no chance of divorce. I need complete and unswerving loyalty. . . . You most likely won't like the [job] after you've gotten into it. Seldom do a President and Vice President get along." Johnson then reminded me that after the first year Vice President Alben Barkley seldom saw President Truman—that hostility, or at least distance, grew between them. And that Truman himself, as vice president, had rarely spoken to President Roosevelt.

He did not have to remind me of President Eisenhower's statement and its implication, when asked about Richard Nixon's contributions as vice president: "Give me a week and I'll think of one."

Of his own experience as vice president, he said: "You know, Hubert, that I was totally loyal to John Kennedy. Whatever John Kennedy wanted me to do, I did. I never tried to upstage him. You keep out of the news. The news belongs to the President. I never went around the country making speeches without the President knowing about it. Even when it came to Democratic party functions, we had a working agreement."

To all this, Humphrey answered: "You can trust me, Mr. President."

Then Johnson got Muriel on the telephone: "We're going to nominate your boy." And he led Humphrey into the next room, where Rusk, McNamara, and the other cabinet members were waiting to meet him. But Johnson, as a parting shot, asked Humphrey to say nothing about his decision, so Humphrey flew with Dodd back to Atlantic City, and it was not until the next day, while Humphrey was being interviewed live on a Minneapolis radio station, that the announcer cut in with a news flash from Washington that the president was on his way to Atlantic City with the recommendation that Humphrey be nominated.

Only then was bedlam loosed in Humphrey's Claridge Hotel suite. People jumped, embraced, cheered. And when Johnson shortly arrived and took the rostrum, he was still dragging out the suspense. Only at the end of his convention announcement did he bellow out the name, "Senator Hubert Humphrey of Minnesota." That was the moment for the Humphreyites to break out at last the boxes of Johnson-Humphrey posters and streamers that had been hidden all over Atlantic City. Then Eugene McCarthy, at Humphrey's request, stepped to the rostrum and nominated his colleague for vice president. Said Humphrey later: "It was a moment of glory. My eyes filled with tears of joy. My whole family was there, and with them I savored every word of praise, every cheer of assent. My body tingled with excitement. I wished my father were alive."

Everett Dirksen said: "He is *the* modern liberal." *Progressive* magazine said: "His record in the Senate has no parallel in the struggle for liberal legislation: he has repeatedly shown extraordinary gifts for leadership in just about every area of legislation designed, in the words of the Preamble of the Constitution, 'to promote the general welfare.' " "Humphrey has earned a magna cum laude," said the *New Republic*. The *Wall Street Journal* called him "an energetic, effective, immensely imaginative politician whose fertile brain sometimes hatches solutions to problems that may not yet exist." "Hubert has had his just desserts at last," wrote Adlai Stevenson to a friend. Humphrey had been given the chance he had thought lost, and at that glorious moment loyalty to Lyndon Johnson did not look like a big price to pay for the perch he had reached.

24

A Moment of Glory

I T W A S Hubert Humphrey who drew the biggest cheers as the candidates accepted nomination in Atlantic City. Johnson, trying to be lofty, seemed hollow and sententious. Humphrey, taking the rostrum first, showed why Jim Rowe had touted his campaign prowess as first of all reasons why he belonged on the ticket.

A president might disdain, as Johnson tried and F.D.R. always did, ever to mention his opponent's name. But not the irrepressible Humphrey. For Johnson's running mate, the identity of the Republican nominee was the irresistibly tempting target of the 1964 contest. At their July convention in San Francisco, Republican delegates had named Barry Goldwater of Arizona, darling of the party's extreme right wing, as their candidate. When Governor Nelson Rockefeller, the moderate contender from New York, tried to present his views, the convention drowned him out with boos. After that, Humphrey wrote Columnist Bill White: "Goldwater and his crew have kidnapped the Republican party." There were votes, millions of Republican votes, to be won if Goldwater could just be tagged and labeled the freaky candidate Humphrey saw him to be. So with deft help from speech writer Bill Moyers, he delivered a classic "man who" speech—in reverse.

Goldwater, he shouted, "has been facing backward against the mainstream of American history. He is not only out of tune with the great majority of his countrymen, he is even out of step with his own party." And with the commanding heights of the American political center lying open before him, Humphrey reveled in repeating the name of the man whose "stridency" and "extreme and radical language" were leading the Republicans away from them:

> Most Democrats and Republicans in the U.S. Senate, for example, voted for the nuclear test ban treaty, but not the temporary Republican spokesman.
>
> Most Democrats and Republicans in the Senate voted for a $11.5 billion tax cut for American citizens and for American business. *(Pause.)* But not Senator Goldwater.
>
> Most Democrats and Republicans in the Senate, in fact 4/5 of the members of his own party, voted for the Civil Rights Act. *(Pause.)* But not Senator Goldwater.
>
> Most Democrats and Republicans in the Senate voted for an expanded medical education program. But not Senator Goldwater.
>
> Most Democrats and Republicans in the Senate voted for an expanded education legislation. But not Senator Goldwater.

By the time Humphrey had repeated the refrain a couple of times, delegates were roaring and slapping their thighs and chorusing the cry along with him. By the time Humphrey had belted out his climactic call to take arms in the autumn battle, the delegates were on their feet, and Convention Hall was a storm of cheers.

The triumph was all the sweeter for being so long withheld, and Humphrey wanted to celebrate it. His entire family had assembled in a rented house on Marion Street, half a block away from the ocean. His brother and sister-in-law, Ralph and Harriett Humphrey, were there from South Dakota. His sister and her children, Mrs. Frances Howard, William Ray, and Ann, had come up from their Virginia home. His children rejoiced with them: Nancy, now twenty-five, and her husband, Bruce Solomonson; Hubert H. III, twenty-two, and his wife, Nancy Lee; Robert, twenty; and Douglas, sixteen. But with practically no advance warning Johnson ordered Humphrey and his wife to fly with him to his ranch.

On arrival at Johnson City the president decided that his running mate should go horseback riding with him. He called Humphrey into his bedroom and handed him an outfit to wear—pants, shirt, and cowboy hat all several sizes too big. Outside, Johnson said: "Hubert, get on that horse. We're going for a ride." The Tennessee walker Johnson put him on was big and spirited, and Humphrey was no horseman. Reporters grinned and cameras clicked as the critter reared, and Humphrey in his ridiculous get-up hung on for dear life. Coming after the scenes at the White House and Atlantic City, it was, Nick Katzenbach remarked later, "almost like Johnson holding Humphrey up by the ears the way he did with his beagle."

Such harsh hospitality turned out to be incidental to the purpose of the visit. The president wanted to plan his partner's campaign. Sitting with Humphrey and Humphrey's friend Dwayne Andreas in the guesthouse, he said:

Humphrey [he always pronounced it 'Umphrey], we've got to get busy right now. I want you to get your own plane. Rent a Lockheed and crew from American Airlines. Make your own plans. Start right now. And raise your own money.

I'll never forget when I started out with Jack Kennedy. After I accepted the vice presidency down there at the convention, that's the last I ever saw of the Kennedy people until after the election was over. I couldn't get in touch with Kennedy. I had absolutely no help from them. Finally in desperation Lady Bird and I went to the bank, borrowed a million dollars, rented an airplane, and went to work. We were entirely on our own. You'll be surprised how well it will work even if you have to improvise. . . .

But Johnson was not a man to let Humphrey go it alone. He marked out eleven states—the big states of the industrial Northeast plus California and Texas—as the ones that would deliver victory. He defined the consensus he'd been proclaiming: "Let's just make it a general rule never to refer to Goldwater as a Republican. A lot of Republicans in this country ought to be Democrats, but we've never given them a chance to come in. This is the best opportunity we're ever going to get." The president handed Humphrey specific orders:

Now I want you to head right for the South. Talk about farms and farming. Don't preach. Just let them see you and make up their own minds that you don't have any horns. We'll win the South. I guarantee you that we'll win Texas big.

The other thing I want you to concentrate on is to go after the confidence of the business community. Hubert, you and I are going to put an end once and for all to the reputation the Democratic party has of being anti-business. I want you to go to every businessmen's luncheon and meeting that you can possibly go to. Tell them, You don't need to be afraid of us just because we're looking after the old people and the kids. We're going to be mighty liberal on things like Medicare, Social Security and free milk for the babies, but we gotta have profitable companies in this country to make it work.

How did we get this anti-business reputation? I'll tell you why we got it, Hubert—that young fellow in the Justice department. And boy, did I have a talk with him about three months ago.

This was a reference to the time Johnson called Bobby Kennedy in and told him he would not get the No. 2 spot on the 1964 ticket:

> I told him: "Young man, you know as well as I do what your crowd is doing over there. You're harassing businessmen all over this country." I told him: "Young man, today is the last damn day for that kind of business."
>
> Hubert, if you and I are going to be in the saddle, we'll get good law enforcement men, and we'll see to it that they behave themselves. That kid has done more damage to this party with those shenanigans than you or I can ever imagine—and it's all over with.

A week before this conversation, Robert Kennedy resigned to run for the Senate from New York. Johnson left his office vacant until after the election, then named Kennedy's right-hand man, Nicholas Katzenbach, to succeed him.

Humphrey followed orders, althought it is not clear that he raised all his own money when both Republican and Democratic businessmen were falling over themselves to contribute to the Johnson-Humphrey treasury. While the president attended to the nation's business in his White House office, his vice-presidential nominee flew around the country in a chartered Electra dubbed "The Happy Warrior." Muriel Humphrey wrote Eugenie Anderson: "This time campaigning is so much easier. We have a wonderful plane to fly in and we seem to have money to operate with. Of course, Senator is helping to get this—we have staffs and everyone is being so good to us that it is truly a pleasure and lots of fun to be part of it. I think the hard years of campaigning were when we first started out in the early years and did as well as we could on little or nothing."

On the first weekend of September a crowd of fifteen hundred turned out at the airport for Humphrey's Minneapolis homecoming, including Republican State Treasurer Val Bjornson, the man he had outpointed when he ran for reelection the first time. Skywriters spelled "HHH" high overhead; Chippewa braves danced on the tarmac; and a mile-long caravan honked Chief Running Water, as the welcomers called him, from the airport to Northrup auditorium. His friend and rival Gene McCarthy introduced him. In a thirty-minute speech interrupted thirty-five times by applause, Humphrey lauded Johnson as a "giant of a man" and lambasted Goldwater as "irresponsible, divisive and unqualified to be president." From the ranch, Johnson wired: "A great beginning. Proud to be on the same team."

Humphrey published two campaign books, *The War on Poverty* and *The Cause Is Mankind*. Actually, he told Eugenie Anderson, the book about poverty was the product of several hands and minds. "The other, primarily a rewrite of statements, speeches and articles that I have given on other days, is more a statement of political philosophy." Reviewers noted the prairie progressive's new praise for big business: "I do not think we have many real grievances to be urged against bigness in business today. For the most part, big corporations are a source of strength and economic vitality. And certainly, big business is here to stay."

Just as John Kennedy faced the clergy four years before in Houston, Humphrey met the businessmen at the Houston Club in September. Governor John Connally, who had opposed putting Humphrey on the ticket, remarked in introducing the candidate that he saw "more distinguished Texans" than had ever been gathered in one room before. Like Connally himself, they were there by Johnson's edict. They applauded twenty-two times in the speech. The question was whether Humphrey would soften his stand against the oil depletion allowance. He certainly seemed to when he said: "If you will just give me a little chance, I am going to feel like a Texan." Then he went on: "Talk about being liberal, there is no more humanitarian and progressive force in American life than the American business community. Why, there aren't any people in the world that have the spirit of adventure, the spirit of progress, the willingness to meet unbelievable challenges that you do. There is no one in the world that can equal you." Afterward, the *Oil Daily* bannered: "Humphrey Will Follow LBJ's Oil Policies." A vice-presidential candidate's campaign effusions however, seldom receive wide attention, and luckily for him this parcel of patent nonsense never came back to haunt the orator.

Humphrey plunged into the South. Pausing at Chattanooga, bastion of the Tennessee Valley Authority that Goldwater talked of dismantling, he told the crowd: "What that man would do to Dixie would make Sherman look like a friend." Marching into Georgia, he stated his views on racial equality before audiences that disagreed strongly with him. The crowd at Moultrie was hostile, but at Tifton next day he ripped off his coat and told listeners: "I didn't come down here to pick magnolias." He proceeded to tackle civil rights head-on—and was cheered.

If consensus was what Johnson claimed, Humphrey helped him get it together. *Life* magazine endorsed him; the *Wall Street Journal* spoke respectfully of his "maturity"; and former Republican Treasury Secretary Robert Anderson, the man Eisenhower wanted to succeed him, said he would vote for Humphrey. George McGovern stumped for him and wrote: "You can count on my friendship and support in the important years ahead." A whole string of professors called him a credit to the ticket, and Joe Rauh and the rest of his old Americans for Democratic Action friends stood by him as, pleading prospective responsibilities, he resigned as ADA's vice chairman.

Of the top four nominees, Humphrey was the least wealthy—Johnson and Goldwater were millionaires. Humphrey's net worth, disclosed by his auditors on September 10, was $171,296, consisting of his Chevy Chase and Waverly homes, his share of the Huron drugstore, his government savings bonds, and three or four small stocks. Of the four, he was also the one who had the most fun campaigning. "Every day was shot through with laughter," wrote Reporter E. W. Kenworthy of the *New York Times*. "There were lots of laughs on the plane," the Minneapolis *Tribune*'s Charles Bailey said later. Of course pressures on the No. 2 man were far less intense than for the top candidates. But Theodore White, who later joined the party in Dakota, found the candidate totally relaxed and not locked into a schedule. He trailed Humphrey into Doland, the old hometown. As they climbed the stairs of the redbrick schoolhouse where the senator had spent twelve years, Humphrey spied a huge silver loving cup on the second-floor landing. Everybody stopped while Humphrey recalled how he and his friend Julian Hartt had taken alarm clocks left for repair at his father's drugstore, set the alarms to go off at intervals, placed the clocks in the big loving cup, then chortled at the din as they disrupted the entire school in mid-morning. "And, boy, did old Jennie Higgins, the principal, shriek at me," said Humphrey.

He took extra relish in addressing young people. At a Princeton rally he quoted Presidents Madison and Wilson against Goldwater's states-rights theories, and at Notre Dame he quoted St. Augustine and Pope John XXIII against Goldwater's leaning toward nuclear weapons. His campus audiences were uniformly friendly—"I have never seen more enthusiasm in young people," he told a fellow Minnesotan. He kidded the occasional Goldwaterites: "We've got a few slow learners here. . . ." And when hecklers at the University of Kansas screeched, "We Want Barry," Humphrey yelled back: "Strawberry or raspberry?" When the first urban riots of the 1960s touched off dire warnings of "backlash" and "frontlash," the Republican candidate began referring sarcastically to Humphrey's middle name. "In the name of charity I must warn him," Humphrey replied: "The hidden middle-name vote—all those youngsters blessed by loving parents with a middle name they choose to convert into an initial—may rise against him. He should beware of the midlash."

As he campaigned, his crowds grew huge. His hands were scratched and swollen from the handshaking. But in Erie, Pennsylvania, where sixty-three teen-age girls lined up, the first one abandoned handshakes for kisses, and all sixty-three kissed the candidate. As he toured Manhattan with the Democratic candidate for the Senate, Robert Kennedy, their car was mobbed. A woman threw him her shoe. He caught it, signed it, and tossed it back. Not until he saw it later on the floor did he realize that another had flung him her girdle. He lost three wristwatches, several tieclasps and uncounted cufflinks to the clutches of well-wishers on his eastern swing.

Of course the insouciant and seemingly free-wheeling campaigner was anything but "unprogrammed." He was following White House orders throughout. Jack Valenti of the president's staff even tried to get him to devise a single, all-purpose speech. But for an orator like Humphrey, that was simply preposterous. A staff of John Stewart, Bob Jensen, and Ted Van Dyk prepared drafts that were cleared at the White House, but the speeches

Humphrey delivered bore little resemblance to them or even to the presumably final versions that aides handed out on the plane. The words, re-phrased, re-arranged, and often amplified to startling length in the delivery, were inimitably Humphrey's.

His dazzling improvisations were performed under wraps. What Humphrey said was not only restricted in subject but sometimes prescribed. Announcing his resignation from the ADA vice chairmanship, for example, followed a prior command by the president. At no point in the campaign did Humphrey speak of the burgeoning crisis in Vietnam, except to cite the Senate resolution upholding the president's action in ordering the U. S. Navy to counterattack North Vietnamese small craft in the Gulf of Tonkin. And when Soviet Premier Nikita Khrushchev tumbled from power in October, Johnson broke into a Humphrey campaign address in Pittsburgh with a telephone call instructing him on what to say.

But Humphrey was free to blast the Republican nominee, and crowds in Akron, Detroit, and elsewhere listened for the moment to join in his mocking litany: "But NOT Senator Goldwater." As public unease grew over Goldwater's supposed nuclear adventurism, it was Humphrey who asked in Cleveland: "Can we trust a man whose idea of foreign policy is to lob a missile into the men's room of the Kremlin?" By then the Johnson-Humphrey ticket was miles ahead in the polls, and Humphrey was pulling such big crowds that local candidates rushed to ride along with him. In dozens of places he stopped to film television programs expressly to help local hopefuls.

On election night he sat with Muriel, herself back from a vote-seeking trip to Hawaii and Alaska, and with Dwayne and Inez Andreas. They waited for three and a half hours in their nineteenth-floor suite at Minneapolis's Sheraton Ritz for President Johnson to claim victory. Humphrey's only disappointment was that Goldwater's home state of Arizona, which he had boldly invaded at the last minute, wound up after a close finish in the Republican column. For the rest, the Johnson-Humphrey ticket swept every state that Humphrey campaigned in except Georgia. Perhaps the most striking feature of the landslide was that five farm states of the Middle West lost by Kennedy in 1960 swung to the Democrats this time, showing what strength the progressive Humphrey brought to Johnson's consensus ticket.

25

In LBJ's Doghouse

Laughter rang through the tract house in Chevy Chase as the vice president-elect downed his morning coffee and eggs on the frosty days of January 1965. Joy filled his heart as he bounded out the door to the black limousine that conveyed him downtown to his Capitol Hill office. For the eighteen-man Secret Service detail dogging his every step, there was a never-ending series of over-the-shoulder quips. To the newspaper reporters who ran beside him as he dashed through the long marble corridors from one meeting to the next, he would exclaim: "Gee, whiz, it's a wonderful time to be alive."

On the twentieth of January, with his wife at his side and his old pinball-parlor friend Freddie Gates holding the Bible, Humphrey took the oath as the 38th vice president, filling the office that had been vacant thirteen months, since Lyndon Johnson left it to replace the murdered President Kennedy.

Once upon a time the office of vice president of the United States had been so lightly regarded that it was the subject of jokes, and a popular Broadway show had mocked and ridiculed it. In the Coolidge-era hit *Of Thee I Sing*, Alexander Throttlebottom was pictured as reluctant to accept the vice presidency because his mother might hear about it. The poor man spent his vice-presidential years feeding pigeons in the park and trying to find two references so that he could obtain a library card. But after the death of Franklin Roosevelt and of John Kennedy elevated first Truman and then Johnson to the presidency, Americans took the office more seriously. In 1965 the memory of the young president's death remained fresh in the national consciousness. President Johnson, who had benefited so palpably by the outpouring of sympathy at his accession, acknowledged the heightened public perception of the vice presidency by his repeated emphasis that he was picking a man above all qualified to succeed him. For the public, the party, and, to an unfathomable extent, the man himself had to take account of the fact that the president had already suffered one major heart attack.

What were the new vice president's thoughts, then, when four days after he had been sworn in, he was awakened at three in the morning and told that the president, suffering chest pains, had been rushed to the hospital? "That's all I was told," he said on the following day at a luncheon in St. Paul, where he had gone to act as grand marshall in the city's winter carnival.

"I don't know whether you can understand the feelings that ran through my mind," Humphrey said. A student as apt as Humphrey could not help remembering that when William Henry Harrison caught cold after his inaugural and died, Vice President John Tyler served an entire four-year term in his place. A senator who had been in Washington as long as Humphrey could not help recalling how Harry Truman had been vice president less than a hundred days when he heard the strangled voice of Roosevelt's secretary Steve Early on the telephone: "The president is dead."

"I didn't know what to do or say," Humphrey went on. He roused his physician friend Edgar Berman out of a sound sleep in Maryland to demand what in his professional opinion "chest pains" signified. Berman growled it could mean anything. Then, Humphrey said: "I just walked around the house for a while." His wife awoke. They both went downstairs and sat for an hour. Then a second call came, and Humphrey learned that it was just a presidential cold—that the doctors thought it best for Johnson to take a four-day rest in the hospital. For Humphrey, it was a jolting reminder how dependent he was on Johnson for any chance at the presidency.

In the weeks and months to come, Humphrey was brutally reminded by Johnson himself how completely—how abjectly—dependent on the president he was. President Johnson was a domineering man. He habitually sought to subjugate those around him by humiliating them. In Humphrey's case, he seized opportunities to remind him of his total dependence, forcing him to behave with a demeaning servility. He had demeaned Humphrey even in the process of selecting him, putting him through the silly charade of trips to the White House before the Atlantic City nomination. He had demeaned Humphrey as soon as he became the candidate, dressing him in a ridiculous cowboy costume at his ranch and parading him on a fractious horse in front of reporters and cameramen. And within a month after Humphrey became vice president, Johnson found a way to put him down again.

If there was one function that any vice president, even a Throttlebottom, could be expected to perform it was to represent the president and the country at funerals of notables abroad. But when Winston Churchill, revered by

a whole generation of Americans, died after long illness that first January of
Humphrey's term Johnson withheld the privilege from his vice president and
sent Chief Justice Earl Warren. If this was Johnson's way of putting down
the man who now stood No. 2 in the nation, it was an act so gratuitous as to
cause public surprise. Asked about it later at a press conference, Johnson
acknowledged that it had probably been a mistake not to send his vice president to London. And that carefully measured admission ought to have ended
it. But sometime later the Humphreys were at dinner at the White House
with the Johnsons, the Larry O'Briens, and the Jack Valentis. There was a
lot of kidding, for Johnson was a great lover of kidding—a form of humor
that could be light-hearted but could also wound and cut down (Humphrey
always referred to it as Johnson's "teasing"). The chaffing had gone on for a
good while when Muriel Humphrey asked: "Mr. President, why didn't you
send Hubert to Churchill's funeral?" The laughter died. The president sat
silent. The evening was at an end.

Humphrey always said that Johnson was such a big man, a nature so large
that it contained a host of inconsistencies. That was one way of saying it,
and if it was true—and it was—it must also be said that Humphrey, too, was
a very big man, capable of rising above resentment of such petty treatment.
In both the domineering Johnson and the forgiving Humphrey was conduct
at times spontaneous, at times calculating. Humphrey said again and again
during his vice presidency: "There's no man alive who knows the president
as well as I do." He would confidently predict Johnson's reactions and counsel others: "Don't approach him that way" or "Let [Bill] Moyers or [Marvin]
Watson bring it up." But Humphrey, in stepping up to the successor's position, made a fundamental misjudgment of the president's character, and it
was to cost him dear.

Lyndon Johnson was indeed a big man. He towered over others as he
talked with them, leaning down "so close over you," as Larry O'Brien once
said, "that your eye-glasses bumped." Johnson's ego towered even higher. It
stood so tall that when Johnson was raised to the highest office, it remained
unsatisfied because of the manner of his elevation. Now Johnson had won
the presidency in his own right, and won by a margin so overwhelming that
only FDR had surpassed it. First his mentor, Roosevelt had become the model
against whom Johnson measured himself. Now he beheld a vision: he would
outdo Roosevelt. In his hands was a nation incomparably richer and stronger
than FDR's. Master of legislative legerdemain, mounting huge majorities in
both houses of Congress, he would build atop the New Deal foundation a
Great Society of vast dimensions. He would turn business loose. He would
put through more measures for the women and children and aged of America
than Roosevelt and his braintrusters had ever dreamed of. He would bring
together the races as Lincoln had never aspired to, or Roosevelt dared to, by
closing the gap of poverty in America that divided them. His great unifier
would be education, which was to be opened wide to every child born in

America. "Every young American," he informed his cabinet in January, was to get "all the education his abilities and background can use."

Less than a month after election, Humphrey, addressing an American Jewish Committee awards dinner in New York, had thrown away his prepared text to plead for education as a way to erase bigotry and hatred. Warning of a "race between education and catastrophe in America," he had forecast that "massive investment" in education would be the "single most important step toward building the Great Society." Johnson had not liked that—the ebullient vice president elect stealing any of his thunder. But in January he told Adlai Stevenson that he was going to pile work on Humphrey, and make Humphrey his close adviser in the public eye. Tireless worker, accomplished legislator, practiced persuader, eloquent evangelizer, Humphrey seemed sure to be a help in putting across Johnson's vision. Even before their inaugural, the President asked Humphrey to prepare a program for coordinating the government's enforcement of civil rights. In February, accepting Humphrey's outline as "wise," he created a new council under the vice president to ride herd on government agencies exactly as Humphrey had proposed. In the opening weeks of the new term, Humphrey was volubly present as the president laid out his master list of bills before congressional leaders. And afterward, when the president began signing Great Society measures and pushing others to passage, his vice president, rushing from last-minute cloakroom persuasion sessions, was close by his side.

In the majestic prospect of domestic progress envisioned by Johnson, there was one small complication: the five-year-old war in Vietnam. By the standards of so flamboyant a cold warrior as Johnson, it was a conflict on the fringe. It posed nothing like the threat that loomed after World War II when Moscow's victorious Communism seemed likely to encroach on the Middle East—and was brought up short by the Truman Doctrine's aid to Greece and Turkey. It represented nothing like the danger to U. S. safety presented by the postwar weakness of western Europe—so dramatically and effectively met by the economic-military mobilizations of the Marshall Plan and the NATO alliance. It was not even the challenge to collective security presented in the Korean Communists' 1950 invasion across the 38th parallel—alertly faced and hurled back by United Nations action under U. S. leadership.

Moscow called it a war of liberation. The Pentagon's term was a brushfire war. But in holding Communism at bay around the world, the United States had guaranteed the security of all sorts of countries. After the North Atlantic Treaty Organization came the Southeast Asia Treaty Organization and Central Treaty Organization, a network of alliances that encircled the entire borders of Communist Eurasia. The system required a lot of policing, and the United States built bases in forty-four countries.

In Indochina there was already a record of American intervention. President Truman had stepped in first with military aid to the embattled French colonial overlords. When the French lost out, President Eisenhower countenanced a peace worked out at a conference in Geneva that divided Vietnam in two; the Communist victors over the French got the northern half. President Kennedy had accepted the responsibility of helping the new state of South Vietnam establish its authority, even to the point of inviting the overthrow of the first president when he appeared to abuse that authority.

Some called the strife that broke out in South Vietnam in the late 1950s a civil war. That was because so many of those who took up arms again the new government, whether they were Communists or not, felt that they were still waging the fight for national independence. They saw among the leaders in the Saigon regime many who had served in the French forces, many who confessed a Catholicism alien to their ancient Buddhist-Confucian traditions. But to John Kennedy, who at his inaugural called on his countrymen to bear any burden, make any sarifice for freedom, the war was a fight against Communist oppression. To lose it was to tip South Vietnam, and with it the neighboring states of Laos, Cambodia, Thailand, and Malaysia, to the Communist side. Before his death, Kennedy sent eighteen thousand members of the U S. armed forces into South Vietnam to prop up the tottering domino.

Still, Saigon was not Berlin. President Kennedy preferred to deal with the threat posed by the guerrilla warfare of the Viet Cong revolutionaries by sending in the irregular operatives of the CIA and the counter-insurgency commandos of the army's Special Forces. Only at the end of his 2 and a half years in office had the failure of the South Vietnamese regime to establish its authority in the countryside begun to force Kennedy and his advisers to consider dispatching regular U. S. forces to ward off its collapse. By that time, Peking had split violently with Moscow for signing the nuclear test ban treaty with the United States, and landing U. S. troops on Communism's Asian flank seemed a good deal less of a risk.

By customary cold war procedure, when armed force might conceivably be needed sooner than Congress could get around to declaring war, presidents would obtain from the Senate resolutions of support in advance for whatever they might have to do. In the summer of 1964, when hostile small craft reportedly attacked U. S. warships in the Gulf of Tonkin, President Johnson obtained just such Senate endorsement for the reprisals he took then—and might take later—against the forces of North Vietnam. As one government succeeded another and the political situation grew ever more unstable in Saigon, Ho Chi Minh in Hanoi stepped up the pressure on the South. He called for the unification of all Vietnamese under his rule, denied him by the Geneva settlement after his victory over the French in the 1950s. General Maxwell Taylor, the former chairman of the Joint Chiefs of Staff made ambassador in Saigon by Johnson, reported that the Viet Cong—supplied over back-country trails by Ho from the North—were inflicting defeat after defeat on a South Vietnamese army sapped by corruption at the top and desertions below. Not only that, the National Liberation Front, political arm of the revolutionaries, was providing the only real government in much if not most of the rural areas. By the beginning of 1965, Taylor was advising that, even with American arms, training, and logistical support, the South Vietnamese army was fast losing ground. There were indications, besides, that Ho Chi Minh, scenting final victory, was moving in elements of the North Vietnamese army for the kill.

A decision therefore pressed upon Johnson at the beginning of his second term just as he was rolling up his sleeves to build the Great Society: should the United States call upon its superpower might to avert the takeover of South Vietnam by this small upstart Communist state on the faraway rim of Asia? As Johnson saw it, each successive president before him had upheld the U. S. commitment to defend freedom in Southeast Asia. President Kennedy had not hesitated to send a substantial number of uniformed Americans into South Vietnam to support that commitment. And Johnson's top advisers, the same Secretary of State Dean Rusk and Secretary of Defense Robert McNamara he had inherited from Kennedy, counseled that it was vital for the United States as guarantor of peace in the region—and, as Rusk said, everywhere—to maintain that commitment.

The president addressed himself to the decision at the same time that he was sending his Great Society measures to the new Congress, in February 1965. The forum for his deliberations was the National Security Council. By law, Vice President Humphrey was a member of the council.

Throughout his sixteen years in the Senate, Humphrey had taken a typically liberal line on Southeast Asia, cheering on the independence movements of Indochina, Malaysia, and Indonesia and objecting loudly when Nixon and other Eisenhower advisers proposed dropping nuclear bombs to rescue the French in 1954. In the Kennedy years he defended the president but said in a Senate debate that the United States should limit its part in Vietnam to "military assistance, to supplies, and to military training." Campaigning in 1964 he had been careful to say as little as possible about Vietnam, except to join in the 98-to-2 Senate vote for the President's Tonkin Gulf resolution. Unlike his Foreign Relations Committee colleague Mike Mansfield, who had traveled and lived in Asia and taught university courses in Asian affairs, he could not be accounted a Far Eastern expert. But with his insatiable appetite for information, Humphrey had formed many ties with people knowledgeable about Vietnam. One important influence was Major General Edward Lansdale.

Lansdale first won a name as the CIA's chief operative aiding President Magsaysay's famously successful efforts to overcome Communist guerrillas in the Philippines. The Dulles brothers then moved him to South Vietnam, where he spent a half dozen years in dogged "nation-building" around President Diem and his successors. Lansdale was unable to duplicate his Philippine success in Saigon. It became his fate instead to be pilloried in Graham Greene's sardonic 1957 novel *The Quiet American*. But nobody on the U. S.

side knew the South Vietnamese civilian scene better than Lansdale. Sent home and retired after General Taylor took charge of the embassy, Lansdale carried away the conviction that the problems in Vietnam were political rather than military, requiring political, not military, solutions. Humphrey, who talked often and long with Lansdale in Washington, tended to share that view.

A more intimate Humphrey counselor was Thomas Hughes, a Rhodes scholar from Minnesota who had served as Humphrey's legislative counsel in the 1950s and was now chief of State Department intelligence and research. Shortly after Humphrey took office Secretary Rusk called in Hughes for a pointed conversation. While acknowledging Humphrey's long interest in foreign affairs, Rusk warned that the Vice President could not expect to be involved in interagency formulations of policy. As vice president, Rusk said, Johnson had served without a foreign-affairs staff of his own, relying instead on information supplied by the State and Defense departments and by the CIA. To Hughes, Rusk assigned the job of briefing the vice president from time to time. But, he made clear, foreign affairs were first and last the president's preserve. In Rusk's eyes and—as Humphrey read this warning signal—in Johnson's eyes as well, the vice president's role was to be limited.

Humphrey had already sat in on a cabinet meeting, taking copious notes, at which Rusk reported the situation in South Vietnam as "critical." He had also attended a first National Security Council meeting, at which he learned that the president had dispatched his national security adviser, McGeorge Bundy, to Saigon for a first-hand look at the situation.

As Johnson prepared to make the decision of plunging deeper into Vietnam, crisis erupted. On February 6, 1965, Viet Cong forces attacked a U. S. enclave at Pleiku, killing nine and wounding one hundred Americans. Humphrey was in Minnesota mending political fences that weekend and missed the tense council session at which the president received cables from both Bundy and Ambassador Taylor urging that the Pleiku outrage demanded prompt and stern retaliation—by bombing North Vietnam.

Humphrey also missed the next day's dramatic, drawn-out session—with McNamara's assistant Cyrus Vance manning the "secure" telephone to Saigon in the next room, the president calling out: "Are they unanimous in Saigon? Have you talked to each one individually?" and Vance answering: "Yes, they are solid and unanimous." It was Mike Mansfield, invited to sit in (and occupying Humphrey's vacant chair across from the president) who said: "I would negotiate. I would not hit back. I would get into negotiations." To the hushed aides around the table, Johnson's dismissal of his old Senate lieutenant sounded unexpectedly brusque. The president did not even ask Mansfield how he might go about negotiating. He said: "I just don't think you can stand still and take this sort of thing." His mind was made up. The bombing of North Vietnam was on.

Three days later, before the generals had time to execute Johnson's reprisal, the Viet Cong struck again at American forces, a mortar attack that killed twenty-three at the coastal base of Quinhon. This time, Humphrey was not only on hand for the meeting but became involved beforehand in a discussion with Secretary McNamara and others. They noted that none other than Soviet Premier Alexei Kosygin chanced to be visiting North Vietnam, and Humphrey thought he had McNamara's agreement that the retaliation should be delayed until Kosygin left Hanoi. But when the president joined the meeting and went around the table asking for opinions, Rusk and McNamara recommended prompt response. Humphrey spoke out strongly for a delay. So did Undersecretary of State George Ball and Ambassador Llewellyn Thompson, the Soviet expert brought in for the occasion. But neither of these bureaucrats had pledged to the president, as Humphrey had when Johnson chose him as running mate a few months before, that though he might "be against me until as president I make up my mind," after that he would "follow [the president's] policies." Now, at the first important occasion of their partnership, Humphrey had broken his pledge.

Why did Humphrey pop off in the presence of others? In his memoirs he implied that McNamara and others went back on what they had agreed to before Johnson came into the room, and in consequence he was left alone in counseling against the president's action. But obviously there was more to it than the ploys of contending courtiers. Asked later, he was vague in his reasoning. "I had misgivings, uneasiness. [It was] by the nature of myself."

The reason was simply that Humphrey, in accepting the office Johnson had offered him, erred in his judgment of the president and their changed relationship. Other Johnson friends and advisers, men such as Jim Rowe, Abe Fortas, and Mike Mansfield, were careful to turn down positions that would have placed them under his control. Certainly Humphrey had experiences aplenty of these lacerating constraints. But they had always been in the context of the Senate, where Humphrey could truly say that his position was "one of creativity, innovation and free lancing," where the process of decision was slow and consensual, and practically nothing was final. The real power resided in the Executive, and as Humphrey himself said later, senators see it only from "outside the fence." Now, coming suddenly into its presence as vice president, he was slow to perceive the guillotine finality with which Johnson, making decisions as president, wielded his power. In advancing to the vice presidency, Humphrey knew that he had become a considerable figure with several substantial constituencies—and views that had a way of prevailing. He thought he could accept Johnson's outbursts as he had in the past and go on upholding views that Johnson would come round to accepting as he had before on some important matters—civil rights, for instance.

He could not have been more mistaken. The following day he asked his aide John Rielly, as if nothing had happened, to "keep a good file on Vietnam. Shortly I shall be sitting down with the president, the secretary of state and others to discuss U. S. policy on Southeast Asia in all its implications."

Rielly had to tell his boss that he had learned from another member's assist-ant that the president was conducting Security Council meetings without notifying the vice president.

In those meetings the bombing reprisals had only doubled the pressures on the president. For now he had two decisions to make: first, whether to continue the bombing of North Vietnam begun as a tit-for-tat reprisal; sec-ond, whether to send U. S. ground forces in to stem the rout inside South Vietnam.

Alone among those Johnson still listened to, Undersecretary of State George Ball opposed both courses. As a member of the U. S. Bombing Survey at the end of World War II, Ball had seen the limited result of trying to knock out Germany from the air. As an international lawyer with clients in highest French circles, he had lived through the futile attempt of the French to pre-vail by arms in the Vietnamese jungles. Still looking for help in persuading the president not to get into a war he profoundly believed the United States could not win, Ball thought of course of Humphrey. Remembering that Rusk had detailed Tom Hughes to brief the vice president about events on occa-sion, Ball therefore left Johnson's next meeting to urge Hughes to bring Humphrey up to date on Vietnam. Using his secure telephone, Hughes called Humphrey, who had flown to the Georgia hunting lodge of the Minneapolis tycoon Ford Bell for a quail-shooting weekend. At Humphrey's suggestion, Hughes flew to Thomasville, Georgia, where they tramped the woods and talked for most of the weekend. Deciding that the only thing to do was to write a memorandum to the president, Humphrey asked Hughes to draft it. Hughes did so on the plane back to Washington. Humphrey put on the finishing touches and sent it to the president.

Unlike Ball's dissent, which was cued to the technical papers before the president, Humphrey's memo was broad and sweeping. And it was shrewd. Here was one political heavyweight speaking to another. Ever talky, ever ready with an opinion, ever prone to see things in terms of "issues," Hum-phrey went right ahead, while protesting his loyalty, to offer his views on the "politics" of the Vietnam decision.

First of all, he said, in thinking to win by bombing and landing troops in Asia, the president was moving Goldwater's way. Why do that, he asked, when we've won so big at the polls that for once we don't have to worry about the Republican right? In the recent campaign, "by contrast, we stressed not enlarging the war"—and won by a landslide.

Second, Humphrey doubted whether the president's proposed course was "politically understandable to the American public." Democrats went to war when they had a clear case, as in the two world wars. They had a pretty good case in Korea, too—rallying for collective security against a straight, across-the-border aggression. But you had to agree, people were confused about Korea before it was over. And in Vietnam, Humphrey said, America did not even have that much of a case. All it had was a thin, politically barren argument about protecting "national interest."

Third, Humphrey said, Democrats had built a record of avoiding World War III. To escalate, to bomb in Vietnam, was to court it, or at least to invite another entanglement with the Chinese of the unpleasant kind that had snarled us up in Korea. "Political opposition will mount steadily," coming not from the Republicans but from new and different sources: from "Democratic liberals, independents, labor."

So, Humphrey counseled, while politically strong the administration should "cut losses." And he offered this final advice:

> President Johnson is personally identified with, and greatly admired for, political ingenuity. People will be counting on him to use on the world scene his unrivaled talents as a politician. They will be watching to see how he makes the transition from the domestic to the world scene.
>
> The best possible outcome a year from now would be a Vietnamese settlement which turns out to be better than was in the cards because LBJ's political talent for the first time came to grips with a world crisis, and did so successfully.

A few days later, Humphrey told Hughes that his memo had only "infuriated" Johnson. It was at once clear that the vice president was now in the president's doghouse. He was frozen out of the president's Vietnam consultations. His plight in some ways bore resemblance to the hazing he underwent when he first arrived in the Senate and, as now, failed to perceive at once the power relationships. But then the treatment was administered by the likes of Harry Byrd, and Humphrey had found allies—notably the senator from Texas—to help win his way to the club's acceptance. But this time the hazing was being administered by Lyndon Johnson himself.

To Progressives, issues matter most. And Humphrey, a Progressive whose very nature, upbringing, senatorial experience, and platform proclivities had driven him to strong stands on issues, found himself required to back down on an issue about which he obviously felt strongly. In a like position an earlier prairie Progressive, William Jennings Bryan, had resigned as secretary of state when President Wilson, against Bryan's deepest feelings, headed toward war. As an appointed official, Bryan was free to do so. Humphrey, elected by the people to a four-year term, had no such choice. The sole constitutional responsibility of the office he had assumed and sworn to fulfill, apart from the ceremonial duty of presiding over the Senate, was to hold himself in readiness to step in as president if that office should become vacant. Only one vice president, John Calhoun, had ever resigned. In an age when the succession to the presidency had come to count for so much, resignation was out of the question.

Formerly, as an outspoken Progressive, Humphrey had counted a number of constituencies, among which Minnesota was but one. As Vice President,

he abruptly realized and belatedly began to remind himself, he had a constituency of one. The president had cast the all-important vote designating him
for his office and would assuredly do so four years hence. To win acceptance
in his job, the sole party Humphrey had to please was the president. Though
he never said it, at least not aloud, he was Johnson's prisoner. He was trapped.
Humphrey, the man of issues, had no choice but to subordinate himself to
the president on *all* issues—starting with Vietnam, which soon became, not
only for Humphrey and Johnson but for all America, the main issue. Humphrey liked to say that he loved being vice president, that "to be elected vice
president was an honor second only to being president." But he also said it
took "a great deal of self discipline . . . to be second man in a two-man team."
One can only imagine what Humphrey's thoughts may have been when, the
day after his dressing down for his memo, he had to assemble five liberal
senators, all of them his good friends, at the president's direction and sit
silent at his office desk while McGeorge Bundy lectured them for their criticisms of Johnson's Vietnam actions.

Humphrey did not give up, at least not right away. He had ended his
February 17 memo with the declaration: "I intend to support the Administration whatever the president's decision." And never again did he raise his
voice at general meetings in disagreement with the president. But as in his
bout with Byrd, he returned a second time to the charge. Admitted to one
more Vietnam meeting in March, he heard the reports of the "pounding of
North Vietnam" and the plans to "put in U. S. combat troops" and sent
Johnson another memorandum. Although the president had given the orders,
Humphrey said: "We do not see yet where we are going. We need a policy
definition." Humphrey's recommendation was to adopt what he called "the
political objective of hanging on" in South Vietnam—subordinating bombing ("a dangerous policy") and troop input while seeking "every indirect means
of sounding out weaknesses on the other side that might lead to negotiations."

"We do not need all these memos," Johnson growled. "I don't think you
should have them lying around your office." And from that time, Humphrey
was banished from important deliberations. He could not be kept from the
National Security Council, of which the vice president is a member by law,
but its meetings grew infrequent and consisted of routine recital. Johnson
reserved the big decisions for his Tuesday luncheons. Only Rusk, McNamara,
Bundy, CIA Director John McCone and Chairman of the Joint Chiefs Earle
Wheeler attended this "Tuesday Cabinet." Humphrey was out.

Accordingly, Humphrey was not around when Johnson without informing the country changed the mission of U. S. troops in Vietnam from support to combat in April 1965. He was also on the outside when Johnson,
responding later that month to a panicky cable from his ambassador that
Communists were about to take over the Dominican Republic, became the
first president to order Marines into a Latin American country since Roose-

velt proclaimed the good-neighbor policy. Humphrey only learned what Johnson was up to when, implored by the Venezuelan ambassador to get word to the White House that his government was opposed to hasty action, he was told by McGeorge Bundy it was too late: "We've had a meeting this afternoon. The intervention is on."

Humphrey was also not present that summer when McNamara and others, flitting back and forth between Washington and Saigon, brought in their plans for pouring three hundred thousand troops into Vietnam. Finally, Humphrey was absent from the climactic meetings on July 27, 1965, at which Johnson accepted the recommendations and then turned the tables on those who had proposed them. Setting aside the program of Secretary McNamara and his generals for calling up reserves and asking Congress for a whopping appropriation, the president required the defense secretary to find the needed men by beefing up draft calls and to submit only a small request for supplementary funds to Congress. Instead of going before a joint session of Congress and summoning the nation to sacrifice, he announced his decision at an afternoon press conference.

If Johnson had no further use for Humphrey's counsel on Vietnam, the vice president could still carry out the more footling tasks in foreign affairs—serve as the president's stand-in on the more perfuctory occasions. So even while cutting him out of top meetings, Johnson arranged through Rusk for Humphrey to receive diplomats and visiting dignitaries for whom he simply lacked time. This Humphrey did with diligence, sending Johnson chatty reports to which he received no replies. Characteristically, he made some lasting friendships during these supposedly formal encounters. Not only that, he exhibited such high spirits dancing in and out of Washington embassies on these assigned rounds that Washington critics began alleging a certain fatuous frivolity among the qualities in Humphrey that detracted from his image as a believable future president.

The foreign-relations freezeout also extended to the kind of overseas trips that Johnson himself had made as vice president to President Kennedy. But one of Humphrey's functions was chairing the president's space council, and there was no keeping Humphrey out of the parades after the astronauts Jim McDevitt and Ed White circled the moon in June 1965. At every reception he kept pestering the president to let him take the pair to the Paris air show, where the Soviets had earlier scored by unveiling a giant new jet and sending in Cosmonaut Yuri Gagarin. At the State Department party, Johnson gave Humphrey a wink and then announced that the vice president would lead the U. S. space troupe to Paris at once. They took off that midnight in a wild scramble, and McDevitt and White and their wives were the hit of the show. Humphrey made the most of his opportunity. President de Gaulle, having decided it was time for some thaw in frosty Franco-American relations, met with Humphrey for an hour and twenty minutes, during which the Vice President made a strong plea for French understanding of U. S.

actions in the Dominican Republic and Vietnam. Humphrey's only other foreign trip during his fall from favor followed when Adlai Stevenson died in London on July 14, and he was permitted to accompany the body of his old friend back to the United States.

Even Humphrey's involvement in domestic affairs was impaired by Johnson's displeasure over his Vietnam advice. The vice president soon saw that legislation beyond the Civil Rights Act of 1964 would be required if Southern resistance to votes for blacks was to be overcome. No sooner had his new rights council held its first meeting than trouble erupted in Selma, Alabama. If anyone could rival Birmingham's Police Chief Bull Connor—with his police dogs, cattle prods, and fire hoses—for race-baiting notoriety, it was Selma's Sheriff Jim Clark. When Martin Luther King, Jr., assembled demonstrators to protest the blocking of black voter-registration in his county, Clark arrested 3,400 of them, including King. The following Sunday his men clubbed and teargassed 600 blacks and whites as they tried to cross a bridge into Selma. King, freed by federal court order, appealed to the nation's clergy for help. When 300 rallied to Selma, one, the Rev. James Reeb of Boston, fell mortally injured by a deputy bludgeon.

Humphrey brought a group of civil rights leaders into the Oval Office. Afterward he told Johnson: "You're not getting across. You've got to speak again on voting rights." And at Humphrey's suggestion the president went before a joint session of Congress to call for enactment of the Voting Rights law. The bill passed, and Johnson, invoking his grand vision of unity before a black audience at Washington's Howard University in May, proclaimed: "We Shall Overcome."

But the persisting civil rights disturbances annoyed and disquieted the president, who became impatient with Humphrey's council. And it was true that Humphrey, inexperienced as yet in how the Executive Branch functioned and not well served by staff, was slow getting on the ball. It was his style to get all parties together to talk out disputes as if he were handling constituents, rather than exerting his power. Johnson was particularly aggravated when the Department of Health Education and Welfare, ruling that Chicago had not made plans to correct racial imbalance in its schools as prescribed by the law, ordered a cut-off of federal funds to Mayor Daley's board of education.

In the next racial blowup the president did not turn to Humphrey. In July, Joseph Califano, one of McNamara's whiz kids at the Pentagon, moved into the White House as the president's coordinator of domestic affairs. Califano was bright, and he was aggresive. When blacks rioted in the Watts district of Los Angeles, the White House sent in a task force headed by the Justice Department's Ramsey Clark. Humphrey's council was not even consulted. That fall an order went out under Califano's prodding to recalcitrant Southern school districts. A subordinate agency, after consultation with Humphrey, had sent them the same word two weeks before. If that was not a flagrant enough mixup, the White House suddenly issued its report on the first year's progress in fulfilling the 1964 act just before Humphrey's council was about to put one out.

The domestic crises happened at the same time that the president, having set his new course for war in Vietnam, was laying out a series of high-level briefings for business and professional leaders at the White House. Dr. Carleton Chapman, president of the American Heart Association, attended an August dinner at which Secretary McNamara explained with flipcharts how American armed might would turn the situation around by 1966. Chapman noted that Humphrey "was present but more or less ignored, not only by the President but by Cabinet members like McNamara. It was quite evident, commented on by guests afterward. He wandered aimlessly among the crowd, trying to be pleasant." Novelist Saul Bellow sadly dropped the idea of doing a piece about his old Minnesota campus friend, "anticipating no pleasure . . . in writing about poor Hubert's misery as LBJ's captive." This was the summer when Tom Lehrer, the Harvard troubadour, was singing in nightclubs:

> Whatever became of Hubert?
> Has anyone heard a thing?
> Once he shone on his own,
> Now he sits home alone
> And waits for the phone to ring.

And it was the period when the vice president, trying to find out what was up with his civil rights council, was kept waiting outside the office of thirty-four-year-old Joe Califano. Unable to get to the president, Humphrey was reduced to asking Johnson's political aide Marvin Watson to relay his "uncertainty" to the president. Finally, in September, Johnson called in Humphrey and Califano. The vice president agreed without protest that his council should be abolished.

Given that Humphrey had never gotten on top of his assignment and given that responsibility finally resides in those charged by statute with a policy's execution, the outcome was probably inevitable. But when the New York *Post*'s James Wechsler entitled a column "Slowdown on Civil Rights," Humphrey wrote to deny it and protested, unconvincingly, that he would still act as "coordinator of civil rights" without title.

The Watts explosion, first of the big urban racial outbursts of the 1960s, marked a turning point. Reflecting the vast shift in the black population from the rural South to the urban North, it signaled a change from the nonviolence preached by such Humphrey friends as Roy Wilkins, Clarence Mitchell, and Martin Luther King, Jr. to calls for direct action from new, younger, more radical black leaders, such as Stokely Carmichael and Rap Brown. It also enormously increased backlash among whites outside the South, and this was felt at once on Capitol Hill and at the White House.

If any proposition is self-evident in politics, it is that a change of structures and a relocation of responsibilities are always accompanied by alterations in policy as well as programs. Johnson, like Humphrey, denied this as the President's Council on Equal Opportunity passed out of existence. Ironically, it was just after the president of the United States had proclaimed "We Shall Overcome" that the government's push for racial justice appeared to let up. The Voting Rights Act of 1965 was the last great civil rights measure enacted in what turned out to be the second Reconstruction of the South. That summer, King, moving north, was stoned as he led a drive for fair housing assurances in Chicago. And Humphrey wound up "loyally" agreeing that the president should not accept his Special Housing Committee's recommendation to extend the Executive Order banning discrimination in federally supported housing to all housing. The white flight to the suburbs spread out from every city. And when Johnson's Commission on Violence in the Cities reported in 1968 that the frenzy of urban resettlement had reached such proportions that the races of the United States seemed likely to live as two nations apart, the president who said "we shall overcome" laid the report on the shelf.

JOHNSON's hazing of Humphrey lasted nearly a year, and in many respects it never ended. Outwardly, Humphrey performed as the busiest vice president in history. Besides overseeing the space and marine programs, he kept a fatherly eye on the poverty program, served as the administration's conduit to mayors and local governments, led the President's Committee on Youth Employment, and headed the "Discover America" program to right the tilting balance of international payments by promoting stateside tourism. On taking office, he received as many as a thousand speaking invitations a month. In his first eight months he took fifty-two trips to places as far away as Alaska and Hawaii, and yet he seemed to turn up at every legislative conference, diplomatic reception, or plumbers' convention in the capital. He was on the phone to Minnesota keeping on top of the cliffhanging election recount that ended only in March with his DFL protégé Karl Rolvaag safely installed as governor by 91 votes. He kept up his usual voluminous correspondence by dictating in cars, on planes, and after midnight at his three offices in the windup of his average sixteen- to eighteen-hour days. Bouncy as ever after a few hours' sleep, he loved to quote his father: "Work never killed anyone."

But Lyndon Johnson, bearing down ever harder on his vice president, seemed only to feel that what he had endured from the Kennedys in that office was treatment too good for Humphrey. Having passed his years as No. 2 in the dark of the Kennedy dazzle, he begrudged any shaft of public light that fell on his own vice president. He often chided Humphrey when he felt the vice president was getting too much newspaper space. And to make sure that Humphrey did not, Johnson forbade him to take any member of the national press with him on his out-of-town trips. Paranoid even by latter-day presidential standards about leaks, Johnson almost invariably blamed them on his vice president's loose tongue. "Goddamit, Hubert, can't you keep your mouth shut?" he would say. "Every time I say something I find your friends writing stories about it." And try as he would to comply, Humphrey sometimes slipped. On one occasion, he told a group of labor leaders, off the cuff, that the administration was about to ask Congress for an increased minimum wage. A newspaper picked up the comment, and at the next congressional breakfast Johnson said caustically: "I see by the papers where I have a minimum wage program." When Humphrey apologized next day, Johnson put his arm around him and said soothingly: "Well, we all make mistakes."

"What does he need all that staff for?" the president asked after the inaugural and barred Humphrey from hiding assistants on other department payrolls, as he himself had done when vice president. Every time Humphrey flew in an official plane, he had to get Johnson's personal okay beforehand. From the moment he took office, the text of all his prepared speeches had to be sent to the White House in advance, and practically all suffered excisions. After Humphrey incurred Johnson's anger by suggesting he hold back in Vietnam, the censorship grew severe. Humphrey's February address at a United Nations conference on Pope John's *Pacem in Terris* encyclical, which naturally contained references to peace, was slashed so ruthlessly that Humphrey's friend Bill Benton remarked: "Hubert, that was the worst speech I've ever heard you give."

Nobody enjoyed delivering speeches more than Hubert Humphrey. He particularly loved riding around the party circuit of Jefferson-Jackson Day dinners and firing up the faithful with calls to work in the political vineyard. As vice president he did so every chance he got, but Johnson did not seem to think such efforts worthwhile. He let the party machinery slide, and scarcely ever saw Democratic Party Chairman John Bailey. But he kept close watch over the President's Club, the campaign-financing device by which he attracted support and contributions from businessmen—particularly the businessmen who had watched him ease Bobby Kennedy out of his cabinet in 1964 and then crossed over when the radical right seemed to be ruling the Republican party.

Early in 1965, Johnson summoned Humphrey and his campaign treasurer. Humphrey was given the task of going around the country thanking President's Club contributors and putting the bite on them to renew their membership (minimum dues: one thousand dollars). Much as he loved speaking, Humphrey detested begging for money. But at Johnson's command, he did it. On his first outing, to Newark, the dinner he addressed took in $304,065. Most of these occasions were small and exclusive, and there was always time after the address for the vice president to share tidbits of high-office thinking in Washington, for questions and answers, and for individual donors to make suggestions and requests that the vice president presumably took back to the White House.

In this way, Humphrey met the chiefs of practically every corporation in *Fortune*'s 500, and inevitably it was *Fortune* that asked the question: "What's New About Humphrey?" Humphrey answered:

> Don't let anyone ever tell you that it's just a change of office. It's a change of life-style, even a change of attitude. For one who is naturally effusive and gregarious and outgoing, it surely require[s] a great deal of self-discipline. But Muriel and I talked it out and . . . made up our minds we would be loyal and helpful to the President.
>
> I've changed. I've become more prudent. I've become more tolerant, too. When you come up the hard way, as I did, you become a bit brittle. Then, when life has been good to you, you become more tolerant.

Humphrey's change of emphasis was not lost on *Fortune* editor William Bowen, who recalled for his executive readership that the vice president had once said: "Who are these high and mighty people who think there is something in this country besides . . . the men who work in the shops, in the factory, on the farms? *They* are the producers." At the president's urging, he now addressed the National Association of Manufacturers and pledged "our faith in you who bear the great responsibility for the success of the [free enterprise] system." Saluting the Johnson-Humphrey "working partnership" with the U. S. Chamber of Commerce, he said: "The Great Society only has meaning in the context of an expanding economy." At Philadelphia's Union League a utility magnate declared: "He certainly increased confidence in this administration," and some forty top corporate officers renewed their financial pledges. In Manhattan, where his hosts at the Fifth Avenue Club were U. S. Steel Chairman Roger Blough and Investment Banker Sidney Weinberg, he talked about "outdated anti-trust laws," and the response was even better. During the year, Humphrey addressed president's clubs in twenty-seven states. At the White House there was a granitic gleam of gratitude. Informed that Humphrey was budgeted to raise $752,000 in a November swing through thirteen states, Johnson wrote at the bottom of the memo: "Half of it would be good."

At the start of the new term both Johnson and Humphrey had expected that the vice president's evangelizing would promote mainly the president's big domestic programs. With every expectation of igniting student and faculty enthusiasm for the administration's gigantic aid-to-education programs, Humphrey sent Johnson a list of eight university appearances he had arranged to make in the first six months. But as soon as the president escalated the war in Vietnam, opposition, though slight at first, arose on the campuses. The "teach-ins," originating with an all-night seminar attended by three thousand students at the University of Michigan on March 24, were the peace movement's first response. The idea proved contagious. Other big universities held them, and Berkeley's lasted two days.

Humphrey's appearances usually included question-and-answer sessions, and of course he had to respond to queries about Southeast Asia. Loyally he hewed to the administration's official line. In April, Johnson himself appeared once on campus to add peace to his Vietnam aims. Speaking at Johns Hopkins University, the president proclaimed that, as part of its commitment to Vietnam his Administration stood ready to enter into "unconditional negotiations" at any time. That raised the question of whether the rebel Viet Cong would figure in any such talks. Humphrey, again following the administration line, assured Michigan State University students that the Viet Cong was "not a great idealistic movement, not at all. These are no reformers. They are destroyers, assassins. The enemy is not in Washington. It's in Hanoi and Peking, and we ought to know it." He always gave the White House reports on his meetings. On July 12, 1965, came his first mention of being heckled: "Only about a dozen or fewer persons among 1200 appeared to show any resistance to our Vietnam policy. Of these dozen, three put down their signs after I had spoken and started to applaud. In other words, they confessed their sins and were saved."

In an address to a western governors' conference—cleared of course with the White House—in mid-June, Humphrey restated the president's goals, adding an almost imperceptible qualifier of his own: "Recognizing that a political solution of the conflict is essential, the Administration stands on these principles honoring our commitment, continuing willingness to seek an honorable political solution, and a massive cooperative development program for friend and foe alike, to give the people of Vietnam a cause for which to fight."

His first interview on Vietnam, given that month to Jack Bell of the Associated Press, showed him still guarded. Asked if his remark that "we'd have to win on the ground" meant with ground forces, Humphrey said: "No, I mean that while I support the bombing, ultimately this conflict will have to be won in Vietnam."

How, it may be asked, was it possible for Humphrey, the man of issues, to move from outspoken opposition in February toward these expressions of support for the war? Part of the answer at least is that Humphrey was a man of many issues and had throughout his political life taken strong stands for both war and peace. Only deep-dyed ideologues should find this ambiguity beyond understanding in a political leader. Even the American author of the cold war, President Truman, at the height of the Berlin airlift crisis was capable, while running for reelection in 1948, of suddenly asking Chief Justice Fred Vinson to undertake a peace mission to Moscow.

Humphrey had entered upon his political manhood as a Roosevelt internationalist in the isolationist Midwest, upholding the League of Nations ideal while preaching armed collective security before Pearl Harbor against fascist aggression. When the United States next went to war in Korea, Humphrey cheered again for armed collective security—this time through the United

Nations against communist aggression. In the 1950s, while compiling an unvarying cold war voting record, he made himself perhaps the leading advocate of disarmament in public office. While regularly introducing resolutions for freeing the "captive nations" of Eastern Europe, he deplored the arms race in repeated speeches, pioneered the nuclear test ban with the Soviets, and pushed for other treaties that were later embodied in the policy known as détente.

It was Humphrey's fate in 1965 to lose this latitude in the administration's plunge toward heavy commitment of troops in Vietnam. One evening in July, after he reviewed the parade at the Marines' Washington barracks, General Wallace Greene, the corps commandant, took him aside. Looking gravely at his guest he said: "Mr. Vice President, you must understand that it will take no less than five hundred thousand troops on the ground to do what we must do to carry out our mission and bring an end in Vietnam." Drawing back in shocked disbelief, Humphrey said: "My God, general, you can't really mean that." Greene replied: "Indeed I do, Mr. Vice President. You should have no illusions."

Humphrey was not present when Greene said the same thing to President Johnson at the showdown meeting a week later. But he caught the force of the president's decision sooner than anybody. He was due to address another governors' conference in Detroit just as Johnson, having made his big commitment, was bent on downplaying its importance. Having to leave a cabinet meeting to keep his engagement, there was no time to clear his speech. An hour or so later, Johnson read Humphrey's speech and the sentence: "The United States must be prepared for a long, ugly, costly war." The president exploded; his instructions sizzled to Detroit: "Hubert better damn sight not use it." Too late, the text had already been released, and Humphrey caught hell. Next day, he sent this message to his constituency of one: "I have a roomful of senators over here at the Capitol, and we thought that the [announcement] was tremendous. I was personally inspired, moved, and I just couldn't be happier if they had Christmas every day and every dream I ever wanted came true."

Following up this bit of groveling with an unbidden note to the president, Humphrey criticized his old friend Wayne Morse, one of the first senators to question the president's war policy. How, he asked, was it possible for Morse to call in the Senate for negotiations at the United Nations "when you are using every opportunity to achieve meaningful discussions" in and out of the United Nations? On Johnson's birthday he told him "how privileged I feel to be your Vice President and partner. You make me prouder of our country and our government every day." And he enclosed a letter from a friend on the Columbia University law faculty: "The great majority of the academic community is in support of the national policy in the distressing state of affairs in Southeast Asia. Most of us are writing and teaching—not 'teaching-in.' "

Early in October an event occurred that may have brought the professed partners a little closer. The president informed Humphrey that he would be entering Bethesda Naval Hospital for a gall bladder operation. "Well, Mother, let me tell you the news," Humphrey said as he walked into the house on Coquelin Terrace that evening. Muriel Humphrey promptly sent a pair of blue pajamas to the hospital room. Next morning as he left the house, the vice president was trailed by a man carrying a briefcase that held the code the president of the United States must have in case of a nuclear war. By further agreement, Humphrey received certain foreign visitors for the president. Johnson made a strong recovery, and when Humphrey paid a get-well call the president was wearing the blue pajamas. Humphrey told him about his visit with Souvanna Phouma of Laos. The supposedly neutralist premier had astonished Humphrey by recommending what he called the sure way to bring the Communists to negotiations speedily: bomb North Vietnam's dikes, thereby loosing floods that would destroy the people's fields and homes.

That was a bit extreme for Johnson. Reports were coming in of peace demonstrations in places like New York and San Francisco. While the president convalesced, Humphrey visited local election contests and met with more picketing. By this time draft calls were coming thick and fast, and pacifists started burning draft cards. Humphrey was criticized by liberals for saying his hecklers were Communists. After a visit to West Virginia State College, he sent the president a declaration of support signed by 1,200 of 2,000 undergraduates with this note: "There is a rising tide of support for your policy on Vietnam among the college students. I have been in touch with many. When they are asked to help their country, they respond whole-heartedly. Our young people give you every reason to be encouraged."

In November, Humphrey had a chance to return the hospitality of Tage Erlander, the Swedish prime minister who had played host to the European Socialist summit Humphrey attended in 1963. Of all European countries none was more outspokenly critical of U. S. armed intervention in Vietnam than Sweden, and when the Humphreys brought the Erlanders to West Virginia's palatial Greenbrier hotel for a weekend, the vice president took occasion to make a strong pitch for President Johnson's policies.

Such loyalty was not lost on the President, who wrote: "There are few matters more important than making our position in Southeast Asia crystal clear to our friends and allies. As a result of your report, I am most optimistic about the success of your endeavors in this direction." And one day near the end of 1965, when a vice-presidential aide brought the text of a Humphrey speech to the White House for the usual vetting, Johnson's response indicated a significant change of heart. McGeorge Bundy relayed the president's instructions: as an elected official, the vice president was free to say whatever he pleased whenever he pleased, and under no circumstances were members of the White House staff either to approve or censor anything he might say. As if this were not a clear enough signal that Humphrey might be returning to favor, when Bundy queried the President about who would represent the United States at the inaugural of Philippine President Ferdinand Marcos on December 30, the note came back from the Oval Office with this reply scrawled below: "Send the VP."

A couple of other factors favored the rehabilitation of Humphrey at this time. For one thing, five senators critical of Johnson's policy and led by Majority Leader Mansfield were about to depart for a look around Asia, and a Humphrey mission might usefully blanket their adverse reports. For another, at Christmas the president announced a "pause" in the bombing of North Vietnam and the launching of a "peace offensive" in quest of negotiations. "We're going to try Hubert's way now," he was heard to say. Finally, and perhaps most important, the president's hospitalization had drawn attention to the vice president; in early December, Gallup released a poll that disclosed the public knew little about the vice president. Worse, 56 percent of those polled said they would prefer that he never be president.

Humphrey's staff was devastated—but not Johnson. Apparently the president, a notorious poll watcher, took the Gallup findings to mean that his denial of the limelight to the vice president had worked exactly as he had wished, and that the public not only viewed Humphrey dimly but was grateful to have Lyndon Johnson in the White House. Wrapping a big arm around Humphrey's shoulder, he said that he had never had a press secretary as vice president, and Humphrey didn't need one either. He advised Humphrey to concentrate on being a good, loyal vice president and not pay attention to his image. It was convenient advice for Humphrey, who had been fretting at the poor quality of news stories about his activities. He went home and fired his press secretary.

The trip to Asia, laid on in part because the president thought Humphrey needed the prestige and exposure, marked the end of the doghouse days for the vice president. It was a trial run. Johnson sent along Jack Valenti of the White House staff to see how it went. Humphrey carried messages to the heads of the Japanese and Korean governments as well as to Marcos. He did all right. The dismal year of 1965 was over. In the new year he would step out and speak out—for the president.

26

The Hatchet Man

Now commences the most startling chapter in Humphrey's life. The vice president who had opposed the president's war policy persuaded himself that Johnson was right, and emerged as the leading spokesman for the president's course in Vietnam.

"My discovery of Asia" was how Humphrey described his first eight-day mission abroad for President Johnson. The reward for his performance was a bear-hug from the president, a broad hint that there would be a return trip soon—and an invitation to attend his first National Security Council meeting in nearly a year. Meanwhile, however, Indian Prime Minister Shri Lal Bahadur Shastri died, in January 1966, and Johnson as part of his peace offensive dispatched Humphrey at the head of a large delegation (including Secretary Rusk and Ambassador Averell Harriman) to represent the United States at the funeral in New Delhi. Representing the Soviet Union was Premier Alexei Kosygin, and the two men met three times in the first major face-to-face encounter between the new Soviet leader and top U. S. officials. Humphrey found Kosygin "a heavy, big-boned, blue-eyed man, a management type, not bombastic like Khrushchev, one of those hard-to-talk-to Russians, reasonable about being unreasonable, going through those insulting comments but never personal, very proper. Dressed well. Healthy. I watched his pulse-beat very carefully—he had his legs crossed—and I could see, very normal. You have to case a fellow by his hands: his hands, I noticed, were never weak and sweaty."

In their first exchange, sitting near one another at an early ceremony, Humphrey congratulated Kosygin on Soviet peacemaking efforts between India and Pakistan; Kosygin murmured: "Thank you, thank you." The second occurred by chance when both went for a stroll the next morning in the presidential palace garden. With Kosygin's daughter interpreting, Humphrey struck up a conversation about weather in Moscow and in Minnesota; he drew from Kosygin the comment that President Johnson's peace diplomacy was "too forceful, too dominating." Before they parted, Humphrey reached in his pocket and presented the Soviet premier with a set of cufflinks displaying the vice-presidential seal. At their third meeting, a formal occasion at which Secretary Rusk did most of the talking, Kosygin was impassively noncommittal about interceding in Hanoi. At the end, Humphrey said: "Mr. Kosygin, I am going to be watching you, and every time you lift your arms I am going to look to see if you have my cufflinks on. And if you do, I know that's the signal that things are better." Even Kosygin laughed.

From the assignments given him, it was evident that Humphrey had returned to the president's good graces. On successive Sunday evenings the Humphreys dined privately with the Johnsons in the White House family quarters. The peace offensive having fizzled, the president confided to the vice president that there was a job for him in the next phase of his Vietnam plans. "Keep your schedule loose, keep your bags packed," he said, and warned Humphrey to tell no one, not even his wife.

Johnson was worried about criticism when he ended the "pause" and went back to bombing the North. Fulbright was holding hearings on Vietnam; Mansfield was returning from a month's visit to Vietnam with a gloomy report; and fifteen senators addressed a letter to the president asking him not to resume the bombing. His old nemesis Bobby Kennedy, stronger than ever in the polls since leaving his cabinet for a seat in the Senate from New York, had begun talking up civil and humanitarian goals in Vietnam. With his military campaign well under way, Johnson decided to take the wind out of his critics' sails by programming a great drive to win "the other war"—to beat out the Communists in the competition for the heart, the votes, the fealty of the South Vietnamese populace. To dramatize America's nation-building effort in Vietnam and to muzzle the dissenting liberals, the president decided to call the leaders of the latest South Vietnamese government to meet him in Hawaii and concert plans to bring the benefits of democracy—schools, clinics, paved roads, and so on—to the South Vietnamese home front.

Inconveniently, the head of government when Johnson decided to add democratic transformation to his war aims in Vietnam was no civilian but a militarist and an extremely gaudy militarist at that. Air Vice Marshal Ky, at the age of thirty-four, was a fighter pilot who wore flashy black uniforms and jumpsuits and went around twirling the pistols he packed in hip holsters. He was, moreover, not a South Vietnamese at all but a Northerner, trained by the French—a Catholic in a country overwhelmingly Buddhist-Confucian by tradition.

In Johnson's grandstand play, the role of his vice president was both diplomatic and political. Historically, the only vice president to receive substantive working assignments had been Henry Wallace. That was during World War II, when President Roosevelt not only gave him important overseas missions but put him in charge of such large bureaucracies as the Board of Economic Warfare. Having humbled his vice president for so long that he was ready to go anywhere and do almost anything the President asked, Johnson proposed to make Humphrey his agent first to carry word of the Honolulu program to Asian capitals and then to tout his war policy to the American people.

Hypersensitive as Johnson was, he did not let Humphrey in on all of this at once. On February 6, the vice president delivered a speech to students in Michigan and was rushing to his fourth address of the day, in Cleveland, when his Secret Service men told him the president was calling from Hawaii. "Get back to Washington," the president said.

The trip was on: the president wanted Humphrey to meet him in Los Angeles on February 7 as he returned from Hawaii; Humphrey should fly to Honolulu, pick up Premier Ky and General Thieu, the chief of state, and assembled brass and newsmen, and proceed on a two-and-a-half week journey to Saigon and eight other Asian capitals.

In a mad rush, Humphrey and his party boarded a Boeing 707 dubbed "*Air Force Two*," and headed for Los Angeles. As John Rielly, his foreign affairs adviser said later: "We left without any briefing papers, any speech drafts. We got our shots in Guam." At Los Angeles, Humphrey went aboard *Air Force One*. While the presidential plane refueled, Johnson hastily filled him in on what had been said and done in Honolulu, and what he wanted Humphrey to accomplish on his trip. This was when Humphrey first heard details of the "democratic social revolution" that, along with the killing of Viet Cong, the United States was committed to delivering to the people of South Vietnam.

At Honolulu Humphrey's plane took aboard the Vietnamese chieftains and their families, Jack Valenti, McGeorge Bundy, and others of the White House staff. The White House press, which ordinarily never covered Humphrey, had been encouraged to ride along.

To Rielly, the trip was a "disaster," but Humphrey did not see it that way at all. For him, it was his chance at last to step out from the shadows and shine in the most prominent theater of American action. Exiled (in his view) from power after expectations of being close by the president's side, he had won his way back into his friend's trust. Now he was carrying out an assignment possibly more important than any a vice president had ever before been given.

On the first leg of the journey he conferred with Ky and Thieu, only to discover, when a copy of Valenti's report went astray and fell into his hands, that the president's aide was also sending back reports of his conversations. On the ground in Saigon he declared: "Yes, indeed, two wars can be won—the war to defeat the aggressors and the war to defeat the ancient and persistent enemies: disease, poverty, ignorance and despair." Self-delusion also suffused his top-secret cable to Johnson, which noted that Ky accompanied him on his field trips and "appears to be learning something about campaigning at the grass roots."

Humphrey was in South Vietnam only two days. At Danang he presented the Presidential Unit Citation to the 3rd marine regiment, whose commanding officer was killed a month later. At Chulai he visited the America division, the outfit involved afterward in the Mylai massacre. With General Westmoreland as guide he flew in an old prop plane along the demilitarized zone that marked the border with the North. Beside him at the window, Westmoreland talked about the terrain, the location of enemy forces, the fierce but invisible battle being fought in the jungle below. Humphrey's Marine aide, Colonel Herbert Beckington, who was also along, said later: "Humphrey was so knowledgable that I used to ask: 'My God, how did he know that?' But militarily, he was not knowledgable. And this man who was at ease with almost anybody, was not comfortable with professional military people. He had had no service experience. He once told me: 'One of my greatest regrets—it's been with me in public and private all my life—is that I never had the opportunity to serve in the armed forces. I cannot say how much that has hurt me.' "

But war made Humphrey think of his own battles with the Communists in the Minnesota DFL party. He told newsmen: "I fought those bastards then and I'm going to fight them now." When he flew on to Thailand the Foreign Minister identified Peking as the fount of Communist aggressiveness and warned that the pattern of subversion in the country's provinces nearest China—fifty police chiefs killed in six months by raiding bands—resembled that of the first outbreaks in South Vietnam in the late 1950s. At Ambassador Graham Martin's request, Humphrey readily signed a strong communiqué pledge of aid to the Thais. In Laos the supposedly neutralist premier Souvanna Phouma again identified China as the No. 1 menace. In India, Mrs. Indira Gandhi told of fears that China would invade. In Karachi, Humphrey said: "The closer one gets to the Communists, the less obscurity there is about their aim to take over the governments of Asia by force."

By the time he got to Australia, Humphrey, the political evangelist looking for a cause all Americans could rally to, was already viewing the Vietnam conflict as merely part of a much bigger battle—a massive struggle for Asia comparable in every way to that America undertook after 1945 when Communism took half of Europe but was stopped in its bid for the rest. Thus he saw it as he began sketching to his staff at a late-night session in Canberra the report he wanted to bring back to the president:

The big picture must be shown, the big picture that Mansfield, Fulbright, Morse all missed. The Vietnam situation is a dramatized, concentrated example of what the Communists intend to do elsewhere.

I want to show that there is a master plan, a designed conspiracy.

I want a report that says that every single official we have seen recognized a threat of Communism in Asia. The public knows that Communism is a danger just like they know that sin is wrong.

The danger of China is a plague—an epidemic, and we must stop that epidemic. . . .

We must lift the whole thing out of the quagmire in Saigon. China has many different plays in the making. This is not a fight about Saigon. If this is only a fight about Vietnam, then you are not going to get my kid. And I will have a helluva time convincing Mrs. Humphrey that he ought to go.

Humphrey's staffers well knew that the vice president liked to try out his ideas in talk. But James Thomson, who was along on the trip as McGeorge Bundy's assistant, and who had lived in China as a young man, took Humphrey at his word. He challenged Humphrey's assertion that the Chinese were coursing down the Mekong, over the Himalayas, and perhaps, as Jack Valenti had said over dinner, across the Pacific to Honolulu and San Francisco. It was late at night; tempers were short. Humphrey, stirred by his brush with the war, had never sounded so bellicose in his life. Angered by Thomson's upstart objections, he threw away the speech that Thomson had written for the next day and—after pushing past a phalanx of jeering antiwar picketers delivered a ripsnorter that Prime Minister Holt, ready to send four thousand Aussies to Vietnam, called "the greatest speech I have ever heard in my years of public life," and that Humphrey's foreign-affairs aide John Rielly later called "just another hard-line harrangue."

And hard-liner was what Humphrey had become. Although he and young Thomson exchanged contrite apologies on the following day, tension ran high as the party flew to their next stop in New Zealand. It was at this moment that the White House reporters who had been traveling with him stopped the vice president on the sidewalk in Wellington to ask him about Bobby Kennedy's latest statement on Vietnam.

Robert Kennedy had been strongly identified with his brother's original decision to send U. S. troops into Vietnam. But since his departure from the Johnson administration he had begun taking positions on issues that endeared him to some in the liberal wing of the Democratic party who were growing restive with Johnson's leadership. Humphrey's concern about Kennedy's rising popularity was as great as Johnson's. In a December Gallup poll of possible future presidential candidates, Kennedy had led Humphrey forty-to-twenty-three, and the Baltimore *Sun* noted that Kennedy's changing views were attracting some of Humphrey's old liberal constituency.

The Kennedy statement being considered was his suggestion that the Viet Cong be included in a South Vietnam government as a way toward peaceful settlement of the conflict. Humphrey's reply:

> Putting the Viet Cong in the Vietnamese government would be like putting a fox in the chicken coop. . . .
> The history of coalition government including Communists or Fascists has been one of either paralysis of that government or the taking over of the government by the totalitarians. We are in Vietnam to see to it that the people of Vietnam have a chance for a free choice of their government. If South Vietnamese who believe in Viet Cong principles wish to stand for election in a free election, let them take their chances. . . . We are not going to permit the VC to shoot their way into power.

That did it. Probably nothing ever said about the Vietnam war—not even President Johnson's admonition to the troops at Camranh Bay to "nail the coonskin to the wall"—ever shocked American liberal opinion as much as Humphrey's "fox in the chicken coop" statement. Maybe the Viet Cong was a Communist front—certainly it became just that. But in early 1966, when the U. S. government was presumably pursuing peace by every avenue, when its own figures showing the VC doubled in size in a year suggested much more than just Communist support, the remark was a harsh and brassy put-down. It haunted Humphrey for the rest of his life. It caused *The Progressive*, the magazine that LaFollette had founded and that had always counted Humphrey one of its Midwest heroes, to label the vice president a "hatchet man" and to say he had become "more royalist than the crown."

As if the New Zealand outburst were not proof enough that Vice President Humphrey had become the president's mouthpiece, he stepped out of a helicopter on the White House lawn three days later and proclaimed: "The tide of battle has turned in Vietnam in our favor." That was the message the president wanted, the message that hit the headlines and traveled by television into every home, the message Humphrey, at the president's bidding, dinned into the ears of Congress at three successive briefings in the next three days. "The vice president was optimistic," Senator Dirksen commented. Senator Frank Church said: "He was on Cloud Nine."

But what of the message of Communist menace that Humphrey had formulated—the message that he so passionately felt was needed to fire up the American people to wage the war to successful conclusion? That was the message Senator Vandenberg had urged in an earlier day when President Truman was preparing to ask backing for aid to Greece and Turkey. In 1947, President Truman took the advice and called on America to unite and throw back the Communism that threatened to engulf Europe; Congress and the country responded.

Two decades and two wars later, that was more than President Johnson wanted. Humphrey's fifty-page report, already considerably toned down after his own staff had split violently over its super-militant themes, was junked. Concerned that Humphrey's call to long-term commitment in Asia would bring "sniping and revitalized criticism" from those who thought the war already intolerable, the president spoke to Rusk. The secretary slashed Humphrey's big paper to ribbons. The "revised" seven-page version dutifully hailed Johnson's Honolulu meeting as a "historic turning point" and passed over Humphrey's "big picture" in two sentences.

Rusk said blandly that the vice president could use the "detailed material" he had excised in speeches around the country. But already the thinking behind Humphrey's cry—that it was Asia's leaders who had identified Chinese aggressiveness as the mortal danger—was challenged. He was forced to acknowledge that Pakistan, virtually allied with China, rated India a greater menace. And his brief visit to Thailand brought out the very political perils back home that Johnson wanted to avoid. Even before Humphrey's return, Senator Fulbright sent word to the White House that his Foreign Relations Committee would like to hear testimony from the vice president on Southeast Asia. Humphrey said he would not answer a subpoena but would respond to a request as Johnson had as vice president after a 1961 Far Eastern trip. They met in executive (i.e., closed) session in Majority Leader Mansfield's office. All the senators had heard Humphrey's White House recitals, but Chairman Fulbright had something quite specific in mind. He was concerned about a possible new U. S. commitment to Thailand. In a testy exchange he got Humphrey to deny that his Bangkok communiqué had pledged any new military aid to the Thais; then he growled that he wanted no more "statements like the Tonkin Gulf statement that later on we are told are commitments that we are all honor bound to live up to."

Humphrey did use the "details" of his Asian findings in subsequent speeches. In fact his theme of stopping the Communist epidemic in Asia ran like a red thread through his utterances over the next months. On March 12 he told a Columbia University forum: "We must be firm in resisting the expansionist designs of the present rulers of China."

The following day he said on "Meet the Press": "It is my view that Communist China is today the militant aggressive force in large areas of Asia, and is using some of this force through her agent North Vietnam into South Vietnam. China must be brought to understand that aggression is not a policy that can be pursued."

The next day he pronounced: "If Americans are willing to die for Berlin, I humbly submit that a commitment of our country to the defense of a small nation—South Vietnam—in Asia is equally honorable and valid."

To an AFL-CIO audience in Washington he said: "Communism in Asia is not a subject of academic discussion. It is a matter of survival. Vietnam today is as close to the United States as London was in 1940."

In Minneapolis he even slipped in a racial dig at those dovish individuals who drew back from the sweeping implications of his big-picture thesis: "Are we to be put in the position of saying that we are able to keep our commitments to white people, not to brown people or yellow people?"

When Humphrey compared Johnson's Honolulu Declaration with Roosevelt's Atlantic Charter commitment, Eric Sevareid asked in a CBS television interview if he was "proposing a relationship between this country and Asia . . . as fundamental, as long-lasting, intimate and possibly expensive as our historic Association with Europe?"

Humphrey answered, yes.

Clearly, in becoming an all-out apostle of the Vietnam war, Humphrey had accepted his lot as Johnson's vice president. His former misgivings about the president's war policy were all but banished. When Ed Morgan of the American Broadcasting Company asked him: "Weren't you in the doghouse a year ago for resisting the bombing?" Humphrey replied: "I felt the bombing had certain limitations. I am still of the same opinion. And the president has taken that position consistently, at least up to now."

But Humphrey went further. He had become convinced of the correctness of Johnson's war policy. Taking George McGovern aside in the Senate cloakroom, he told him—"as an old friend" and one he had "never tried to mislead"—that he supported the war because "it's right." When Columnist William Shannon, a long-time liberal Humphrey backer, published a piece in *Commonweal* defending the vice president against the charge that he had flipflopped, Humphrey wrote to him:

> There is a suggestion in your article that I may well have a different viewpoint on Vietnam from the President, but that I cannot express differences with the President because it would be highly irresponsible. I agree that it would be highly irresponsible, but I must tell you privately that I am thoroughly in agreement with the President.
>
> If somehow I should become President tomorrow, I would follow essentially the same pattern, I believe, on the basis of the evidence I now have.

Humphrey sent a copy of this letter to Valenti at the White House. Valenti replied: "The President thought your letter was 'excellent.'" The following week Humphrey was invited for the first time to join the president at one of his top-level Vietnam lunches.

Humphrey's advocacy of Johnson's war policy cost him the support of his old friends on the left. At first the *New Republic* explained that Humphrey had simply behaved like Humphrey and gone overboard for "a kind of export ADA—Asians for Democratic Action." His new fervor, the liberal journal said indulgently, was "compassionate in intent but unsophisticated and excessively optimistic. It is inevitable that our overcommitment in Vietnam should be matched by Humphrey's overcommitment to the overcommitment. To expect him to moderate his enthusiasm is to expect sobriety from an alcoholic."

When Phil Potter of the Baltimore *Sun* polled former ADA chairmen to see how the vice president stood with his old "spiritual kinfolk," the replies were almost forgiving. While opposing the war as immoral, Joe Rauh stood by Humphrey personally: "He believes in the Administration's policy, God bless him. Hubert is a congenital liberal, and always will be." Arthur Schlesinger, equally in disagreement but troubled most of all by the "tone" of the vice president's utterances, replied: "Given the complexity of the issues, I do not think that the Vice President's views have resulted in his excommunication by the liberal community." But as Humphrey went about preaching Johnson's war gospel before university students, business groups, and labor rallies, practically all his old ADA friends expressed shock at things he was saying. His old admirer Columnist James Wechsler wrote: "His righteous rhetoric is almost reminiscent of Richard Nixon." Wechsler, Schlesinger, Rauh, and Jim Loeb all received aggrieved letters from the vice president. Reciting his long record and protesting that he did not deserve their "unfair and unwarranted" criticism, he ended by saying: "There is an old scriptural saying that carries me through these days: 'This too shall pass.' "

It did not. When he went to New York to address a dinner honoring Reinhold Niebuhr, founding father of ADA, two hundred of Niebuhr's seminary students paraded outside in protest. In April, Humphrey's old friends arranged for him to address the ADA convention. Uncompromisingly he repeated: "Saigon is as close to this ballroom tonight as London was in 1940." At the close of his speech the audience rose and applauded, Wechsler wrote, "in what can only be called an ovation." But it was a gesture to the past. With Humphrey's knowledge and consent, the convention had already debated and passed its anti-war resolution before Humphrey spoke.

Humphrey insisted that his differences with his friends were only over the tactics of upholding freedom in Asia; he continued to protest that their attacks were unfairly personal. When Wechsler wrote an article entitled "Humphrey At War with Himself," the vice president denied the assertion and told him: "It is not Hubert Humphrey who became personal. It was not I who criticized or condemned. . . . It was not Hubert Humphrey who cast the first stone. But constantly I receive reports that people who once claimed to be friends of mine in the liberal community now attack me viciously, accuse me of selling out, aping Johnson, violating liberal principles."

A few days later, twenty-four liberal writers calling themselves "the conscience of America" arrived in Washington. Calling a press conference, they proclaimed: "Vice President Humphrey has betrayed the liberal movement." "Does he have to agree with such damned rapture?" asked Essayist Irving Howe. Author Alfred Kazin said: "He suffers from the Hemingway syndrome: you can never be tough enough, and you have to prove your masculinity." The attacks were turning bitter and, like it or not, personal.

Outwardly and inwardly, Humphrey was surer now than ever of himself and of the president's confidence. He was totally immersed in his job. In March the Harris poll reported that 54 percent of those asked gave him a favorable rating on the way he was doing the job—not as high as the president's 62 percent but evidence enough that working loyally for the president could yield a personal political payoff.

Several of his close friends in the Senate had warned him that, bird-dogging bills for the president, he had perhaps become too involved in the day-to-day legislative process in the Senate. He therefore told his staff that in his second year he hoped to work with Congress "at arm's length." He was one year away from tenure as a senator, he said, and antagonism was greater. "I am in the club but not a member." Then the president announced in his State of the Union message: "We can continue the Great Society while we fight in Vietnam," and he proposed a dozen more major domestic measures. Once again at the president's legislative leadership breakfasts, Humphrey was handed his lists of doubtful Senators and congressmen before every tight vote. Having junior members of the Senate preside on the rostrum, he charged back into the cloakrooms. Meeting with civil rights leaders, he echoed the president's assurances that defense was taking only 7.6 percent of the GNP and that the nation could expand education, widen welfare, and—a new urgency—rebuild its cities.

It was by "creative federalism," the president said, that he would build the Great Society. In the partnership between federal and local government that was crucial to the operation of the anti-poverty programs, former Mayor Humphrey was Johnson's man-between. Very early it became apparent that the programs were vulnerable politically. To Republican mayors the anti-poverty effort looked like a drive to register discontented (and mostly Democratic) voters. And when influential Democratic mayors ran into trouble with the new Community Action agencies, Mayor Daley of Chicago led a deputation to confer with Humphrey. The vice president assured them that the Johnson administration had no intention of bypassing city hall, and early in 1966 it came out that the Office of Economic Opportunity was letting the mayors have an informal veto over Community Action projects. Welfare militants denounced this as a sellout. As Chairman of OEO's Advisory Council, Humphrey conferred often with Sargent Shriver, the program administrator. On one occasion, as welfare mothers marched up and down outside, Shriver passed Chariman Humphrey a note: "Excuse me a moment while I go talk to my constituents."

Of course the thrust of the Community Action agencies was political. Their loosely drawn programs were inherently prone to scandal. The agencies, effective only by engaging in pressures and antagonisms, stirred up landlords and merchants. They challenged those who held local power, and Congress soon began asking questions. As resistance rose, Johnson toyed with the idea of stripping OEO of all but planning functions and handing the programs over to the Department of Housing and Urban Development and the Department of Labor. Humphrey, citing New Deal experience, counseled against this. Great programs, he said, ought to be kept out of the oldline departments "because the departments absorbed the energy and enthusiasm of the programs and quickly brought them down to the level of the departments' long-term functions and responsibilities." The president seemed to agree and appointed Humphrey head of a cabinet task force to find jobs for youths fast, before the expected summer troubles in the cities.

Instead of a tax increase to finance his guns-and-butter budget, the president rigged up a patchwork fiscal program that required no sacrifices. Faithfully Humphrey lobbied senators on behalf of such makeshifts as raising cash by selling off the strategic stockpile. After another meeting with the president, he carried the word to mayors and county officials that Washington was cutting back on capital programs in their communities. Still, inflationary pressures mounted. One night in April, Humphrey flew to New York to meet with two hundred top corporate heads assembled by the Cowles publishing group. When the vice president appealed for a holddown on business outlays, the businessmen's response was to ask a cutback in Great Society programs and to invite the vice president to talk labor into restraint on wage demands.

Between such assignments, Humphrey kept up his frantic round of speaking coast to coast for the president's war policy. "I guess I am Lyndon Johnson's Eleanor Roosevelt," he said one day as he prepared to fly to a session of county educators in Atlanta. The remark prompted Columnist Mary McGrory to comment: "The Vice President is not a proud man." James Reston of the *New York Times* was more pointed. In a column headed "Alas, Poor Hubert," he wrote: "He is not using the opportunities in the Vice Presidency to establish himself as the natural successor. He is not acting like a President. He is running around to every meeting in town as if he were campaigning for mayor of Minneapolis. His speeches are thin, repetitious and interminable." Reston proceeded to describe a Humphrey oration at an Associated Press luncheon that was "not one speech but three—one on Vietnam, one on foreign aid, and one on leadership. For the first ten minutes he was witty and disarming, and for the next twenty he was impassioned and effective on Vietnam, and then he began to ramble and repeat, so that by the time he had been talking for over an hour he had lost the attention of most of his audience."

Humphrey, of course, read such strictures and complained mildly about them to friends. But he was much too bouncy and much too busy to brood over them. And when *Time* magazine put him on its cover, he was "pleasantly relieved at what they wrote about [him]," even though the article said that lately he had "added to his image as a White House Uriah Heep."

Besides, he was looking always to his constituency of one. At the very time these arrows whistled around him, he wrote these notes "for the files, for historical purposes":

> The month has been a very active one with the President. My relations with him have become cordial, intimate and extensive. From time to time we've had long visits. Frequently these visits take place in the late afternoon when he retires to his bedroom to get an afternoon nap.
>
> On at least two occasions this month I have been at the White House for lunch or a morning cup of coffee. Mrs. Humphrey and I have been at the White House also from time to time for an evening get-together of a private nature. We were over to the White House one Sunday evening for dinner and movies. On my birthday—May 27—the President gave me a watch, a razor and three wonderful photos.

That may seem pathetic coming from a man of Humphrey's attainments, but it has to be recorded that the constituency of one could be fickle. Within a month, the president took sudden umbrage at something his vice president said or did—his staff never quite understood, and Humphrey left no record of it. Bill Moyers of Johnson's staff, recalling it in an interview with Humphrey ten years later remembered, "He wouldn't speak to you, and ordered us not to speak to you." Then, as Humphrey proceeded to relate, came "that quick thaw." It was a month later at the wedding of Johnson's daughter Luci:

> I was sitting there with Muriel right on the aisle and now President Johnson and Luci come in—Luci's on her father's arm coming down the aisle. . . . And as he's coming down he gives me a wink—and it's like two cymbals coming together in this clash. You could almost feel it in the church. He looked at me and right away I said to Muriel: "I'm back in good standing with the man."
>
> He'd forgiven me in one flick of the eyelid. Why, he'd apparently forgotten why he'd been angry with me—and I was in good shape.
>
> When we went back over to the White House after the wedding for the reception, why he had his arm around me. My goodness, I was just like his son, you know.

So it went. But even though the president had authorized a buildup to 383,000 men, things were not going well in Vietnam. The hopes for a turnaround on the civilian front suffered a severe setback when Ky, by firing a general with a strong Buddhist following, provoked religious uprisings in Hue, Saigon, and other cities that had to be put down by force. In June, Johnson moved to step up the bombing. This time, as the vice president's notes record, he was not only on hand for the decision but had gone over the pros and cons beforehand with the president. At the meeting, "I told him I thought we had to be firm and resolute. I reluctantly went along with the extension of bombing to the key targets, the petroleum depots [in Hanoi]."

At home or in Vietnam, the question was whether the tide was really turning, and the summer of 1966 brought disquieting signs to the administration that events within the United States were not running its way. The dozen new Great Society proposals stalled in Congress. The decade-long civil rights drive seemed to have lost its momentum. In the midst of a supposedly nonviolent march into Mississippi, Stokely Carmichael stepped out and proclaimed "Black Power." A new group of young redhots who wanted nothing to do with Martin Luther King, Jr., called for armed defense and an end to integration.

Humphrey fought back. He reported to the president that his crash program had "identified 880,000 summer jobs," and that youth unemployment in June was down to 16 percent from 27 percent the year before. At the NAACP convention in Los Angeles he seemed to touch a deep chord among delegates by appealing: "Do not deny me the chance to walk with you." And at a county officials' meeting in New Orleans he said: "There will be open violence in every major city and county in America as long as people are forced to live like animals in filthy, rotten housing, with rats nibbling on the kids' toes, with garbage uncollected, with no swimming pools, with little or no recreation." And he added: "If I lived in such conditions, I could lead a mighty good revolt."

It was the declaration of a man with a heart, of course, interpolated on the spur of the moment into his script. But it was also a declaration made just a week before black riots erupted in the Hough district of Cleveland, and thereafter in New York, Chicago, and Los Angeles—and plenty of whites thought the vice president of the United States had no business talking about leading revolts. The Paterson, New Jersey, *News* front-paged the sardonic headline: "Crack of the year." The Republican National Committee took occasion to proclaim that crime had increased 46 percent under Kennedy and Johnson and charged—there was no need to mention names, plenty of people remembered Humphrey's remark—that "high officials of this Administration have condoned and encouraged disrespect for law and order." The second of the issues that would bring down Hubert Humphrey in 1968 had been born.

By that time, Congress had adjourned. Ardor for his Great Society legislation had ebbed so far that the President, lamenting to Valenti that he had "lost Congress," arranged for the vice president to do all his campaigning for the fall elections. Johnson took himself right out of the picture in early October when he announced that he would attend a conference with Asian leaders at Manila at the end of the month. Humphrey, getting out to campaign in thirty-seven states, proclaimed it as his opinion that home-front issues such as civil rights would not be decisive in 1966. Without quite wrapping himself in the flag, he gave this advice to Democratic candidates standing for reelection: "Run on Vietnam."

It was not a year for Democrats. In Humphrey's own state, his DFL party went through a devastating split. Younger elements rebelled against Governor Rolvaag, who had gained office only after a three-month-long recount and provided uncertain and plodding leadership thereafter. Unable to hold the line for his old retainer, Humphrey held back through a twenty-ballot convention donnybrook between Rolvaag and Lt. Governor Alexander Keith, 33. When Sandy Keith finally wrested the party's endorsement, Humphrey flew in and blithely announced his support for the winner. "You can't live forever on the older generation," he said. Then the governor, winning sympathy by an underdog campaign, toppled Keith in the September primary. It was a blow for Humphrey, and would have been worse if the president had not met with a like setback in Texas when his old adversary Ralph Yarborough won renomination for senator.

Campaigning, Humphrey called attention to his crowds—forty thousand at the national plowing contest in Iowa, one hundred thousand at a downtown rally in Cleveland. But the Los Angeles *Times* reported that where "two years ago he was constantly on the offensive, now he's mostly on the defensive."

Yet there's no one around, including the Kennedys, who can match Humphrey in the delicate art of infusing party workers with a fighting spirit. When the Vice President is in top form, which isn't always, he is par excellence as a political evangelist.

In Chicago, lending a hand to Paul Douglas, he had 1200 precinct workers literally in tears as he exhorted them to work their hearts out for "one of the giants of our times." Douglas was so overcome by a moving appeal by Humphrey at a downtown outdoor rally earlier in the day that he rose sobbing and embraced the Vice President. Humphrey returned the embrace and the two old friends stood on the platform with tears running down their cheeks. There were few in the crowd who were not visibly moved. Of course Humphrey is also storing up debts he can cash when he sees fit.

The television cameras that were beginning to bring the blood of the Vietnam war into the nation's living rooms also focused at Humphrey's meetings on what was already a familiar phenomenon of the 1960s—the generation gap. As Johnson's ambassador to liberals, Humphrey had reached robustly across this gap in innumerable appearances on the nation's campuses. Now television turned its unblinking eye on the young people trying increasingly to disrupt Humphrey's meetings. As the vice president arrived to address a Boston College forum, viewers saw the youthful pickets and heard their cries of "Get off our campus." They saw the young woman rise during a Humphrey speech in Portland, Oregon, and squirt red ink up and down her arm to protest the bloodletting in Vietnam. Inevitably, Humphrey tried to say that the cameras were giving a misleading impression of the dissidents' numbers. The day came when the vice president told a Minnesota businessmen's luncheon how the television crews, tipped off beforehand, ignored his speech and his four thousand attentive listeners at a Rutgers University convocation. Instead, they kept their cameras riveted on a walkout by "this handful of unwashed and bearded beatniks." At that point, Humphrey seemed not only to concede but to claim that he had fallen back to the far side of the gap. It was the point at which *Esquire* magazine stated: "Humphrey is going out of style."

Former Vice President Richard Nixon, who knew what it was like to be a vice president not only heckled but spat upon, wrote Humphrey: "I have nothing but sympathy and respect for you when I read stories like this. The first duty of a Vice President is to be loyal to a President and you have met that responsibility in admirable fashion. . . . Needless to say, this letter requires no answer." No doubt Nixon scented a Republican victory. When the voters spoke in November, the Republicans were big winners. The Democrats lost forty-five House seats, and the important Senate races in Texas, Massachusetts, Michigan, and Illinois, where Paul Douglas, most prominent of Humphrey's old friends to stick with him on Vietnam, went down to defeat. And they lost eleven governorships, including Minnesota's—a foregone conclusion Humphrey said to friends. In California, where voters were upset over student riots as well as Vietnam, they turned out Governor Edmund Brown for an avowed right-wing Republican, Ronald Reagan.

No sooner were the elections past than the president announced he was entering Bethesda naval hospital for surgery to repair his gall bladder operation of the year before. He had complained of pain to Humphrey earlier and alerted him of his intention days in advance. Forewarned, Humphrey cleared his schedule to stay close to Washington. On the night of November 16 he was with Johnson at a congressional reception until the president left for the hospital. Next morning, Bill Moyers telephoned him when the operation started and again when it was completed. Humphrey was at home, where he talked with newsmen and cameramen. He noted: "The press said I looked grim. I was not frightened nor was I tense. I had no reason to doubt that all would be well." Once again the surgeon was Dr. James Cain of Minnesota's Mayo Clinic, who kept Humphrey steadily informed of the president's convalescence. Two days later the vice president and his wife visited the hospital: "We had a good talk. He asked me to work out the pay legislation for the postal workers, and try to keep the increase within the guidelines. I told the postal workers that if they did not stay within the guidelines, the President would veto it. My efforts paid off, the increase was within the guidelines."

About this time the Humphreys moved from the suburban Maryland tract house they had occupied since coming to Washington in 1949 to a six-room condominium in a new high-rise apartment building overlooking the Potomac in southeast Washington. Welcomed by some two thousand people at three neighborhood gatherings, Humphrey said: "Like most husbands, I resisted the whole operation. When I protested, my wife told me to leave town. I did—for the period known as the campaign." To his old friend Tony Thompson he wrote: "Yes, we've moved. Muriel has gone high-hat, aristocratic. She is beginning to show the Republican instincts of her upbringing. She was afraid I wasn't moving up in the world fast enough. So she got me an apartment on the eighth floor. There are nine floors in this apartment building, but as you know I never dare think, talk or even dream about getting to the top!" On that note, Humphrey entered his third year as No. 2.

27

The Great Adventure

Midway through his vice presidency, Humphrey was willing to acknowledge that he had changed. Mellowed is hardly the word for it since he had never spoken in harsher accents during his sixteen years in Washington. For the pioneer of disarmament who had emerged as the leading spokesman for Johnson's war, there seemed no limit to the lengths he would go in defending the president. At a time when U. S. planes were dropping a greater weight of bombs on Vietnam that had been dropped in the whole of World War II in the Pacific, Humphrey spoke of the exquisite care they took to spare civilian lives. Not long before the My Lai massacre he told University of Pittsburgh students: "In Vietnam only the Viet Cong commit atrocities." While anti-war demonstrators in Manhattan's Central Park flaunted buttons that asked: "Lee Harvey Oswald, where are you now that we need you?" Humphrey assured Baptists in Denver: "There is no man who seeks peace more diligently than Lyndon Johnson."

The vice president told reporters, as if it explained everything: "I am Vice President because he made me Vice President." Still, Lyndon Johnson remained a hard man to please. One morning in January 1967, just after the administration had moved to send more troops to Vietnam, Tom Hughes, Humphrey's former aide now in charge of State Department intelligence, arrived to give the vice president another one of his periodic briefings. Humphrey said: "Let's go for a run in Rock Creek Park." It turned out to be a fast walk.

With the Secret Service men a safe distance behind, Humphrey said: "This is the only place I feel free to talk." And he told how Johnson was constantly after him about his staff. Concerned about the Secret Service men repeating his conversations at the White House, Humphrey also thought his new residence might be bugged. The FBI, he said, tried to please the president by their bugs, their wiretaps, their electronic eavesdropping. On top of this, Jack Valenti and others on the White House staff, he said, were forever keeping tabs on Humphrey staffers, and Johnson, paranoid about leaks, would upbraid the vice president about "the wild people" who worked for him. His latest "I'll bet you didn't know that . . ." was to tell Humphrey that his foreign policy assistant John Rielly had had lunch that week with a KGB agent from the Soviet embassy. Humphrey was convinced that this information had been obtained through electronic eavesdropping, though the lunch itself took place in a big public restaurant.

As he strode along, Humphrey unburdened himself further. He told Hughes: "I've just had another unpleasant experience with the President of the United States." He related that, having moved their residence, "Muriel and I thought it would be fitting to invite him and Lady Bird to see our new apartment. They decided they'd come—last night." And it seemed that while the wives were in the kitchen fixing the steaks, Johnson suddenly said:

Hubert, I hear you make the best speeches in explaining our country's effort in Vietnam. From the reports I get, you are our greatest national resource for dealing with members of the public who do not seem to understand the need for a patriotic commitment to the defense of freedom in Southeast Asia. Here we have the riots in our cities, demonstrators raising their clamor, and the President himself cannot move through the streets. Yet you can go out and make these addresses to the people. I don't know what we'd do without you. Now, Hubert, I'd like to hear one of your speeches. I'd like to hear what you say. He was lying on the sofa scratching himself as he talked.

Humphrey tried to make light of the matter. "Oh, I just say the usual things. . . ." But Johnson said: "I'd like to hear." So Humphrey ticked off a few of the stock arguments he used. Johnson interrupted. "No, I know these things. I'd like to hear what you say. Give me one of your actual speeches." Humphrey was getting thoroughly uncomfortable. Johnson went on: "You've made some of these speeches, I know. Now, come on, let me just hear you say it."

So the vice president got to his feet, and in his own living room started to comply with his guest's demand. As he began, Johnson got up and went to the bathroom. "Keep talkin', Hubert," he called over his shoulder. "I'm listenin'." Mercifully, the steaks were ready—and the torture ceased.

At that very time, presumably in fear of leaks, the president gave firm orders that Humphrey was not to be given any prior knowledge of the contents of the State of the Union message, and Joe Califano, as coordinator of domestic affairs, carried out the command to the letter. To Humphrey's usual blizzard of suggestions the White House made utterly no response. Humphrey got no copy of the address until after the White House press had been briefed on its contents. "Every newspaper in Washington knew the contents before the Vice President of the United States," wrote the Washington *Star*'s Douglas Kiker.

To a White House aide, Humphrey confided: "If I could only find a way to convince this man of my loyalty." And he wrote the president: "This message was the most impressive of any of the State of the Union messages. The people like its frankness and candor, and the respect for the President was greatly increased. I have not heard a single derogatory comment."

Most of this was simply the inside stuff of life around the court of a vain and suspicious president. Humphrey, throwing off comments on that morning race through the park, said he was sure that people on the White House staff played games with the Johnson appetite for intercepts. Knowing their wires were tapped, their conversations eavesdropped, they would tell others on the phone or even in talk across their desks of what they had done last night, or what they would do tomorrow—things they knew would please the president, expecting that Johnson would hear it later and their standing in his eyes would be correspondingly advanced. They would order bogus errands for the president, he said, and even plant rumors, counting on Johnson's notorious credulity for "intercepts."

This was courtier's talk—but was the vice president a courtier? Did the vice president serve only the president and not the electorate too? The public was watching the spectacle. Columnist Henry McLemore ran an item stating that in Las Vegas, where bookmakers were willing to bet 126,000 to 1 that the sun would not set in the East, a new wager commanded even bigger odds. It was now possible, he said, to get odds of 34,000,000 to 1 that vice president Humphrey "would, just once, disagree with President Johnson." Humphrey thought that such a good joke that he sent the clipping to the White House.

By this time representatives of the Johnson administration visited campuses at their peril. At Harvard, Defense Secretary McNamara was jeered, then literally shaken up when students stopped his car and rocked it from side to side for ten minutes. Ambassador Lodge was shouted down at Wesleyan University. And the vice president, who was used to student barracking in his frequent university appearances, met with violence at Stanford. Four hundred anti-war demonstrators mobbed his car, pushed placards in his face, and shrieked: "War criminal," "Murderer," and "Burn, Baby, Burn." Several tried to crash through the cordon of police, and one emptied a can of urine on a Secret Service man defending the vice president. Another threw himself under the front wheel of Humphrey's car but was dragged back by a policeman.

As such incidents became more frequent, Humphrey compared the "foul language and physical violence" of the students with "Hitler youth breaking up meetings in Germany." When he delivered an address at the National Book Award dinner in New York, a group of writers walked out. "This is what we mean by free speech," snapped Humphrey. As the interruptions increased he said he was being denied his right to be heard. While strongly defending the right of dissent, he declared: "But dissent must be responsible, and we must have the equal right to state our position." To this his old friend Morris Rubin, editor of the *Progressive*, retorted: "It is ridiculous to suggest that the Administration with its considerable army of yea-sayers, its instruments of propaganda and persuasion," lacked opportunity to "speak up as often and as forcefully as they want."

In March, when there was still no light at the end of the Vietnam tunnel, the president flew to Guam for another war meeting. General Thieu had won out over Marshal Ky as top dog in Saigon; the United States had sent in a new team headed by Ambassador Ellsworth Bunker; and Johnson's Guam publicity heavily stressed the administration's non-military programs in South Vietnam. Thereafter, while ordering even stronger bombing of the North, Johnson decided it was time to allay anxiety and anger over his war policy in Europe. Once again, Humphrey was handed the job.

Except that he had broken a wrist tripping over the family cat and had his arm in a cast, Humphrey found this a more comfortable task than his journeys to the Far East. Asia had been practically unknown terrain for him, and he had been rushed off unprepared. In Europe he knew his way around. The people were his kind of people. The Socialist leaders of government in Britain and Germany, Prime Minister Harold Wilson and Vice Chancellor Willy Brandt, were his personal friends. Moreover, less was expected of him this time. The president had long since ceased to look for European help in the war: all he desired now was a little understanding.

The press not only expected but looked for trouble involving the traveler. To Geneva, one of the vice president's first stops, the following cable went out from UPI in New York: "Aren't there any Vietnam demonstrators around shouting abuse at Humphrey, or don't such things happen in Switzerland? If so, or they turn up later, they should of course be ultra-up in the story."

If the Swiss proved uncooperative, the press's expectations were not disappointed in Italy. When Humphrey went to the opera in Rome, anti-war demonstrators threw paint, deluging the opera manager (but not Humphrey). At Florence young protesters hurled eggs—and also missed. During one session with leaders, Humphrey himself reported "a thousand Communist-led demonstrators" massed outside the palace. "However, I did not see them as I left," he told Johnson. The following day he met alone with Pope Paul VI for more than an hour. The pope told him he often prayed for the president. "I explained our bombing pauses," he reported, but the pope "returned to his concern over the bombing several times," When Humphrey recited the social programs proclaimed for Vietnam at Guam, the pope protested that all Vietnam news seemed to come from the Americans. "Why doesn't the government in Saigon be the spokesman for South Vietnam?" he asked. On the other hand, President Giuseppe Saragat told Humphrey that President Johnson had plenty of support in Italy and compared his position with Truman's—"making decisions which would look twenty years from now even greater than Truman's."

Humphrey's best show was probably in Britain, where he could debate critics on their own terms and talk to his good friend Wilson as could no other American. Pointing to his bandaged arm he said with a grin: "I told the President I got this defending his policies." Meeting three hundred members of parliament, including many Labour leftists, the man from Minnesota fielded their questions as fast and deftly as any minister at question-time in the House of Commons. "How can the United States justify its presence in Vietnam—is it just a matter of holding a line against Communist aggression?" asked left-winger Anne Kerr. "If that were the one reason it would be reason enough," Humphrey shot back to cheers. In private he warned Wilson, whom Johnson distrusted, against "jeopardizing his relationship with the President" by backing away from U. S. Vietnam policy; and after dinner with Queen Elizabeth he passed a convivial night as a fellow guest with the prime minister at Windsor Castle. Fetching a bottle from down the hall, Wilson hoisted a glass and said: "Here we are, a couple of ordinary fellows, the son of an English schoolteacher and the son of a smalltown druggist, in Windsor castle drinking the Queen's whiskey. Not bad for a couple of boys trying to make good."

In Bonn and Berlin the leaders seemed most concerned to hear from Humphrey that in its Asian adventures the United States had not forgotten "Germany's vital interests." In Brussels and Paris the vice president met more eggs, paint, and angry slogans. Demonstrators tore down the U. S. flag and burned it, broke windows in U. S. buildings, and injured forty-six police. But Humphrey delivered his message. Arriving unscathed at the Elysée palace, he rose to propose the last toast of his trip. He threw away a State Department text that recited all the instances of U. S. aid to France. He delivered instead one of his own that enumerated everything, from Lafayette to de Grasse, that France had done for America. By the time he got to the Statue of Liberty, tears coursed down the cheeks of President de Gaulle.

"A success," the Washington *Post* summed up. "Humphrey was straightforward but never simplistic, his speeches were emotional but not cloying. The words were pedestrian but the contents were not. They were 'idealistic' but not offensive. They were everyday, full of uncomplicated and almost routine value judgments, but not corny. His disarming directness had a stunning reception. His prime accomplishment was checking in top government circles a persistent, nagging, indefinable malaise about American intentions."

Even before the vice president returned, Johnson cabled him: "I have read your reports to me, every line. I want you to know that we think you've done a perfectly wonderful job for the country. Your presence, your political skill, your good will and good humor have, I believe, helped us turn an important corner in our relations with Europe. I want you to know how grateful I am." The president told Humphrey's friend Bill Benton he would cheerfully die the next day if he could be assured that the vice president would succeed him for eight years. And from Fred Smedley, the most exacting of New York liberal businessmen and one of the vice president's most punishing correspondents, came what after previous blasts had to be the ultimate accolade: "Warmest congratulations on the way in which you handled yourself in Europe. It considerably reduced my disappointment at your absence from the ADA's 20th national convention."

Back in Washington, Humphrey whirled out at once on President Johnson's circuit. In the shifting political scene, as the Republicans looked southward and Alabama's Governor George Wallace prepared to lead a 1968 bolt, this meant buttering up the Southerners. After the vice president finished stroking Democratic backs in North Carolina, the Raleigh *News & Observer* hailed him as "the best bridge builder in the party." The difference was that the bridge no longer arched, as in Humphrey's Senate days, to the left. Humphrey had changed, and now the bridge arched the other way. The man who had been their "black beast" the North Carolinians now called their "darling," especially to be preferred over Bobby Kennedy, who now said sharper things about both civil rights and Vietnam than did the vice president. Humphrey went on to Georgia, where he was photographed with his arm around the shoulder of Governor Lester Maddox, a notorious racist who carried pick handles to show how he dealt with blacks. To Johnson the vice president reported: "I made a strong effort to convince him that under all circumstances he should remain in the Democratic party next year, and not bolt to Wallace." But those in the North who saw the vice president embracing a black-baiter wondered what had become of the straight-arrow civil rights pioneer.

The old liberal who loved late-night bull sessions was even getting harder to talk to. When aides persuaded him to meet with academic experts on Asia to get sharp, new pointers, he turned the evening into one long monologue on the Johnson line. In April his old worshipper Joe Rauh assembled ten leading liberals at his house for a last-try dinner with the vice president. Those present, besides Rauh, were Arthur Schlesinger and Kenneth Galbraith of the Kennedy camp, Columnists James Wechsler and Clayton Fritchey, Gilbert Harrison and Alex Campbell of the *New Republic,* and Robert Bendiner of the *Nation.* At first everybody tried to maintain an atmosphere of friendliness and nostalgia, and the vice president went into almost interminable detail about unrest among the farmers and the difficulties of holding on to their vote in 1968. Then he discoursed about his audience with the pope, and how the pope repeatedly voiced personal sympathy with the president. Finally Wechsler asked whether the pope had expressed opposition to the Vietnam bombing. There was a brief silence, then Humphrey said tersely: "Yes. he did." When Humphrey went on to brag how he had boned up on history for his toast to de Gaulle, he was once more interrupted. Fritchey asked what the French president said about Vietnam. Humphrey replied: "I didn't want to bring it up. From what I knew of de Gaulle's position, it would have been like trying to discuss atheism with the Pope."

When Humphrey finally got around to Vietnam, the listeners opened up, and the exchanges grew hot, especially when Humphrey mentioned Indonesia. The vice president made the standard White House pitch that the U. S. fight for Vietnam had been the key factor in swinging the Indonesian government from pro-Peking neutralism to the anti-Communist side. Schlesinger blew up: "Hubert, that's shit and you know it. Those generals were just fighting for their lives, and would have done so whether we were in Vietnam or not."

Humphrey seemed determined to hold his temper. In a wrangle about the Vietnam bombing, he said, you had to listen to the generals. With some derision, Schlesinger retorted that the generals had been outrageously wrong about the Bay of Pigs. When Humphrey then asked if Schlesinger thought he was better equipped than the generals to evaluate these matters, Schlesinger said: "I damn well do." But when the argument shifted to the role of the State Department and Schlesinger kept demanding its overhaul, Humphrey finally raised his voice and said angrily: "Arthur, these are your guys. You were in the White House when they took over. Don't blame them on us." Schlesinger did not answer back.

Late at night, after the tension had subsided somewhat, Humphrey dropped the only remark that even faintly suggested he might not go all the way with LBJ. Several times he referred to Vietnam as a "morass." Later he asked those at the table whether the United States should stop bombing, and when all said yes, he said very quietly: "On balance, I think you are right. But the President's advisers don't agree."

Humphrey was extremely friendly as he left. He went out of his way to put his arm around Schlesinger, and when Schlesinger apologized for using such strong language to the vice president, Humphrey said that was the way old friends could talk to each other. But his friends went away convinced that if Humphrey had to choose between his old liberal constituency and supporting the president, he would support the president. As Rauh said later: "Most of us were struck by the sense that he was increasingly conscious of the dead-end into which his own political life might be headed as the result of the war." And Rauh wondered, of course, why he inexorably headed toward that dead end.

In June of 1967 another Middle East war broke out, and the vice president attended all the big meetings at the White House to cope with the crisis as Israel threw back Nasser's Soviet-made tanks and in seven days took Gaza, the Sinai peninsula, and all Egyptian territory up to the banks of the Suez

Canal. But for Humphrey, June was also the month he first experienced symptoms of the bladder ailment that would ultimately kill him. He discovered blood in his urine. His friend and personal physician, Dr. Edgar Berman, arranged for him to enter Bethesda hospital, where on June 9 he was anaesthetized. A tube was inserted in his penis, and the surgeons found multiple small polyps growing on the inside of his bladder. Snipping them off, they took a biopsy and the probe was over. Painful though it was, Humphrey was out that afternoon, as he told Johnson, and back at the office after three days.

The exploratory surgery was a minor ordeal, but one of the polyps was found to be malignant. Dr. Berman sent slides to eleven consultants for an opinion. Only one of the eleven recommended surgery to remove the bladder. Berman put the findings to the vice president, who of course asked what he thought. "I could not go against the weight of opinion," Berman said fifteen years later. "But had the bladder been removed then, he would very likely be alive today." Humphrey decided to go with the experts and rely on semi-annual examinations thereafter to watch for any recurrence. An additional deciding factor, Dr. Berman said later, was Humphrey's extreme personal sense of cleanliness. The urostymy, which would have been a major operation, would have required discharging his urine thereafter into a bag worn externally.

The minor surgery may have been responsible for holding the vice president down to only five major out-of-town addresses that month. It did not keep him from five White House dinners for visiting heads of government, three National Security Council meetings, and a couple of leadership breakfasts and cabinet meetings with the president. It also did not keep him from leading the U. S. delegation to the inaugural of Korea's President Park Chung Ho at the end of June.

THAT summer the nation's cities exploded. On the night of July 13 police in Newark, then the one U. S. city besides Washington with a black majority, beat up a black taxi driver; looting and burning broke out. With much of the city in flames on the following day, police began using live ammunition, and five people were killed. Humphrey, of course, was supposed to be the president's liaison with the cities. He telephoned the white mayor and learned that, with the situation out of control, New Jersey's Governor Richard Hughes was sending in the National Guard. At that point, Humphrey was over Indiana aboard the vice-presidential Lockheed *Jetstar* bound for a speaking engagement in Missouri. He telephoned his friend Hughes from the plane and had a brief conversation. President Johnson, who was determined to keep the federal government aloof from the disturbances, heard that the vice president had offered Washington's help and raised the roof. Unable to get to the president, Humphrey was reduced to writing a letter: "I know from my conversations with Joe Califano that you have been disturbed over certain news reports coming from Newark about my conversation with Governor Richard Hughes. . . . I said to him these words: 'If you feel that I can be of help to you, do not hesitate to call on me.' At no time did I suggest federal aid. I deeply regret that my action may have caused you worry." Johnson's wrath was not assuaged until Humphrey sent him a transcript of his telephone conversation.

On the night of July 23 still more violent rioting broke out in Detroit. Mayor Jerome Cavanaugh at once called the vice president, and Governor Romney joined them in a three-way phone conversation. The mayor, worried that the National Guard was not trained for such duty, wanted to ask for federal troops. Humphrey told Cavanagh that "the Vice President has no authority," and that "in the light of our Newark experience," he should call Attorney General Ramsey Clark. Frustrated, Humphrey watched the rioting go on for six days. Much of the city was destroyed, and forty-three people died. Most of the deaths were caused, as in Newark, by the National Guard. In the end the president had to climb down and send in the Army to restore order.

Johnson finally brought the vice president back into the action by making him chairman of a cabinet task force to review federal legislation for the cities. Humphrey's group advised the president that "the character of the riots suggests widespread rejection of our social system" rather than "simply dissatisfaction with conditions"; he urged Johnson to make "a major television appeal to the nation to repair these deep wounds in our society." Along with recommending enactment of a dozen Great Society bills stalled in Congress, Humphrey stressed increased funding for measures already enacted. Specifically, he singled out the Model Cities program. This was the administration's urban development bill. It had gained narrow approval in May after being rebaptized with the more acceptable "model cities" name and broadened to include not just the problem ghettos but, in porkbarrel fashion, just about every populated area in the United States.

The president never made the recommended appeal for racial reconciliation. Faced with the immense cost of the war and stiff resistance in Congress, he hunkered down in the White House through that 1967 summer of America's most violent urban storms. It was Humphrey, addressing a meeting of local government officers amid the smoking ruins of downtown Detroit, who struck the audacious note: "Our commitment to the building of free, safe and just communities must be no less than the commitment we have made in the past to military defense of our country, to the exploration of outer space, to the rebuilding of devastated Western Europe after World War II. We have a commitment in the Model Cities Act. It is for our cities a Marshall Plan for the impoverished areas of America. Yes, call it that if you wish. . . . The 89th Congress, by adopting President Johnson's Model Cities Act, has already given us most, if not all, the mechanism we need to carry out the plan." Back in Washington, Johnson berated Humphrey for talking about a Marshall Plan for the cities when he could not even get money for existing programs from Congress. Humphrey dutifully called one hundred mayors to Washington to brief them on the need to curb requests for federal funds.

Summer ended, and so did the racial riots. But the student protests went on, and public opinion began to swing. People who had not done so before asked, Why should we be in Vietnam? What's it all going to accomplish? Newspapers, newsmagazines, and television commentators explicitly began to convey a sense of stalemate in Vietnam. Television, which had brought the frightening scenes of downtown arson and pillage to the suburbs, also delivered from night to night the blood and mud of Vietnam to American living rooms. It was the first war ever reported by television, and the shock was great. The frustration of a seemingly endless war at a time of enveloping violence and fear for public safety in the streets—the combination was altogether too much for many Americans.

So it was that the president's popularity plummeted. From a solid 62 percent in January his job rating sank to 39 percent in October. His advisers told him that the summer's events were responsible—riots much more severe than in previous years, heavy casualties in Vietnam. But since a majority of those polled still supported the war, it appeared that their criticism of Johnson was more personal. The press spoke openly of the president's "credibility gap"—begun that moment in 1965 when he decided to widen the war without saying so and now enlarged daily as the administration tried, in William Bundy's rueful phrase, to "win the war with figures."

As one who lived by the polls, Johnson grew obsessed with the problem of how to "get it across to the people we're making progress." In South Vietnam there had been no coups in two years; orderly elections had been successfully carried out in September; and Robert Komer, the man Johnson had sent to Saigon to win the "other war," was writing Humphrey as "one optimist to another" that "we have finally invested enough men, blood and treasure to achieve our aims in Vietnam—if we are willing to stay the course."

At almost every point in his life "optimist" had been the term pinned on Humphrey. He believed in all his causes with all his heart, which was big, and with all his mind, which was quick. In combination these attributes equipped Humphrey with a gift that his friends and detractors alike agreed he possessed to excess—the gift of gab. And in these months when many of those who had voted for President Johnson were turning against him and arriving at the view that the whole Vietnam war might have been a ghastly mistake, in this season of rage and disgust, Vice President Humphrey's tongue seemed to run away with him.

As protests grew more strident, so did Humphrey. On a weekend in October young and old from all parts of the country walked and rode to Washington to take part in a mass demonstration against the war. At the climax of the protest, militants assaulted the Pentagon in scenes described brilliantly by Norman Mailer in *Armies of the Night*. The following afternoon the vice president addressed the National Defense Executive Reserve, a kind of businessmen's auxiliary to the Pentagon. He dismissed the marchers as "incredibly ridiculous." He said that while they gave aid and comfort to the Communist enemy, the president, who was "pained, unhappy, burdened," was leading a war that was beneficial for the Vietnamese, crucial to Asian security, and fundamental to the existence of the United States. He continued, "I think it is time that all Americans realized that we are in the midst of a protracted, costly struggle . . . which . . . will probably not end until Hanoi comes to believe that we have the will, the determination, the perseverance, patience and strength to see it through." How fortunate, said Humphrey, that in its president, America had a man who put principle above popularity. Citizens could be thankful that in the White House was a president as resolute as Washington, Lincoln, Roosevelt, Truman, and Kennedy. At the end of this outpouring, Nancy Dickerson, Lady Bird's secretary, rushed back to the White House to report that the vice president had delivered "the very best speech he has ever made." But the Washington *Post* termed it "sarcastic, emotional."

At this point, when the administration was drawing up its wagons in a defensive circle, the president sent Humphrey on his second trip to Southeast Asia. This time he was to represent the United States at the inauguration of General Thieu as the lawfully elected president in Saigon, and to stop off in Malaya and Indonesia on his way back. Just as he entered the palace grounds in Saigon, the first of three mortar shells burst near the gate, wounding an admiral's driver. "What do we do now?" Humphrey asked. "Hunker down," roared Westmoreland. Two more shells exploded in quick succession. There were no further casualties, but it was the Viet Cong's way of signaling that the conflict would be "protracted." Once again, the vice president had an avuncular talk with Thieu and Vice President Ky. He cabled Johnson: "Both are determined to move strongly not only militarily but in building a responsive, representative government. Both feel that the Viet Cong can hold out no longer than our November 1968 elections but will fight strongly, if in smaller units, until then. Both were concerned as much as anything else with U.S. opinion. I assured them of our continued support, in the face of unfavorable public opinion." Once again, with General Westmoreland he toured the forward bases—Phu Bai, Danang, Chulai—they had visited eighteen months before. Once more he visited hospitals, and wept over the wounded. And once more he spoke as if loyalty to the President had led him beyond his own common sense.

The scene itself lent drama to Humphrey's speech. Assembled before a rustic podium in the U.S. embassy's tree-shaded courtyard were the entire U.S. staff in Saigon, from file clerks and messengers to Ambassadors Bunker and Lodge and, baton under his arm, General Westmoreland. Looking down upon this dedicated gathering, the vice president threw away his prepared speech. He delivered instead an impassioned, hour-long outburst on American history "as proof of the right of a man to be optimistic. . . ." "Our business is to make history. It's all right to study it—and I did. It's all right to teach it—and I have. But it's wonderful to make history in our own way and our own time." Humphrey felt certain that he and present company were doing just that.

Turning to the proud past, he invoked the memory of Washington holding firm at Valley Forge while troops deserted and the Continental Congress refused to send food or supplies. He spoke of the defectors, of Arnold and Burr. He recalled that at Yorktown Americans took surrender of Cornwallis and prevailed after all. He went on to recite how Lincoln bore up in the trying times of 1864, how Truman stood fast in near-defeat in Korea, and how the British persevered at Dunkirk in 1940. And, just as America was born for freedom, he said, "in the last third of the twentieth century" the infant Republic of Vietnam was to be "nourished into maturity" by Americans, preserved and "sacrificed for," all in the cause of freedom: "I believe that Vietnam will be marked as the place where the family of man has gained the time it needed to finally break through to a new era of hope and human development and justice. This is the chance we have. Ths is our great adventure—and a wonderful one it is!"

Even for some present it was embarrassing to be told that muddling through in the morass of Saigon was "our great adventure." But to soured dissenters back home, this was the Humphrey verbiage they called "obscene." In the excess of their own vehemence they called him "truthless," "swine," and "totally dishonest."

The vice president had to hurry back to Washington. Johnson wanted him present early enough on a Monday morning to put him through the usual White House performance before the House of Representatives convened at eleven o'clock. Years later, Humphrey recalled what this required of him:

> Yes, I know what jet lag is. Coming back with no long breaks on the return, I land[ed] at Andrews Air Force base, incredibly tired, feeling slightly wobbly, and to say the least [with] mental processes not too clear or active.
>
> The Presidential helicopter met me, delivered me to the White House launching pad, where I was met by the President and Cabinet. Then [I] met with the leaders of Congress [and this was] followed by a press conference. It's in situations like that that you make mistakes of judgment, particularly in how you word your sentences. Never meet the press after a long flight. You are bound to make mistakes.

It may have consoled Humphrey that on his return to this particular ordeal, President and Congress were too preoccupied with another crisis to hear more than his first message: "Our military progress is clear." The dollar was in a spin, and desperate consultations took place at the White House to stop the hemorrhage of gold flowing to Europe—the result of Johnson's not having gotten the tax boost through Congress that he finally proposed in 1967. The international balance-of-payments had gone heavily against the United States in the latter part of the year, and the gnomes of Zurich, presidential aides growled, coldly refused to believe in America's inflationary way of life.

Johnson's popularity had sunk so low that Eugene McCarthy announced his candidacy to oppose the president's renomination in the 1968 Democratic primaries. Humphrey, "very much upset" and heeding the president's request, made an attempt to dissuade McCarthy but had to report: "I guess I have no influence on these friends of mine."

On November 22, the anniversary of President Kennedy's assassination and the end of Johnson's fourth year in office, night had fallen on the capital when a whirring noise was heard on the White House grounds. Only when the helicopter rose in silhouette against the Washington monument did Humphrey aide Doug Bennet, working late in the vice-presidential office across the street, see and comprehend: it was the president of the United States taking off under security conditions so extreme that departure took place in a blackout. Again, venturing to New York for Cardinal Spellman's funeral in December, he landed by helicopter in Central Park out of fear for his security. On the cathedral steps, massed pickets held up signs: "Johnson's Baby Powder—Napalm" and "Burn, Baby, Burn" while Secret Service agents spirited him in and out through a rear door.

The chief executive could not risk being seen in public, but the vice president kept filling university speaking engagements. The students, the young people, turned off by his repeated appearances on television and infuriated at his Kiwanian garrulity, gave their hearts over to Bobby Kennedy, who told them the war had to stop. The day came when Martin Luther King, Jr., himself left off advocating civil rights at home to speak for peace in Vietnam. So far had his constituency of two decades parted from Hubert Humphrey.

One day Humphrey addressed the National Grocery Manufacturers in Manhattan. Making his Johnsonian pitch that America had no choice but to hang on in Vietnam despite all criticism, his arguments fell so close to what Richard Nixon had been saying that he got a congratulatory phone call from his vice-presidential predecessor and a friendly reminder that grocerymen were Nixon's audience: "My dad was a grocer. You came up the pharmacy way." It was fair warning: Nixon and the Republicans now stood in good position to harvest the discontent in 1968. They backed the war, as the public still did; but in the shock at black and student rioting, they demanded law and order.

His consensus having vanished, could the president muster a majority when he ran again? The Left had abandoned him; the Republicans were resurgent. Johnson was holed up in a kind of hedgehog position in the middle—a good spot in American politics but not a good posture. Humphrey was irrevocably tied to Johnson and his war policy, and he knew it. On his Asian tour he had said to reporters: "If the war in Vietnam is a colossal failure, I know what happens to me."

PART
FIVE

The Year
1968

28

"Johnson's Not Going to Make It Easy"

I T   W O U L D   be going too far to say that everything went downhill for the Johnson administration after the president decided to plunge into Vietnam. The nation continued to enjoy the prosperity that had rolled steadily onward since President Kennedy's time. The economy grew to such gigantic proportions that Johnson could speak of the war as costing "only" $17 billion per year. But his comment revealed that, simultaneously, the dollar was losing its value. In fact, inflation had become a concern for the president second only to the war as the 1968 election year began. With the international balance-of-payments sharply against the United States, the fabled gold reserves of Fort Knox seemed to have melted away. Having failed to raise taxes, the government wound up in effect paying for the war by printing money. The bankers and traders of Europe lost confidence in the administration's conduct of affairs. The dollar, emblem of American hegemony, weakened in world money markets until its stability hung by a thread.

Even at the summit of his power in 1964, Lyndon Johnson had told Humphrey he might not run for reelection in 1968. He was, as none knew better than his vice president, a mercurial man. As he began to meet setbacks, as resistance began to rise in Congress, as prospects of a quick outcome in Vietnam faded, he sometimes talked of handing over his office before his term ended. More than once he spoke of it to Humphrey, who dismissed these remarks as the outbursts of a moody, frustrated, and egotistical man. Others also heard such talk. In September 1966 the president said to Valenti over lunch: "I won't be around then [1968]. . . . They would say I was playing politics if I resigned and gave the job to Humphrey. My own party has turned against me, and the Republicans are chiming in. We probably need a fresh face. Humphrey would start with a clean slate, he would be fresh. As it is now, I have lost Congress." At his ranch in October 1967, Johnson dictated a draft resignation letter to George Christian, his press secretary, and instructed Christian to show it to Governor Connally.

True, Johnson had lost the vaunted consensus that won his election landslide victory and propelled his bundle of Great Society measures through Congress in 1964 and 1965, but the Democrats had not utterly lost control of Congress. The midterm elections of 1966, as Humphrey said, merely reduced the Democratic majorities. But the Great Society programs ran into heavy resistance. Appropriations for the war against poverty were slashed. The only significant new measure enacted thereafter, the Model Cities program, was seriously weakened before passage. Denied adequate funding, it never got off the ground.

In the tenth year of fighting, a bare majority of Americans still backed the effort in Vietnam. Opposition had grown virulent. To the obscenity, as they saw it, of endless Vietnam bloodshed, the anti-war students responded with obscenities of their own. To what they called the barbarity of wholesale bombing, they replied with barbarities of behavior toward police, politicians, and authority in general. In Congress, in newspapers, on television, the spreading talk of stalemate threw the president on the defensive. The administration tried to counter with statistics of Viet Cong slaughtered, of roads cleared, of villages "pacified." Then, on January 31, occurred the event that was to bring Lyndon Johnson, and then Hubert Humphrey, to judgment in this election year.

It was the first day of Tet, Indochina's lunar New Year's festival. Early that morning the supposedly decimated and jungle-bound Viet Cong boiled out of the boondocks to launch attacks on every major South Vietnamese city. Some eighty-four thousand men were involved in these assaults. In Saigon, nineteen Viet Cong sappers penetrated the U. S. embassy compound, where three months before Humphrey had proclaimed "the great adventure." Seven embassy personnel were killed; Ambassador Bunker took refuge in a CIA hideaway. Before U. S. and South Vietnamese soldiers regained control of the capital, large areas of the city were leveled. The Viet Cong were not driven out of Ben Tre, a town of thirty-five thousand, until artillery and air attacks demolished at least half of the town's structures. "It became necessary to destroy the town to save it," an American officer explained in a memorable oxymoron. It took twenty-eight days before the last Viet Cong were driven out of Hue, the ancient capital on the North coast.

General Westmoreland announced the rout of the attackers as if the United States had won a famous victory. The Viet Cong had suffered heavy losses, but if 32,000 had been killed, as the U. S. command asserted, and if three were wounded for each one killed, this would have meant that the 84,000 attackers suffered more than 120,000 casualties. Whatever the military score in Vietnam, the real setback for the president was at home. Stunned by the manifest ability of the Viet Cong to exert power, the U. S. public took the Tet offensive to mean that the United States was not getting anywhere in Vietnam. And while the public still reeled back in surprise and dismay, newspapers reported from Washington that the military command in Saigon was asking for 206,000 more troops.

The shock waves from Tet and the popular reaction converged with other forces bearing down upon the president. On one side, Treasury Secretary Henry Fowler was pleading for an emergency tax boost to keep the dollar from collapsing under the withdrawal of confidence abroad. On another side, recently appointed Defense Secretary Clark Clifford, completing a review of U. S. strategic commitments, was recommending that General Westmoreland's call for more troops could not be accepted. In the White House, aides began drafting a speech for the besieged President.

The approaching presidential primaries also demanded urgent decisions of the president. The Johnson-Humphrey ticket had been duly entered in New Hampshire and Wisconsin. But when the vice president arranged for Governor Roger Branigin of Indiana to stand in for the president as a favorite son in the Indiana primary, the president put off talking with the governor to seal the arrangement. Despite Humphrey's urging, the president also made no move to line up their 1964 manager, Larry O'Brien, to run the 1968 campaign.

When the voters of New Hampshire went to the polls in the year's first primary, the president won, as expected. But Senator Eugene McCarthy, aided by an outpouring of student volunteer doorbellringers from all over the country, took a stunning 46 percent of the vote. That was enough to make Bobby Kennedy, too, declare his candidacy against the president. Suddenly it was apparent that Johnson had a real fight on his hands for the party's nomination. Humphrey wrote Lawyer Morris Ernst: "We are in a tremendous swing . . . back from the policies that have kept the nation safeguarded for the past generation."

For Humphrey it was the worst time of the war. "I'm worried," he wrote, that Martin Luther King, Jr.,'s vocal opposition to the president could jeopardize the black vote. Of this lowest point, Walter Mondale said later: "I think Humphrey thought his political career was destroyed."

The next primary was April 2 in Wisconsin, where McCarthy's chances were better than in New Hampshire. Seven thousand young volunteers fanned out across the state to turn out votes for the man who dared to say: Johnson must go. Humphrey persuaded the president to fly to Minneapolis to address the National Farmers Union, which was influential in Wisconsin. But reports flooded in that the Johnson-Humphrey ticket would take a beating in Wisconsin. Jim Rowe, now the president's political strategist, sent him warning that he would have to do "something startling and dramatic" before the Wisconsin primary.

Was there anything the president could do at this late date to break the impasse in Vietnam? The North Vietnamese had spurned his overtures, and when Johnson had discussed this earlier during a visit by Ne Win, the neutralist premier of Burma, Ne Win had told him in Humphrey's presence: "You are doing wrong in asking for peace; the North Vietnamese interpret that as weakness." So Johnson, himself, had always thought. But now his advisers obviously had to come up with some alternatives for the president to consider. In early March the idea of proposing a halt in bombing North Vietnam above the 20th parallel popped up as a gesture that might induce the Communists to enter into negotiations.

No aspect of the Vietnam war had drawn greater criticism from other governments and world opinion than the relentless plastering of the North by huge, high-flying B-52 bombers. By the spring of 1968 these giant planes based in Guam, Taiwan, and three Thai airfields were dropping up to a million pounds of explosives each day on North Vietnam. When their original mission—"to break the will of North Vietnam"—was seen to be fruitless, it was soon changed to "cutting the flow of men and supplies" from North to South and, after U. S. combat forces moved in, supporting "the growing number of U. S. ground troops." But truck factories, marshalling yards, and military depots were not plentiful in a small and backward country like North Vietnam, and it appeared that the enormous quantity of explosive dropped (one million tons) was dictated less by the number of suitable targets than by the sheer availability of large numbers of these monster planes.

One night in the privacy of the president's bedroom, Humphrey said later, he ventured to put in his own recommendation: "Mr. President, from a political view here at home, that [the pullback to the 20th parallel] is not going to do much good. What you should do is stop it all. You should cease bombing north of the 17th parallel, the border demilitarized zone." Humphrey thus made his first recorded statement at variance with the president's policy since his luckless dissent at the start of his tenure as vice president. It happened also to be almost exactly the position he adopted six months later when he attempted to cut loose as candidate in his own right for president.

Yet another force bore down upon the president at this time. After the appalling violence that had devastated the heart of some of America's biggest cities, he had named a blue ribbon committee, the National Advisory Commission on Civil Disorders, under the chairmanship of former Governor Otto Kerner of Illinois. The commission now turned in its report. At a moment when shouts for "black power" were drowning out the civil rights leaders' call for racial integration, and when Alabama's Governor George Wallace was touring the North and winning white backing for his insurgent racist candidacy for president, the findings were political dynamite. The commission reported that racism—white and black—was polarizing the country, that America was fast splitting into two nations, one black and penned up in the inner city, the other white and ensconsed in a surrounding surburban ring. How to handle this report was a matter of the most extreme political delicacy, and his ultimate solution was to shelve it. When Humphrey discussed and even appeared to criticize it in Milwaukee, he again angered the president. Humphrey tried to assuage the president's wrath by claiming press reports were "a serious distortion of what I said." But by this time events were moving too rapidly for the president's freezeout of the vice president to last long.

So it was that Humphrey was on hand for a pivotal meeting shortly before the Wisconsin primary. It had been the president's habit to bring to the White House a group of elders such as Dean Acheson, John McCloy, and Omar Bradley to consult on the conduct of the war. On Tuesday, March 26, they met again at the president's request. The White House briefings reflected the changes since their last meeting in November and prompted the "wise men," as the newspapers called them, to tell the president: 1) more force was not the answer; 2) the South Vietnamese must be asked to do more; and 3) "if you can think of something to do toward peace, do it."

On March 27, the president's principal advisers gathered in Secretary Rusk's office to go over the draft of the speech the president was to deliver. At this fateful meeting, Humphrey was not included. Here it was Defense Secretary Clifford's role that was crucial. In the past he had counseled force, but now he said it was time to change. Rusk and the others fell in with him. While skeptical that Hanoi would respond, they agreed that the speech must take a "peaceful tone." The suggestion to end U. S. bombing south of the twentieth parallel, which had meanwhile received Ambassador Bunker's qualified assent, was inserted in a new draft, and Johnson accepted it. The president would offer the new proposal in the course of a nationwide telecast Sunday evening, March 31.

On Sunday morning, having telephoned beforehand, the Johnsons stopped off at the Humphreys' Potomac-side apartment on their way home from church. The vice president was on the point of leaving for Mexico City, where he was to sign for the United States a protocol of the nuclear nonproliferation treaty the following morning. The President, his aide Jim Jones, and Humphrey went into the study and closed the door. Johnson handed a copy of his speech to Humphrey, who read it, noted the proposal for a limited bombing pause, and said: "That's just great, the best thing I ever heard you say." Humphrey also suggested a few changes, which the president inserted in the speech. Then the president handed him another piece of paper. It was an alternative ending to the speech that he had had the Secret Service go back and fetch from his bedside table. The vice president read on to the last line: ". . . Accordingly, I shall not seek, nor will I accept, the nomination of my party for the Presidency of the United States." The words, Jim Jones said later, "put a time-warp on Humphrey. His face flushed, and tears ran from his eyes."

"You're kidding, Mr. President," said Humphrey. "You can't do this, you can't just resign from office. You're going to be reelected." Johnson replied that he had not yet decided which ending to use. But he also said: "Hubert, nobody will believe that I'm trying to end this war unless I do that. I just can't get them to believe I want peace." And Johnson told Humphrey: "If you're going to run, you'd better get ready damn quick." Humphrey, Jones said later, was dejected at the news. He said: "There's no way I can beat the Kennedy machine."

Johnson replied: "You've got to get moving."

But would Johnson actually renounce? In January, unknown to all but two or three aides, he had had such a concluding paragraph ready when he delivered his State of the Union address—but had kept it in his pocket and not used it. Now he advised Humphrey to listen to the speech. Thus he left Humphrey on tenterhooks, just as he had when dangling the vice presidency before him in 1964. "Not a word to Muriel," he said and took his departure. The visit had lasted exactly an hour.

Muriel Humphrey thought the president's behavior strange as he embraced her on the way out. "Is he ill?" she asked. In the car on the way to the airport she kept asking questions, and Humphrey tried to put her off by saying that the president was very discouraged and did not want to run and might not.

Arriving at the plane, Humphrey also behaved uncharacteristically. Boarding *Air Force Two*, he brushed past reporters and aides without stopping to visit and locked himself in his office at the front of the plane. On arrival in Mexico City, he broke away from his wife and aides at the hotel, and went for a walk in the park with his physician, Dr. Berman. Visibly nervous, he walked straight ahead with his short-paced, quick stride, saying little and paying no attention to the throngs of Sunday strollers. That evening, in the midst of a U. S. embassy dinner with Mexico's President Gustavo Diaz Ortiz, he insisted on getting up and going into another room to listen to Johnson's speech. Midway through the broadcast, about the time that Jim Rowe and a few others were getting the word in Washington, he got a phone call from Marvin Watson: the president would use the second ending, the one announcing his withdrawal.

As the president spoke the actual words, Muriel Humphrey burst into tears, crying: "Why didn't you tell me?"

He answered her: "I've been trying to prepare you for it all day, but I didn't know myself." In notes he drew up a day or two later, he wrote: "She was very shaken and emotionally upset. To say the least, I felt the same way. I resolved however to say little or nothing except to commend the President in my toast at the dinner."

What thoughts passed through the vice president's mind that day of harrowing suspense? The presidency he had sought and despaired of, the presidency to which he had drawn so near while suffering frustration and ignominy during his years of indenture to Lyndon Johnson, that prize was at last within his grasp. Up to this time he had believed, he said then and later, that Johnson would be renominated and reelected despite all. Now Johnson had stepped aside—or had he? Now the presidency was in sight—but he would have to win it.

For Humphrey, though he did not want to say so right away, there could be but one course. After returning to the dinner and even staying to dance with some of the Mexican wives, the vice president excused himself. "I called in the members of the staff who traveled with me—Van Dyk, Sherman, Rielly, Cahn, Gartner, and Dr. Berman. I also called Bill Connell, my son Skip, and Fred Gates. I told each and every one to play it cool, to make no statements." He took a telephone call from Margaret Truman Daniel, the former president's daughter, who urged him to declare his candidacy. There were some fifty other calls, but he refused them all. He needed time to assess his strength against the snowballing candidacies of Gene McCarthy and Bobby Kennedy.

> And before I could make any move I would have to ascertain the view of the President—where did he stand—what, if anything, he would do. Second, where did some of the key political leaders stand, i.e, Dick Daley, Dick Hughes, some of the top California Democrats, Frank O'Connor, and the Southern governors.
>
> In other words, did I have a chance if I were available, or would I just be a punching bag for Kennedy, only to be humiliated and defeated in the Convention?
>
> I wanted to have some time to think this through. I explained I am not anxious. Quite frankly, I am not sure that I have the stomach for it, knowing the ruthless methods that are employed by both Kennedy and Nixon.

He was still musing about Lyndon Johnson while getting ready for bed that night in Mexico City. As Dr. Berman later recounted what Humphrey said: "I felt so sorry for him. He said the saddest thing. He said 'As much as I've tried to do for the Negroes and the poor, even they're against me. Now don't get me wrong. If I want that nomination, I can get it. There's no two ways about it. But the only way I can unite the nation is to do something about Vietnam now.' And then he made the strangest statement: 'Maybe the people just don't like my face.' When Berman asked: "What do you think right now?" Humphrey said only that the mayors and governors and labor chieftains knew what he had done for them. "We'll wait and see, we'll know in a week or so. . . . If I run, Johnson's not going to make it easy."

29

The Politics
of Joy

T H E first thing Humphrey said when he got off the plane in Washington was: "Has Bobby got it locked up yet?"

His aide Bill Connell had spent the night after Johnson's speech by making some fifty telephone calls, starting to line up the troops. It seemed none too soon. People kept telling him that Robert or Ted Kennedy had just called. He had to say: "I'll be honest with you. I haven't got word from Humphrey. Just hang tough."

Returning, Humphrey plunged into the vortex. Waiting at the plane were two senators, a few congressmen, a cabinet member (Orville Freeman), and some two hundred friends. That evening his closest advisers met with him at his apartment and said he must run—Connell, Kampelman, Welsh, Gus Tyler of the Garment Workers. Humphrey wanted to wait. He did not want to rush headlong into another Kennedy meat-grinder. And he had to check with Johnson. At a press conference, Johnson had already called his withdrawal "irrevocable"—but was it?

Next day, the day Gene McCarthy defeated Johnson in the Wisconsin primary, two Southerners, Hale Boggs and Russell Long, took Humphrey aside at the congressional leadership breakfast and said he should declare at once, "or Kennedy will wrap it up." George Meany came to him and urged him to announce for president right away. Oklahoma's Mike Monroney telephoned to say he feared a Kennedy blitz: Bobby had already offered Fred

Harris, the attractive young junior senator from Monroney's state, second place on the ticket. Bobby had urged Harris to stand as Oklahoma's favorite son, then withdraw in Kennedy's favor. But Harris, Monroney said, had held back, friendly to Humphrey. That set Humphrey's mind working: both Robert Kennedy and Gene McCarthy were drawing excited support from young people, and if he could bring Fred Harris, thirty-seven, to his side, it would prove that he too could appeal to the young.

Meanwhile, Kennedy had gone in to see the President to ask whether the president meant to cut his throat. On first hearing that Kennedy had requested a meeting, Johnson said: "I won't bother answering that grandstanding little runt." But the meeting took place, attended and recorded by Johnson aides Walt Rostow and Charles Murphy, and was friendly enough. Johnson said: "You and I weren't meant to be vice presidents," and then held forth at length about how he had continued the work of Kennedy's brother. When Robert Kennedy then asked if Johnson intended to dictate his successor, Johnson answered that he had no such intention. He said he felt closer to the vice president, but did not know if Humphrey intended to run. As stated in his speech, Johnson wanted to keep the presidency out of the campaign and had withdrawn because as president he simply could not pursue the great issues—peace in Vietnam, the cities' racial crises, the tax bill—while subjected daily to attacks from Nixon, McCarthy, and Robert Kennedy. He said if he had thought he could engage in politics and still "hold the country together," he would have run, and added, "if I campaign for someone else, it will defeat what I am trying to do."

After Kennedy left, Humphrey, waiting in an anteroom, was ushered in. Johnson informed his vice president of what he had just told Kennedy. And he said Humphrey had been a great and loyal vice president. In fact, he would rate him an A plus vice president, whereas he would rate himself as only a B plus.

But for all his loyal service, Humphrey got no invitation to run in Johnson's place, and certainly no pledge of support. When Humphrey said he had considered announcing his candidacy immediately but feared that to do so might "demean" the president's statement, Johnson said only that it was up to him. And he even added that if Humphrey ran, "he must do a better job than he was able to get organized in Wisconsin"—a gratuitous thrust at his vice president and the first suggestion that the president now chose to blame the vice president for the humiliating Wisconsin defeat. Then, as if washing his hands of the business, he proceeded to give Humphrey some less-than-reassuring advice. Money, along with organization, would be Humphrey's big problem if he ran—a clear signal that Johnson intended no help on the financial side, where he might have been able to help most. And he said not the South, which might well support him, but six Northern states—New Jersey, Pennsylvania, Illinois, Michigan, Ohio, and Indiana—would be those Humphrey had to win. The vice president said he had been in preliminary contact with Mayor Daley of Chicago, Governor Richard Hughes of New Jersey, and other party leaders: "They appeared not yet to have made up their minds. He had the impression that they were not willing to be 'blitzed' and had not yet committed themselves." To this, Johnson replied heartlessly that in the end Daley and Hughes would go with Kennedy.

Now began a strange turn in Humphrey's life, for Johnson proved to be wrong about the money, at least the "early" money. In 1960, Humphrey had been done in by Kennedy money. This time it appeared he could have as much money as he wanted if he ran against a Kennedy. That night he flew to New York for a dinner at the Waldorf. It had been arranged by Gardner Cowles of *Look* magazine for his advertisers. But after dinner, Gardner Cowles took Humphrey upstairs for a private chat with some of his rich friends. Besides the two Cowles brothers, Henry Ford was there, and Sidney Weinberg and John Loeb, investment bankers who had backed the president. After a long talk they adjourned to the Waldorf Towers hideaway of Dwayne Andreas. No one was asked for a pledge but lo and behold, everyone present urged Humphrey to run. Before the night was over a Citizens for Humphrey committee took shape, to be led by Loeb and former Commerce Secretary John Connor, with the influential Weinberg, the "director's director," as vice chairman. What spurred on the corporate chieftains was a determination above all to stop Kennedy. That was the talk in the boardrooms. Suddenly Humphrey was the beneficiary of all the established powers that felt threatened by the swirling currents of radical dissent that Robert Kennedy was trying to ride into the White House. The Citizens Committee for Humphrey promised to be an imposing lineup. "I've got every establishment in America against me," Robert Kennedy told a reporter on the plane the night the fatcats at the Waldorf asked Humphrey to run.

Humphrey's consuming passion to be president was further stimulated when he flew to Pittsburgh to address the state AFL-CIO. Mayor Barr introduced him as "the next president," and two thousand unionists cheered and interrupted his speech with shouts of "Tell us what we want to hear." Humphrey shouted back: "I know what you want" and was on the point of declaring his candidacy as he headed back, exultant, to Washington.

Instead, he returned to the first terrible night of a murderous spring. As he learned at a fund-raising dinner that evening, Martin Luther King, Jr., apostle of nonviolence and the greatest black figure of the age, had been fatally shot by a white assassin in Memphis. At word that King had been murdered, all the rage and despair of America's blacks gushed out of the ghettoes. Riots erupted in eighty cities that night, in places as big as Chicago and as small as Port Chester, New York. In Washington the glare of burning stores and tenements lit the sky as Humphrey rode home through the city. Looting and burning spread to within two blocks of the White House, where President Johnson went on television to plead in vain for public order: "I ask every American to reject the blind violence that has struck down Dr. King." The rioting went on the next night, and the next, and the next. Before it was over, 21,000 federal troops and 34,000 state guardsmen were called out—the biggest military deployment for a civil emergency in history. In all, forty-six persons died, all but five of them black. The explosion left blacks embittered; it appalled those whites it did not terrify. President Johnson proclaimed Sunday, April 7, a national day of mourning and ordered the U. S. flag lowered to half mast over all federal buildings.

The death of King put an end to all campaigning and knocked out Humphrey's thoughts of an immediate announcement. Along with the declared candidates Kennedy and McCarthy and a host of notable Americans, the vice president went to the funeral in Atlanta and joined Coretta King and the throngs of mourners. In Washington he issued this statement: "The blight of discrimination, poverty and neglect must be erased. . . . An America full of freedom, full and equal opportunity shall be his living memorial."

These events, shocking and foreboding as they were, could not dissuade Humphrey from running. Six months before, chained fast to an administration's sinking ship, the vice president had seemed ruined as a political force. Now Johnson had withdrawn from the race—and Humphrey could thank his friend Gene McCarthy for that. But the president's withdrawal had also eliminated the war as the big campaign issue for McCarthy and Kennedy, and Humphrey, stepping out from behind Johnson to survey the scene, could see for the first time in his life a clear shot at the top. By all appearances, Kennedy was now the front runner. But he already knew that the Kennedy blitz had not succeeded, and when Kennedy sent Kenny O'Donnell to propose that he stand down in return for a high post in a Kennedy administration, Humphrey dismissed it as a brazen ploy. McCarthy's victory in Wisconsin heartened him, because it promised that McCarthy and Kennedy would weaken each other in head-on primary confrontations in Indiana, Nebraska, Oregon, and California.

If he were to make the most of his chances, it would be better to stay out of the primaries. More than enough delegates to give him the nomination could be found in the non-primary states, where delegates were chosen by state conventions and caucuses in which political leaders made the decisions. It was too late, anyway, to file in primaries except in South Dakota and New Jersey. "I didn't have time to raise the money and to get organized for them. I thought it would be rather foolish to enter," Humphrey said later. For if he had sought a primary fight, it would inevitably have restored the war as the leading issue—used against him, of course.

Forgoing the primaries involved risks. In this of all years, when public opinion expressed in votes had already forced one president out, bypassing all primaries invited the charge of avoiding a popular test. But according to Rowe's law—formulated first for Humphrey in advance of his 1960 race and confirmed soon afterwards in Wisconsin and West Virginia at his expense—

primaries served only to inform the professional politicians who would later make the selection at the convention which of the candidates looked like having winning ways. Toward Robert Kennedy, Humphrey was finding out, there was a surprising amount of distrust among the line politicians; there was also, as James Reston noted in the *New York Times*, "a very large body of anti-Kennedy voters in the country at this time." Taking his name for his slogan, Robert Kennedy had stormed across the country against the president, calling out the disaffected young in frenzied rallies as if to win the nomination in the streets. But now the president was out of it, if anything a figure of sympathy for what some called a "noble" act of renunciation. "Up to now," McCarthy remarked, "Bobby was Jack running against Lyndon. Now Bobby has to run against Jack." McCarthy seemed sure that among the suburban middle class he appealed to, Bobby simply did not stack up with Jack.

Humphrey had a good deal going for him. Incumbency carried with it recognition, prestige, and, for the holder of such a high office, a certain acceptance on the part of many voters. His nineteen years of federal performance had won such esteem, James Reston wrote, that "if presidents were elected by the thousand best-informed men in Washington on the basis of who would make the best president, he would be number one." Whatever else this encomium implied, it underlined that the "ins" of the administration were on his side, the officeholders in a powerful and ubiquitous government. The vice president also stood high with those in the national and state party organizations who would choose delegates. He commanded loyalties. He had made speeches for these people. Sitting up late talking and drinking with them, he had endeared himself in his way to many of them. Significantly the president, in notifying him of his neutrality, had signaled that the vice president could expect to win the delegates of the South, including his own state of Texas. And when it came to the crunch in those Northern states where the contest might be close, it seemed a pretty fair assumption that the president would use his still considerable influence to see that his "persecutors" McCarthy and Kennedy—above all, Kennedy—would not prevail. Taking all this with the first polls' suggestion that he would not fare badly, it appeared as if the vice president had a chance to corral the 1,231 delegates needed to win nomination at the Convention without entering a single primary. That was the Humphrey strategy as it emerged almost at once: the man who had fought and defeated the Organization in 1948, would run as the Organization's man in 1968.

For Humphrey these were hectic days. A kind of command committee formed and met in his office—Connell and Welsh from the staff, Kampelman and Rowe from their law offices, Andreas flying in and out from New York and Minneapolis, and one or two others every day or so. But Humphrey had not yet signaled "Go"—and there was no one in charge but himself. While the New York committee extracted Johnson's "no objection" to its fund-raising plans, the vice president's office across the street from the White House was a madhouse of yacketing squawk-boxes, jangling telephones, milling messengers. Connell was on the line to the network of operatives that he had quietly built up since 1964 for just this moment. Welsh was working his congressional contacts. Eiler Ravnholt was assembling the "200 list" and "400 list" of key supporters—coded for age, sex, office, nationality, interest, and amount of money or talent contributed in the vice president's 1960 and 1964 campaigns. Dave Gartner was taking Andreas's almost hourly reports—a long talk with Walter Reuther (doubtful), another with Farm Leader Oren Lee Staley (enthusiastic), another with Publisher DeWitt Wallace (who promised a big contribution and favorable articles in the *Reader's Digest*). In the midst of the melee sat the vice president, shirtsleeved, feet propped on the desk, telephone cradled in his shoulder. He talked to all twenty-four Democratic governors, to mayors, to labor chieftains. And as he worked he lined up backers for the United Democrats for Humphrey organization, making these notes:

> A long talk with President and Mrs. Truman—he agreed to be honorary chairman. . . . . A long talk with Charlie Murphy [top political adviser at the White House]—raring to go. . . . a long talk with Governor Connally of Texas. It appears he will be favorite son unless we have objections. . . .
>
> Talked with Jack Arvey, Chicago—OK . . . with Jim Farley, he will serve . . . with Matt McCloskey, influential in Philadelphia—he is for us but we should touch him up again . . . with [ex-Gov.] Ned Breathitt of Kentucky—likes me, wants to be for me, but said he would clear it with the President. . . . Mayor Sam Yorty, Los Angeles, he is for us, will be making a statement. . . .

Humphrey's first thought without question was to get Postmaster General Larry O'Brien, who had run the victorious campaigns of 1960 and 1964, to manage his race. Best of the pros, O'Brien was an organization man's organization man. But O'Brien, explaining that his prior loyalty was to the Kennedys, resigned from the Cabinet to take charge of Bobby's race. Jim Rowe, who might have had the job, preferred the role of counselor. While the vice president hesitated, Kampelman and Connell brought in Richard Maguire, an old Kennedy worker from Boston who had served Johnson for a time as treasurer of the Democratic National Committee, and set up temporary campaign headquarters in Maguire's Washington law office.

Humphrey had other ideas. If his campaign was going to make any headway against the New Politics that had brought down Johnson, it had better look new too. As soon as he heard that Fred Harris had resisted Kennedy's blandishments he invited the young senator and his Comanche wife, LaDonna, to breakfast. They agreed to help him. Humphrey went off to tell audiences in Louisiana and North Carolina that it was time to look—past the two candidates in the field—for "maturity of judgment." But even while he thought to present himself as a candidate offering a mature and calming influence in troubled times, the conviction grew that to compete he had to put a younger look on his race. He told a group of academics whose advice he sought: "I'm old hat. I've been around in the Vice Presidency since 1965. I have to break out of it. I can't look back."

The DFL party that Humphrey led to power in Minnesota was noted for the talented people it produced—Humphrey, McCarthy, and Freeman, for example. And out of this party that was at once wide-open and highly organized, not only active before elections but busy hammering out issues at year-round meetings, a younger generation of leaders had come forward. Not formed in the dust bowl days of the Depression, they showed the same gift for identifying and defining progressive issues. They were lively, attractive, and some had already reached Washington.

Walter Mondale, a Methodist minister's son from Elmont (population, 580) was the most prominent of these young DFLers. He had risen phenomenally through the ranks. Freeman had recruited him as a Macalester College doorbell ringer for Humphrey's second mayoral race. The following year, aged nineteen, Mondale was Seventh Congressional District manager for Humphrey's senatorial campaign. From law school at the University of Minnesota he entered the attorney general's office in St. Paul, where his diligence, thoroughness, and courtroom dash won attention. When his boss resigned in early 1960, Governor Freeman named him attorney general, at the age of thirty-two. Just four years later, when Humphrey's seat fell vacant by reason of his election to the vice presidency, Freeman's successor, Governor Karl Rolvaag, appointed Mondale to Humphrey's place.

Though Humphrey played a part in the key appointments in Mondale's rise, it would be wrong to say that Mondale was Humphrey's boy. In Washington, Mondale moved into Humphrey's old committees, took advice from Humphrey, and cast votes like Humphrey's. He fought Humphrey's fight to seat black Mississippians at the 1964 Democratic convention. He favored a strong U. S. position in the world, including Vietnam. But he spoke in his own accents from the first. In the Senate he took a backrow seat alongside two other newly elected members, Robert Kennedy of New York and Fred Harris of Oklahoma, both of whom became his good friends. One day toward the end of their first year the time finally came when a Senate vote ended in a tie, and Humphrey, presiding as vice president, got his first chance (of only two, as it turned out) to cast a deciding vote. A page skipped up to the dais with a note signed by the three backrow freshmen: "Mr. Vice President, you have arrived."

Even before he returned from Martin Luther King, Jr.,'s funeral, Humphrey talked to Mondale about a role in his campaign. A few days earlier the young senator had been sure that Humphrey would not get the nomination.

Watching the Johnson speech on television with Senator Henry Jackson, Mondale exclaimed at the end: "Bobby's nominated. Hubert shouldn't even get into the race." But when it became evident that Kennedy would not walk away with it, Mondale was receptive to the vice president's asking him to lead the United Democrats for Humphrey. At thirty-nine, he fell right in with Humphrey's accent on youth. He agreed to ask his good friend Fred Harris, only thirty-seven, to serve as UDH co-chairman. The Mondales and Harrises summered together on Delaware Bay, their children played together. Harris agreed to join Mondale as co-leader.

Offering himself as the one man who could unify party and country while dividing the direction of his campaign betrayed, however, an old Humphrey failing. His campaigns tended to split up under several leaders for a simple reason. Sooner or later aggressive lieutenants would take a proposal or complaint to Humphrey. Almost invariably, Humphrey would respond: "You do it" or "You fix it." The vice president already had one campaign being run by Bill Connell—with his eight-foot shelf of black books breaking down each state by region, by city, by county, by power brokers, by union control, by delegates. Maguire and Kampelman had started another, tapping into old Johnson networks in some sort of loose confederation with Connell and his battery of contacts. The vice president had also called in his old Minnesota operatives—Orville Freeman and Bob Short, both of whom had outspoken views on how to mount the campaign and both of whom, of course, could and did talk to the candidate at any time.

Determined to put a new face on his Old Politics entanglements, the effervescent vice president now summoned his co-commanders to Florida, where the Humphreys had gone as they always did at Eastertime to spend a few days' rest with the Andreases. The two senators arrived Sunday evening at Key Largo and went aboard the Andreas cabin cruiser berthed at Key Largo's fancy Anglers club. Humphrey insisted that two such spirited young chieftains, making due allowance for their Senate duties, could manage his drive better than one. He told them: "We're going to have a close campaign. The biggest hunk of gold is the President's power, which is in our hands. But it could turn to lead—this campaign will be won or lost not on the positive things we do but on the mistakes that will be made."

It was agreed that Mondale would whip together the organization and lead the convention planning; Harris would head the delegate hunt. Each, with Senate burdens in mind, would have a deputy—Larry Hayes, Mondale's twenty-eight-year-old lawyer from St. Paul, running the shop; Bob McCandless, Harris's thirty-year-old lawyer from Oklahoma, chasing delegates. Old stagers such as Rowe, Connell, Kampelman, and Maguire would have to take second place. Even as UDH's first ad appeared in the newspapers proclaiming the candidate's "MATURITY . . . INTEGRITY . . . EXPERIENCE," youth was put in charge. Humphrey told the two senators: "I'm giving you carte blanche. I'll meddle as little as possible," then added with a laugh, "and as much as necessary." At the end it was agreed that Humphrey would announce his candidacy at a big Washington sendoff, and the Senators would introduce him jointly.

Would such patchwork management work? One after another Connell, Kampelman, and Maguire bent the vice president's ear to say that neither the senators nor their deputies had any national political experience. And within days, Humphrey was fretting that they were losing Iowa, that he would call headquarters Saturday night and find no one there, that they had omitted to invite multimillionaire Jacob Blaustein, one of his biggest contributors, to the announcement party. Mondale assured him that they had all worked until midnight Sunday, and would more than make up for Iowa when Maryland chose its delegates.

Somehow things shaped up. Announcement day arrived—Saturday, April 27—the day Humphrey had aimed for all his life. The night before he had dined privately at the White House with a seemingly benevolent president. As a *Life* photographer snapped pictures that morning in his office, Humphrey was "almost irrepressible, buoyant, kicking up his heels." Picking up the text of his speech he insisted on adding to its list of credentials ("Maturity, restraint, responsibility")—"a loving family." At Washington's Shoreham Hotel he waded gaily into a ballroom packed with friends who had come from as far as Hawaii—two thousand at the luncheon tables, another twelve hundred pressing at the doors. The crowd hummed with high spirits. The two young senators provided a lively buildup. Mondale said he was the bright one, Harris the hard worker. Harris, adlibbing adroitly, brought the audience to its feet precisely as the national television came on and the vice president launched into his declaration.

The speech had been in preparation since four days after the president's withdrawal. Willard Wirtz from the cabinet, Harry McPherson and Charles Murphy from the White House, New York editor Norman Cousins and Long Island editor Bill Moyers had all contributed drafts. Brief (only twenty minutes long), it was polished and honed to the last comma. It presented the candidate as man and statesman, a leader of wisdom and compassion. Humphrey, resolutely refusing to smile as his friends chanted "We Want Hubert" at every pause, stuck all the way through to his text, so deliberately dignified. But rapport with his audience was everything to this orator, and the roar of applause called irresistibly. The peroration drew on some impressive words of Victor Hugo that he had been carrying around in his pocket: "The future has several names. For the weak, it is the impossible. For the faint-hearted, it is the unknown. For the thoughtful and the valiant, it is ideal. The challenge is urgent, the task is large; the time is now. On to victory!"

Humphrey followed his lines to their resounding end. Then, carried away by the friendly cheers, he went on extemporaneously. Rubbing his hands with glee, he shouted: "Here we are, the way politics ought to be in America, the politics of happiness, the politics of purpose, the politics of joy. And that's the way it's going to be, too, all the way, from here on out." The whole day—the luncheon, the introductions, the big party afterward, the exquisitely prepared speech itself—had gone off with a precision unusual in any candidate's campaigning and unprecedented in Humphrey's. His wife looked great, and he posed with her. He skipped about, shaking hands and blowing kisses, "knowing," as a bystander said, "that he had done well."

But it was his impulsive words, uttered in an outburst of shared exhilaration, that took the headlines next day: "Vice President a Candidate, Proclaims the Politics of Joy." It was pure Humphrey, bubbly, extemporaneous. But it was an inappropriate note to strike when the wooden boxes were arriving back from Vietnam, when flags still flew at half-mast for the murdered Dr. King, when wild-eyed students were occupying the president's office at Columbia University, when cities ripped by racial hatred quaked in fear of renewed arson and looting. Editorialists clucked disapproval, and Robert Kennedy, campaigning in Indiana, cried: "It is easy to say this is the politics of happiness—but if you see children starving in the Delta of Mississippi and despair on the Indian reservations, then you know that everybody in America is not satisfied."

At that moment the battle for the Democratic nomination seemed as close as Humphrey had predicted, and Kennedy appeared to be in the lead. Eugene McCarthy was also an enormously appealing figure, leonine, fearless, acerb. First to take up the fight, he was the hero of the young activists—idealists who saw in his candidacy the chance to stop the war and change things after all within the system. The candidate, however, seemed enigmatically reluctant. A liberal who was anything but a believer in "causes," he was also an Irish Catholic politician of a style no one had ever seen before. German on his mother's side, he had been reared in solidly German farm country north of Minneapolis. He had gone for schooling to the German monks at nearby St. Johns University, largest Benedictine abbey in North America. The ideas and traditions he absorbed there traced to ancient continental roots quite distinct from those of the dominant Irish-American hierarchy. The monks of St. Johns bridled at the impatient push of their fellow Catholics to assimilation. Through college and a year's novitiate thereafter, Benedictine pride in rules, in scholastic superiority, in aloofness from things modern, industrial, and "American" shaped McCarthy's outlook. They influenced his entry into politics. In ten years in the House and another decade in the Senate, McCarthy thought of politics as a process of enlightened adjustment, of what the French philosopher Jacques Maritain called "the mutable application of immutable moral principles in the midst of the agonies of an unhappy world." The pessimism of this outlook gave bite to his wit—and clothed his liberalism in a conservative style.

That a man so contemptuous of impetuosity should have become the leader of a popular insurgency must seem ironic. But the McCarthy character was forged of rare mettle. Having as a Foreign Relations Committee member watched the nation lose its way in Vietnam, he said: "There comes a time when an honorable man simply has to raise the flag." He may also have been willing to stand forth when the likes of Robert Kennedy quailed because he burned with resentment at Lyndon Johnson for lightly dangling the vice presidency before him in 1964 and then prodding him into nominating his colleague and rival Humphrey for the office.

In twenty months in the Senate, Robert Kennedy had also made himself a Democrat of the dissenting left. Not content to wait as the Kennedy-in-the-wings, he moved aggressively into the arena as an impatient critic of his brother's successor. Impassioned where John Kennedy had been cool, he spoke out for the two groups most militantly dissatisfied: the young and the blacks. He called his early espousal of the war "a mistake," and having ended his cabinet stint dispatching marshals to break white-supremacist resistance in Southern universities he did not have to apologize for his early reluctance, as his brother's attorney general, to press civil rights legislation. By 1968 he had taken such strong positions on the war and minority rights that he looked like running off with Humphrey's old constituency on the left.

His candidacy had certain flaws. By declaring after New Hampshire, Kennedy seemed so brazenly opportunistic that he invited Murray Kempton's brutal analogy—a scavenger come down from the hills to shoot the wounded. And to a damaging extent, Kennedy never overcame the force of this accusation, especially among the young idealists who had rallied to McCarthy. What appeared more like a pounce than a leap into the race also refreshed Kennedy's reputation for "ruthlessness" both among businessmen still nursing bruises from his midnight subpoenas to executives in a 1963 steel strike and among politicians still bleeding from his hatchetry in John Kennedy's campaign.

Still, Kennedy was a Kennedy, heir to the nation's martyred hero, and now at forty-two the same age as his brother when John Kennedy captured the minds and hearts of the young on his way to the White House. He had celebrity, great wealth, a famous family, a high-powered organization. When he started his campaign he had zoomed around the country and stirred up such a hullaballoo of enthusiasm that it doubtless played some part in the president's decision to withdraw. Even after Johnson backed out, he continued to play for the nomination on the basis of crowd appeal. Exploiting the glamor of his name and the appeal of his tousled, turned-on personality, he tried to create a groundswell across the nation for his candidacy so strong that the politicians, like it or not, would have to accept him at the nominating convention. This early resort to the New Politics, however, while registering on Johnson, failed in its purpose. It stiffened rather than swayed Chicago's Mayor Richard Daley and other Irish chieftains who had backed Jack Kennedy's rise in 1960 but now felt threatened by such a blatant attempt to bypass them.

So Kennedy entered the primaries, and it was essential for his candidacy that he win every single one. For a starter he descended on the campuses, where the massed students who turned out for him seemed more like fans than political activists. Wherever he went the excitement of his crowds was almost frightening, sometimes threatening to people's safety. Teenage girls surged close, squealing: "Sock it to 'em, Bobby." The candidate himself suffered torn clothes, bleeding hands, a tooth chipped when he was shoved against the side of his car. Such fervor inevitably pushed him to the edge of demagoguery. Speaking before a huge U. S. flag in Nashville, the astronaut John Glenn at his side, he accused the administration of "calling upon the darker impulses of the American spirit."

When Kennedy invaded Indiana for his first primary, he threw in everything he had. "It's our money, and we're free to spend it any way we please," said his mother, Rose. It helped especially in clinching the Senator's new position as the candidate with the strongest appeal for blacks. Although Humphrey had tried to line him up, Major Richard Hatcher of Gary, Indiana—first black mayor of a sizeable American city—plumped for Bobby and toured the streets with him. Organized labor backed Governor Roger Branigin, favorite son entered earlier as Johnson's stand-in, but the rank and file—many of them members of ethnic groups disturbed by the recent outbreaks of rioting and demonstrations—preferred Bobby. When Kennedy proclaimed "I was the chief law enforcement officer of the United States," they cheered it as a signal that as president he would brook no street disorders. On this unlikely alliance of ghetto and blue-collar precincts, Kennedy carried Indiana. His 44 percent of the vote, however, fell short of a majority in a race that pitted him against Branigin and McCarthy, and the win was compared with his brother's opening victory in the 1960 Wisconsin primary: impressive but indecisive. McCarthy's 27 percent made a respectable showing, especially since he scored well in the suburbs, among college graduates and older folks—a hint that he could draw Republican votes too.

Democratic National Committee Chairman John Bailey had said that Bobby could get the nomination only if he swept the primaries. He won Nebraska by a clear majority. But he lost Oregon to McCarthy. This was a grievous blow—no Kennedy had ever before lost an election. It became absolutely necessary to win California, or, as he himself acknowledged, he would be knocked out of contention.

Humphrey, meanwhile, traveled around making speeches as if he too were contesting primaries. Sometimes, as in Omaha on the eve of the Nebraska voting, he addressed the same rallies as his two rivals. And because they too were out to corral delegates in non-primary states, Kennedy and McCarthy gave the vice president occasional knocks. Kennedy accused him of offering the country "pablum"—talking of the "politics of joy in times of rioting, violence, disorder." But for most of these decisive weeks of the pre-convention campaign, several factors worked to Humphrey's advantage. Kennedy and McCarthy were locked in fierce man-to-man primary contention, while

Humphrey was free to concentrate on bagging the far more numerous delegates from non-primary states. Moreover, to his great benefit, the Vietnam war—by far the most telling issue that could be used against him—was removed from the debate when, after Johnson's speech, Hanoi agreed to hold peace talks. It was almost mid-May before the parties fixed upon Paris as the place to meet, and Averell Harriman, assisted by Cyrus Vance, actually sat down for the first formal conversations with Hanoi's chief delegate, ex-Foreign Minister Xuan Thuy. During the six-week interval the candidates, both Democratic and Republican, fell silent on the issue of war in Vietnam. More time passed before it became evident that the sides were deadlocked, and the war was going to drag on. Even then, the vice president was able to protest that he ought not to comment lest his words upset the delicate negotiations.

As things turned out, these were precisely the weeks during which the vice president collected most of his delegates. For while everybody watched the primaries, the Organization rolled in the other states. At times the Old and New clashed within the Humphrey machine. At the first meeting after Key Largo, one of former party treasurer Maguire's men explained that the co-chairmen would have to keep a promise made to deliver forty-five thousand dollars in cash to two operatives in West Virginia who happened to be under indictment. Mondale leaped from his chair, "almost foaming at the mouth," as Harris later described it. He shouted: "Out of the room! Out! Out!" then turned to the others and said: "I don't want to hear that kind of talk again." Some of the oldtimers thereafter referred to the Mondale-Harris team as "the boy scouts." The two young chairmen cut dashing figures as they zipped around the country, each in his little jet. But, once on the ground they worked in the style of Roosevelt's Farley and Flynn, of Truman's Hannegan and Kennedy's O'Brien, currying governors, cosseting county chairmen, egging on their ninety-five local coordinators. Having divided the country into eight regions, they placed these regional operatives under the whip of McCandless and eight hard-driving lawyer-volunteer lieutenants.

Predictably too, the co-chairmen soon found staffers explaining that Humphrey's aide Bill Connell had ordered them to Idaho or Dick Maguire had called them into a deal in New Jersey, and it always turned out that Humphrey had flashed a green or at least an amber light to his old friends. McCandless said later: "I spent as much time cutting Bill's interfering hands off as on the job I was supposed to do." Prodded by Mondale, Humphrey contritely dictated a memo to Connell: "I am bringing this to an abrupt end— I do not want you, Maguire, Kampelman or anyone else bypassing the two senators." Nothing changed. Humphrey kept adding campaign aides, and McCandless kept getting Humphrey's memos, dictated on a plane late at night: "Why were the calls of two delegates from Pennsylvania not returned?" "A friend of mine in South Dakota told me two weeks ago he would like to be of help. Why has he not been contacted yet?"

The machine rolled on. Just as Johnson had predicted, the Southerners wanted no part of Kennedy or McCarthy, and Humphrey, the civil rights firebrand who drove the Southerners to bolt in 1948, found himself with some five hundred Dixie delegates that could be classified as his. In the North and West, the new team zeroed in on the "structured" Democrats and on labor. Harris said later: "If there was a Democratic governor or lieutenant governor who might be for us, we started with him. If there was no one in the statehouse we tried the mayors, and if there was no one in city hall we tried the union halls."

"We went into the state conventions like the Hun," McCandless said later. In Maryland they rode right over Kennedy's friend Senator Joseph Tydings, and by a few parliamentary maneuvers and some brisk arm-twisting got the state committee to deliver all Maryland's 49 votes to Humphrey under the unit rule. Delaware's delegation came over in a body after the Humphreyites chartered a plane and airlifted all 22 delegates and their spouses to Washington for a convivial evening that included a chat for each with the vice president.

The machine rolled most implacably in Pennsylvania. It happened at the state convention in Harrisburg on May 27 while everybody else was watching the big primary battle in California. McCarthy had the previous month run away with a non-binding primary vote in Pennsylvania. Kennedy had formed an alliance with William Green's organization in Philadelphia that was thought to make him a formidable contender. But Mondale flew to Pittsburgh, where Mayor Barr and former Mayor David Lawrence had lined up the troops for Humphrey, and Harris was on top of the scene at Philadelphia's City Hall. As he later described it: "First Mayor [Jim] Tate assembled [the Philadelphia delegates] in a meeting room and gave them a speech. Then he marched them in lockstep to two buses. Every one of them wore a Humphrey hat and carried a Humphrey banner."

Bill Green's insurgency had been squelched. According to Harris "He [Tate] seated Green up at the front of one of the buses, with a seven-foot-tall black delegate sort of sealing Green off from the others. Why, Tate wouldn't even let those delegates go out to the bathroom by themselves. When they got to Harrisburg, he marched them out in lockstep to cast their votes for Humphrey." The co-leaders telephoned Humphrey in Minnesota. The vice president, surrounded by fund raisers, was at that moment carving the cake at his fifty-seventh birthday gala. They told him the news that Pennsylvania Democrats had given him two-thirds of their 130-vote delegation. McCarthyites screamed: "Pennsylvania Railroad." Harris said later: "Humphrey was nominated in Harrisburg."

The climax, however, came in California after all, and it was shattering. There the candidates of the New Politics fought to lead the movement to sweep away the Old and change party, government, country. Kennedy, smarting from the sharp words hurled by McCarthy in Oregon, thought the artillery of discontent should have been trained on the real enemy, Humphrey. Playing his version of the New Politics, he made the cause of the grape pickers his own, went to mass with their chief, Cesar Chavez, and won over the Mexican Americans as well as the blacks. Along the way he also accepted the support of the backlashers brought him by the old-style organization of his local ally Jesse Unruh, Speaker of the state assembly. At one other phase of the politics of the past Kennedy excelled: he drew huge crowds. McCarthy, however, neatly offset this seeming edge by shrewd resort to New Politics technique. Conceding the streets to Bobby, he went around to the television stations, where he talked leisurely and seriously about the issues. In consequence he came across nightly on the TV news as a serious man while Kennedy was pictured being mauled by mobs, losing his shoes. The final television debate turned out to be decisive. Billed as a slugging match, it showed McCarthy holding back his punches as if regretting the earlier sharp swings, and Kennedy throwing little love taps as if not caring who won. The result, as Bobby hoped, was that California Democrats decided Kennedy was not perhaps so ruthless after all, and that made the difference.

On the last, bone-crushing day, Kennedy traversed twelve hundred miles of the state, won Mexican-American cheers in Fresno, Delano, and Mexicali, and made a triumphant last visit to Watts. At the final appearance in San Diego, where he had to address successive audiences of twenty-five hundred in the same hall, he collapsed temporarily between speeches. The following day votes flooded in, and it was apparent that Kennedy had won the race he had to win in the biggest state of the union. He was making his way through a kitchen passageway that evening from the ballroom where he claimed victory when shots rang out. Kennedy fell to the floor, mortally wounded by a bullet in the brain. The assassin was one Sirhan B. Sirhan, a Palestinian-born drifter down on his luck but with no discernible motive to shoot the senator other than his private quarrel with an indifferent world. Thus the primaries that so many hoped would open the way to change ended abruptly and violently with the extinction of the man who gained their mandate. It was the second dreadful blow to fall upon a nation trying to steady its course in the murderous spring of 1968.

30

The Oldest Son

MURIEL HUMPHREY said: "The bullet that killed Bobby Kennedy also wounded Hubert." This was true in more ways than one.

Partly because it was so late, partly because he feared another popular contest with a Kennedy, Humphrey had refrained from entering any primaries at all, and now Kennedy, having emerged on top in the primary competition, was suddenly and violently struck down. If politics is the struggle for power, it is also conducted as a game, at least in the United States, a game in which all are supposed to play. The death of Kennedy broke up the game—before the issue was decided, but after the people, in the only contest in which they could, had spoken, and spoken for Kennedy. It could be argued, as Fritz Mondale did, that in non-primary states the people also spoke—"in the caucuses, in the precincts." But the testing that the public awaited, that it felt entitled to expect on the strength of the votes given Kennedy in the primary battles, was abruptly denied. For millions of Americans the senseless extinction of one so charged with charisma was a disorienting, estranging event. The effect, as Humphrey said later, was to "sour the whole public, and particularly the Democratic party, on the election and on the democratic process." In consequence, the value of the nomination Humphrey now stood to win was diminished. Indeed, much of the resentment and frustration that people, especially young people, felt was vented upon Humphrey, as the contender who had so obviously—and, it seemed, unfairly—benefited by the breakup of the game. "I was doing everything I could to get the nomination," Humphrey said later, "but God knows I didn't want it that way."

Second, with Kennedy out of the race, the flow of campaign funds to Humphrey promptly dried up. At the early New York luncheons—the first at Le Pavillon restaurant, the second at "21"—Humphrey's finance committee had raised more money than all the contributions he had received in his life up to that time; other rallies in Washington and New York had boosted his campaign fund to more than $3 million. Now, relieved of the fear that Kennedy would come out on top, the big givers felt free to follow their inclinations and to direct their contributions once more to the Republican campaign chest. Humphrey's finances never recovered.

Third, with the Kennedy candidacy eliminated, Johnson's personal stake in ensuring Humphrey's nomination subtly altered. The president no longer felt compelled, as he had in March, to modify his war policy to keep his nemesis Kennedy from prevailing at the convention. His most urgent incentive to mollify the left and thus help Humphrey re-unite the Democratic party was gone; the president would stonewall change on the Vietnam issue all summer, however that might hurt Humphrey.

Finally, the end of the Kennedy candidacy, though practically assuring Humphrey's nomination, occasioned a concentrated scrutiny that he had hitherto escaped, and that disclosed damaging evidence of his predicament as vice president in a beleaguered administration—and of the personal qualities that contributed to his "entrapment" in that position. The disorganization of his campaign, the weaknesses of his staff, the dimness of his television image, and especially, his fatal dependence on the president, all came into public view.

As the original insurgent, Eugene McCarthy should have emerged as the candidate of the nation's discontents, the standard-bearer of all the anti-war and anti-administration forces that he had hitherto divided with Kennedy. But he did not. He stopped campaigning. And when he returned he was a ravaged man, looking and acting as if he thought he were responsible for Kennedy's murder. He said: "It's like a football game without a goal line." He had often likened politicians to tragedians—Act I men being posers of problems; Act II men, analyzers; Act III men, those leaders like Hitler, Stalin, and, he had hinted, Robert Kennedy who solved them all too summarily. He had called Humphrey an Act I man and now pronounced himself the in-between type, stuck in the "involutions and complexity" of Act II. Why, oh why, would he not seize the hour, his young backers cried, when California's Democrats had cast 90 percent of their vote for him and Kennedy—Nebraska's 80 percent, Pennsylvania's 90 percent, Oregon's 84 percent—in a manifest outpouring of popular protest against Washington's leadership? McCarthy stayed in the race, but with almost ostentatious reluctance. He let it be understood that he was staying in out of loyalty to those who believed in and rallied to him—not out of any driving personal conviction that he could and must win the nomination.

Humphrey, too, seemed unhinged, his campaign thrown into disarray. It was not intimations of mortality that jarred Humphrey, though he knew it might as well have been he as Bobby whom the assassin gunned down. Since the night in 1947 when someone took a shot at him in Minneapolis he had known that his life was at risk; he had received three times as many death threats in his three and one-half years, the Secret Service informed him, as Dwight Eisenhower had in his eight years of high office.

The vice president wept, visibly stricken, at the funeral of Martin Luther King, Jr. But he never allowed King's assassination to deflect his driving pursuit of the nomination. When word reached him at midnight in Colorado of the attack on Kennedy, he telephoned Washington to dispatch a plane to rush Kennedy's doctor from Boston. He then broke off his campaign, informed the commandant that there would be no speech from him to the Air Force Academy's graduating class that afternoon, and returned to Washington. He was a pallid, grieving presence at the Kennedy rites in New York. But afterward he excused himself, flew ahead, worked in his office, then finally rejoined the mourners for the late-night interment at Arlington.

Humphrey did not resume campaigning for two weeks. After Kennedy's death he saw the president. For three hours, he said afterward, they "talked about everything"—the nomination (it was Humphrey's, no question, and "the President knew it would be that way"), McCarthy (no problem), the vice-presidential nomination, the convention. The president was "1 million percent" for Humphrey and "would do exactly what Humphrey would wish." Humphrey had feared that if they discussed the No. 2 spot, Johnson might get down to names—specifically the name of Texas Governor John Connally. Instead the president said loftily: "Don't let people talk you into any vice-presidential candidate, and remember how I chose you." He advised Humphrey to be mysterious about it as he himself had been in 1964—not just to enliven a dull convention, he now said, but "also to take some of the play away from Robert's memorial address" about President Kennedy. "You may have to make a similar play," Johnson said, to keep Teddy Kennedy from taking too prominent a convention role. This time there would be "three memorials—one to John Kennedy, one to Robert Kennedy, one to Martin Luther King." But even though he repeated the president's "1 million percent" remark several times afterward, Humphrey worried that Walt Rostow or Joseph Califano or some other White House assistant would be on his back asking: Did you really mean what you said yesterday, and won't it hurt the administration? And before long the president, who had said he would do exactly as Humphrey would wish, was vetoing Humphrey's proposal that the convention be switched from Chicago to quieter Miami, taking personal charge of all the arrangements, and rejecting all the names that Humphrey put forward for convention officers.

It was ironic—and it must be said, pitiable—that in the period from Kennedy's death to the convention in August, this most voluble of American politicians had almost nothing to say about the issues that troubled his fellow citizens most. As he himself said, he "ducked and bobbed." His critics charged that even his syntax went bad, his sentences failed to scan. He was the man in the middle: tied to a president who dominated him, pulled by all the forces on the Democratic left that demanded a candidate who stood for anything different from Nixon.

Even before the death of Kennedy the disquiet in the cities had set loose dark currents of fear and distrust. Alabama's Governor George Wallace, who had invaded the North in the 1964 campaign and found plenty of disaffected workers ready to vote for him, was a candidate again. "Let 'em see you shoot down a few of 'em and you got 'em stopped," he said of ghetto rioters that spring, and drew a steady 14 to 17 percent in all the national polls. Addressing Northern crowds, he could talk about law and order, folks running their own schools, protecting property rights, and never mentioning race except to say: "Whole heaps of folks in this country feel the way I do." When he campaigned in New England, Norwood, Massachusetts, Police Chief James M. Murphy, father of ten (one killed in Vietnam), said: "Wallace thinks like I do." Unions were supposed to be the backbone of Humphrey's support, but Joe Beirne, chief of the Communication Workers, told Humphrey: "Half of my members are for Wallace," and I. W. Abel said as many as a third of his Steelworkers wanted Wallace. With the Alabama governor running on a third-party ticket this time, neither Democratic nor Republican candidate stood to gain a popular majority, and Humphrey's staff held meetings on what to do if the contest were thrown into the House of Representatives.

Humphrey knew that his candidacy was in trouble. Resuming the race, he told aides:

> The President didn't run because he knew he couldn't make it. And he clothed me with nothing. I've been subjected to the worst type of calumny and humiliation. On college campuses they've not only insulted and spit on me but thrown filth at me.
>
> To pull ourselves up from these ashes and the humiliation of this awful job is the most difficult thing in the world. We must begin in but not repudiate the past. I'm going to break out of this cocoon without repudiating my father. . . .

The McCarthyites dealt two damaging blows—Humphrey was the candidate of the bosses, not the people; and Humphrey offered nothing on Vietnam policy different from Johnson. In Minnesota, where DFL regulars led by Mondale captured most delegates at the state convention after anti-war forces had carried the big-city caucuses, the McCarthyites yelled "steal." McCarthy forces swept New York, where Humphrey received only 3 percent of the vote; but organizational maneuvers then shifted many of the delegates to Humphrey. As the Humphrey regulars beat down the insurgencies in Montana, Utah, Delaware, Connecticut, the McCarthyites denounced the vice-presidential "steamroller." That democracy was about to be betrayed in a "bossed convention" was the cry of the New Left, those partisans of McCarthy and Kennedy who vowed that nominees must be picked by delegates representative of all the people, men and women, black and white, young and old. The cry was taken up by the National Mobilization to End the War in Vietnam and by the Youth International party, both of which announced plans to hold demonstrations when the Democrats met in Chicago.

The few trips that the vice president essayed while amassing more delegates only added to his troubles. The Washington *Post* reported his crowds "thin, apathetic and ominously hostile." In Cleveland he blamed his poor reception on inept advance men, who had somehow failed to notify the unions he was coming. "Without labor in Ohio, you're dead," he snapped. But slack staffwork was only partly responsible for what happened when he visited California. Young blacks yelling "Honky, go home" drove him out of a hall in Watts—"like a rat running across the street with everyone shouting, 'Throw something at it,'" a press report jeered. Five thousand anti-war demonstrators, all white, ringed his Los Angeles hotel for an entire day waving "Dump the Hump" signs, pouring blood into the hotel fountain, and shrilling the cry of California "free-speech" protest: "To the wall, mother-fucker." In San Francisco there were more obscenities. Ragged, head-banded hippies trailed him through Chinatown, picketed his every meeting, and when he rode a cable car they hopped aboard yelping: "Wash the blood off your hands." In Philadelphia only fifty hecklers hounded him, but his crowd was so small that he talked too much, as he always did when trying to win over an audience.

There were boos in Detroit too, but his harshest encounter was in private. A group of black leaders, angrily notifying him that their city was now 42–45 percent black, scoffed at "the joke of an OEO [Office of Economic Opportunity]," and demanded "an open-labor bill just the same as the open-housing bill." When Humphrey remonstrated that Walter Reuther's United Auto Workers had "done a lot for the Negro cause," they jumped on him for saying "Negro" instead of "black," and Congressman John Conyers said: "Reuther doesn't understand the black problem any more than you do. You're behind the times." At the end most of those present applauded the vice president. But Humphrey, shaken, wondered aloud: "What do you think of that, after all I've done?"

Of course with Kennedy out of the race, blacks had nowhere to go but with Humphrey. But like union members, blacks would have to vote in big numbers if Humphrey were to prevail, and there were disquieting signs that the organization to make sure they did so was flagging. Mondale, complaining bitterly of all the "factions" around the vice president, was about ready to throw in the sponge. "When you set out to deal with something, you find it's being done by four other people," he growled. Johnson's intended campaign manager, Governor Terry Sanford, called in to help, gave Humphrey a memorandum: "Your campaign is badly organized, badly run and lacks sharpness; you are not catching the imagination of the people; and you are failing to grasp the initiative." Fund-raising lagged badly, and Humphrey, so worried he could not sleep after meeting with his finance men, finally appointed his Minneapolis friend Fred Gates controller to ride herd on dispensing of what dollars there were. The vice president's best workers, the young lawyer-volunteers lining up delegates, grew so confused and alarmed at the campaign's "lack of coherence" that they asked the candidate to meet with them one Sunday evening. Humphrey was shocked to hear them say they would have to fold up the entire regional operation unless he established some order. Politely but pointedly they suggested he put Larry O'Brien in charge. As it happened, after Kennedy's death the vice president had set about doing just that. But he could not bring himself to tell Mondale and Harris they were superseded, even though he was heard to say that naming two senators as campaign chiefs had been a mistake. Nor could he keep old friends such as Kampelman and Connell, Freeman and Short, from horning in on decisions big and small. If O'Brien, ambiguously designated "convention coordinator," now took command it was because he was an old campaigner and knew how to do it, not because of clear orders from Humphrey to that effect.

But none of these troubles, not even running out of money, was as threatening to Humphrey's candidacy as the mounting pressure to declare whether he was in the race on his own or just—as *Esquire* magazine's cover cruelly pictured him—a ventriloquist's dummy in the president's lap. On this fundamental question as to whether the vice president should go his own way, Humphrey's campaign staff was split right down the middle. Harris and Mondale, along with such young aides as Van Dyk, Welsh, and Rielly, argued that the president's war policy no longer corresponded to the best interests of the nation, and unless the vice president declared himself committed to United States withdrawal from Vietnam, the party's nomination would not be worth much because he would have lost the votes of liberal Democrats needed to beat Nixon and Wallace in November. Connell, Kampelman, and Rowe on the other hand believed that the vice president should and must stand as the administration's candidate; Connell, in particular, citing polls, kept insisting that the public still backed the war. And when in July a Washington column forecast a Humphrey-Johnson split over Vietnam, the vice president himself called the White House to say he felt "heartbroken" at the story, "had no intention of breaking in any way with the president," and "would rather lose the election than let [it] appear he is double-crossing or repudiating the president he has been proud to serve."

The vice president's actual view was hopelessly complicated by the role he had so enthusiastically embraced as administration mouthpiece over the past years. Back at the beginning of his term he had urged a contrary course on the President. But he had been overruled, and, as his wife related: "They sat down one night in 1965, right after the inauguration, and made a pledge: this was going to be a new era for them. They were going to be absolutely loyal to Lyndon Johnson, come what may." In all public statements, from that day, Humphrey had loyally upheld the President's war policy. He had out-Johnsoned Johnson. By the summer of 1968, after Johnson himself had pulled back, Humphrey's close friend columnist Carl Rowan could write: "In February, after Tet, he is known to have argued vehemently against sending 207,000 more combat troops to Vietnam." But when Bill Moyers, who had resigned from Johnson's staff because he felt so strongly that policy must change, said that Humphrey privately agreed and "would emerge on his own in the next week or so," the vice president roundly denied it: "I may be wrong or stupid, but I'm not a hypocrite." And indeed this time it was Rowan, not Moyers, who had spoken with Humphrey. To the embarrassed Moyers he sent placating word: "I know you were trying to help me."

A vice president standing for office as the chosen successor to an immensely popular president—a Van Buren succeeding an Andrew Jackson—might contrive to conform in every word and act to his patron's wishes. But this president had lost his mandate. He was a lame duck. As Humphrey himself said, he had pulled out of the race because "he knew he couldn't make it." Why, then, trying to succeed him, should the vice president persist in backing the president's discredited policies?

The answer lies only partly in the crass political considerations of Humphrey's immediate predicament. Granted, the president still possessed a lot of power. Granted, he held the chief executive's capability to transform the outlook for Humphrey's candidacy by actions on the all-important issue of Vietnam. Granted, he held the old politico's power to sway Southern governors and such Northern leaders as Mayor Daley and thereby influence the chances of Humphrey's nomination. Moreover, Humphrey's decision to shun popular primaries undoubtedly increased this residual political leverage of the president, so that even with a majority of delegations "committed" to him Humphrey could never be sure until the actual voting that the nomination was his.

Yet the decisive reasons why Humphrey appeared "trapped," as Mondale put it, in a dependency upon Johnson could be traced to the candidate's own nature.

In the midst of her husband's ordeal that summer, Muriel Humphrey recalled how he had worshiped his father. When they broke away from the drugstore to go to Minneapolis in 1937, she said, "it was the father cutting off the boy to be out on his own," and "though he went out on his own," as sons must, "Hubert was still closely attached—just hung on to him"; and when H. H. died twelve years later, she "never saw anyone so forlorn." Those who had served with Humphrey would remember how he quoted his father on almost any subject in almost any circumstances. He justified dictating letters after midnight with the remark: "My Dad said if you wanted to stay heathen, you had to work harder." He was always appealing to his father's judgments. Even publicly he seemed to protest too much how good, how beneficent Dad was—once in a 1964 television program on "My Childhood," and again in a 1966 *Readers Digest* paean "My Father."

In his study *Young Man Luther*, Erik Erikson notes that in later life the fiery reformer, upholding the authority of the German princes and condemning the peasants' rebellion, "abnegated much of his post-adolescent identity." The rebel who had dramatically cut loose from his father "expressed the opinion that Moses' commandment 'Honor thy father' applies to these princes and is, therefore, equivalent to an injunction against political rebellion."

It has to be said that in the presence of President Johnson, Hubert Humphrey could not maintain the independent posture that had been his hallmark ever since he burst into public life as a reforming mayor, party leader, and senator. As vice president he surrendered his autonomy and gave absolute loyalty. More than deferring, he demeaned himself. In Erikson's language, he was still giving in compliantly to his father. He was hooked in the age-old dilemma: betray yourself or betray your father.

In the summer of 1968, having practiced total subservience for nearly three years, he commenced the struggle "to get out from under." His wife said: "It's very difficult now. It's very tough to get out of. You can't break these things overnight."

Humphrey was caught in the toils. As Nixon said to Simmons Fentriss of *Time* magazine: "Humphrey's problem, one he can't escape, is that he carries on his back the past. He is the candidate of the past no matter how much he talks about his programs and the future."

Some around the vice president thought they sensed a loosening of the reins. It seemed that at their meeting following Kennedy's assassination the president had told Humphrey: "We'll find a way out of this Vietnam situation and maybe make it easier for you. Things are happening in Paris—and, on the Q.T., the [South] Vietnamese are rebuilding their army so well that we may even be pulling some troops out soon."

Still, Humphrey deferred. He told staffers: "I can't be constantly speaking without an occasional bobble. I can't talk without some settlement with the White House. Politically and otherwise, it would be hazardous for me to get out of line. . . . I'm in the position of walking on a tightrope." When Moyers blurted that Humphrey did not really believe in the president's war policy and might say so "within a week," Johnson, furious, telephoned Humphrey from the ranch: "You can't trust him. Stay away from him as far as possible," he roared.

After that there was a long interval in exchanges between President and Vice President. During the first week of July, Humphrey fell ill. He awoke one morning with a stomachache and diarrhea. He tried to keep up his appointments and television appearances but felt achy and ran a low temperature—"a grippy condition," Dr. Berman thought. But it persisted for days, and finally Humphrey had to call off a Western trip. He telephoned the president, who told him not to fret: "Don't go to California, they're just a bunch of kooks out there. Somebody'll kill you just to even up the situation with Kennedy." Humphrey replied: "You shouldn't be saying that, Mr. President." Johnson said: "I mean it." The president took note that the Humphrey forces were conceding some delegates to McCarthy to offset the steamroller charge: "The trouble with you, Hubert, is that you're just too damn good. Somebody comes along and kicks you in the face, and you pat their leg. I give them nothing." The night before, Humphrey, complaining that he felt hot and jittery, had been unable to sleep. After the president's jocular reassurance, Dr. Berman noted: "The Vice President fell asleep. He slept the sleep of a man who had undergone a crisis. I finally awakened him a little after 11 A.M."

By week's end, after a restorative outing for golf and skeet-shooting at Greenbrier, West Virginia, the vice president felt ready to return to action. It was about time. He had been out of the firing line for the better part of six weeks and had not yet begun to stake out a position. Under the headline "Humphrey Failing to Inspire Voters," the *New York Times*'s Max Frankel reported: "The Vice President's warmest supporters fear he is winning by default." Tom Wicker wrote that Humphrey's "politically painful identification with the administration and the war is the primary reason the vice president's campaign is not catching fire with the public." Meanwhile, President Johnson flew to Honolulu to consult with his Vietnam commanders, and what he heard increased his suspicions that the North Vietnamese were determined to fight on. When on his return he assailed Hanoi's "irreconcilability," Governor Hoff of Vermont said Humphrey would have to resign to establish his independence.

U N D E R the leadership of economist Robert Nathan no fewer than thirty task forces had formed to develop ideas for Humphrey's presidential campaign. One, dubbed the "Post-Vietnam Task Force" and including such eminent academic experts as Edwin Reischauer and Samuel Huntington of Harvard and Zbigniew Brzezinski and Doak Barnett of Columbia, was at work preparing just what everybody wanted: a statement defining Humphrey's own position on Vietnam. Appearing at New York's Waldorf, the vice president vowed a quest for peace and said he would have a statement on Vietnam in ten days. Outside, demonstrators yelled: "Keep America Hump-Free," and police arrested thirty youths. On his return to Washington the vice president said: "I don't want anything this week but Vietnam. I want it concentrated. I want to have the task force on it."

A major difficulty was that the president kept the vice president on a starvation diet for information, especially about Vietnam and the Paris negotiations. Paranoid about leaks, he gave orders that certain messages be shown to only three, four or five persons. The vice president was cut out almost invariably from the highest military and diplomatic messages. "We simply can't let this in that other building," Johnson would say with a gesture toward Humphrey's office across the street. Humphrey's experts from the universities knew even less of what was really going on.

By the afternoon of July 25, Humphrey's force had worked through to a fifth draft, entitled: "Vietnam: Toward a Political Settlement and Peace in Southeast Asia." It called for a ceasefire in Vietnam and talked more about what to do after the war than what to do right away. But it did call for "de-Americanizing" the fighting, and included the following paragraph: "I am encouraged by recent reports of a lull in the fighting, a decline in the infiltration rate from North Vietnam, and at least a temporary curtailing of the shelling of Saigon. If these trends should continue, they might at some point approximate the reciprocal action that our Government has called for on previous occasions. If this should develop I would favor an immediate halt in the bombing of North Vietnam." The drafters thought this declaration, by establishing Humphrey's independent position, would take the vice president out from Johnson's shadow and win him election. When he read it and told them he liked it, they hoped he would go right ahead and issue it. Instead, as Reischauer recalled later, he said meekly: "I'll have to show it to the President."

He did so that evening—and was with the president for an hour and eleven minutes. When he returned to his office he was cross and went straight to the washroom. His public relations aide Ted Van Dyk followed him into the washroom and recalled later:

> He was furiously washing his hands, a nervous habit he had when he was worked up. I said, "What happened?" He said, "Oh, Johnson had guests and I couldn't get in to talk." I said, "You're kidding." He said, "Well, the truth is that Johnson said I would be jeopardizing the lives of his sons-in-law, and endangering the chances of peace. If I announced this, he'd destroy me for the Presidency."

Van Dyk put out the story that Humphrey had not got the chance to speak to the president, and Columnist James Reston, while accepting this version, noted the "savage pressures" on Humphrey and correctly reported the formal argument Johnson had used to squelch his vice president: that if Humphrey came out for a bomb halt, he faced the risk that the administration might subsequently have to step up the bombing to meet a renewed Hanoi offensive.

Persuasive this argument may have been. But it was Johnson's personal assault that packed the wallop—that Humphrey's proposal might cost the blood of the marine lieutenant and army captain who were married to his daughters, and that the president would "destroy" his vice president if he issued the statement. Humphrey could not bring himself to tell anyone else of these threats for months afterward.

Cowed, Humphrey handed the draft to John Stewart, his research director, for "revision." And since the Democratic National Convention was by then only weeks away, he also asked his old friend from ADA days, Washington Lawyer David Ginsburg, to take a hand with it. The vice president had designated Ginsburg his chief carpenter in the all-important task of shaping a Vietnam plank for the party platform. Ginsburg warned, however, that if the vice president left it for the platform committee to define his Vietnam stand, delegates would judge he had abdicated his leadership. Humphrey, still asking his staff "Would it hurt to wait a little while?" retreated to his Waverly, Minnesota estate, while the Republicans convened in Miami. Governor Nelson Rockefeller having failed to attract votes for a more moderate candidacy, Nixon took the Republican nomination on the first ballet and named Governor Spiro Agnew of Maryland as his running mate.

On August 8, explaining that Nixon and Agnew would be arriving for a visit the next day, the president called Humphrey and invited him to his Texas ranch on the ninth. With draft eleven of his Vietnam statement in his briefcase, Humphrey flew down with his wife, his son Douglas, and Bill Connell, his most hawkish aide. At lunch the vice president was embarrassingly deferential to the president. Reminiscing about Senate days he went so far beyond the facts in heaping praise on Johnson as "unsung leader" of the civil rights fights of the 1950s that one guest, the young historian Doris Kearns, felt "saddened," and Johnson himself began tapping the table until Humphrey stopped.

The president's purpose that day was to brief the candidate, and he told the vice president much that Humphrey had not heard before. In the course of the exchange, Humphrey had a chance to show his revised Vietnam statement. The president read it through twice and "said it was perfectly all right." In the revised version, Humphrey's proposed bomb halt carried the simple qualification: "I for one am willing to take that step now if North Vietnam is willing to offer an appropriate act of reciprocity." The president said that "reciprocity" was too hard a word, and accepted Humphrey's substitute phrase "restraint and reasonable response"—a change, if anything, toward accommodation.

But the president again advised against putting out the statement. This time he said: "You can get a headline with this, Hubert, and it will please you and some of your friends. But if you'll let me work for peace, you'll have a better chance for election than by any speech you're going to make. I think I can pull it off." And the president went on to tell him, as Humphrey recounted it a few days later: "There are situations afoot that he expected within the next week to become imminent, which would not only clarify but advance the peace negotiations. It was not the bombing pause that was going to do this, or anything I'm going to do, but events are going to fashion it.

The President said he wasn't at liberty to tell, but there was a third country, a third party, that was going to be in touch with Hanoi to provoke [it]."

It speaks volumes about how little the vice president was told that he was ignorant of the administration's ongoing exchanges with the Soviet Union for disarmament talks and their expected effect in softening the North Vietnamese negotiating stance in Paris. Though he had no idea how it would come about, he went away from this meeting so persuaded that a breakthrough was imminent in Paris, so sure that within a few days all the pressure on him for a declaration would be lifted by the kind of action only a president could take, that he withheld his statement once more.

The vice president left the ranch feeling much better about his relationship with Johnson. The coolness left by the July blowup appeared to have ended. Connell reported that his boss now felt "that they had good communication." Mrs. Humphrey wondered aloud whether that same feeling in which "he just hung on" to his father, would operate here. Could the vice president, after indoctrinating himself for years to be this man's son, try to break away? She "had a funny feeling" that "things were not as before," that "a certain sense of freedom" was present now, "that the Vice President had really cut the cord." "You could almost feel that the way he bounced off the plane when he arrived in Corpus Christi," Dr. Berman noted. A few nights later, Humphrey sat down for a beer with his doctor before turning in. "What would you think if the President should nominate me?" Humphrey asked suddenly. Berman waved a glass in answer, and Humphrey went on: "He asked me—if I wanted him to nominate me—and I said no."

In the absence of Humphrey's promised declaration, his candidacy drifted. When South Dakota's Senator George McGovern joined the race in expectation of picking up support of Kennedy delegates, Columnist Tom Wicker wrote that it only showed how "flabby" was Humphrey's frontrunner position. As the convention neared, the McCarthyites released their Vietnam platform demands—an unconditional bombing halt, a coalition bringing the Viet Cong into the South Vietnamese government, and "downgrading" claims for the Johnson administration's performance in the war. Still holding back, Humphrey waded through mingled cheers and boos in Boston. When he stopped to rest at the hotel, Berman wrote, "Davy Gartner came in and said the president had called, and would the vice president call him back. The vice president was gone about fifteen minutes. When he came back he looked as if he had been kicked. He just seemed to sag all over. He said he had just had some very bad news."

The president had just called to say he was sorry, but things had not worked out as he had expected when they talked at the ranch. The North Vietnamese were unshakeable at Paris and pouring "hundreds" of truckloads toward the frontlines in Vietnam. So Johnson was going to renounce the whole notion of a bomb halt in a tough speech to the Veterans of Foreign Wars in Detroit next day.

Swallowing this disappointment as best he could, the vice president delivered his speech that night, only to receive some more bad news: a Gallup poll, taken right after the Republican convention, showed Republican nominee Nixon leading him by sixteen points. Up to then, the vice president had either matched or led all rivals in these polls. Suddenly, he had skidded sixteen points. The worst of the new results was that only Humphrey showed such a phenomenal drop—McCarthy ran as strongly as ever. On the plane back to Washington, Humphrey sat poring over the report. Dr. Berman said he "looked like he could have just cried."

In these straits advisers urged all sorts of drastic action upon the candidate, and it seemed that Humphrey scarcely knew what to do. Larry O'Brien placed midnight calls imploring Senator Edward Kennedy, less than three months after laying his brother in his grave, to join with Humphrey as the vice president's running mate. At the same time, Ted Van Dyk opened a channel through Massachusetts' former Governor Endicott Peabody to Nelson Rockefeller with a view to inviting Nixon's defeated Republican rival to go on the ticket with Humphrey. And some of Humphrey's oldest friends began laying elaborate plans for the vice president to resign his office in mid-convention as proof he was his own man and quits of Lyndon Johnson.

But the president had other plans for the nominating convention. Originally it had been set for the last week of August to suit his convenience as the incumbent president needing only the shortest possible campaign for his reelection. Even after he withdrew the president preferred the late date because his sixtieth birthday fell that week. Chicago's Mayor Daley and Johnson's representatives on the scene planned to make the celebration on the twenty-seventh the convention's biggest event—and were openly hoping that his appearance that evening might lead the convention to draft him as the party's nominee after all. This might have been more of a hope had Moscow not jettisoned the joint U. S.–Soviet announcement set for August 20, that disarmament talks were about to begin at the highest level, and marched troops into Czechoslovakia instead. But for the Kremlin's abrupt reversal, the president would have been able to proclaim, possibly when he appeared before the delegates, that he would be flying to a summit in Leningrad in September to negotiate with Kosygin the detente between East and West that must signal peaceful resolution of the Vietnam conflict.

With or without this option, the president kept close control of convention arrangements, rejecting Humphrey's and McCarthy's suggestions alike, and handpicking Congressman Hale Boggs of Louisiana as chairman of the Platform Committee that would frame the all-important plank on Vietnam. Boggs began by telling the vice president and his representative, David Ginsburg, that he "wanted the plank to be a Humphrey statement." And though Johnson had vetoed Humphrey's idea of holding open sessions on the platform around the country, Boggs announced a series of public hearings to be held in Washington and Chicago just before the convention. Humphrey, in a decision that was to have some bearing on his ultimate choice of a running mate, picked Senator Edwin Muskie over his top delegate hunter, the more dovish Fred Harris, to speak for him at these sessions.

When Muskie testified he presented a statement carefully phrased to leave plenty of room for the McCarthy and Kennedy forces to enter into negotiations over the Humphrey Vietnam draft. On his Chicago hotel room bed, David Ginsburg laid side by side the latest versions put forward by the peace forces and was impressed by the "narrowness of the gap" separating them from the version he and Humphrey aide Bill Welsh had worked up. Ginsburg paid particular attention to a speech that Senator Edward Kennedy had delivered the night before in Massachusetts: it slightly qualified the insistence upon a bomb halt and left out the demand for an imposed coalition government in South Vietnam. "There's not ten cents worth of difference from the Vice President's policy," he said, and set out to close the remaining distance in negotiations with Theodore Sorensen, White House counsel to President Kennedy and now the senator's designated representative. By the Saturday evening before the convention opened, Ginsburg had a draft that he told Humphrey he thought would be acceptable to almost all the Kennedy-McGovern people and a great many of the McCarthyites. Delighted at the prospect of something approaching unity on this most contentious of all issues, Humphrey took the agreed text down word by word on the telephone in Washington. Late that night he called Secretary Rusk, who listened to the version as Humphrey read it, suggested a few word changes, and then said: "We can live with it, Hubert." Exultant, believing that he might be home free after all, the vice president checked the draft with White House Security Adviser Walt Rostow. Rostow, too, gave his okay.

But it was Lyndon Johnson himself who called the shots for Chicago. While his Postmaster General Marvin Watson watched over everything else, the president's senior political aide, Charles Murphy, stood guard over the platform. Charlie Murphy had submitted the original pro-administration outline on Vietnam as long ago as July. He attended and reported on Boggs's Washington hearings, and when the Platform Committee moved to Chicago, so did Murphy. There, from his perch in the Conrad Hilton, he noted the feverish efforts of the peace forces to reach agreement among themselves on bedrock demands and the delicate Sorensen-Ginsburg negotiations that culminated in the Humphrey draft. On the Saturday night Humphrey was clearing it in Washington, Murphy asked, without comment, for the agreed text in Chicago and, presumably, telexed the draft to the ranch. Murphy was in contact with the president by telephone, and the following evening asked that Boggs call a meeting with the Humphrey draftsmen.

It was the evening before the convention opened, the same evening that the vice president arrived in Chicago. The meeting took place in Boggs's room at the Congress Hotel. Present were Boggs, his son Tom, Ernest Lefever of Boggs's staff, as well as Murphy, Ginsburg, and Welsh. As soon as the

Humphreyites arrived, Boggs said: "The ranch wants to speak with us." Then Murphy and Ginsburg took turns at the telephone, speaking directly with Tom Johnson, the President's young aide. Ginsburg recalled later: "I could hear the President's voice in the background instructing Tom Johnson what to say. We went over the sentences and the words. It was not possible to get agreement. Johnson was speaking—that's an understatement—telling us what we could not say."

Late that night, Ginsburg went to Humphrey's suite. The place was aroar with festive excitement, newsmen coming and going, politicians shouting greetings on all sides. The vice president took Ginsburg into a bedroom and closed the door. Together they went over the differences and their implications. Staff members had been complaining that the vice president had become so indecisive that he seemed to take his opinions from the last person he talked to. Now Humphrey vowed to stand firm. And at breakfast next morning the vice president said: "I can't go further—they're [the White House] going to have to take it."

Humphrey's drafter David Ginsburg went back to three hours' more haggling with Johnson's man Charlie Murphy. The variations they fought over may seem slight. However, they made all the difference to the forces at and around the convention demanding change. By this time the seven points of the peace advocates had boiled down to four, and of the four a single one became the crux for change in Vietnam— the demand that the United States, which had already ended bombing attacks on 78 percent of North Vietnam, now pledge to cease bombing north of the border altogether.

The Humphrey version, all but unconditional, read: "Stop the bombing of North Vietnam. The action and its timing shall take into account the security of our troops and the likelihood of a response from Hanoi." Twice Murphy called the ranch. Twice Jim Jones, another Johnson aide, stood adamant against the Humphrey phrasing. Insisting on what became known as the "when clause," the president decreed the following: "Stop all the bombing of North Vietnam *when* this action would not endanger the lives of our troops in the field; this action should take into account the response from Hanoi." Emerging briefly for lunch, Ginsburg reported: "They played with these words, and the President at the other end of the line down on the ranch just hung on to every inch as if he had nothing else to do."

Then Johnson's top aide Postmaster General Marvin Watson stepped in. Watson had been holed up in a secret White House communication center a few floors below Humphrey's headquarters. He informed Humphrey that the president absolutely refused to accept Humphrey's draft plank. "Upset and angry at this outrageous turn of events," Humphrey wrote in his memoirs, he went to the telephone and, "in the gentlest words I could muster," told the president that there would be trouble at the convention if the Humphrey draft was not put forward. Johnson spurned his plea: "That plank undercuts our whole policy and, by God, the Democratic party ought not to be doing this to me, and you ought not to be doing it—you've been part of this policy."

With that Humphrey knuckled under. When Platform Committee Chairman Boggs said what was unacceptable to the president was unacceptable to him, the vice president withdrew his draft. And so it came about that the convention that nominated Humphrey for president was presented with a majority plank shaped to suit the president and a minority plank offered by the McCarthy-McGovern forces—and no Humphrey plank at all. As Humphrey himself said six months later: "I had become like the oldest son—and I couldn't make the break."

31

Catastrophe at Chicago

T HE consensus briefly won by the Johnson presidency had vanished. The Vietnam war had divided the generations. The miscarriage of the Great Society had split the cities. The administration had lost the confidence of the nation. By polls, by primaries, by street manifestations so hostile as almost to drive the president from sight, Americans demanded change in the election year 1968. When Lyndon Johnson announced in March that he would not run again, they seemed to be getting the change they most urgently wanted. But when the Republicans proceeded to nominate Richard Nixon, who backed the war, the chance for a change in Vietnam policy narrowed. Then, in the summer of 1968, other forces demanded change: elements from both North and South whose fear and loathing of black advancement in general and of ghetto riots in particular made the third-party candidacy of Alabama's racist Governor Wallace a major factor in the presidential race. The Democrats tried to meet the demand for tightened "law and order" by passing the Safe Streets Act. Nixon's response was to choose as his running mate Governor Spiro Agnew of Maryland, a man known for his rough, almost brutal stand on racial disturbances and urban crime. But the selection of Agnew, calculated to attract Southern support away from Wallace, was repellent, even frightening to those independent and Democratic forces most actively casting about for alternatives. For them—the liberal, the young—the only vehicle for reversing the government's war policy became the president's own party.

But that chance, too, threatened to be closed off. Of the candidates for Vietnam change, Kennedy had been murdered, McCarthy spurned by the party regulars. Meanwhile, Johnson was still obstinately waging his war. For the forces seeking change in America, the forces that had driven Johnson to renounce his office and, indeed, modify his policy by concessions that started peace talks in Paris, the Democratic convention of 1968 therefore became a showdown.

The man in the middle was Hubert Humphrey. In times past, clashing views had met at the nation's nominating conventions and somehow fused into improbable coherence under new leadership, which then set the new consensus forth so persuasively, so dynamically, that it carried the country in the following election. Truman, Eisenhower, Kennedy—Truman with vital help from the young Humphrey—had all managed to do this. But could Humphrey, twenty years later and now Johnson's loyal vice president, achieve such a miracle?

Humphrey had a solid liberal record on domestic issues, but he had supported Johnson all the way on his war policy. As a candidate must he not, as younger aides pleaded, "come out from under?" Must he not, standing for president in his own right, assert his own position, an independent position, on the Vietnam war? The vice president himself seemed to think so. But he had already tried in July, and quailed before the president's displeasure; tried in early August, and quailed again. Now, as the convention met to choose the nominee, would he still present himself as a candidate offering no change? It was a choice that might gain him the nomination, although even that was not absolutely sure. It flew in the face of all the pent-up forces pressing for change. It courted the kind of confrontation that no reconciliation could transcend. It invited the kind of convention that no candidate looking to win election in the turmoil of 1968 could want.

On the morning of his departure for the convention the vice president faced a last-minute test on "Meet the Press." Six publishers grilled him on all the big questions—on Vietnam, on law and order, on being his own man. He was firm, even tough, against breaking with the president, and his answer made headlines: "I think the policies the President has pursued are basically sound." To the hawkish, the answer affirmed that the vice president still stood by the president and his policy. Yet for the last-ditch fighters for a peace plank, the interview conveyed a hint that Humphrey still thought the president would accede to some sort of compromise statement on Vietnam. At that moment, in fact, Humphrey thought he had such a green light. Having spent the night getting an okay from top Johnson advisors on his own Vietnam plank, Humphrey felt good about his performance. He had kept his place on the tightrope. He had given his rivals nothing to pounce on. He joked with his valet Ray Young as he packed his own bags to make sure that certain shirts and suits went along.

On the elevator to the street he kissed his wife, danced a little two-step, and punched his friend Dr. Berman on the arm. "Off we go, into battle—and I can hardly wait," he said. He was ready. He had been building up for this trip through trials, tribulations, assassinations, riots, pleadings, spurnings, support, lack of support, kicks in the pants, whacks on the back, desertions, embarrassments. Even now he trod the tightrope: any incautious aside at a caucus, any unconsidered retort to a cranky delegate, any ill-timed signal to a big-state chairman could wreck his convention chances. During a year when the nation's capital had been set afire, a hundred ghettoes torched, a great university seized and shut, and presidential candidates shot, spat upon, and driven from meeting halls, anything could happen.

And did. The convention was a catastrophe, for Humphrey, for the Democratic party, for the nation. By the decisions he made, or failed to make, Humphrey the candidate brought disaster upon himself. But his troubles were compounded by the fact that the convention was in the hands of President Johnson and the mayor of the host city.

Watching and wirepulling from his Texas ranch was the unabdicated Johnson. The president dictated the city, the date, the officers, the program of the convention. His control of its arrangements was so complete that Humphrey's son-in-law had to line up every morning for tickets for members of the Humphrey family. Drawn up in the convention city as if for combat were Mayor Richard Daley and his police, backed by five thousand National Guardsmen in five armories and five thousand federal troops bivouacked on the edge of town. The city's lakefront convention facility having been destroyed by fire, Mayor Daley had offered instead the smaller International Amphitheatre on the site of the old stockyards, five miles west of the Loop, and ringed it with barbed wire and guards. At their downtown hotels were the McCarthy-Kennedy-McGovern contenders, flushed with the force of the latest anti-administration polls, joining to fight off a fresh commitment to "Johnson's war," and knowing that nothing was settled until the votes were cast. And outside the convention, already gathering in city parks, were thousands of young protestors mobilized from all over America by eighty-three anti-war committees for 1968's last-stand chance to compel change.

Sunday the twenty-fifth was a beautiful day, coolish for August, and Humphrey was in a happy mood as he flew to Chicago. Newspapers were predicting his first-ballot victory. But landing at the airport, he met with his first disappointment: though the mayor had sent out a bagpipe band to planeside, Daley himself was not there to welcome him. There was almost no crowd at the airport or, he noted, along the way into the city. McCarthy, he said grumpily, had been met by five thousand supporters.

The vice president went directly to the Sherman Hotel caucus of the Illinois delegation, at which Mayor Daley was expected to announce for him. Waiting nervously in a small room, Humphrey brushed off small talk, paced up and down, turned on a television set and immediately snapped it off. When the call came, he strode unsmiling down a long hall lighted for television, ignoring reporters' queries, and looking straight ahead as the cameras ground away. Inside, he finally found Daley. Humphrey delivered a deft speech—"not hawkish, not dovish, just Daleyish." But the meeting was not the stampede-starter that Humphrey had looked for. Instead, Daley reserved decision on Illinois' endorsement.

At once the convention was thrown into suspense. It seemed that Daley had breakfasted the day before with Jesse Unruh, leader of the California delegation. "Humphrey's a lousy candidate," Daley was said to have remarked. "If we're going to have another Lyndon Johnson, let's draft the real thing." When Unruh said Johnson was unacceptable to a state that had voted for Robert Kennedy, the two men had agreed to turn instead to the surviving Kennedy. When Daley telephoned, Ted Kennedy told him he was not a candidate. Daley said: "Give me two days." Kennedy said the mayor could contact his brother-in-law Stephen Smith in Chicago.

Pressing on to the Conrad Hilton Hotel, Humphrey got his first taste of what his Secret Service man Glenn Weaver had been warning him about. Hundreds of young people jammed the lobby and surged toward the vice president yelling, "We Want Gene." With Weaver's men running interference, Humphrey slipped into his private elevator and was whisked up to his twenty-fifth-floor eyrie. This was his headquarters; but he also had a hideaway across town in the Astor Towers, where his wife and family stayed and where he ate dinner once during the hectic week.

Humphrey met immediately with his top aides—O'Brien, Harris, Mondale, Rowe, Connell, Andreas—to consider the changing situation. Without Illinois' 118 votes, the vice president still held a commanding lead, and McCarthy, as he himself conceded, was out of the running. The threat of a Kennedy candidacy was chilling to Humphrey, who had good reason to fear Kennedys. But O'Brien had talked with Kennedy and insisted that the senator would not change his mind. Brightening, Humphrey recalled the senator's speech five days before and declared that Kennedy's Vietnam views and his own draft plank "practically agree—hell, it's a matter of semantics." Extolling his draft, at that point cleared with Rusk and Rostow, he exclaimed: "It won't get us into trouble in high places, and it's progressive."

With the nomination in balance, Humphrey felt compelled to seek support among Southern delegations. To skeptics such as O'Brien and Mondale, who felt that a forward-looking party could only win by concentrating on the big Northern states, he said: "I've got a lot of friends in the South. They aren't all bad. You can deal with them like I did in the Senate with Eastland and Stennis. They're not so tough." His problem with the South was over the proposed abolition of the convention's unit rule, the rule that required all of a state's delegates to vote for a single candidate. That was what the U. S. Constitution prescribed for presidential elections, and Southern governors, notably John Connally of Texas, had been using the unit rule to keep command over their delegations at Chicago. But the McCarthyites, Humphrey went on, "have backed us up against the wall on the open convention." They were chorusing "one man, one vote," and calling the unit rule the last refuge of "bossism." So Humphrey with his huge lead had dashed off a letter to the Credentials Committee saying he favored jettisoning the unit rule.

Loosely drawn, the letter had called for action "at this Convention." Now, looking South, Humphrey said; "Hell, I wish I hadn't written that sentence." It had mightily angered John Connally. And to make matters worse, by another of those Humphrey staff snafus, Mondale had announced the vice president's call for abolition of the rule the same day Connell was informing Connally that Humphrey would uphold Texas's unit vote at Chicago. Trying to clarify his stand, Humphrey had protested to Connally that he favored abolition for the future but not retroactively—not for delegates already chosen for this convention. In fact he had been on the phone day and night, he said—not only to Connally but to the other Southern governors who controlled similar block votes as their states' favorite sons. But the effort might have been too late. Making the most of the Humphrey booboo, Connally had called governors representing 528 Southern votes and advised Johnson at the ranch to "get to Daley and get him to withhold his endorsement until Monday or Tuesday—that would give the Southern states time to show their strength to Humphrey."

The next morning, Humphreyites heard that former Ohio Governor Mike DiSalle had set up Kennedy for President headquarters in Chicago, and Michigan's Senator Philip Hart and Chairman Sandy Levin had come out for Kennedy. As the convention met to hear Senator Daniel Inouye's keynote address, the press and television networks buzzed with talk of a Kennedy "boom." In Humphrey headquarters, August 26—first day of the convention—became "payoff day." That was the day Humphrey, as he said, heard "rumbles from the ranch in Texas—the President didn't like the platform." Distraught over Johnson's refusal to accept his platform plank, he resumed telephoning Southern governors. He ducked out for three television appearances. He was, Dr. Berman wrote in his diary, "just waffling all over the place." Sensitive he might well be, deeply bruised by his vice-presidential experience and conscious of the antagonisms of the jeering young in the lobby below and the estrangement of liberal friends such as Hart, McGovern and his old ADA comrades. But the biggest source of his torment was not the alienation of old associates or the derision of the young but the baffling intent of Lyndon Johnson. That afternoon, as Ginsburg and Welsh poured out their drafting woes to O'Brien, Humphrey came up and said: "I don't want to hear any more of it—they're just quibbling over words."

Humphrey still lacked the votes for nomination. Even after Ted Kennedy had his Washington office announce he was not a candidate and had no intention (as the television men were reporting from the convention floor) of flying to Chicago, Mayor Daley continued to withhold his declaration.

Johnson's top aide Marvin Watson then appeared and gave Humphrey the bad news that the president absolutely rejected his draft Vietnam plank. And it was then that the vice president, quailing again before the president's displeasure, for the third straight time withdrew his own statement on Vietnam. The Platform Committee and the convention had, therefore, no Humphrey draft to consider—only what was now called a Humphrey-Johnson draft, which Chairman Boggs promptly rammed through the committee by a 65-to-35 vote. This now became the Vietnam statement embodied in the committee's majority report.

The irony of Humphrey's situation is stunning. Twenty years before, as the fiery young challenger to the Establishment, he took a minority report before the Democratic Convention and won a famous victory for a civil rights plank far more sweeping than the one Truman and his cohorts wanted. Then, bright-eyed and brash, he scorned the power of the Southerners, and the spectacular success of his revolt catapulted him to the role of darling of the liberals. Now, as the cautious middle-of-the-roader who could not bring himself to "step out from under," he truckled to the president and relied upon old Southern dignitaries and the relics of city machines to combat the restless and the discontented. To win nomination, he presented himself after all as the candidate offering no change.

From this decision everything followed. The next morning, maneuvered into the convention's only debate between candidates, Humphrey delivered an uncompromising defense of the war before California's delegate caucus, and it was George McGovern who stole the show with a bold plea for peace. But Governor Connally paid a back-slapping visit to the vice president's headquarters and told Bill Connell: "We've been playing games. Let's forget all this nonsense; we're with you." One after the other, Southern governors released their delegations to Humphrey. Although the vice president could not repudiate his 1964 pledge to seat Mississippi's freedom fighters, his position blurred on the other liberal convention fights. His backers voted to bar black contestants from Alabama's delegation and to seat rival delegations, one lily-white and the other integrated, from Georgia. And notwithstanding the McCarthyites' clamor that Texas Democrats had given scant representation to blacks and Mexican-Americans, Humphrey forces helped seat Connally's delegation "as is."

That afternoon a call came from the ranch for the vice president. Humphrey talked first with Johnson's assistant Jim Jones. It was the president's sixtieth birthday, and Mayor Daley had laid on a monster birthday party for the amphitheatre that evening. With his speech written and his Starjet poised on the runway, Johnson was prepared to go to the convention. But Marvin Watson, Charlie Murphy, Arrangements Chairman John Criswell all advised against the trip. The conversation that followed between the president and vice president was brief. Johnson was still watching the platform closely, and when Humphrey hung up he wheeled on his platform advisers and chided them for "fighting with" Johnson's draftsmen and thereby "embarrassing the

President." Then he added: "If he comes up, it will be just as embarrassing for me." It was the closest Humphrey came that week to acknowledging the heavy price he paid for Johnson's support.

The vice president's nomination was now assured, but the convention was far from over. There remained one more option open to Humphrey, another decision to make: to use his acceptance speech to declare his independence. O'Brien had urged it ("Disclaim the plank in the acceptance speech"); Ginsburg had urged it ("Say in your acceptance speech you have your own plank reading thus-and-so"); even Valenti, the former Johnson aide, said the president could not expect to hold Humphrey once he had been nominated. But the aides also told the vice president: "To show the country that you are now in the lead, the acceptance speech would have to be a shocker."

Unbeknownst to Humphrey, unbeknownst to all those who had been conferring with the vice president in Chicago, another group of advisers had been preparing a speech with the required wallop. A group of old Humphrey friends, political science associates from University of Minnesota campus days, had met in Washington to analyze polling data for the vice president. They included Evron Kirkpatrick of the American Political Science Association, his wife, Jeane, of the Georgetown political science faculty, Herbert McClosky of the University of California at Berkeley, and on occasion their old colleague Max Kampelman. Looking over the findings McClosky saw that the vice president's weak point was that he was perceived as President Johnson's handy man. Well before the convention, McClosky got the idea that to separate himself from the president, Humphrey should resign as vice president.

Others had made the same suggestion, including Averell Harriman. But McClosky's idea, worked out in great secrecy with the Kirkpatricks, Kampelman, Robert Nathan, and Bill Welsh of the vice president's staff, was that Humphrey should announce his resignation in his acceptance speech. When Ted Kennedy still looked like the choice for the No. 2 spot, the group's scenario called for Humphrey to fly first to Hyannisport to get his agreement. Then he would fly to Washington, and while his plane was en route he would give out his speech to the press—in sealed envelopes to be opened later when he spoke. In Washington he would lay the speech before Johnson, saying: "Mr. President, I want you to see this. But it can't be retracted. It has already been given to the press. I shall deliver it tonight in Chicago." And this was the speech, as McClosky wrote it: "I must give thanks for the confidence that you have bestowed upon me in choosing me as candidate to lead the country. And I must pay tribute to our great President. But for his selflessness, but for his determination not to risk the lives of more Americans in Vietnam, *he* would be the man who would be here accepting this nomination; the candidate for next president would be Lyndon Johnson. This great man, this man of courage, of selflessness, my patron—out of his immense love for his country, stood down from his presidential duties to win peace." What Humphrey would then say would have impact like no other acceptance speech—since it was without precedent. "I can do no less. If I remain vice president, every word I utter will be questioned: is this Humphrey the Vice President speaking, or is it Humphrey the candidate? I therefore offer my resignation, and today have handed it to the President. Under the new 21st amendment we can now have a new Vice President in a few days, chosen by constitutional succession—and I shall be free to offer myself, Mr. and Mrs. America, as YOUR candidate for President."

Because to have proposed the plan earlier might have rattled the vice president, the group waited until nomination was assured to make their move. Then they took the idea to Larry O'Brien, sagacious veteran of nominating conventions, who listened and said: "I'll try it." On the morning of August 28, O'Brien took the proposal (but not the speech draft) to Humphrey. The vice president listened carefully, mindful that such high-powered political figures as Governor Harriman thought resignation both feasible and desirable. He thought hard. His jaw squared. Finally he said: "Well, it would not look like an act based on principle or conviction; it would look like a gimmick. It would seem strange. And it will enrage the President."

With this last decision not to turn from Johnson, the lines were drawn. The president stayed away from the convention, and Humphrey, for all practical purposes his surrogate, stood forth as the lame-duck administration's candidate, offering no change.

After this the Johnson forces controlling the convention machinery had put off the Vietnam debate overnight to noon of the twenty-eighth, when it was assumed fewer voters would be at their television sets to hear the speeches of the dissenting minority. But this delay also left time for just about everybody who had come to Chicago to see what was taking place. To all appearances, the convention's business was settled. Behind Daley's barbed wire the delegates would drone through their debate to its foreordained end, then go right to the nominating speeches and balloting for surviving candidates—all in one day and with but one result: nomination of Johnson's man Humphrey.

The National Mobilization to End the War in Vietnam, which had already organized the 1967 march on the Pentagon, vowed to bring masses of demonstrators to Chicago to put pressure on the delegates to repudiate the Johnson Vietnam policy. Students, for idealistic reasons and because they resented being drafted to fight in Vietnam, responded in greatest number to the Mobilization's call. They were the vanguard of young anti-war dissenters who began gathering in Chicago's northside Lincoln Park on the convention eve. But not all were partisans of the New Left. There were hippies in their love beads and long, flower-decked hair, along with their exhibitionist offshoot: the blood-throwing, money-burning, traffic-stopping members of the Youth International party, known as "yippies." The yippies' kooky notions, raptly reported by television, included a "Festival of Life" in the park's fountains and a mock "unbirthday party" for the president. It was no mighty turnout that the Mobe mustered for their Chicago protest—the demonstrators never numbered more than ten thousand at any one time.

But the widely publicized threats of mass disruption of the city and convention had put Mayor Daley and top party officials on edge. During the April riots touched off by Martin Luther King, Jr.'s, assassination, the mayor had rebuked his police chief for not taking strong enough action. Police, he said, ought to "shoot to kill arsonists and shoot to maim looters." Chicagoans, especially inner-city white ethnic groups who feared for their lives and property, approved such talk. Just before the convention met, police raided southside ghettoes near the International Amphitheatre and rounded up a dozen Blackstone Rangers, leather-jacketed proponents of "black power" said to be plotting attacks on the presidential candidates.

In the circumstances, there is no doubt that Mayor Daley and his forces overreacted. They turned the city into an armed camp and the convention, in Arthur Krock's words, into a "garrison Convention." The night before the Democrats met, there were no more than a thousand young people in Lincoln Park. Shortly before midnight, police pushed them off the grounds, then chased them through nearby streets indiscriminately clubbing the demonstrators and anybody else who got in their way. According to the Walker report prepared later for the National Commission on the Causes of Urban Disorders, "it was the clearing of demonstrators from Lincoln Park that led directly to the violence" during the convention. The following night, when the Lincoln Park crowd was bigger, the scene was repeated. This time reporters and cameramen were present, and the cops slugged twenty-one of them, too.

David Dellinger, the middle-aged radical who was the Mobe's chairman, tried to negotiate permission to march downtown. Daley refused. Dellinger sought a permit to march peaceably through the ghettoes to the convention hall. Daley refused. Bullhorn in hand, Tom Hayden and Rennie Davis, two young Mobe organizers, raced around between parks and "mobile centers" in churches and YMCAs bellowing new directions. But wherever the demonstrators tried to form up, Daley's police poured out of trucks to turn them back. Frustrated and furious over the beatings, the demonstrators yelled obscene epithets at the hefty lawmen lined up shoulder to shoulder. When the cops caught the youngsters in side streets they got their own back, smashing arms and bloodying heads with a few choice obscenities of their own.

The violence crested on Wednesday. By then everybody knew that Humphrey had swallowed Johnson's Vietnam plank, that the Democrats like the Republicans intended to stonewall any change on the war. At noon that day, Daley threw Illinois' support at last to Humphrey, more than assuring the vice president's nomination in the balloting that evening. Everything seemed foreclosed. That day the biggest crowd, some ten thousand young protesters, massed angrily in Grant Park across Michigan Avenue from the Conrad Hilton headquarters of Humphrey and McCarthy. Some broke up park benches and collected concrete chunks. Some had bags of excrement, others balloons they filled with paint or urine. Dellinger and others delivered stop-the-war speeches at a bandshell. While radios blared the Vietnam debate from the convention hall, a young man climbed a flagpole and pulled down the U. S. flag. Dellinger ordered it placed at half-mast. "Pigs! Pigs!" the kids jeered at police. Thereupon the cops charged, sticks swinging. The bandshell crowd broke and ran.

By four-thirty the convention debate ended as the peace plank went down to defeat, 1567¾ to 1041¼. Dellinger called on everybody to start a march on the hall from an intersection west of the park. Some five thousand headed across Michigan Avenue. Police met them on an overpass and hurled them back with a barrage of mace and teargas. Frustrated and angry, some two to three thousand surged down Michigan toward the Hilton. The crowd had now become a mob. Humphrey was inside; police feared they might storm the hotel or rush southward along Michigan Avenue and turn toward the amphitheatre. The Secret Service got an anonymous call that the amphitheatre was to be blown up.

The kids moved from the park and pressed against the police lines, chanting: "What's holding us up, let's go, let's go." From the rear, rocks, sticks, bags of urine pelted the cops. There were shouts of "Fuck you, LBJ," "Hump Sucks," "Daley Sucks Hump." Then from among the trucks in the street a hurtling column of police cleaved through the mob. Thrusting a yellow barricade like a battering ram, another wedge of cops lunged at the massed protesters. Kids ran into the park, across bridges, into hotel lobbies. Everywhere cops caught boys and girls, pounded them, grabbed them, and hauled them, heads bumping on the ground, to paddy wagons. Some demonstrators, pushed against the front of the Hilton, toppled back through windows as the plate glass smashed.

There were more confrontations later that night and next day, but that seventeen-minute episode was the fiercest. Nobody was killed, but more than two hundred were hurt, including fifty cops; 600 were arrested. And television cameras on the street and in hotel windows had caught it all.

In his suite high above, Humphrey had only fragmentary knowledge of these events. "I did not witness all of this. I was busy receiving guests," he said afterward. And earlier that day he had received Mayor Daley, the Southern governors, and the press, eaten a sandwich with black athletes Jackie Robinson and Elgin Baylor, and conferred with Mayor Joseph Alioto of San Francisco, who was to nominate him. But his Secret Service man Glenn Weaver had told him some of the demonstrators below were armed with spiked golf balls and potatoes with razor blades embedded in them; and of course, peering out the window, he saw the ominous massing in Grant Park. Between callers he stopped occasionally to watch the Vietnam debate and complain of the way television was "playing up the kooks and rioters" instead of the convention. He snorted when the New York delegates, defeated on the peace vote, donned black armbands and began singing "We Shall Overcome." Irritably, he began tidying up the room, gathering up stale beer glasses, emptying ashtrays, picking matchsticks off the floor.

Toward evening, as deputations from Illinois and Pennsylvania were ushered out, the vice president submitted to the ministrations of his chiropractor—a rubdown that lasted an hour. His wife came in before leaving for the convention hall. With Andreas and Dr. Berman he stood at a window watching the crowd below. Suddenly everybody in the suite started coughing and sneezing at once—tear gas from the street had been sucked up through the Hilton's air-conditioning system. Humphrey retreated into the shower.

The vice president, already Lyndon Johnson's prisoner, was now Mayor Daley's. At the convention the nominating speeches began, and Humphrey sank back into a chair to watch. Just as Carl Stokes, the black mayor of Cleveland, rose to second Humphrey's nomination, the networks finished editing their films of the Hilton violence and put them on the air. To Humphrey's dismay, Stokes's speech was switched off entirely; for seventeen minutes, before the startled eyes of the nation, Daley's police were shown gassing and brutally beating the youthful protesters and dragging them bloody-headed to their vans. It was a shocking sequence, shown over and over that night. When the cameras flicked back to the convention, the viewers' eyes jumped to the damning conclusion: there on the podium was Connecticut's Governor Abe Ribicoff of the peace forces assailing the "Gestapo tactics" of the police, and there, sitting granite-faced amidst the Illinois delegation, was Boss Daley, self-evidently the heavy villain who had loosed the cossacks on their rampage and was now stonily railroading the nomination of Hubert Humphrey.

Many of the 89 million Americans watching the appalling spectacle of violence on their television screens that night exclaimed: "The Democrats are finished." Five thousand telegraphed their disgust and outrage to the vice president the following day. And what was Humphrey's reaction? After all the indignities he had suffered on the way to this moment, he said simply: "I'm not going to worry—I'm either going to get it or I'm not." At first, angry at the networks for blotting out Stokes's seconding speech to show the riot scenes, he cried: "I'm going to be President some day. I'm going to appoint the FCC—we're going to look into all this!"

Humphrey was not much of an actor, but there were reporters present; the night of his nomination ought to have been one of the transcendent times of his life. As the balloting proceeded, the vice president sat back and with a great show of satisfaction penciled on his score sheet the 112 votes that Illinois cast for him. But did he already know, did he really feel, that the night's events had betrayed his dearest ambitions? In the midst of the balloting, he rose suddenly and excused himself. When Dr. Berman followed his friend into the bedroom, he found him weeping.

Humphrey was back in his chair when Pennsylvania gave him the ninety-two votes that put him over for a first-ballot victory. He said: "I feel like jumping." Orville Freeman, who had shared his every victory since 1945, jumped up and down with him. His wife appeared on the screen. He said:

"I wish Momma were really here. Look at how pretty she is. I'm going to give her a big kiss." And in an outburst of cornballism that delighted the photographers, he went to the screen and planted one on her image. "I wish my Dad were here now," he told Freeman. Then the president called to congratulate him ("Bless your heart," gushed Humphrey). Nixon called too.

A few hours later reporters found the vice president at a victory party. He had rejected the suggestion of his friend Miles Lord that he take his children and go down and talk to the young people in the park. To the newsmen he defended Mayor Daley. Both he and Mrs. Humphrey, he said, had received "half a dozen" assassination threats: the mayor had no choice but to set up a heavy guard. Humphrey spent more time criticizing the demonstrators than the police: "It is very disheartening to see that a mob on the outside should feel they could control the Convention. They think they can pick and choose the laws they want to change. We might just as well draw the line here and now. You cannot have anarchism, you cannot have nihilism in this country."

Humphrey did not even get to bed that night before eight Southern governors, led by John Connally, called with their IOUs. They wanted a vice-presidential nominee then and there. Names were mentioned, including that of one Northerner, Cyrus Vance, but the vice president was noncommittal. He had practically decided on Senator Muskie. If Kennedy was out, Muskie was also a Catholic, and his Polish blood more than offset the ethnic pull of Nixon's Greek-descended man, Agnew. Muskie was solid and steady. As Humphrey said later: "I know I talk too much. I wanted someone who makes for contrast in styles." Waking after only three and one-half hours sleep, he called his young aides into his bedroom, lay back on the bed with his arms folded behind his head, and said: "OK, boys, who's it going to be?" They all knew his short list, which had been printed in the newspapers—Muskie, Harris, Hughes of New Jersey, Ambassador Sargent Shriver. The aides argued for their favorites; somebody brought up Alioto. The vice president cut it short: "Listen, it's going to be Muskie."

But it almost wasn't. While he sent Bill Welsh to fetch Muskie, he began making phone calls. First to Johnson's man Marvin Watson. Watson listened, then proposed Senator Inouye. Humphrey brought up Vance's name; Watson downgraded it. The vice president was now ready to call Johnson. The president listened, anything but enthusiastic about Humphrey's choice. He named two Southerners, Governor Terry Sanford of North Carolina and Governor Carl Sanders of Georgia, and one Northerner, Hughes of New Jersey. Meanwhile, Humphrey aides called senators, governors, labor chieftains for their reactions. Mayor Daley came in, looking grim. Outside, the vice president could see many young people sleeping on the grass. About this time the Poor Peoples March, for which the Rev. Ralph Abernathy had somehow obtained a permit, approached the Hilton with two mule-drawn wagons in front and a horde of marchers behind, very few of them black—blacks stayed on the sidelines throughout the week's demonstrations. He made a great exhortation, and Humphrey could hear the cheers.

Muskie arrived, but after forty-five minutes with him Humphrey came out and said: "I need Jim Rowe right away." It had been Rowe whom President Johnson assigned to grill Humphrey before his 1964 nomination to see if he had any skeletons in his closet. And, sure sign that Humphrey was disturbed, the vice president began tidying up his bedroom: getting the laundry together, placing the soiled shirts neatly one on the other. Before Rowe arrived he took Berman into the bathroom, locked the door, and said: "I want to talk to you not as a friend but as a physician" and told the doctor of the Muskies' "grave problem"—an unmarried daughter was pregnant. "What would you do?" asked Humphrey. "It seems as if my path to the White House is fraught with one crisis after another."

The noon press conference to announce the vice-presidential choice had to be put off as Humphrey anguished. Rowe, when he arrived, advised against taking Muskie on the ticket. But O'Brien and Daley thought he should. "It's your decision," said Johnson, with whom Humphrey spoke four times. But the president made no bones that he preferred Terry Sanford. The announcement was put off to 2, to 2:30, then 4, then 4:30 while Humphrey hesitated. Muskie waited below in his hotel room. At 2:30 New Jersey's Dick Hughes was called in. Instead of asking Hughes to go on the ticket, however, Humphrey asked his advice on the Muskie problem. Forthrightly Hughes replied that he would have no compunction over it. As Hughes left, Humphrey came out with tears in his eyes, exclaiming what a wonderful man the governor was and how thankful he was for his counsel.

The vice president had made up his mind. By then he had Fred Harris and Muskie waiting in two bedrooms. He went first to tell Harris of his decision. It had been a difficult one, he said: "In an equal way you are just as good a man. I could just as easily have taken you but for a few fine differences." And he asked Harris, who had wanted it so badly, to nominate Muskie. "What else could I answer?" Harris said next day. His reply: "You're still my leader. If that's your decision, I'll be glad to nominate him."

Humphrey went into the other bedroom and told Muskie he was, after all, his man. Without a word, Muskie threw his arms around the vice president and hugged him. The harrowing decision made, Humphrey was jubilant. He said: "Well, I've got the best man, that's what counts," and rushed off to make the announcement.

Back in the suite, he turned to the speech that writers such as Secretary Wirtz, Norman Cousins, Bill Moyers, Jack Valenti, John Stewart, Doug Bennet, and Ted Van Dyk had been slaving on for weeks and, in a few minutes, tore the pages apart and began writing rapidly with his black felt pen, putting the speech into his own words. There was an interruption when George McGovern came in, saying he was ready to help and promising to appear on the platform with Humphrey that evening. No such word had been received from McCarthy. "Too bad Gene is acting the way he is," McGovern said.

Humphrey then told the writers that the speech simply would not do, not after last night's violence. Dissident delegates, Humphrey had been warned, might stage a walkout when he rose to speak. In the brief time remaining, amid the tumult about him, the vice president began dictating in relays to his two secretaries the speech that would have to save the situation. After perhaps an hour of this, he gathered up his papers, fixed his eyes on Berman, and recited his revised speech to the doctor. Finally, the last pages typed over by Vi Williams, sitting on a stool in the bathroom, he gave the draft to Van Dyk for polishing, retyping, mimeographing.

As he dressed he fussed about what he should wear—what type shoes, what necktie, whether his shirt was too large. He knew people said he did not look "presidential." He was especially sensitive about "my wattles." He was also self-conscious about his hair, which he himself dyed to look blacker than it really was. He had his wife's hairdresser come in to fluff up his skimpy locks; his television adviser Bob Squier had told him his hair looked too slick and plastered. And because the television camera was using a new type of tinted lens, the vice president switched to a new makeup man, the fellow Humphrey thought had done such a good job the week before when he appeared on Irv Kupcinet's show in Chicago.

At the amphitheatre a memorial to Robert Kennedy ended, and the convention, running two hours late, took up the nomination of Muskie for vice president. It was the signal for Humphrey to head for the hall. Wound tight as a spring he rose, looked long in the mirror, then said gingerly: "We're off." There was no motorcade this time, just Humphrey and Berman in the limousine (Mrs. Humphrey had gone on ahead); the Secret Service went behind in their follow-up car with mace, teargas, and machine guns. The moon was out as they rolled along the expressway. Overhead, following a strobe light beamed upward from the Secret Service car, an army helicopter flew close cover. The authorities were on guard.

The vice president's thoughts, however, were on what he could possibly say to heal the ghastly wounds opened at Chicago. Suddenly he exploded: "The prayer of St. Francis!" He had wanted it in; the writers had taken it out, and in all the frantic recasting and rewriting he had forgotten to put it back. He reached for the Secret Service intercom phone to call back to the hotel for the missing words.

At the amphitheatre, while Muskie accepted nomination, someone obtained the prayer from the Chicago Public Library. Once again the vice president read his speech aloud to Berman. Then it was time to step to the podium.

"My moment of triumph," as Humphrey later called it without conscious irony, was what the occasion should have been. The best platform orator of his day, Humphrey had been kept by conservative rivals from addressing Democratic conventions for years after his speech that swung the delegates in 1948 until, accepting nomination as vice president in 1964, he delivered by far the most effective speech at Atlantic City. Now, having finally gained the opportunity he had lived for all his days, Humphrey had no chance to savor his victory. Recalling the moment later, he could only say: "I have never had a more difficult assignment." His candidacy, though he would not admit it, was in ruins. His party, split over Vietnam, lay in shambles around him. Many of the thirteen thousand faces looking up at him were bitterly hostile.

The situation demanded, and Humphrey delivered, a highly emotional speech. He was florid, repeating statements in the style of the old-fashioned orator. He was good, but he was not good enough.

He began, as he had to, by acknowledging "my sorrow and my distress" at "the troubles and the violence which have erupted . . . tragically in the streets of this great city." His voice solemn as a preacher's, he called at once upon his listeners to "pray for our country—quietly and silently, each in his own way"—the prayer of St. Francis of Assisi:

> Where there is hate, let me sow love;
> Where there is injury, pardon;
> Where there is doubt, faith;
> Where there is despair, hope;
> Where there is darkness, light.

Like all acceptance speeches, Humphrey's was meant to be inspiring, and by all the usual standards it was. "Within a short time they were responding. I knew I was safe," Humphrey recalled. He spoke for 48 minutes, won 71 bursts of applause, and received three standing ovations; and it was reported later from the floor that at the end even the McCarthyite delegations of Wisconsin and New York were on their seats yelling and screaming with the rest. But for Democrats battered and reeling under the calamity of Chicago, only an oratorical spell such as that cast but once in history, by William Jennings Bryan, could have bound the party together. Even so, Bryan's Cross of Gold speech, while it gained the nomination, was not enough to win the election of 1896.

Coming as it did right after the Chicago violence, Humphrey's address packed drama—though nothing like the sensational sock the proposed resignation announcement would have delivered. What the speech lacked was substance. Humphrey identified the three "basic realities" of 1968: "the necessity of peace in Vietnam," of "peace at home," of unity in the nation. But he still had nothing new to say about Vietnam. He had accepted the president's plank as his own. He had rejected the counsel to declare his independence.

And so, face flushed, eyebrows arching, voice rasping, he turned—in the roundhouse style of party orators on declamatory occasions—to the Democrats' great past. One by one, getting great gusts of applause at each name he mentioned, he recited the roll of those the party had raised to lead the nation—Roosevelt, Truman, Kennedy. And when Lyndon Johnson's turn came, he named Johnson and affirmed: "I truly believe that history will surely record the greatness of his contribution to the people of this land, and tonight to you, Mr. President, I say thank you. Thank you, Mr. President." It was the one moment in the speech when boos were heard in the hall.

For the rest, the vice president spoke of the need to pull the shattered party together: "I call upon my good friends Gene McCarthy and George McGovern . . . those two good Americans: I ask your help for America and I ask you to help me in the difficult campaign that lies ahead. And I appeal to those thousands, yea millions of young Americans to put aside recrimination and dissension [and] join us. . . . Believe, believe in what America can do, and believe what America can be." It was standard political oratory— not enough.

And while McGovern went to the platform to stand by Humphrey's side, McCarthy did not. Instead, after witnessing the television clips of the scene at the Hilton, McCarthy had gone out among the young demonstrators in Grant Park and in a characteristically wry speech proclaimed a "government in exile."

By contrast, Humphrey, as the convention adjourned, gave an interview with CBS's Roger Mudd that placed him on the far side of the generation gap:

> Goodness me, anybody that sees this sort of thing is sick at heart, and I was. But I think the blame ought to be put where it belongs. I think we ought to quit pretending that Mayor Daley did anything wrong. He didn't. . . .
>
> I know what caused these demonstrations. They were planned, premeditated by certain people in this country that feel all they have to do is riot and they'll get their way. They don't want to work through the peaceful process. I have no time for them. The obscenity, the profanity, the filfth that was uttered night after night in front of the hotels was an insult to every woman, every mother, every daughter, indeed, every human being, the kind of language that no one would tolerate at all. You'd put anybody in jail for that kind of talk. And yet it went on for day after day. Is it any wonder that the police had to take action?

That was the authentic Humphrey speaking, in accents that doubtless found echoes in the hearts of many who were more disturbed at the blacks demanding too much too fast in the cities, and who were just as glad to see the upstart young given a few knocks. But to the young, he was both ridiculous, with his "goodmess me's" and "good griefs," and infuriating, with his "the police had to take action." At fifty-seven, the man who had always been ahead of his time had been overtaken by changing attitudes and opinions. He sounded out of date.

It was a glum conclusion to a dismal week. The nomination was his, but what was it worth? The party that had dominated politics for decades emerged so divided by the war, so discredited by the chaotic convention, that the public lost confidence in its capacity to lead the country. After Chicago there was no chance that its candidate could carry a majority. His only chance was to put together something like 40 to 43 percent of the vote and hope that this remnant portion of the vast outpouring of four years before might be just enough to top the Nixon and Wallace returns. Even Lawrence O'Brien, the man he now asked to head the Democratic National Committee and manage his campaign, thought that hope far-fetched. Thus Humphrey left Chicago—and Chicago left Humphrey—with defeat staring him in the face.

32

Out of the Grand Canyon

AFTER the fiasco of Chicago, Humphrey floundered. He had failed to resolve the relationship with the president. He had not come to grips with what kind of a campaign he would run against Nixon and Wallace. He had not even sorted out his thoughts about the ghastly denouement of his nomination. First, as a gut reaction, he had defended the police and Mayor Daley. At this his liberal friends jumped in anger. Thereupon he started saying the police had overreacted—repeated the remark four times in a television session only twenty-four hours later. That led some to question what he really believed, and those doubts were not quieted when he then said the subject should be left to official investigation.

To the candidate, too, the moment was appalling. Shown the letters flooding in, he exclaimed: "My God, the incredible intensity of the feeling. Woe is me!" Overnight, having held up well in the polls all year, his Gallup rating plummeted to just a few points above Wallace's. As he withdrew to Waverly, he said to his wife: "It's as if we've been pushed off the rim of the Grand Canyon—and now we have to claw our way up the sides."

It was already Labor Day weekend—traditional time to launch a Democratic campaign. So far down in the dumps, he scarcely dared launch in Detroit, as Democrats always did, because half the United Auto Workers were sporting Wallace buttons. He contented himself with flying to Manhattan and marching up Fifth Avenue in a union parade that brought out 150,000 marchers but only a thin line of spectators. Not even New York looked like Humphrey country.

Back at his lakeside homestead, he had to take a few days out to get organized for the drive itself. A few weeks before he had asked Orville Freeman, who had managed three campaigns for him in Minnesota, to "think about what I should be doing after the convention." Tough and decisive, the secretary of agriculture drew up a full program almost as detailed and expensive as Nixon's elaborately crafted scheme. But others, notably Connell, Kampelman, and Maguire, had different ideas. The candidate, having failed to delegate clear authority earlier, could not keep down the savage infighting for control of the campaign. Mondale said later: "I didn't leave Chicago; I escaped it." As for Harris, Humphrey himself explained: "Fred wanted to be vice president. He was terribly disappointed when I didn't pick him." O'Brien, who had agreed to serve only through the convention, thought Freeman's plan unworkable. Humphrey was heard to say: "Orville is too much like a marine colonel for the job." More importantly, not in the farm belt but in the big states of the Northeast lay the hope of an electoral college victory. To induce O'Brien to carry on, Humphrey made him both campaign manager and chairman of the Democratic National Committee. As gloomy about the prospect as other professionals ("Frankly, it looked like a hopeless task," he said later), O'Brien took the assignment. When Freeman then threatened to quit, Humphrey asked him to take over issues, scheduling, and advancing. Gritting his teeth (but keeping his cabinet post), Freeman consented.

Assembling in the Waverly guesthouse, the new "team" scarcely knew where to begin. Joe Napolitan, O'Brien's ex-business partner and media expert, sat up all night typing out what passed for a plan. About all we had time for, O'Brien said, was "just getting on the telephone and seeing where we could send [Humphrey] to kick off the campaign." There was never a moment to sit back, try to define issues, lay out a strategy. O'Brien said later: "My God, it was just an unbelievable nightmare, and it stayed that way through the campaign."

What really drove Humphrey up the wall was his money problem. The vice president figured he needed $10 million to $15 million to wage a proper campaign. Bob Short, the Minnesotan he had named treasurer of the Democratic National Committee, told him absolutely no money was coming in: the big givers had seen the convention debacle and the bad polls and were holding back. Napolitan said they would have to put off any media push until the final weeks of the campaign. But surely the administration, and especially such a master of political fund-raising as Johnson, had resources to make available to its candidate? At the least, Humphrey asked, what about the President's Club, for which he had made so many appearances over the past three years—couldn't these funds be tapped now? No, Short said, the $600,000 in that account was out of reach, controlled by President Johnson.

In alarm, Humphrey and O'Brien tried to telephone the president and Arthur Krim, head of the President's Club and Johnson's chief fund-raiser. Their calls were not returned.

September 3 was the Humphreys' thirty-second wedding anniversary, and Dwayne Andreas, Humphrey's commodity-king friend and finance chairman, had laid on a quiet dinner at a yacht club near Waverly. But the vice president was in a grim mood, his mind on his financial plight. Without cash, O'Brien and his man Napolitan could not buy television time. Unable to get on television, they could not put the candidate and his message across. Appalled at this prospect, Humphrey broke away from the party and finally reached Arthur Krim through the White House switchboard. "What's wrong?" Humphrey barked. "There's no communication with the man, and now you're not coming up. What the hell's happened now? It couldn't have been the platform, he's talked to me since, and I've done nothing out of the way."

Krim answered: "Well, it's the little things." It seemed that the president was upset because Humphrey's press aide, Norman Sherman, asked some question about Lyndon Johnson at a post-convention briefing, had replied jocularly: "Lyndon who?" The remark had gotten back to the ranch. And Humphrey's choice of his friend Short as treasurer in place of Johnson's man Criswell had irked the President. Even Humphrey's selection of Larry O'Brien as campaign manager and National Committee chairman had displeased Johnson, who had not forgiven O'Brien for leaving his cabinet back in April to run Bobby Kennedy's ill-fated campaign.

"Screw the President, you've taken enough from that man," Bill Benton had counseled during the first foray to New York on Labor Day. "Only way to treat a bully is to ram it down his throat," Dr. Berman had advised. Now, with Johnson's chief fund-raiser on the phone, Humphrey stiffened. Well knowing that the call was being recorded, he shouted: "Goddamit, Krim, nobody's indispensable. If you're not going to help me, okay. If I have to raise money myself, I'll do it—and it will make the goddamnedest story you ever heard. I have the Communists, the Republicans, and now the White House against me. Goddamit, I'll go it alone." Humphrey was no great shakes at asking for contributions, though like all candidates he did it. That night he telephoned Mondale to appeal to his Twin City friends. He sat up late penciling a list of the hundred most obvious names to solicit. The notes he scribbled for Andreas were almost pathetic. "Here's a potential contributor—Mrs. H. J. Heintz, of the 57 varieties." He had met the lady, of course, but she belonged to one of the most Republican families in Pittsburgh. When he finally turned in, he could not sleep for worrying about money. He was up before dawn, muttering: "Do I really have to go back?" "Back" was to Washington—in the midst of his frantic efforts to throw together a campaign. But he saw no other choice: he had to rush back to "iron things out" with the President.

Arriving for an evening National Security Council meeting, he missed his first chance to talk with Johnson but stayed on to tell White House aides:

"I'll take an auto across the country and raise funds myself. I'm not going to let this chance go just because the Administration"—i.e., Johnson—"doesn't want it." Next morning the president was ostentatiously attentive. After the congressional leadership breakfast, he called in photographers and for the first time had the vice president stand next to him for the group picture. Then he took Humphrey into the Oval Office for a ninety-minute tête-à-tête and promised—so Humphrey related next day—"to work with me closely, to do everything I wanted, and to release the cabinet to help me."

That was a minimal assurance for Humphrey, who had been troubled at reports Johnson was going to dump him on convention eve and who had not forgotten how, in August, the president forbade him even to mention his visit to the ranch but next day received Richard Nixon with full panoply of newspaper and television coverage. Humphrey was not satisfied with the conversation. True, Johnson's money man Krim telephoned Humphrey the following day in Waverly to say he had already gotten in touch with Andreas and offered help. But it was only as a consultant. Krim proceeded to dismantle the fund-raising apparatus on which Humphrey had counted for emergency aid: the $600,000 in the President's Club was never freed for Humphrey's use. His campaign simply had to start out without television spots, newspaper ads, brochures, buttons, bumper stickers. In these straits, Bob Short told the anxious group at Waverly that he would go out and borrow $2 million— getting twenty people to sign for $100,000 apiece—so Humphrey could start campaigning.

It took all the resources of Humphrey's optimistic nature to call the takeoff of his campaign auspicious. Since Detroit was deemed doubtful, he had to start some place else. Humphrey had initially burst on the national scene in Philadelphia in 1948, and it was in Philadelphia's John F. Kennedy Plaza that he launched his drive on September 9, 1968. Even by Humphrey standards, the day was chaotic—the advance work was sloppy, bands and pretty girls were missing, Humphrey buttons and pennants unavailable, the crowd thin—and the hecklers thick. "Dump the Hump," they chorused. The candidate's speech, too long, struck no ringing themes—an address to a Jewish group the day before in Washington was far more telling. Terming his candidacy "a referendum on human rights," he had proclaimed himself the consummate liberal, charged that reaction and extremism were leagued against him, and accused Nixon and Wallace of exploiting the "fears and hates" raised by the issues of social justice.

But it was the millstone of the Vietnam war that dragged him down. Answering a question from a University of Pennsylvania student panel he said he thought that in early 1969, and possibly as soon as late 1968, American troop units might begin to return from Vietnam. During another give-and-take at his next stop in Denver, Humphrey said the doves' plank at Chicago was "so mildly different" from the one the convention adopted that he could easily have run on it. Before the day was over, Secretary of State Rusk had put down his statement about troop withdrawals, and he himself had to take back his remark about the doves' plank with the lame explanation that he had never read it and seen that it contained a call for an unconditional bombing halt that he could not accept. The very next day, picking up a newspaper in Houston headlined "Troops to Come Home," and brandishing it as proof, he repeated his forecast that American soldiers would soon be pulling out of the war in Asia. In his excitement, however, he had neglected to read the story's second paragraph, which stated that a marine unit was being routinely returned to be replaced by another. Retreating to his hotel room, Humphrey sagged, crestfallen. "I guess I just made a mistake," he muttered. Before he had time to issue a correction, the president himself, growling "When is he going to learn that I'm still President?" did so. That night, addressing the American Legion in New Orleans, Johnson went out of his way to say "nobody can predict" when American boys might come home. It was a rum start for the vice president, who smouldered at "the President pulling the rug out from under me." "Not an act of friendship," Humphrey told friends.

The Vietnam war may not have been wholly responsible for the American people's displeasure with Democratic rule in 1968, not when so many white voters were disturbed at the rising impatience of blacks for justice long denied. But it was his Vietnam policy that made Lyndon Johnson a lame-duck president. And within his administration were men profoundly concerned that the Democratic nominee to succeed him was being dragged down to defeat by the unpopular president. Nicholas Katzenbach, Ball's successor as undersecretary of state, and Benjamin Read, executive secretary of the State Department, felt that they had to help the candidate out of his entrapment. They saw him stumbling badly. They shuddered at the great gaps of knowledge evident in his groping efforts to state his position on the war. After the convention they began drafting a Vietnam statement. Knowing that Johnson would pounce if given the slightest opening, they made it immune to his attack by focusing strictly on what Humphrey would do upon taking office. If Humphrey talked only about events after his election, he could not be faulted. That would be beyond Johnson's term, hence a proper and responsible statement for a candidate to voice.

Their first paper, titled simply "Themes," was not couched in any ringing rhetoric. But it was truly informed. These men were privy, as Humphrey was not, to every cable from Saigon, every signal from Paris, every hint from Moscow. They proposed "to give the Government in Saigon our own hard schedule for U. S. troop withdrawals . . . starting in 1969"—just what Humphrey was trying to say—terming the process "de-Americanization of the war" (Nixon got around to it much later as "Vietnamization.") And they proposed "stopping the bombing," with the proviso that such action would depend on "evidence—direct or indirect, by word or deed—of Communist willingness to restore the demilitarized zone" between North and South Vietnam.

Ben Read was an old friend of Humphrey's administrative assistant Bill Welsh from days when he served as aide to Pennsylvania's Senator Joseph Clark. Read showed the draft to Welsh, who had just fought the losing fight with Johnson's men over the platform at Chicago. "I wish you'd been here two weeks ago," exclaimed Welsh. Welsh brought Read to Humphrey, who read the paper and said: "My God, this is what I need."

An even more senior administration official who wanted to help extricate the candidate from his trap was George Ball. Up to this time, Johnson had kept Humphrey in the dark about the negotiations Harriman and Vance were conducting in Paris, sometimes warning him against issuing statements on Vietnam because they might jeopardize the talks, sometimes persuading him to hold off on such statements by tantalizing hints of imminent breakthrough in Paris. Ball, preparing to resign as ambassador to the United Nations to assist Humphrey, now told the candidate that the Paris talks were "sterile," and that it would not hurt, and might even help, for Humphrey to say his piece about Vietnam. Averell Harriman himself, when he saw Humphrey during a brief visit home at this time, affirmed that the talks had gotten nowhere.

Meanwhile the candidate was taking such a barracking from young antiwar protesters at his every campaign stop that, far behind though he was, he could not get off the defensive and mount an effective attack on Nixon. Aides pleaded that he break with the president, but even after Johnson men stayed conspicuously away during his unlucky visit to Houston, Humphrey insisted that Johnson still meant too much for his campaign, especially in Texas. His campaign manager Larry O'Brien was not a man of issues, but he knew that the war issue was hurting the candidate most; in mid-September he sought out Humphrey in the privacy of his Washington apartment to say "Let's face it, Mr. Vice President, as of now we've lost. It's on every newsman's lips. It's on everybody's lips. You're not your own man. Unless you change direction on this Vietnam thing, and become your own man, you're finished."

Humphrey did not deny it. "I guess we're at 3 to 1 odds right now," he told O'Brien; and he acknowledged his poor start at Philadelphia, "my mistake" at Houston, "the President's undercutting me" at New Orleans. But still Humphrey persisted in his loyalty to Johnson. "The press wants to divide us—me and the President. That makes their stories." He said: "Now hear my view."

What he needed, Humphrey said, was "some[thing] positive," some compelling stroke that would turn things around so that he could hammer home the three strong points by which "we must win":

[First] most Americans don't want Nixon. We must show what happens if Nixon takes over. When people begin to believe [the] trouble with

Nixon, there will be a change. He represents resistance and apathy. And Wallace represents apartheid.

The second thing I offer is the economy. People will vote their pocketbooks.

And the third thing I can offer them is peace. I can give them hope to get their boys home. . . . I will tell them we have to start pulling our ground forces out as soon as the Vietnamese are ready—de-Americanizing it.

Listening, O'Brien broke in: "How can you say that without a break? Johnson hasn't said, 'Phase out.' Listen, we have to make a clean break this week or never. Do it now—maybe even a white paper." Humphrey said only: "Well, I don't know. . . . "

Early next morning the vice president submitted to another painful bladder treatment. When he arrived at the plane to fly to Boston to campaign with Ted Kennedy, he was as cross as a bear. He had read the morning columnists. In the Washington *Post*, David Broder had said nasty things about his ties with LBJ. In the *New York Times*, Max Frankel had ticked off his lack of discipline, his gabbiness, his wind-on-Capitol-Hill fatuities ("Most of us are going to spend our time in the future. . . . My father used to tell me most of your troubles are in your mind.") That day the peaceniks booed him in Boston. And they heckled him at every airport, shopping center, hotel, and courthouse square on his swing across the country. They nearly shouted him off the platform in Flint.

Returning to the capital, he met again with the president. There was still no hint of a break. But the longhand notes Humphrey made that day record a mutual acknowledgement of an ineluctable fact: the candidate would be the man who would have to make the decisions after January 20, no matter how belligerently the president defended his constitutional turf meanwhile:

Johnson: I do not think proper for the VP or an ex-VP or an ex-President to play commander in chief.

Humphrey: [Agree] Mr. Nixon or I or Ike* will not have anything to do between now and January 20.

Johnson: Tactics, strategy, peace conference, troop movements [are] very delicate things. . . . Three hours a day President reads cables.

Humphrey [as if to himself]: When I become President, I'll spend every day finding peace. Re-examine everything.

The very next day, while addressing a waterpower conference in Sioux Falls with George McGovern at his side, Humphrey said it aloud: "I'm going

*Eisenhower, ailing at Walter Reed hospital since May, had issued a statement that America must not accept "camouflaged surrender" in Vietnam, and Johnson was scheduled to visit the former President the following day.

to seek peace in every way possible, but only the President can do it now. Come January, it's a new ball game. Then I will make peace." At the mention of peace, the engineers and farmers jumped to their feet and cheered. The following day, in the midst of berating Nixon ("his stands make Jell-O look like concrete") at a Louisville fund-raiser, he said it again: starting January 20 he would somehow get peace in Vietnam "so we can get on with business here at home." Once again, a thundering, standing ovation. Frankel, watching it happen over and over, wrote that Humphrey had touched a national chord. Jim Rowe, the Johnson man in Humphrey's entourage, told O'Brien's next meeting: "Peace—every time the Vice President said that was his No. 1 priority, he got an explosive response."

If that was the comment of observers, what were the thoughts of the speaker who played on an audience as if it were a symphony orchestra? Humphrey knew he had found an issue. By September 21, a re-drafted Katzenbach-Read paper was in his hands. Between rallies, Humphrey sent it to O'Brien. O'Brien, reacting to the post-Chicago polls that showed Humphrey fifteen points behind Nixon, had refused to accept the vice president's brushoff of his first appeal. He had collected three "white papers" of his own, including one by Ted Sorensen and another thought to have been the work of the repentant hawks McGeorge Bundy and Robert McNamara. On the plane westward, Humphrey handed over the Katzenbach-Read draft to Ted Van Dyk for the speech writers; and walked back from his stateroom to tell reporters that he would have to make some decisions soon.

Touching down in Minnesota he still did not sound like a man moving out from under. Shown the interview article he had given *Life* magazine, he exclaimed: "I didn't say enough about the President here, he may be mad." In Los Angeles, where he tangled with more college students, he heard from O'Brien and Short that funds were so tight that if he decided to speak out, he might not be able to afford buying television time and might have to settle for some press conference setup the networks might not cover. At the Sacramento airport he was told that O'Brien had gone ahead and pre-empted a half-hour for him on NBC for Monday evening, September 30. As he landed in San Francisco, O'Brien's assistant told him they had to have a decision in half an hour. "Well, suppose we decide not to do it?" Humphrey countered. At that moment, Van Dyk rushed up to report that Bob Short had said he would get the $100,000 to pay for the broadcast. Humphrey said: "Okay, then let's do it."

On September 27 Humphrey flew on to Portland. There, four hundred young anti-war protesters, nearly half the Reed College student body, interrupted his Civic Center speech with shouts of "Murderer," "Racist," "Stop the War." Back at the hotel, the vice president, who had bet Dr. Berman he would be even with Nixon by mid-September, got the worst news yet: the latest Gallup poll showed that he had slipped further, trailed Nixon by fifteen points, and at 27 percent was only seven points ahead of George Wallace. White-faced, he turned to Berman and said: "I don't understand it. If the polls are really what they stand to be, I don't stand a chance. I don't give a shit any more, I'm saying what I want to say." That was the night that George Ball, having resigned office to become Humphrey's chief foreign policy adviser, flew in with Bill Welsh to take a hand with the Vietnam statement. Distraught, Humphrey said: "Now just tell me, George, how do I handle this thing? Jesus, anything to get peace for the people. The people have to understand that I'm for peace, and if this will do it, that's what I want to do." Ball's arrival helped steady the shaken candidate. As second man in the State Department, Ball had opposed the Vietnam adventure from the first. With Humphrey he had spoken against Johnson's first decision to bomb North Vietnam in 1965, and unlike Humphrey he had been telling Johnson ever since—the president styled him his "devil's advocate"—that the war was a mistake. Now he had joined Humphrey as the first and only official of cabinet rank to quit the government over its war policy. In Humphrey's worst hour he was reassuring. "Mr. Vice President, I think you can still win," he said. And when Humphrey replied: "I've loused up the situation a couple of times when I should have stood firm, especially on the troop withdrawal and on the bombing pause," Ball told him: "But you were right, you should have stuck to your guns."

Ball and Welsh had started working on the Vietnam statement on the flight west. They had already cut it in half, Ball said, and would now recast it to give fifteen minutes to Vietnam and fifteen minutes for "a general, worldwide policy statement." "Does it say the basic thing—'When I am President?' " Humphrey asked, and when Welsh said yes, he set Salt Lake City as the place from which he would broadcast. He asked: "Can Nixon say this will destroy negotiations?" Ball had an answer for that question too. He told the vice president he had talked with both Averell Harriman and Cyrus Vance, the two U. S. negotiators in Paris, "and they're willing to come out for you 1,000 percent if you do it." Ball said he had already arranged for a Lehman Brothers friend in New York who knew Harriman to courier the completed draft to Paris and get Harriman's okay back by Monday morning. Meanwhile, Ball himself, after staying up to work with Welsh on the draft statement, would fly back to the East Coast keep a Sunday "Meet the Press" date—then return in time to brief the press on Humphrey's statement before it went on the air Monday. Senator Harris, who had come in from California, asked if the vice president was going to clear the statement with Johnson. Humphrey said: "Hell no, I'm not going to ask—I did that once."

Then, while Ball and Welsh worked on the statement and Van Dyk went over the next day's arrangements, the vice president retired to his small bedroom—"just totally shot," Dr. Berman said. Pacing in his underwear, Humphrey could not get the ghastly polls out of his mind. "I just don't understand it," he kept repeating. Berman gave him a tranquilizer and a sleeping pill, and he turned in.

At this low point, battered by the polls, the press, the protesters, Humphrey was joined by his wife, who broke off her own campaigning in Idaho to be with him. She found him terribly depressed that his life should have culminated so ignominiously. At breakfast he said to Berman:

> Muriel and I have been talking it over this morning and we've decided on one thing. I'd kill myself to win if I thought I had a chance. But if I don't have a chance, it's no use.
>
> I'm going to go like hell for the next two weeks, see what happens, and if it's no better I'm just going to take it easy and maybe go out two days a week.

Saturday, September 29, was one more heartbreaking day for the candidate. He flew in a small plane to dedicate one of the big Columbia River dams. He delivered a plodding address on conservation and recreation, not what people want to hear from a presidential candidate. Unhappy afterward, just as he began giving Van Dyk hell for not producing something better, a call came through to the riverside construction shack from O'Brien in Washington. The campaign manager had already read the Portland version of the proposed statement. "The Ball draft is an abomination," O'Brien shouted. Humphrey said O'Brien had better come out.

Humphrey flew to Seattle. That night he ran into the worst heckling of the campaign. Four thousand Humphrey supporters filled the Civic Arena; hundreds outside were unable to get in. But wedged into a balcony corner to the right of the platform were some two hundred well-organized protesters. Their boos and shouts of "Stop the War" drowned out Senator Warren Magnuson when he rose to introduce the vice president. As the television cameras swiveled to the balcony, one of the demonstrators pulled out a bullhorn. Through the din, Humphrey cried: "There's a man that wants to make a speech—let's listen to him." The bullhorn boomed: "In Vietnam there is a scream that does not end. . . . " The bullhorn paused, began again. The interruptions grew louder, ruder. Humphrey shouted: "Oh, for God's sake, shut up and let the decent people listen." Finally the police and Secret Service men waded in, collared the ringleaders, and shoveled them out; the rest followed. Humphrey went on to give a good speech. But his heart was not in it; afterward at the hotel, "beat and dejected," he said: "I don't know what to do." Dr. Berman gave him another tranquilizer and a stronger sleeping pill.

Sunday, September 30, was to have been a day of rest. But Humphrey, with the Vietnam broadcast on his mind, canceled out of the salmon-fishing trip on Puget Sound. He was shaving, looking in the mirror with the lather on his face, when Van Dyk walked in. "I've come to report to you on the speech drafts," Van Dyk said. "There are umpteen of them." Ball's draft—the one O'Brien had called an abomination—seemed to Van Dyk "totally about the importance of Europe with a little statement about Vietnam tacked at the end." Humphrey said: "Well, I don't want to see the drafts. Go and write something quick and bring it back before everybody shows up."

Then, while the vice president breakfasted with his wife, Van Dyk went back to his briefcase and pulled out the original paper that the president had stopped Humphrey from using before the convention. "I dictated some language before and after," Van Dyk said later, but the draft he now laid before Humphrey was essentially the statement worked out in July and early August—and it included a virtually unconditional pledge to stop the bombing in Vietnam. The only qualification was that the demilitarized zone would be viewed as a test of good faith. That is, if the Communists violated it, the United States would reserve the right to start bombing again.

Through the rest of the day, Humphrey sat at a table with Van Dyk, mostly cutting and slashing the non-Vietnam portions of the speech that Ball had wanted in. Staff and secretaries moved in and out carrying penciled additions, re-typed pages. Off and on, Humphrey, still in dressing gown and slippers, watched the football telecast from the East—but not with real interest. To all appearances the candidate, in frontal challenge to Johnson, was going to come out for the end of the bombing that the McCarthy and Kennedy forces had asked in vain at Chicago. Arthur Goldberg called from New York, Dick Hughes from New Jersey, to say a complete and unconditional bombing pause was absolutely essential if the candidate was to carry their states. At mid-afternoon, O'Brien arrived and pronounced the new version emerging much better. Fred Harris looked at it and liked it.

Then Welsh went off to telephone his friend Read and learned that George Fitzgibbon, the courier Ball had dispatched to Paris to confer with Harriman and Vance, was already back. Harriman, it seemed, had said it was only "a fifty-fifty proposition" whether he could accept the statement shown him. That left a considerable margin of risk for the vice president. Accordingly, what Humphrey would say on the morrow was still up in the air when at the end of the day his party left Seattle.

At Salt Lake City, Jim Rowe and former Democratic National Chairman John Bailey showed up, and the hotel room debate resumed. Humphrey said later that he wrote 90 percent of his Vietnam statement himself, and this turned out to be literally true. Everybody had a copy of the text as the meeting started. Humphrey began reading, line by line. He kept changing phrases, words, punctuation. Arguments broke out. Finally Humphrey would make the decision, and everybody would pencil in the changes. Through most of the speech, even the part about troop withdrawals and de-Americanization of the war, the process went fairly quickly. But whether the candidate liked it or not, stopping the bombing was still the crux of his speech. When the vice president came to the three short paragraphs on the bomb halt, arguments grew angry and mean. The struggle raged for five hours and was not finally settled when Humphrey went to bed at 4:30 A.M. Connell opposed any statement that did not leave America free to resume bombing if necessary. Rowe wanted some bombing to continue but was willing to compromise. O'Brien and Harris fought bitterly for an outright halt in U. S. bombing of the North as the dramatic stroke that would bring the McCarthy and Kennedy peace partisans back into the fold. They wanted the version that Van Dyk had prepared earlier in the day.

But Welsh kept insisting that such a pledge went beyond the declaration that Harriman had seen and pronounced risky. And Humphrey, while he had made up his mind to bypass the president, was loath to take responsibility for a statement that might be unacceptable to the negotiators in Paris. Several times the vice president broke off the dispute and leafed ahead to less contentious parts of the statement. But finally he returned to the bombing paragraphs and wrote in the passage that Ball and Welsh had prepared the day before in Portland. This included the seminal paragraph that Katzenbach and Read had written into their first paper in early September—that any halt in the bombing must depend on evidence—direct or indirect, by word or deed, of Communist willingness to restore the border demilitarized zone. O'Brien and Harris fought bitterly against this proviso, protesting that it negated any chance that Hanoi would agree to a mutual pullout of troops.

At 2:30 A.M., O'Brien, having said his piece with finality, rose and left in unconcealed disgust; Harris, not quite so angrily, departed soon after. But the fight was not over. Sherman, the press aide, said the newsmen were expecting a strong declaration and anything less would diminish the impact of the statement. Welsh struggled to re-word the point while still keeping the pre-condition. Van Dyk, after holding out for his version, finally gave in and accepted what his chief had accepted. Connell stayed to the end, watchful lest Dr. Berman, the man in a position to have the last word with the vice president, might somehow put in his oar and get the condition removed. For Humphrey, having accepted the qualification on his pledge to halt the bombing, was now uncertain again and terribly tired. This time, when he went to bed, he got no sleeping pill because he had to get up at eight for breakfast with Utah Democrats.

On the day of the big broadcast, Humphrey operated, as it seemed, on nerve alone. Though he and his advisers had pretty well written off Utah and other mountain states to the Republicans, he fired up the local party people with a slambang speech at breakfast; then he delivered a measured and statesmanlike address on national unity to an overflow audience of ten thousand at the Mormon Tabernacle. He did not return to the hotel until 1:45 P.M., too late to rest even for a moment before the taping of the evening broadcast.

By then, Van Dyk and Welsh had put the finishing touches on the speech. To make sure that the statement on the bombing halt was "something that Harriman can live with," Welsh had actually strengthened the qualifier by adding to the crucial paragraph the phrase "before taking action." The declaration now read: "As President I would be willing to stop the bombing of the North as an acceptable risk for peace. . . . In weighing that risk—*and before taking action*—I would place key importance on evidence—direct or indirect, by deed or word—of Communist willingness to restore the demilitarized zone between South and North Vietnam."

Shown the final version, O'Brien snorted that it was "not worth a damn." He had not spent the Humphrey campaign's last dollars for a half-way speech that could blow their comeback chances for good. The vice president, eating a hasty lunch, could see that his campaign manager was displeased. O'Brien paced the floor, dragging deeply on cigarette after cigarette, barking orders in a side-of-the-mouth, clubhouse style of delivery. Van Dyk was to call Goldberg before the speech, Connell the governors, O'Brien himself would call Ted Kennedy, Harris the other senators. The candidate was now firm about what he was going to say. When Berman asked him about the last change, he replied that Welsh had explained it to him and he was sorry, "but this is the position I have to take. This is my position, and it has nothing to do with Johnson. We'll just let the chips fall where they may."

Ball, flying in from Washington, was enthusiastic about the final draft. He now said he had sent a telegram to Harriman and Vance saying everybody was counting on them to respond positively to Humphrey's statement. It was agreed that after the taping, but before the actual statement, Ball would brief the press and Humphrey would call the president to tell him the main points of his speech. Then, as Ball recounted later, he would telephone Johnson "and get him down off the ceiling." But it didn't happen that way.

The making of the telecast was a grueling hour and a half for Humphrey. He was at his limit, knowing that the speech had to come off just right—and he was not at all sure. For the first time, to show the public and the president that he was speaking in his own right, he ordered the vice-presidential seal removed from the stand as he spoke. He dispensed with the Teleprompter. And conscious that he always came across shorter than he was on television, he spoke standing at his full five feet eleven inches. Berman gave him a tranquilizer before he went on.

Dissatisfied with his first run-through, he called for a second taping. And as he sat fidgeting nervously to go on again, Berman made a last try at changing the speech. "Mr. Vice President," he began, "you have to come on a little stronger." Humphrey gasped: "Jesus, everybody tells me this and that." The director came up, and Berman backed away. At the end it was decided to use the first taping after all. But in the delay, Humphrey, pleading lack of time, asked Ball to make the telephone call to President Johnson. When Ball called, the President's line was busy—he was talking to Nixon. When the call went through and Ball gave the gist of the speech, Johnson was noncommittal. Later, when Humphrey finally called, the president was colder and carped: "You know, we have other qualifications than the DMZ—the infiltration rate and others."

If Johnson sulked, the overall reaction to Humphrey's "half-way" speech was surprisingly positive. In his "deep briefing," Ball passed lightly over the pre-condition in Humphrey's pledge to end the bombing, and with few exceptions the newsmen accepted his interpretation. As he said later, "they wanted to believe" Humphrey was taking an independent stand. The immediate headline in the Salt Lake City *Deseret News:* "HHH to Halt Bombing." The following day the State Department announced that the Humphrey statement was compatible with the broad outlines of U. S. policy.

Humphrey, not overly elated at first, had a drink. But after boarding the plane for the East and getting congratulatory calls from Kennedy, Muskie, and others, he was in high good humor. "I feel good inside for the first time," he said. He had taken down the vice-presidential seal for good and would not display it again in the campaign. He had finally said what he felt about the war in Vietnam, what he had sought to say in July, in August, in the platform, in his acceptance speech. It was late, but he had come off the defensive at last. As the Boeing 707 bored through the night, he summoned his aides to a strategy meeting in his little bed compartment. He had given his pledge for peace, he said. Now, backed by an economy in which incomes stood at a record high and unemployment at 2 percent, it was time to go over to all-out attack on Nixon.

33

The Halloween
Peace

PSYCHOLOGICALLY, Humphrey turned a corner with his Salt Lake City speech, and that may have been its chief benefit for his lagging campaign. A big load lifted off the candidate's mind. "He felt good," Larry O'Brien said and added hopefully: "He's his own man." Relaxing on the plane winging East, Humphrey warbled the lines of a Negro spiritual: "Ain't gwine study war no more" and laughed appreciatively when LaDonna Harris cracked: "That's the new party line." The very next day in Nashville the anti-war hecklers who had dogged him everywhere before, were gone. Instead young people waved signs: "If You Mean It, We're With You," and "Stop the War—Humphrey, We Trust You."

Freed at last of his defensive posture and certain that doves would now return to the party cote (three days later he won the ADA board's endorsement, 73-to-13), Humphrey went over to the attack. At Nashville and Knoxville he lambasted George Wallace as "a political plunger," "apostle of hate and racism," "a creature of the most reactionary underground forces in American life"—and reminded those who thought the governor the arch-defender of law and order that his state of Alabama had the highest murder rate in the nation. And since Nixon's Southern strategy drove at capturing the very states drawn to Wallace, Humphrey lumped Nixon in the same unsavory bag. "My Republican opponent, he shouted, "appeals to the same fear, the same passions, the same frustrations which can unleash in this country a torrent of unreasoning hate and repression."

In the fall of 1968 the American people were moving amid the trauma of war in Vietnam and civil strife at home on to the downward slope of a long wave of military and economic expansion that had lasted since World War II. It was the end of an era, and such times are not apt to call forth heroic leaders. Certainly there was nothing epic about the 1968 presidential contest. Both Humphrey and Nixon were No. 2 men competing for the succession. Both had run for the top before and lost. Nixon offered himself as the candidate of what had been, ever since the Great Depression, a minority party. Humphrey, though the designee of the majority party, had fallen so far back after Chicago that he was a minority candidate. Not in his wildest dreams could he aspire to more than a slim plurality of the nation's votes.

It would be going too far to say that the underdog Humphrey, foremost orator of his generation, rose to his greatest and most persuasive eloquence after the turn at Salt Lake City. But by his impassioned invocations of peace, he stirred thousands of dissident liberals to return to the Democratic ticket. By his powerful preachments to unionists to search their consciences before casting a vote for a racist, he moved masses of factory workers to desist from crossing over to Wallace. And by fire-breathing tirades in sweaty halls and steamy banquet rooms, he roused local Democratic workers to get out and organize again after the torpor of the Johnson years.

The nearly three hundred thousand dollars in small contributions that flooded in was the most palpable evidence of the Salt Lake City speech's effectiveness. Hoping to build momentum, O'Brien used the money to buy time for a second big telecast. Both Humphrey's campaign manager and his old political-science mentor Evron Kirkpatrick, who now served as his chief opinion analyst, agreed that law-and-order was the toughest remaining issue of the campaign. Kirkpatrick pronounced it "the major issue, no doubt." On the basis of party surveys that canvassed many more voters and asked many more questions than ordinary political polls, Kirkpatrick reported that "Humphrey is soft in the area of law and order, and this softness is hurting him more than anything else. Crime prevention is at the top of what people— as many as 89 percent—want."

As trumpeted by Nixon and Wallace that year, "law and order" was a code word for putting blacks in their place. How could Humphrey, who had made his whole life a fight for civil rights, join the parade to close down America's Second Reconstruction? Freeman, brooking no nonsense, said: "The objective of this speech is to identify Humphrey with the lower, middle-class whites." Rowe, Kampelman, and others advised that the vice president had already said enough about "justice," the code word for giving blacks access to long-denied schooling, housing, jobs. So Humphrey and his speech writers, led by John Stewart, his chief aide in the historic fight to pass the Civil Rights Act of 1964, struggled and strained to strike a balance between what the public wanted to hear after three years of urban rioting and what the candidate believed.

Eighteen million Americans tuned in the telecast. And though the taped format permitted none of the usual Humphrey spur-of-the-moment flights, the orator could and did bear down heavily on how firmly he would enforce the law. His wattles shook as he cried: "As President, I would stop these outrages at whatever cost." And, promising to widen federal aid to communities already expanded by the administration's Safe Streets Act of 1968, he pledged a billion-dollar program to help hire more police, speed trials, upgrade prisons and "train our police far better than we do." But he made clear he had no easy solutions: "Anyone who tells this country—as Mr. Nixon has—that poverty and crime have little or no relationship—is fooling you and himself."

Humphrey simply could not and would not hide his deep conviction that there could be no turning back from the drive to integrate the races of America. The October 12 speech had no such impact as the Vietnam telecast and brought in no comparable outpouring of five- and ten-dollar checks. Yet on law and order the tide turned for Humphrey in October too. Organized labor forced the turnaround.

The AFL-CIO, recognizing the Wallace surge as a revolt against its own leadership, threw all its power behind the Humphrey candidacy. Labor had propelled Humphrey into public life twenty-five years before, and Humphrey had fought labor's battles in Congress when at times it seemed the unions were almost unheeding. In the hour when Humphrey needed labor's help most in 1960, the unions had succumbed to Kennedy's appeal and abandoned him in the Wisconsin and West Virginia primary battles. But now, when Humphrey would have been lost without it, the AFL-CIO and its eighty international unions went to work for his presidential campaign as never before in history.

They poured out money, possibly $10 million's worth. But cash was not their weightiest weapon. Led by George Meany, organized labor gave Humphrey their formal endorsement. From first to last, Al Barkan, grizzled director of labor's redoubtable Committee for Political Action (COPE), sat in on the candidate's most intimate planning sessions. As the race heated up, labor's leaders, recognizing Wallace's candidacy as a naked challenge to the loyalty of their following, mounted an all-out drive quite separate from that of the Democratic National Committee, for whose neglect and disarray under Johnson they had unconcealed contempt. Task One was to stop the big slide of their members to Wallace. Task Two, undertaken as soon as the first job was done, was to deliver every last union vote for Humphrey in November. Barkan said later:

> Our polls showed 30 percent of this Wallace infection. And we countered. We put the fear of God into them.
> We had this computer. It had 13 million names on it. And it was pumping out our mailings non-stop. We showed that Wallace was a phoney.

We gave 'em the numbers—how busdrivers in Birmingham make thirty bucks a week less than in Northern cities, carpenters forty bucks less, schoolteachers $2,000 to $4,000 a year less in Alabama. We asked: "Do you want Alabama wages and Alabama working standards in Michigan? in Pennsylvania? in Ohio?"

Business agents of the steel, auto, and electrical unions marched out to plant gates. They handed out fliers that told how Alabama siphoned off union plants from the North to fill them with non-union workers; how Alabama was one of only sixteen states in the country with no minimum-wage law; how Alabama ranked forty-ninth in the nation in welfare payments to dependent mothers; how Wallace used his state police to bust unions.

Under this kind of gut-punching, with shop stewards bugging the men at every assembly-line break, and with Humphrey appealing to their consciences at every union-hall stop, the defiant enthusiasm for Wallace in Northern union locals began to ebb. It showed in the polls, as Wallace's strength, rising as high as 20 percent in August, fell five points and more by mid-October.

By that time labor's mighty machine was really rolling. Its impact was felt in every state. Between them COPE, the big unions, and the state labor federations put out sixty million pieces of campaign literature. Driving to register members and then pushing to turn out the union vote for Humphrey, labor may have fielded more volunteers than the Democratic party itself. Unhappy at the official party's disorganization, the AFL-CIO assumed responsibility for getting out the black vote—and set up special units in thirty-one black communities across the country. Altogether organized labor registered 4.5 million voters that fall. In the last weeks of the campaign, COPE had 19,232 unionists and family members manning 6,539 telephones in 638 localities, and 58,474 more out canvassing house to house for Humphrey-Muskie. On election day, in a climactic get-out-the-vote push, COPE sent out 67,272 volunteers to act as baby-sitters, watch polls, pass out sample ballots, and haul voters to the polls. Labor, more than making up for past inconstancy, really delivered for Humphrey in 1968.

The administration helped, too, by handing Humphrey the peace issue at the last minute. It was a neat trick for the vice president who stood in the Saigon embassy compound proclaiming the war as "the great adventure" to turn in less than a year into the apostle offering to "bring the boys home" from Vietnam. Perhaps few of the young folks who slammed the president's mouthpiece in January as "war criminal" and "truthless hypocrite" could stomach such a scrambling shiftabout—though by November, if they wanted to vote, they had no place to go but with Humphrey. And as Nixon's pollsters reported in alarm, when Humphrey got the chance finally to hold out the hope of peace, he touched the hearts of a great many Americans, particularly women.

From the time President Johnson, withdrawing from the 1968 race in March, ordered limits placed on U. S. bombing of North Vietnam, it had become obvious that the next step in the American pullback must be the total cessation of such bombing. World opinion demanded it, U. S. doves clamored for it, and the representatives of Hanoi who met thereafter with Averell Harriman and Cyrus Vance, the U. S. negotiators in Paris, expected it. But Johnson, before entering into substantive peace talks, said the Communists must first give proof they would bargain in good faith.

All summer long, to the mortification of the candidate Humphrey, the president held fast to his demand. He thought the Communists, far from tendering the olive branch, were preparing yet another offensive. But when the Vietnam dry season drew to a close without any such attack, and with little time left to wind up the Vietnam conflict to his satisfaction, Johnson on September 7 authorized Harriman and Vance to probe privately for Hanoi's terms for a deal. He soon conceded that serious talks, once begun, would have to include the National Liberation Front, the political arm of the Viet Cong, alongside the North Vietnamese, and on the American side South Vietnam as well—in effect, two parties on each side. The Communists' well-publicized position was that they would not bargain with the South Vietnamese government and certainly would not deal unless Johnson agreed to a complete halt in bombing North Vietnam.

Inevitably, the U. S. political campaign figured in these exchanges. The North Vietnamese well knew that time was running out on Lyndon Johnson, and their resistance was stiff. But Humphrey's declaration at Salt Lake City on September 30 that as president he would end the bombing, though publicly dismissed by Hanoi, quickened Communist thoughts about Johnson's possible successor. In North Vietnamese eyes, the Democratic candidate might after all be preferable to the hawkish Nixon.

Whatever the North Vietnamese reasons, a break came at Paris on October 11. In previous exchanges they, by ceasing to raise objections, had in effect accepted the two demands to which the United States had narrowed on the military side—respecting the border demilitarized zone and refraining from shelling South Vietnamese cities. They now made President Johnson's representatives an offer: if the United States would halt the bombing, they would drop their resistance to Saigon's participation that had been their other reason for refusing to sit down at the peace table. To Harriman and Vance this appeared to add up to a firm deal. It became clear that this was a significant opening when next day the Soviet minister in Paris, Oberenko, paid a visit to Vance. The Soviet government could say on good authority, he told Vance, that if the United States stopped the bombing, the North Vietnamese were ready in good faith to discuss all the questions of a political settlement. And Oberenko added that Moscow thought the moment opportune—and one that should not be lost.

But then the to-ing and fro-ing began. The president cabled the terms to

Ambassador Ellsworth Bunker, who obtained what he thought was President Thieu's assent. Johnson then pressed for more specific commitments. On October 16 he had his negotiators in Paris put forward a list of check points, asking once more if the North Vietnamese would promise to respect the DMZ and refrain from shelling Saigon and other cities. As before, the North Vietnamese responded: "Well, we understand that the halt in bombing is unconditional"—meaning that the understanding on these two points, like Washington's assent to the presence of the NLF at the bargaining table, was tacit. Then Harriman and Vance, fully expecting that the substantive peace talks could start within twenty-four to forty-eight hours after the United States stopped the bombing, asked for a date that could be inserted in the announcements being drafted for parallel release in Washington and Hanoi. At this the North Vietnamese drew back.

The immediate problem was that when the Americans insisted on a definite date, the North Vietnamese asked for a memorandum on it. But a declaration in writing of such indirect and contingent commitments would have been awkward. A memorandum of understanding would have been hard to put across in Saigon because it would have made the bomb halt appear unconditional and would also have required the United States to be explicit about admitting the Viet Cong to the Paris talks.

Harriman and Vance were all for going ahead, leaving the date for the talks open; had this been agreed to, Washington could have announced the big move for peace on October 16. That was what Humphrey was hoping for, and indeed on that day rumors were rife in Washington that a bombing halt was in the works. At the State Department, Bill Bundy and Ben Read took turns sleeping by the secure telephone to Paris.

But Johnson was strongly persuaded that the negotiators had to run the deal by the North Vietnamese once more and extract a Russian guarantee. Instead of making the announcement, the president decided to place one of his conference calls that day to the three presidential candidates. After giving them an extremely superficial briefing on the difficulties holding up agreement, he warned them sternly against saying anything that would cut across his path. Humphrey, who had broken away from a morning rally in St. Louis to hurry to the telephone, was crushed. His fidelity to the president, his position as the administration's candidate, seemed at that moment to count for nothing. Political considerations had been spurned. Johnson had given him the arm's-length treatment. What seemed important to the president, Humphrey confided to Dr. Berman, was his own place in history.

It certainly did seem, as the vice president flew from St. Louis to try to lure the fractious Democrats of New York to his side, that the president was not looking out for his man. Humphrey's campaign treasurer Bob Short was in a stew because the president continued to withhold $700,000 in sorely needed funds that the party had raised back in 1965 by selling corporations space in a party advertising book. And when Johnson's old friend Jim Rowe came to ask him to campaign for Humphrey in New Jersey, Texas, and key border states, the president refused. He was still miffed at Humphrey's effort at independence in his Salt Lake City speech. "You know that Nixon is following my policies more closely than Humphrey," he told Rowe. As the vice president pressed on into Michigan and Connecticut, two more states he had to carry to stand any chance of winning, his young aide Ted Van Dyk urged him to go and see the president. Newspapers were filled with stories of how a dramatic shift at Paris could lift Democratic chances in the election. "See if some momentum can't be started for the peace table," Van Dyk said.

After an evening meeting at New York's Madison Square Garden, Humphrey had Van Dyk call the White House on the Secret Service line. Johnson's aide Jim Jones said the president would see him the next day, Saturday, at one o'clock sharp. The vice president had a rally scheduled at noon at a Landover, Maryland, shopping center and was late. Even so, ever respectful of the president, Humphrey stopped momentarily at his apartment to shave and change his shirt. At one, Van Dyk answered the telephone at the vice president's office. It was Jones barking: "Cancel the appointment." From his window, Van Dyk could see the vice president scurrying through the White House gate. He said: "Jim, as I'm talking, he's there. I'm telling you what I see." A little later, Humphrey came storming back, furious that the president had cancelled the meeting. "That bastard Johnson," he shouted. "I saw him sitting in his office. Jim Jones was standing across the doorway, and I said to him: 'You tell the president he can cram it up his ass.' I know Johnson heard me."

The following night, Johnson invited Humphrey to the White House but kept him waiting a good hour. Years later, Jim Jones recalled: "The expression on the Vice President's face told all about his campaign troubles. Finally he saw the President. A couple of times I went in and out. It was a long session, lasting till about midnight. The Filipino houseboys who brought drinks in and always brought the President his scotch-and-soda with just a quarter-jigger, brought Humphrey his with full jiggers. By the end Humphrey was a good four sheets to the wind. But I think they really got some things settled."

That was when the president arranged for Mrs. Johnson to appear at Dallas on Humphrey's next swing through Texas. That was also when Humphrey asked Johnson to help out at his big windup rally at the Houston Astrodome. But the president was guarded as always with his vice president about developments in Paris.

As events turned out, it took twelve more days of tough talking in Paris for Harriman and Vance to get agreement. The North Vietnamese, suspicious that Johnson's list of double-check items harbored new American conditions, insisted on going back to Hanoi on everything. Officials in Washington agonized as the parties in Paris haggled over bits and pieces of procedural detail. As agreement took shape, word-play broke out over the text of the announcement. Adjectives were inserted one day, removed the next. Said one participant later: "We were at the point of dancing on the head of a pin." Finally, on Sunday, October 27, the North Vietnamese agreed to waive all remaining procedural details and fix November 6—day after the U. S. elections—for the start of the peace talks. That night Vance telephoned the State Department: "We've got everything we asked for."

Thereupon President Johnson went into action. First he fetched his commander, General Creighton Abrams, back from Saigon to give assurance that the halt in bombing would not hurt U. S. troops in Vietnam. Abrams, traveling secretly, dressed and identified as a sergeant, arrived at two in the morning and at four spoke the required words to Johnson: "My forces can take care of themselves all right. You can stop the bombing of North Vietnam without hurt to our men." Johnson then went round the circle of his advisers and exacted similar assurances.

At last, late in his term but well before its end, the president could glimpse light at the end of his tunnel. The break had occurred. Peace loomed. He could look forward to leaving office having begun to extricate his country from its Vietnam morass. And now the president could make all this known to the nation—before the end of October and well before the voters went to the polls to elect his successor.

It was an Olympian prospect—but it was not to be. During the drawn-out procedural hassle in Paris, President Thieu in Saigon had begun suddenly raising a lot of captious objections that Ambassador Bunker and other U. S. officials had thought already disposed of. Now, when the president was all set for his big announcement and ordered his ambassador to obtain Saigon's compliance, Bunker could not even get to see Thieu, who was being evasive. But in something as delicate as what Johnson planned, Thieu's presence at Paris was essential—otherwise it would not look like the start of peace at all. After a frantic thirty-six hours, Bunker had to report that the puppet was talking back. The South Vietnamese government was not going to send representatives at this time to the scheduled Paris talks. On the contrary, Thieu had summoned the National Assembly into session for the purpose of announcing this decision.

What had derailed Saigon's prior agreement? What had caused Thieu to renege? The answer—and Johnson knew it but could not prevent it—was that the China Lobby had struck again.

In the presidential contest of 1948 this shadowy coterie of exiles and lobbyists had won notoriety by trying without success to oust Harry Truman in hopes that a Republican taking over at the White House might reverse U. S. policy and rescue Generalissimo Chiang Kai-shek's tottering regime from disaster. The 1968 intervention was again for the purpose of electing a Republican president in hopes of shoring up a shaky Asian regime. The ploy in 1968 worked like this: by staying away from the Paris peace talks and thereby blunting their favorable impact for the Democratic candidate Humphrey, Thieu could help elect Nixon, from whom he could expect a better deal.

The China Lobby's instrument of intervention was a petite, attractive, China-born woman who had intimate connections with the Saigon government and a high position in the Nixon campaign. Madame Anna Chan Chennault, vice chairman of the Republican finance committee and co-chairman with Mamie Eisenhower of Women for Nixon-Agnew, had long played a role of intrigue on the right wing of U. S. politics. Born in Peking and educated in Hong Kong, in 1947 at the age of twenty-three she married General Claire Chennault, dashing leader of World War II's Flying Tigers and founding owner of China Air Transport. She bore the general two children and became an American citizen in 1950. After he died of cancer in his native New Orleans in 1958, she sold the airline to the CIA and moved to Washington. There, stunningly gowned in long, high-collared Chinese dresses, she entertained lavishly and met all the top people. Two or three times a year she traveled through the Far East, visiting such personages as Korea's President Park, South Vietnam's Vice President Ky, Taiwan's President Chiang Chu-kuo. The godmother of her two daughters was Madame Chiang Kai-shek. Returning from a Saigon trip in the fall of 1967, Madame Chennault briefed Richard Nixon in New York on Vietnamese developments. A woman of strong views, she was alarmed by the McCarthy and Kennedy candidacies and felt that America would grow weary of the war and abandon her friends in Saigon to the North Vietnamese. Early in 1968 Madame Chennault brought Bui Diem, Saigon's ambassador in Washington, to meet with Nixon and his campaign manager, John Mitchell. "I know you consider [Anna] a friend," the candidate told the ambassador, "so please rely on her from now on as the only contact between myself and your government." As the campaign warmed up she continued to send Nixon notes beginning "Dear Dick" and to meet frequently with Bui Diem and Senator John Tower, chairman of the Republican Key Issues committee.

The Johnson administration was aware of Thieu's interest in the U. S. election campaign because the National Security Agency was intercepting Bui Diem's messages to his government. As early as September 27, Humphrey's aide Bill Welsh informed him that these intercepts disclosed South Vietnamese apprehension over his efforts to take a softer stand on the war, and Madame Chennault's role in stirring up these fears. Humphrey's response was: "The President will do nothing about it." But when the break occurred in Paris and the North Vietnamese, interested equally no doubt in the outcome of the U. S. election, offered Johnson the firm deal he had been looking for, Madame Chennault set out to abort it. On October 15, having learned the outlines of the deal probably through Bui Diem, she wrote Nixon to protest the arrangement of an election-eve bombing halt. And as Bui Diem kept cabling her advice to Thieu, Bunker in Saigon found the going stickier and stickier. On October 27, Bui Diem cabled Thieu: "The longer the present situation continues, the more we are favored. . . . I am still in contact with the Nixon entourage. If Nixon is elected, he would first send an unofficial representative to Saigon, and consider going himself to Saigon before taking office." And on October 30 another intercepted message, citing Madame Chennault, urged Thieu to delay going to the Paris talks because he could get a better deal from the Republican Nixon.

At this point, President Johnson ordered an FBI wiretap at the embassy, as well as surveillance of Madame Chennault. The evidence in administration hands of Republican interference in the peace process was enough to have blown the Nixon candidacy out of the water; it may well be supposed that had Johnson been Nixon's opponent, that is exactly what he would have done next. But the president, though angry, was not running against Nixon. His overriding concern was to get the last major initiative of his administration started at Paris—and he determined to go ahead and announce the bombing halt with or without a pledge of South Vietnamese participation. As for the political impact of his peace move, his role in the campaign all along had been ostentatiously above the battle, all but nonpartisan. And Nixon, shrewdly refraining from statements critical of Johnson's war policy while Humphrey edged away from it, did his best to show the president that on Vietnam he really stood closer to Johnson than the vice president did.

The president set the night of October 31, Halloween, for his announcement that the United States, starting peace negotiations with the Communists at last, would halt all further bombing of North Vietnam. A few hours before going on television with his big news, Johnson conducted another of his three-way conference calls with the presidential candidates. As aides sat listening in the Oval Office, Johnson outlined his deal to the contenders. Then he said certain problems had developed. First, he said, speeches had been made that the United States ought to withdraw troops or stop the bombing with almost nothing in return. That was a slap at Humphrey, and an almost gratuitous one since what Johnson had extracted from the North Vietnamese was little more than the vice president had asked in his Salt Lake City speech. Second, he said, there were implications "by some of our folks, even including some of the old China lobbyists, that a better deal might be made with another president." That was a slap—but only a slap—at Nixon, and as Johnson delivered it, Harry McPherson said later, "he looked around the room at us with a wicked grin."

Then, declaring that the plan he was about to announce had nothing to do with the election, Johnson asked for comments. First to speak was George Wallace, who exclaimed: "Mr. President, I just pray that everything you do works out fine, and I'm praying for you." Nixon spoke next and when he said: "We'll back you," Johnson looked around the room again and grinned. Humphrey, last of all, echoed: "We'll back you, Mr. President."

Thus the Humphrey candidacy seemed caught again in the toils of the president's purposes as Johnson carried through his last major decision in office. Before the president spoke, the National Security Council was to deliberate; but when Humphrey asked if he might attend, the president said no.

At 6:15 P.M. Humphrey was ending a hard day's campaigning in New Jersey, a state he already knew he had probably lost. Registration was sharply down, notably in the black neighborhoods of the state's biggest city. But he stopped to speak in a schoolyard in Newark's ghetto, burned-out scene of recent rioting and looting. All around on tenement roofs stood white police. In front of him stood a thousand blacks who had just booed their white mayor, Hugh Addonizio. And Humphrey spoke his words that day not only because he believed them but because he thought they needed to be said: "We have learned a lesson in this city. Divided, we can do absolutely nothing. United, we can do what ought to be done. All of us, black and white, must learn to live together or else we shall live in a country that is divided and destroyed." He ended the afternoon at Elizabeth, New Jersey, saying much the same to a crowd of white factory hands.

Humphrey's mind was on the president's speech, which could do so much to sway a campaign in which he had almost caught up. Something like a hundred reporters would be at his heels, and he knew they would demand comment on what was developing at Paris. But when he called the White House, first one aide and then another said he must limit himself to "no comment." Humphrey replied, almost pleading: "I can't say that. If Nixon or Wallace say something and I say nothing, I'll look like a damned fool." Finally the president himself came on the line, and between them they worked out an innocuous statement that Humphrey could give the press. As for the NSC meeting, the vice president was to say he was staying away so as to do nothing that could in any way be called partisan in a matter of such high national importance. Humphrey's comment as he turned away: "I hope I can keep my Vice President in line as well as he does."

Humphrey heard the big speech on the radio that evening as he sat in his limousine at Newark airport. Hangers-on crowded close. Television cables coiled past the car to cameras set up by his plane, twenty-five feet away. When Humphrey got out, Secret Service men moved in as people yelled questions. The candidate stood on the plane steps, gave out the statement he had cleared with Johnson, and went into the plane. The whole sense of a suddenly close election was in the air. After all the buffeting, Humphrey at last had the issue he wanted—peace. Elated, he walked up and down the aisle of the plane, trading quips with the newsmen.

He landed at Battle Creek and went along the airport fence shaking hands with a big crowd before going to the downtown rally. The crowds were bigger now. This one had been waiting four hours—a labor rally, a packed hall. When they sang "The Battle Hymn of the Republic," Humphrey joined them in his cracked baritone. Afterward he was chipper, very alive, kidding everyone, in high spirits; he stayed up until three although he had to be on his way at eight-thirty. He talked about being dis-invited to the NSC meeting: "No, the President did it just right. This is the way the peace announcement should be done." Five days before the vote, he still followed the leader: "Everything has been worked out, but it won't be until after the election. . . . It can help tremendously. The aura of peace will be salutary to anyone connected with the Administration."

His next stop was Chicago, scene of catastrophe. All his advisers, doves and hawks alike, insisted he should not go. The public memory was too fresh. At breakfast he said: "I've been quaking all week about it." He made a shivering motion and laughed: "It's just one of those decisions you have to make." The staff had worked up elaborate plans for Humphrey to be summoned back to Washington. Humphrey said: "Forget it, we're going. You just can't disregard a major city. We're not going to give this into the hands of the enemy." Illinois' twenty-six electoral votes were too important to ignore.

On the way to the airport, Humphrey saw a high school band practicing. He stopped the motorcade and walked into the field to listen. The principal let everybody out of school. That made Humphrey late for his first Illinois stop—Peoria. In the heart of Republican country he was only trying to cut back the downstate vote, but the crowd of eighteen thousand to twenty-five thousand massed in the square was one of his biggest. With his son-in-law Bruce Solomonson holding the microphone for him, he shouted: "Two–three weeks ago I was reading the election was all over. Mr. Nixon was taking afternoon naps, his campaign cool and efficient. We've cooled it off plenty, and there's going to be a Democratic victory on November 5."

A Secret Service man drew Jim Rowe out of the crowd, explaining that the president was calling. There had been a morning-after huddle at the White House. Word had been received from Saigon that President Thieu was summoning the National Assembly into session to hear his decision not to send representatives to Johnson's Paris peace talks. When Rowe went to a telephone rigged up beneath the speaker's stand, the president said: "I want you to tell Hubert we've got a problem. I'm not going to work out this Vietnam peace negotiation early enough to help him."

Johnson did not have to explain about Anna Chennault to Rowe: the China Lobby worked both sides of the political fence. Mrs. Chennault was a close friend and business associate of Rowe's law partner and fellow ex-braintruster Thomas Corcoran. Johnson said: "We found out that Anna Chennault had told the Vietnamese ambassador to tell the Vietnamese government to hold off—Nixon would give them a better deal." Rowe asked: "Can't we pull it off?" Johnson said: "It's too late."

Late or not, when Rowe gave Humphrey the news, the vice president asked him to fly back to Washington and pass word through the Corcoran channel that he expected to be elected president, and that the South Vietnamese would shun the Paris talks at their peril. As Rowe left, Bill Connell brought the candidate a fresh poll at the Rockford airport stop that showed him just three points back now in Illinois. Then it was on to Chicago and, of course, Mayor Daley was waiting for him at the foot of the airplane ramp. The flashbulbs popped, a picture every newspaper in the country wanted. Daley told Humphrey: "It's going to be tough, but it was tough in 1960 and we beat it. Wait till you see tonight's torchlight parade." Touring Chicago, Humphrey pulled no punches. In a hard-hitting speech he called for more democracy in America, more democratization of the Democratic party, hardly what Daley and his minions wanted to hear. Huge crowds surrounded the candidate in the streets. The Secret Service had a tough time keeping people off Humphrey's car (for obvious reasons, the candidate wanted no police around). But the torchlight parade that night drew only fourteen thousand to the big Daley stadium show that had brought out twenty-six thousand four years before—telltale sign that the mayor's men had given up on the state and national contests and were concentrating on getting their own local tickets elected.

President Thieu's announcement was not the only last-minute news. Gene McCarthy finally endorsed the vice president on the twenty-ninth. Humphrey's position on Vietnam, he said, "falls far short of what I think it should be," but he felt the vice president had shown "a better understanding of our domestic needs and a strong will to act." Humphrey, who had all but given up hope of winning McCarthy's support, said: "I am a happy man." He had reason—the newest Gallup polls showed he had pulled to within two points of Nixon, 42 to 40. Starting westward on what was the final leg of his campaign he shouted over the roar of the airplane's jets: "There's going to be a happy time in the Humphrey ranks next Tuesday night."

One could not be sure he believed it, though, because earlier in the day he had gotten further word about the blow Madame Chennault had dealt his hopes for peace. At the president's direction, William Bundy of the State Department visited him in his apartment and filled him in on details of how the administration had learned through intercepts and wiretaps of Madame Chennault's meddling. Afterward when Humphrey, Van Dyk, and his press secretary Norman Sherman discussed what Bundy had related, Sherman wanted to blast Nixon. But Humphrey said evidence linking Nixon to Madame Chennault's intervention was lacking, and besides "it would have been difficult to explain how we knew about what she had done." Immediately afterward, on ABC's "Issues and Answers," Humphrey appeared to build the groundwork for coming defeat: "We have no regrets. We think we have done the best we could have, given it all we have, and what is more, we have said what is in our hearts as well as in our minds. We have made some mistakes but we think we've done a pretty good job."

He flew to Texas; if there was any place in the country where the situation had turned around, it was Texas. Under the canny leadership of Congressman Jim Wright, the warring factions of that state had been dragged together and an organization seemingly put together by baling wire—part regulars, part volunteer Citizens for Humphrey, part local free lances—brought Democrats back to life in 254 counties. Though the oil money that always backed Johnson went to Nixon, Wright and his co-workers whistled up $150,000 in small contributions and made it stretch. Their climactic effort was a Houston Astrodome extravaganza. To fill the 58,000 seats, Wright said afterward, "we exacted ironclad promises, written figuratively in blood, that totaled almost $100,000." And though Johnson had not promised, Wright touted the event to his local workers: "Of course we can't say it, but we are expecting that a famous Texan may be there."

A full hour before the appointed time, every seat was taken. And when President and Mrs. Johnson appeared with Humphrey for the first time since the campaign began, the crowd whooped it up. Side by side the two leaders went around the playing field waving to the stands while the astrodome scoreboard spelled out HHH in four-story-high letters and exploded in imitation fireworks. Humphrey gratefully accepted the president's belated endorsement. Of the man he had virtually ignored during the campaign, the president said: "A progressive and compassionate American is seeking the office of President. That man, my friend and co-worker of twenty years, is a healer and a builder and will represent all the people all the time. Hubert Humphrey has worked all his life not to generate suspicion and not to generate fear among the people, but to inspire them with confidence in their ability to live together." Then, motioning Muriel Humphrey to his side, he put his arm around her and told the crowd: "You'll never find a better first lady than this one, and I hope you'll put her there Tuesday."

Humphrey's address was one of his most thoughtful of the whole campaign. He spoke of his gratitude for all that his country had given him, saying he was asking only for the chance to return some of those blessings. He said:

> Nineteen sixty-eight has been no normal campaign year. There has been almost too much pain, too much shock, too much violence, too much uncertainty for the American people to sustain.
>
> I have told you the hard truths about our nation's problems at home and abroad. I have told you exactly where I stand, so if you vote for me you will know not only whom but what you're voting for.

Then, in an eloquent re-affirmation of the faith of the prairie liberal, the nation's best lawmaker summed up his bid to become the nation's chief lawgiver:

> I have always believed that freedom was possible. I have always believed that the basic decency within this nation would one day enable us to lift the veil from our eyes and see each other for what we are as people—not black or white, not rich or poor, not attending one church or another— but as people standing equally together, free of hate or suspicion.

I have believed that within the sharecropper, the son of the immigrant, the grandson of the slave, lay such human potential that America need only call it forth to see its full realization.

And he came back to his theme of trust—the theme of a two-month campaign that had taken him from almost certain defeat to the point where the election was too close to call: "No one man can alone lead this country out of crisis and into a certain, happier future. But if you will trust me, I tell you that I shall call forth from America the best that lies within it."

Challenging it was—and worthy of the occasion, delivered before by far the largest crowd of Humphrey's campaign. But it was the speech of a troubled man. Before the president departed, the candidate had a chance to tell him his worries. Back when all seemed lost he had said he needed three things to win: the economy, the specter of a Nixon presidency, and peace. Tough talk about seventy straight months of Democratic prosperity had finally pulled the bulk of labor away from Wallace to his side. The accent on "trust" and the chance to point to Nixon's choice of the egregious Agnew as exemplifying the kind of administration his opponent would form, had widened the extensive anti-Nixon vote. But to win he still needed all three. The president had delivered peace—but had he? The people were confused. Thieu, Humphrey feared, had dashed the public expectation of peace.

Johnson said he was "concerned," that he was still putting the heat on Thieu. But he had made his move, and there was not much more he could do. That left it up to Humphrey.

At Houston the vice president's aide Ted Van Dyk got word from Rowe about the effort to warn the South Vietnamese through Corcoran that they had better cooperate. Rowe said: "No use. They [the South Vietnamese] are locked in." On the plane for Los Angeles, Van Dyk gave Humphrey the message with the comment: "Well, the old China Lobby's coming back for one more time." At this Humphrey leaped from his seat, pounded his fist on the table, and shouted: "I'll be damned if I'm going to let the China Lobby of all people steal the election from me." In his anger and frustration he dictated a statement to be handed out when the plane landed: "As President, I would sever all relations with the South Vietnamese and leave them on their own. . . ." After a bit the vice president walked back to find Van Dyk. "Say, what did you do with that statement?" he asked. Van Dyk said: "Why, we reproduced it and gave it to all the press on the airplane." Humphrey said: "No, you didn't." Van Dyk said: "No, I didn't." On second thought, the vice president now toned down his statement to read: "If the Vietnamese do not come to the conference table as promised, the United States should go on without them." And he decided to withhold even this statement until Van Dyk could check with Bundy at the State Department to see if Thieu had changed his stand.

At Los Angeles the vice president was met by all the big Southern California Democrats, including Assembly Speaker Jesse Unruh, the only man in public life Humphrey is ever known to have personally condemned. "A doublecrosser" Humphrey once called him, then ordered his editor to expunge the phrase before it reached print in his memoirs. Nearest thing to a boss in California, Jesse Unruh controlled the Kennedy delegates that the state sent to the Chicago convention. Neither then nor later did he ever lift a finger to help carry California for the vice president. Joe Rauh, Humphrey's old ADA partner, had considerable success in rounding up eleventh-hour McCarthyite converts in California. But neither he nor anybody else could loosen up Unruh, who would not forgive Humphrey for asking San Francisco Mayor Joe Alioto, the man Unruh figured he had to beat for governor, to nominate him at Chicago. Almost the first thing Humphrey heard on landing was that the highly touted Muchmore poll, which had last shown Humphrey ten points back in California, now placed him a scant point behind Nixon. Unruh, standing in the background but well within earshot of the vice president, told reporters he still thought Humphrey would lose the state by 150,000 votes.

At Los Angeles, Humphrey issued his mild rebuke to Thieu—and passed up his chance to land the last-round haymaker on Nixon. Van Dyk said later: "Ninety-nine out of a hundred men with the Presidency at stake would have had no inhibitions—they would have demagogued it." When word of the Chennault episode leaked out months after the election, Theodore White wrote of Humphrey's forbearance: "I know of no more essentially decent story in American politics than Humphrey's refusal to [exploit it]; his instinct was that Richard Nixon, personally, had no knowledge of Mrs. Chennault's activities; had no hand in them; and would have forbidden them had he known."

What Humphrey did not know was that on the previous day the FBI's wiretap detected the lady again calling the embassy and assuring Bui Diem that the South Vietnamese would get a better deal from Nixon if they held out. This time the ambassador asked if Nixon knew that she was calling. "No, but our friend in New Mexico does," she replied. This was an allusion to Agnew, campaigning that day in Albuquerque. Years later, especially after Madame Chennault's earlier contacts with Nixon became known, it seemed likely that if Agnew knew, Nixon knew. Alas for the trusting Humphrey, he could not know that his opponent, rushing to clear himself after Johnson's warning tipoff, was sending John Mitchell that very weekend with frantic messages to Madame Chennault to hush up. Nor did Humphrey know that Johnson was reluctant to pursue the Nixon link lest discovery that the Republican had sabotaged the peace talks would impede his ability later to govern. The Democratic candidate could only shake his head at his plight. Having claimed peace as his indispensable issue, Humphrey was reduced to hoping that Johnson's gesture to the foe, even with Thieu hanging back, might satisfy just enough of the nation's yearning for peace to lift him past

Nixon's fading finish. Whatever the vice president's instincts, they certainly did not include the instinct for the jugular.

On this last day of campaigning, Connell's chart gave Humphrey an extravagant 420 electoral votes. O'Brien was not so optimistic. But the final Harris poll came out showing Humphrey in the lead, 42 to 40. The vice president climbed on the back seat of an open car to take the Robert Kennedy trail through downtown Los Angeles streets, and his reception was tumultuous. Blacks and Mexican Americans were out in huge numbers. Secret Service men had to hang on to Humphrey's legs to keep him from being hauled overboard by enthusiasts. One black woman yelled: "I wish I could vote for you a thousand times." From the tops of tall buildings fifty hired auxiliaries dumped confetti on the motorcade inching through the crowd. Some fell in big wads and caught fire from the exhaust pipes of the cars. A tall black man leaped forward and doused the flames before they set fire to Humphrey's automobile. It was a wild mob, twice as large as Chicago's, everybody screaming for Humphrey and Muskie.

Back in his hotel Humphrey closed the door, carefully took off his coat, and with a sudden "Yeow" threw it in the air. He went into a little dance and yelled at Berman: "Edgar, we might just do it." He had a sandwich and a beer, took a nap, and got a rubdown from his chiropractor. Then he went to the studio for his telethon finale.

It was a four-hour effort, paralleling Nixon's, and the two shows crystallized the differences between the Humphrey and Nixon campaigns. Nixon's was highly structured—and dull. "Democrats," a British reporter remarked, "have more fun." Humphrey had Muskie at his side, and the pair were like a top tennis doubles team at the net, returning calls with ease and, for Humphrey, unwonted brevity. Staffers monitoring the Nixon show fed notes to Humphrey, and as fast as Nixon said taxes were up or wage earners earning less, the vice president blew the assertions out of the air. Paul Newman acted as showmaster, and other stars took turns. An early and unexpected caller was Gene McCarthy, who said: "I hope I have cleared the way so my friends are free to vote for you—not only free but a little moved by what I've said." There was a filmed tribute from Senator Kennedy on his Cape Cod beach, and finally a sentimental documentary that Joe Napolitan had brought in showing the candidate playing with his mentally retarded granddaughter, Vicky, and explaining how the little girl's affliction "taught me the meaning of true love."

Afterward the vice president was completely relaxed, knew he had done well, and sat down for back-slapping reminiscences with a couple of old Dakota friends who dropped by. He went to a Hollywood party and danced until long past midnight.

The campaign over, he flew home to Minnesota.

34

Day of Defeat

T HE chartered TWA Boeing 707 landed at Minneapolis at 7:55 A.M., November 5, election day. Despite the chill rain a cheering crowd of fifteen hundred awaited the candidate. "I was tired, more tired than I ever dreamed possible," he said later. He hurried the forty miles westward to his twenty-three-acre Lake Waverly spread, showered and shaved, and then went out to be photographed casting his vote early.

Even at nine the Maryville Township Hall, a plain white clapboard building with a single, uncurtained voting booth inside, was filled with Wright County people; at least a hundred cameramen and reporters waited by the door. Humphrey said later:

> It was difficult for me to walk in. I knew it was the moment of my life.
>
> When I marked my ballot I had a feeling that it was more or less life and death. I sort of stood in silence and I guess I made a little prayer—ecumenical, nonpartisan prayer—that my efforts would be successful.
>
> I wanted very much to win, and yet I knew it was almost beyond my reach. I had a feeling even then that I might not quite make it. I knew our Monday night broadcast had been very successful. Would it be just the thing needed to put us over the top? I had a feeling that it might just do it. And yet we'd been so far behind for so long, I just couldn't bring myself to that level of confidence that the election would be ours.

The vice president went home and went to bed. At four that afternoon he got up and drove five miles to the little town of Buffalo to get a suit pressed. Back at the house he walked around, fidgety. "Muriel and I did very little talking that day. We knew we'd given it everything we had, and we knew that our fate was literally in the hands of the gods and the voters. . . . I had climbed up the ladder of politics, and many times I had slipped and almost fallen back. And then it appears that I was just within reach of the top rung of the ladder. but never did I feel I had a secure hold on it. I was quiet during the day—tired, worried." Then the candidate and his wife went off to Dwayne Andreas's Lake Minnetonka home, where they were joined by the rest of their family for dinner. The first returns were already coming in from the East: the very first, from Dixville, New Hampshire, had Humphrey ahead, 8 to 4. Then another New Hampshire hamlet reported, and Humphrey lost that one, 11 to 0.

At Humphrey headquarters in Minneapolis's Leamington Hotel, Bob McCandless had set up a complete "boiler room"—a bank of telephones and boxes for each state. Bill Connell and his team took the reports and charted them. John Bartlow Martin, the Stevenson speech writer who had joined Humphrey in the closing weeks and written some of his strongest speeches, had prepared three statements for the vice president: one each if he won, if he lost, and if the election went to the House of Representatives.

Earlier, John Bailey of the National Committee had broken open a box in Connecticut—and reported that it showed Humphrey well ahead, a hint that proved correct for his state and a harbinger that Humphrey was going to run strong in the urban Northeast. Other early returns were telephoned from the South. Very quickly Humphrey lost North Carolina and Virginia, and losing them to Nixon was telltale: the Republican "Southern strategy" had broken into the South. But Humphrey stacked up well in the popular vote, running 41 to 43 percent right along.

Arriving at the Leamington headquarters at a little after eleven the candidate was met with wild cheers. As he later recalled: "The crowd was so enthusiastic—and yet for some reason, I couldn't feel that same enthusiasm. Maybe it was just that I didn't dare believe that we could win; maybe it was because if I lost I didn't want to be disappointed. It's very unusual for me because I'm an enthusiastic person, and the enthusiasm of other people is contagious. But not this time."

Humphrey went to his fourteenth-floor suite and asked Dr. Berman for a tranquilizer; his stomach was upset. His wife was also upset. Though his children, his sisters Frances and Fern, and his close friends Fred Gates, Miles Lord, and the Andreases clustered around, he soon withdrew to his own room: "I was quiet. I listened to the returns. And of course there were moments of encouragement." Indeed there were. A week earlier, *Time, Newsweek, U.S. News,* and the *New York Times* had written Humphrey off, none of them conceding him more than 66 electoral votes. Now he was carrying virtually the entire Northeast. He was winning New York, the state he had stumped seven times, with its 43 electoral votes, and he was way ahead in Pennsylvania, with its 29. He was turning back the Wallace challenge and edging out Nixon in Michigan. When it appeared he was behind in Maryland, he asked someone to telephone the governor, who reported he had carried that state by 15,000 votes.

At midnight, McCandless thought Humphrey would win with 294 electoral votes. Connell raised his estimate of 313 to 340. O'Brien was more guarded. Texas returns were good, and Delaware, Alaska, and Wisconsin were all tight races. Wisconsin, the state he lost to Kennedy in the 1960 primaries, was one Humphrey had given up on. Now he told O'Brien: "My God, we should have gone there. One visit would have done it."

But New Jersey was not coming through. And Nixon, besides taking the border states that Connell had counted on, was running ahead in crucial Ohio and California. Humphrey was especially depressed over New Jersey and California. "What Jesse Unruh did to us no Republican could have done," he exclaimed. Unfriendly to Humphrey throughout, California's Democratic leader announced just after the polls opened that Nixon would carry the state. The remark, sure to reach many voters before they went to the polls, was one of the cruelest blows Unruh could have struck the vice president.

Watching these late trends and well aware that Illinois was going to run worse as more of the downstate returns were reported, Humphrey saw his chances slipping away. By 2:00 A.M., he said later, "it looked as if we had lost it." He had wanted to go below to speak to his troops. Twice Van Dyk restrained him. Finally at 2:15 A.M. he went down to the yelling mob in the big Hall of States and, amid the bright party decorations and television cameras, "tried to give the people a bit of a pep talk. But the truth is that I knew it would take more than a miracle to pull it out."

Shouting "We're full of optimism," he told his friends he was going upstairs to bed. By then, he said later, "I knew that the odds were two to one that I wouldn't make it." O'Brien did not have to tell him that even a House of Representatives finish was out of the question. He had lost. He was extraordinarily nervous but dry-eyed. He said to the Marylander Berman: "Edgar, at least we took your state." Berman replied: "Mr. Vice President, you can still take this country." Berman gave Humphrey a sleeping pill, and the candidate went to his bedroom.

He could not have slept much. Waking and switching on the news, he thought of his friend Fred Gates asleep in a room nearby—the Fred Gates who met his plane, ran his errands, watched over his children, raised his campaign money since he first ran for mayor. When Joe Napolitan, the campaign media expert, bumped into the vice president in the corridor in the gray dawn and asked what he was doing up at such an early hour, Humphrey said: "I'm going to wake Freddie Gates. I don't want him to hear it first on the radio."

As the grim morning broke over the city of Minneapolis, Humphrey had his juice and coffee and watched television for a while. It was all over. One after another, the states the vice president had to win slid into the Republican column: California, Ohio, even Missouri. Humphrey sat at a table with Van Dyk putting finishing touches on the speech conceding to Nixon. Mayor Daley telephoned to say he was still fighting in Illinois, holding some votes back. But Illinois was going for Nixon too. Humphrey said later: "I talked to Mr. Nixon. That was a very difficult assignment for me. He was, of course, gracious. But even then I didn't feel any strength in the man, any sense of greatness. I don't say that to be unkind or critical. It's just the way he came through to me."

At one, the vice president went down by the back elevator to the big hall to make the speech of concession: "It was the most difficult assignment of my private or public life. What made it so difficult was that I knew we could have won it—and that we should have." Under chandeliers, tinsel, and red-white-and-blue bunting that now looked tawdry, his faithful followers chanted: "We Want Humphrey" as he stood with his family behind him. A tear glistened in his eye and he tried to smile. "It's nice to know," he said in a quavering voice.

He went through the ritual of thanking his supporters, his family and his wife, his campaign staff, and his running mate Ed Muskie. He read the telegram he had sent Nixon pledging cooperation in "unifying and leading the nation." Then he squared his shoulders, thrust out his chin, and said: "I shall continue my commitment to the cause of human rights, of peace, and to the betterment of man. If I have helped in this campaign to move these causes forward, I feel rewarded. I have done my best. I have lost. Mr. Nixon has won. The democratic process has worked its will, so let us get on with the urgent task of uniting our country. Thank you."

He went back upstairs. For a time he stood alone in the hallway, looking out over the city where he had begun his political climb twenty-five years before. Dr. Berman came up, stood beside him, and then put a hand over his shoulder. After a while, Humphrey broke his silence. "I have a lot of thinking to do," he said. Then he said: "Jesus, I think I would have done a good job in the White House."

The president called. Humphrey said: "Well, Mr. President, it looks like I didn't make it. I'm sorry I couldn't do it for you. I just want to thank you for all the help." Then Lady Bird came on the line, and Muriel talked to her. Then the vice president talked to Lady Bird. His voice was thick, his heart heavy.

Others drifted in. Van Dyk looked like he had lost his best friend. Connell came in with his statistics. It had been so close: a few votes changed in Delaware, Alaska, New Jersey would have sent the election into the House of Representatives, where Humphrey would have won. The candidate groaned: "Sold down the river in New Jersey and California." Turning away he exclaimed: "Jesus, we just lost by a little. That's what I'll go down in history with—I got the popular vote."

It *was* close: 31,785,480 votes (43.4 percent) for Nixon to 31,270,533 (42.7 percent) for Humphrey. Thus, a single vote changed in each of the nation's 250,000 precincts would have given Humphrey the popular plurality. In the electoral college the outcome was not nearly so close: Nixon 301, Humphrey 191, Wallace 46 (all in the South). Humphrey carried twelve states—Maine, Massachusetts, Rhode Island, Connecticut, New York, Pennsylvania, Maryland, West Virginia, Michigan, Minnesota, Texas, Washington, plus Hawaii.

No doubt the *New York Times* reporter R. W. Apple, who had dogged Humphrey through many of the 116 cities and 36 states he traversed clawing back up after Chicago, paid the candidate a just tribute: "Almost by himself, with a little help from the party organization, only sporadic contributions by an erratic staff, and indifferent support from many old friends [and that would include the President] the Vice President pulled his campaign together and made it very nearly work."

But Humphrey himself knew better. A year later, looking at his 1968 candidacy from the perspective of a Virgin Islands retreat, he cast this self-judgment:

> After four years as Vice President . . . I had lost some of my personal identity and personal forcefulness. . . .
>
> It would have been better that I stood my ground and remembered that I was fighting for the highest office in the land.
>
> I ought not to have let a man who was going to be a former President dictate my future.

All true, and the candidate, trapped finally by what must from one standpoint be accounted his sheer decency and from another his want of that reach for the jugular that he called "forcefulness," went down to defeat.

Yet even when the drive and eloquence of Humphrey, calling the old New Deal coalition back to the polls one more time, made it a close race, the thrust of history that had raised him to the vice presidency in the landslide victory of 1964 had passed him by. In those stormy four years of stalemated war, of ghetto riots and campus rebellion, Humphrey had suffered a loss larger than the diminution of his identify in the shadow of Lyndon Johnson. Hubert Humphrey, the pioneering Progressive who had for three-fourths of his career been way ahead of public opinion, went down to defeat in 1968 because he had fallen behind American attitudes and American opinion.

Humphrey's defeat, in which 57 percent of the votes were cast against him, could be seen as a virtually inevitable outcome given the recurrent Progressive syndrome in modern American politics. Two centuries after the American Revolution, Progressivism holds power in the United States only for brief spells—as in a cataclysm like the Great Depression. In its first twentieth-century surge, Teddy Roosevelt, after taking the Progressive nomination from LaFollette, lost the election of 1912, and Woodrow Wilson came on as a minority winner. After enactment under Wilson of the first set of laws regulating corporations, banks, and insurance companies, Progressivism suffered an eclipse. In his second term Wilson became as good a warmonger as anybody and invited the corporate chiefs he had frightened to join him in Washington to wage World War I. The second surge ended when Franklin Roosevelt said Dr. New Deal had to give way to Dr. Win the War. The brief upwelling of 1963–64 was made possible only by the shock of John Kennedy's death and the accession of the Texan Johnson, which broke up the Southern Democrat-Republican congressional coalition that blocked Truman's Fair Deal and guillotined all postwar efforts to expand the New Deal.

By all signs, the Progressive surge of 1963–64 was already so sundered and spent that one big mistake like the Vietnam "adventure" was enough to bring down the 1968 candidate with a crash. Failing to keep their 1964 campaign pledge to stay out of war in Vietnam, Johnson and Humphrey were charged with "betrayal" and routed from office in 1968. By contrast, promising to get the United States out of Vietnam in one election year and failing to do so by four years later did not cost Nixon his constituency when he stood for reelection in 1972.

For Hubert Humphrey there was no such constancy of support. The social scientists who had had such a big hand in the programs he sponsored in the 1960s did not have the answers. The economists for their part did not know how to control inflation touched off by simultaneous financing of the war and the Great Society. The educators' nostrum of college-for-all seemed to produce mainly rebellion, and the helping professions, having obtained the welfare state, seemed helpless as the young rebelled, the poor rioted, older folks bolted their doors, and churches and other institutions tottered amid the fear and fury. Once again the Progressive wave ebbed: voters turned away or, in ominously large numbers, simply stayed away from the polls. The majority assembled for reform and renewal had dissolved. Not Vietnam but the inability of Progressivism to command more than a fleeting majority in the dynamic of the conservative country's politics, appeared to have done in Hubert Humphrey.

PART
SIX

Aftermath

35

Back to Minnesota

A FTER the disappointment of losing to Nixon, Humphrey made a brave show of confidence and humor when he led the Muskies and many of his staff to a postelection vacation at Caneel Bay. But when away from public view, his posture sagged, his voice trailed off into awkward silence, his eyes turned toward some distant, inner vision. Back in Waverly, he walked about the grounds endlessly picking up twigs. In Washington he busied himself wading through stacks of mail. And he caught the flu.

He tried to sum up his feelings in a letter dictated to his youngest son, Doug, a student at Hamline University in St. Paul:

> Well, we surely enjoyed having you with us for Christmas. I was tired, achy, irritable, restless; and I suppose my problem wasn't just the flu.
>
> It was also the emotional letdown from the campaign, and the realization that your Dad had been reaching for the stars and had not quite made it. To put it more directly, . . . the climax of a man's career in public life is of course the Presidency. Dad came so close to gaining that high and honorable position, I could almost feel it. At least, I thought I almost touched it. It was like reaching for the top rung of a ladder, and your fingernails scratch the surface, but you fail to put your fingers around it and to hang on to it. You just slip away. That's the way it seemed.
>
> Now I must design a whole new life for myself. This is the first time

in 25 years your Dad has not held an elective public office. In many ways
it seems like a relief not to have that responsibility. And yet I like public
office so much that not to be in it leaves me with a sad feeling.

Oh, by the way, your Dad straightened up your room . . . didn't throw
anything out you would want. . . . It looks mighty nice. And just remember I love you very much.

He simply could not forget that he had missed the goal of his life—"by just
a handful of votes," he kept saying to Dr. Berman. And as if there were any
chance he would forget, Lyndon Johnson invited him and his wife to the
Executive Mansion for dinner one Sunday night in December and told the
vice president in no uncertain terms that he had lost the presidency by dis-
regarding Johnson's advice.

Worst of all, Humphrey kept coming back to his deepest foreboding: he
could see no political future for himself. Certainly, political oblivion was all
that stared him in the face when President-elect Nixon met him at a Florida
airfield and invited him to accept the ambassadorship to the United Nations.
Humphrey, who had truckled to Johnson, was not ready to serve Nixon. He
refused and wrote wryly to his friend Tony Thompson: "I always told you
Nixon would increase unemployment. He has—by one—me."

Offers came in. Max Kampelman, who resumed the intimate counseling
from which he had been shunted during the campaign, told him the presidency of Columbia University was open, and Brandeis University wanted to
make him a life professor. His old friend Bill Benton offered him a place as
a roving ambassador for his Encyclopedia Britannica enterprises, and Humphrey liked that. DeWitt Wallace of the *Readers Digest* promised a handsome
stipend if he would go back to teaching where he had started—at Wallace's
alma mater, little Macalester College in St. Paul. And Minnesota for Humphrey was home. Malcolm Moos, his old debating teammate and later Eisenhower's speech writer, was now president of the University of Minnesota.
After a football game that fall, Moos invited Humphrey back to his house.
Another old Republican friend, Regent Les Malkerson, went along. Malkerson said later: "Humphrey was lower than a snake's heel. He was depressed.
It's a rough go when you think you're a failure. But right there in Mac's
basement den we worked out the arrangement for Hubert to teach at the
University. We'd get outside money through the Minnesota Foundation. As
we saw it, the kids would have the opportunity to talk to the Vice President,
and Humphrey would be kept involved."

By these arrangements, Humphrey stood to earn more money than he
ever had in his life. He was entitled to a federal pension of $19,500 per year.
The endowed Macalester professorship paid $30,000 per year; the University
of Minnesota appointment, some $10,000. The job with Britannica brought
him $75,000 per year plus generous payments for travel and other expenses.
The contract for his memoirs carried an advance of $70,000. Fees for speeches

on the lecture circuit, especially for Jewish organizations, would push his total income past $200,000 in 1969.

All such rewards at this point were no more than ashes in Humphrey's mouth. As midnight struck on New Year's eve he put down his drink, marched into the bathroom, turned down the handle on the toilet, and in a gesture of disgust, flushed 1968 away. The transition between administrations was painful. When Humphrey went to the Washington airport to board the small jet he was routinely assigned, a huge air force Boeing 707 stood waiting nearby for another VIP. It had been specially ordered by President Johnson for Vice-President-elect Spiro Agnew. In the final month of Humphrey's tenure the president as a consolation gesture asked him to represent the United States at the funeral in Oslo of the United Nation's first secretary general Trygve Lie. Humphrey took along his Aunt Olga and Uncle Tollef, and the day after the Oslo rites boarded the train for Kristiansand, birthplace of his mother, their sister. He looked up the family homestead, still occupied by a cousin, drank coffee and sang songs with a lot of relatives, and tried to explain to them why he had not been elected president.

Back in New York for his last days in office, he attended a book and author luncheon, autographed copies of his 1968 book *Beyond Civil Rights*, and signed contracts for still another book, a volume on foreign affairs. Saying his farewells at the United Nations he ran into Soviet Ambassador Jakob Malik. This stiff and humorless apparatchik asked Humphrey if he had ever been in the Soviet Union. "Oh, two or three times," the Vice President responded. Then a vagrant memory flitted through Humphrey's head.

Five years earlier, on a trip to Moscow for the signing of the nuclear test ban treaty, he had been invited to return to Russia—but nothing came of it. After the signing ceremony that day everybody had repaired for dinner to the Kremlin's cavernous Hall of St. Catherine. The place next to Humphrey's remained empty until halfway through the banquet. Finally General Alexei Grechko, then chief of the Soviet missile force, slid into the chair. "Why are you late?" barked Humphrey. "I've been making a speech," said the burly general. "What about?" asked Humphrey. "Imperialism," said the general. "Ours or yours?" Humphrey shot back—and the general laughed. The two hit it off and were soon chatting about hunting pheasant in Dakota and wild boar in the Urals; and of course the general said, you must come back and hunt with me.

Years went by as the two rose to high position, Humphrey as vice president, Grechko as defense minister. Now Humphrey bethought himself of the 1963 conversation and said in an offhand way: "Your defense minister once invited me to hunt with him, but he's a deadbeat and has forgot all about it." Malik took this sally so seriously that he reported it to Moscow. When a week or so later a group of ambassadors visited the Hill to say their goodbyes to the vice president, Russia's Anatoli Dobrynin came up to Humphrey and whispered: "I've got your invitation from Grechko."

The following July the Humphreys and Andreases set off together on a leisurely trip to Europe. Humphrey asked Ben Read, the former State Department official who now ran the Woodrow Wilson International Center for Scholars in Washington, to go along. Ostensibly Humphrey was traveling on Encyclopedia Britannica business. But, as he wrote Eugenie Anderson: "Muriel and I are going to be regular tourists on this trip. We're not going to commit ourselves to anything other than the Investiture of the Prince of Wales in London and the American Independence Day celebration in Denmark on July 4." With Britannica footing the bill he stopped at Claridge's in London and hosted a party whose forty guests included Tricia Nixon, Happy Rockefeller, and a hatful of junketing senators. He made an unannounced stop in Geneva, where he was almost persuaded to join the board of Investors Overseas Services, Bernard Kornfeld's speculative bubble that collapsed less than a year later. But his destination was always Moscow, where he hoped to see the Soviet chieftains and shoot boar with Marshal Grechko.

Arriving in Russia, the party toured Leningrad, Odessa, Kiev, then spent some days sightseeing in Moscow, where Humphrey struck up conversations with young strollers in Gorky Park. Then one afternoon, just after a heavy lunch at the Hotel National, in the usual abrupt Soviet style word came from Marshal Grechko that the hunt was on. Up rolled the black limousines of the Red Army. Humphrey, Andreas, and Read were whisked off on a two-hour ride to a huge wooded military preserve north of Moscow. Deep in the forest they came to a big hunting lodge. The marshal and his officers stood waiting. "You must have your hunting clothes," he roared. Upstairs they found Red Army fatigue uniforms laid out for them. The head gamekeeper asked if they wanted a little target practice first, but Humphrey declined.

The hunstmen rode off in different directions. Humphrey's car came to a big clearing in the middle of which was a sort of tree house. Climbing the circular stairway, he found his perch furnished with stores of vodka and beer. On the ground below he watched the gamekeeper scatter a trail of grain back into the woods. Further back in the woods he could hear pigs being discharged from pens. Soon what looked to Humphrey like little pigs, big pigs, huge pigs came snuffling out into the clearing. The gamekeeper said: "Shoot." The mosquitoes were thick, so Humphrey, swallowing his distaste, took aim at the biggest. The boar died almost instantly. Humphrey climbed down and rode to the lodge with the critter in the back of the car.

The others returned, each with his "boar." It was dark as Grechko led the way into the lodge. The guests saw a banquet table laid with seven glasses of varying sizes set by each place. Never in his life, Read said later, did he have so much to drink. At the slightest pause in the conversation one of the Red Army hearties signaled a toast: bottoms up. "Jabber, jabber, jabber," an early co-worker said of Humphrey, and that night the huntsman from Minnesota surpassed himself, babbling frantically about his first meeting with

Grechko, his pheasant shooting in Dakota, his salmon fishing in New Brunswick, his trolling Lake Superior for whitefish. Read and Andreas talked themselves silly, chattering to avert the lull that would demand yet another toast. At midnight they got unsteadily to their feet. The iron-bellied hosts were prepared to go on drinking longer. They said, be sure to be ready for the elk hunt in the morning. Unable to answer the hunting horn at dawn, the guests rose later and rode blearily back to Moscow passing through villages where collective-farm hands were being dragged in, some to have their heads held under pumps, soaking out *their* hangovers after Saturday-night binges.

At the hotel the marine guard assigned to Humphrey had turned on a short-wave radio. It was the night of July 20. The U. S. astronauts were about to land on the moon. Like a barker, Humphrey began giving a play-by-play from the U. S. radio report for the little crowd that gathered around him in the hotel lobby. All, including a couple of secret police, were fascinated by the epochal event taking place.

The following morning came the call to the Kremlin. Humphrey found Premier Kosygin, who had been so stiff and formal in Delhi three years before, not only relaxed but warm and cheery, as excited as anybody over Neil Armstrong's walk on the moon. Said Kosygin: "We feel that this is our event too. We feel the same pride as if they were Soviet cosmonauts." Humphrey, briefed beforehand in Washington, said that the United States was ready for talks to reduce the nuclear arms race. And afterward, when Humphrey walked out to the inevitable press conference, he never doubted that he would be asked about his exchange with the Soviet chieftain. Instead, the first question was: "What do you think about Senator Kennedy driving off the bridge at Chappaquiddick?"

It was the first Humphrey had heard of it. The little radio at the Hotel National had not brought this particular piece of news. At the time all the polls rated Ted Kennedy as the likely next president of the United States. All Kennedy had to do was hold himself ready to stand for the 1972 Democratic nomination. Humphrey, called upon for comment about the midnight drowning of the senator's female companion in the midnight waters of Cape Cod, could only murmur that he wanted to give the consequences "a great deal of thought." The whole political equation for his own future had been dramatically altered. He rushed off to his room to write a cable to Nixon reporting that Kosygin favored détente between the two nations.

Suddenly for Humphrey the way was clear. After his 1968 defeat he had been for months, in his wife's words, "not what he was." He refought his campaign, brooded over his mistakes. "Can you think of a politician other than Harold Stassen with more experience in losing?" he asked. And when he met his classes, his friend Geri Joseph recalled later: "You could see that he was struggling and wasn't confident the kids would like him. The kids were rough on him. They didn't accept his experience, and they constantly questioned him, sometimes in very cruel ways. I think he had to swallow his pride every morning with his coffee." The day came when one of his students approached him after class and suggested bluntly that he seemed to be wallowing in self-pity and that he should stop dwelling on the past. A major reason he looked back, of course, was that he could see no political future for himself, and a major reason he could not glimpse such a future was that, once again, a Kennedy stood in his way. Humphrey had apparently resigned himself to this outcome after his 1968 defeat. When Congress reconvened in 1968 he had backed Kennedy's successful bid for Humphrey's old post of Senate majority whip as a likely springboard for the expected leap in 1972 to the White House.

Now the scene was transformed. Even as Humphrey flew home, Gene McCarthy called a press conference in Minneapolis and announced that he would not seek reelection to his Senate seat in 1970. "A fantastic week for Humphrey," summed up the St. Paul *Pioneer Press*. "He got to see Kosygin, Teddy gets knocked out of the national picture, and Gene took himself out of the Minnesota picture." Suddenly Humphrey could see a pathway open wide before him that had been closed before: return to the Senate with a big Minnesota win in 1970, and then try for his party's nomination to finish off Nixon in a rematch in 1972.

Surveying the scene so suddenly transformed, Humphrey sounded almost like his old self. On hearing that McCarthy had stepped aside he shouted: "It's a resurrection. I'm high as a kite. I'm on the run. I'll win in a walk." And he fired off a breezy note to Tony Thompson in California: "There's a rumor around that I may run for the Senate. Could be." Though he acknowledged to Eugenie Anderson, "that presidential election took something out of me," he assured her, "I heal rapidly." This was his attitude when shortly afterward his bladder ailment flared up, and he spent a couple of weeks convalescing after surgery to correct an infection. "An agonizing period, both in worry and discomfort," he wrote Lyndon Johnson, "but everything came out fine." And indeed his doctors, removing more small polyps, found no sign of malignancy. As the fall teaching term drew near he announced he would spend more time in Minnesota than ever; he scheduled all his classes on Wednesdays and Thursdays so as to be free other days for reinserting himself into state politics. His closest counselors continued to be members of the 1968 losing team—Connell and Kampelman, Andreas and Gates. But all four agreed that in 1970 he would have to field a fresh lineup and display a new "image."

"Image" was contrived appearance, treated with utmost seriousness in the age of mass advertising and managed television. Goldwater had striven to "shape a popular conservative image," Nixon had offered a "new Nixon." Though "image" bore only the most approximate resemblance to the real person, the "real" Humphrey had in fact changed as he reached for the heights—affable, cheerful, voluble as ever but indubitably rounded and smoothed by the years of proximity to power and wealth. Now, in the spirit of the times the Humphrey image was to be crafted to emphasize yet more "moderation."

Because of his past identification with the Vietnam war, his new posture required that the war soon disappear as a political issue. But since he had held high office, it was also necessary that he assume the lofty stance of statesman. To that end he tried to recreate at the highest level the post-World War II tradition of bipartisan agreement on foreign policy. In the fall of 1969 he arranged through Henry Kissinger, Nixon's national security adviser, to visit the president. His attempt at agreement was not a success. His next day's record of the conversation opened with the declaration: "The President expressed his appreciation of my attitude to his effort on Vietnam," but Humphrey's try at resurrecting bipartisanship on so rending an issue did not come near to closing the gap:

> I had to tell him that Vietnam had given the country a sickness. That I had come to realize since being out of office that the depth of bitterness about the war was much more than I previously realized. It wasn't just college kids, it was everyone.
>
> To which he replied: "Yes, this is the feeling, but if we get out at once and then the Communists win, take over, assassinate thousands, the same Americans that asked 'Get out' will turn on the government, indeed on him, and say: 'Why did you let this happen?' . . . He was a troubled man.

Humphrey wanted to believe, and when Nixon replied that U. S. casualties, lowest in three years, "would continue at a very low level" as he "Vietnamized" the war, Humphrey noted: "I have reason to believe he is giving consideration to a ceasefire. He didn't say so, but in my talk with Kissinger there was some inkling of it."

When Humphrey emerged to insist that Nixon "wants to get out just as fast as he can and a lot sooner than some people think," the press ran headlines "HHH Praises Nixon" and "HHH Supports Nixon War," and liberal Democrats hooted it was the same old Humphrey spouting off. In his role as Democratic Policy Council chairman, Humphrey then endorsed a resolution calling for a "firm and unequivocal commitment to withdrawal" of all U. S. troops from Vietnam in eighteen months. But when he added: "The issue that is going to determine the elections in 1970 is the economy, not Vietnam," he got no credit for statesmanly vision. His critics saw only the same old Humphrey wishful-thinking. In April 1970, Nixon launched his invasion of Cambodia, and with that Humphrey's last hope of taking the war out of politics vanished. Having already been jeered off the stage when he ventured East to the University of Massachusetts, he arrived one morning at his Macalester office to find the door barricaded by barbed wire placed by student protesters; and shortly afterward he was booed when he spoke at the nearby Hamline University commencement.

By that time, Humphrey had already made fund-raising appearances in every congressional district in his state—and done his best to show off the rest of his new image. He had taken off twelve pounds, refitted himself in sharp, New-York–tailored suits from William Fioravanti, and dyed his sparse hair a blacker hue. A new manager, Minneapolis lawyer Jack Chestnut, thirty-six, was introducing an unprecedented degree of planning into the helter-skelter Humphrey campaign operations. A New York ad agency produced a Madison Avenue slogan: "You Know He Cares." And an Eastern speech writer, Ben Wattenberg, furnished neo-conservative ammunition to neutralize the crime issue that had bedeviled Humphrey in his 1968 campaign. It was Wattenberg's view, set forth in a 1969 book *The Real Majority*, that the deciding votes in the next election would be cast by the unyoung, the unblack, and the unpoor. In an August speech, written by Wattenberg for delivery to the American Bar Association and entitled: "Liberalism and Law and Order— Must There Be a Conflict?" Humphrey declared that liberals "must let the hardhats, Mr. and Mrs. Middle America, know that they understand what is bugging them, that they too condemn crime and riots and violence and extreme turbulence, that they scorn extremists of the left as well as extremists of the right. . . ."

Humphrey won the DFL state convention's endorsement, but not before 20 percent of the delegates cast their votes for Earl Craig, a young black university instructor who had worked actively for McCarthy in 1968. In what the *New York Times* called "the culminating irony of Humphrey's move from left to right center of the Democratic spectrum," the state chapter of Americans for Democratic Action that he had helped found as a fiery young Progressive a quarter-century before then endorsed Craig. For Humphrey, writing to Eugenie Anderson, the irony was that "after a lifetime of championing the cause of the black man, I should now be faced by an opponent who is black and says that I am not sufficiently liberal. If this is a way of testing a man's character, believe me, mine is being tested." Yet, chatting over a late-night beer with a reporter, the candidate acknowledged that he might have changed a bit: "We've got to conserve our gains and plan for new advances. There have got to be people on the left pushing you all the time— but that may not be my role. I think my role will be to try to learn how to reconcile our differences, to be a healer but also to show a better way."

The old campaigner now claimed left, right, and center, and there was no stopping him. His Republican opponent, Congressman Clark MacGregor, complained privately that he would not have entered the race had he known that not McCarthy but Humphrey was to be the DFL candidate. Publicly he conceded that Humphrey was "a likeable cuss" and said: "I suppose he is an institution." To dispose of the charge that he no longer knew the state's problems, Humphrey attended every county fair, showed up for every crossroads corn roast or sauerkraut festival, and shook (his estimate) 150,000 hands.

Spinning across the state in Andreas's helicopter, he spoke to twenty-three Iron Range communities in one day. At a Veterans of Foreign Wars picnic in Blaine, he spotted children standing nearby and cried: "When I see these little ones here, I think what are we going to do for their future, what kind of America are they going to have?" Then, stopping short, realizing he had talked ten minutes, too long and too seriously for people enjoying a lazy Sunday afternoon, he said: "Well, I guess I got a little wound up there"; then he walked to the helicopter and whirled off as the crowd gawked and waved. He could even joke about 1968. Touching down at Anoka, he said: "Why, just a change of less than 80,000 of the 73 million votes cast two years ago, and we'd have this picnic in the White House rose garden." (shout from the crowd: "That's all right, Hubert, we'll get you there next time.")

This time he had plenty of money, and the $500,000 he spent just about matched the Republicans' outlay. In-depth polls indicated almost 30 percent of the voters disliked Humphrey's gabbiness, so his handlers seldom featured him in his television commercials. Humphrey himself saw it differently: "To some politicians standing in shopping centers is a bore, but I like it. I like people, and when they see me in person, they tell me I look younger or taller than I do on television. You know, television tends to make me look squat." Meeting a housewife in curlers at Winona, he said: "You'll be the belle of the ball tonight." Greeting seven-year-olds at Rochester he said: "You tell your mom and dad to vote for me." One morning after a prior event in a down-town hotel, Humphrey's super-efficient managers had arranged for him to attend a fund-raiser at the Minneapolis Club. Humphrey said: "I'd like to walk." Tom Kelm said later: "It was twenty minutes to twelve, and the club was only a few blocks away. I thought there was time. But Humphrey walking up the Nicollet Mall simply couldn't resist talking to people. He was in his element. It took us an hour and twenty minutes—tugging at his sleeve—to go those few blocks."

Popularity contest though it was, Humphrey would not have been Humphrey if he had not had lots to say about issues—and as the balloting drew nearer, about bread-and-butter issues. His old Populist boilers throbbing, he denounced high interest rates in almost every speech and called the sales tax "the most regressive tax that's ever been written." He trotted out his "Marshall Plan" for the cities, restyled as a proposal for an Urban Development Bank. He put forward a fifteen-point health program as ambitiously detailed as the plan Senator Kennedy introduced in the Senate a few months later. He had pungent things to say about an issue just beginning to claim popular attention: "Pollution is a form of aggression. Just as we condemn military aggression we must condemn the aggression of persons—nations and businesses alike—that destroy the life-giving resources of air, water and land. As in other forms we applied economic and political sanctions, we need to apply economic and political sanctions upon international pollution of the air, water and land." He may have been accepting big business's contributions at the

Minneapolis Club, but he still held that government must intervene to assure the good life and promote the good society.

At the last minute, President Nixon came into the state to say a good word for MacGregor, who was to serve as his campaign manager in 1972. It was of no avail. Humphrey swept the state by more than 200,000 votes and carried Wendell Anderson into the governorship and other DFLers into Congress and state legislature seats. Humphrey had begun his comeback saying he had no intention of seeking the Democratic presidential nomination in 1972. But he carefully avoided ruling it out, saying: "I would be less than candid if I tried to pretend I would turn away from the nomination if it came my way."

By still another resurrection in his down-and-up career, he had risen from the depths. He was a contender again.

36

Again, Defeat

WHEN Humphrey lost the race in 1968 and went back to Minnesota, Democrats around the country did not even invite him to speak at their meetings for almost a year. It was not just that he had gone down to defeat while other Democrats were capturing Congress and winning many state races. Some could not forget his acceptance as party standard-bearer of contemptuous treatment from a lame-duck president. Bitter memories of the calamitous Chicago convention and the frustrating contests that led up to it filled other party members with a "never again" mood that made them want to blot Humphrey out of all future consideration.

It had been up to Humphrey to choose the new Democratic chairman. But even this did little to improve either his standing in the party or such hopes as he may have harbored for 1972. Because he wanted to make amends after passing him over for the vice presidency in 1968, Humphrey picked Senator Fred Harris of Oklahoma. Harris proved an impossible choice—he aimed to run for president in 1972, and resigned as Democratic chairman after little more than a year. But Harris was young and assuredly not wedded to the old order. As it happened, the ill-starred convention that nominated Humphrey, the convention so largely dominated—bossed—by President Johnson and Mayor Daley, had made one mollifying gesture toward the new. By a narrow, 1,350-to-1,206 margin it had passed a resolution proposed by the minority whose primary votes for McCarthy and Kennedy had been otherwise ignored—a resolution to revamp the rules by which delegates to future Democratic conventions should be chosen. To Harris in his brief tenure fell the assignment of selecting the commission that would draw up the new rules.

For its chairman he chose George McGovern, the man who had offered himself after Robert Kennedy's death as the stand-in candidate at Chicago for Kennedy's delegates. Humphrey, who had first gotten his fellow South Dakotan to stand for public office and later helped obtain for him the White House post from which he could run for the Senate in 1962, heartily approved.

That "all Democratic voters should have full and timely opportunity to participate" in nominating candidates was how the authorizing resolution read, and McGovern moved at once to see that this charge was obeyed to the letter. First of all, he insisted on the appointment of Senator Harold Hughes of Iowa, a McCarthyite, as his vice chairman and named young graduates of the McCarthy campaign to his staff. Then, bypassing regular party officers, the commission took testimony in state after state. It heard six hundred witnesses, few of them party regulars. It established that one-third of all delegates to the 1968 convention had been elected two years beforehand, and that only 13 percent had been women, still fewer under thirty years old, and only 5.5 percent black—though blacks cast 20 percent of the Democratic vote.

If Humphrey, heeding the outraged cries of the regulars, had cared to restrain McGovern's reforming vigor, he was undermined by events surrounding Chairman Harris's sudden resignation. Party sentiment favored reinstalling Larry O'Brien in Harris's place. But Humphrey, operating from the banks of the Mississippi, let events back in Washington get away from him. He spoke to O'Brien but was unable to persuade him. Satisfied that O'Brien would not take the job, he turned to ex-Governor Matt Welch of Indiana, a choice so uninspired that the National Committee, when it met, took matters out of Humphrey's hands. Telephoning O'Brien, members convinced O'Brien that the party needed and wanted him. Summing up what happened the Washington *Post* observed that O'Brien, "having extricated himself after earlier wins from his only loser, Humphrey," now gained the chairmanship "on his own terms and not as any man's candidate," whereas Humphrey, by his "administrative sloppiness," had "dimmed the lustre" of his leadership.

Almost the first thing that came before Chairman O'Brien was the McGovern commission's report. Its recommendations were sweeping: that the delegate selection process be thrown open so that women, youth, and blacks be represented at the next convention in full proportion to their number among Democratic voters. When O'Brien then secured the adoption of these far-reaching changes, the rebels of 1968 gained all they had asked and more. The reforms made it easy for the insurgents, among whom McGovern now had to be classified, to go after the presidency. By midsummer of 1969, when the Chappaquiddick scandal knocked Senator Kennedy out of the 1972 campaign, it was already clear that McGovern intended to run. By then Senator Muskie, who had made such a favorable impression as Humphrey's running mate in 1968, had emerged as the front-runner. But McGovern, undaunted by the fact that his base was one of the nation's least populated states, went ahead and announced his candidacy long before anybody else, in January 1971.

Chappaquiddick brought a turnabout for Humphrey, too, both in his thinking and in his political fortunes. Where previously he had brushed off advice of counselors such as Jim Rowe and Bill Connell on how to position himself to run again, he now wrote Eugenie Anderson: "I want to think through very carefully what I ought to do, both for '70 and '72." With new caution, he put off his memoirs, shelved his book on foreign affairs, and signaled his friend Dr. Berman not to proceed with the book he had commissioned him to write about the 1968 campaign. Belatedly he took up Rowe's suggestion: to bring together a Democratic Policy Council that would serve the same way the earlier Democratic Advisory Council had when, after Adlai Stevenson's 1956 defeat, that group defined the issues on which a candidate such as Humphrey could run against the Republicans in 1960. But the council members, split over Vietnam, could not come up with an agreed program. When the Democrats were asked to nominate a spokesman to reply to a Nixon television speech on the eve of the 1970 elections, Humphrey, with uncharacteristic reticence, suggested that O'Brien ask Muskie to do the job. It was Muskie's finest half-hour.

After his own big win in Minnesota that fall, Humphrey suggested that Democrats spend the next year looking over the field and then rally around one candidate, taking care to avoid divisive primaries like those of 1968. Liberals pounced on this advice of a man who hoped that the past would be forgotten as wholly out of spirit with the wide-open convention they were promoting. It was the opening gambit of a strategy that counted on other contenders to fade until Humphrey loomed as the qualified, electable, consensual choice. Replying to this criticism he said: "I see little reason why it is incumbent on me to disavow any possibility for 1972 when others whom I consider less able not only do not disavow their intentions or hopes but affirmatively state them."

Back in the Senate, Humphrey was greeted coolly. The man who had guided important legislation through the Senate and then presided over it for four years, found himself ninety-third among one hundred on the seniority list. Nothing could be done about that, but Humphrey expected that, like Barry Goldwater returning as Arizona's senator after his earlier try for the White House, he could at least be restored to his old committees. It was not to be. There was never a chance, after their stormy disputes over Vietnam, that his Foreign Relations colleagues would have him back. But Humphrey was also denied re-admission to Appropriations, where the task of allocating funds had been especially congenial to his wide-ranging interests. Majority Leader Mansfield and his Steering Committee even ruled against Humphrey's return to his old Government Operations post as well. But crotchety old Chairman John McClellan, who hardly shared Humphrey's Progressive outlook, protested: "He's so productive. I want him." So the freshman from Minnesota ended up on Government Operations and Agriculture and, because nobody else wanted it, on the Joint Economic Committee.

In other ways Humphrey found the new Senate less to his liking. The clublike intimacy in which he had basked, after the initial freezeout, seemed to have vanished with the passing of men such as Richard Russell. There were many new faces. And the Senate was no longer a place where, when a member had something to get off his chest, he simply rose and said it. One of the first afternoons after his return, Humphrey strolled on to the floor to do just that and was gaveled down by the presiding officer. Under new rules, senators had to notify Majority Whip Robert Byrd of their desire to speak, after which he might assign them a fifteen-minute slot a day or two hence. Taken aback, Humphrey wrote Eugenie Anderson: "The way they run this Senate now leaves it anything but an exhilarating and inspiring experience. Really, you can get quite bored with it all. . . ."

Humphrey, however, had no intention of accepting boredom. Once again he was up to all hours preparing bills and running errands for constituents. Unready to heed Kenneth Galbraith's appeal for "the reappearance of the old, reckless, quixotic, dangerous Humphrey," he nonetheless told Richard Gilmore, his foreign policy aide, as he went over a draft speech on his old subject of arms control: "You know, Rick, I've returned to the Senate now and I can afford to be irresponsible." He introduced a billion-dollar bill to extirpate cancer. He called for new programs in support of the arts. He proposed a revenue-sharing measure under which the federal government would have footed the entire nation's welfare bill. If in fact he could not wangle his way on to Foreign Relations, he could tell Jacob Javits, his old Republican friend on the committee: "Keep me in mind on legislation on Latin America and economic developments. I want to become your junior partner in this Latin American area." Even though Muskie now chaired his old disarmament subcommittee, there was no stopping Humphrey from appearing as a witness before it and winning headlines by calling for a nuclear freeze pact with the Russians. And it was not lost on Galbraith and Humphrey's old ADA associates that he at once declared his support for the Hatfield-McGovern amendment calling for withdrawal of all U. S. troops from Vietnam by the end of the year.

"I think we ought to get the whole Vietnam thing on the back burner," he told his staff. In his zeal to be quits of the Vietnam issue, Humphrey seized upon the platform that nobdy else wanted—the Joint Economic Committee. To Chestnut, who had managed his Senate campaign and would manage his 1972 campaign, he wrote: "The economy is the Achilles heel of the Nixon Administration, This is where he is vulnerable. This is where he's not going to succeed in time. We've got to keep hammering on it. This is much more important than a lot of ordinary politics."

Once again Humphrey pored over abstruse reports as he had twenty years earlier when boning up for his tax reform fight. Once again he proved to be the Senate's quickest study. Enlisting the help of his old friend Walter Heller, the Minnesotan who headed Kennedy's Council of Economic Advisers, he put on several "presentations"—hearings at which he drummed on unemployment, deficits, the dollar drain, the administration's "lack of monetary restraint" in fiscal policies. Before the session ended he made twenty major speeches on economic and disarmament issues.

Inevitably, such exertions set the pundits of press and television talking comeback and prospects for another Humphrey run in 1972. When they noted that he was still his party's titular leader he scoffed: "That's a joke." But he began to appear at party gatherings again, and as James Reston observed: "When the politicians invite him, almost as a courtesy, the old pro steals the show." The public began to take notice too. Two months after Humphrey's return to the capital, a Gallup poll showed him close behind Muskie and Kennedy, "winning back the support," the *New York Times* commented, "of Democrats who deserted him over the last year."

At these signs that the strategy of outwaiting his rivals might work, Humphrey brought Chestnut to Washington for a strategy meeting with such counselors as Connell, Kampelman, and Harrison Dogole, a financial backer from Philadelphia. If Vietnam (so embarrassing to Humphrey) could be kept on the back burner, he said, Nixon could be brought down by his mishandling of the economy. "Since January I've been on target on the subject," he said. To test the waters, Dogole offered to raise funds for a party in Washington on May 27, Humphrey's sixtieth birthday. Some two hundred came, and cheered uproariously when the singer Edie Adams toasted the guest of honor: "Sixty—going on '72." But what impressed the Washington *Post* columnists Evans and Novak, mindful of Humphrey's past fund-raising problems, was that

> there was a half billion dollars in the room, and much of it carried a reserved-for-Humphrey label.
>
> He returns vounteered checks. He intends to enter the 1972 primaries late or not at all. But Muskie must enter and win, he must unlock the centrist money locked in by Humphrey.

As a candidate at that point, Humphrey was still wary, still holding back. And he told Dr. Berman that he had good reason to be:

> I'm not at all sure that I ought to be interested in any way in this presidential business. I've been around so long, and so many people have

analyzed and re-analyzed me, that there's very little left to look at that hasn't been exposed in its full nudity and at times ugliness.

This is not self-pity; it's just an honest evaluation. No man can be on the political scene in the front line of fire as long as I have and not get scarred and battered. I know it. It doesn't really make me happy. It's just one of those facts of life.

And he was right. No sooner had the polls established Humphrey as a contender again than the old animosities broke out and his old vulnerabilities—the identification with the war and Johnson—were exposed anew. "He was a swine in '68 and he's worse now," hissed the counter-culture's Hunter Thompson. He "should be put in a goddam bottle and sent out with the Japanese Current." Roused to vituperative fury at "the return from the graveyard of Hubert Humphrey," Pete Hamill wrote in the New York *Post:*

> He was apparently finished and behind us, a wormy artifact from a wormy year. He has returned, he is running, and it's not a joke: he can win the nomination.
>
> There was a time when Humphrey was a reasonably brave liberal politician, but he lost that somewhere along the line. It's possible to salute the record of his youth: all whores were once virgins. In the unlikely event that there were War Crimes trials in this country, Humphrey would be in the dock. The destination would not be 1600 Pennsylvania Avenue, it would be Leavenworth.

Humphrey not only shrugged off this savagery ("Rather cruel and tough, but I can take it," he wrote a friend), he seemed to think it might help him. Referring to certain New Yorkers, identified by an aide as "limousine liberals," who shared Hammill's disenchantment but recoiled from his language, Humphrey told the *New York Times:* "I know I'll have trouble with a very articulate, minute minority, which I consider an asset, not a liability, given the mood of the country." At this Columnist James Wechsler commented: "That translates: he's abandoned the hope of recapturing much of his one-time liberal constituency and now sees himself rallying the law-and-order legions and George Meany." And Wechsler warned that these liberals, especially the young, would be crucial to any Democratic nominee.

After the long ordeal over Vietnam, the event that followed was even more upsetting to Humphrey. Whatever hopes he had entertained that the U. S. public might forget about his links to the war and to Johnson were crushed when in June 1971, the Pentagon Papers, the secret history of the Vietnam intervention that Secretary McNamara ordered before leaving office, leaked to the press.

The hysterical reaction of the Nixon administration left the impression that the Republicans had a lot to lose by disclosure of these documents. It undertook a series of unlawful acts that began with the ransacking of the California home of Daniel Ellsberg, the suspected leaker, and led on to the break-in at the Watergate offices of the Democratic National Committee. But in the end, the papers convicted Democrats, not Republicans. They laid bare as never before the Johnson administration decisions to expand the war without admitting it. As vice president, Humphrey had shilled for Johnson. This man who now presumed to ask for the nation's trust and confidence once again, had not he shared in the deception too?

Humphrey's first response, at a press conference in St. Paul, was to deny that Johnson had deceived the country. But then he appeared to shift, and the actual dimensions of his contradictory position as Johnson's vice president began to come out publicly for the first time. What some knew and many suspected he now told the Baltimore *Sun*'s Philip Potter: "To tell the truth, I didn't have a helluva lot to say about things." He proceeded to give Potter permission to disclose for the first time that he had written a memorandum to Johnson opposing the president's crucial February 1965 decision to expand the air war to North Vietnam. And to Al Eisele of the St. Paul *Pioneer Press* he said: "I was informed about key Vietnam decisions [but] I've always said that when the decisions were made by the government it was my job as Vice President to support those decisions." Humphrey continued to insist that "everything that was harmful to my political life has already been said," yet troubling questions returned with painful new point. For the acknowledged inconsistencies of his actions now called attention to aspects of his nature that raised doubts about his capacity for independent decision and command. The Minneapolis *Star*, which had backed him in 1968 and 1970, resurrected these concerns and addressed them to 1972: "Humphrey's agony over the Pentagon Papers evokes more sorrow than anger, . . . He was the supersalesman of the Johnson 'peace' policy. It was his fear, many assume, of crossing Johnson that cost him the White House in 1968. The long shadow cast by the brooding, domineering, devious man in Texas seems able even now to dim Humphrey's future White House hopes."

Humphrey's answer—"I supported the president's policies because I sincerely believed and still do that his objective was peace through a negotiated settlement"—did not allay these misgivings. The truth was out, Vietnam was back on the front burner, and Humphrey appeared to accept his handicap: "I know some people won't forgive me for the war and for being with Johnson. I am not sure I forgive myself for that, but I have a right to grow and learn."

At this point Humphrey was for withdrawal from Vietnam, all the Democratic contenders were for withdrawal—and so, as evinced by the steadily diminishing U. S. troops there, was President Nixon. There was also disconcerting evidence that the president as incumbent could control the issues of political combat. Well before the end of 1971 he took action to shore up the country's shaky economy. By a sudden stroke he devalued the dollar, exactly as a Joint Economic Committee report had urged. To check the war-stoked fires of inflation he imposed an emergency wage-price freeze. This too conformed with a Humphrey recommendation, though when labor let out a howl and Emil Mazey of the United Auto Workers wrote: "With your usual overenthusiasm you blindly endorsed the freeze," Humphrey was happy to be able to say he was not responsible for the order. The president's action, he said, "was only part of what must be done—unemployment must be foremost in our mind." All the same, the President had wrecked Humphrey's strategy. Ruefully, Humphrey concluded: "Nixon is tough and has many resources at his command, including that valuable resource, surprise."

As late as September, Humphrey had thought to wait until the last big primary in California before entering the 1972 race. He began his preparations that month with an understated letter from Pennsylvania's former Governor George Leader informing fifty thousand Democrats he was available. In October the friends who had hailed Humphrey on his birthday met again at Minneapolis's Hotel Radisson East and pledged a cool $800,000 if he would run. His wife informed him: "Daddy, as long as I have to campaign for a Democrat for president, I'm sure I want you as my candidate."

Rocked by Nixon's surprises, Humphrey began to shed his studied patience. He took to traveling around the country to check on his rivals' progress and his own prospects. The familiar sounds of his barnstorming left the press in little doubt that the old campaigner was back on the trail and sprinting for his third go at the White House. Reporting his appearance at an Arkansas gathering, *Time* magazine noted his mod clothes and a new reddish hue to his black-tinted hair. *Newsweek* said he spoke at eighty miles an hour with gusts up to one hundred. Almost everywhere he went local leaders kept telling him they loved him but did not think he could win the nomination. Reluctantly—fighting primaries was an "ordeal" he told Eugenie Anderson— he decided he would have to abandon the waiting game. There was no choice but to bow to the spreading democratization of the party ordained by the McGovern reforms and battle the other eleven aspirants for a popular mandate. Back in the capital he declared on November 19: "Whoever gets the nomination will have to be in the primaries—a representative sampling of them."

It was late. Up to now his preparations had consisted chiefly of leisurely strategy sessions with Jack Chestnut and close friends in Washington. McGovern had been organizing for more than a year already. Muskie had commitments from sixteen senators and top Democrats in every state. Senator Henry Jackson of Washington had already assured himself of important backing in the labor movement that had gone to Humphrey in the past. Opening a headquarters in Washington, Humphrey wrote Eugenie Anderson:

> I know I'm not the new man on the scene, and many of the Democratic leaders are hungry for a new face even if there isn't much behind it.

I have a reservoir of good will and affection amongst many people. But it's one thing to know that and another to translate those emotions into solid political support.

I can't afford to have the organizational troubles we had in 1968. Everything depends on whether we can put together a good organization—without it, it's a hopeless task.

There simply was no time to pull together the people and money to implement the battle plan that Humphrey now set for himself—to run in fifteen primaries. Still, nobody else had made seven trips to California and lined up the party's best fund-raiser, Hollywood lawyer Eugene Wyman, to shake the money tree. Nobody else could count as many friends in Pennsylvania, where the Steelworkers stood ready to work for him again whatever George Meany and his AFL-CIO Executive Council might decide this time. And nobody else could, or would, go out and address fifteen meetings each day. Humphrey told Kampelman, who took charge of his speeches: "I think I have a better chance of bringing the party together than most of the rest of them. Scoop [Jackson] is a little too tough; the rest of them a little too soft. We've got to walk a very delicate and sensitive line but I think we can do it." A Gallup poll of Democratic voters released on December 26 encouraged him: Humphrey led the pack with 36 percent, outpacing Muskie (31 percent) for the first time.

The remaining days before Humphrey announced were frantic. A playing manager to the last, he peppered Chestnut with memos and messages: "We need to get aboard a top qualified woman leader, also a labor coordinator, a youth coordinator, an agricultural coordinator. . . . I talked with [Cleveland Millionaire] Joe Cole, [former California Governor] Pat Brown, [former Democratic chairman] John Bailey today. . . ." "I want you as my strong right arm, handling key people, following up letters, being on the telephone—and just being my alter ego," he told Kampelman. "We cannot wait any longer to get regional people—I talked to [West Virginia's former Governor] Hulett Smith, as good as any. Let's move," he told Chestnut. Finally, only three days after Muskie's formal launch, he went before the television cameras at the Poor Richard Club in Philadelphia. It was the place where the United States began—and the city where in 1948 his own national career began. With three famous black Minnesota Viking linemen standing behind him, Humphrey proclaimed that he was a candidate again—and this time, in contrast to 1968, "I'm going to take my campaign to the people." Indeed his slogan, also visible on the wall behind him as he spoke, was: "We the People." He roundly acknowledged that he had lost time and again before—but always came back to win the second time. The reception was mixed. "Disappointing," wrote fund-raiser Wyman in his diary.

Jack Chestnut said later that Humphrey's 1972 campaign was not ill-organized—"or he couldn't have kept a schedule three or four times as heavy as any other candidate." But the late switch and the need to prove popular appeal left little room for planning. Both Chestnut and Humphrey later acknowledged that too much of the organizational effort, and far too much of the money, were poured into the opening stages of the race. The Humphrey strategy was to preempt the center, and this required knocking Muskie, the favorite, out of the competition. Leaving McGovern to contest the New Hampshire primary on Muskie's own Yankee turf, the Humphrey team went all-out to beat Muskie in the Florida primary immediately thereafter. As it happened, Muskie hurt himself badly in New Hampshire when he lost his statesman's cool in public and wept at a local publisher's criticism of his wife. But Florida was Humphrey's first outing, and even though Alabama's Governor George Wallace, back in his spoiler's role, was certain to get the most votes, Humphrey felt he had to best the rest.

Declaring, "This is it for me. It's now or never. I've gotta go, go go," he campaigned in the state for twenty of the twenty-six days before the vote. Playing for black, Hispanic, and elderly votes, he stumped the beaches, walked the ghettoes, and ate knishes at the retirement condos of south Florida. By lavish television, radio, and newspaper ads he reached out to the Wallace following farther north, and some of the messages reached too far. One radio plug for the old battler for civil rights and foreign aid promised: "Humphrey will stop the flow of your tax dollars to those who chisel their way on to the welfare rolls through fraud. . . . Humphrey will spend tax dollars on Americans before sending them to foreigners."

"This isn't the Humphrey I'd have died for," protested his old friend Hy Bookbinder of the American Jewish Committee. Such trimming for racist votes, though Humphrey soon repudiated the ad, did not stop him from being engulfed by Wallace, who polled twice as many votes in the primary as anybody. Humphrey came in second, but the six delegates he won hardly repaid the prodigious effort and the $1.5 million expenditure—especially when the result, betraying the conservative middle-class mood on race in '72, signaled Nixon as the real winner.

A few days later, Nixon delivered a speech opposing compulsory busing of school children to achieve racial balance. Humphrey, asked for comment on his way to the next primary fight in Wisconsin, hailed the President for backing "the things that some of the rest of us have been trying to do." Once again Humphrey, who had waffled on the red-hot busing issue in Florida, seemed to be pulling back from his lifelong beliefs, because Nixon had called for a moratorium on such court-ordered busing. Like the Florida commercial, Humphrey's busing blurt, an "error" he attributed to not reading "the fine print" in the president's speech, persuaded many liberals that Humphrey was a horse who had gone to the well too often. "The trappings of a man who would rather be president than right," huffed the *New York Times*.

Wisconsin was next. Of all the fifty states, none was more consistently unrewarding to Humphrey. Though it shared his own state's record of hospitality to enlightened reform, when Humphrey needed its votes to make his

1960 race, Wisconsin had deserted him for the Eastern outlander John Kennedy. In 1968 when he tried again, Wisconsin preferred McCarthy in the spring and took Nixon over Humphrey in the fall. A legacy of Wisconsin's early readiness to experiment was its uniquely open primary: a voter had always been free to vote either ticket. The crossover option thus created— Republicans crossing over to vote in the Democratic contest—was Humphrey's bane. He always attributed his 1960 defeat to this, and he feared a repetition in 1972, this time by masses of Republicans crossing to give Democratic delegates to George Wallace.

As things turned out, he was right. But Wisconsin was also where organization paid off, and it was not Humphrey, denounced as the organization man in 1968, but the insurgent McGovern, who cashed in on it. With campaign teams in place more than a year in every county, with young volunteers manning phones and ringing doorbells, and with a strong core of leaders working the auto plants of Kenosha and the tool factories of Milwaukee, McGovern, as he himself said later, "organized rings around" the sketchy Humphreyites. Lacking either regular support or grassroots presence, Humphrey made a race of it by valiant personal effort. As Columnist James Kilpatrick reported:

> He starts at 7, popping like a cork from champagne. And he never stops bubbling. The effervescence has its drawbacks: he is promising too much, talking too much, pausing too seldom.
>
> But such wamrth and vitality evoke spontaneous response. He may be Golden Bantam corn, hot and buttered, right off the cob. But my goodness, he is honest corn. He is gee-whiz, by-gosh and by-golly.
>
> Accepting an invitation for a TV interview, he says: "Boy, I can use the free time." Before a Catholic school for the deaf he delivers a 20-minute speech that is a small gem of homespun inspiration. He talks to a hundred oldsters at a home for the elderly and a veteran TV newscaster is moved to tears.

The conservative Kilpatrick thought Humphrey might pull ahead. Not so. On April 5, as Humphrey feared, thousands of right-wing Republicans crossed over to Wallace. But the blue-collar voters in the factory towns and the Polish wards of Milwaukee gave Wisconsin to George McGovern. McGovern, not Humphrey, knocked the early front-runner Muskie out of the race. Wallace placed second. And Humphrey, outorganized, finished a discouraging third.

With Wisconsin, McGovern acquired a momentum that never abated. He sent out a huge mailing for help, and the outpouring of small contributions that flowed in enabled him to mount the campaign of a major contender. Humphrey carried Pennsylvania as expected, and he edged out McGovern in Ohio and Wallace in Indiana. But he lost Michigan and Maryland to Wallace.

The Humphrey effort had peaked. His campaign, having emptied its coffers early, had nothing left now to contest for New York and had to concede its 278 delegates to McGovern. The candidate himself had to break off in the midst of scheduled speeches and fly with his finance director, Harrison Dogole, to Manhattan and negotiate a $150,000 loan from a wealthy supporter to meet payroll, settle hotel bills, and pay for the campaign plane. After the narrow win in Ohio, Humphrey had to spend an entire day telephoning his friends around the country for emergency cash. New prospects were wary, and it was necessary to ask those who had already given to give more. In the process, Humphrey learned that his managers had quietly shelved plans to campaign in New York. "I was furious," he said later, "but they told me they just didn't have the money."

As Humphrey and McGovern started for the showdown primary in California, *Newsweek* magazine projected McGovern with 900 delegates on the first ballot at Miami, and Humphey at 760, with 1509 needed to win. Thus if Humphrey captured California, the balance might yet tip to him. It was a gamble, but Humphrey, his aides chorused, was "a strong finisher." Asked whether he might, if he ran second, claim a share of the delegates under the new rules, Humphrey dismissed the possibility as the act of a spoilsport. In California it was winner-take-all. To his leading labor backer, the Steelworkers' I. W. Abel, he wrote: "California is the Superbowl of Democratic politics. If we win, we go on to win in Miami. If we lose, that will be like falling in a ditch with a bulldozer filling it in."

High as the stakes were, Humphrey now ran low on both money and organization. But McGovern, offering himself as a voice for change, had given the old scrapper some issues to fight on. To raise them was to put Humphrey on the side of the status quo, of big business, of the military-industrial complex. But Chestnut and Kampelman insisted that California, having elected Ronald Reagan governor, was a "moderate" state, filled with defense plants and dead-set against change. Lacking funds to counter McGovern's expected media blitz and door-to-door volunteer onslaught, they urged carrying the fight to the new front-runner. Humphrey, who had given his staff "strict instructions not to attack McGovern personally—he's my friend and I'm proud of his success," now agreed with his advisers that to carry California he would have to throw some hard punches.

Arriving in Los Angeles he at once challenged McGovern to debate. Rushing out to a Lockheed aerospace plant at Palmdale, he told workers at their lunch break that he, unlike McGovern, had voted for the Space Shuttle. "Proud" to have cast the deciding vote for the $200 million loan to rescue Lockheed from insolvency, he was also "proud to have played a role in protecting your jobs." He charged that a McGovern proposal to replace the welfare program with a one-thousand-dollar income supplement for everybody would empty the federal treasury. "I'll be damned if I'm giving everybody in the country a thousand-dollar bill," he shouted. "People in this country want jobs, not handouts."

McGovern accepted the debate challenge, and each of the three networks offered the free time Humphrey's managers hoped for. But this, Gene Wyman wrote in his diary, was "the only bright spot" in a grim week. On May 24, Wyman faced an excruciating decision: whether to use the $200,000 he had raised locally for television and get-out-the-vote commitments in the California climax—or send it back to Washington, where national headquarters faced a $317,000 overdraft. As Wyman wrote a few days later:

> We asked for an appointment to see the senator.
>
> At 9 at breakfast in the Beverly Hilton Ted Rogers pulled me aside and told me that if I did not give him $900 immediately the plane would not take off on a campaign hop. I wrote the check, I was then advised that unless $16,000 was wired to Washington today, the telephones would be shut off. I wired the $16,000.
>
> At 1 P.M. I spoke to Dwayne [Andreas]. He said he made at least 19 phone calls, all without success.
>
> At 2 the senator arrived . . . Jack Chestnut detailed our plight. The senator sat calmly and listened without expression. Without hesitation he commented that our principal duty was to meet the overdrafts. Even if it broke us here in California, we had to do it. He said that he would never quit. If necessary, he would win in this campaign on free time in the debates.

Wyman gritted his teeth and sent California's money east to pay Washington's bills.

The campaign rolled toward its climax without Humphrey television spots and without the get-out-the-vote drive. While McGovern limited himself to careful studio television appearances with individual workers and housewives, and gave thoughtful interviews to the news people who interpreted him to the public, Humphrey, too rushed to see reporters, dashed about addressing small crowds of blacks, chicanos, and oldsters, and cut a less-than-imposing figure when the evening newscasts pictured his perspiring, gesticulating old-school oratory. Instead of resting before the first debate, Humphrey worked the telephones trying vainly to get the support of Martin Luther King, Jr.,'s widow, Coretta, and the United Farm Workers' Cesar Chavez, both of whom wound up endorsing McGovern. Then he went off to a noisy sixty-first birthday party at Disneyland.

The press, though anything but sympathetic to him, conceded that Humphrey won the first debate. He was incisive and commanding as he ripped into McGovern's proposed defense cuts as "reckless" and ridiculed the thousand-dollars-for-everybody alternative to the welfare system as "preposterous." He warned that the income supplement scheme could cost $72 billion. These were heavy shots, and McGovern tried lamely to explain that his thousand-dollar figure referred to a proposal of the National Welfare Rights Organization that he had introduced in the Senate "to provoke discussion." But Humphrey, irked by the slick McGovern slogan "Right from the Start," made the mistake of bringing up Vietnam. It was quite true that McGovern had not opposed the war from the outset. Indeed, on February 17, 1965, the very day Humphrey was secretly protesting to President Johnson against starting air attacks on North Vietnam, McGovern had made a Senate speech praising Johnson's "restraint." But Humphrey had given McGovern the opening, and in reply McGovern struck back with what Columnist Tom Wicker called "the single most devastating blow" of the debate. He simply recited the effusive description of the Vietnam war that Humphrey had intoned for the Americans in the Saigon embassy compound in 1967: "Our greatest adventure—and a wonderful thing it is."

There were three more debates, and in each of them Humphrey tore gaping holes in McGovern's ill-considered welfare and tax reforms. Commentators with a taste for paradox observed that in this campaign it was McGovern who had the ideas, whereas Humphrey, the idea man, had none. And McGovern, after his defeat, wrote of the "destructive" California debates. For by his hammering assaults, Humphrey, exposing the inadequacies and inconsistencies of the bold McGovern tax, defense, and welfare proposals, raised doubts far beyond California about his rival's soundness—and the Republicans exploited them to crush him that fall.

But Hubert Humphrey was not the master of events. Once again Richard Nixon moved in, and with a mind to ending what had grown to be America's longest war, went beyond anything countenanced by his predecessors and ordered the mining of Haiphong, the harbor through which war supplies flowed to North Vietnam from Russia. Among California's frightened and infuriated Democrats, Vietnam was back, to Humphrey's woe, on the front burner.

Shortly afterward the Field poll came out showing Humphrey twenty points behind McGovern. "Unbelievable," Humphrey cried. Of course the numbers were the lead story that night on Walter Cronkite's TV news. The Los Angeles *Times* headlined: "McGovern Appears Near Big Primary Victory." Wyman wrote: "Our campaign slowed to a walk. The momentum of the first debates faded. Many commitments that had been given to me were not fulfilled. Morale dropped, and we all became somewhat despondent. From Thursday on, whenever Senator Humphrey was mentioned, it was always, 'Humphrey, who is trailing Senator McGovern by twenty points.' " The rest was anti-climax. By court order the fourth and final debate was widened to include the minor candidates, and the drama dissipated. On June 6, Humphrey lost California—not by twenty points but by the narrow margin of 5 percent. A shift of eighty thousand votes would have put him on top. "If we had had our media allocation of $150,000, the results would have been different," Humphrey wrote Eugenie Anderson.

Even after California, Humphrey did not give up. At a Washington meeting his chief delegate hunter Mike Maloney reported that McGovern was still several hundred votes shy and could not make it. Joining the Jackson and Muskie remnants in an ABM—Anybody but McGovern—movement, Humphrey swallowed his words about "spoilsport" and asked the Credentials Committee for a proportionate share of the California delegates. The committee accepted the appeal, but Humphreyite hopes were short-lived. On convention eve, Chairman O'Brien, ruling that the 120 undisputed McGovern delegates from California could vote on the committee's recommendation, gave the McGovern forces votes enough on the floor to assure victory. Weeping, Humphrey announced his withdrawal from the race. McGovern then won nomination on the first ballot.

McGovern proceeded to run into trouble when he picked Senator Thomas Eagleton of Missouri to run with him for vice president, only to discover that Eagleton had a record of mental illness. After vainly trying to get Edward Kennedy as a replacement, McGovern asked Humphrey to be his No. 2. The invitation was more than Humphrey ould bear. Declining, he told McGovern: "I just can't take the ridicule any more. You know that if I take that nomination, they'll just say: 'There goes old Hubert over the track again. He just can't resist running.' "

Ernest Furgurson of the Baltimore *Sun* commented: "He was, it is true, the easiest politician in recent times to deride and make fun of. He was also the easiest to love, for the simple reason that he himself was full of love. You might say he based his whole career on it."

In an interview, Humphrey confessed that the presidency "was a tremendous goal in my life, one that I'm not going to achieve. Errors cost the nomination. I can't help but remember that I got more votes in the primaries than anybody else [3,807,726 to McGovern's 3,583,667]. I can't help but feel I could have done better. To be honest about it, I was more disappointed in losing the nomination this year that I was in losing the election in 1968."

After the California loss, Roger Kent, one of Humphrey's most steadfast friends, a progressive San Francisco lawyer who had wavered in his loyalty only when the vice president went overboard for the Vietnam war, wrote Humphrey:

> Somehow a false picture of you emerged. In spite of your fantastic drive, energy and stamina, which were on view every day, people still talked of you as a tired old representative of the establishment. I cannot understand such widespread feeling but it was there.
>
> In my view it probably stemmed more than anything from your close and loyal association with Johnson. Unfortunately, a lot of Johnson rubbed off on you, and that was the critical poison.

In the wake of the Pentagon Papers revelations, a correspondent had asked Humphrey if he thought he would ever escape the unpopularity of Lyndon Johnson. "Never," Humphrey exclaimed. In the bitter hour of defeat, Humphrey, appearing to acknowledge that subservience to Johnson had cost him the "tremendous goal in my life," wrote Kent: "It is not easy for me to accept the analysis that you have given but I am afraid that it is true." Then he added: "There is a mood in the country—a mood of resentment, of change. There is little sense of direction. That's what I had hoped that I might give the country. I shall keep at it—regrettably, not from the vantage point of the White House. But I will keep pounding away at what I believe is right from the rostrum of the Senate. I'll be damned if defeat is going to shut me up. I have something to say, and I'm going to say it even if no one will listen."

37

The Money
Problem

I F there is one theme that runs like a red thread through Humphrey's auto-biography, *The Education of a Public Man*, it is a plaint about money—not hunger for money but simply the lack of it. For much of his life he was short of money to live on, and his relentless drive to attain the White House seemed at times like one long, losing struggle to raise enough campaign funds to get there. It was Humphrey's misfortune to run for the prize in the years when campaign spending reached such levels that it exploded in scandal and crime. He never transgressed the law as Nixon did, but was soiled nonetheless by the corrupting demands for the huge electioneering sums that only the biggest givers seemed able to provide. Subtly but perceptibly his own notions about money changed. The prairie Progressive who had once excoriated bankers for their grasping foreclosures stopped make speeches exposing the loopholes through which the rich avoided their taxes and grew not only tolerant of but comfortable with great wealth.

In his early years he had been so poor that he swabbed toilets, sold five-cent sandwiches made by his wife to fellow students, and often had to borrow to meet bills. When he arrived in Washington as senator in 1949 his furniture sat in the van for two days until his father in South Dakota could send funds to get the stuff unloaded. Thereafter the only way he could make ends meet was by accepting out-of-town speaking engagements for fees.

Labor unions and small businessmen provided the bulk of his campaign contributions in the early years, and members of the Jewish community were also generous with their gifts. A loan from Morris Ebin of Minneapolis had helped him finance the house he bought in Chevy Chase when he arrived in Washington, and another Minneapolis friend, Ray Ewald, sold him (for a giveaway two hundred dollars) the Lake Waverly plot west of the Twin Cities on which he built a second home in the 1950s. Two other friends, Bill Benton and Dwayne Andreas, took care of the expense of educating his sons at the Shattuck military academy in Minnesota.

Finding funds for the Waverly house, which he built from plans for Lyndon Johnson's Texas ranch guesthouse, strained Humphrey's finances. He told his accountant Darrell DeVilliers it left him "flat," and he had to borrow money from Freddie Gates and other friends to furnish it. "I had a tough summer until I started to earn money [by making speeches] in the fall," he wrote.

In 1959 when his income from speechmaking rose to $27,648, he still had to ask for an extension on paying his income tax ("Jail, jail, jail," he fumed to his secretary Vi Williams), and wrote DeVilliers: "If anyone asks you how a man in public life acts, just reply: 'Like a damn fool, particularly when it comes to his personal affairs.' This statement characterizes the way I treat my personal business." He had an even tougher time in 1960 when Kennedy wealth overpowered him in the presidential primaries, because the campaigning left no time to go out speaking for fees. He was dismayed at an "unbelievable" $225 boost in his local taxes at Waverly and heard that someone in the county assessor's office had said "Humphrey is rich, so why not?" Humphrey was so incensed that he called on his friend Gates in Minneapolis to rush to the courthouse and protest.

Throughout these years, Humphrey's income tax returns looked like those of any other harassed middle-class striver—deductions for getting children's teeth straightened, interest on home mortgages, and travel expenses. He had bought some government bonds and picked up a scattering of stocks, and when in 1964 a public statement of his assets seemed called for, his aides Bill Connell and Norman Sherman thought it needed to be padded upward. Humphrey's wealth (far below that of the other candidates, Johnson, Goldwater, and Republican vice-presidential nominee William Miller) totaled $171,396 net assets. These consisted of a $36,000 equity in his Chevy Chase house, $28,000 in the Waverly property, a $3,900 share in the family drugstore at Huron, and what the New York *Journal American* described as a "helter-skelter list" of securities adding up to some $40,000.

Then Humphrey took office as vice president, and everything changed. His life-style rose dramatically as, at Johnson's orders, he started shuttling around the country addressing fatcat contributors to the President's Club and currying favor with corporate executives. He sold his Chevy Chase tract house and bought a fancy cooperative apartment in downtown Washington. Also, following Johnson's example, on January 15, 1965, he placed his stocks and bonds, by then worth some $80,000, in a blind trust and appointed Dwayne Andreas—"the one man of wealth who had been closer to me and more generous than any other in my life"—as trustee. From the money-making standpoint, handing over his assets to Andreas turned out to be a smart move. The following year, Humphrey wrote DeVilliers: "When I saw the staggering figure of over $100,000 for 1965 I could not imagine where all that income came from." DeVilliers, saying he too was "staggered," listed it for the vice president:

Salary	40,730
Book and article royalties	24,733
Trust income ("also a surprise")*	7,500
Fiduciary income	6,484
Personal interest income	4,253
Net long-term capital gain	875
Dividends	344
Unexpended expense-account funds (from V.P.'s regular expense fund)	1309
	$81,618

That was before exclusions, and DeVilliers added: "With exclusions and expenses this figure reconciles with the total income of $76,789 reported on federal income tax return."

The following year, though as vice president Humphrey could no longer speak for fees, his income rose to $93,513, including $22,318 income from the blind trust; in 1967 trust income amounted to $25,927—a third of his total income. This requires explanation. In managing Humphrey's trust, Andreas took the advice of his Republican friend and lawyer Thomas E. Dewey, and instead of handling Humphrey's money separately pooled it with other Andreas family trusts in an entity called the Mutual Income Fund. In 1965, Andreas was invited into Archer-Daniels-Midland, the giant Minneapolis agribusiness firm, which was then ailing. Andreas acquired a 10 percent interest and in 1966 took control. Thereafter something like half of Mutual Income Fund assets were invested in A-D-M stock, which rose phenomenally under Andreas's astute management.

When Humphrey ceased to be vice president, he made an important decision. Out of public life for the moment, he was in a position for the first time to earn substantial sums of money. Besides drawing a large salary and a sizeable expense account from Benton's Encyclopedia Britannica enterprises, he was free to accept pay for speaking, writing, and teaching. The blind trust was performing strongly and though he no longer had to give thought to possible conflicts of interest, he decided to leave things, as before, in Andreas's skillful hands.

---

*The comment is DeVilliers'.

From that time on, as the commingled fund grew (the A-D-M stock alone increased twelvefold in value over the next decade), Humphrey's piece of the golden pie grew proportionately. It grew so fast that, like Andreas himself, he began setting up trust funds for his children and grandchildren and transferring to them annual gifts up to the maximum tax-free limit of $3,000 per year. Within a few years these trusts grew to be quite substantial, those for the children from $100,000 to $200,000. His own trust grew more slowly, partly because of these annual transfers but also because he tapped the trust to meet some heavy expenses. In 1975 he withdrew $240,000 to pay taxes and penalties after the Internal Revenue Service decided he had not been entitled to take $199,000 deductions over the years 1969–73 for donating his vice-presidential papers to the Minnesota Historical Society. Humphrey dipped into the blind trust a second time in December 1971 when he withdrew and sold 2,500 shares of A-D-M stock and contributed the $110,000 realized to his 1972 presidential campaign chest. He drew on it again in 1974 to purchase title to fourteen acres of land surrounding his Waverly house that Andreas, through the Andreas Foundation, had acquired in 1965. There were other withdrawals to make payments on the $59,000 mortgage on his Washington apartment and later for medical bills.

The Hubert H. Humphrey trust remained blind to the end. Until the day of his death, Andreas said later, Humphrey never knew how much money was in it. His style was to ask Andreas if he had "enough" to cover this outlay or that, and Andreas would answer: "You have enough." During his 1976 reelection campaign in Minnesota, Humphrey's lawyers drew up a disclosure of his net worth for public release. At that time his share of the Mutual Income Fund was given a value of $388,000. By the time of his death eighteen months later, however, the Mutual Income Fund, including trusts for some eighty-eight persons, had grown to a value of well in excess of $100 million. Humphrey's share was about 1½ percent of the pie—or roughly $500,000. This was exclusive of the sums he had transferred over the years to his four children and ten grandchildren, and exclusive also of the proceeds—close to a million dollars—of sale after his death of the Waverly estate and the Washington apartment.

Humphrey died, after all, a rich man.

OF COURSE influence often translated into money in the Washington world, and while Humphrey helped people, they sometimes took advantage of his helpfulness. Through twenty-two years and four terms in this environment, Humphrey cultivated and enjoyed the reputation among his constituents as "the senator who gets things done for Minnesota." Ironically, some of the things of which he was so proud came back to plague him later, especially when he ran for president.

In one extremely embarrassing case, Herbert Waters, for six years his administrative aide and campaign manager, had to resign a position in 1967 as assistant administrator of the Agency for International Development. President Kennedy had named Waters to this key foreign-aid post at Humphrey's behest. The resignation, which was requested, was handled with great reserve. The official charge was that three Waters aides had accepted gratuities, including the favors of women, from a Belgian firm that held a $2.8 million AID contract.

A second case involved Napco Inc. of Minneapolis and Max Kampelman, Humphrey's legislative counsel before entering private practice in Washington in 1955. Napco's president, Max Rappaport, began negotiations in 1959 for establishment of a firm that would buy the plant and equipment of the Detroit Bevel Gear Co., a Napco subsidiary, ship it to India, and establish a gear works there. Humphrey was a great friend of India, and Rappaport had been a financial contributor to Minnesota's DFL party. So when Napco, with Kampelman as its Washington counsel, sought an AID loan to finance the purchase, Humphrey wrote identical letters to the AID administrator, the chairman of the Export-Import Bank, the assistant secretary of the treasury, the undersecretary of state, and the director of the Development Loan Fund, all of whom had a voice in the decision. His purpose, he said, was "to bring to your attention my interest in the Napco loan that will shortly be presented to the board of directors of the Development Loan Fund." He added. "I am not in a position to appraise the economic justification of the project, but I am in a position to say that the American businessmen who are participating in it are reputable constituents of mine in Minnesota." He wrote Ambassador Kenneth Galbraith that Rappaport was traveling to New Delhi, and that "our mutual friend" Kampelman might be with him. He followed this up with a letter to Galbraith, saying that Rappaport had departed and asking Galbraith to help him. Six months later, when things seemed to bog down, he cabled the New Delhi embassy: "Would appreciate your personal inquiry on status of collaborating agreement Napco Bevel Gear of India. AID loan already granted requiring final approval of Indian government. Napco, my constituents and friends cannot understand delay. Project important to Indian defense and economy particularly considering present crisis [with China]. Thank you." When Humphrey wrote congratulating Rappaport on Napco's increased sales and profits as reported in a newspaper article, Rappaport replied: "Our team of Napco experts has just returned from their trip to India where our project seems to be progressing satisfactorily, so all seems to be falling into place nicely here. I certainly hope the same is true for you."

The joint Indian-Napco venture foundered. One result was that when President Johnson in 1967 nominated Kampelman to be chairman of the new District of Columbia city council, that is, mayor of Washington, Republicans attacked the Napco deal as a foreign-aid "bungle" and criticized Kampelman's role as director of the parent firm. Kampelman withdrew as candidate for the city council job, and Walter Mondale, assuming direction of Humphrey's 1968 campaign, insisted that Kampelman be kept in the background throughout the campaign.

Still another case was that of the Universal Fiberglas Co. of Two Harbors, Minnesota, which received a $13.3 million government contract in 1965 for producing three-wheel "Mailster" trucks for the Post Office department. To Humphrey, an unflagging advocate of small business, it seemed a timely opportunity to create jobs in a small town hard hit by the closedown of iron-ore mining. The Humphrey aide most directly involved was Neal Peterson, who had been Humphrey's nominee to the Senate Small Business Committee staff. Republicans condemned this contract as "boondoggling" and charged that political meddling led to its award. At the outset, Humphrey wrote two letters to the SBA's regional director in Minneapolis urging him to "start working" on Universal's application for a loan "as soon as possible." Universal got its first loan, and when it sought to bid on the Mailster contract, Humphrey wrote Bernard Boutin, General Services administrator, asking postponement of bids until Universal, "advised late of the availability of this procurement," could have time to bid. Universal submitted the low bid but the GSA, after a survey, recommended against an award to the Minnesota firm. At this point two meetings occurred at the GSA at which Peterson represented Humphrey. One month later Small Business Administrator Eugene Foley, another Humphreyite, overruled a contrary field-staff recommendation and issued a "certificate of competency" that enabled Universal to get the job.

The deal went sour. Universal ran into trouble with production and shut down after building fewer than a third of the promised 12,714 Mailsters. The Republicans lambasted the affair as a fiasco, and Congressman Charles Gross of Iowa criticized Peterson's role on grounds that his brother, a Minneapolis lawyer, was working for Universal.

Asked point-blank about these cases at a publishers' dinner by the Minneapolis *Tribune*'s John Cowles, Jr., Humphrey roundly defended all four aides. As senator, he said, he worked for his constituents and would do anything legally possible to help them. He implied that his aides had been helping Minnesota in the same way. But Mrs. Katharine Graham of the Washington *Post*, taking exception to Humphrey's defense of his aides, said her staff had looked into each of the cases. She said the actions of Humphrey's associates raised troubling doubts, and the vice president's loyalty to these men was a bit extreme. Later both newspapers ended up endorsing the Humphrey presidential candidacy. But others pointed to these cases as examples of how Humphrey's staff, advisers, and friends had used him for years without his knowledge.

Four years later, Humphrey, his staff, and his friends were caught up in the hot blast of the Watergate firestorm. One of the first names to hit the headlines after the scandal broke was that of his friend Andreas. It came out that funds used by the White House aides who broke into Democratic National

Committee headquarters at the Watergate included a twenty-five thousand dollar check contributed to the Committee to Reelect the President by Andreas. Humphrey should not have been surprised because Andreas, a great friend also of Republican Tom Dewey, was one of a number of politico-business-men identified at the time as "swingers": men who hedged by contributing to both sides. But Humphrey was hurt, as he acknowledged afterward to Orville Freeman.

Two attorneys general and thirteen White House aides went to jail, and seventeen others, including the President, resigned as the result of the Watergate investigation. Inevitably, what the Senate committee learned about improper Republican campaign practices led to scrutiny also of Democratic fund raising. On June 17, 1973, the committee subpoenaed Humphrey's 1972 campaign records.

First, the committee's minority staff found out that Humphrey's campaign manager Jack Chestnut, like his Republican counterpart Maurice Stans, had destroyed all records of contributions before April 7, the date a new law took effect requiring, among other things, that candidates report all contributions to the General Accounting Office. When they looked at post-April 7 records, two items leaped to their attention. The first concerned Humphrey's old friend John Loeb of Loeb, Rhoades, the New York investment banking firm. At Humphrey's specific request, he had come to his aid when the campaign suffered a sudden cash shortage. Finding checks for five thousand dollars apiece from nine Loeb employees, the investigators quickly established that Loeb had supplied the funds for his subordinates' contributions, which was contrary to the new law. Loeb's only defense was that he was not up on the new law and had simply acted as in 1968, when he raised a lot of money for Humphrey and no questions were asked. He pleaded no contest and paid a three thousand dollar fine.

The second item took longer to unravel. It involved the so-called milk funds that had already entangled John Mitchell, John Connally, and several other Nixon stalwarts. In the 1970s two or three large dairy cooperatives, anxious to persuade the government to raise milk-price supports, made large contributions to the Nixon campaign and had the satisfaction of seeing the administration lift prices soon afterward. Checking, the senate investigators found that Associated Milk Producers Inc. (AMPI), largest of the co-ops, had made donations to Humphrey too. That was hardly surprising, since Humphrey had worked hard in the Senate ever since 1949 for high milk-price supports.

But the committee's findings drew a picture of links between AMPI and Humphrey aides that appeared far from casual. After Humphrey left office in 1969 two of his aides, Bill Connell and Ted Van Dyk, became consultants to the company. In 1970, Connell recommended that Jack Chestnut, the young lawyer organizing Humphrey's Senate comeback campaign, be retained to handle AMPI's legal business in Minnesota. Still another Humphreyite,

Norman Sherman, had formed a Minneapolis company Valentine-Sherman Associates to supply computerized voter lists to political candidates. Chestnut, impressed by Valentine-Sherman's work in the 1970 campaign, decided to hire them to work up lists in other states when he took charge of Humphrey's race for the presidency in 1972. His plan: get AMPI to pay for Valentine-Sherman's part in the campaign.

Like the labor unions, AMPI had its own political action fund, called TAPE, which raised voluntary contributions from members and could make donations lawfully to political candidates. But the cooperative's officers, anxious to conceal help to Democrats while making their pitch for aid from a Republican administration, chose to funnel their aid to Humphrey by direct but unreported contributions. Accordingly, AMPI's checks went directly to pay the Humphrey campaign's obligations to Valentine-Sherman. Though Valentine-Sherman tried to help by drawing up false invoices for their services, the Watergate investigators had little trouble establishing that AMPI's $82,000 checks to Valentine-Sherman were a corporate contribution and therefore unlawful. They also found Chestnut's memos setting up the deal. Brought before the committee, Chestnut pleaded the Fifth Amendment and declined answer to all questions. He was tried, convicted, and in 1974 sentenced to four months in prison. Sherman, tried separately, was fined $500.

Documentation of Humphrey's pre–April 7 fund-raising efforts had been destroyed, but during the Florida primary his office had issued what it claimed was a record of all contributions received up to mid-March. When the Watergate investigators persisted in asking where Humphrey got funds to launch his campaign in the first place, his lawyers reluctantly came forward with the answer. And that was when it came out that in December 1971, to provide funds to support his last-minute decision to enter the primaries, Humphrey had tapped his blind trust and contributed a sum totaling $116,000 to Humphrey for President committees. At the same time, to assure Humphrey a running start, Andreas, his daughter, and a friend of the daughter had sold blocks of A-D-M stock that added a further $348,000 for the Humphrey treasury. When asked about all this, Humphrey made a great show of protesting that he was perfectly entitled to spend his own money on his campaign—but of course that still did not answer the question why he or his helpers omitted the gifts from the March campaign statement.

Although 1972 campaign abuses were supposed to be the subject of inquiry, the Watergate committee did not hesitate to look back at 1968, especially when it found that all or part of a 1968 Howard Hughes contribution to Nixon had lodged mysteriously ever since in a safe belonging to Nixon's great friend, Bebe Rebozo. In the midst of the outcry over the Nixon money, a Hughes aide, Robert Maheu, asserted that he had given Humphrey fifty thousand dollars in cash during the 1968 campaign. When Humphrey denied recalling any such gift, Maheu testified in a Nevada court that on July 31, 1968, as Humphrey was leaving Los Angeles's Century Plaza Hotel after a rally, he jumped into the vice president's limousine and left a briefcase with the cash at Humphrey's feet. Humphrey carefully refrained from denying that a contribution from Hughes might somehow have found its way into his campaign chest. And indeed, on April 25, 1968, Hughes wrote Humphrey asking his help in getting nuclear tests stopped near his residence in Las Vegas. The Watergate investigators duly put in the record Maheu's hand-written notes of a July 31, 1968, meeting with Hughes' associate Bill Gay:

> "$25,000　　Kennedy
> 50,000　　Nixon
> 50,000　　Humphrey"

and a canceled check dated June 27, 1968, to Robert Maheu Associated signed Howard Hughes, along with a Maheu note marked "received for non-deduct-ible contributions." Although a "smoking gun" was not found, it seems a fair assumption that the Hughes contribution, like many another in the free and easy days when presidential candidates were not obliged to report individual gifts, reached the Humphrey campaign treasury.

Humphrey was greatly upset by the Watergate fallout that hit him. "I've been embarrassed to tears by the revelations of the milk fund," he wrote Denver publisher Palmer Hoyt. Later he said bitterly: "There's no way you can live this kind of thing down." Only one of the Watergate committee's twenty-five volumes of findings had much to say about Humphrey; his lawyers obtained an advance text of that one and got any slight suggestion that he was a party to wrongdoing removed. It was highly unlikely that Humphrey knew anything about the milk-fund hanky-panky, and as for being influenced, as he told Hoyt: "I didn't need that. I've been for 90 percent of parity since 1949." On receiving his first milk-fund contributions in 1968, his first thought, he said later, was: "The dairy farmers in politics? It's like getting money from church."

But Humphrey was not innocent. In his 1968 campaign diary, Edgar Berman recorded a moment when Pat O'Connor, treasurer of several Humphrey fund-raising committees, bustled into the vice president's presence and pulled out a huge roll of bills, and Humphrey said: "I don't want you to bring cash contributions to me." He detested soliciting campaign funds, but he did it. He tried to avoid accepting them, but he did that too. He told Hoyt: "Clean up the whole business of campaign financing—that's what I've been trying to do for the last three years. I was one of the first to advocate that we have a checkoff on our income tax [to establish] public financing." After Watergate he told interviewers: "Campaign financing is a curse. It's the most disgusting, demeaning, disenchanting, debilitating experience of a politician's life. It's stinky. It's lousy. I just can't tell you how much I hate it." But as he added: "When you are desperate, there are things you just have to do."

The red thread of money persisted. When various corporations began owning up to unlawful contributions, Humphrey's name was usually on the list—Gulf Oil, Ashland Oil, American Airlines, and so on. As a rule he got less. A typical example was Minnesota Manufacturing and Mining, one of the biggest corporations in his home state. Three M's illegal benefactions went on for a decade and were so flagrant that in the aftermath of Watergate they forced the resignation of the company's chairman, Harry Heltzer. Of Three M's unlawful $635,000, Humphrey received $1,200, the rest went to Republicans. In 1978 when the gaudy doings of the Korean importer-exporter Tongsun Park made headlines, Humphrey's name popped up again. Park bribed several House members to win contracts to export rice to Korea, and one congressman was convicted and went to jail. But several lists of Washington figures were found in the course of the investigation, and Humphrey's name appeared on a list with some mysterious numbers after it. Members of the Senate Ethics Committee decided they had no choice but to look into the matter. By then Humphrey was dying of cancer, too ill to be interviewed, but the senators learned that Park had been keeping company with Humphrey's niece and had given $10,000 to Humphrey's 1972 campaign so that the niece could fly west and help out in the California primary battle. The senators concluded that there was no evidence that Humphrey knew of the contribution or that he ever helped the Korean land contracts.

The senators all liked Humphrey—as who did not? Their view was that he always had money troubles and would take campaign contributions from anybody, giving little thought to where it came from. He was the kind of man who assumed that nobody he knew had bad motives. And these were the sort of considerations that were in the minds of Humphrey's colleagues at the time the unusual honors were paid him near the end of his life. When, after he suddenly withdrew from his last bid for the White House in 1976, and Congress then voted him "presidential perks" (money, chauffeured limousine, and the rest), it was not a tribute to a visionary and reformer but a recognition of Humphrey as one of their own. The question, profoundly pertinent to Progressivism's lack of staying power, is whether he could have done the good things without becoming one of the boys.

38

The Last Campaign

T H E debacle of his 1972 defeat at the hands of his former protégé George McGovern was not the end for Humphrey. Having gone down for the third time, he yet would bob back to the surface—once again in the presidential swim. But that came several years later and was far from his thoughts as he wrote Lyndon Johnson in disgust after getting steam-rolled by the practitioners of the New Politics at the Miami convention: "Many who were on the outside raising hell in 1968 were on the inside running things—and I have to hand it to them. They sure know how to use the old politics of power." While privately viewing McGovern's election prospects as "catastrophic," he went to bat for his vanquisher, sent out three hundred thousand letters for McGovern, and spoke up and down the land for his candidacy. When one Ida Larson of Fairmont, Minnesota, protested that "you have turned traitor and backed the soundrel you so ably denounced earlier," he replied mildly: "My disagreements with Senator McGovern are small compared with [my disagreements with] Mr. Nixon."

He took time to help his son Skip, now thirty and standing for state senator from a Minneapolis suburb. He wrote out instructions in longhand:

> Tie yourself to Mondale—for example, your ad copy should read: "Vote for two good senators—Hubert H. (Skip) Humphrey, state senator; Walter F. Mondale, U.S. senator.

You and your committee pick the date for the final door-knocking and Mom and I will put on the party that day or night to thank your helpers. And I want to go with you to shopping centers. Mom can do the same. . . .

In November, while McGovern was losing every state except Massachusetts, Skip won his race, and the DFL captured control of the state legislature for the first time since Humphrey led it.

In January 1973, President Johnson died. Publicly, Humphrey lauded him for his domestic achievements ("a leader who struggled to bring dignity and hope to all the American people"). Privately, he set forth his defense of Johnson's war policy in a letter to his friend, the retired banker William Biggs: "Had we not gone into Vietnam we would see today Indonesia in the hands of the Communist party, and surely all of Southeast Asia would have been taken over by the North Vietnamese Communist forces." But for America the war that had divided the nation and split Humphrey away from his liberal friends was over, and when the Senate convened, Humphrey had the profound satisfaction of being re-admitted to the Foreign Relations Committee. He was on especially good terms with Secretary of State Henry Kissinger, remarking that had he won in 1968 he would have appointed Kissinger, as Nixon did, national security adviser. He backed Kissinger on East-West détente, and Kissinger backed Humphrey's proposals for expanding the Food for Peace program through the Third World. He continued to speak out for disarmament, opposing the deployment of anti-ballistic missiles, and trying, unsuccessfully, to keep the Pentagon from placing multiple warheads on U. S. missiles until the administration had first tried to negotiate an end to the arms race. Given the chairmanship of the subcommittee on foreign assistance, he threw himself into redrafting the aid program to help uncommitted as well as allied nations.

But 1973 was not Humphrey's year. The Watergate fires that engulfed the Republicans showered sparks on Democratic rooftops, too, the most prominent of which was Humphrey's. The smoke that curled up at once after the Senate committee subpoenaed Humphrey's campaign records at the Republican minority's behest only added to the general public revulsion at Washington politicians and their fund-raising tricks. Humphrey, the ever accessible senator, retreated almost as much as Richard Nixon into defensive huddles with lawyers as he maneuvered to keep the flames from enveloping him. His aide David Gartner later remarked that the stress Humphrey felt in these unhappy months was exceeded only by what he underwent when torn between the president and his liberal friends at the height of the 1968 campaign.

During the fending off of Watergate fires, Humphrey went to Bethesda for one of his biannual checkups—and ran into a more serious problem. For the first time tissue samples extracted from his bladder suggested to Dr. Berman the presence of cancer. One of the tiny tumors that grew inside looked "suspicious." "I didn't like it at all," Berman said later.

Berman sent samples to ten leading urologists. Only one recommended radical surgery. Berman presented the options to Humphrey, who chose X-ray treatment—eight intensive weeks of it. Humphrey broke the news that he might have cancer to his wife a few days later during a walk by the lake at Waverly. She said: "Well, Daddy, that's all I need to know. We'll work together."

Humphrey went to the Washington municipal hospital near the Capitol for therapy. It was devastating. He would stumble out, double up in the back seat of the car gasping: "Take me home," and the young driver would rush Humphrey, sometimes screaming, to his apartment. There, after an hour or two, the pain would subside. Then Humphrey would head for the office and, as if nothing had happened, chaff with visitors and in the afternoon stroll on to the Senate floor to manage the foreign aid bill. He even broke away for a ten-day trip to Europe.

But in December 1973, at the end of the eight weeks, the painful experience of X-ray treatment caught up with him. Dr. Berman said later: "He got a helluva reaction right before Christmas. He became anemic. He had to go to the hospital and have 4 or 5 blood transfusions." For this he was admitted to Bethesda. But after sixteen days he was released; forty-eight hours later, looking vigorous as ever, he was on television denouncing the chairman of Nixon's Council of Economic Advisers for paying no heed to unemployment. In April 1974, after further tests, Berman announced that the troublesome tumor had disappeared—"destroyed by the treatment last winter." And Humphrey, describing his ordeal, told reporters he felt "better than I have in five years." He went off to China, and produced a 756-page committee report titled "China Economic Assessment." He squared off for what looked like the Senate's principal business of the year: sitting in judgment on the impending impeachment of the man who had defeated him for president in 1968. "I must say that I find the whole situation terribly depressing," he remarked after Nixon sacked Special Prosecutor Cox, thereby provoking the resignations of his attorney general and deputy attorney general. But he told his friend Geri Joseph: "The nation desperately needs relief from this continued tension, suspicion and disillusionment," and he was pleased when Nixon resigned to avoid facing trial.

That fall he broke away to attend the World Food Conference in Rome. His one companion was his son Skip. Having already extracted Secretary Kissinger's pledge for a bigger U.S. commitment to Food for Peace, Humphrey felt he had things well in hand. But it was Dad who, rising at six after dinners that lasted until 2 A.M., rushed to morning meetings. "I was flaking out," Skip said later. Between sessions they flew to Vienna, where Humphrey led his son through Hapsburg palaces and looked in on the U. S.– Soviet missile talks. When the session ended, father and son took off for four days in Israel, toured the Sinai front, and visited with Golda Meir in her living room. On the way home they stopped for a day with Humphrey's friend Prime Minister Harold Wilson and an obligatory visit to the House of Commons. "C'mon, we're going," Humphrey said, but when they arrived at Westminster somehow they got separated. Instantly recognized, the senator from Minnesota was escorted on to the floor while the senator-elect from Brooklyn Center got to view the mother of parliaments from the gallery.

Finally, as Congress met in January 1975, Humphrey succeeded to the only chairmanship he held in all his years on Capitol Hill—the Joint Economic Committee. No post could have been better suited to his breadth of experience and interests. Holding hearings in Washington and around the country that ranged from energy to cartels to medical care, he took up what seemed like the ultimate issue for the most accomplished lawmaker of his generation—the productive involvement of the government in the nation's economy. "It's hard to sum up succinctly," his veteran staff director John Stark said later, "but at the risk of being oversimple I think Hubert aimed to make our economic society the parallel of our political society, serving the people."

For the involvement of government did not abate with the passing of the Vietnam war and the Great Society. It continued to grow under Nixon and Ford. By the time Humphrey assumed his chairmanship, the federal government took in and spent 20 percent of the national income. When state and local revenues were added, one in every three dollars passed through a public till. Interdependence with other national sovereignties had grown meanwhile to the point where international trade amounted to 15 percent of the gross national product. And if other power centers within the economy—giant corporations, big unions, huge banking combines—made important decisions, the federal government's responsibility for some $300 billion in credit shaped them all. Add government's mighty hand in housing, and its myriad regulations for practically every gainful activity, and the dimensions of Washington's involvement in the economy appeared nothing less than overwhelming.

Humphrey, the master legislator, grasped the scale of the change. He had come to the Senate when proposing to raise Social Security benefits above $50 per month was called spendthrift. He had fathered great social programs—Medicare and food stamps, for example. He had served on the Appropriations Committee, where all the departmental allocations passed in review. He had sat with the president when the ultimate priorities for spending were established. From the vantage point of his years, he looked on the tremendous expansion, the crippling rigidities in both the public and private sectors—and saw the need for some kind of general government planning. He had sensed this need for years but, ever the sensitive man of politics, he knew that "planning" was a word that raised hackles in Congress. As he circled the big issue, he trotted out many of his earlier ideas—the urban bank, the Marshall plan for the cities, a rural development bill—and his proposals evolved only gradually.

Finally, in 1974, he introduced the bill, inevitably weakened on its way to passage after his death, that became known as the Humphrey-Hawkins Full Employment and National Growth Act of 1978. Humphrey's measure could not guarantee jobs for all, of course. Its equally generalized forerunner, the Employment Act of 1946, had said for the first time that national policy must be guided by such goals, and Humphrey's idea was to set a goal of no more than 3½ percent unemployment in five years. As finally enacted the new law, the one measure that carried Hubert Humphrey's name, set only general guidelines and a framework by which the nation could—if it would— coordinate political and economic growth to enhance the promise of American life.

Most Americans by the 1970s thought government had grown too big. Not Humphrey. When Democrats came roaring back to victory in the 1974 congressional elections, one of the newly elected senators, Gary Hart of Colorado, made a point of saying: "We're not a bunch of little Humphreys." To this Humphrey replied roundly: "Only a government that is big and strong can possibly stand up against the powerful corporate interests that control our economy. . . . Not to spend, that's not the answer. That's just political bunkum." At that point he wasn't thinking of himself as leading another charge up the mountain. "I'm kind of a part of history now," he told a reporter, and as if he had raised his last hurrah he encouraged Mondale, now Minnesota's senior senator, to run for president. He talked at length with Mondale, then wrote state DFL chairman David Roe: "I am pleased to join in your endorsement of Fritz Mondale for President." But after a time, Mondale, saying he had no liking for the primary ordeal ("all those nights in Holiday Inns"), pulled back.

It was after this that Humphrey's stock began, improbably, to rise. Bright as Democratic chances seemed after Watergate, there were no strong new contestants in sight. As Humphrey's old ADA friend John Roche wrote jovially: "The '60s are over, Vietnam never happened, and you are the man who divides the Democratic party the least." Asked on his sixty-fourth birthday if there was pressure on him to run again, Humphrey answered: "Indeed, yes." When this brought a warning shout from Bill Connell ("I heard it three times today: 'Old Hubert, that itch is too much for him' "), Humphrey said: "I told them I'm not a candidate—they know it." But then he added: "Bill, I'm trying to keep in touch with the AFL-CIO leaders and with [Party Chairman] Bob Strauss. I'm not making any concerted effort. I'm just doing what is natural."

Humphrey a candidate? It seemed preposterous even to the loyalist who had worked for him through three campaigns. But press and politicians spoke of it. A web of draft-Humphrey committees, coordinated through Governor Rudy Perpich's office, spread through Minnesota's eight congressional districts. One day George McGovern dropped by Waverly to propose a Humphrey-McGovern ticket for unity in 1976. With tears in his eyes, Humphrey replied—his campaign manager Jack Chestnut had just been sentenced to prison—that he could not bear the squalor of fund-raising again. At the end of an August vacation he wrote his friend Marvin Rosenberg: "Yes, I'm worried about this so-called Humphrey Boom. I have nothing to do with it. It has been as natural as a rainstorm. I spend most of my time telling people I'll not be a candidate. I shall stick to my position, and we'll see what happens."

In an October Gallup poll the old stager placed first among a dozen Democrats, and James Reston wrote from Washington: "The idea is getting around this town that Hubert Humphrey is going to be the Democratic party's nominee for 1976." President Ford was reported confident that Humphrey would be his opponent. To all this Humphrey said: "The longer I am not a candidate, the more support I have," and when he appeared on NBC's "Meet the Press" for a record twenty-fifth time he said: "I shall enter no primaries, but if the Convention should turn to me, no clear winner having been found, I would readily accept the nomination." He told Eugenie Anderson: "I'm not at all sure that's going to happen—the odds are that it won't."

But as 1976 began he flew across the country addressing Democrats, then launched into attention-getting efforts in Congress to put over his full-employment bill and a national food plan. Senator Muskie described him as a "very active" candidate—"he was not as excited in 1968 as he is now." George Meany volunteered that Humphrey was 1976's "most electable" Democrat. The *Progressive*, the liberal Midwest journal that had wrung its hands over his Vietnam apostasy, now proclaimed "Humphrey's Second Coming." Muriel Humphrey said: "We don't need the presidency at this stage of our lives, and yet I know he would be the best president for our country at this time."

The contender who first pulled out in front of the 1976 pack was Georgia's Governor Jimmy Carter. His pitch was that he had nothing to do with the Washington goings-on exemplified in Watergate. He was a peanut farmer, Annapolis-trained. Well-organized and single-mindedly bent on winning, he started out by making off with the most delegates at January precinct caucuses in the unlikely state of Iowa. Then, after taking first place even farther north in New Hampshire's primary, he broke George Wallace's lock on the South with a win in Florida. Democratic regulars shrank from Carter for his being as much of an outsider as Wallace, but had trouble finding anyone who could stop him. When he won Illinois and proceeded to polish off Scoop Jackson in the Pennsylvania primary, it was plain that unless he were stopped in at least one primary, Carter would sew up the nomination before Humphrey's wait-for-the-convention strategy had a chance to work. Jim Rowe wrote: "The only way to prevent Carter's nomination is for Humphrey to enter the New Jersey primary on June 6 and beat him. My own feeling is that you will once again try."

To file in time for the Jersey contest, Humphrey had to make his decision known by April 30. Old friends gathered. Two party wheels, Joe Crangle of New York and Paul Simon of Illinois, were already beating the bushes for support, and polls told him he would win Jersey two-to-one. His office booked the big Senate Caucus Room, where Kennedy and others had announced, for a declaration on April 30. He told family and friends he was all set to go. As late as midnight on the twenty-ninth he told Dr. Berman he would run. But on the morning of decision day he sat at home talking long with his wife. Time passed. The press conference was postponed. Finally at 11:30, Humphrey walked into the packed room and announced that he would not be entering his name as a candidate in New Jersey.

Tears filled his eyes as he told friends and supporters the decision had been "an exceedingly difficult one." He knew he had health problems. He knew that the old charges of improper fund-raising by his aides would be hurled against him. ("They would have torn me apart," he told Eugenie Anderson.) He knew, and said: "I have no organization, no committee, and no campaign funds." He also knew that if he should take the nomination in this fashion, it would divide the party, lose the South, and probably hand the election to Ford. All in all, he told James Reston: "It's ridiculous—and the one thing I don't need at this stage of my life is to be ridiculous." He would stand instead as candidate for reelection to the Senate.

Humphrey's announcement was more valedictory than anyone listening in the Senate Caucus Room or watching on television could know. In June he published the memoirs that had been timed to appear just before the convention. In July he had the satisfaction of seeing Carter make Fritz Mondale his running mate at the convention in New York. In September he swept the Minnesota primary with more votes than all other candidates combined. But on September 27, out stumping in western Minnesota, he had to stop short. Dr. Berman said later: "One night he called me. There was real worry in his voice. He said: 'Edgar, I'm really peeing blood.' "

This time it was cancer, invasive cancer. Berman said later that he "spent two days with him going through the whole business. It called for an ostomy on his abdomen . . . with a bag to void his urine . . . one helluva operation. And no one can understand a man of such impeccable cleanliness about himself having an ostomy. It's smelly, uncomfortable, messy. But he was resigned to it. He thought he would beat it like he beat everything else."

The operation was performed at New York's Memorial Sloan Kettering Hospital Center. As Berman recalled: "He went in as if he were going to a Yankee game. He went in giving cheers to all the patients."

In the six-hour surgery, Dr. Willet Whitmore removed Humphrey's bladder, an inch-long tumor attached to its base, and his prostate. Humphrey was left with an external pouch in place of his bladder.

He made a remarkable recovery. President Ford and Vice President Rockefeller came to see him. Berman said: "He was up and made the rounds—the patients looked forward to his rounds rather than the doctors'. One day Kissinger came in and the three of us made the rounds, joking like the Smothers brothers." Dr. Whitmore announced: "As far as we are concerned, the patient is cured." But in the postoperational tests, cancer was detected in nearby lymph glands. Whitmore recommended chemotherapy. On October 30, Humphrey was discharged, and on November 4 won his fourth Senate term, defeating Republican Gerald Brekke, a college professor, by eight hundred thousand votes.

Pale, a dozen pounds lighter, and now utterly white-haired, Humphrey returned to Washington vowing to contest for Majority Leader Robert Byrd's job. But he came down with the flu on his way back from a Caneel Bay vacation and when the Senate met in January had to telephone Byrd he was withdrawing from the contest. Thereupon the other Democrats together invented a new post for Humphry—deputy president pro tem of the Senate. It carried the perks of the job he had missed—$8,000 added to his $60,000 salary, a limousine, a Capitol office. It also placed him in the Senate leadership, which made him eligible for invitation to the leadership breakfasts at the White House as in the old days.

The fortnightly chemotherapy bouts in New York hit Humphrey hard: "Worse than the X rays," he told friends. His hair fell out. He wrote Eugenie Anderson:

> The treatments make me feel lousy for 4 or 5 days. That interferes with my appetite, and causes me to lose weight. Just about the time I've regained that weight, I take another treatment. It's kind of a roller-coaster.
>
> But I'm determined not to let this get me down. When I stay busy I feel much better.

After the first leadership breakfast, he peppered Carter with memos on foreign aid, energy, more schools for Indians, relief for honey producers. His hair began to grow back in—curly. He told his chemotherapist: "You may not be able to cure my cancer but at least you gave me curly hair." He was working fourteen hours a day, refusing to nap. In late February his right leg began to swell up. Berman examined him and found a tumor mass in his abdomen: "Told him exactly what it was. And he was sitting at three-hour committee meetings. I said, 'Jesus, put your leg up. You don't have to tell anybody.' "

The *Readers Digest* printed a Humphrey article: "You Can't Quit." President Carter, who had sniffed at Humphrey as a "has been" in his campaign, found that Humphrey could tell him how to get things done in Washington. Kampelman relayed word from three different White House aides: "You're always pulling them out of holes." *Newsweek* watched him "bound" out of his limousine into the White House for breakfast and quoted a fellow senator: "Anybody else and you'd say 'incredible.' But with Hubert, well, that's the way he is." His old friend Eppie Lederer (Ann Landers) saw him on a two-hour television special and wrote: "I don't give a damn if your hair is thinner, you're the best damn speaker in the U. S." Humphrey stayed on the job to adjournment, speaking up for Carter as the president moved toward a Mideast settlement between Israel and Egypt.

Then in August, Humphrey went back to Minnesota. Berman said later:

> He called me every night provided he had a free WATS line, and if he didn't I called him. One night [in September] he called me and said he had stomach cramps. I said, "Get yourself into a hospital."
>
> He did, and that's when they did the colostomy. With that he had two ostomies—one of stool, one of urine. Imagine that with that man.

It was an emergency surgery for intestinal blockage, performed at the University of Minnesota medical center in Minneapolis. Compared with his first, it was simple. He was on his feet the next day. But the operation also disclosed that the abdominal tumor Dr. Berman had found earlier had spread through his entire pelvis. "Terminal," said the Minnesota doctors' communiqué, and with that bald word all America knew that Humphrey was dying.

Emerging from the hospital he looked so gaunt and shriveled that one newspaper described him as "a skull on a stick." In his hollowed features his sister Frances saw a sudden likeness to his Norwegian sea-captain grandfather. The senator himself vowed cheerily that he would soon be back at his Senate desk. A week later he walked on to the stage at the Minnesota AFL-CIO convention. He began: "I may start out a little wobbly, but I am going to end up damn strong." Then he spoke for forty-six minutes—about the future, about the needs of the cities, about the need for jobs, pounding the lectern until it jumped. On October 23, President Carter stopped in Minnesota to pick up Humphrey in *Air Force One* and return with him to Washington. There Humphrey addressed the Senate, the House. He attended the dedication of a new Health, Education and Welfare building named for him and joined two thousand friends at a two-hundred-dollar-a-plate dinner for the projected Hubert Humphrey Institute of Public Affairs in Minneapolis. President Carter invited him to Camp David—in all his years in Washington Humphrey had never been there. For two days they talked long, just the two of them (only Humphrey's urologist, Dr. Dabney Jarman, was present) about the economy, the Middle East. One day Prime Minister Begin asked to see Humphrey. It took until noon to get Humphrey ready, then when Begin arrived with Secretary Vance, maps of the Sinai and Gaza were spread and Humphrey went over the terms to be offered Egypt's President Sadat.

On December 22, Vice President Mondale took Humphrey home. With cameras watching he walked unaided to the plane. At Waverly his family gathered. Their Christmas present to him was a WATS line, and for the next week scores of people around the country—Nixon was one—picked up the telephone and heard with astonishment that Senator Humphrey was calling to wish them well. After New Year's he asked Dr. Berman to come. By then, though he told his receptionist in Washington he would be returning,

David Gartner had to lift him from bed to a chair by the fire. Berman reported that the Washington *Post* had asked a thousand people on Capitol Hill to name the top congressman of the past seventy-five years and they chose Sam Rayburn. "And they voted Hubert Humphrey the top senator." Humphrey murmured: "Jesus Christ, Lyndon Johnson's going to be sore as hell about this." Pharmacist to the last, he scrutinized every pill. But the day came when it was necessary to dull the pain. He lapsed into a coma and died at 7:35 P.M. on the evening of January 13, 1978. He was sixty-six.

Toward the end he had been willing to discuss his funeral. He insisted that it not be a memorial but a "celebration," and even, half fancifully, named three Minnesota hamlets where it might well take place. But the family and the White House decided otherwise. The body was flown to Washington to lie in state at the Capitol. It was at the Rotunda service, thronged with friends of high and low estate, that Vice President Mondale spoke the lines: "He taught us how to hope and how to love, how to win and how to lose. He taught us how to live, and, finally, he taught us how to die." Then the body lay in state at the state capitol in St. Paul, where forty thousand Minnesotans lined up in freezing cold to pay respects.

The funeral at St. Paul's House of Hope Presbyterian church, Dr. Calvin Didier pastor, was as solemn a ceremony of state as church and state in America could contrive. Three television networks covered it. The president of the United States spoke in tribute. Two former presidents, Nixon and Ford, stood among the mourners. Opera stars, concert artists, and a black chorus provided music. But the Humphrey style broke through. Toward the end, at Humphrey's express wish, the Rev. Robert Schuller, television preacher from California, took the pulpit. For years Humphrey had listened admiringly to Bob Schuller's thundering sermons. Aroused, Schuller spoke so long it began to get dark. The three thousand packed in the church squirmed. But that was Humphrey, himself a lifelong evangelist, and prone to go on. He was buried, in the dark, at Minneapolis's Lakewood Cemetery.

39

The Man and His Legacy

Hubert Humphrey was a prairie Progressive in the tradition of Bryan, Norris, LaFollette. In personal style, origins, traits, and career trajectory, he stands as the foremost modern example of the Progressive leader in America, and, with his cry of "more" for all, a symbolic figure of his times.

He differed from earlier midwestern examples of this distinctly American type in being, after the tradition of Franklin Roosevelt, an ardent internationalist. Humphrey was essentially a man of the left, but in the post–World War II years when he was catapulted to prominence, this meant being a cold warrior—a backer of the Truman Doctrine, the Marshall plan, NATO, the defense of Berlin, the war in Korea. The anti-Communism of his cold war belligerence grew directly out of his precocious experience back in Minnesota of fighting and ousting local Reds from control of his leftwing Democratic-Farmer-Labor party.

His was a prairie personality—warm, cornballish, open, short on dignity, filled with a strong desire, strong even for a politician, to be liked. But greatly as his farm-country background influenced his character and beliefs, Humphrey was no provincial midwesterner. The breadth of his principles was proclaimed when, as the young Minneapolis mayor, he stormed on to the Democratic Convention stage in 1948 and successfully fought to commit the party to a radical civil rights plank. That fight immediately lifted Humphrey out of the stereotype of the regional Populist from the plains. He had his

personal, regional passions—high support prices for dairy farmers, love for
the small-business man. But Humphrey from the start was attractive to the
labor unions, and his stand on nuclear arms control evoked popular support
in New York and Los Angeles. Elected senator, he was at the forefront on
all the great issues of his time.

Though no intellectual, he had not only been to college but had taught
there. As a sometime political scientist, he was uncommonly accessible to the
ideas put forward in those post–World War II years by the social scientists:
the gospel of economic growth; the doctrine that education was everybody's
ladder to fortune; the School of Social Work teachings that the poorest families could be raised to schooling, training, jobs, and good housing by the
helping professions; and the theory of the political scientists, which seemed
to cut to the heart of the matter, that Southern blacks could be integrated
into the national life if enabled to vote.

Humphrey-the-Progressive was orator, leader, legislator, politician. He
thirsted to be president, but the only executive office ever granted him was
mayor of a large city. As vice president he was close to power, observed and
understood its use, but never got to wield it. In the end, he asked to be
remembered as an "effective man of government."

So he was and so he must be judged. His were the politics of principle.
Issues were uppermost. And here he differed from his great midwestern predecessors, outsiders all their lives whose Progressive influence had to be
transmitted indirectly. By the ingratiating force of his personality, Humphrey carried his Progressive principles into the mainstream of American
politics. For this many-sided man who could speak with the eloquence of a
Bryan and define issues with the pioneering prescience of a LaFollette, had
also the gift of compromise. He was a pragmatic Progressive. The friendliness and good humor that led colleagues to say "he can disagree without
being disagreeable" commended him to members of the Senate and voters of
Minnesota alike. Having called for change, he lived to enact it.

In doing so, as the political scientist Nelson Polsby said, Humphrey more
or less invented the modern senator as we know him: creator, innovater,
educator, using his place and prominence to define issues for the wider public—and, ultimately, through mastery of the interminable process of committee, cloakroom, and floor maneuver, translating these issues into law. So
important was this role in Humphrey's time, so central were the issues he
dramatized with his endless bills and amendments, that he was almost constantly in contention for the presidency.

AS AN ORATOR, Humphrey was the standout platform speaker of his
time. In Australia, in Rhode Island, in West Virginia, prime ministers, senators, party workers left the hall exclaiming: "Best speech I ever heard."
Morris Udall, another presidential contender, said of Humphrey: "The best
of his time. He could make you feel good about yourself going away." In

thirty years of public life, Humphrey must have delivered ten thousand speeches in that "razzberry" voice of his. The magic worked to the end. Thousands of Minnesotans believed—and scores kept treasured tapes to prove it—that his last fifty-minute address to the state's AFL-CIO convention in the fall of 1977 was the most stirring of all his speeches.

A man so extravagantly oral may never have had an unuttered thought. "Jabber, jabber, jabber," said a co-worker in his early Works Progress Administration days. In public or private, he never seemed to stop talking. Speeches were both the locus and focus of his intellectual development and no matter how high the office he held, they were his ninety percent of the time. The words became still more originally and creatively his own as he spoke. Aides recall that he worked up one of his most substantial legislative ideas—to turn the surplus food crops overflowing the nation's postwar granaries into an instrument of U. S. foreign policy by selling them for local currencies in the Third World—in a series of shirtsleeve harangues to Minnesota farmers in the summer of 1953.

If some thought this style of refining ideas in speeches was responsible for his tendency to platform repetition, Humphrey himself did not. He held that the purpose of speaking was to educate and inspire. Acknowledging that he "frequently" had to repeat to persuade his hearers, he explained: "Education is essentially saturation." He also advised: "Enjoying your audience is important—you either have it or you don't. It comes from natural endowment. No amount of training can make a gifted speaker." Humphrey had that gift.

The striking thing about Humphrey's speeches is that they sounded so much better than they read. There was nothing literary about them; they are not destined for anthologies. His ear was not very sharp to begin with, and his South Dakota schooling and land-grant university years imparted no great degree of polish to his rampant style. Norman Mailer, listening to him at the 1968 Chicago convention, could complain of "slovenliness of syntax which enables him to shuttle phrases back and forth like a switchman who locates a freight car by moving everything in the yard." Humphrey addressing delegate caucuses, of course, was not Humphrey in full cry, and Mailer's comment ignored the crucial difference between the written and the spoken word. The stuff of Humphrey's speech was in his energy, passion, fire, personality, all difficult to translate to the printed page. What he conveyed to his hearers as truth was apt to come out as truism on paper.

For all his unprogrammed virtuosity, Humphrey was forever asking people to draft speeches for him; often he had two or three working on the same subject without their knowing it. What he was looking for was not structured texts but ideas, preferably "grabbers," as he called them. And what he got, he transformed. In a few minutes he could knock any proposed speech into a cocked hat. As he skipped through a text on the plane, his felt pen would strike out whole paragraphs, whole pages, and he would scribble in what he wanted. The transmutation did not stop there. When he arrived and stepped before his audience, his speech changed shape again. Speech writer Douglas Bennet tried to explain the process he so often witnessed in the 1968 campaign: "You tossed in a piece of dross and"—Bennet snapped his fingers—"a wonderful idea would flower forth." Once, leafing through a draft late at night, Humphrey remarked: "Bennet, the difference between you and me is that I'm a great artist and you're a barn painter." "It's okay," he told the future director of U. S. Foreign Aid, "but you just don't capture the way I speak." Of course nobody did, though over the years dozens of writers listened to Humphrey tapes and then tried vainly to match his untrammeled raptures. "You never could get the cadence of his spoken discourse," said Arthur Naftalin, his 1945 city-hall aide and first speech writer. Bennet, valiantly trying to do so decades later, had to say the same: "You couldn't translate it into writing, it was so discursive, and so unbelievably repetitious. What was impossible to capture was the audience rapport he was achieving precisely by these changes and repetitions."

But as his wife, his friends, his foes, practically everybody in the United States said, he did go on and on. His media adviser, Robert Squier, always held that Humphrey was a figure out of the old Chautauqua circuit who felt that if he could not hold an audience for an hour he was somehow less of a man. And Humphrey grew up in a Dakota small town where people, coming to meetings from a distance, expected and demanded more than a fifteen-minute performance. Yet some on his staff thought he might not have developed such a lifelong propensity to keep spouting but for the pangs and frustrations of his early Washington years. Made miserable by the deep-freeze treatment of his fellow senators and strapped as always for money, he felt driven to accept out-of-town invitations to speak for fees. Humphrey loved nothing so much as making speeches, but in the long run speaking for fees hurt him. For when his audiences responded, he was drawn to speak longer, and to accept invitations more often. Gratifying as these nightly successes seemed, it would have been better if the speeches had been half as long and half as frequent. He won the wrong kind of attention—and a lot of people thought of him as a windbag.

As a legislator, Humphrey's preeminence was not quickly or easily established. Entering the Senate as a dynamic big-city chief executive used to acting decisively and seeing immediate results, he found it awkward to shift to the pace and style of the legislator who might never see the results of his efforts and could get them only after long debate and persuasion. Arriving as leader of a successful convention revolt against the party hierarchy, he started by making cocky, challenging, chip-on-the-shoulder speeches that sounded as if he were out to make a reputation with the public at the expense of the Senate higher-ups. He demanded that the seniority system be scrapped. He appeared to turn all issues into moral issues. His speeches castigated conservatives for being in bondage to special interests.

Reacting to these assaults as insults, the Senate elders virtually ostracized

Humphrey. To a man who wanted so much to be liked, this was wounding. In his first session he spoke on 450 topics, filled the pages of the *Congressional Record* with insertions, many of them speeches and letters by his ADA friends. He introduced fifty-seven bills (including Medicare), offered seventeen amendments and five resolutions. But not one item passed, and indeed no bill Humphrey offered in his first four years went through. Then as his friend Jane Freeman recalled later he gritted his teeth and vowed: "I'm going to learn to do it their way."

The Eisenhower years, when Johnson won his reputation as Senate leader, saw little legislative achievement; most of what Humphrey did for Johnson was to help pass money bills to keep the government going. But by forever introducing bills of his own, holding committee hearings, and waging ceaseless floor debate, he began opening the hitherto private world of the Senate club to the great forces of mass politics. Session by session he turned the ritual of Senate process into weapons for mobilizing constituencies for civil rights, Medicare, nuclear disarmament, and his dozens of other causes. Defeated year after year, his bills eventually passed, monuments to his tenacity and skill.

"I like every subject," he exclaimed. The initial idea for a bill might or might not have been his, but it was invariably Humphrey who would shape it. Having sketched the solution broadly, he would invite comment from his colleagues, for he was anything but a prima donna about his bills. He welcomed others pitching in. For example, having earlier introduced his Wilder-

~~ Frank Church and Henry Jackson,
ke to be co-sponsor with you."
became law in 1964, it did not

bills, was utterly unlike John-
Humphrey, and he twisted no
personal ties with the others
not have one enemy." Instead
ting, an understanding word
. He said later: "I knew every
nily." That went for Republi-
1964 campaign he called his
siness Administration, to put
a goddam Republican, what
y said: "I never met him but
me on the floor if you would
back on."
d Humphrey moved up to
ity and skill began to pay off
the president, White House
the most forceful of all those

around the breakfast table." With Humphrey mobilizing his constituencies outside and mustering his majorities on the floor, the Kennedy administration put through measures he had proposed long before: the Peace Corps, the Arms Control and Disarmament Agency, the nuclear test-ban treaty. When Kennedy died and, at Humphrey's urging, Johnson proclaimed: "Let us continue," Humphrey broke the back of the Southern filibuster at last and won passage in 1964 of the civil rights program he had offered as a rank insurgent in 1949. Finally, as vice president, he saw enactment in the Great Society programs of the agenda he had pioneered over the years: federal aid to education, Medicare, Job Corps, vocational training, and welfare.

The master legislator did not neglect a senator's other tasks. He was indefatigable in small things as in big—got jobs for people, won advantages in Washington for constituents, sent thousands of "clip" letters every time the newspapers reported a boy joining the air force, a girl exhibiting a prize heifer. In the midst of his 1968 presidential campaign he could take time to see a St. Paul widow's pension restored within a week. His clout got the Minnesota River dredged to Port Savage, enabling corn to be shipped over water from west of the Twin Cities and saving millions for farmers—and for Cargill, which bought and shipped out their crop. In 1956, Eisenhower put through the interstate highway system, and Humphrey voted for it. But when the bureaucrats set out to elevate the link between the Twin Cities in the neighborhood-blighting style of the Los Angeles freeways, Humphrey bustled into a meeting with Federal Highway Administrator Rex Whitton. He quickly extracted the admission that the engineers had chosen the elevated design to avoid having to haul away excavated earth and won agreement that, at least between Minneapolis and St. Paul, there would be a sunken right of way.

Humphrey was in on almost everything, whether in committee, in floor debate, or in final appropriation of funds. Along with the civil rights and other measures that changed America, he saw to aid for Sri Lanka, research in solar heating, federal help to the arts. In the field of agriculture alone he introduced 119 bills in his first dozen years in Congress, important elements of which found their way later into the statute books. A fair example is food stamps. With Representative Lenore Sullivan of Missouri, Humphrey first pushed for an experimental program in the early 1950s. His was the seminal idea: why should the federal government get up warehouses around the country to dish out the surplus foodstuffs to the needy when a fabulously efficient food distribution system was already in place at the local supermarket? But when the time came to introduce the plan he said: "Not me. Let's get Bob Dole. If he proposes it, it will be different." Humphrey got the conservative Republican Senator Dole to touch base with the National Association of Retail Grocers. Dole then took up the bill in the Agriculture Committee and, together with Democrat George McGovern, lined up other committee members. Enacted into law in 1964, the food stamp program grew into the biggest instrument for transferring benefits to those who need them since the Social Security Act of 1936. One last example: at the end of his life, Humphrey tacked on an amendment to the Tax Reform Act of 1976 that slashed the inheritance tax when farmland passes from father to son. With this all but unnoticed change, Humphrey may have struck the most effective blow in his long fight to save the family farm in America.

AS A POLITICAL LEADER, Humphrey aimed for the presidency as early as his first election as mayor in 1945. His ambition was not the manipulative kind that showed its seams, as in a Harold Stassen or John Connally, but one that drove him to run not walk and to work, where possible, harder than all rivals.

Speechifier that he was, Humphrey led by inspiring others. He built a strong and enduring political party in Minnesota that adhered to the Progressive principles he proclaimed; it brought forward a remarkable group of honest, effective, and visionary public servants. At least two, McCarthy and Mondale, also stood for president and all—from Orville Freeman in the statehouse to Don Fraser in Humphrey's city-hall office forty years later—were, in their highly individual ways, extensions of their great teacher.

Humphrey believed that political democracy rests on the informed awareness of the electorate, and toward this end he excelled in hortatory leadership. He had an ability to express issues in the language of common understanding. He could see and say how a budget affected a grandmother, a ten-year-old, a baby. His friend Jane Freeman thought he came by this gift listening to ordinary people in a drugstore. He never worked on a farm, but he knew farmer talk. He never worked in a factory, but he knew that language as well. He could empathize and used to say: "I learned more about economics from one South Dakota dust storm than I did in all my years in college."

The vision Humphrey proclaimed was that people of good will working together could make a better society. When others were jeering at the welfare state as a socialist featherbed for free-loaders, Humphrey retorted that it was what the founding fathers had in mind for the land of the free when they wrote "to promote the general welfare." New Dealer, Keynesian, unreconstructed believer in the power and duty of government to help widows, orphans, the handicapped, and the unemployed—he fought his fight at a higher, generalized level. If he had to, he could manage the minutiae of precinct caucuses, buttons, and bumper stickers, but he soon left such business to others. As a political scrapper he drew back from eyeball-to-eyeball combat. As mayor he was never a Richard Daley (he hadn't a dictatorial bone in his body), and he never was much of an organizer. He was "the prominent guy," the famous fellow, the senator in Washington. Freeman, Heaney, and others organized, lined up volunteers, formed the county committees. Not taken up with nuts and bolts, Humphrey was the glue that kept everybody together. When the party needed him he was there, arriving to give the battle speech.

Humphrey's efforts to move toward higher political office were always dogged by organizational weaknesses, and these traced to the same friendly, forgiving nature that made him so effective at winning colleagues' assent to his Senate bills. As a national contender he was pained and puzzled that he could not create a regional base in the Midwest such as Kennedy's in New England. Because Humphrey was simply incapable of holding a grudge, politicians and labor chieftains could cross—and doublecross—him with impunity. After he allowed his Minnesota protégé Robert Short to help Estes Kefauver take the vice-presidential nomination to his great personal cost and humiliation, Eugene McCarthy said to him: "Hubert, I know you're not going to be rough on Short after what he did to you. But Hubert, couldn't you at least be mad at him for two weeks?"

Humphrey's gifts did not include the disciplined coolness and detachment needed to do what he had to do to knock heads together for a well-organized campaign. He worked so hard himself that he did not notice that people had to be supervised. He was not quick to see what had to be done, to spot the weak in his entourage and promote the strong. He liked everybody.

Observers could not help thinking he was indiscriminate about it. As senator he could keep a delegation waiting because a seven-year-old in the corridor asked to snap his picture, and when the camera jammed Humphrey spent a quarter-hour fussing at trying to fix the boy's machine. Jim Rowe related that once when Humphrey failed to show for a Salt Lake City meeting with Utah Democratic chieftains he went looking for him and found him in the hotel lobby sitting beside an old prospector. "Give us fifteen minutes," Humphrey pleaded. "Listen to him, fascinating fellow."

Of course it was this feeling for people that made Humphrey so possessed and effective a campaigner. He couldn't shake enough hands, join enough lodges, send enough Christmas cards. He was forever late on the trail because of his desire to please his last audience—end all their doubts, answer all their questions, convert them totally to him. Wanting to be loved, he was unable to be cruel. He could make neither his allies nor his adversaries fear that his anger would have long-term consequences for them. "It was his fatal flaw, it was what killed him in the 1968 race," said the old Democratic National Committee hand, John Hoving.

AS A HUMAN BEING, Humphrey was so impulsively outgoing and spontaneous that he could never be called disciplined. But he did change over the years, and in the most important ways he grew and continued to grow to the end. As a young mayor he quite evidently felt his importance at times. Out socially with Minneapolis businessmen, he would often end up reading them a bit of a lecture. He sounded brittle, tinny, mouthy, and—a word often hurled at him—brash. After his put-down by the Senate, friends noted that he was a pretty realistic judge of his own place and influence in the scheme of things political. He loved the spotlight but never got inflated under its heat and glare. When Orville Freeman in 1958 asked: "My God, Hubert, how can you contemplate becoming president—doesn't it scare you?" Humphrey answered, neither boastful nor modest: "I can't see anybody doing it any better." Up against John Kennedy, the first thoroughly "packaged" candidate, Humphrey was the least synthetic of men. He resisted efforts to make him other than he was.

James Michener said: "If I had to summarize this man in one sentence it would be: 'He knows.' " That was a plausible judgment when Michener wrote it in 1968, reflecting as it did not only Humphrey's ability as a leader to sense and say what others felt but also his personal capacity for steady growth. Along with a good mind, Humphrey had a compelling drive to learn and a memory like a computer. All around him remarked on his "off the track" knowledge. Bill Connell said: "In conversation you would see something click. He was storing it, a good idea." By briefings and night study he got on top of the issues that gripped him. He tapped the Library of Congress for his legislative forays. He talked to bureaucrats. His contacts with foreign statesmen were extensive. He "knew."

Yet there remained more than a trace of the naïve about Humphrey. A child of the Depression, he confessed that when he stayed at Windsor castle he worried about wasting hot water. Until the last fifteen years of his life he wore chainstore clothes—Bond suits, Thom McAn shoes. He felt uneasy when he addressed his Eastern ADA intellectual friends. Meeting him in the Senate in the early 1950s Bill Benton said: "He had never been anywhere. He was the strangest combination of brilliance, great natural gifts, extraordinary ability—and inexperience in the world at the simplest level." Benton had to show him how to use a dictating machine, how to order food in a French restaurant. Muriel Humphrey, having obviously discussed the subject with her husband, once said that if Humphrey had only been able to afford graduate study at Princeton instead of Louisiana State he would have been president of the United States.

A man who threw himself at so many subjects invited the criticism that he lacked a sense of priorities. True, Humphrey had no inclination to delegate. But for a man with Humphrey's gifts this was in many ways a good characteristic. People always compared his staff unfavorably with those of the Kennnedys. John Kennedy, as Dwayne Andreas remarked, "had total staff—he could go out and play tennis. But he was a prisoner of that staff." Humphrey could pull his ideas out of his own notebooks, generate his own initiatives, and, being able like a sailor to sense the weather, could pick his own best time to launch them.

Even if Humphrey was never as superficial as his multitude of projects suggested, he ran so fast and worked so hard that he left himself no time for reflection. An early co-worker, watching him sprint from meeting to meeting, exclaimed: "Jesus, if the guy would only sit down with himself and say, 'What am I all about?' " Both Naftalin and Eugenie Anderson warned him in vain to make time to think. Mrs. Anderson's advice was to go off by himself before the 1956 convention for two weeks and read Sandburg's life of Lincoln. Paradoxically enough, the hyperactive Humphrey did have the thinker's gift to see connections, to tie things together—only this tended to happen while he was talking. It was early observed that this busy man, burning the candle at both ends as he did, seemed to positively dislike privacy, that he had to have somebody to talk to.

Humphrey was fun to be with. He was lively, warm, bursting with affirmation of life, magnetic, a man in touch with his own gut feelings. Naftalin said: "He could come into a room, and was at once everybody's friend, above all in this capacity to be interested in you." He was always giving himself to people. Instead of saying like other politicians "I've got five minutes to spare," he would reach out a hand and say: "Now we have a little time. . . ." He could be extremely sensitive to the hard and soft spots in others. If he fell into conversation he found out about one's family, one's interests, even what one thought to do in the next ten years. When others said he cried easily, he said: "If you haven't any tears, you haven't any heart." Yet within this same man burned a huge ego: let a bundle of newspapers arrive at the office, and Humphrey would drop whatever he was doing to read them—to read about himself.

As the years passed, Humphrey grew to curtail and repress his impulsiveness to some degree. When Bill Moyers, in an interview a year before Humphrey's death, reminded him that President Johnson had said his vice president trusted his enemies too much, Humphrey responded: "I'm a man that has matured later in life emotionally. Now I'm at about the fifty-year maturity," by which he meant that he had been taught some harsh lessons in restraint.

Optimistic, gregarious, endaemonian, Humphrey seemed so open that many said he was exactly as you saw him, in private as in public. So unreservedly the self-proclaimed "public man," he seemed continuously on stage. As such, he was every man's friend, ready not only with a handclasp, a joke, a shouted greeting, but willing to put himself out enormously for others. But the fact was, as he told Moyers, "I don't have many deep, real, intimate friends." Norman Sherman, who helped him write his memoirs, went further and said Humphrey had no close friends at all.

No one in later life was ever such a counselor—or alter ego—as Evron Kirkpatrick had been in the days when Humphrey was making up his mind to run for mayor. Humphrey shared confidences with Max Kampelman and Edgar Berman that were not limited to legal and medical matters, but theirs were still the relationships a man might have with a trusted lawyer and physician. Freeman and Humphrey were never so close after Humphrey, by backing Stevenson at the 1960 convention, disappointed his friend's hopes of getting on the ticket with Kennedy. Fred Gates, who knew and understood him so well, was never privy to Humphrey's larger ambitions. Dwayne Andreas was—and counseled Humphrey on many more matters than money—but theirs was for both essentially a friendship of convenience. Even Humphrey's wife did not share in all of her husband's thoughts. She had to be, and was, a tough person to survive life with a politician who drove so hard for his career and his causes. Friends knew she was not a political person and watched admiringly as she adapted to Washington, kept her family together, and not only faced up to campaigning but did a good job of it. Humphrey knew it, said "Muriel is my greatest political asset," and was loyal to her all the way. But while she did turn out for some of his evening meetings, she passed up many. Again and again she was home alone, and lonely. Norman Holmes, who helped Humphrey in his 1970 campaign, brought some papers to their St. Paul house early one Saturday morning as Muriel was fixing breakfast, and was invited to have some bacon and eggs with them. In her dressing gown at the stove Muriel asked: "Hubert what are you doing today?" He had the whole day lined out: an hour at a Catholic church, then a visit to two synagogues, then lunch in Minneapolis. She went back to frying the eggs. "Hubert, what are you going to do tomorrow?" He pulled out the little cards he always kept in his pocket and read off: early morning mass, another meeting, another lunch, a list extending into the evening. Then Muriel, spatula in hand, said: "Hubert, you really know how to louse up a weekend."

Humphrey was a sports fan. He liked to dance and go to parties. He drank socially—by preference, beer. After narrowly surviving pneumonia at six and wearing a chamois vest against chills all through childhood, he was grateful for robust health, stopped smoking after a scary stomach upset in 1957, and drove his body hard as ever to his early end. His passion for neatness and order was so pronounced that Dr. Berman called it "microbe phobia." He liked raunchy jokes however. Sample from his notebooks: "Chicken blood transfusions make men cockier, women lay better."

Reared in small-town Protestant traditions, Humphrey remained essentially religious, filled with faith in the brotherhood of man. Arthur Naftalin always remembered the argument Humphrey made in 1945 for the existence of God: "The proof that God exists is that all men are brothers." Kampelman felt this was so fundamental to the Humphrey character that it explained why he kept forgiving people who did not deserve it. The faith also undergirded his Wilsonian devotion to peace and his Rooseveltian commitment to government helping those who, through no fault of their own, met economic distress.

In practicing the politics of principle, Humphrey's pragmatism brought him much nearer Roosevelt than Wilson. Ambivalences thronged his political life, and while he managed his contradictions with great skill they finally overtook and defeated him. A perceptive fellow political scientist early identified Humphrey as a natural-rights thinker—but also a great believer in majority rule. As senator, Humphrey found it perfectly possible at one and the same time to advocate direct election of presidents while insisting on the right of corner druggists to hold their place by "fair trade," that is, price-fixing laws, as well as the right of dairymen to hang on to their farms by subsidized milk prices.

When Humphrey first entered politics he astonished Kirkpatrick and Naftalin by his accommodating of Republican businessmen, his flexibility with Communists, his mysterious ease with the smalltime union leaders and café owners on the fringe of Minneapolis's "shadow world." He was always ready to make human allowances. Later, having purged the Reds from his DFL party, he went to Washington a blazing anti-Communist. More contradictions appeared, but in general he handled them well. He developed separate and conflicting constituencies. He was on good terms with both Zionists and Arabists. He worked for disarmament treaties with Russia at the same time he raised his voice for the captive nations of Eastern Europe. He was at once for defense and détente.

The Humphrey duality, otherwise so successful, was glaringly illuminated in one embarrassing flash at the height of the cold war. Facing reelection and declaring himself disgusted with Republicans scheming to pin the "soft on Communists" label on Democrats, Humphrey brought in a bill to outlaw the Communist party. Outrageously opportunist, it outdid the Republicans and was swiftly adopted as the Communist Control Act of 1954. Though shocked, liberals wrote it off at the time as a momentary aberration on the part of the liberal battler for civil rights, and forgave him. But out in South Dakota, George McGovern, then a young instructor at Dakota Wesleyan, heard a grizzled University of South Dakota historian make a prediction about Hubert Humphrey that he never forgot. Sooner or later, Professor Herbert Schell said, a leader who would play fast and loose with liberal standards, ignoring the Holmes doctrine that ideas, however odious, are dealt with in the competition of the marketplace and in no other way, would stumble on some other issue. Humphrey's espousal of a measure so out of spirit with American constitutional principles, the old man said, revealed "a flaw in Humphrey's political character that will keep him from becoming president of the United States."

With his gift for compromise, his knack for being ambivalent about things most Americans were ambivalent about, Humphrey left the Communist Control Act far behind as he moved forward winning victory after victory for progressive reform in the years thereafter. Persuasive, persevering, he finally gained enactment of the breakthrough civil rights legislation in 1964. Having insisted through every compromise that every citizen must be free, he at last made it an official law of the land.

The prairie Progressive had indeed arrived in the mainstream of American politics, and a stunning thing happened to him: the goal of the presidency that he had thought lost forever when Kennedy flattened him, now reappeared bright and beckoning. By becoming Lyndon Johnson's vice president, he at last pulled within sight of the White House.

For this the free spirit from the Dakota prairies paid a great price. The exciting capacity to go in unexpected directions he had displayed as mayor, the creative pragmatism he had shown as a rising senator, the treasured privilege of open options he had gloried in for sixteen years in Washington—all these he lost irretrievably. As vice president he forfeited the liberal essence that was the source of his commanding autonomy. Lyndon Johnson took his measure—and took him captive.

Back in 1945 his father, reading in the newspapers that the young mayor had eaten with bankers, telephoned next day to warn him not to succumb to the flatteries and attractions of these men of wealth, but to remember how many farmers the bankers had foreclosed in the Depression. Now Lyndon Johnson sent him out to make friends with Wall Street. And the challenger changed, becoming part of the establishment. He hobnobbed with bankers, praised big corporations as a "source of strength," and remarked that antitrust laws should be "modernized." *Fortune* magazine saluted "the new Humphrey."

These were changes more in emphasis than essence. They had been prefigured in his conduct as mayor joining with businessmen to deliver good government in Minneapolis, and they occurred at the time that the pent up budget of Humphrey's reforming legislation was being enacted in the Great Society program. Humphrey was entitled to say, as he did when asked what had become of the liberal program of the 1940s: "We passed it." If he had changed, the country had too.

But a much more glaring contradiction loomed ahead: Vietnam. A vice president can go along, or keep quiet. Humphrey did neither. Banished from presidential favor for early dissent, he persuaded himself that Johnson's war policy was right and became its loudest proponent. In so doing, Humphrey stumbled as fatefully as the old man in South Dakota had predicted. For when, by the vicissitudes of politics, he and not Johnson stood for the White House in 1968, he could not wrest free of his unpopular chief. The resulting riots and party split in Chicago doomed the Humphrey candidacy.

As a man reaching for the ultimate office, Humphrey lacked the necessary quality of ruthlessness. He was a terrific fighter but no killer. Men were not afraid of him. Though he might be the best speaker, the most accomplished lawmaker of his time, nobody stood in awe of him. But if others betrayed him (and were forgiven) Humphrey himself gave loyalty, loyalty that blurred into submission. The rout he suffered when he stood for vice president in 1956, the harsh defeat inflicted when he ran for president against Kennedy in 1960, these were the elements that created Humphrey's subsequent loyalty to Lyndon Johnson. He wanted to be president—and after his hopes had been crushed Johnson gave him the vice presidency. It was giving Humphrey the chance he thought he had lost; it was, as Gene McCarthy said, giving him life. He felt obligated to Johnson for the rest of his days.

By the margin imposed by this burden—the price paid when, at the height of his Progressive achievements, he agreed to be Johnson's No. 2—Humphrey missed the prize. And so he passed into history as one of those eminent politicians such as Clay and Webster, Bob Taft and LaFollette, who shaped the nation but never governed it.

Had Humphrey won he would at least have spared the nation the iniquities of his vanquisher. And for all his compassion, he probably would have run up deficits no bigger than Nixon's. Chances are he would have handled Congress about as well as Johnson, and foreign affairs infinitely more knowledgably. Like Nixon he would have pushed for détente. Above all he would have been a doughty sort of president, using Teddy Roosevelt's bully pulpit to exhort the people. But most likely, they would not have heeded him. Had he won, it would have been by the slimmest plurality. The times had already passed him by. The tide for Progressive change had ebbed.

As it happened, Nixon was stayed in his plan to dismantle the Humphrey legislation by the persisting Democratic majorities in Congress, shortly reinforced by the return of Humphrey to the Senate. But the war on poverty remained unwon; unemployment, especially among the inner-city young, ran high. Meanwhile the cycle of American postwar imperial expansion hurtled on to the final defeat in Vietnam and disgrace to the presidency. The calamity in Vietnam, far from having merely influenced Humphrey's defeat in 1968, buckled the seams of the American economy—not by an old-style Depression but by a vast slide during which the nation lurched out of the age of growth into an uncertain new era of limits. Inflation raged unstaunched, the dollar went through two devaluations, and in the unrelenting dynamic of change the nation was overtaken in the 1970s by a crisis of energy supply that seemed the conclusive signal that the years of heedless plenty were over.

In the new era of limits the old American innocence that Humphrey spoke for appeared out of date. Opinion *had* passed him by, and one looked at him as a kind of earth-father giving out more goods, or words of hope to make yet more goods come true—a symbol, one saw, of his times. He was a casualty of Progressivism's lack of staying power. And however painful the lapses and losses that followed Nixon's accession, the Humphrey enactments of the 1960s afforded the nation enough domestic tranquility, or respite, to give some time for working out the arrangements by which, under the constraint of limits, America—with, very probably, the rest of the world following after—will make its way into the twenty-first century. And if Progressivism returns to play a part in this process, it will be because the dispossessed millions go on to use the franchise, the schooling, the social facilities that Humphrey helped win them. That remains the promise of American life.

Notes

Shortened titles are used below, with the complete titles listed in the Bibliography. Abbreviations have been used in citing from the Humphrey Papers, not all of which have been processed. Citations have also been abbreviated for papers at the Johnson Presidential Library, in accordance with the library's usages.

HUMPHREY PAPERS (HP)

AAF71	Administration, Administrative Files, 1971, also AAF72 up to AAF76
CF68	Campaign Files, 1968 Campaign
CF68 PP	Campaign Files, 1968 Campaign, Personal Political
CF6870	Campaign Files, 1968 and 1970 Campaigns
CF70	Campaign Files, 1970 Campaign
CF72	Campaign Files, 1972 Campaign
CF u/p	Campaign Files, unprocessed
CO70	Control Files, 1970
DNC	Democratic National Committee (Files), 1969–73
MSF	Master Speech File
M u/p	Miscellaneous, unprocessed
PFPA	Personal and Family, Personal Alphabetical
PFPC	Personal and Family, Personal Correspondence
PFPF	Personal and Family, Personal Financial
PFPM	Personal and Family, Personal Miscellaneous
PFPMB u/p	Personal and Family, Personal/Miscellaneous/Biographical, unprocessed
SFM	Staff Files, Memos, 1971–77
VIP Corr.	VIP Correspondence
WHM u/p	White House Files, Miscellaneous, unprocessed

JOHNSON LIBRARY (JL)

NSF	National Security Files
NSC	National Security Council meeting notes
NSC/VP	Name file (Vice President)
WHCF	White House Central File Subject File

Exec FG 440	Executive (FG 440 denotes Vice President)
Exec PL/HHH	Executive-Political Affairs (Humphrey)
Exec PL	Executive-Political Affairs
Exec PL-1	Executive-Conventions
WHCF CF	White House Central File-Confidential File
CF Exec FG 440	Confidential File-Executive-Vice President
CF Exec PL	Confidential File-Executive-Political Affairs
WHDD	White House Daily Diary
WHDC	White House Daily Diary Cards
WHDD Backup	White House Daily Diary, Backup file
WHFN(HHH)	White House Famous Name File (Hubert Humphrey)

OTHER ABBREVIATIONS

COLLECTED PRIVATE PAPERS

AP	Eugenie Anderson Papers
BP	Chester Bowles Papers
CLU	Minneapolis Central Labor Union (Papers)
CP	William Connell Papers
DFL	Democratic Farmer-Labor (Party Papers)
FP	Orville Freeman Papers
KP	Max Kampelman Papers
LP	Herbert Lehman Papers
MP	Stephen Mitchell Papers

LIBRARIES

KL	Kennedy Presidential Library
RL	Franklin Roosevelt Presidential Library
TL	Truman Presidential Library

NEWSPAPERS AND MAGAZINES

CR	*Congressional Record*
MJ	Minneapolis *Journal*
MS	Minneapolis *Star*
MSJ	Minneapolis *Star Journal*
MT	Minneapolis *Tribune*
NYT	*New York Times*
PRO	*Progressive* magazine
STPD	St. Paul *Dispatch*
STPPP	St. Paul *Pioneer Press*
WP	Washington *Post*
WS	Washington *Star*

Prologue: "THE SUNSHINE OF HUMAN RIGHTS"

11. "**were jumping on their chairs . . .**": M. W. Halloran *MS*, July 16, 1948; *STPPP*, July 15, 1948; *MT*, July 15, 1948; *NYT*, July 15, 1948. Eugenie Anderson (July 10, 1980), Orville Freeman (April 9, 1980, April 15 and May 9, 1981), Ione and Douglas Hunt (July 31, 1980), Dorothy Jacobson (April 6, 1981 and Sept. 16, 1982), James Loeb (April 4, 1981), Arthur Naftalin (April 22, 24, 25 and July 28, 1980, June 8 and 12, July 8, Aug. 14, and 27, 1981), Joseph Rauh (Nov. 12, 1980) and William Simms (Oct. 31, 1981) interviews. Oscar Ewing (May 1, 1969) and Matthew Connelly (Nov. 28, 1967) interviews for JL.

12. "Hubert has the greatest coordination . . .": Doris Kearns, 366–67.
"We have those in Minnesota . . .": Humphrey in Proceedings of the ADA Committee," Chicago, May 1, 1947, Box 19, series 1-E, Anita McCormick Blaine Papers. "Agenda for ADA Midwest conference," Mar. 1, 1947, Box 60, folder 4, series 2, ADA Papers. Arthur Naftalin to James Loeb, Mar. 6, 1947, Box 60, series 2, ADA Papers. Frank McCulloch letter, Aug. 22, 1983. Rauh letter, June 7, 1983. Chicago *Tribune*, Mar. 2, 1947. Madison *Capitol Times*, Mar. 4, 1947. *PRO*, Mar. 1947.
"dazzled": Joseph Rauh interview. Eugenie Anderson, Dorothy Jacobson, James Loeb, Arthur Naftalin interviews.
"self-survey": L. H. Bennett to Reuben Youngdahl, Mar. 11, 1946, PFPA (civil rights speech), HP. Minneapolis *Times*, Mar. 27 and Dec. 27, 1946. *MT*, Sept. 5, 1949. John Harding, "Community Self-Survey," *Congress Weekly*, Mar. 5, 1948.
"capital of anti-Semitism in America": Carey McWilliams, *Common Ground*, Spring 1946.
13. "government in exile": A. L. Hamby, *Beyond the New Deal*, 161. Rauh letter, June 7, 1983.
Democrats in disarray: Humphrey to Loeb, Mar. 24, 1948, Box 51, HP. Bowles to Humphrey, Mar. 17, 1948, Box 39, BP. Humphrey to Gael Sullivan, April 19, 1948, Box 51, HP. *MS*, July 4, 1948.
"The Democratic party must lead . . .": *PRO*, Apr. 1946.
Humphrey to Democratic notables: Humphrey press release, July 5, 1948, Box 50, HP. Humphrey to Lehman, June 10, 1948, Humphrey file, LP.
14. Administration plank: Rauh memo, n.d., Rauh files. Eugenie Anderson memo, n.d. July 1948, Box 1, AP.
"Who does this pipsqueak . . ?": *Education*, 111–12.
15. "protect my rights": Biemiller interview, May 13, 1980. Rauh memo, Rauh files. Anderson memo, AP.
"Practically everybody thought . . .": Anderson memo, AP.
"afraid we were going to lose . . .": Freeman interview. Freeman letters, May 11 and June 9, 1983.
"this may tear the party": *Education*, 113.

"We got Humphrey away . . .": Anderson memo, AP.
"Humphrey thought the wording . . .": Ibid.
16. "We highly commend . . .": *Democracy at Work, Official Report of Democratic National Convention*, Philadelphia, July 12–14, 1948, 181–82.
"the good phrases were his": Milton Stewart interview, Nov. 15, 1980.
Dougie was "fussing": Muriel Humphrey, July 10, 13, PFPM, HP.
"More than I have ever seen": Anderson memo, AP.
"Joe, you won't get fifty . . .": Rauh memo, Rauh files.
"Our argument was . . .": Rauh interview.
Arvey "all right": Rauh memo, Rauh files.
"In this fight, Wallace . . .": Rauh interview.
17. "Your rights are protected . . .": Biemiller interview.
"Look, you kids are right . . .": Ibid.
"courtesy and forthrightness . . .": Humphrey speech, July 14, 1948, text in Box 53, HP.
19. "Whatever it is about . . .": Anderson memo, AP.
"Here goes": Rauh memo, Rauh files.
"Can you beat that?": Anderson memo, AP. *WS*, July 15, 1948. *NYT*, July 15, 1948.
Heard by estimated 60 million: *Broadcasting*, July 19, 1948.
Post-convention overtures: Clifford Bouvette, Mayor Humphrey request for appointment with Truman (Note: "No"), July 16, 1948, file 300 (Minnesota), TT. Humphrey to Truman, July 28, 1948, and Truman to Humphrey, Aug. 4, 1948, General file (Humphrey), TL.

PART ONE
1: FRONTIER FOREBEARS

23. "Our branch has been preeminently . . .": Dr. Harry B. Humphrey, "Some Notes on the Humphrey (Humphreys) family," Box 5, PFPM, HP.
"Humphreys are of mixed . . .": Humphrey to Mrs. Aleen McNeel, Oct. 23, 1977, PFPMB u/p, HP. Humphrey to Morton Puner, Oct. 3, 1966, M u / p, HP.
24. Humphrey ancestry: Gilbert Nash and Otis H. Humphreys, "The Dorchester

and Weymouth Families of Humphrey (vol. 3 of *The Humphrey Family in America*, N.Y., Frederick Humphreys print, 1883. *A Report of the Record Commissioner of the City of Boston*, vol. 28 (1890), 107; vol. 21, 146. Frank P. Rice, *Vital Records of Dudley, Mass.*, Worcester, 1908. *American Genealogist*, vol. 34 (1958), 101. Clarence Winthrop Bowen, *History of Woodstock, Conn.*, *Genealogy of Woodstock Families*, vol. 7 (1943), vol. 2 (1930). Lucius Barnes Barwood, *Families of Early Hartford Conn.*, 1977. *D.A.R. Lineage Book*, vol. 156 (1937), 221. J. E. Ames, *Leadbetter Records*, 1917. Boston *Evening Transcript*, July 24, 1935. Charles Goodell, *Black Tavern Tales*, Brooklyn, Willis McDonald, 1932.

Humphrey westering: Seth K. Humphrey, Nash and Humphreys, vol. 3, H. B. Humphrey, "Some Notes."

25. **Union Lakes, Minn.:** Rev. Edward D. Neill, *History of Rice County, Minnesota. Minnesota Territorial Census Records*, 1857. **"was limited solely to a few months":** H. B. Humphrey, "Some Notes."
Granite Falls, Minn.: Edward D. Neill, *History of the Minnesota Valley*, Minneapolis, North Star Publ. Co., 1882. Carl and Amy Narvestad, *History of Yellow Medicine County, Minn.*, Granite Falls, Yellow Medicine County Historical Association, 1972.

26. **Regester ancestry:** Gilbert Cope, *Genealogy of the Smedley Family*, Lancaster, Pa., Wickersham Publ. Co., 1901. H. B. Humphrey, "Some Notes." *MJ*, Mar. 16, 1910.
"I followed my mother . . .": H. B. Humphrey, "Some Notes." Hubert Humphrey, "Notes for Bicentennial Celebration at Elk River, Minn., June 28, 1976," Box 16, PFPC, HP. H. B. Humphrey to Humphrey, Nov. 21, 1941, Box 16, PFPC, 1939–47, HP. Humphrey, "The Legacy My Father Left Me," *Atlantic Monthly*, Nov. 1966.

27. **"I believe I would have stopped . . .":** H. B. Humphrey, "Some Notes". F. E. Balmer, "The Cooperative Movements in Minnesota," 1930, Arthur McGuire Papers. John R. Humphrey, *Patronage Dividends in Cooperative Grain Companies*, Bulletin 371 (1916), U. S. Dept of Agriculture. John R. Humphrey, *A System of Accounts for Farmers Cooperative Elevators*, Bulletin 236 (1919), U. S. Dept of Agriculture.
"rammed-earth" house: *Montgomery County Billboard*, "Famous Mud House," June 16, 1971. Frances H. Howard interviews, Nov. 18, 1980, and Sept. 25, 1981.

28. **"Your grand letter fortified my faith . . .":** H. B. Humphrey to Humphrey, Nov. 21, 1941, Box 16, PFPC 1939–47, HP.
"Go to it": H. B. Humphrey to Humphrey, Mar. 23, 1945, Box 16, PFPC 1939–47, HP. Humphrey to H. B. Humphrey, May 29, 1945, Box 16 PFPC 1939–47, HP.

2:   THE NORWEGIAN CONNECTION

30. **Captain Sannes:** "Engebretsen-Sannes Family History," booklet, n.d., *Sannes Family*, Booklet, n.d., Box 5, PFPM, HP. "A. G. Sannes," memo, n.d. "Sannes genealogy," trans. from Norwegian, memo, Aug. 7, 1963, Box 5, PFPM, HP. Andrew Sannes naturalization record, June 30, 1890. Andreas and Tomine Sannes family Bible, Roger Sannes files. O. E. Rolvaag, *Giants in the Earth*, 62.
Also Rose A. O'Connor, *Sioux City, a true story. Iowa State Census, Woodbury County*, 1885. Sioux City *Journal*, "River Notes," Mar. 7–July 21, 1885. Dana R. Bailey, *History of Minnehaha County, S. Dak. Pioneer History, Minnehaha County's Norwegian Pioneers*. L. G. Ochsenreiter, *History of Day County*.
Also Julia Harshner letter, Dec. 23, 1980. Sherman Holland letters, Jan. 13, and May 11, 1981. Roger Sannes letters, April 17, 1981. Thorlief Sannes letter, June 3, 1983. Olga Burge (Sept. 29, 1980), Roger Sannes (Oct. 1, 1980) interviews.

31. **"He never was told . . .":** *Education*, 19. Humphrey, "Memo for files," Box 5, PFPM, HP, "Special Tribute to Hubert Humphrey," Watertown *Public Opinion*, Jan. 1978. Barry Lopez, "The Indians' Cottonwood," Minnesota *Volunteer*, April 1978.

33. **"My earliest recollection . . .":** Mary Engebretsen in "Sannes, Early Family History," n.d., Box 5, PFPM, HP. Mrs. Ruth Hagen interview, Sept. 30, 1968.
"Humphrey is coming . . .": Raymond Callsen, Watertown *Public Opinion*, Jan. 1978. Oliver Wanglie interview, June 2, 1981.

34. **Doland:** Best sources are Humphrey interviews with Producer Arthur Barron for TV film *My Childhood,* also Humphrey interviews with Norman Sherman for his memoirs.
35. "**Come on in, is mother after you too?**": *NYT,* April 29, 1968.
36. "**My mother said she . . .**": Humphrey, "Book Tapes," 16, Box 8, Autobiography files, HP.
37. "**I was very sick and . . .**": Humphrey interview with Sherman, n.d., prob. 1969, Box 2, Autobiography f., HP.
    "**I was brought up to . . .**": Ibid.
    "**I'd keep my money in . . .**": Humphrey interview with Barron, Oct. 31, 1963, Box 698, HP. Transcript Humphrey speech at Doland high school, April 1969. PFPMB u/p, HP.
38. "**and he would do things for them . . .**": Olga Burge interview.
    "**looked sideways at Helen . . .**": Mrs. Irven Herther interview, Watertown *Public Opinion,* Jan. 1978.
    "**When I went out of church . . .**": Humphrey interview with Arthur Barron, Oct. 31, 1963, Box 698, HP. Julian Hartt interview, Feb. 2, 1981.
39. "**Showed great tact in discussing . . .**": Doland *Times Record,* Mar. 15 and April 12, 1928. See also Doland *Times Record,* May 19, 1924; April 19, 1928; April 4, May 9, and 17, 1929. *NYT,* Aug. 28, 1964. Chicago *Tribune,* Feb. 23, 1968. Humphrey to Ruth Ewing, Feb. 20, 1946, Box 6, HP. Humphrey to Bob Fryer, Feb. 27, 1948, Box 6, HP. Humphrey to Rev. Albert Hartt, Feb. 27, 1948, Box 6, HP. Humphrey to Edna Holmes, Feb. 27, 1948, Box 6, HP. G. W. Cook to Humphrey, April 16, 1946, Box 3, HP. Humphrey to Blaine Rowlee, Mar. 7, 1946, Box 3, HP. Humphrey to G. W. Cook, Jan. 20, 1948, PFPA, HP. Humphrey to Janette Higgins, Jan. 3, 1946, Box 3, HP. Humphrey to Julian Hartt, Oct. 15, 1945. Humphrey to Claire Lovelace, Aug. 14, 1945, Box 2, HP. L. R. Hayes to Humphrey, Feb. 28, 1946, Box 3, HP. Humphrey to Hilda Gross, Box 2, HP. Humphrey to Merle Else, June 12, 1945, Box 2, HP. Tillie Ueland to Humphrey, July 2, 1945, Box 2, HP. Humphrey to Claire Lovelace, Aug. 14, 1945, Box 2, HP. Olive Doty to Humphrey, Sept. 17,

1945, Box 2, HP. Humphrey to Mrs. Herbert Gosch, June 25, 1945, Box 1, HP. Berwyn James to Humphrey, July 29, 1959, Box 51, HP. Humphrey to Michael Amrine, Sept. 29, 1959, HP. Mrs. Olive Doty in Doland *Times Record,* Nov. 9, 1950. Humphrey interview, *Parade* magazine, Oct. 1977. Humphrey speech at Doland high school, April 1969, PFPMB u/p, HP. Huron *Plainsman,* Jan. 15, 1978. Watertown *Public Opinion,* Jan. 1978. Rev. William R. Ellis letter, Jan. 14, 1981. Julian Hartt letter, March 11, 1981. Also Humphrey to E. S. McIntyre, June 27, 1974, PFPA, HP. Humphrey to Mrs. A. G. Sannes, Feb. 10, 1919, PFPMB u/p, HP. Humphrey to Ralph Henneman, Oct. 23, 1968, PFPA, HP. Aberdeen, S. D. *American-News,* Sept. 30, 1964. Juanita Decker to Humphrey, June 10, 1964, Box 694, HP. Humphrey to Juanita Decker, Aug. 22, 1964, Box 698, HP. "This is Humphrey," n.d., PFPMB u/p, HP. Berwin Schrader to Humphrey, Oct. 12, 1947, PFPA, HP. L. C. Ferguson to Humphrey, Dec. 28, 1974, Box 6, AAF74, HP. E. J. Eccleston to Humphrey, Oct. 20, 1968, PFPA, HP. Humphrey to Don Hofsommer, June 16, 1972, PFPA, HP. Humphrey to Bernice E. Webb, Sept. 9, 1947, PFPA, HP. Dolly Kline to Humphrey, Mar. 29, 1977, PFPA, HP. Humphrey to Ruth S. Anderson, July 26, 1971, PFPA, HP. Humphrey to John Egan, Dec. 14, 1976, PFPA, HP. Russell Ewing to Humphrey, July 18, 1972, Box 5, AAF72, HP. Humphrey to Vi Williams, Oct. 4, 1968, PFPMB u/p, HP. Lori Hjermestad to Humphrey, Dec. 15, 1977, PFPA, HP. Also Frances Howard, Deschler Welch (Sept. 30, 1980), Gordon Twiss (Sept. 30, 1980), Walter Hofer (Sept. 30, 1980), Robert Fryer (Sept. 29, 1980), Olga Burge interviews.

4: HIS FATHER

40. "**He never sells you a pill . . .**": *Education,* 26.
    "**Before the fact is the dream**": *Education,* 25.
    Father as youth: St. James (Minn.) *Plaindealer,* Sept. 26, 1968. Dr. Harry B. Humphrey, "Some Notes on the Humphrey (Humphreys) Family," Box 5, PFPM, HP. "A Dream Fulfilled," *Northwestern Druggist,* June 1947.

41. "No brother could have been . . .":
Olga Burge interview. Charles E. Gilbert, 22. Humphrey interview with
Norman Sherman, Nov. 25–30, probably 1969, Box 2, Autobiography files,
HP. *Education*, 24.

42. "a rebel in a politically othodox . . .": Humphrey, "My Father,"
Atlantic Monthly, Nov. 1966.
"My best friends are my children . . .": Ibid.
"Mother, you sleep for all of us":
Education, 27.
"Never go to bed . . .": Humphrey,
"My Father."
"I had normal ideas to . . .": Humphrey interview with Barron, Oct. 31,
1963, Box 698, HP.
"I heard things . . .": Humphrey, "My
Father."
"I place a lot of responsibility":
Humphrey interview with Barron.
"You know, my son Hubert . . .":
Ibid.
"Dad set such high standards . . .":
Ibid.
"Son, you're not half as smart . . .":
Ibid.
"Acti-vitty, boys . . .": Humphrey
speech at Doland high school, Frances
Howard interview.

43. "Now you treat your mother . . .":
Humphrey, "My Father."
"the city of God on earth": Julian Hartt
interview. Rev. William R. Ellis letter,
Jan. 14, 1981. *Education*, 29.
"Dad, Jonathan here . . .": *Education*, 26. Hazel Van Dyck interview Sept.
30, 1980. Humphrey, "My Father."

44. "I was a junior in high school . . .":
Humphrey interview with Barron.
Humphrey, "My Father."
"Through the years I carried . . .":
Ibid.
"You can't make a living . . .":
Humphrey interview with Barron.

45. "I put 25 cc of the serum . . .": Ibid.
Humphrey to Debbie Drain, Mar. 18,
1970, PFPA, HP. *MT*, April 28, 1946.
Watertown *Public Opinion*, Jan. 1978.

5: WILDERNESS YEARS

46. "From here on, it's on you": *Education*, 38.
"Now you go down to the Marigold . . .": Ibid., 38–9.

47. "I was awfully sweet on . . .": Ibid.,
39. Connie Nyman to Humphrey, Dec.
20, 1968, PFPA, HP. Lee Loevinger
interview Nov. 19, 1980.
"Something to start you back . . .":
Education, 42.
"I've just got to get out . . .": Ibid.,
43.
"Humphrey's Advantages": *Daily
Huronite*, Mar. 19 and April 2 and 30,
1931. Edgar Berman, "1968 Campaign
Diary," May 11, 1968, Berman files.
Humphrey to Willard Morrow, May 13,
1974. Willard Morrow to Humphrey,
May 17, 1974, Box 6, AAF76, HP.
Frances Howard, John Kildahl (Jan. 30,
1981 and Nov. 8, 1982), Jeffrey Boyd
(Feb. 8, 1981) interviews.

48. "Get the hell out . . .": Humphrey
interview with Norman Sherman, June
29, 1969, tape transcripts, Autobiography files, HP. *Education*, 44.
Scoutmaster: Humphrey, "My Scouting Past," *Scouting*, Jan. 1966. Humphrey speech at Emmanuel Luth. church,
Minneapolis, n.d., Box 24, HP. Hazel
Van Dyck interview. Humphrey to Vi
Williams, Dec. 31, 1972, PFPM, HP.

49. "Such a nervous person": Margaret
Hahn (July 3, 1982), Caroline Beatty
(July 3, 1982), Deschler Welch, and
Hazel Van Dyck interviews.
"It looked like a terrible . . .": *Time*,
Feb. 1, 1960. Huron *Plainsman*, Jan. 3,
1935. Humphrey tape transcripts, n.d.
"Book Tapes," Box 8, Autobiography
files, HP.
"Respect   them,   what   they
spend . . .": *Education*, 48. Humphrey
interview with Norman Sherman, June
24, 1969, Box 2, Autobiography files,
HP.
"Those who know you . . .": H. B.
Humphrey to H. H. Humphrey, Sr.,
Mar. 19 and Sept. 25, 1933, Aug. 20 and
Oct. 16, 1934, PFPMB u / p, HP. Also
J. H. Humphrey to H. H. Humphrey, Sr.,
Nov. 18, 1936, PFPMB u / p, HP. Hubert
Humphrey to Franklin D. Roosevelt,
Aug. 23, 1936, Box 24, OF 200 FF, RL.
Evening Huronite, Aug. 29, 1936. *Daily
Huronite*, Jan. 8, 1931.

50. Capitol College of Pharmacy: *Education*, 44–5. Humphrey interview with
Norman Sherman, June 24, 1969, Box
2, Autobiography files, HP. San Bernardino *Sun*, Aug. 28, 1964. *Drug News
Weekly*, Aug. 25, 1964. L. J. Maher
interview, Sept. 29, 1980.

"some of the emotional and spiritual . . .": Frances Howard interview.
Shouting match: Eisele, 23.
"Shapely, attractive, shyly . . .": Humphrey interview aired KTCA-TV, St. Paul, Jan. 14, 1978, quoted Cohen, 50.
"so young, unbelievably skinny": Muriel Humphrey interview with William Connell, April 30, 1978, 11, Connell files.
"The store came first": Ibid., 4.

51. Humphrey's mother: Ibid., 10–11. Frances Howard interview *Education*, 29. Julian Hartt, Hazel Van Dyke interviews.
"Hazel, there's too much family . . .": Hazel Van Dyke interview. Harry B. Humphrey to Humphrey, Sept. 25, 1933.
"This trip has impressed . . .": Education, 53.

52. Wedding: *Educatiion*, 55. Muriel Humphrey interview with Connell, 18. Humphrey interview with Norman Sherman, June 24, 1969, Box 2, Autobiography files, HP. Ravnholt memo, Oct. 1, 1965, PFPMB, u / p, HP.
"Hubert hated the wind": Muriel Humphrey interview with Connell, 12, 20, 21.

53. "It went right into postal savings": Ibid., 21.
"If we don't do something . . .": Hazel Van Dyke interview.
"Hubert, let's go for a ride": S. P. Glanzer interview Sept 29, 1980, *Education*, 57. Frances Howard interview.

PART TWO
6: MINNEAPOLIS, CITY ON THE SKIDS

57. City Background: Charles R. Walker, *American City;* "The Twin Cities," *Fortune*, Aug. 1936; I. Bernstein, 229–53; Theodore C. Blegen; Mildred Hartsough, "Transportation as a Factor in the Development of the Twin Cities," *Minnesota History*, Sept. 1926.
58. State background: C. R. Walker, "Minneapolis," *Survey Graphic*, Oct. 1936; Blegen; Kramer, *The Wild Jackasses;* Crampton; Mayer; Morlan.
59. "I hope the present system . . .": C. R. Walker, *American City*, 62.
"I am not a liberal, . . .": Minnesota *Leader*, Mar. 30, 1934.

"We declare that capitalism . . .": *MT*, Mar. 29, 1934.
"The businessmen are organizing . . .": I. Bernstein, *Turbulent Years*, 231.
The Dunne brothers: Tselos, 202; Draper, 316; V. H. Jensen, 317; Kramer, in *Harpers*, Mar. 1942.

60. "Not a wheel turning": *MJ*, Feb. 8, 1934.
"Shut tight as a bull's eye . . .": I. Bernstein, *Turbulent Years*, 234.
61. "organize and fight for . . .": C. R. Walker, *American City*, 86.
62. Battle of Deputies Run: Cannon, *History of American Trotskyism*, 151.
"For sale, one half bushel . . .": *The Organizer*, July 16, 1934.
"They had been shot while . . .": Sevareid, *Not So Wild a Dream*, 58.
"Suddenly I knew what fascism . . .": Ibid.
63. "the Citizens Alliance dominates . . .": I. Bernstein, *Turbulent Years*, 247.
"appointees of the federal . . .": Ibid., 248.
64. "suggested getting in touch . .": Ibid., 249.
"a very far-sighted . . .": J. Clay, 68.
65. Strike aftermath: D. Kramer, *Brothers;* G. D. Tselos, 485, 532. J. P. Cannon, *Socialism on Trial*, 72. Pahl. *MT*, July 21, 1980. *NYT*, May 17, 1982, D-14.

7: RETURN TO THE CAMPUS

66. Re-entry was "difficult": Muriel Humphrey interview with Connell, April 30, 1979, 22.
"I hadn't really made up . . .": *Education*, 58.
67. "He'd been away for so long . . .": Muriel Humphrey interview with Connell, 22.
"I will not bear arms . . .": Sevareid, 60. Richard Scammon (Sept. 23, 1981), Frank Adams (Sept. 10, 1980), Naftalin, Freeman, C. Donald Peterson (June 5, 1981) interviews. Mayer, 272.
"I didn't have much time . . .": Humphrey interview with Richard Heffner, June 3, 1968, Box 8, Autobiography files, HP. Humphrey, "Résumé of Experience," n.d. probably 1942, PFPA (M, for military), HP. New York *Post*, July 17, 1968. *MS*, Jan. 16, 1978. Humphrey interview, n.d. probably 1969,

"Book Tapes," Box 8, Autobiographical files, HP. Muriel Humphrey interview with Connell, 22.

68. **"a review of the basic political . . .":** Evron Kirkpatrick interview April 21, 1980 and Dec. 2, 1982. *Education*, 59.
"You sit down": Benjamin Lippincott interview, June 17, 1981.

69. **"More than anything else . . .":** Freeman interview, Kirkpatrick interview.
"I want to know who that . . .": Kirkpatrick interview.
"I swabbed toilets . . .": *MS*, Jan. 16, 1978. P. Kenneth Peterson (July 13 and Aug. 5, 1981), Herbert McClosky (Nov. 6, 1982), William Kubicek (July 23, 1980), Anton Thompson (Feb. 19, 1983), Freeman, Kirkpatrick, Jane Freeman (Mar. 10, 1982) interviews. *Education*, 61. *Minneapolis City Directory*, 1937–47, lists successive Humphrey residences.
"a slim, dark-haired . . .": F. Manfred, in *Minnesota History*.
"taken aback by the way . . .": Ibid. Scammon interview. Humphrey to L. F. Brown, Sept. 21, 1950, Box 88, HP. Frank Boddy to Humphrey, Aug. 13, 1945, Box 1, HP. Anne Kunkel to Humphrey, Mar. 21, 1948, Box 2, HP. Mildred Gillespie to Humphrey, June 21, 1945, Box 1, HP. Colin Lovell to Humphrey, Oct. 8, 1945, Box 2, HP. Gerald Barron to Humphrey, Aug. 21, 1945, Box 1, HP. Connie Davis Nyman to Humphrey, Nov. 26, 1968, PFPA, HP.

70. **"He was a liberal Democrat . . .":** Lippincott interview.
Moderates "socialist" conference: Lippincott interview. C. Donald Peterson interview. Elmer Benson to C. Donald Peterson, Oct. 26, 1938, Peterson files. *MS*, Mar. 1, 1938. Arnold Canfield to Humphrey, May 3, 1974, Box 1, HP. *MJ*, April 11, 1938. Frank Adams, Burton Paulu (June 19, 1981) and Dr. Harold Margulies (Feb. 26, 1983) interview.
"Had the poorest physical . . .": R. A. Siggelow to Humphrey, May 11, 1965. Box 4, PFPA, HP.

71. **"Gave the impression of . . .":** Ibid.
"He jammed the epiglottis down": *The Persuader*, Nov. 1941. Mrs. Ralph (Melba Hurd) Duncan to L. P. Devlin, May 16, 1966, PFPMB u/p, HP. L. P. Devlin, "Hubert H. Humphrey: His Speaking Principles and Practice."

72. **"How could we? We had no money":** Muriel Humphrey interview, with Connell.

Asher Christianson: Ibid., 23–4.
"The press orientation would have . . .": Ibid., 28. Humphrey's university transcript: PFPMB u/p, HP. Freeman, C. Donald Peterson, Kirkpatrick, Lippincott, Frank Adams, Kubicek, Frederick Manfred (June 6, July 10 and Aug. 23, 1981), Scammon interviews.

8:   IN HUEY LONG COUNTRY

73. **Living in Louisiana:** *Education*, 63. C. W. Bailey, in Sevareid, *Candidates 1960*, 178. Muriel Humphrey interview with Connell, 31, 34, 35. Humphrey on Huey Long, n.d., probably 1969, Box 2, Autobiography files, HP. Baton Rouge *Advocate*, Aug. 28, 1964. Charles Hyneman interview for American Political Science Association oral history project, Nov. 15, 1979
"Sweeping into the chamber . . .": *Education*, 64.

74. **"a pledge of 5-cent laundry":** Ibid, 63.
"They were well-organized . . .": Robert J. Harris interview, *Daily Reveille*, Nov. 18, 1939. Humphrey to Curtis Johnson, May 10, 1977, PFPA, HP.
"the great thrill of . . .": Robert J. Harris interview Feb. 3, 1981.
Masters thesis: *The Political Philosophy of the New Deal*, received M.A. 1940, published 1970.

75. **"The main characteristic of the pragmatist . . .":** Ibid., 13.
"is scientific in temper . . .": Ibid, 14.
Fascism "sacrificed" freedom Ibid, xxi. Humphrey to Rudolf Haberle, June 28, 1976, PFPA, HP.
"the essential features of . . .": Humphrey's Political Philosophy, 16.
"wrote one of the great compromises . . .": Ibid, 100.

76. **"ever-increasing concentration . . .":** Ibid., 108.
Not "negative" but "positive" liberty: Ibid., 88.
"apply social values in place of . . .": Ibid., 52.
"Democracy and socialism are . . .": Ibid., 105.
"Hubert was what in Europe . . .": Evan Thomas interview Feb. 25, 1980.
"This son of a smalltown druggist . . .": Jeane Kirkpatrick, "On the Cele-

bration of Hubert Humphrey," Woodrow Wilson Center, 1980.

77. "the six new rights . . .": Humphrey, *Political Philosophy*, 95–6.
"the blunder of isolationism . . .": Ibid., xxiii.
"there can be no peace . . .": Ibid., xxii.

78. "Humphrey, we're going to fail you . . .": Harris, and Kirkpatrick interviews. Charles Hyneman interview, Mar. 11, 1969, Autobiography files, Box 1 HP.
"Terribly upset" at war in Poland: W. Griffith, *Humphrey; a Candid Biography*, 67.
"Why, it's uneconomic": *Education*, 66. Gilbert, 33. Julian Hartt interview, Louisiana State transcript of grades, PFPM, HP.

9: WORKING FOR THE W.P.A.

80. "Thought of himself as a Democrat": Kirkpatrick and Freeman interviews. G. T. Mitau, *Politics in Minnesota*, 10, 22, 24. A. Naftalin, "History of the Farmer Labor Party," 127.
"I am frank to say . . .": Minnesota *Leader*, Mar. 30, 1934. Howard Y. Williams, interview, n.d., for Minnesota Historical Society.

81. For "enlightened capitalism": I. Hinderaker, 24, 59, 103, 272. McDermott 539. Stassen, *Where I Stand*, 1, 3, 53.
"Are They Communists or Catspaws?" Box 8, Ray P. Chase Papers.
"Here is the Proof": Hinderaker, 260, 352.

82. "Who is this man?" Naftalin, "History of the Farmer Labor Party," 352. J. M. Shields, 100. Joseph Ball interview, Feb. 7, 1981. *STPPP*, Oct. 14 and 17, 1938. Youngdale, *Populism*, 170.
"the turning points of the campaign": Joseph Ball interview.
"gloom in the Benson caravan": Shields, 101. STPPP, Oct. 17, 1938.
Stassen ascendancy: McDermott,401.
"The lights are going out . . .": Stassen, *Man Was Meant to be Free*, 5.

83. Humphrey's first job: Robert Harris, Kirkpatrick, Freeman, Naftalin, Dorothy Jacobson interview. *Education*, 68. William Anderson to Humphrey, Oct. 4, 1940, Box 16, PFPC, HP.
"They seemed to like me": *Education*, 67.
"broke, married, a daughter": Ibid.,

68. Humphrey to Colin Lovell, July 30, 1947, Box 5, PFPC, HP.

84. "It's just too much of a hardship": Freeman interview.
"I never thought I'd find . . . ": *Education*, 70.
"I've contacted hundreds of . . .": Humphrey to Charles Hyneman, Jan. 30, 1942, Hyneman files. Tom Berry to Humphrey, Sept. 20 and Oct. 17, 1940, Box 16, PFPC, 1939–47, HP. Albert J. Maag to Humphrey, Oct. 15, 1940, Box 16, PFPC 1939–47, HP. John G Rockwell to Humphrey, Sept. 27, 1940, Box 16, PFPC, 1939–47, HP. Helen Aaberg to H. L. Richards, Oct. 28, 1940, Box 16, PFPC 1939–47, HP. Glenn W. Thompson to Humphrey, Nov. 19, 1940, Box 16, PFPC 1939–47, HP. Ernestine Friedman to Humphrey, n.d., Box 16, PFPC 1939–47, HP. Hilda Smith to Humphrey, Mar. 24 and 27, 1941, Box 16, PFPC 1939–47, HP. Humphrey to Theodore Brameld, May 15, 1941, Box 16, PFPC 1939–47, HP. Humphrey to Reuben Latz, May 16, 1941, Box 16, PFPC 1939–47, HP. Helen Aaberg to Humphrey, Aug. 8, 1941 Box 16, PFPC, 1939–47, HP. Helen Ervin to Humphrey, Aug. 18, 1941, Box 16, PFPC, 1939–47, HP. H. A. Swanson to Humphrey, Sept. 8, 1941, Box 16, PFPC, 1939–47, HP. George Sundberg to Humphrey, Sept. 2, 1941, Box 16, PFPC 1939–47, HP. Humphrey to R. B. Fairbanks, Oct. 13, 1941, Box 16, PFPC, 1939–47, HP. Humphrey to William Coffey, Dec. 3, 1941, Box 16, PFPC 1939–47, HP.
"We missed his jabber, jabber . . .": Ruth McPartlin, "The St. Paul Labor College and Worker Education, a personal account," n.d., probably 1941, Box 1, HP.
"I was out on speaking . . .": Humphrey to Robert J. Harris, April 15, 1942, Box 16, PFPC, 1939–47, HP.
"The majority of Americans do not . . .": *Labor World*, Feb. 27, 1942.

85. "At any time you need . . .": Humphrey to Committee to Aid America by Defending the Allies, Minneapolis, May 16 1941, Box 16, PFPC, HP.
"This is our war": Humphrey to Robert Farmer, Sept. 30, 1941, Box 16, PFPC, HP.
"I've been doing a lot . . .": Humphrey to Charles Hyneman, Jan. 30, 1942, Hyneman files.

"He demolished me . . .": McClosky interview. McClosky interview with Arthur Naftalin, Feb. 2, 1978, Naftalin files.

"dull and inconsequential": Humphrey to Hyneman, Jan. 30, 1942, Hyneman files.

"We are in the baby business . . .": Ibid.

Job-seeking: "Personal Data sheet, Application for Federal Employment," PFPA (F-O), HP. "Résumé of Personal Experience," n.d., probably 1943, PFPA (M for military), HP. Humphrey to Dan West, Jan. 21, 1942, Box 16, PFPC 1939–47, HP. Jonathan Daniels to Humphrey, Feb. 9, 1942, Box 16, PFPC 1939–47, HP. R. G. Scobey to Humphrey, Feb. 10, 1942, Box 16, PFPC, 1939–47, HP. Humphrey to Halvor Haugen, Feb. 14, 1942, Box 16, PFPC 1939–47, HP. E. B. Young to Humphrey, Feb. 28, 1942, Box 16, PFPC 1939–47, HP. Philip Jessup to Humphrey, Feb. 26, 1943, Box 16, PFPC, HP. Humphrey to Frances Howard, Feb. 16, 1943, Box 16, PFPC, HP. J. Zamrazil to Humphrey, Mar. 1, 1943, Box 16, PFPC 1939–47, HP.

86. "I've found work . . .": Humphrey to Hyneman, Jan. 30, 1942, Hyneman files. "Report on Minneapolis Labor School on 'The World Today' Series," n.d., Box 27, CLU Papers. "Report on Open House," Jan. 28, 1941, Box 27, CLU Papers. "Report on Workers Education conference in Illinois," Oct. 6, 1941, Box 27, CLU Papers. "Report of 40 Unions Participating in Minneapolis Labor School," Oct. 14, 1941, Box 27, CLU Papers. Paul Hendrickson to Rebecca Barton, May 13, 1942, Box 2, CLU Papers. Minutes of Educational and Legislative Committee, Mar. 10, 1942, Box 25, CLU Papers. M. Finkelstein to Humphrey, Mar. 12, 1942, Box 16, PFPC 1939–47, HP. Humphrey to P. E. Lerman, Mar. 3, 1942, Box 16, PFPC 1939–47, HP. Humphrey to Claude Sheldon, Mar. 19, 1942, Box 16, PFPC 1939–47, HP. Humphrey to W. J. Doescher, April 8, 1942, Box 16, PFPC 1939–47, HP. Herman Erickson to Humphrey, Sept. 24, 1942, Box 16, PFPC 1939–47, HP. Humphrey to Max Lerner, Dec. 28, 1942, Box 16, PFPC 1939–47, HP. Humphrey to H. H. Humphrey Sr., Nov. 2, 1942, PF/PMB u/p, HP. Humphrey to Hilda Smith, Jan. 4, 1943, Box 16 PFPC 1939–47, HP. Frank Gannon to Humphrey, Jan. 10, 1943, Box 16, PFPC 1939–47, HP.

"I thought Hubert ought . . .": Kirkpatrick interview.

87. "All of us here . . .": Robert J. Harris to Humphrey, June 25, 1942, Box 16, PFPC, 1939–47, HP. Humphrey to Harris, April 15 and 24, 1942, and Harris to Humphrey, July 28, 1942, Box 16, PFPC 1939–47, HP.

"looked unbeatable": *Education*, 74.

"with him and the baby . . .": Humphrey to Frances Howard, Aug. 17, 1942, Box 16, PFFC, 1939–47, HP.

"I am reporting a change . . .": Humphrey to Local Board No. 2., Aug. 22, 1942, Box 16, PFPC 1939–47, HP. Stassen, *Man Was Meant to Be Free*, 45.

10: DASHING OUT OF NOWHERE

88. "Just listen to what . . .": Kirkpatrick and McClosky interviews.

"Fresh, funny, striking off . . .": McClosky interview. McClosky interview with Arthur Naftalin, Feb. 2, 1978, Naftalin files,

"Hubert was always in . . .": McClosky interview.

89. Judge Day: *Education*, 74. Haynes, 292. Frank Adams interview.

Naftalin as aide: *Education*, 74. Kirkpatrick, Freeman, McClosky, Naftalin interviews.

"My father was a total . . .": Dr. Walter H. Judd interview. Judd letter, April 15, 1981. Humphrey interview, with Norman Sherman, Nov. 25–30, probably 1969, Box 2 Autobiography files. HP. "In a very brave move he [Ball] had supported Roosevelt in 1944. In fact I was one of his strongest supporters at that time, and supported Joe Ball for election in 1942." Niels Nielson letter to *MT*, n.d., April 1943. Orville Freeman letter, June 18, 1981.

"Have you thought about . . ?" Judd interview.

"It takes $50 to file . . .": Ibid. Harlan Strong (June 1, 1981), Walter Bush Sr. (June 1, 1981), Harold Stassen (Jan. 5, 1983), Fred Manfred, Orville Freeman, Kirkpatrick interviews. Manfred letters, July 16 and 18, 1981.

90. "Gee, they're really hot . . .": Naftalin interview.

"New blood": Adams interview *MT*,

April 10, 1938. Haynes, 292. Judd and Naftalin interview.

Labor endorsement: *Education*, 74–5. Political Committee Executive board minutes, Mar. 13, and 15, April 5 10, 19, 16, May 24, 1943, Box 36, CLU Papers. CLU payment for Humphrey broadcast, June 14, 1943, Box 36, CLU Papers. William Simms letter, March 8, 1982.

"a new star is born": "Election News," n.d., probably April 1943, Box 47, HP. *MSJ*, May 11 and 27 1943. *MT*, May 28, 1943. Minneapolis *Labor Review*, April 8, 1943.

"Yes, but what about . . .": Fred Manfred interview in Luverne (Minn.) *Herald*, n.d. Haynes, 292. *Education*, 76.

91. **"Make Minneapolis Hum—Humphrey":** Kubicek interview.
"I'd hear the kind of . . .": McClosky interview. McClosky interview with Naftalin.
"He was so powerful . . .": Ibid. Manfred interview. Humphrey campaign speech texts April 10, 27, 30, May 1, 3, 5 (10-point program), 7, 8, 9, 14, 27 and June 1, 6, 9, 12, Box 24, HP.

92. **"What are these doing . . .?"** Naftalin interview. "Leadership for Minneapolis." brochure June 14, 1943, Box 47, HP.
"We were desperately short . . .": Humphrey to John H. Humphrey, July 1, 1943, Box 47, HP.
"The Fourth Ward fell down": G. Jensen report n d June 1943, Box 47, HP. *MSJ*, July 22, 1942. Freeman to Humphrey, May 8 and 23, and June 21, 1943, Box 16, PFPC 1939–47, HP. Bradshaw Mintener to Humphrey, June 14, 1943, Box 16, PFPC 1939–47, HP. Gene O'Brien, Naftalin, and P. Kenneth Peterson interviews. Humphrey to Melanie Conover, July 3, 1970, PFPA, HP. Humphrey to Douglas Hall, July 5, 1943, Box 16, PFPA, HP. Humphrey to Bradshaw Mintener, July 5, 1943, Box 16, PFPC 1939–47, HP. Harold Seavey to Humphrey, July 16, 1943, Box 16, PFPC 1939–47, HP.

11: FUSION ON THE LEFT

93. **His "spectacular" campaign:** *MSJ*, July 22 1945.
"Look, we'll make you governor . . .": McClosky interview. McClosky interview with Naftalin, Feb. 2, 1978. *Education*, 79–80.
Hubert was offered this . . .": Muriel Humphrey interview with Connell.

94. **"I can't do it, I'm a . . .":** *Education*, 80. McClosky interview. Muriel Humphrey interview with Connell.
"I'm going to be immodest . . .": Humphrey to Simmons Fentriss, June 27, 1973, Box 2, Autobiography files, HP. Humphrey to Allan P. Sindler, May 31, 1961, PFPA, HP. Naftalin, "History of the Farmer Labor Party." Gieske, 325. Haynes, 316–46. Shields, 262. Oscar Ewing to Elmer Kelm, Mar. 31, 1943, Box 1129, Democratic National Committee Papers, RL. Elmer Benson to Oscar Ewing, June 29, 1943, Box 1129, DNC Papers, RL. Oscar Ewing interview. April 29, 1969, TL. Douglas Kelm (Aug. 28, 1980) and Tom Kelm (July 21 and Oct. 5, 1981) interviews.

95. **Republicans a "plurality" party:** *Education*, 81–2. H. H. Humphrey, Sr., to Frank Walker, July 7, 1943, Box 1129, DNC Papers, RL. John J. Exon to Frank Walker, July 7, 1943, Box 1129, DNC Papers, RL., John R. Coan to Frank Walker, July 9, 1943, DNC Papers, RL. George E. Clifford to Ambrose O'Connell, "Memo re Hubert Humphrey, Jr.," July 21, 1943, Box 1129, DNC Papers, RL. Ambrose O'Connell to John J. Exon, July 22, 1943, Box 1129, DNC Papers, RL.
"By God, inside of 5 minutes . . . : Eisele, 54.
"Get into politics . . .": Bradshaw Mintener and Charles Turck interviews. Mintener letter April 29, 1981. Larry Nye to Charles Ficken, Aug. 14, 1943, Box 16, PFPC 1939–47, HP. Charles Ficken to Humphrey, Aug. 15, 1943, Box 16, PFPC 1939–47, HP. Humphrey to Charles Ficken, Sept. 1, 1943, Box 16, PFPC 1939–47, HP. D. Cohen, 99.
"Unity" was entirely possible: Humphrey to Ambrose O'Connell, Aug. 23, 1943, Box 1129, DNC Papers, RL.
"Let's call it the DFL party . . .": Ibid.

96. **"Progressive forces look to you":** Humphrey to Henry Wallace, Mar. 1, 1944, Box 16, PFPC 1939–47, HP. "Legal Aspects in Minnesota of Attempted Fusion or Merger of Political Parties," Aug. 5, 1943, Box 1, Francis M. Smith Papers, *STPPP*, Aug. 8 and 11, 1943. Viena Johnson outline of choices, Sept. 26, 1943, Farmer Labor

Association Papers, cited in Gieske, 326. *MT*, Nov. 28, 1943. Gene O'Brien (June 24, 1981), Naftalin, Kirkpatrick, and Meridel LeSueur interviews. Humphrey to Charles B. Cheney, Jan. 16, 1944, Box 16, PFPC 1939–47, HP. D. J. Smilow to Humphrey, Feb. 5, 1944, PFPC 1939–47, HP. Humphrey to Francis M. Smith Feb. 11, 1944, Box 1, Francis M. Smith Papers. Roger Rutchick and Francis M. Smith, "Minnesota Legal Aspects of Proposed Change of Party Names," Feb. 21, 1944. Box 1, Francis M. Smith Papers. Humphrey to H. C. Kiehn, Feb. 16, 1944, Box 16, PFPC 1939–47, HP. Harold Young to Humphrey, Feb. 24, 1944, Box 16, PFPC 1939–47, HP. Madeleine Long to Humphrey, Feb. 26, 1944, Box 16, PFPC 1939–47, HP. *MSJ*, Feb. 22, 1944. E. F. Selling to Humphrey, Feb. 22, 1944, Box 16, PFPC 1939–47, HP. Barney Allen to Humphrey, Feb. 29, 1944, Box 16, PFPC 1939–47, HP. Humphrey to William Neale Roach, Sept. 28, 1945, Box 2, Hp. Theodore S. Slen letter, May 6, 1981.
"got so cockeyed mad . . .": Humphrey to Charles Hyneman, April 22, 1944, Hyneman files.
"Since the fusion committee . . .": Ibid. Humphrey DFL convention keynote speech text, April 14, 1944, Box 24, HP. *Education*, 85. *MSJ*, April 14, 1944.
97. **Military servie status:** E. G. Perine to Humphrey, Nov. 6, 1943, Box 16, PFPC 1939–47, HP. W. D. Donahue, to Humphrey, Dec. 14, 1943, Box 16, PFPC 1939–47, HP. E. G. Perine to Humphrey, Feb. 17, 1944, Box 16, PFPC 1939–47, HP. Humphrey to Barney Allen, May 15, 1944, Box 16, PFPC 1939–47, HP. Humphrey to Werner Levi, May 31, 1944, Box 16, PFPC 1939–47, HP. Humphrey to Tom O'Brien, April 6, 1944, Box 16, PFPC 1939–47, HP. Harold Young to Humphrey, May 25, 1944, Box 16, PFPC 1939–47, HP. Humphrey to Charles Hyneman, May 26, 1944, Box 16, PFPC 1939–47, HP. Humphrey to Otto Silha, May 26, 1944, Box 16, PFPC 1939–47, HP. *MSJ*, June 9, 1945. Humphrey transcript "Book Tapes," Box 8, Autobiography files, HP. E. G. Perine to Humphrey, July 11, 1944, Box 16, PFPC 1939–47, HP. *Education*, 85–6. Humphrey to Selective Service Local Board No. 2, Dec. 9, 1944, Box 21, HP. Harry B. Humphrey to

Humphrey, Dec. 29, 1944, Box 21, HP.
Landlord: Humphrey to David E. Anderson, May 31, 1944, Box 16, PFPC 1939–47, HP. Humphrey to Frances Howard, Oct. 17, 1945, Box 16, PFPC 1939–47, HP.
"No man seemed more closely . . .": *Education*, 87–8.
"I was busier than a cat . . .": Humphrey to Charles Hyneman, Dec. 1, 1944, Hyneman files.
"weak, polluted, devoid of . . .": Hokah (Minn.) *Chief*, Sept. 7, 1944.
"We have not seen the like since . . .": Thomas L. Hughes interview, March 3, 1981 and July 8, 1983.
Benson calls Humphrey "fascist": *Education*, 85.
98. **Truman "without force":** Ibid., 87–8. Ellis Arnall to Humphrey, Jan. 7, 1945, Box 16, HP.
"I am deeply concerned . . .": Humphrey to Henry Wallace, Dec. 19, 1944, Box 1, HP.
"You typify to my mind . . .": Henry Wallace to Humphrey, Dec. 27, 1944, Box 1, HP. Humphrey to Joe Cloud, Dec. 5, 1944, Box 1, HP. *STPD*, Dec. 5, 1944.

12: "I'M MAYOR!"

99. **"My life is in a kind . . .":** Humphrey to Mrs. Barney Allen, Feb. 9, 1945, Box 1, HP.
"I am to report for induction . . .": Humphrey to Evelyn Petersen, Feb. 6, 1945, Box 1, HP.
"He has made such plans . . .": Mrs. H. H. Humphrey, Sr., to Muriel Humphrey, Jan. 23, 1945, Box 16, PFPC 1939–47, HP.
"I am a lousy 4-F . . .": Humphrey to Robert Gannon, Feb. 16, 1944, PFPC 1939–47, HP. *STPD*, Jan. 19, 1945. Humphrey to Lt. K. G. Boggs, Feb. 8, 1945, Box 20, HP. Notice of Classification cards from Local Board No. 2: Sept. 27, 1944, "classified II-A until April 1, 1945"; Jan. 10, 1945, "classified I-A"; Feb. 15, 1944, "classified IV-F"; Sept. 20, 1945, "classified IV-A"—Box 21, HP. Elmer Kelm to Robert Hannegan, Jan. 8, 1945, Box 1129, DNC Papers, RL. *Northwest Industrial News*, Sept. 1964, 4.
Labor support: Minutes of Political Committee, Jan. 20, 1945, Box 36, CLU Papers. *STPD*, Jan. 25, 1945. Hum-

phrey to Sander Genis, Feb. 5, 1945, Box 1, HP. Humphrey to Earl Bestor, Feb. 6, 1945, Box 1, HP. Humphrey to Robert Wishart, Feb. 7, 1945, Box 1, HP. Humphrey to Lester Covey, Feb. 8, 1945, Box 1, HP. Robert Wishart to Humphrey, Feb. 15, 1945, Box 1, HP. Humphrey to Paul Tinge, Feb. 8, 1945, Box 1, HP. Haynes, 361. Sander Genis (July 14, 1981), Anthony (June 30, 1983), and Ernest (July 4, 1983) DeMaio interviews.

100. **"I intend to be community . . .":** Humphrey to John Cowles, Sr., Feb. 14, 1945, Box 1, HP. A. E. Bowman to Humphrey, Jan. 19, 1945, Box 1, HP. John Cowles, Sr., to Humphrey, Feb. 25, 1945, Box 1, HP. F. P. Heffelfinger to Humphrey, Jan. 16, 1945, Box 1, HP. **"the gangsters of Chicago . . .":** Bradshaw Mintener interview May 13, 1980.
"reminiscent of gangland . . .": *MT*, Jan. 23 and May 16, 1945. William Simms interview.
"the most corrupt within . . .": *The Public Press,* Dec. 1944. Humphrey to Evelyn Petersen, Feb. 6, 1945, Box 1, HP.
"I am no blue nose . . .": Humphrey to John Cowles, Sr., Feb. 14, 1945, Box 1, HP.

101. **"I was born in a little Norwegian . . .":** Humphrey to Rev. Tenner Thompson, Mar. 1945, Box 1, HP.
"the militancy of labor . . .": Humphrey to Robley Cramer, Mar. 12, 1945, Box 1, HP. Humphrey to Ellis Arnall, Mar. 22, 1945, Box 1, HP. Haynes, 364. George Killion to Gael Sullivan, Mar. 8, 1947, Box 1129, DNC Papers, RL. 1945 financial donors listed: Box 47, HP.
Fred Gates: *Education,* 90. William B. Horn letter, June 28, 1943. William Simms letter Mar. 8, 1982.

102. **"Do you want gangsters . . . ?":** Mintener interview.
"Businessmen are coming to . . .": P. H. Carr to Humphrey, May 18, 1945, Box 1, HP. George K. Belden to Humphrey, April 18, 1945 and Humphrey to Belden, May 1, 1945, Box 1, HP.
"14" and "Hooligan" games: *MT*, May 16, 1945.
"a boner": H. H. Humphrey, Sr., to Humphrey, May 20, 1945, Box 16, PFPC, 1939–47, HP.
"Every gambling joint in . . .": Humphrey to Capt. Orville Freeman,

May 23, 1945, Box 1, HP. Haynes I, 371.
103. **"Bob, I know what's bothering . . .":** *Education,* 96. Mintener interview. Ed Ryan interview with Naftalin, July 11, 1978, Naftalin files. Haynes, 370.
"What do you mean, what do I want?" Simms interview. Susan Berman, "Memoirs of a Gangster's Daughter," *New York* magazine, July 27, 1981.
104. **"We will enforce the law":** Ryan interview with Naftalin, Naftalin files.
"Our job of closing down . . .": *MT*, July 6, 1946.
"I know you are paying off . . .": Max Kampelman in *NYT*, Jan. 18, 1978; *Education,* 99–100.
"The gangsters are out . . .": Mintener to Humphrey, July 30, 1945, Box 1, HP. *MSJ*, July 27, 1945. Des Moines *Register,* July 28, 1945. *STPD*, Aug. 1, 1945. *MSJ*, Mar. 19, 1948. Mintener interview.
"The Police Department will . . .": Humphrey to Ed Ryan, Oct. 17, 1945, Box 2, HP.
105. **"In this testing time . . .":** Humphrey to Julian Hartt, Oct. 15, 1945, Box 2, HP.
"If you want to run a hotel . . .": *CWA News,* July 1967, 11.
"I did not enforce the law . . .": *MSJ*, April 30, 1947.
"I didn't send the police . . .": Humphrey to John Cowles, Sr., May 6, 1947, Box 49, HP.
"Members of the Jewish faith . . .": Henry Piper to Humphrey, June 24, 1945, Box 2, HP.
"I fully recognize . . .": Humphrey to Nell Russell, July 27, 1945, Box 29, HP. Minneapolis *Spokesman,* Aug. 25, 1945, and Jan. 15, 1946.
"I have already learned . . .": Humphrey to Grace Langley, Feb. 26, 1946, Box 4, HP.
Race the most "ticklish" matter: Humphrey to Russell Nye, Nov. 9, 1945, Box 2, HP.
106. **"capital of anti-Semitism . . .":** McWilliams, in *Common Ground.*
"self-survey": L. H. Bennett to R. K. Youngdahl, Mar. 11, 1946, PFPA (civil rights speech), HP. Minneapolis *Times,* Mar. 27 and Dec. 27, 1946. *MT*, Sept. 5, 1949. John Harding, "Community Self Survey," *Congress Weekly,* Mar. 5, 1948.
FEP ordinance passed: Minneapolis *Times,* Jan. 21, 1947. Hyman Berman in

Jewish Social Studies, Summer-Fall 1976.
"an office or position . . .": Humphrey to John Cowles, Sr., Feb. 14, 1945, Box 1, HP.
"We have a very large . . .": Humphrey to Ken Byerly, Oct. 5, 1945, Box 1, HP. *MSJ*, Sept. 20, 1945.
"We are not used to a mayor . . .": Emmet Salisbury to Humphrey, Sept. 25, 1946, Box 4, HP. John H. McMillan to Humphrey, Sept. 7, 1945, Box 2, HP.

107. "We need you": Humphrey to Croil Hunter, Feb. 14, 1946, Box 4, HP.
"I cannot tell you how pleased . . .": Humphrey to Paul O. Solum, April 22, 1946, Box 4, HP.
"What a bum player . . .": Mike Finkelstein to Humphrey, Aug. 19, 1946, Box 3, HP.
"Thanks for attending . . .": Harry Bullis to Humphrey, Mar. 25, 1946, Box 3, HP.
"Every item marked 'Rush' ": Naftalin and Simms interviews.
"Harry Carlson told me . . .": H. H. Humphrey, Sr., to Humphrey, Feb. 21, 1946, Box 3, HP.

108. "You are getting a reputation . . .": Frank Rarig to Humphrey, Mar. 1, 1946, Box 4, HP.
"What there is left of it": U.P. dispatch, Aug. 1, 1945.
"Are you the City Attorney?" Robert O. Naegele interview, Aug. 27, 1980.
"What the hell are you doing, Kelm?" Douglas Kelm interview.
"Dear Doc . . . I'm mayor": Humphrey to Robert J. Harris, Oct. 8, 1945, Box 1, HP.
"a hilarious house party . . .": Humphrey to John Seabert, Jan. 7, 1946, Box 3, HP.
"I literally live for the job": Humphrey to Gideon Seymour, July 15, 1946, Box 4, HP.
"I know that is inexcusable . . .": Humphrey to Frances Howard, May 26, 1947, Box 17, PFPA, HP.
"grown in stature . . .": Frances Howard to Humphrey, May 18, 1947, Box 17, PFPA, HP.

109. Reelected: Humphrey to George Phillips, Feb. 27, 1947, Box 6, HP. Humphrey to A. C. McIntosh, April 17, 1945, Box 5, HP. Humphrey statement re charter: Mar. 5, 1947, Box 8, HP. H. H. Humphrey, Sr., to Humphrey, May 14, 1947, Box 17, PFPA, HP. Harry B. Humphrey to Humphrey, June 10, 1947,

Box 17, PFPA, HP. Olga Burge to Humphrey, June 15, 1947, Box 17, PFPA, HP. Humphrey to Frances Howard, June 23, 1947, Box 17, PFPA, HP. Humphrey to Harry B. Humphrey, May 26, 1947, Box 17, PFPA, HP. Humphrey to Guy Alexander, Jan. 8, 1947, Box 36, CLU Papers. Political Committee minutes Jan. 20, 1947, Box 36, CLU Papers. Humphrey to Henry Moen, May 2, 1947, Box 17, PFPA, HP. Humphrey to Tom Davis, May 2, 1947, Box 17, PFPA, HP. Humphrey to Charles Ward, May 5, 1947, Box 17, PFPA, HP. Humphrey to Croil Hunter, May 5, 1947, Box 17, PFPA, HP. *MT*, Jan. 6, April 22 and May 6, 1947 *MSJ*, May 13, 1947. *Education*, 107. Press release Ray Ewald appointed finance committee chairman, May 16, 1947, Box 17, PFPA, HP. Humphrey to Harry H. Leonard, May 20, 1947, Box 17, PFPA, HP. Robert Wishart to Humphrey, May 1, 1947, Box 17, PFPA, HP.
"I hope you feel that I . . .": Humphrey to Mintener, Oct. 28, 1947, Box 5, HP.

13: FISSION ON THE LEFT

111. cold war: Solberg, *Riding High*, 7, 32.
112. "As far as I'm concerned, Orv": Humphrey to Freeman, Jan. 10, 1945, Box 1, HP. Naftalin, Freeman, Eugenie Anderson, Kubicek, Genis, Meridel LeSueur, Anthony and Ernest DeMaio interviews. Haynes, 395. *Education*, 96, 105.
"I simply can't conceal . . .": Humphrey to Henry Wallace, April 12, 1945, Box 1, HP. Wallace to Humphrey, April 21, 1945, Box 1, HP. Humphrey to Wallace, April 19, 1945, Box 1, HP. Wallace to Humphrey, April 24, 1945. Box 1, HP. Walton, 32.
"There will be an attempt . . .": Humphrey to Robert Hannegan, Dec. 19, 1945, Box 1, HP.
"Wished not to become . . .": Elaine Cox to Humphrey, Feb. 21, 1945, and Humphrey to Elaine Cox Feb. 26, 1945, Box 1, HP. Humphrey to Cyrus Barnum, Feb. 14, 1946, Box 3, HP. Handbill, Feb. 3, 1946, Box 1, FP. Minneapolis *Times*, Feb. 9, 1946.
Second ward caucus: *MT*, Mar. 13, 1946. Minneapolis *Times*, Mar. 13, 1946.

Minutes, Feb. 19, 1946, meeting of United Labor committee, *Labor*, Box 36, CLU Papers. Naftalin, Kubicek, Anthony DeMaio interviews.

113. "Sit down, you son of . . .": *Education*, 104. *MSJ*, Feb. 20, Mar. 11, 16, 1946. *MT*, Mar. 26, 30, 31, 1946. Minneapolis *Times*, Mar. 31 and April 1, 1946. *STPPP*, Mar. 31 and April 1, 1946. *STPD*, April 1, 1946. Minneapolis *Labor Review*, April 4, 1946. Minnesota *Leader*, April 1946. Kubicek, Naftalin, and Gene O'Brien interviews. J. M. Shields, 297.
"Humphrey tempted to run for Congress . . .": Humphrey to Dudley Parsons, Aug. 19, 1946, Box 4, HP.

114. Loeb letter: *New Republic*, May 13, 1946, 699. Eugenie Anderson interview.
"struggling with the same problem": Eugenie Anderson to James Loeb, July 25, 1946, Series 3, Box 23, ADA Papers. Loeb to Eugenie Anderson, July 25, 1946, and Eugenie Anderson to Loeb, Aug. 18, 1946, ibid.
"the position we had been pleading": Eugenie Anderson to James Loeb," ibid.
"Not only must we say . . .": *MS*, Sept. 7, 1946.
"a very personal friend": Humphrey to Mrs. Barney Allen, Sept. 24, 1946, Box 53, HP.
"Mr. Wallace says . . .": *MT*, Sept. 22, 1946. Valley City (N.D.) *Times-Record*, Sept. 27, 1946. Humphrey to Charles Turck, Oct. 29, 1946, Box 53, HP.
"Whatever happens in any part   ": Humphrey to Mrs. Barney Allen, Sept. 24, 1946, Box 53, HP.
Wallace in Minneapolis: Humphrey to Harold Young, Oct. 31, 1946, Box 49, HP. Eugenie Anderson report, Oct. 1946, Series 3, Box 23, ADA Papers. Eugenie Anderson and Cecilia Wallace (Aug. 25, 1981) interviews.

115. "We seemed to be fighting . . .": Eugenie Anderson interview.
". . . for your encouragement": Douglas Hall to Humphrey, Nov. 20, 1946, Box 48, HP. Robert Wishart to Humphrey, Aug. 26, 1946, Box 4, HP. Wishart to Humphrey, Nov. 13, 1946, Box 49, HP. Freeman memo to Humphrey, "The Doug Hall Problem," n.d., Box 48, HP.
"This organization is not . . .": *NYT*, Nov. 17 and 24, 1946. CIO, *Daily Proceedings of the 8th Constitutional Convention*, Nov. 18–22, 1946, Atlantic City,

113–14. M. M. Kampelman, *The Communist Party and the CIO*, 226.
Humphrey at ADA founding convention: *Education*, 105, 108. Brock, 51. Naftalin, Eugenie Anderson, Joseph Rauh, Loeb interview.

116. Benson calls Truman "imperialist": Box 15, Benson Papers.
"We're not going to let the totalitarians . . .": *Education*, 106. *MT*, Mar. 19, 1947. *STPD*, Mar. 19, 1947.
"them or us": Humphrey to Gael Sullivan, June 10, 1947, Box 52, HP.
"a political party that has to . . .": Humphrey to C. O. Madsen, Mar. 26, 1947, Box 49, HP.
"unfortunately for the success . . .": Humphrey to Dudley Parsons, April 1, 1947, Box 5, HP.
"Exhilarating" meeting: *Education*, 107. Humphrey to James Carey, Mar. 23, 1948, and Humphrey to Walter Reuther, July 15, 1947, Box 56, HP.

117. "They were begging for . . .": Freeman interview. Naftalin interview.
"I recruited five young men": Freeman interview.

118. "We had created such a steamroller . . .": William Kubicek interview. Freeman to Stephen Harrington, Aug. 12, 1946, Box 52, HP. William Simms to William G. Rhodes, Sept. 23, 1947, and Humphrey to William G. Rhodes, Nov. 16, 1947, Box 47, HP. Donald Fraser (July 7, 1981), Douglas Kelm, Freeman interviews.
"Goebbels types". Kubicek interview.
"If these are rightwingers . . .": Douglas Kelm interview.
"It's all over; we've won": Freeman interview.

119. "May I suggest as one friend . . .": Humphrey to Gottfried Lindsten, et al., Dec. 31, 1947, Box 48, HP.
"The only ones I have ever . . .": Humphrey to Henry Olson, Dec. 29, 1947, Box 6, HP.
"If he's not one, he's gypping . . .": Freeman and Karl Rolvaag (Sept. 20, 1980), interviews. Walter Mondale interview with Connell, CP.
"Your associations with . . .": Minnesota *Leader*, Mar. 1948. For pre-election polls, Humphrey to J. Howard McGrath, Jan. 6, 1948, Box 52, HP.

120. "with only 300 members": Minnesota *Outlook*, April 1, 1948. "Proposed Procedure for Regular DFL Precinct Caucuses and Ward Meetings," leaflet, April

30, 1948, in Box 3, DFL Party Papers. Freeman interview.

"legally entitled to participate": Minnesota Committee for Wallace memo, April 23, 1948, Box 48, HP. James Shields memo, n.d. 1948, Box 48, HP.

"Bill said he told Henry . . .": Humphrey to Barney Allen, Jan. 15, 1948, Box 53, HP. Harold Barker and Humphrey to J. Howard McGrath, Feb. 21, 1948, Box 49, HP. Freeman and Gerald Heaney (Oct. 9, 1980 and March 5, 1982) interviews.

"We may lose": Humphrey to Gael Sullivan, April 19, 1948, Box 52, HP.

"the leftwing is planning . . .": Minneapolis *Times*, April 29 and 30, 1948. *MT*, April 29, May 3 and 9, 1948. *MS*, May 4, 1948. McCarthy in Haynes, 603. Iron range outcome, Haynes, 603.

121. "one of the most vicious . . .": Mitau, in *Minnesota History*, Spring 1955, 192.

"an illegal delegate from . . .": Ibid.
1948 DFL convention: *MS*, June 12 and 14, 1948. *STPPP*, June 12, 1948.
leftwing "rumped": *MS*, June 14, 1948. Ione Hunt, Rolvaag, Naftalin, Eugenie Anderson, Freeman interviews.

122. "If Humphrey had only . . .": Heaney interview.
"We were the organizers . . .": Ibid.

123. "We forgot about the ADA . . .": Ibid.

14: VICTORY OVER BALL

124. "His views are too much like . . .": Humphrey to H. H. Humphrey, Sr., as reported by Ben Williamson to *Time*, Jan. 2, 1949.
"I don't think anybody else . . .": Humphrey to Gael Sullivan, Jan. 7, 1948, Box 52, HP.
"We not only face defeat . . .": Humphrey to James Loeb, Mar. 24, 1948, Box 52, HP.
"The reelection of the President . . .": Humphrey to Chester Bowles, April 9, 1948, Box 51, HP.

125. Visit to Roosevelt Junior: Humphrey to Franklin D. Roosevelt, Jr., Feb. 25, 1947, Box 6, HP. William Simms interview.
"Would it be wise for me . . . ?" Rauh, Eugenie Anderson and Joseph Lash (Oct. 21, 1982) interviews.
"Mayor Humphrey asks your advice . . .": Ibid.

"Bill Simms informed me . . .": H. H. Humphrey, Sr., to Humphrey, July 2, 1948, Box 48, HP.
Triumphal return: *Education*, 116. *MS*, July 16, 1948, 6.

126. Wallace endorsement: *MT*, Oct. 2, 1948.
"I disagreed with him . . .": *MS*, Aug. 6, 1948.
Humphrey at Farmers Union convention: *STPD*, Oct. 14, 1948. Truman to Humphrey, Nov. 12, 1948, VIP corr., HP. Dr. Robert Thatcher interview, Feb. 28, 1983.

127. "if American policy had been . . .": *MT*, Sept. 27, 1948.
"He could talk a bird . . .": Joseph Ball interview.
"We have tried to slant . . .": Freeman to David Weber, Oct. 19, 1948, Box 11, DFL State Central Committee Papers.
"I want to break up these . . .": Humphrey keynote speech, Bemidji, Minn., Oct. 5, 1948, Box 55, HP. Press Release, "A Day in Humphrey's Campaign Cavalcade," Oct. 1948, Box 57, HP. Thomas R. Hughes interviews, Nov. 21, 1980, and Sept. 24, 1981.
"In his speeches he lets the corn . . .": *New Republic*, Oct. 18, 1948.
"What did I say of . . . ?" Press release, Oct. 1948, Box 57, HP. Humphrey schedule, Sept. 26, 1948, Box 12, HP.

128. "He wore us 25-year-olds . . .": Douglas Kelm interview. Walter Mondale interview with Connell.
Labor support: Smaile Chatek to Humphrey, Oct. 28, 1948, Box 55, HP. Wishart to Humphrey, Oct. 5, 1948, Box 56, HP. Lee, 149. Haynes, 681, 688, 715. *UE Local 1146 Shop News*, Mar. 1948, Box 53, HP. Humphrey to Lester Covey, Mar. 13, 1948, Box 6, HP. Humphrey to Hugh McElroy, Mar. 24, 1948, Box 7, HP. George Phillips to A. F. Whitney, Feb. 3, 1948, Box 36, CLU Papers. *MT*, June 12, 1948. Minnesota *Labor*, June 4, 1948. *MS*, June 12, 1948. Jacob Potovsky to Humphrey, June 22, 1948, Box 49, HP. Humphrey to Walter Reuther, July 15, 1948, Box 56, HP.
"virtuoso performances": *MT*, Oct. 30, 1948.

129. 1948 contributors list: George Totten and Howard Gelb, "Humphrey's Personal Campaign Committee 1948," report to Minnesota Secretary of State, Box 58, HP. Also unannotated list in Financial

Contributors 1948 file, HP. Humphrey to Ray Ewald, Oct. 20, 1948, Box 55, HP. Simms to H. H. Humphrey, Sr., Aug. 13, 1948, Box 17, PFPC, HP. Morris Ebin to Milton Kronheim, Nov. 8, 1949, Box 17, PFPC, HP.
Gene McCarthy or any of . . .": Freeman interview.
"His name is anathema": quoted *MT*, Dec. 3, 1948.
"defiance of the entrenched . . .": Ibid.
"Druggists are the finest talkers . . .": St. Louis *Post-Dispatch*, Jan. 2, 1949.
130. Sendoff to Washington: *MS*, Dec. 7 and 17, 1948. *MT*, Dec. 23, 1948.
"You have given expression to . . .": H. H. Humphrey, Sr., to Humphrey, Nov. 7, 1948, Box 17, PFPC, HP.

PART THREE
15: THE UNHAPPY WARRIOR

133. "glib, jaunty spellbinder . . .": *Time*, Jan. 17, 1949, 13. Lowry.
134. made chairman ADA: *NYT*, Jan. 13 and April 11, 1949. Humphrey to Herbert Lehman, Feb. 18, 1949, Humphrey file, LP. *Trade Union Courier*, Jan. 17, 1949. Hamby, *Beyond the New Deal*, 284.
Senate club: *Education*, 121–23. W. S. White.
135. "There are enough votes . . .": *STPPP*, Jan. 14, 1949.
Taft-Hartley & the club: Humphrey to Robley Cramer, Jan. 10, 1949, Box 726, HP. Evans and Novak, *LBJ*, 28.
136. "No longer content with . . .": *MSJ*, Dec. 11, 1948.
"You and Lyndon are not permanently . . .": Gorman, 67. *CR*, Vol. 119, Jan. 24, 1973 (Humphrey tribute to Johnson). Humphrey interview with Walter Cronkite, CBS Special Report, Jan. 24, 1973.
"dark days—I despaired": Harris, 153. *Education*, 147.
"How in hell could the people . . .": *Education*, 124.
"He was this brash and . . .": Carl Auerbach interview with Naftalin, July 13, 1978, Naftalin files. Rauh interview.
"Once when he was in the Senate . . .": Auerbach interview, Naftalin files.
"Hubert never felt at home . . .": Rauh interview.
137. "I'll knock his block . . .": James Rowe interview, Nov. 13, 1980 and Feb. 21 and

March 29, 1983. *NYT*, Feb. 22, 1949, 22. Chester Bowles to Humphrey, Mar. 7, 1949, Box 88, HP.
"I think you are a man . . .": Kirk Bates to Humphrey, Mar. 8, 1949, Box 16, PFPC, HP.
Cyril King incident: *Education*, 121.
"Mr. President, I rise . . .": *CR*, 95, 1713, Mar. 2, 1949. Humphrey newsletter, Mar. 3, 1949, Box 2, KP.
138. Civil rights defeat: *CR*, 95, 2260, Mar. 11, 1949. *NYT*, Mar. 3 and 16, 1949. *STPPP*, May 12, 1949.
"I am going to remember . . .": Humphrey to Robley Cramer, Jan. 10, 1949, Box 726, HP.
"That's not the right way . . .": U. S. Senate, 81st Congress, 1st session, *Hearings to repeal the Taft-Hartley Act*, Feb. 1, 1949, 183.
"I don't want to make . . .": Ibid., 317. *MT*, Feb. 25, 1949.
139. "Have you ever heard . . . ?" *CR*, 95, 1334–35, Feb. 17, 1949. *MT*, April 11, 1949.
"royally trimmed": *MT*, Feb. 21, 1949. Los Angeles *Times*, quoted in *MT*, Feb. 25, 1949.
"who first loomed . . .": Thomas Sancton, *Nation*, Mar. 26, 1949, 351.
"You are simply . . .": Gideon Seymour to Humphrey, April, 1949, Box 726, HP.
140. "Senators, listen to this": *CR*, 95, 4027 April 7, 1949.
"I've never worked so hard . . .": Humphrey to Freeman, Mar. 2, 1949, Box 88, HP.
"purely and simply an undemocratic . . .": Howard University speech reprinted, *CR* 95, A1259, Feb. 5, 1949.
"rotten political bargain . . .": New York *Post*, April 10, 1949.
141. "because it then becomes . . .": *NYT*, June 10, 1949.
"public ownership and development . . .": *Christian Science Monitor*, April 11, 1949.
"an honorable word in . . .": Wheeling *Intelligencer*, Aug. 22, 1949.
His first Congressional Record: See *CR* index, Vol. 95; Humphrey's items fill 12 columns. *STPPP*, April 30, 1949, *NYT*, July 22, 1949.
"I am battling my heart out . . .": Humphrey to Emil Krieg, April 29, 1949, Box 726, HP.
"I have been the Administration's . . .": Ibid.

Taft-Hartley repeal speech: *CR*, 95, 7542, 7623, June 10 and 14, 1949, reprinted as "The Case for a Fair Labor Policy," by AFL-CIO, 68 p. PFPMB u / p, HP. Lee, 181. *NYT*, June 11, 1949. Pomper, in "The Repeal of Taft-Hartley," 323. Humphrey newsletter, June 12, 1949, Box 2, KP.

142. "Does the senator think . . . ?" *CR*, 95, 7561, June 10, 1949.
"We have taken quite a beating . . .": Humphrey to Roy Blakey, July 1, 1949, Box 88, HP.

143. "The Republicans and Dixiecrats . . .": Humphrey to Cormac Suel, Aug. 8, 1949, Box 726, HP.
"took up the smear job": Ibid. Dodge County (Minn.) *Independent*, Aug. 25, 1949.
"He has introduced or . . .": *CR*, 95, 12637, 12450, Aug. 29, 1949.
"I don't want to brag, Phil . . .": Humphrey to Philip S. Duff, Jr., Aug. 31, 1949, Box 726, HP. David Lloyd to Humphrey, Aug. 30, 1949, Box 626, HP.

144. "This committee's very existence . . .": *CR*, 96, 2328, Feb. 24, 1950, *Education*, 129–31.
"I have mentioned nine . . .": *CR*, 96, 2610, Mar. 2, 1950. Sherrill and Ernst, 92.

145. "a violation of the intent . . .": *NYT*, Mar. 20, 1950. *STPPP*, Feb. 25, 1950. Lawrence Rogin interview, Jan. 4, 1982.
"Harry Byrd was a phony . . .": Eisele, 93.
Labor subcommittee report: Humphrey press release, April 27, 1950. Box 2, KP. Kampelman interview. Sept. 17, 1981.
"This may be the biggest . . .": *CR*, 96, 9233, June 27, 1950.

146. "got to learn about taxes . . .": Kampelman interview with Connell, Mar. 27, 1979. Connell files. Kampelman interview.
"He was the quickest study . . .": Joseph Pechman interview with Connell, April 24, 1979, Connell files. Kampelman and Walter Heller (June 16, 1981) interviews.
"Is it true that . . ?" Heller interview.

147. Tax loopholes speech: *CR*, 96, 13671–13705, Aug. 23, 1950. *Education*, 149. *NYT*, Aug. 24, 25, 28, 30, 1950. Humphrey, *Tax Loopholes*. Douglas, "The Problem of Tax Loopholes," 21–43. Lehman to Humphrey, Aug. 25, 1950, Humphrey file, LP.
Chevy Chase household: *Education*,

123. Humphrey to Vanita Beidler, Sept. 7, 1950, Box 88, HP. *Pathfinder*, Jan. 26, 1949. *MSJ*, Dec. 7, 1948. William Simms interview. Humphrey interview with William McGraffin, Chicago *Daily News*, June 13, 1964. *WP*, April 3, 1960.
"We have a big grocery bill . . .": Humphrey to Vanita Beidler, Sept. 7, 1950, Box 88, HP.

148. "All the way home . . .": Robert Humphrey interview, Aug. 12, 1981.
"Your difficulty is purely . . .": Dr. Luther Terry to Muriel Humphrey, June 17, 1949, PF/PMB u/p, HP. Humphrey to H. H. Humphrey, Sr., June 23, 1949, PF/PMB u/p, HP. Humphrey income tax returns 1949, Box 6, PFPF. Muriel Humphrey interview with Connell, April 30, 1979, 56. Connell files. Fentriss interview with Humphrey, Box 2, Autobiography files, HP. Humphrey to Fred Gates, Jan. 2, 1950, Box 88, HP. Gates to Humphrey, Mar. 20, 1950, Box 88, HP. Skip Humphrey, (June 17 and July 23, 1981), Orville and Jane Freeman interviews.

149. "my best friend": *Education*, 126. MS, Oct. 25, 1949. Humphrey to William Green, Dec. 31, 1949, Box 88, HP. Guy W. Cook to Humphrey, Dec. 20, 1949, Box 88, HP. Humphrey, "My Father," *Atlantic Monthly*, Nov. 1966. Humphrey to Truman, Jan. 2, 1950, PPF, Folder 4232, TL.

16:   COLD WAR CAPER

150. "I don't care if . . .": *MSJ*, Dec. 7, 1948. Simms, Freeman, Atherton Bean (Sept. 3, 1980), Lester Malkerson (June 4, 1981) interview.

151. "thought at first . . .": *MT*, July 11, 1951. Humphrey to Darrell DeVilliers, Mar. 11, 1954, Box 6, PFPC, HP. Humphrey to DeVilliers, April 5, 1955, Box 6, PFPC, HP. Humphrey to Earl Larson, Oct. 5, 1955, Box 6, PFPC, HP. Humphrey to Anton Huseby, Nov. 28, 1955, Box 6, PFPC, HP. Chicago *Tribune*, Oct. 20, 1968. *NYT*, Oct. 31, 1968.

152. "Ewald opened the subject . . .": Robert O. Naegele interview. Humphrey to Freeman, Jan. 6, 1949, Box 1, Freeman Papers. *Education*, 173, Kampelman interview
"Don't even tell . . .": Kampelman interview.
"Looks as if our judgeship . . .":

Truman to Humphrey, July 6, 1951, PPF, folder 4232, TL.
"It has surely been of help . . .": Humphrey to Truman, July 12, 1951, PPF, folder 4232, TL. Truman to Humphrey, July 16, 1951, PPF, folder 4232, TL. Humphrey memo to himself, Jan. 16, 1973, u/p, HP. Kampelman to Eugenie Anderson, July 11, 1951, Box 61, HP. Gerald Heaney to Humphrey, July 5, 1951, Box 88, HP. *MT*, July 5, 1951. *NYT*, July 5, 6, 8, 9, 15, 1951. *Christian Science Monitor*, July 11, 1951. *Time*, July 16, 1951.

153. "You stay out . . : William Benton, 1968 interview for Columbia University Oral History Project, 210. Humphrey transcripts "Book Tapes," n.d. Box 8, Autobiography files, HP. Honolulu *Star-Bulletin*, June 17, 1951. Humphrey to Emory Lingle, June 21, 1951, Box 63, HP. Benton report on McCarthy, *CR*, 97, 9498–9500, Aug. 6, 1951. Humphrey to Benton, Aug. 27, 1951, Box 51, HP. Benton to Humphrey, Sept. 1, 1951, Box 61, HP. Humphrey to Benton, Aug. 9, 1951, Box 60, HP. Humphrey to Eugenie Anderson, Aug. 10, 1951, Box 60, HP. Benton to Humphrey, Aug. 15, 1951, Box 61, HP. Humphrey to Benton, Aug. 31, 1951, Box 61, HP. Hyman, 22.
"I am an old hand . . .": Benton to Humphrey, April 11, 1951, Box 60, HP Benton to Humphrey, July 23, 1951, Box 60, HP.
"the kind of story you like . . .": Benton to DeWitt Wallace, July 18, 1951, Box 60, HP.
"I'm working on one . . .": Benton to Muriel Humphrey, Sept. 26, 1957, Box 560, HP. Humphrey to Simms et al., Nov. 1951, Box 701, HP.
"thrilling and exciting experience": Humphrey to "Dear Folks," longhand Nov. 1951, Box 701, HP. *Education* 157–58. Benton to Humphrey, Nov. 5, 1951, Box 701, HP.
"made myself a terrific bore . . .": Humphrey to Kampelman, Nov. 12, 1951, Box 701, HP.
"the French are truly artists . . .": Ibid.
"Water, plain water . . .": Ibid.
"the weak pillar of NATO": Ibid.
"I say the German question is . . .": Humphrey to Kampelman, Nov. 22, 1951, Box 701, HP. *MSJ*, Nov. 13 1951.
"Brother, if you ever appreciate . . .": Humphrey to Kampelman, Dec. 4, 1951, Box 701, HP.

Humphrey for president 1952: Kampelman and John Lane (Jan. 4, 1982) interviews. Naftalin, "Minnesota." Humphrey to Lehman, Sept. 30, 1952, Humphrey file, LP. Humphrey to Bowles, May 10, 1952, Box 86, BP. Humphrey to Eugenie Anderson, May 19, 1952, Box 4, AP. STPPP, May 2, 1952. Hamby, *Beyond the New Deal*, 487.

155. "Politics is a strange admixture . . .":
Humphrey to Benton, Sept. 30, 1952, Box 66, HP.
"thrilling letter": Benton to Humphrey, Oct. 6, 1952, Box 66, HP.
"heartbroken": Humphrey to Benton, Nov. 18, 1952, Box 66, HP.

156. "the Dept. of Peace is located . . .": Truman to Humphrey, Jan. 3, 1952, Box 70, HP.
"Your proposed 15-point program . . .": Truman to Humphrey, Aug. 31, 1950, General file, (Humphrey), TL. Humphrey to Truman, Aug. 18, 1950, General file (Humphrey), TL.

157. Anti-Communist subcommittee: Subcommittee on Labor and Labor-Management, *Hearings* (1952) and Report, (1953): *Public Policy and Communist Domination of Certain Unions*. Kampelman, Ph. D. dissertation, "The Communist Party and the CIO:" Graham Dolan, "Who Is This Guy Humphrey?" in *Union*, Jan. 28 and Feb. 25, 1952. *American Communist Association News*, Mar. 1952. *Labor*, Mar. 22, 1952. "Senator Humbug," *March of Labor*, April 1952. Sherrill and Ernst, 73–84. *U.S. News & World Report*, Dec. 28, 1951. "Humphrey Introductory Remarks," Subcommittee Hearings, Mar. 17, 1952, Box 1, KP.
Butler bill: CR, 100, 14192, Aug. 11, 1954.
"and we can have one . . .": Ibid, 14148. A. R. Smith, 273.
"I am tired of . . .": Eisele, 98.

158. "cleverly conceived . . .": New York *Herald-Tribune*, Aug. 11, 1954. *NYT*, Aug. 13, 1954. *PRO*, Oct. 1954. *I. F. Stone's Weekly*, Sept. 6, 1954. Parmet, *Jack*, 306. (Sept. 22, 1981).
"unconstitutional and unconscionable": Gerald Siegel interview, Sept. 22, 1981.
"On McCarthy, my opponent . . .": Humphrey to J. C. Stiepan, Aug. 18, 1954, Box 109, HP.
"I'm tired of hearing this talk . . .": *CR*, 100, 14210, Aug. 12, 1954.
"The Communist Party isn't really

. . .": Humphrey to David B. Leonard,
Sept. 20, 1954, Box 104, HP.
"the violent capture": Communist
Control Act text, *CR*, 100, 14208ff, Aug.
12, 1954. Kampelman, Siegel interviews. Siegel interview, Feb. 11, 1977,
for JL. McAuliffe, 134.

159. **"superpolitical ploy . . .":** Rauh
interview.
"grave doubts": Schlesinger to Hum-
phrey, Sept. 14, 1954, Box 104, HP.
"personally": Rosenberg to Hum-
phrey, Aug. 23, 1954, Rosenberg files.
Humphrey to Rosenberg, Aug. 27, 1954,
Box 104, HP.
"It's not one of the things . . .":
Humphrey interview, 1957, for Colum-
bia Uiversity Oral History Project.
Humphrey to Mrs. Herman Brandt,
Aug. 14, 1954, Box 109, HP. Hum-
phrey to Anabel Bancroft, Aug. 18, 1954,
Box 104, HP. Kampelman memo to
Herbert Waters, Aug. 19, 1954, Box 104,
HP. Carl Chrislock to Humphrey, Aug.
21, 1954, Box 104, HP. W. H. Smith to
Humphrey, Aug. 24, 1954, Box 104, HP.
Humphrey newsletter, Aug. 30, 1954,
Box 104, HP. Humphrey to James W.
Holliday, Sept. 2, 1954, Box 104, HP.
Humphrey to Ned O'Neill, Sept. 7,
1954, Box 104, HP. Humphrey to
Charlton Dietz, Sept. 11, 1954, Box 104,
HP. Humphrey to Warren Haggstrom,
Sept. 11, 1954, Box 104, HP. Hum-
phrey to Rev. George Lapoint, Sept. 11,
1954, Box 104, HP. Humphrey to K. L.
Shishler, Sept. 16, 1954, Box 104, HP.
Humphrey to Mrs. L. H. Lackore, Sept.
18, 1954, Box 104, HP. Humphrey to
Joseph Goldberger, Sept. 25, 1954, Box
104, HP. Leo Marx to Humphrey, Sept.
27 and Humphrey to Leo Marx, Oct. 9,
1954, Box 104, HP.
"These rats will not get out . . .":
CR, 100, 15108, Aug. 19, 1954.
"adored" Humphrey: McGovern
interviews. Sept. 17, 1981, and June 15,
1983.

17:   LEARNING THE HARD WAY

160. **"The Southern Democrats ought
. . .":** Humphrey to Dudley Parsons,
Dec. 17, 1947, Box 6, PFPC 1939–47,
HP.
161. **"He knew the senators . . .":** Humphrey interview with Joe Frantz Aug. 17,
1971, for JL. Kampelman interview with

Naftalin, Jan. 17, 1978, Naftalin files.
William C. Simms letter, Jan. 19, 1982.
"that Minnesota is a great . . .":
Eisele, 94.
"He wanted to crossbreed me . . .":
Kearns, 139.
"He didn't enjoy talking . . .": Hum-
phrey interview with Frantz for JL.
"Do you think you can help me?"
Ibid.
162. **"(Thanks) for your support . . .":**
Humphrey to Lyndon Johnson, Sept. 13,
1951, Box 63, HP. Humphrey to John-
son, Oct. 4, 1951, WHFN (HHH),
Container 2, JL.
Long and the inner dining room:
Education, 161.
"Exhilarating" hint: Ibid., 163.
"Let me tell you . . .": Ibid., 164.
Humphrey interview with Norman
Sherman, n.d., probably 1969, Box 2,
Autobiography files, HP. W. Griffith
213–14. Baker, with King, 61. W. S.
White, *Citadel*, 111. Evans and Novak,
LBJ, 55–6. W. S. White, *The Professional
Lyndon B. Johnson*, 63.
163. **"Hubert, come over . . ."** McGaffin
in Chicago *Daily News*, June 13, 1964.
"you and your fascists . . .": Kampelman, "HHH, Political Scientist."
"by this time . . .": Humphrey interview with Frantz for JL.
164. **"I've stopped kicking the wall":** *Time*,
Sept. 4, 1964.
"foremost Zionist": Kampelman interview in Connell, "Notes of Foreign Policy Discussion," June 21, 1978, Connell
files. Humphrey re. NATO: *CR*, 95,
9777–8, July 20, 1949. *NYT*, Jan. 22,
1951. Humphrey Senate speech "Essen-
tials of American Foreign Policy," April
25, 1951, Box 4, AP. J. W. Fulbright
interview, Nov. 14, 1980.
**Secretary Benson's "disaster insur-
ance" speech:** Gilbert, 309. Herbert
Waters, Burton Joseph, Dwayne Andreas
interviews. Humphrey interview with
Kampelman, Dec. 14, 1964, for JL. *Education*, 184. *STPPP*, Jan. 12, 1953. Humphrey to Lyndon Johnson, Mar. 12, 1954,
WHFN(HH), JL. Humphrey to Tru-
man, June 8, 1953, Post-Presidential files
(Humphrey), 1953–59, TL. Humphrey
to Mrs. W. C. Christopherson, June 16,
1953, Box 724, HP. Humphrey speech
for overseas food aid, June 30, 1953, Box
724, HP. Drew Pearson in *WP*, July 15,
1953. Humphrey to James Markham,
July 20, 1953, Box 94, HP. Humphrey

newsletters Aug. 24, Sept. 14, 21, and 28, 1953, Box 8, Minnesota Republican State Central Committee Papers. Lyndon Johnson to Humphrey, Sept. 13, 1954, WHFN(HH), JL.

165. **"Had fun pitching bundles . . ."**: Humphrey newsletter, Oct. 19, 1953, Box 8, Minnesota Republican State Central Committee Papers. Herbert Waters interviews, May 12, 1980, April 20 and May 10, 1982. Wesley McCune interview, Sept. 17, 1982.

Humphrey and P. L. 480: Waters and Andreas interviews, May 6 and 27, 1982, June 11 and 29, 1983.

"You are certainly entitled . . .": Walter George to Humphrey, July 11, 1953, Box 94, HP. Willard Cochrane interview, Sept. 18, 1982.

166. **Andreas background**: Unannotated list 1948 campaign contributors, Box 58, HP. Simms letter, Mar. 8, 1982. *NYT*, Jan. 20, 1954. *WP*, Jan. 29, 1955. *Time*, Jan. 25, 1954.

"We kept after them . . .": Humphrey to Andreas, April 22, 1954, Box 115, HP.

"You bet we're pleased": Andreas to Humphrey, April 28, 1954, Box 115, HP. Andreas to Kampelman, June 22, 1954, Box 70, HP. Simms to Andreas, June 29, 1954, Box 70, HP. Humphrey to Andreas, Jan. 18, 1955, Box 208, HP. Andreas to James McConnell, Mar. 1, 1955, Box 115, HP. Humphrey to Andreas, April 28, 1955, Box 560, HP. Kampelman to Gerald Heaney, May 31, 1955, Box 560, HP. Andreas to Humphrey, July 19, 1955, Box 115, HP. Andreas to Humphrey, Nov. 10, 1955, Box 75, HP. Humphrey to Andreas, Mar. 31, 1954, Box 115, HP. Charles Bailey in Sevareid, ed. *Candidates 1960*, 166–67. Val Bjornson interview, June 11, 1981.

167. **"If you say as much . . ."**: Val Bjornson interview. Humphrey interview, June 21, 1977, JL. Tom Davis to Humphrey, Jan. 25, 1954, Box 71, HP. *STPD*, Feb. 9, 1954. Humphrey to Lehman, Feb 23, 1954, Humphrey file, LP. Humphrey newsletters Mar. 1, 8, and 29, 1954, Box 8, Minnesota Republican State Central Committee Papers, Humphrey to H. O. Sonnesyn, Mar. 26, 1954, Box 74, HP. Humphrey to Anton Thompson, Mar. 31, 1954, Box 89, HP. Freeman to Humphrey, April 9, 1954, Box 88, HP. Humphrey to Mitchell Perrizo, April 19,

1954, Box 88, HP. Humphrey to Freeman, April 19, 1954, Box 88, HP. Freeman to Humphrey, April 20, 1954, Box 88, HP. Gilbert, 292. Humphrey to Doris Kirkpatrick, July 20, 1954, Box 89, HP. Humphrey to Lehman, Aug. 3, 1954, Humphrey file, LP. Humphrey to Walter Cramond, Aug. 11, 1954, Box 12, CLU Papers. Humphrey to Lehman, Oct. 7, 1954, Humphrey file, LP. Humphrey to Benton, Oct. 14, 1954, Box 89, HP.

Parity: Wilcox and Cochrane, *Economics of American Agriculture*, 497.

"He's the only one who . . .": Anton Thompson letter, Mar. 21, 1983. Andreas interview.

"I disagree with most . . .": Humphrey interview, June 21, 1977, JL.

168. **George letter** to *MS*, Ibid.

"Orv was the ornery Marine . . .": Kubicek interview.

"If Humphrey had had Orville . . .": Heaney interview.

"Any country that can . . .": Eugene Foley interview, Dec. 26, 1980 and Nov. 10, 1982.

"Hubert was throwing his arms . . .": Val Bjornson interview.

"an earthquake": Val Bjornson to Leonard Hall, Nov. 17, 1954, Bjornson files. *MT*, Nov. 8, 1954. Official vote tally: Humphrey 642,193; Bjornson 479,619; Frank Ryan 12,467; Vince Dunne 4,683, *Minnesota Legislative Manual, 1955*.

18: COMPROMISE IS NOT A DIRTY WORD

169. **"Mellowed . . ."**: Humphrey to Robert R. Humphrey, Jan. 14, 1955, Box 89, HP. Humphrey to David Ginsburg, April 28, 1955, James Wechsler files. Humphrey to Lehman, Jan. 10, 1955, Box 3, KP. Humphrey to Kefauver, Jan. 11, 1955, Box 3, KP. Humphrey to Thomas Stokes, Jan. 14, 1955, WHFN, Container 2, JL. Humphrey to Walter White, Jan. 13, 1955, WHFN, Container 2, JL. Humphrey to Cecil Newman, Jan. 18, 1955, Box 3, KP. *PRO*, Feb. 1955.

"abject surrender": Walter White press release, Jan. 13, 1955, WHFN, Container 2, JL.

170. **"political sops"**: *NYT*, Feb. 13, 1955.

**"You have always talked straight

. . .": Humphrey to Johnson, Feb. 14, 1955, Box 3, KP.

Warnings to colleagues: Humphrey to Lister Hill, Mar. 14, 1955, Box 560, HP. Humphrey to Thomas C. Hennings, May 17, 1955, Box 3, KP.

"I needle him . . .": Humphrey to Paul Butler, Mar. 14, 1955, Box 560, HP. Humphrey to Butler, June 1, 1955, Box 560, HP. Humphrey to Roy Wilkins, June 1, 1955, Box 560, HP. Johnson to Humphrey, June 9, 1955, VIP corr., HP.

171. **"In the light of . . .":** *STPPP*, June 12, 1955. Humphrey to Dorothy Jacobson, July 14, 1955, Box 560, HP.

"I miss having you . . .": Humphrey to Johnson, July 30, 1955, VIP corr., HP. Johnson to Humphrey, Sept. 26, 1955, WHFN(HH), JL.

"Program with a heart": *WS*, Nov. 23, 1955.

"mere slogans and promises": Evans and Novak, *LBJ*, 152–53.

"I really hope, Lyndon . . .": Humphrey to Johnson, Nov. 28, 1955, VIP corr., HP.

"Don't you cut, shuffle or . . .": Gene O'Brien interview.

"Lyndon is no battling . . .": Humphrey to Markham, Dec. 28, 1955, Box 89, HP.

"When Johnson stepped in . . .": *CR*, 105, 1853 (Feb. 5, 1959). Also *CR*, 103, 2607 (Feb. 26, 1957) and *CR*, 104, 10876 (June 11, 1958). Humphrey to Markham, July 2, 1956, Box 89, HP.

172. **"I propose to enter . . .":** *NYT*, Nov. 17, 1955. J. B. Martin, *Stevenson*, vol. 2, 220. Stevenson to Ray Hemenway, Nov. 15, 1955, Box 560, HP. Walter Cramond to Paul Butler, Sept. 29, 1955, Box 12, CLU Papers. Humphrey to Heaney, Nov. 28, 1955, Box 560, HP.

"Orville Freeman ran a . . .": Heaney interview. Freeman, Miles Lord (Feb. 24, 1981 and Sept. 22, 1982), Tom Kelm interviews. Humphrey memo for the file, Dec. 27, 1955, Box 560, HP. Humphrey to Cecil Newman, Feb. 8, 1956, Box 560, HP.

"I'm Estes Kefauver . . .": Patrick O'Donovan, in *The Reporter*, April 5, 1956. *New Republic*, Mar. 5, 1956.

"The situation is all fouled . . .": Humphrey to George Totten, Feb. 9, 1956, Box 560, HP. Stevenson to Humphrey, Jan. 30, 1956, Box 560, HP. *NYT*, Mar. 21, 1956.

173. **Crossover voting:** Richard Scammon

letter, Mar. 10, 1982. J. B. Martin *Stevenson*, vol. 2, 281. Martin and Plaut, 21. Ray Hemenway to Humphrey, Mar. 28, 1956, Box 560, HP. Humphrey to Alden Bye, April 12, 1956, Box 560, HP. Eric Sevareid interview, 1968, for Columbia University Oral History Project, 22. William Kubicek to Humphrey, Mar. 24, 1956, Box 560, HP. Eric Sevareid column, May 3, 1956, Box 560, HP.

"heartsick": Humphrey to Norman Dahl, April 12, 1956, Box 560, HP. Humphrey to Drew Pearson, Mar. 25, 1956, Box 89, HP. *WP*, Mar. 24, 1956.

"Those Republicans really . . .": Humphrey to Eugenie Anderson, Mar. 21, 1956, Box 6, AP.

"disaster": Stevenson to Humphrey, May 14, 1956, Box 560, HP.

"I'm walking around in . . .": Humphrey to Stevenson, May 14, 1956, Box 560, HP.

"Old Humphrey had to go around . . .": Eisele, 103. Humphrey to Heaney, May 5, 1956, PFPA "Vacation Trips," HP. Heaney to Humphrey, May 14, 1956, Box 560, HP. Humphrey to Freeman, May 23, 1956, Box 560, HP. Humphrey to Heaney, May 23, 1956, Box 560, HP. Heaney to Humphrey, May 31, 1956, Box 560, HP. Humphrey to M. F. Sweeney, May 28, 1956, Box 560, HP. Humphrey to Ione Hunt, April 12, 1956, Box 560, HP. Humphrey to Curtiss Olson, May 8, 1956, HP.

"already forgotten . . .": Benton to Humphrey, May 23, 1956, Box 89, HP.

174. **"greatest political speech . . .":** "Memo on Vice Presidential candidacy," probably by Kampelman, July 2, 1956, Box 89, HP.

"wonderful": Benton to Humphrey, Dec. 19, 1955, Box 89, HP.

"I expected it": Humphrey to Eugenie Anderson, July 10, 1956, Box 6, AP. Charles Hamilton to Humphrey, July 19, 1956, Box 560. *Journal of Proceedings*, Democratic National Committee, April 25, 1956, DNC Files 1956, National Archives.

"thing I had in my craw": Humphrey interview with Kampelman, Dec. 16, 1964, KL. Parmet, *Jack*, 357. *NYT*, July 10, 1956.

"Well, Hubert, why don't . . . ?" *Education*, 188.

"Hubert, if you are acceptable . . .": *Education*, 188. Humphrey interview with Kampelman, Dec. 16, 6 KL. Humphrey to Edith Weiss, July 30, 1956, Box 560, HP. *Congressional Quarterly*, July 30, 1956. Eugene McCarthy to Joseph Clark et al., July 30, 1956, Box 560, HP. Humphrey to Eugene McCarthy, July 23, 1956, Box 560, HP. Humphrey to Johnson, July 30, 1956, Box 560, HP. Humphrey to John Kennedy, July 30, 1956, Box 560, HP. Martin and Plaut, 22–3. Willard Wirtz interview, Sept. 22, 1981.

"left the hotel with stars . . .": Humphrey interview with Kampelman, Dec. 16, 1964, KL. Humphrey to A. L. Marovitz, July 23, 1956, Box 560, HP. Humphrey to Eugene McCarthy, July 23, 1956, Box 560, HP. Humphrey to Edith Weiss, July 30, 1956, Box 560, HP. *STPPP*, July 31, 1956. Herbert Waters to Marvin Rosenberg et al., Aug. 2, 1956, Box 560, HP. "A Fighting Candidate for Vice President," n.d., Box 560, HP. Johnson to Humphrey, Aug. 3, 1956, Box 562, HP. Humphrey to Johnson, Aug. 8, 1956, Box 562, HP.

175. "I've never seen him so upset": Sevareid interview, 1968, for Columbia University Oral History Project, 31. "Hubert, I'm for you": Humphrey interview with Kampelman, July 30, 1964, KL. Martin and Plaut, 23. "We told him the delegates . . .": Martin and Plaut, 23.

176. "It's all over": Gorman, 251. John Sharon interview. Nov. 7, 1967, KL. Chester Bowles interview, 1968, for Columbia University Oral History Project, 684. J. B. Martin, *Stevenson*, vol. 2 343. Evans and Novak, *LBJ*, 237. Humphrey to Robert Short, Aug. 9, 1956, Box 560, HP. *NYT*, June 25, 1956. John Bystrom memo, Aug. 14 and 15, 1956, Box 560, HP. Mitchell Perrizo Memo, Aug. 15, 1956, Box 560, HP. Henry Arens to Humphrey, Aug. 17, 1956, Box 560, HP. Humphrey to Mrs. J. E. Wasche, Sept. 4, 1956, Box 560, HP. *NYT*, Aug. 18, 1956. Neil Staebler to Gerald Heaney, Aug. 21, 1956, Box 562, HP. Herbert Waters to John Kennedy, Aug. 21, 1956, Box 560, HP. William Connell to Herbert Waters, Aug. 21, 1956, Box 562, HP. Martin and Plaut, 88. Freeman, Waters, Heaney, Martin Agronsky (April 4, 1983), Eugenie Anderson interviews. "I'm for Kefauver": Martin and Plaut, 88. "That was the worst . . .": Muriel Humphrey to *Time* reporter, Sept. 11, 1960.

"I've never seen a guy . . .": John Sharon interview, 1970, for Columbia University Oral History Project, 32. "I dreamed about you . . .": Humphrey to John Kennedy, Sept. 8, 1956, Box 560, HP.

177. "You would have been the best . . .": Kennedy to Humphrey, Sept. 18, 1956, Box 560, HP. "felt very low . . .": Humphrey to Johnson, Sept. 10, 1956, WHFN(HH), JL. "You certainly have had a rough . . .": Johnson to Humphrey, Sept. 18, 1956. WHFN(HH), JL. "They build character . . .": Humphrey to Clara Sarvala, Sept. 8, 1956, Box 560, HP. Humphrey to Mrs. Clara Nielsen, Sept. 10, 1956, Box 560, HP. Humphrey to D. J. Isman, Sept. 10, 1056, Box 560, HP. Humphrey to Albert Gore, Sept. 6, 1956, Box 560, HP. Humphrey to Bowles, Sept. 4, 1956, Box 138, BP. Humphrey to Mrs. Olive Humphrey, Sept. 9, 1956, Box 89, HP. Humphrey to Hazel and Dewey Van Dyck, Sept. 9, 1956, Box 560, HP. Humphrey to Lehman, Sept. 4, 1956, Humphrey file, LP. Humphrey to Llewellyn Humphrey, Aug. 24, 1956, Box 89, HP. Littlefork (Minn.) *Times*, Aug. 23, 1956. Steve Nehotte to Humphrey, Aug. 29, 1956, Box 560, HP. Humphrey to Robin Lord, Aug. 31, 1956, Box 560, HP. Bowles to Humphrey, Aug. 26, 1956, Box 138, BP. Thomas Corcoran to Humphrey, Aug. 31, 1956, WHFN(HH), JL. Humphrey to Leonard Eriksson, Sept. 15, 1956, Box 560, HP. "Politics is a cold, hard . . .": Martin and Plaut, 71. "A young friend named . . .": Humphrey to F. J. Rarig, Nov. 19, 1956, Box 560, HP. "I put everything . . .": Humphrey to J. L. Markham, Nov. 19, 1596, Box 560, HP.

178. "You broke faith . . .": Pearson in *WP*, Jan. 13, 1957. Humphrey to Paul Butler, Dec. 7, 1956, Box 560, HP. Gorman, *Kefauver*, 289. "Now Lyndon, you know . . .": Eisele, 104. Humphrey to J. L. Markham, Jan. 23, 1957, Box 89, HP. "We've got to change . . .": Humphrey interview, July 23, 1957, for Columbia University Oral History Project. John Howe to Benton, Dec. 11, 1956,

Box 89, HP. Sundquist, *Politics and Policy*, 230. Clark, *Congress: The Sapless Branch*, 1.

179. **"We wanted someone in . . ."**: Humphrey interview, for Columbia University Oral History Project. C. Anderson, 137.

"a wonderful omen": J. L. Markham to Humphrey, Jan. 9, 1957, Box 89, HP. "Senate Resolution 29, submitted by Sens. Humphrey, Anderson, Clark, and Douglas," Jan. 3, 1957, Box 647, HP.

"Motion to Table . . .": Jan. 4, 1957, Box 647, HP. Johnson to Humphrey, Jan. 23, 1957, WHFN(HH), JL.

"What do you want me . . . ?" Gerald Siegel interview JL. Johnson to Humphrey, June 7, 1957, VIP Corr., HP.

"That comes out, by God": Gerald Siegel interview, JL.

"You've gutted the bill . . .": Gerald Siegel interview, JL.

"Auerbach's suggestion": Carl Auerbach, "Jury Trials and Civil Rights Cases." Carl Auerbach letter, Dec. 31, 1981. George Reedy int. Feb. 14, 1972, JL.

"most exhausting and at times . . .": Humphrey to Eugenie Anderson, Aug. 14, 1957, Box 8, AP.

180. **"a pallid little measure"**: Clark, *Congress: The Sapless Branch*, 7.

"Not as good a bill as . . .": Humphrey to Anton Thompson, Aug. 17, 1957, Box 89, HP.

"I did not yield on . . .": Humphrey to Eugenie Anderson, Aug. 14, 1957, Box 8, AP.

"Last night during the closing . . .": John Stennis to Humphrey, Aug. 2, 1957, Box 567, HP.

"Compromise is not a dirty word . . .": *Education*, 136. Gerald Siegel and Lee Loevinger interviews.

19:   LIFTED OUT OF THE PACK

181. **"defensive about junketing"**: Kampelman and Thomas L. Hughes interview, June 21, 1978, in Connell, "Notes on Foreign Policy Discussion," Connell files. Kampelman, Hughes, Betty Goetz Lall (Feb. 9, 1981 and April 9, 1982) interviews.

182. **"He prided himself"**: Excerpt Humphrey Senate remarks on Air Force

appropriations bill, 1953, Box 724, HP. Kampelman and Hughes interviews. Connell, "Notes on Foreign Policy Discussion." Kampelman interview with Naftalin, July 27, 1979, Naftalin files.

"Going around like Fearless Fosdick . . .": *CR*, 101, 3385–88, Mar. 22, 1955.

"We really took Mr. Knowland . . .": Humphrey to Eugenie Anderson, Mar. 29, 1955, Box 6, AP. Humphrey to Eugenie Anderson, July 5, 1955, Box 6, AP. *NYT*, Jan. 13, 1956. Bowles to Humphrey, Jan. 13, 1056, Box 138, BP. *CR*, 102, 394, Jan. 12, 1956. *NYT*, Feb. 18 and 25, 1956.

183. Humphrey speech: *Bulletin of International Peasant Union*, May 1952. Benton to Humphrey, Jun. 24, 1952, Box 66, HP. Humphrey resolution commending East German freedom fight, June 1953, Box 724, HP. Humphrey to Eleanor Moen, June 25, 1953, Box 46, HP.

184. **"The stocks of food . . ."**: "Report on the Middle East and Southern Europe to the Senate Foreign Relations Committee," June 10, 1957. Humphrey newsletters May 10, 17, and 31, 1957, Box 701, HP. Humphrey trip itinerary, April 25–May 15, 1957, Box 701, HP. "Humphrey Talks with Nasser," *U.S. News and World Report*, May 17, 1957. Mankato *Free Press*, May 23, 1957. Humphrey to Andreas, May 31, 1957, Box 701, HP. James A. McConnell to Andreas, June 5, and 13, 1957. Humphrey to Mark Najar, June 13 and 24, 1957. *Time*, June 10, 1957, 24. M. W. Thatcher to Humphrey, May 14 and Humphrey to Thatcher, May 27, 1957, Box 701, HP. Humphrey to Rev. Tenner Thompson, May 31, 1957, May 31, 1957, Box 701, HP. Milwaukee *Sentinel*, June 4, 1957. Humphrey to Karl Baehr, June 5, 1957, Box 701, HP. Humphrey to Abe Marovitz, June 24, 1957, Box 701, HP. Thomas Christie to Humphrey, June 31, 1957, Box 701, HP. Bowles to Humphrey, July 20, 1957, Box 701, HP. Humphrey to Johnson, July 3, 1957, WHFN(HH), JL. Andreas and Waters interviews.

184. **Humphrey in Foreign Relations Committee:** Fulbright, Rowe, Kampelman, Hughes, Carl Marcy, and Betty Lall interviews. Koskoff, 423. Humphrey interview with Kampelman, Dec. 16, 1964, KL.

185. **Disarmament subcommittee:** Humphrey press release, April 3, 1955, Box

3, KP. Verner Clapp to Humphrey, Dec. 6, 1955, Box 76, HP.
Stassen, Murray testimony: U.S. Senate, 84th Congress, 1st session, Subcommittee on Disarmament, "The Executive Branch and Disarmament Policy," Feb. 20, 1956, Box 644, HP. Stassen quoted, Jan. 25, 1956, Box 644, HP. Divine, 67. Norman Thomas to Humphrey, Mar. 18, 1956, Box 560, HP. Humphrey to Norman Thomas, Mar. 18, 1956, Box 560, HP. Humphrey to Walter Lippmann, April 12, 1956, Box 72, Lippmann Papers. *NYT*, April 13 and 22, 1956. Eugenie Anderson to Humphrey, July 18, 1956, Box 6, AP. Humphrey to Walter Lippman, July 18, 1956, Box 72, Lippmann Papers. Betty Lall interview, *NYT*, Oct. 16 and Dec. 16, 1956..

186. **"They think the Soviet . . .":** Stassen and Lall interviews, *NYT*, Feb. 4 and Mar. 17, 1957. Humphrey to Johnson, Mar. 8, 1957, WHFN(HH), JL. Dulles testimony, May 23, 1957, 521, 548, and Stassen testimony, 526, 551, U.S. Senate, 85th Congress, 1st session, *Executive Sessions of Senate Foreign Relations Committee* (Historical series), IX. *NYT*, June 19, and July 8, 1957. Humphrey to Johnson, Oct. 14, 1957, WHFN(HH), JL.

187. **Humphrey speech:** "Foreign Policy and Disarmament," *CR*, 104, 1607, Feb. 4, 1958. *NYT*, Feb. 5, 1958. *Daily Worker*, Feb. 9, 1958. Lall interview. Humphrey to Johnson, Feb. 4 and 10, 1958, WHFN(HH), JL.
Speech reaction: *NYT*, Feb. 6, 1958, 26. Humphrey Easter week speeches: *CR*, 104, 5557, 5744, 5895, 6074, 6221, (Mar. 27, 31, April 1, 2, 3, 1958). *NYT*, Mar. 1, 2, 10, 12, and April 4, 1958. *CR*, 104, 6304, 6306, (April 14); 8574 (May 13); 9835, (May 29, 1958).

188. **"Fairbanks, Alaska, distance . . .":** Lall interview. Humphrey notes for unpublished book, Box 1411, HP.
"gives the impression . . .": Lall interview. *NYT*, Mar. 29, 30, 1958. Stassen interview. *NYT*, May 7, 12, 14, 25 and June 1, 1958.
Confirming leads: Humphrey to Cyrus Barnum, Mar. 4, 1958, Box 726, HP. Humphrey to Robert N. Barr, Mar. 10, 1958, Box 726, HP. Robert N. Barr to Humphrey, Mar. 21, 1958, Box 726, HP. Humphrey, "Turning Point for Disarmament," *PRO*, Aug. 1958. Humphrey to Johnson, Oct. 8, 1958, WHFN(HH), JL.

189. **Humphrey at Soviet embassy:** Thomas L. Hughes and Julius Cahn (Nov. 17, 1980) interviews.
Humphrey to Herb Waters: "European trip schedule," n.d., probably Nov. 1958, Box 702, HP. Humphrey to Bowles, Nov. 22, 1958, Box 138, BP. Humphrey to Eugenie Anderson, Nov. 22 and 23, 1958, Box 8, AP. Johnson to Humphrey, Nov. 5, 1958, Humphrey to Johnson, Nov. 6 and 12, Johnson to Humphrey, Nov. 22, 1958, WHFN(HH), JL. *Time*, Nov. 17 and 24, 1958. Benton to Humphrey, Nov. 5, 1958, Box 89, HP. Humphrey to Eugenie Anderson, Nov. 10, 1958, Box 8, AP. Benton to Lester Markel, Nov. 12, 1958, Box 89, HP. *STPPP*, Nov. 6, 1958.
"Now of all times . . .": Humphrey to Eugenie Anderson, Nov. 22, 1958, Box 8, AP.

190. **"It was total Iron Curtain":** Cahn interview. Humphrey, "Notes, Trip to Moscow," Nov. 1958, Box 703, HP.
"Munchausen fairy tales": *Time*, Jan. 12, 1959.
"I had no small talk . . .": Humphrey interview with John Osborne, Dec. 15, 1958, HP, Box 703.
"As if I were talking to a fencepost": *Education*, 199.

191. **"But I must thank . . .":** Humphrey longhand notes, Dec. 2, 1958, Box 702, HP.
"You know we have trouble . . .": Humphrey, "Conversation between Sen Humphrey and Khrushchev," Dec. 1, 1958, Box 703, HP.
"If you are having . . .": Humphrey interview with John Osborne, Dec. 15, 1958, Box 703, HP.
"Who are you trying to fool?" Humphrey, *Life*, Jan. 12, 1959.
"I'll tell you a secret . . .": Humphrey interview with John Osborne, Dec. 15, 1958, Box 703, HP.
"bone in my throat . . .": Humphrey longhand notes, Dec. 2, 1958, Box 702, HP. *Education*, 199.
"dont' threaten me": Humphrey, "Conversation," Dec. 1, 1958, Box 703, HP.
"I know you do not decide . . .": Ibid.
"If you just keep talking . . .": Humphrey interview with Osborne, Dec. 15, 1958, Box 703, HP.
"W will never bomb Minneapolis": *Education*, 198.

192. **"Defensive in an offensive way . . .":**

Humphrey interview with Osborne, Dec. 15, 1958, Box 703, HP.

"**the old order . . . incompetent . . .**": Humphrey longhand notes, Dec. 2, 1958, Box 702, HP.

"**as English gentlemen . . .**": *Education*, 202. Eiler Ravnholt for record, May 5, 1966, PFPMB u / p, HP.

"**People should come in here . . .**": Humphrey interview with John Osborne, Dec. 15, 1958, Box 703, HP.

193. **Humphrey the pharmacist:** Humphrey, "Trip to Moscow," Nov. 1958, Box 703, HP.

"**I don't know much about that**": Humphrey interview with Osborne, Dec. 15, 1958, Box 703, HP.

"**You are a subtle man . . .**": *Education*, 201.

194. "**Khrushchev Meets Senator**": *NYT*, Dec. 9 and 12, 1958. Humphrey longhand notes with Pres. Eisenhower, Dec. 9, 1958, Box 702, HP.

"**Humphrey in 1960**": *MT*, Dec. 10, 1958. Humphrey, "My Marathon Talk with Russia's Boss," *Life*, Jan. 12, 1959.

"**Mr. Humphrey will now . . .**": Reston in *NYT*, Dec. 10, 1958.

"**lifted him out of the pack**": *Economist*, Dec. 20, 1958.

"**Circumstances have suddenly . . .**": Doris Fleeson in New York *Post*, Dec. 10, 1958. "Candidate in Orbit," *Time*, Dec. 22, 1958.

195. "**the spark of greatness**": Eleanor Roosevelt on ABC-TV "College News Conference," quoted *NYT*, Dec. 8, 1958.

"**As it worked out . . .**": Muriel Humphrey to Eugenie Anderson, Dec. 29, 1958, Box 8, AP.

"**I'd say something while . . .**": Humphrey family interview, Nov. 13, 1981.

"**the voices all fuzzy . . .**": Muriel to Hubert Humphrey, n.d., probably July 13, 1948, Box 6, PFPC, HP. Muriel Humphrey interview with Connell.

"**is a great homemaker**": Humphrey to Eugenie Anderson, June 30, 1951, Box 60, HP. June Hendrickson to Humphrey, Nov. 14 and 21, 1951, Box 701, HP.

196. "**Muriel helped out a lot . . .**": Humphrey to Doris Kirkpatrick, Nov. 26, 1954, Box 89, HP. Skip, Robert, and Douglas (Aug. 17, 1981) Humphrey interviews. Humphrey family interview. "Log of Senator Humphrey," Feb. 1955, Box 208, HP.

"**boys and their dad . . .**": Humphrey to Benton, Oct. 30, 1959, Box 89, HP.

"**I have not had supper . . .**": Humphrey to A. A. Boyd, May 28, 1956, Box 560, HP.

197. **Waverly home:** *NYT*, Oct. 31, 1968. Humphrey press release, Oct. 30, 1968, M u / p, HP. WP, April 3, 1960.

"**a lovely place . . .**": Humphrey to Gordon Buck, Oct. 1, 1957, Box 89, HP. Humphrey interview with Drew Pearson and Jack Anderson, April 22, 1960, Box 3, PFPA, HP.

198. **daughter Nancy:** *NYT*, Jan. 5, 1960. Humphrey to June and Carl Faler, Jan. 27, 1958, Box 89, HP. Humphrey to Benton, Aug. 4, 1958, Box 89, HP. Humphrey family interview.

Shattuck school: Humphrey to Benton, Aug. 4, 1958, Box 89, HP. Larry Lynch to Humphrey, Sept. 9, 1958, Box 17, PFPM, HP. Humphrey to S. W. Goldsmith, Mar. 24, 1959, Box 17, PFPM, HP. Benton to Andreas, Sept. 22, 1960, Box 17, PFPM, HP. Humphrey to D. B. Purrington, Oct. 19, 1960, Box 17, PFPM, HP. Humphrey to S. W. Goldsmith, Feb. 1 and Aug. 12, 1961, Box 17, PFPM, HP. J. M. McKee to Humphrey, Sept. 16, 1963, Box 17, PFPM, HP. Humphrey to William F. Kummer, Mar. 22, 1958, Box 17, PFPM, HP.

Lecture fees: "Personal finances file," n.d., Box 17, PFPF, HP.

"**man of modest means**": Humphrey to Goldsmith, June 21, 1960, Box 17, PFPM. HP.

"**Your willingness to sit down . . .**": Humphrey to Goldsmith, Oct. 19, 1960, Box 17, PFPM, HP.

20:   FLATTENED BY THE KENNEDYS

199. **Humphrey for President:** Kampelman interview. H. H. Humphrey, Sr., to Humphrey, Nov. 7, 1948, Box 17, PFPC 1947–48, HP. Naftalin, "Minnesota," 180. John Lane interview. Walter Cramond to Paul Butler, Sept. 29, 1955, Box 12, CLU Papers.

"**I didn't think we could win . . .**": Humphrey interview with Kampelman, Dec. 14, 1964, KL.

"**I don't think a party . . .**": Eisele, 104.

200. **Wisconsin preliminaries:** James Loeb to Humphrey, June 10, 1959, Box 734,

HP. Humphrey to McCarthy, Mar 9, 1959, Box 567, HP. *WP*, June 13, 1959. Milwaukee *Journal* June 17, 1959. Waters interview. Kampelman to Humphrey, Jan. 28, 1959, Box 734, HP.
Election gains 1958: Humphrey to Eugenie Anderson, Oct. 30, 1958, Box 8, AP. Benton to Humphrey, Oct. 30, 1958, Box 89, HP. Joseph Alsop in *WP*, n.d., Box 3, KP. Johnson to Humphrey, Nov. 6, 1958, WHFN(HH), JL. Humphrey to Benton, Nov. 3, 1958, Box 89, HP. Waters to Benton, Nov. 24, 1958, Box 89, HP. Benton to Humphrey, Nov. 25, 1958, Box 89, HP. *Time*, Dec. 22, 1958, Benton to Waters, Dec. 10, 1958, Box 89, HP. William Shannon in *PRO*, Dec. 1958. "Schedule note for Sen. Humphrey," Dec. 6, 1958. Box 89, HP. *Christian Science Monitor*, Dec. 11, 1958. Reston in *NYT*, Dec. 10, 1958. Humphrey to Benton, Dec. 16, 1958, Box 89, HP. Eugenie Anderson to Humphrey, Dec. 21, 1958, Box 567, HP. Benton to Waters, Jan. 28, 1959, Box 89, HP. J. B. Martin, *Stevenson*, vol. 2, 449–50. Eugenie Anderson to Humphrey, Feb. 10, 1959, Box 727, HP.

201. **James Rowe, "Strategy of Hubert Humphrey,"** Rowe interview. Abell, Feb. 7, 1959, 514. Pat O'Connor to Waters, Feb. 16, 1959, Box 570, IIP. Naftalin to Humphrey, Feb. 18, 1959, Box 567, HP. Bailey in Sevareid, ed., *Candidates 1960*, 156. Duluth *News Tribune*, Mar. 6, 1959. *The Reporter*, May 5, 1959. Waters to Benton, Mar. 30, 1959, Box 89, HP. Humphrey to Waters, April 8, 1959, Box 715, HP. Humphrey to Waters, May 8, 1959, Box 715, HP. William S. White in *MT*, May 28, 1959. Benton to Waters, June 11, 1959, Box 89, HP. Griffith, 241.
"**If he does not take . . .**": Eisele, 138–39. John Blatnik interview, Feb. 4, 1966, KL.

202. "**the first foot forward . . .**": Eisele, 138–39.
"**unbelievably good**" Kennedy publicity: Humphrey interview with Kampelman for KL, Dec. 14, 1964. Humphrey to Robert Barrie et al., Nov 13, 1959, Box 734, HP. Humphrey to Barrie, Jan. 5, 1960, Box 185, HP.
"**the Kennedy people moved in . . .**": Humphrey to McCarthy, Mar. 9, 1959, Box 567, HP. Joseph Robbie memo, Mar. 13, 1959, Box 734, HP.

203. **Not "gotten off the ground":** J. B.

Martin, *Stevenson*, vol. 2, 456.
"**Details . . .**": Humphrey to James Rowe, Sept. 23, 1959, Box 567, HP. Humphrey to Eugenie Anderson, Sept. 24, 1959, Box 8, AP. Andreas to Waters, Sept. 30, 1959, Box 567, HP.
"**Of one thing I am sure . . .**": Humphrey declaration of candidacy, Dec. 30, 1959, *MT*, Dec. 31, 1959.
"**Old Bob LaFollette would . . .**": Reston in *NYT*, Dec. 31, 1959.
"**I have no illusions . . .**": *NYT*, Dec. 31, 1959.

204. **Campaign preparations:** Robert Barrie to Humphrey, Oct. 2, 9, and 23, Nov. 29, 1959, Boxes 715, 734, and 575, HP. Eugenie Anderson to Humphrey, Oct. 17, Nov. 21, and 29 and Dec. 18, 1959, Box 8, AP. Pat O'Connor to Humphrey, Oct. 5 and 30, 1959, Box 572, HP. David Ginsburg to Humphrey, Nov. 25, Dec. 1, 2, and 27, Box 575, HP. "Agenda for Meeting at Home of Ed Rhetts," Oct. 13, 1959, Box 715, HP. "Meeting at Home of Ed Rhetts," Dec. 22, 1959, Box 715, HP. Humphrey to Barrie, Nov. 5 and 13, 1959, Box 185, HP. Humphrey to Barrie, Nov. 11, 1959, Marvin Rosenberg files. John Kennedy to Lloyd Frakes, Oct. 7, 1959, Pre-presidential, pre-convention, W.Va., 1959–60, Box 969, KL. Humphrey to Jim Schwinden, Oct. 15, 1959, Box 567, HP. Walter Butler to Humphrey, Oct. 29, 1959, Box 572, HP. Frank Wallick memo on Wisconsin, Oct. 29, 1959, Box 567, HP. Humphrey to Connell, Oct. 30, 1959 Box 567, HP. Johnson to Humphrey, Nov. 6, 1959, WHFN(HH), JL. Humphrey to Fred Weinberg, Nov. 30, 1959, Box 567, HP. Humphrey to N. M. Shapiro, Nov. 30, 1959, Box 567, HP. Humphrey to Karl Rolvaag, Nov. 30, 1959, Box 715, HP. Connell to Humphrey, Dec. 9, 1959, M u/p, HP. Gerald Heaney to James McDevitt, Dec. 10, 1959, Box 567, HP. Barrie to Rolvaag, Dec. 14, 1959, Box 570, HP. James Loeb to Humphrey, Dec. 21, 1959, M u/p, HP. Omaha *World Herald*, Dec. 20, 1959. Gerald Heaney memo, Jan. 11, 1960, M u/p, HP. Eugenie Anderson report, Feb. 17, 1960, Box 560, HP. James E. Harrington to James Rowe, Feb. 15, 1960, M u/p, HP. Connell to Humphrey, Mar. 8, 1960, Box 567, HP. Heaney, Rolvaag, Waters, Connell, Rowe, Foley, Robert Barrie (May 27, 1982), E. Anderson interviews.

"go for broke": Rowe interview. Harris poll, Sorensen, 107. Parmet, *Jack*, 517. Schlesinger, *Robert Kennedy*, 198.
"not the Pope but the Pop": Koskoff, 429. Rowe to Humphrey, Feb. 10, 1960, M u / p, HP.
"acting like a spoiled . . .": Sorensen, 141. Humphrey to Rolvaag, Feb. 2, 1960, Box 570, HP.

205. "I hate to do this but . . .": Eisele, 143. Barrie to Humphrey, Jan. 7, 1960, M u / p HP.
"spontaneously . . .": Connell to Humphrey, Jan. 11, 1960, Box 567, HP.
"We ought to get Herblock . . .": Humphrey to Bill Sturdevant, Feb. 18, 1960, Box 185, HP.
RFK-Hoffa money charges: Humphrey interview with Drew Pearson, April 22, 1960, Box 3, PFPM, HP. Heaney to Gaylord Neslon, Mar. 17, 1960, Box 734, HP.
"I feel like an independent merchant . . .": Humphrey speech at Madison, Mar. 30, 1960, MSF, HP. *Education*, 208. Longview (Wash.) *News*, April 12, 1960.
Humphrey campaign disarray: Rauh interview, Feb. 23, 1969, JL.

206. "Let's stop . . .": Heaney interview.
"One of us": Ibid. T. H. White, *Making of the President 1960*, 86.

207. "Bitter at the use . . .": J. B. Martin, *Stevenson*, vol. 2, 487. Humphrey interview with Drew Pearson, April 22, 1960, Box 3, PFPA, HP.
"Unconscionable appeals . . .": Eugenie Anderson to Humphrey, April 13, 1960, Box 8, AP.
"Protestants, a leading . . .": West Salem (Wis.) *Journal*, Mar. 31, 1960. *NYT*, April 1, 1960. Milwaukee *Sentinel*, April 1, 1960. LeRoy Dalton (May 11 and 12 and July 6, 1982), Irving Davidson (July 5, 1982), Barrie, Eugene Foley, and Gerald Heaney interviews.
"devastated . . .": Heaney interview.
Charlie Greene: LeRoy Dalton, Irving Davidson, Eugene Foley, Gerald Heaney interviews. Humphrey interview with Pearson, Box 3. PFPA, HP. LeRoy Dalton letters, May 25 and June 16, 1982.
Wisconsin outcome: Richard Scammon to Kampelman, April 8, 1960, Box 735, HP. "Analysis of Wisconsin returns," Box 973, pre-presidential, 1959–60, Wisconsin primary, KL. "Analysis of Wisconsin Primary Election," April 5,

1960, Box 735, HP. James Loeb, "Memo on Wisconsin," n.d., Box 734, HP. Carl Auerbach to Humphrey, April 8, 1960, Box 735, HP. Humphrey press release, "Religion the Most Important Factor," n.d., Box 734, HP. Humphrey to James Benson, April 12, 1962, PFPA, HP. Humphrey to Eugenie Anderson, April 18, 1960, Box 8, AP. Humphrey to Rolvaag, April 18, 1960, Box 735, HP. Humphrey to Darrell Smith, April 18, 1960, PFPA, HP. Humphrey to Robert Humphrey, April 19, 1960, Box 734, HP. Humphrey to Arthur Schlesinger, April 18, 1960, Box 8, AP. O'Donnell and Powers, 147. Ira Kapenstein interview, Dec. 15, 1965, KL.

208. "I have talked this over . . .": J. B. Martin, *Stevenson*, vol. 2, 487.
"I talked with Arthur . . .": Ibid. Humphrey interview with Kampelman, Dec. 14, 1964, KL.
"I've paid a $1,000 filing fee . . .": Rauh, Marvin Rosenberg (Dec. 17, 1980, Jan. 4 and May 6, 1982) interviews, Rosenberg letter, April 21, 1982.
"very gratifying . . .": Humphrey to Robert Humphrey, April 19, 1960, Box 734, HP. Humphrey speech, Beckley W. Va., April 8, 1960. MSF, HP. Humphrey speech, Morgantown, May 5, 1960, MSF, HP.

209. "Is anyone going . . . ?" Ernst, 7.
"No one can tell me that . . .": Ibid.
"My preacher's been preachin' . . .": Snider, 41.
"I don't know where he was . . .": *WP*, April 27, 1960.
Debate: *NYT*, May 5, 1960.

210. "What's a hundred million . . .": Koskoff, 433.
"This costs money . . .": David Ginsburg to Humphrey, Mar. 15, 1960, Box 575, HP. Ernst, 24. Claude Ellis interview, Sept. 9, 1964, KL. *NYT*, Aug. 10, 1981.
"We decided what church . . .": *Education*, 217.
"The election was bought . . .": Rowe interview. Ernst, 30.

211. "Over the hump with . . .": T. H. White, *Making of the President 1960*, 109. James Loeb to Vi Williams, May 3, 1960, Box 185, HP.
"I need people not miles . . .": Humphrey to Barrie, April 26, 1960, Box 575, HP. Paul Andrews to Marvin Rosenberg, n.d., April 1960, Rosenberg files.

"Most of the staff is on the bus":
Barrie to Humphrey, April 30, 1960, Box
575, HP.
"I think I can win . . .": Humphrey
to Ralph Humphrey, May 1, 1960,
PFPM, HP.
"All right, I'll pay . . .": Rowe inter-
view. T. H. White, *Making of the Presi-
dent 1960*, 110. Eliot Janeway interview,
April 29, 1982.
West Virginia outcome: *NYT*, May 6,
1960. *MT*, May 22, 1960. St. Louis *Post
Dispatch*, Aug. 7, 1960. Eugenie Ander-
son to Humphrey, May 2, 1960, Box 570,
HP. Humphrey to Philleo Nash, May
11, 1960, File 2, (Humphrey), Nash
Papers. *NYT*, May 12, 1960. Connell to
Humphrey, May 18, 1960, Box 567, HP.
"Meaning of the W. Va. Primary," n.d.,
Box 575, HP. Barrie to Humphrey, May
26 and 27, 1960, Box 185 and 734, HP.
Humphrey to Mrs. Carroll Binder, May
30, 1960, Box 570, HP. Humphrey to
Viola Berle, May 30, 1960, Box 570, HP.
Humphrey to P. J. Creasy, May 30,
1960, Box 575, HP. Humphrey to Arthur
Koontz, May 30, 1960, Box 575, HP.
Humphrey to Elmo Roper, May 30,
1960, Box 575, HP. Humphrey to Con-
nell, Sept. 11, 1960, Box 185, HP.
212. "I swear to God . . .": Rauh inter-
view. Mary McGrory, *WS*, May 11,
1960.
"We were three in the car . . .": Geri
Joseph interview, June 4, 1981.
"I am no longer . . .": *NYT*, May 11,
1960.
"I'm going to do whatever . . .": Geri
Joseph interview.
"It was a mistake . . .": Humphrey to
Eugenie Anderson, June 17, 1960, Box
8, AP.
Wedding: Humphrey to Ralph Hum-
phrey, May 16, 1960, Box 4, PFPM, HP.
Humphrey to Eugenie Anderson, May
14, 1960, Box 8, AP. Bruce Solomonson
interview, July 30, 1981.
"You might be the strongest . . .":
Marvin Rosenberg interview.
"I never could see why . . .": Eisele,
151.
"I do not want it": *NYT*, June 28 and
29, 1960. *WS*, June 26, 1960. Freeman
to Humphrey, May 23, 1960, PFPA, HP.
213. "Stop Kennedy" movement: Patrick
O'Connor (Sept. 20 and 22, 1982), Rowe,
Rauh, Freeman, Eugene McCarthy (Nov.
11, 1980) interviews. J. L. Markham to
Humphrey, June 24, 1960, Box 570, HP.

J. B. Martin, *Stevenson*, vol. 2, 513. Mrs.
Ernest Ives interview, 1960, for Colum-
bia University Oral History Project.
Robert S. Hirschfield interview, April 1,
1981. John Sharon interview, 1970, for
Columbia University Oral History Proj-
ect. A. S. Monroney, Jr., interview,
1970, for Columbia University Oral
History Project. Humphrey to J. L.
Markham, July 16, 1960, Box 570, HP.
T. H. White, *Making of the President 1960*,
36. Arthur Schlesinger letter July 26,
1983.
"Less fire in your speech . . .": P. K.
Peterson interview.
"Well, that's politics . . .": Ibid.

21: MASTER LEGISLATOR

215. "They want me to be majority . . .":
Humphrey interview with Sherman,
n.d., probably 1969, Box 2. Autobiog-
raphy files, HP.
"I can't tell you one thing and . . .":
Ibid. *Education*, 242.
"I am sad when I think . . .", Dec.
15, 1965, Rowe to Humphrey, M u / p,
HP.
"I am in the thick of things . . .":
Humphrey to Ralph Humphrey, Feb 5,
1961, Box 4, PFPC, HP. Humphrey to
Anton Thompson Jan. 30, 1961, PFPA
(T), HP. Humphrey to Dewey and Hazel
Van Dyke, Jan. 30, 1961, PFPM u / p,
HP. Humphrey to Mike Mansfield, Jan.
6, 1961, M u / p, HP. Humphrey to Win
Griffith, May 10, 1961, M u / p, HP. John
F. Kennedy to Humphrey, May 29,
1961, M u / p, HP. *STPPP*, Jan. 10, 1961.
"because you can explain . . .":
Humphrey interviews with Sherman.
216. "Knew these men better . . .":
Humphrey interview with Sherman,
n.d., probably 1969, Box 2, Autobiog-
raphy files, HP.
"I don't have to prove . . .": *STPPP*,
Sept. 9, 1962.
Peace Corps: *CR*, 106, 12634 (June 15,
1960). *Public Papers of John F. Kennedy*,
Mar. 1, 1961, 136.
Youth Conservation Corps: *CR*, 96,
2458 (Feb. 28, 1950). Humphrey memo
to self, Aug. 7, 1961, M u / p, HP.
Food for Peace: *CR*, 99, 10081 (July
27, 1953). Humphrey to Jack Flynn, Jan.
9, 1961, M u / p, HP. Humphrey to
Fowler Hamilton, Oct. 29, 1961, Box
705, HP.

217. **OSHA:** *CR*, 95, 7221 (June 1949).
War on Poverty: *CR*, 107, 138 (Jan. 5, 1961) for S-1, 43 senators co-sponsoring.
Medicare: *CR*, 95, 4956 (April 25, 1949).
Berlin trip: Humphrey to Kennedy, "Memorandum to the President," July 14, 1961, no. 30 Presidents Office file, Special Corr., Memo, KL.
Kennedy Berlin speech: *Public Papers of John F. Kennedy*, July 26, 1961, 533.
"skinnydipped": *Education*, 251. "Book Tapes," n.d., Box 8, Autobiography files, HP.
"At this very hour when . . .": Humphrey interview with Sherman, Box 2, Autobiography files, HP.
ACDA: Polsby, 13 (first proposed 1960). *Public Papers of John F. Kennedy*, Sept. 25, 1961, 626.
Humphrey to Kennedy: Feb. 6, 1961, No. 30 Presidential Office Files, Special Corr., KP.

218. **"limited" test ban:** Polsby, 13 (first asked for in 1956). *Public Papers of John F. Kennedy*, June 10, 1963, 459. Johan Nykopp to Humphrey, n.d., M u / p, HP. Two Humphrey memos of White House breakfasts, Jan. 14, 1963, M u / p, HP. William C. Foster to Humphrey, Feb. 5, 1963, Box 709, HP. Humphrey to Mrs. Herbert Marks, Mar. 7, 1963, Box 709, HP. O'Brien to Kennedy, Feb. 25, 1963, Box 23, White House staff files, O'Brien Papers, KL. Humphrey remarks, *CR*, 109, 3724 (Feb. 27, 1963), 109,8272 (May 15, 1963), 109, 13800 (July 31, 1963), 109, 13741–46 (Aug. 2 and 8, 1963). Bowles to Humphrey, Aug. 5, 1963, Box 31, BP. Humphrey to Eugenie Anderson, Aug. 9, 1963, Box 14, AP. Humphrey press release, Sept. 10, 1963.
Moscow trip: *Education*, 253.
"Hubert, this is yours . . .": *Education*, 253. *Public Papers of John F. Kennedy*, Oct. 7, 1963, 765.
"Oh, how we botched it": Humphrey to Anton Thompson, May 3, 1961, PFPA(T), HP.
Latin America trips: Itinerary, Humphrey Notes and Notes for Miami speech, Nov. 9–Dec. 5, 1961, Box 706, HP. Humphrey to Stevenson, Jan. 23, 1962, Box 706, HP. Andreas interview. John T. Flynn interview, May 26, 1982. Itinerary and Humphrey trip notes, Nov. 28, Dec. 19, 1962, Box 708, HP. Andreas to Humphrey, May 8, 1963, Box 709, HP. Humphrey to Andreas, Apr. 23, 1963, Andreas files.

219. **Harpsund meeting:** Reuther to Humphrey, June 26, 1963, Box 709, HP. Fulbright to Rusk, July 3, 1963, Box 709, HP. Gartner trip diary, July 1–17, 1963, Box 709, HP. "Participants at Harpsund," July 13–14, 1963, Box 1401, HP. Humphrey longhand notes, Harpsund, July 1963, Box 709, HP. Andreas memo on Harpsund, n.d., 1963, Andreas files. Guy Nunn letter, May 15, 1982. B. J. Widick interview, May 10, 1982. Norman Thomas to Humphrey, July 29, 1963, Box 709, HP. Humphrey to W. R. Biggs, July 31, 1963, PFPA, HP.
"We stand on the eve . . .": Andreas memo, n.d., 1963, Andreas files.

220. **"Though Wilson had nothing like . . .":** Ibid.
"It could create . . .": Ibid.
"He was always learning more . . .": Ibid.

221. **"My God, no.":** Gartner interview, Nov. 10, 1980, and Aug. 12, 1983.
"leadership for civil rights": Humphrey, "Memo on the Civil Rights bill," June 10, 1964, PFPM, HP. George Smathers interview, July 10, 1964, KL.
"We are confronted primarily . . .": M u / p, HP. *Public Papers of John F. Kennedy*, June 11, 1963, 468.

222. **"one of the nation's . . .":** Mansfield, *CR*, 110, 2774 (Feb. 17, 1964). Lyndon Johnson, 159.
"This is your test": Humphrey interview, June 21, 1977, JL.
"I realized it would test . . .": Humphrey, "Memo on the Civil Rights bill," June 10, 1964, PFPM, HP. John Stewart (Oct. 26, 1981), Rauh interviews.

223. **"I am in favor of . . .":** Stewart, "Independence and Control," 185. *Public Papers of Lyndon B. Johnson, 1963–64*, 457. Evans and Novak, *LBJ*, 379.
"reasonably against the bill": Stewart "Independence and Control," 203. Humphrey, "Memo on the Civil Rights bill, June 10, 1964, PFPM, HP.
"I'd ask him, 'Well, Dirk . . .' ": Ibid. Rauh interview, Aug. 1, 1969, JL. George Smathers interview KL.
"If you don't get a whole loaf . . .": New York *Herald Tribune*, April 10, 1964.
"What would you like?" Humphrey, "Memo on the Civil Rights bill," June 10, 1964, PFPM, HP.

224. **"I would have kissed Dirksen's ass . . .":** Rauh interview and letter, Oct. 12, 1983.
"Clarence, you are three feet . . .": Unpublished manuscript, n.d., Rauh files.

"a pattern or practice": Stewart, "Independence and Control," 237.

"not too many Americans . . .": Humphrey speech, May 16, 1964, Box 698, HP.

225. "I feel like someone . . .": *NYT*, May 14, 1964.

"Don't knock his talking": Nicholas Katzenbach interview, April 5, 1983.

"to meet the real evils . . .": Stewart, "Independence and Control," 258.

"stronger than the House bill": Humphrey, "Memo on Passage of the Civil Rights act of 1964," n.d., M u / p, HP.

"puts Charles Sumner to shame . . .": *CR*, 110, 11537–8.

"beginning tomorrow . . .": Stewart, "Independence and Control," 270.

226. "Well, Dick, you haven't . . .": Ibid., 277.

"All we want is the chance . . .": Ibid., 269.

"Stronger than an army . . .": *CR*, 110, 12866.

"Dad, I guess I've had it": Eisele, 194.

"My greatest achievement": *Education*, 289.

227. "The Civil Rights act is without . . .": Humphrey to Walter Lippmann, June 19, 1964, Box 726, HP. John Stewart, David Filvaroff (Sept. 3, 1982) interview.

22: PRIVATE MOMENTS OF A PUBLIC MAN

228. "He never crossed anybody": Naftalin interview.

"Being around him was . . .": Miles Lord interview.

229. "Fred is sitting right here . . .": Simms, Naftalin, Miles Lord, P. K. Peterson, Les Malkerson interviews. William B. Horn letter, June 24, 1983. Olga Burge interview, Don Shelby interview, Aug. 17, 1981. Dan Brennan letter, Oct. 1, 1981. *MS*, May 21, 1981. *Education*, 90, 453. Charles L. Horn to Humphrey, Feb. 2, 1971, Box 5, AAF71, HP. *MS*, Feb. 1, 1971. Gates to Humphrey, April 5, 1949, June 24 and Dec. 29, 1951, Box 480, HP. Gates to Humphrey, Jan. 15 and Mar. 11, 1955, Box 5, PFPA, HP. Marie Gates to Humphrey, Feb. 20, 1956, Box 5, PFPA, HP. Humphrey to Gates, Sept. 28, 1955, Box 5, PFPA, HP. Humphrey to Stuart Symington, Dec. 20, 1955, Box 2, PFPA,

HP. Gates to Humphrey, Jan. 4, 1956, Box 2, PFPA, HP. Humphrey to Marie Gates, Feb. 20, 1956, Box 2, PFPA, HP. Humphrey to Gates, June 25, 1957, Box 2, PFPA, HP. Humphrey to Gates, Jan. 8, 1958, Box 2, PFPA, HP. Gates to Humphrey, Aug. 17, 1959, Box 2, PFPA, HP. Gates to Humphrey, Jan. 23, 1960, Box 2, PFPA, HP. Gates to Thelma Abbot, Mar. 26, 1961, M u / p, HP. Humphrey to Gates, June 11, 1962, M u / p, HP. *CR*, 109, 4945, April 1, 1963. Humphrey to Vi Williams, Feb. 2, 1971, Box 2, PFPA, HP. Humphrey to Fred Gates, Jr., Jan. 29, 1973, Box 2, PFPA, HP.

"I'm the mayor . . .": *Education*, 471, Lord, O'Connor, Gaylord Nelson (Sept. 25, 1981) interviews.

231. "We were family friends . . .": Andreas interview. Humphrey to Andreas, April 22, 1954, Box 115, HP. Andreas to Humphrey, April 28, 1954, Box 115, HP. *WP*, Jan. 29, 1955. "Financial contributors 1948," Box 58, HP. Barrie to Humphrey, Dec. 31, 1959, M u / p, HP. Memo, "Trip to Germany," Oct. 24–27, 1963, Box 709, HP.

"My farmers vote too": Andreas interview.

232. "How much I appreciate . . .": Andreas to Humphrey, Nov. 1961, Box 705, HP.

"Someone who has benefited . . .": Freeman to Johnson, Dec. 9, 1965, WHFN (IIIII), JL.

"Andreas, right or wrong . . .": Humphrey to Freeman, Dec. 15, 1965, M u / p, HP.

"Notes": 10 trips with Humphrey, 1957–69, Andreas files. *MT*, Jan. and Feb. 20, 1966. *NYT*, Oct. 5 and 22, 1966. "Affair with the Soybean," *Business Week*, June 2, 1973. Irwin Ross, in *Fortune*, Oct. 1973. *STPPP*, Oct. 20, 1973. James P. Hertzog letter, Sept. 23, 1981. Jeff Gerth, in *NYT*, July 26, 1978. Eric Pianin, in *Washington Monthly*, April 1981. Sue Shellenbarger, in *Wall Street Journal*, Jan. 19, 1981. Ben Raskin (Sept. 25, 1981), Dan Morgan (Sept. 23, 1981), Atherton Bean, Waters, Gartner interviews.

233. "a teenager, likes to drive . . .": Humphrey to June and Carl Faler, Jan. 27, 1958, Box 89, HP. *NYT*, Jan. 5, 1960. New York *Herald Tribune*, Feb. 28, 1960, *NYT*, May 14, 1960, and June 14, 1965. Humphrey to Elva Renne, Oct. 5, 1962, PFPM, HP. Humphrey to Hazel and

Dewey Van Dyke, Dec. 26, 1962, PFPM, HP.

234. **"My whip duties have . . .":** Humphrey to Anton Thompson, April 3, 1961, PFPM, HP.

"You should have seen me . . .": Humphrey to Anton Thompson, Dec. 26, 1962, PFPM, HP.

"I feel guilty about . . .": Humphrey to Ralph Humphrey, Feb. 25, 1962, PFPC, HP.

"I want to go right back . . .": Humphrey to Anton Thompson, April 3, 1961, PFPA, HP.

"Skip is over in . . .": Humphrey to S. W. Goldsmith, July 31, 1963, Box 7, PFPM, HP.

"Skip has returned . . .": Humphrey to S. W. Goldsmith, Aug. 18, 1963, Box 7, PFPM, HP.

235. **"May very well determine . . .":** Humphrey to Eugenie Anderson, May 7, 1964, Box 14, AP. *Education*, 285. Humphrey to Herbert McClosky, Aug. 12, 1964, Box 1046, HP. Humphrey to Eugenie Anderson, PFPA, HP. Humphrey to Johnson, June 22, 1964, WHCF CF, JL. Humphrey to Judith Stryker, Box 3, CF 1969–77, HP. Muriel Humphrey to Eugenie Anderson, Sept. 17, 1964, Box 14, AP. Humphrey to Mrs. George Schaa, Aug. 15, 1966, PFPM, HP.

"Work out a trip . . .": Humphrey to Gartner, June 21, 1966, Box 1400, HP. Gartner to Humphrey, Aug. 11, 1966, Box 1400, HP. *NYT*, Aug. 29, 1966. Robert Humphrey interview. Humphrey to Gartner, May 5, 1966, Box 1400, HP.

"I had my own schedule . . .": Robert Humphrey interview. Longhand notes on Humphrey's doings, Aug. 27, 1968, M u / p, HP. Humphrey to Spivak, Oct. 10, 1968. M u / p HP.

236. **Humphrey regarding sons' draft status:** Betty Goetz Lall to Humphrey, May 13, 1964, PFPA, HP. Humphrey to R. Bullock, Aug. 15, 1972, PFPA (M for military), HP.

23: "YOU CAN RELY ON ME, MR. PRESIDENT"

239. **"I simply can't conceal . . .":** Humphrey to Henry Wallace, April 12, 1945, Box 1, HP.

"I was at the Chilean embassy . . .":

Humphrey for the record, "Death of Pres. Kennedy," Nov. 23, 1963, PFPMB u / p, HP.

240. **"What have they done . . . ?"** Patrick Moynihan newsletter, May 1981.

"eyes red with weeping": T. H. White, *Making of the President 1964*, 8.

Bowles to Humphrey: Dec. 6, 1963, Box 331, folder 104, BP. J. B. Martin, *Stevenson*, vol. 2, 783.

"Come down on Thursday": Marvin Rosenberg interview.

"All four of us . . .": Ibid. Connell to Humphrey, "What We are Doing," July 3, 1964, CF68, HP.

241. **"How many votes do you have?":** Humphrey memo for the record, "On Lyndon B. Johnson," Jan. 19, 1964, PFPMB u / p, HP. *Education*, 264–66. Humphrey interview, CBS Special News Report, Jan. 24, 1973, Box 4, HP. Humphrey tape for Minnesota broadcast, Nov. 26, 1963, Box 696, HP. L. F. O'Brien, 161. Evans and Novak, *LBJ*, 360–61. Fortas to Humphrey, Nov. 27, 1963, VIP corr., HP. Humphrey, "President Johnson's Address to Congress," *CR*, 109, 2016–22, Dec. 3, 1963.

242. **Latin America:** Humphrey to Johnson, "Executive Personnel Changes in Latin America," Dec. 14, 1963, PFPMB u / p, HP. Humphrey to Johnson, Dec. 16, 1963, "Followup Memo," Executive file (HH), JL. Evans and Novak, *LBJ*, 395.

Other subjects: Humphrey, "Memos to be prepared for President," Nov. 28, 1963, VIP corr., HP. Humphrey to Johnson, Nov. 25, 1963, WHCF CF(HH), JL. Walter Jenkins to Johnson, Nov. 23, 1963, WHCF CF(HH), JL. Humphrey to Johnson, Nov. 25, 1963, WHFN, Container 3, JL. Valenti to Juanita Roberts, Nov. 29, 1963, WHCF, CF(HH), JL. Johnson to Humphrey, Dec. 10, 1963, WHFN(HHH) Container 3, JL. Humphrey to Johnson, Dec. 18, 1963, WHFN(HHH), Container 3, JL. Humphrey to Johnson, Dec. 13, 1963, VIP corr., HP. Humphrey to Johnson, Dec. 18, 1963, VIP corr., HP.

"Hubert, you tell him . . .": *Education*, 290–93.

"The President calls on me . . .": Humphrey to Eugenie Anderson, Feb. 1, 1964 and Eugenie Anderson to Humphrey, Jan 14, 1964, Box 14, AP. Kampelman to Humphrey, Jan. 16, 1964, Box 1046, HP. Humphrey to Johnson, Jan. 23 and 28, 1964, WHFN(HHH), Container 3, JL.Humphrey press release, Jan. 28, 1964, file 2, Philleo Nash Papers. Humphrey to Fortas, Feb. 4, 1964, Box 14, AP.

Signals from Johnson: Rowe interview. Evans and Novak, *LBJ*, 443. Humphrey to Johnson longhand, Feb. 1964, WHCF CF(HH), JL. Humphrey press release, Jan. 28, 1964, File 2, (Humphrey), Philleo Nash Papers. W. L. Clayton to Humphrey, Jan. 23, 1964, file 2 (Humphrey), Philleo Nash Papers. Ted Van Dyk to Humphrey, Jan. 29, 1964, M u / p, HP. Kampelman and Connell interviews. Humphrey to Cornelius Reid, April 13, 1964, PFPA ("Vacation trips"), HP. Kampelman to Humphrey, Dec. 16, 1963, PFPA, HP.

243. **"It was like giving him life":** McCarthy interview.
"In the week ending . . .": Dick Nelson to Johnson, April 16, 1964, WHFN(HHH), JL.
"Johnson always had . . .": Rowe interview. Rowe interview with Connell, n.d., Connell files. Rowe interview, Sept. 30, 1969, TL.
"Mr. President, the party won't   .": Rowe interview.

244. **"This means Humphrey":** J. B. Martin, *Stevenson*, vol. 2, 803. Evans and Novak, *LBJ*, 446.
"I asked him every . . .": Rowe interview. Rowe interview with Connell, n.d., Connell files. Hugh Sidey, "The Horse-Shedding of Hubert Humphrey." *Education*, 298.
"right now has universal . . .". Humphrey to Eugenie Anderson, May 7, 1964, Box 14, AP. Connell to Humphrey, July 3, 1964, CF68, HP.
"Johnson said he liked both . . .": *CR*, 110, 15758, July 1, 1964. Rowe interview. Evans and Novak, 449–50. O'Donnell and Powers, 398. Jenkins to Humphrey, July 27, 1964, M u / p, HP.

245. **"I am going to call . . .":** Rowe interview J. B. Martin, *Stevenson*, vol. 2, 803. Rowe to Johnson, "Oh Behalf of Hubert Humphrey," Aug. 20, 1964, CF68PP, HP. *WP*, Aug. 24, 1964. *Education*, 298. Rowe to Humphrey, Aug. 21, 1968, 1946, HP. Humphrey to Naftalin, Aug. 14, 1964, Box 1046, HP. T. H. White, *Making of the President 1964*, 270, Humphrey to Eugenie Anderson, Aug. 22, 1964, Box 14, AP.
"Joe, the President . . .": Rauh interview. Rauh, unpublished memo on 1964

convention, Oct. 28, 1977., Rauh files. *Education*, 299. Rauh interview, July 30, 1966, JL. *WP*, Aug. 23, 24, 25, 1964.
"Each night before I . . .": Rauh, unpublished memo on 1964 convention, Oct. 28, 1977, Rauh files. *WP*, Aug. 26, 1964.

246. **"I was playing a game . . .":** McCarthy interview.
"horsing around . . .": Rowe interview. *Education*, 300.
"Like you, I have had a heart . . .": Rowe to Johnson, Aug. 20, 1964, Rowe files.
Johnson on vice presidency: Carroll Kirkpatrick in *WP*, Aug. 25, 1964. Garnett Horner in *WS*, Aug. 25, 1964.
"Get Humphrey and tell him . . .": Rowe interview.

254. **"Humphrey just blew . . .":** Ibid.
McCarthy telegram: McCarthy to Johnson, Aug. 26, 1964, Box 25, WHCF, Ex PL / HHH. JL. *MT*, Aug. 26 and 27, 1964. Lyndon Johnson, 101.
"How would you like your Dad . . . ?": Eisele, 216.
"What, is Tom Dodd . . . ?": Rowe interview.

255. **"Senator, the President wants . . .":** *MT*, Aug. 27, 1964. T. H. White, *Making of the President 1964*, 271.
"If you didn't know . . .": Eisele, 219.
"Hubert, do you want . . . ?": *Education*, 301. Frances Howard interview.
"This is like a marriage . . .": *Education*, 301–3.

256. **"We're going to nominate . . .".** *Education*, 304.
"It was a moment of glory . . .": *Education*, 304.
"He is THE modern liberal": New York *News*, Aug. 23, 1964.
"His record in the Senate . . .": *PRO*, Aug. 1964.
"an energetic, effective . . .": *Wall Street Journal*, Aug. 27, 1964.
"his just deserts . . .": J. B. Martin, *Stevenson*, Vol. 2, 814–15.

24: A MOMENT OF GLORY

257. **"Goldwater and his crew . . .":** Humphrey to William S. White, July 28, 1964, Box 726, HP.
"Has been facing backward . . .": *NYT*, Aug. 28, 1964. *MT*, Aug. 28, 1964.

258. **"Most Democrats and Republicans . . .":** *NYT*, Aug. 28, 1964.

"Hubert, get on that horse": *Education*, 307–8. *NYT*, Sept. 1, 1964.
"Almost like Johnson holding . . .": Katzenbach interview.

259. "We've got to get busy . . .": Andreas, "Johnson ranch notes," Aug. 29, 1964, Andreas files.
"Let's just make it . . .": Ibid.

260. "giant of a man": *MT*, Sept. 6, 1964
"a great beginnimg": Johnson to Humphrey, Sept. 6, 1964, VIP corr., HP. *MT*, Sept. 12, 1964. *NYT*, Sept. 12, 1964.
"the other, primarily . . .": Humphrey to Eugenie Anderson, Aug. 22, 1964, PFPA, HP.

261. "I do not think we . . .": *The Cause Is Mankind*, quoted in *U.S. News and World Report*, Aug. 28, 1964.
"This time campaigning is . . .": Muriel Humphrey to Eugenie Anderson, Sept. 17, 1964, Box 14, AP.
"If you will just give . . .": Memo, "Humphrey's Texas Trip," Sept. 17 and 18, 1964, Box 699, HP. Transcript, Houston meeting, Sept. 18, 1964, Box 699, HP.
"Humphrey will follow . . .": *Oil Daily*, Sept. 22, 1964. New York *Journal American*, Sept. 24, 1964.
"What that man would do . . .": *MT*, Oct. 18, 1964. John Stewart interview. Humphrey speech at Tifton, Ga., Sept. 1964, MSF, HP.
"Maturity": *Wall Street Journal*, Aug. 27, 1964. *Life*, Sept. 4, 1964.
"You can count on . . .": McGovern to Humphrey, Oct. 15, 1964, M u / p HP. Humphrey to John Roche, Sept. 2, 1964, Box 1046, HP. ADA release, Aug. 30, 1964, Box 1046, HP. *NYT*, Oct. 9, 1964. *MT*, Oct. 10 and 11, 1964.

262. "Every day was . . .": *NYT*, Nov. 4, 5, 6, 1964.
"There were lots of . . .": Charles Bailey interview, June 23, 1982.
"Boy, did old Jennie Higgins . . .": T. H. White, *Making of the President 1964*, 324–25.
"I have never seen more . . .": *NYT*, Oct. 26, 1964.
"We've got a few slow . . .": *MT*, Oct. 10, 1964.
"Strawberry or . . . ?": *MT*, Oct. 11, 1964.
"Beware of the midlash": Sam H. Johnson, 171–72. *MT*, Oct. 8, 1964. Humphrey interview with L. J. Hackman, Mar. 30, 1970. RFK Oral History

Project, KL. *MT*, Sept. 25, 1964.

263. "Can we trust a man . . . ?": *MT*, Oct. 22, 1964. MSF, Jan.-Sept. 1964, HP. *Pentagon Papers*, Gravel, ed., vol. 3, 12 (for Tonkin Gulf references). T. H. White, *Making of the President 1964*, 382 (for farm-state gains). *MT*, Sept. 22, 1964, reports candidates' assets. Alexander, *Studies in Money and Politics*, no. 17, 44–45. *MT*, Sept. 16, 20, 1964, for polls. *MT*, Oct. 16, 1964, for Khrushchev's fall and Johnson phone call. *Education*, 309.
"Humphrey on campaign 1964": Transcript, n.d., Box 8, Autobiography files, HP.

25: IN LBJ'S DOGHOUSE

264. "gee whiz, it's a wonderful time . . .": Eisele, 236. *Education*, 314. *NYT*, Jan. 21, 1965.

265. "I don't know whether . . .": *NYT*, Jan. 24, 1965.
"I didn't know what to do or say . . .": Edgar Berman interviews, Aug. 14, Sept. 25, Nov. 21, and Dec. 8, 1982, Mar. 7 and Oct. 3, 1983. *Education*, 314.

266. "Mr. President, why didn't you . . . ?": Humphrey "book tape," transcript, n.d., Box 8, Autobiography files, HP. *NYT*, Feb. 5, 1965.
"There's no man alive . . .": Herbert Beckington interview, Nov. 18, 1980. New York *Journal American*, Jan. 17 and 20, 1965.
"so close over you . . .": Toby Solberg interview, Nov. 7, 1980. New York *Post*, July 25, 1965.

267. "Every young American . . .": Humphrey notes of cabinet meeting, Jan. 13, 1965, WHM u / p, Box 48, HP.
"single most important step . . .": Humphrey speech, in New York, Nov. 24, 1964, *NYT*, Nov. 25, 1964, 26.
"going to pile work on Humphrey": J. B. Martin, *Stevenson*, vol. 2, 824.
Civil Rights Council: Johnson to Humphrey, Dec. 2, 1964, WHCF Exec FG 440, JL. *NYT*, Feb. 7, 1965. Johnson to Humphrey, Feb. 7, 1965, *Public Papers of Lyndon B. Johnson (1965)*, 152. Katzenbach interview. Humphrey present at 5 meetings with LBJ, Jan. 21–22, 1965, WHDC, JL. Humphrey to Johnson, Feb. 2, 1965, Box 764, HP.

269. "limit aid to military assistance . . .": *CR*, 108, 3860 (Mar. 12, 1962).
Humphrey on Vietnam 1964: Hum-

phrey to Johnson, June 8, 1964, Vietnam box 1965–71, HP, *CR*, 110, 14295, June 23, 1964. L. B. Johnson, 114–16.
Lansdale influence: 6 Lansdale memos, 1958–64 in Vietnam box, 1965–71, u/p, HP, *Education*, 316–17. Humphrey "book tapes" transcript, n.d., Box 8, Autobiography files, HP.

270. Rusk warned "Humphrey could not expect . . .": *Education*, 317–18. Thomas L. Hughes interview.
Rusk on "critical" situation: Humphrey memo for record of cabinet meeting, Jan. 22, 1965, WHM u/p, Box 48, HP. National Security Council minutes Feb. 1, 1965, NSF NSC Box 1, JL.
Humphrey absent: *MS*, Feb. 6 and 8, 1965.
"Are they unanimous?": William Bundy interview with Paige Mulhollan, May 29, 1969, JL. "Summary Notes of 545th NSC meeting, Feb. 6, 1965, NSF NSC, Box 1, JL.
"I would negotiate . . .": Bundy interview for LJ library.
"I just don't think . . .": Ibid.

271. Humphrey speaks out for delay: "Summary Record of NSC Meeting #548," Feb. 10, 1965 and attachment, Tab A, prior "Meeting of Principals," Feb. 10, 1965, NSF NSC, Box 1, JL. *Education*, 318–19. L. B. Johnson, 130. G. Ball, 390. *Pentagon Papers*, vol. 3, 686. Ball (Nov. 18, 1982), William Bundy (June 7, 1983), Bromley Smith (Aug. 23 and Sept. 17, 1982, Jan. 29, 1983), Chester Cooper (Feb. 4 and Oct. 20, 1981) interviews.
"I had misgivings . . .": Humphrey transcript "book tapes," n.d., Box 8, Autobiography files, HP.
"keep a good file . . .": Humphrey to John Rielly, Feb. 11, 1965, Box 764, HP. Rielly, Smith interviews.

272. Ball dissent: Ball and Thomas L. Hughes interviews.
Georgia weekend: Humphrey daily schedule, Feb. 12, 1965, M u/p, HP. WHDC Backup, Feb. 12, 1965, JL. Hughes, Rielly interviews.
Humphrey to Johnson: "Memo on Vietnam," Feb. 17, 1965, Hughes draft of memo, also Hughes longhand notes for memo, Feb. 15, 1965, Hughes files. Humphrey to Johnson memo dated Feb. 15, 1965, *Education*, 320–24. Philip Potter in Baltimore *Sun*, June 26, 1971. Laurence Stern, *WP*, May 9, 1976. *NYT*, May 10, 1976.

274. "to be elected vice president . . .": Humphrey transcript "Book tapes," n.d., Box 8, Autobiography files, HP.
"Meeting with five senators": George McGovern interview with Naftalin, n.d., 30, Naftalin files. Eisele, 234–35.
"pounding of North Vietnam . . .": Humphrey to Johnson, "Memo on South Vietnam," Mar. 31, 1965. M u/p, HP. *Education*, 319. "Valenti Notes, Presidents Meeting on Vietnam," May 16, 1965, Office files of the President, JL.
"We do not need all . . .": Eisele, 232. Graff, 46–47. Humphrey transcript "book tapes," n.d., Box 8, Autobiography files, HP. Bromley Smith interview. July 29, 1969, for JL.

275. "We've had a meeting . . .": Ted Van Dyk interview with Connell, Mar. 12, 1979, 14, Connell files. Van Dyk interview. J. B. Johnson, 195.
July 1965 decision: L. Berman, 130. *Public Papers of Lyndon B. Johnson*, 1965, 794.
Humphrey daily schedules: 1965, PFPMB u/p, HP. Humphrey to Johnson, Feb. 3, 1965, M u/p HP. Humphrey to Johnson Feb. 17, 1965, M u/p HP. Humphrey to Johnson Mar. 3, 1965, Box 764, HP. *Public Papers of Lyndon B. Johnson*, 1965, 152.
Paris air show trip: Norman Sherman, "Memo for the files," June 22, 1965, PFPBM u/p HP. *Economist*, June 26, 1965. Humphrey interview with Robert Sherrod, n.d., Sherrod files. *Public Papers of Lyndon B. Johnson*, 1965, 685.

276. "You're not getting across . . .": Eisele, 237. *Education*, 493–94. Humphrey to Johnson, Mar. 10, 1965, M u/p HP. Humphrey to Johnson Mar. 11, 1965 M u/p HP. Humphrey memo, "Meeting at White House with President and Civil Rights Group," Mar. 12, 1965, M u/p HP. Humphrey to Johnson, Mar. 12, 1965, M u/p HP. Humphrey to Johnson, April 30, 1965, M u/p HP. Humphrey to Johnson May 4–5, 1965, WHFN (HHH), Container 3, JL. Katzenbach interview. Humphrey to Johnson, Aug. 6, 1965, M u/p HP. Humphrey to Johnson Aug. 11, 1965, M u/p. Humphrey to Marvin Watson, Aug. 26, 1965, M u/p HP. Humphrey to Johnson, Sept. 17, 1965, WHCF CF, Box 346, JL. Marvin Watson to Johnson, Sept. 20, 1965, WHCF CF, Box 346, JL. Humphrey to Johnson and Johnson to Humphrey, Sept. 24, 1965, *Public Papers*

of Lyndon B. Johnson, 1965, 1017. Meeting with Humphrey, Califano, and Johnson, Sept. 22, 1965, WHDC, JL.

277. **"Anticipating no pleasure . . ."** Saul Bellow letter, Nov. 22, 1983.
"Was present but more or less . . .": Dr. C. B. Chapman interview, April 1, 1982.
"Whatever became of Hubert?": Tom Lehrer, *That Was the Year That Was* (album), Reprise Records, July 1965.
"Slowdown on civil rights": New York *Post,* Oct. 19, 1965. Humphrey to Wechsler, Oct. 20, 1965, Wechsler files.

278. **Housing committee recommendations:** Humphrey to Johnson, June 9, 1965, M u / p HP. Humphrey to Johnson, n.d., 1965, M u / p HP. Humphrey to Johnson, June 3, 1965, M u / p HP. Humphrey to Moyers, July 6, 1965, WHCF CF, Box 346, JL. Humphrey memo on Committee recommendations, Nov. 10, 1965, WHM, Box 48, HP. Humphrey to Johnson, Dec. 2, 1965, M u / p HP. Evans and Novak in *WP,* May 14, 1965. Humphrey memo, May 14, 1965, M u / p HP.
Humphrey, "busiest VP in history": Johnson to Humphrey, Jan. 26, 1965, WHFN (HHH), Container 3, JL. Moyers to Humphrey, Jan. 26, 1965, M u / p HP. "Memo for George Reedy," Feb. 13, 1965, WHCF Exec FG 440, JL. Humphrey to Johnson, Mar. 3, 1965, Box 764, HP. Humphrey to Johnson, Mar. 23, 1965, M u / p, HP. Humphrey to Johnson, May 5 and 10, 1965, M u / p, HP. Humphrey to Johnson, June 10, 1965, WHCF CF, Exec FG 440, Box 346, JL. Jim Cross to Johnson, Sept. 16, 1965, Ibid. Ravnholt for record, Oct. 15, 1965, PFPMB u / p, HP. Ravnholt memo, Nov. 3, 1965, PFPMB u / p, HP. Humphrey to H. G. Lohman, Jr., Dec. 17, 1965, Box 928, HP. Neal Peterson interview, Nov. 20, 1980.
"Work never killed anyone . . .": Ravnholt interview, Sept. 21, 1981.

279. **"Goddamit, Hubert, can't you . . . ?:** James Wechsler interview, Jan. 27, 1982.
"I see by the papers . . .": Eisele, 237. Cross to Valenti, Nov. 10, 1965, WHCF, CF, Exec, Box 347, JL.
"What does he need all that . . . ?: *NYT,* Jan. 26, 1965. Califano to Clifton, Jan. 14, 1965 and C. V. Clifton to Humphrey, Jan. 14, 1965, WHCF CF, Exec, FG 440, JL. Clifton to Valenti, Jan. 28,

1965 and Valenti to Johnson, July 8, 1965, WHCF CF Exec FG 440, Box 346, JL. Connell to Valenti, May 17, 1965, Ibid. Hayes Redmon to John Stewart, Jan. 26 and 28, 1965, Box 1, Humphrey speeches, JL. Redmon to Stewart Feb. 1, 3, and 21, 1965, Box 1, Humphrey speeches, JL. *NYT,* Feb. 18, 1965. *Time,* Feb. 26, 1965. Weschler in New York *Post,* Feb. 18, 1965. *Education,* 325.
"Hubert, that was the worst . . .": Humphrey interview transcript, n.d., probably Dec. 1969, Box 2, Autobiography files, HP. WHDC, Feb. 4, 1965, JL. Alexander, *Studies in Money and Politics,* no. 6, 44, re Humphrey fund-raiser, Feb. 5, 1965.

280. **"Don't let anyone . . .":** Humphrey interview with *Fortune,* Aug. 1965, 141.
"Book tapes," n.d., Box 8, Autobiography files, HP. Loevinger interview.
"The Great Society only has meaning" and **"Our faith in you who bear . . .":** *Fortune,* Aug. 1965, 144. See also Humphrey speeches, Feb. 3, 1965 and May 11, 1965, MSF, HP. Humphrey schedule, Oct. 13–Nov. 20, 1965, WHCF CF, Exec, Box 346, JL. New York *World Telegram,* May 13, 1965.
"Half of it would be good": Watson to Johnson, Sept. 15, 1965, WHCF CF Exec and Gen FG 440, Box 346, JL.
Campus appearances: Humphrey to Johnson, Feb. 15, 1968, M u / p HP, Ted Van Dyk to Humphrey, April 5, 1965, M u / p HP. Johnson speech at Johns Hopkins, April 7, 1968, *NYT,* April 8, 1965.

281. **"Not a great idealistic movement":** AP bulletin, June 2, 1965.
"only about a dozen . . .": Humphrey to Valenti, July 16, 1965, WHCF CF, Exec FG 440, Box 346, JL.
"Recognizing that a political . . .": Humphrey speech, June 11, 1965, Vietnam box 1965–71, HP.
"Ultimately this conflict . . .": Jack Bell in AP dispatch, June 4, 1965.

282. **"My God, general . . .":** Herbert Beckington interview.
"Hubert better damn sight . . .": July 26, 1965, WHDC, JL. Humphrey schedule, July 1965, PFPMB u / p, HP. L. Berman, 130. Bromley Smith interview, July 29, 1969, JL. Humphrey Detroit speech, July 26, 1965, MSF, HP. Eisele, 238.
"I have a roomful of senators": Humphrey to Johnson, July 28, 1965,

WHFN (HHH), Container 3, JL. Humphrey to Johnson, Aug. 13, 1965, WHCF CF, Exec, FG 440, Box 346, JL.
"how privileged I feel . . .": Humphrey to Johnson, Aug. 28, 1965, M u / p, HP.
"the great majority . . .": Monrad Paulsen to Humphrey, Aug. 23, 1965, M u / p, HP.

283. "Well, Mother, let me . . .": *Life*, Oct. 8, 1965. Oct. 5, 1965, WHDC, JL. Humphrey to Johnson, Oct. 10, 1965, M u / p, HP. New York *Herald Tribune*, Oct. 8, 1965. Valenti to Johnson, Oct. 12, 1965, WHCF CF, Exec, Box 347, JL. Humphrey to Johnson, Oct. 19, 1965, WHFN (HHH), Container 3, JL. *Education*, 327–28.
"There is a rising tide . . .": Humphrey to Johnson, Nov. 9, 1965, WHCF CF, Exec, Box 347, JL. Wechsler in New York *Post*, Oct. 27, 1965. Humphrey memo, Nov. 12, 1965, WHM u / p, Box 48, HP. Andrew Glass in *The Reporter*, Nov. 18, 1965.
"There are few matters . . .": Johnson to Humphrey, Nov. 9, 1965, WHCF, CF, Exec, Box 347, JL. Humphrey to Johnson, Nov. 8, 1965, M u / p, HP.
Van Dyk to Humphrey: Nov. 24, 1965, PFPMB u / p, HP.

284. "Send the VP": Bundy to Johnson, Nov. 27, 1965, WHCF CF, Exec, Box 347, JL.
"We're going to try . . .": Valenti Notes of Presidents Meeting, Dec. 17, 18, and 21, 1965, JL. Graff, 65 Wechsler, "Humphrey at War with Himself," *PRO*, July 1966.
Gallup poll: "Humphrey, His Public Image," in *WP*, Dec. 12, 1965. Gallup, 1975. Redmon to Moyers, Dec. 10, 1965, WHCF, Exec FG 440, Box 347, JL. Connell to Humphrey, Dec. 13, 1965, M u / p, HP. Evans and Novak "Polls Produce a Humphrey Tour," Des Moines *Register*, Dec. 19, 1965. Humphrey press release, Dec. 23, 1965, PFPMB u / p, HP. New York *Post*, Dec. 23, 1965. New York *Herald Tribune*, Dec. 23, 1965. Saul Bellow letter, Nov. 22, 1983.
Philippine inauguration trip: *Education*, 329. Jack Valenti, 369. Unsigned memo, Dec. 27, 1965, WHCF CF, Box 347, JL. Valenti Meeting Notes file, Dec. 28–Jan. 3, 1966, Box 1, JL. *Asahi* (transl.), Dec. 30, 1965. Humphrey to Johnson, Memos on Manila trip, Jan. 5, 1966, M u / p, HP.

26: THE HATCHET MAN

285. "My discovery of Asia . . .": Humphrey interview with Norman Sherman, n.d., Box 2, Autobiography files, HP. Humphrey to Johnson, Jan. 5, 1966, WHFN (HHH), Container 3, JL. Humphrey "Notes on NSC meeting," n.d., Jan. 1966, WHM u / p, Box 48, HP. Valenti to Johnson, Jan. 7, 1966, WHCF CF, Exec, FG 440, Box 347, JL. Humphrey to Valenti, Jan 10, 1966, M u / p, HP.
"a heavy, big-boned man . . .": Humphrey to file, Jan. 15, 1966, WHM u / p, Box 48, HP.

286. "thank you . . .": Humphrey summary of Kosygin conversations, Jan. 17, 1966, Box 928, HP. Humphrey to file, Jan. 19, 1966, WHM u / p, Box 48, HP.
"Mr. Kosygin, I am . . .": Humphrey summary, Jan. 17, 1966, Box 928, HP. Humphrey to file, Jan. 19, 1966, WHM u / p, Box 48, HP. Humphrey memo of conversation with Aldo Moro, Jan. 11, 1966, and Humphrey of conversation with Pres. Radhakrishnan, Jan. 12, 1966, Box 928, HP. *NYT*, Jan. 12, 13, 14, 15, 1966.
"Keep your schedule loose . . .": *Education*, 329. Jan. 16 and 23, 1966. WHDC, JL.
"win the other war": Lyndon Johnson, 245. Valenti Notes of White House meetings, Jan. 25–30, 1966, JL. Humphrey, "Notes on White House conference," Jan. 15, 1966, WHM u / p Box 48, HP. Wechsler in New York *Post*, Jan. 26, 1966. Humphrey to Wechsler, Jan. 28, 1966, Wechsler files. Mansfield "gloomy report," *NYT*, Jan. 8, 1966, 1. Fifteen Democrats' letter for longer pause, *NYT*, Jan. 28, 1966, and Jan. 31, 1966. Notes on NSC meeting, Jan. 29, 1966, WHM u / p Box 48, HP. Ravnholt memo, Feb. 7, 1966, PFPMB u / p HP. Philip Potter in Baltimore *Sun*, "Humphrey Eyes Kennedy Rise": Jan. 8, 1966.

287. "get back to Washington": Feb. 7, 1966, WHDC, JL. *NYT*, Feb. 4, 5, 6, 7, 8, 1966. Humphrey statement at Washington airport, Feb. 8, 1966, PFPMB u / p, HP.
"We left without any . . .": Rielly and Chester Cooper interviews. At Los Angeles airport: Feb. 8, 1966, WHDC, JL. Marianne Means column, Feb. 14, 1966, WHCF CF, Exec, FG 440, Box 345, JL. *NYT*, Feb. 10, 1966.

"democratic social revolution": *Public Papers of Lyndon B. Johnson*, 1966, 152–53.

trip "a disaster": Rielly interview.

288. "Yes indeed two wars can . . .": Eisele, 242. *NYT*, Feb. 11, 1966. Humphrey to Johnson, Feb. 13, 1966, Box 928, HP.

"appears to be learning . . .": Humphrey to Johnson, Feb. 12, 1966, Box 928, HP.

"Humphrey was so knowledgable . . .": Herbert Beckington interview.

"I fought these bastrds . . .": Eisele, 243, *NYT*, Feb. 13, 1966.

"the closer one gets . . .": Baltimore *Sun*, Feb. 15, 1966. Bowles to Johnson, Mar. 9, 1966, WHCF CF, Exec, Box 347, JL. *WP*, Feb. 15, 1966. *NYT*, Feb. 14, 15, 1966. Chester Cooper, Rielly, Connell interviews. Philip Potter letter, July 27, 1982.

289. "the big picture must . . .": Nell Yates, "Notes on staff meeting in Canberra," Feb. 18, 1966, Box 928, HP. James Thomson interview, Nov. 23, 1982.

"the most magnificent . . .": Baltimore *Sun*, Feb. 20, 1966. USIS release, Humphrey-Holt press conf., Feb. 19, 1966, Box 928, HP.

"just another hard-line . . .": Rielly interview.

290. "fox in the chicken coop . . .": *NYT*, Feb. 20, and 21, 1966. Connell (Aug. 24, 1982), Sherman (Dec. 6, 1982), Potter (July 27, 1982), Lloyd Hand (June 27, 1983), Valenti (May 27, 1983) letters. Thomson and Rielly interviews. Transcript of Senate Foreign Relations committee executive session, Mar. 2, 1966, 45. Humphrey to Johnson, Feb. 20, 1966, Box 928, HP. AP bulletin, Feb. 20, 1966, Vietnam box, u/p, HP. Humphrey to Johnson, Feb. 23, 1966, Box 928, HP.

"more royalist than . . .": *PRO*, Feb. 1966.

"the tide of battle has . . .": White House release, "Remarks of the President and Vice President," Feb. 23, 1966, PFPMB u/p, HP. Lyndon Johnson, 246. Valenti Notes, "Meeting in Cabinet room," Feb. 24, 1966, JL. Humphrey, "Background Briefing at White House for Committees of Congress," Feb. 24, 1966, Box 928, HP. Humphrey, "Background briefing at White House for Cabinet and other members of Congress," Feb. 25, 1966, Box 928, HP. Manatos to Johnson, Feb. 19, 1966, WHCF CF, Exec, Box 347, JL. *WP*, Feb. 25, 1966. *Time*, April 1, 1966.

291. "sniping and revitalized . . .": Valenti to Johnson, Mar. 4, 1966, WHFN, (HHH), Container 3, JL.

"historic turning point": Humphrey to Johnson, 50 pp., Feb. 25, 1966, WHCF CF, Exec Box 347, JL. Humphrey to Johnson, 7 pp. Feb. 25, 1966, WHCF CF, Box 346, HP. *Education*, 337. Ravnholt memo for file, Mar. 16, 1966, PFPBM u/p, HP.

"use the detailed materials . . .": Valenti to Johnson, Mar. 4, 1966, WHFN (HHH), Container 3, JL.

"No more statements like Tonkin . . .": Transcript of U.S. Senate, Foreign Relations committee, executive session, Mar. 2, 1966, 99. Kirkpatrick in *WP*, Feb. 15, 1966. *NYT*, Feb. 22, 1966. *WP*, Mar. 13, 1966. Chester Cooper and Carl Marcy (July 10, 1981) interviews. Humphrey speech at Union seminary, *NYT*, Feb. 26, 1966.

"We must be firm . . .": Humphery speech to Columbia Scholastic Press Association, Mar. 12, 1966. Washington *WS*, Mar. 13, 1966.

"If Americans are willing . . .": Humphrey on "Meet the Press," Mar. 13, 1966, New York *Herald Tribune*, Mar. 14, 1966. Transcript, Vietnam box, u/p, HP.

breakfast with overseas writers: Mar. 9, 1966, PFPMB u/p, HP. Ravnholt memo on staff meeting, Mar. 19, 1966, PFPMB u/p, HP.

"Communism in Asia is . . .": *Time*, April 1, 1966.

292. "Are we to be put . . .": *MT*, Mar. 20, 1966. Wechsler in New York *Post*, Mar. 30, 1966.

"proposing a relationship . . .": CBS Special Report, April 19, 1966, transcript, 6.

"weren't you in the doghouse . . .": Connell notes, Mar. 9, 1966, in PFPMB u/p, HP. Wicker in *NYT*, April 17, 1966.

"as an old friend . . .": McGovern interview.

"There is a suggestion . . .": Humphrey to William Shannon, Mar. 5, 1966, M u/p, HP.

"The President thought . . .": Valenti to Humphrey, Mar. 25, 1966, M u/p, HP. April 5, 1966, WHDC, JL.

"a kind of export ADA": *New Republic*, Mar. 12, 1966.

293. "spiritual kinfolk": Wechsler memo, Mar. 22, 1966, Wechsler files.
"He believes in . . .": Rauh interview with Lansing Lamont, Mar. 26, 1966.
"Given the complexity . . .": Wechsler memo, Mar. 22, 1966.
"His righteous rhetoric . . .": Wechsler in New York *Post*, Mar. 1, 1966.
"There is an old scriptural . . .": Humphrey to Wechsler, April 5, 1966, Wechsler files. Humphrey to Doris Fleeson, Mar. 19, 1966, Wechsler files. Humphrey speech at Union Seminary, Feb. 25, 1966, transcript, WHFN (HHH), Container 3, JL.
"Saigon is as close . . .": Wechsler, New York *Post*, April 25, 1966.
"It is not Hubert . . .": Humphrey to Wechsler, April 5, 1966, M u / p HP.
"has betrayed the liberal . . .": *Esquire*, Nov. 1966, 106.
"such damned rapture . . .": Ibid.
"Prove your masculinity . . .": Ibid. Van Dyk to Humphrey, Mar. 22, 1966, Box 1059, HP.

294. "creative federalism": Roger Davidson "Evaluating the War on Poverty," *Annals*, Sept. 1969.
"I am in the club but . . .": John Stewart to Ravnholt, Jan. 12, 1966, PFPMB u / p, HP.
"We can continue . . .": Lyndon Johnson, 245. Speech, Jan. 31, 1966, Box 1058, HP. Johnson to Humphrey, Mar. 2, 1966, Box 912, HP. Califano to Johnson, Mar. 25, 1966, WHCF CF, Box 347, JL. Humphrey notes of White House meeting, Mar. 18, 1966, WHM u / p, Box 48, HP. Humphrey interview with Al Friendly, Jan. 17, 1966, M u / p HP. Memo, Humphrey meetings with civil rights leaders, Jan. 19 and 20, 1966, M u / p HP. Humphrey to Johnson, Jan. 24, 1966, WHCF CF, Exec, FG 440, JL. John Stewart memo, Jan. 29, 1966, PFPMB u / p, HP. Humphrey to Johnson, July 27, 1966, WHM u / p, Box 48, HP.
"Excuse me a moment . . .": Shriver note to Humphrey longhand, July 26, 1966, M u / p, HP.

295. "because the departments absorbed . . .": John Stewart memo, Jan 12 1966, PFPMB u / p, HP. Neal Peterson memo, April 2, 1966, M u / p, HP. Humphrey to Vi Williams, April 4, 1966, WHM u / p, Box 48, HP. Humphrey to Johnson, April 5, 1966, WHCF CF Exec, Box 347,

JL. Humphrey to Marvin Watson, April 6, 1966, M u / p, HP. Neal Peterson memo, April 7, 1966, M u / p, HP. Ravnholt memo, April 27, 1966, PFPMB u / p, HP.
"I'm Johnson's Eleanor . . .": *NYT*, July 26 and 29, 1966.
"This Vice President is not . . .": McGrory in New York *Post*, July 29, 1966.
"He is not using . . .": Reston in *NYT*, April 29, 1966.
"pleasantly relieved . . .": Humphrey to Wechsler, April 5, 1966, Wechsler files.
White House "Uriah Heep": *Time*, April 1, 1966.

296. "The month has been a . . .": Humphrey memo for files, July 2, 1966, WHM u / p Box 48, HP.
"He wouldn't speak to you . . .": Moyers, "Hubert Humphrey, a Conversation," Bill Moyers Journal, April 11, 1976.
"I was sitting there . . .": Ibid. *NYT*, Aug. 7, 1966.
"I told him I thought . . .": Humphrey memo for files, July 2, 1966, WHM u / p, Box 48, HP. Humphrey longhand notes of special NSC meeting, June 17, 1966, WHM u / p HP. Humphrey, "Cabinet meeting notes," June 17, 1966, HM u / p Box 48, HP. Humphrey, "Leadership meeting with President," July 19, 1966, WHM u / p Box 48, HP. Humphrey to Johnson, July 27, 1966, WHM u / p Box 48 HP. Carmichael and Hamilton, 48.

297. "Identified 880,000 summer jobs . . .": Humphrey to Johnson, July 19, 1966, WHM u / p Box 48, HP.
"Do not deny me . . .": Marsha Shepard memo, July 13, 1966, M u / p, HP.
"There will be open . . .": Humphrey speech, New Orleans, July 18, 1966, WHCF CF, Exec Box 347, JL. Humphrey to Wechsler, July 20, 1966, Wechsler files. *NYT*, July 19, 1966. *WP*, July 19, 1966.
"crack of the year": Paterson (N.J.) *News*, Aug. 19, 1966.
"high officials of this administration": Republican National Committee press release, Oct. 3, 1966.
"lost Congress": Jack Valenti, 154–56. Humphrey to Johnson, Dec. 17, 1966, WHCF CF, Exec, FG 440, Box 347, JL.
"Run on Vietnam": *Christian Science Monitor*, Aug. 16, 1966. Humphrey,

"Memo for record," Sept. 1, 1966, WHM u / p, Box 48, HP. "September schedule of Vice Pres." Sept. 20, 1966, WHCF, CF, Exec, FG 440, Box 347, JL.

298. "You can't live forever . . .": Lebedoff, *Twenty-First Ballot*, 137.
"Yet there's no one around . . .": Los Angeles *Times*, Nov. 3, 1966. Humphrey to Abe Marovitz, Nov. 3, 1966, Box 1063, HP.
"Get off our campus": *The Heights*, Oct. 21, 1966.

299. "This handful of unwashed . . .": Rochester (Minn) *Post-Bulletin*, Oct. 4, 1966.
"Humphrey is going out . . .": *Esquire*, Nov. 1966, 106.
"I have nothing but sympathy . . .": Nixon to Humphrey, Oct. 17, 1966, VIP corr., HP. Connell to Humphrey, Nov. 11, 1966, Box 1056, HP. *NYT*, Nov. 13, 1966. UP bulletin, Nov. 13, 1966 in M u / p, HP. Humphrey, Memo for record, Nov. 28, 1966, WHM u / p Box 48, HP. Nov. 17, 24, and 25, 1966, WHDC, JL.
"We had a good talk . . .": Humphrey memo for record, Nov. 28, 1966, WHM u / p Box 48, HP.
"like most husbands . . .": Rochester (Minn.) *Post-Bulletin*, Dec. 12, 1966.

300. "Yes, we've moved . . .": Humphrey to Anton Thompson, Nov. 17, 1966, Anton Thompson files.

27: THE GREAT ADVENTURE

301. "In Vietnam only the VC commit . . .": *PittNews* May 17, 1965.
"Oswald, where are you?" *WP*, Jan. 25, 1967.
"There is no man who seeks peace . . .": Rocky Mountain *News*, Sept. 11, 1967.
"I'm Vice President because . . .": *Time*, April 1, 1966, 23.
"Let's go for a run . . .": Thomas L. Hughes interview.

302. "This is the only place . . .": Ibid.
"I've just had another . . .": Ibid.
"Hubert, I hear you make . . .": Ibid.

303. "Every newspaper in Washington . . .": Douglas Kiker, *Atlantic Monthly*. June 1967.
"If I could only find a way . . .": Ibid.
"This message was the most . . .": Humphrey to Johnson, WHCF CF, Exec, FG 440, Box 348, JL.

"Would, just once, disagree . . .": Henry McLemore in Toledo *Blade*, Sept. 30, 1966. Humphrey to Marvin Watson, Feb. 10, 1967, WHCF CF, Exec FG 440, Box 348, JL.
"war criminal . . .": Humphrey to Johnson, Feb. 23, 1967, WHM u / p, Box 48, HP. Michael Novak, "Humphrey at Stanford," *Commonweal*, Mar. 24, 1967. Glenn Weaver interview, April 30, 1983.
"foul language and physical . . .": Humphrey interview. *Christian Science Monitor*, Feb. 27, 1967.

304. "This is what we mean by . . .": *NYT*, Mar. 12, 1967.
"But dissent must be responsible . . .": *PRO*, June 1967.
"It is ridiculous to suggest . . .": Ibid.
"Aren't there any . . . ?" UPI bulletin, n.d., WHFN (HHH), Container 3, JL. Dr. G. G. Burkley to George Christian, Mar. 17, 1967, WHCF CF, Exec, Box 348, JL.
"a thousand Communist-led . . .": Humphrey to Johnson, April 1, 1967, Box 935, HP. Humphrey to Johnson, Mar. 30, 1967, Box 935, HP.
"I explained our bombing . . .": Humphrey to Johnson, April 2, 1967, Box 935, HP. *NYT*, April 3, 1967.

305. "making decisions which would look . . .": Humphrey to Johnson, April 1, 1967, Box 935, HP.
"I told the President . . .": *NYT*, April 6, 1967.
If that were the one reason . . .": *NYT*, April 5, 1967.
"jeopardizing his relationship . . .": Humphrey to Johnson, April 4, 1967, Box 935, HP. Humphrey to Johnson, April 5, 1967, Box 935, HP.
"Here we are, a couple of . . .": *Education*, 417.
Germany's "vital interests": Humphrey to Johnson, April 6, 1967, Box 935, HP.
Brussels, Paris: Humphrey to Johnson, April 9, 1967, Box 935, HP. *Education*, 416. *NYT*, April 8, 1967. Andreas interview.
"a success . . .": *WP*, April 9, 1967.
"I have read your reports . . .": Johnson to Humphrey, April 7, 1967, WHM u / p, Box 48, HP.

306. "Warmest congratulations": Smedley to Humphrey, April 10, 1967, Smedley Papers, Columbia University.
Benton quotes Johnson: Benton to Humphrey, May 10, 1968, CF68, HP.

David Bruce to Johnson: April 10, 1967, WHCF CF, Exec, FG 440, Box 348, JL.
"best bridge builder in the party": Raleigh *News and Observer*, Feb. 27, 1967.
"I made a strong effort . . .": Humphrey to Johnson, April 17, 1967, WHM u / p Box 48, HP.

307. "Yes, he did . . .": Wechsler memo, April 26, 1967, Wechsler files.
"I didn't want to bring it up . . .": Ibid.
"On balance I think you are right": Ibid.
"Most of us were struck . . .": Rauh interview.

308. "I could not go against the weight . . .": Edgar Berman interview. *NYT*, June 10–14, 1967. Humphrey memos of conversation with Prime Minister Sato, President Park, July 2, 1967, WHM u / p, Box, 48, HP. Humphrey to Johnson, July 5 and 6, 1967, WHM u / p, Box 48, HP.

309. "The Vice Pres has no authority . . .": Humphrey memos for record, July 24 and 21, 1967, WHM u / p, Box 48, HP.
"The character of the riots . . .": Humphrey to Johnson, July 27, 1967, WHM u / p, Box 48, HP. *Education*, 409. Humphrey to Johnson, Aug. 12, 1967, WHM u / p, Box 48, HP.
"Our commitment to the building . . .": Humphrey to Johnson, Aug. 3, 1967, WHM u / p, Box 48, HP. Van Dyk, John Stewart, Connell interviews. Humphrey interview, *NYT*, Aug. 20, 1967. Humphrey to Johnson, Aug. 23 and 25, 1967, WHCF CF, Exec FG 440, Box 348, JL.

310. Polls plunge: *NYT*, Nov 6, 1967. Gallup, 2075. Connell to Marvin Watson, Sept. 6, 1967, Box 1081, HP.
"credibility gap": *NYT*, Jan. 1, 1967.
"win the war with figures": William Bundy interview with Paige Mulhollan, May 26, 1969, JL.
"one optimist to another . . .": Robert Komer to Humphrey, Oct. 27, 1967, Box 936, HP.

311. "I think it is time that . . .": Humphrey speech Washington, Oct. 23, 1967, Vietnam box 1965–71, M u / p, HP.
Nancy Dickerson to Marvin Watson: Oct. 23, 1967, WHCF CF, Exec, Box 349, JL.
"sarcastic, emotional": *WP*, Oct. 23, 1967. Rauh to Wechsler, Oct. 26, 1967, Wechsler files.

"What do we do now?" Glenn Weaver interview. Weaver to Humphrey, Oct. 31, 1967, PFPA, HP.
"Both are determined to move . . .": Humphrey to Johnson, Oct. 30, 1967, Box 937, HP. Herbert Beckington interview. Beckington to Van Dyk, Nov. 6 and 8, 1967, M u / p HP.

312. "Our business is to make history . . .": Transcript of Saigon speech, Oct. 31, 1967, Vietnam box 1965–71, M u / p, HP.
"our great adventure": Ibid. UPI bulletin, Saigon, Oct. 31, 1967.
"obscene, truthless, swine, totally dishonest . . .": *Ramparts*, Sept. 1968; *Rolling Stone*, Mar. 1972; New York *Post*, May 10, 1971.
"Our military progress is clear": Humphrey to Johnson, Nov. 7, 1967, Box 936, HP. Andreas to Humphrey, Nov. 6, 1967, CF68, HP. Watson to Johnson, Nov. 2, and 4, 1967, WHCF CF Exec, FG 440, Box 349, JL.

313. "very much upset": Humphrey to Johnson, Nov. 28, 1967, Vietnam box, 1965–71, M u / p, HP. McCarthy press release, n.d., Nov. 1967, Box 1064, HP. Humphrey to Miles Lord, Feb. 5, 1968, CF68 u / p, HP.
"I guess I have no influence . . .": Humphrey to Johnson, Nov. 28, 1967, Vietnam box 1965–71, M u / p, HP.
"Johnson's Baby Powder": *NYT*, Dec. 8, 1967. Douglas Bennet interview. Nov. 21, 1980.
"My dad was a grocer . . .": Humphrey memo for record, Nov. 21, 1967, WHM u / p, Box 48, HP.
"If the war in Vietnam is a failure . . .": Eisele, 255.

28: "JOHNSON'S NOT GOING TO MAKE IT EASY"

317. "only" $17 billion a year: Humphrey notes, "Cabinet balance of payments meeting," Dec. 20, 1967, WHM u/p, Box 48, HP. *Wall Street Journal*, Nov. 27, 1967. Humphrey notes "Tax on Tourist Travel," n.d. 1967, WHM u / p Box 48, HP. Humphrey transcripts, n.d., Box 7, Autobiography files, HP.

318. "I won't be around then . . .": Jack Valenti, 154–55. *Education*, 361. Lyndon Johnson, 425. Kearns, 342. Christian, 259. Rostow, 521, Lady Bird Johnson, 706. McPherson, 428.

"It became necessary to . . .": Gelb, 171.

Lansdale "To the Old Team": Feb. 10, 1968, M u/p, HP. Lansdale to Bunker, Mar. 4, 1968, Box 1082, HP. Dick Hunt to Humphrey, Mar. 4, 1968, M u/p, HP. S. Hersh, *My Lai Four*, 21. *NYT*, Mar. 10, 1968, re more troops for Vietnam. *MT*, Mar. 13 and 19, 1968. *NYT*, Mar. 17, 1968. Humphrey to Johnson, Mar. 25, 1968. Box 1082, HP.

319. **N. H. primary**: *NYT*, Mar. 13, 1968.
Preparing LBJ speech: McPherson interview. William Bundy interview with Paige Mulhollan, May 26, 1969, JL. Schandler, 293. *NYT*, Feb. 2, 9, 11, 20, 21, 29, 1968.

320. "**Something startling and dramatic . . .**": Schandler, 224.
"**You are doing wrong to . . .**": *Education*, 346. Schandler, 253.
"**to break the will of North Vietnam . . .**": William Bundy interview, JL. Ball, 390.
"**Mr. President, from a political view . . .**": *Education*, 357.

321. "**a serious distortion of what . . .**": Mar. 23, 1968, WHDC, JL. *WP*, Mar. 23, 1968. *NYT*, Mar. 25, 1968. Wilbur Cohen press conference report, Mar. 25, 1968, M u/p HP.
"**If you can think of . . .**": William Bundy interview, JL. Mar. 26, 1967, WHDC, JL.
"**peaceful tone**": William Bundy interview, JL.
"**That's just great, the best . . .**": Humphrey "Book tape" transcripts, n.d., Box 8, Autobiography files, HP.
"**Accordingly, I shall not seek . . .**": *Public Papers of Lyndon B. Johnson*, 469.

322. "**Put a time-warp on . . .**": James R. Jones interview, Nov. 23, 1982.
"**You're kidding, Mr. Pres . . .**": Ibid. Eisele, 323.
"**Hubert, nobody will believe . . .**": Humphrey "Book tape" transcripts, n.d., Box 8, Autobiography files, HP. Eisele, 323.
"**If you're going to run . . .**": Jones interview.
"**There's no way I can beat . . .**": Ibid.
"**Not a word to Muriel**": Ibid.
"**Is he ill?**": Eisele, 323.
"**Why didn't you tell me?**": *Education*, 59–60. Berman diary, Mar. 31, 1968, Berman files. *Public Papers of Lyndon B. Johnson*, 469.
"**She was very shaken . . .**": Hum-

phrey, "Notes on Mexico," n.d., 1968, WHM u/p, Box 48, HP.

323. "**I called in the members . . .**": Ibid.
"**And before I coulld make any . . .**": Ibid.
"**I felt so sorry for him . . .**": E. Berman, 156–57.
"**Johnson's not going to make it easy . . .**": Ibid.

29: THE POLITICS OF JOY

324. "**Has Bobby got it locked up yet?**": Chester, Hodgson, and Page, 144.
"**I'll be honest with you . . .**": Connell interview. Humphrey "Notes on Mexico," n.d., WHM u/p Box 48, HP. Gartner to Humphrey, April 1, 1968, M u/p, HP. Win Griffith to Connell, April 1, 1968. Box 1082, HP. Berman diary, April 1, 1968, Berman files.
"**Irrevocable**" **decision**: *Public Papers of Lyndon B. Johnson*, 476.
"**or Kennedy will wrap it up**": Humphrey, "Notes on Mexico," n.d., WHM u/p Box 48, HP.
Meany, Monroney: Humphrey, "Memo for record," April 2, 1968, WHM u/p Box 48, HP.

325. "**You and I weren't meant . . .**": Walt Rostow interview, Nov. 5, 1981.
"**If I campaign for someone else . . .**": Murphy, "Notes on Meeting of President with Sen. Robert Kennedy," April 3, 1968, Box 65, Murphy Papers. Rostow memo, April 3, 1968. WHFN (RFK), 1968 Campaign, JL.
"**He must do a better job than . . .**": Rostow, "Memorandum of Conversation, President and Vice President," April 3, 1968, and Rostow memorandum, April 5, 1968, WHD Backup, JL.

326. "**They appeared not yet to have made up . . .**": Ibid. Tom Finney to Connell, April 3, 1968, Box 1149, HP. Ravnholt to Connell, April 3, 1968, Box 1149, HP. Alfonso Cervantes to Humphrey, April 3, 1968, Box 1082, HP. Connell to Humphrey April 4, 1968, Box 1150, HP. Oren Lee Staley to Humphrey, April 4, 1968, Box 1079, HP. Willard Wirtz to Humphrey, April 4, 1968, Box 1150, HP. Bill Welsh to Humphrey, April 4, 1968, Box 1082, HP. Charles T. Jackson to Humphrey, April 4, 1968, Box 1096, HP. *NYT*, April 4, 1968.
"**I've got every establishment . . .**": Chester, Hodgson, and Page, 143–44. Jay

Schwann to Connell, April 2, 1968, Box 1062, HP. *NYT*, April 28, 1968. Andreas, O'Connor interviews.
"I know what you want . . .": *NYT*, April 5, 1968. Berman diary, April 4, 1968, Berman files.
"I ask every American . . .": *Public Papers of Lyndon Johnson*, 493. Berman diary, April 3 and 4, 1968, Berman files. O'Connor interview.

327. "Blight of discrimination": *WP*, April 5, 1968. Berman diary, April 5, 1968, Berman files. *NYT*, April 5–10, 1968. Marvin Watson to Johnson, April 8, 1968, WHCF CF, Exec PL., Box 1, *JL*.
"I thought it would be rather foolish . . .": *Education*, 360–61. Humphrey to Mrs. Jack Schillinger, June 4, 1968, Box 1081, HP. Benton to Humphrey, April 8, 1968, Box 769, HP. Bill Welsh to Humphrey, April 8, 1968, M u / p, HP. Humphrey to Al Barkan, April 8, 1968, WHCF Exec PL, Box 1, JL. Godfrey Sperling interview with Humphrey, *Christian Science Monitor*, June 24, 1968.

328. "a very large body of anti-Kennedy voters . . .": *NYT*, April 24, 1968. David Broder in *WP*, April 10, 1968. Evans and Novak in *WP*, April 10, 1968.
"If presidents were elected by . . .": *NYT*, April 5, 1968. Benton to Humphrey, April 11, 1968, Box 779, HP

329. "Two hundred list, 400 list": Ravnholt notes, April 7, 1968, Box 1150, HP. Welsh to Humphrey, April 8, 1968, Box 1082, HP. Gartner to Humphrey, April 5, 1968, Box 1400, HP. Connell to Humphrey, April 4, 1968, Box 1150, HP. Martin McNamara interview, May 14, 1980.
"a long talk with Pres. Truman . . .": Humphrey to Ken Birkhead, April 8, 1968, Box 1150, HP. Connell memo "Conversation with John Bailey," April 10, 1968, Box 1081, HP.
"maturity of judgment . . .": Humphrey memo to self, April 8, 1968, CF6870 PF, HP.

330. "I'm old hat . . .": Berman diary, May 21, 1968, Berman files. *NYT*, April 11, 1968. Mondale interview with Connell, Mar. 28, 1978, Connell files. Lewis, 175. Lawrence O'Brien (March 10, 1981). Freeman, Lord, Thomas R. Hughes interviews.
"Mr. Vice President, you have arrived . . .": Stinnett to Ravnholt, Aug. 24, 1965, PFPMB, HP.

331. "Bobby's nominated": Eisele, 329.

"We're going to have a close . . .": Berman diary, April 14 and 15, 1968, Berman files. O'Brien to Humphrey, April 16, 1968, CF68 PP, HP.
"maturity . . . integrity . . .": *NYT*, May 12, 1968.
"I'm giving you carte blanche": Berman diary, April 17, 1968, Berman files.

332. "Almost irrepressible, buoyant . . .": Ibid., April 27, 1968.
"The future has several . . .": *NYT*, April 28, 1968.
"Here we are, the way . . .": Ibid. Norman Cousins, Bill Moyers drafts, n.d., April 1968; Wirtz to Humphrey (Wirtz draft), April 22, 1968; Humphrey note, April 8, 1968, CF6870, HP. Van Dyk to Edgar Berman, April 30, 1968, CF68 (incl. speech drafts), HP. Russell Baker in *NYT*, April 30, 1968. Joseph Kraft in *WP*, April 30, 1968.

333. "knowing that he'd done well . . .": Berman diary, April 27, 1968, Berman files.
"VP a candidate . . .": New York *Journal American*, April 28, 1968.
"It is easy to say . . .": *NYT*, May 16, 1968. Benton to Truman, April 29, 1968, Box 779, HP.
"the mutable application of . . .": Larner, 21.

334. "There comes a time when . . .": O'Neill, 361.
"a mistake": Newfield, 110.
McCarthy: Stephen Mitchell, "McCarthy memo," April 22, 1968, Box 100, MP. Larner, 25.
Robert Kennedy: Newfield, 220, 226, 241, 244. *NYT*, May 5, 13, 14, 1968.
"calling upon the darker impulses . . .": O'Neill, 364.

335. "It's our money . . .": Koskoff, 397.
"I was the chief law enforcement officer . . .": Chester, Hodgson, and Page, 164.
"talking of joy in times of . . .": *NYT*, May 16, 1968.

336. "almost foaming at the mouth . . .": Harris, 162.
"I spent so much time cutting . . .": McCandless interview (Oct. 15, 1982).
"I am bringing this to an abrupt end . . .": Berman diary, April 12, 22, 23, 24, May 1, 1968. Connell to Humphrey, April 25, 1968, M u / p, HP. Kampelman to Humphrey, April 25, 1968, Box 779, HP. Maguire to Connell, May 11, 1968, M u / p, HP. Humphrey to Connell, May 16, 1968, M u / p HP.

"Why were the calls of . . .?":
McCandless interview.

337. "If there was a Democratic governor
. . .": Eisele, 331.
"We went into the states like . . .":
McCandless interview. Valenti to Hum-
phrey, May 31, 1968, Box 1082, HP.
Humphrey to Connell, May 16, 1968, M
u / p, HP. Humphrey to Mon-
dale / Harris, May 16, 1968,
M u / p, HP. Anthony Howard, "Last of
the Homespun Heroes," London
Observer, May 12, 1968, *NYT*, May 19,
1968. Berman diary, May 22, 1968, Ber-
man files.
"first Mayor Tate assembled . . .":
McCandless interview.
"Pennsylvania railroad": Eisele, 331.
"Humphrey was nominated in Pa.":
Ibid. Alsop in *WP*, June 1, 1968.

337–8. California primary: Newfield, 286.
Schlesinger, *Robert F. Kennedy*, 907.
Chester, Hodgson and Page, 334.

30:   THE OLDEST SON

339. "The bullet that killed Bobby . . .":
Chester et al., Cleveland Plain Dealer,
Mar. 28, 1972.
"In the caucuses, the precincts . . .":
NYT, July 1, 1968. Berman diary, June
26, 1968, Berman files.
"sour the whole public . . .": Eisele,
332.

340. "I was doing everything I could . . .":
Humphrey interview with Marquis
Childs, *WP*, Sept. 9, 1968.
Humphrey's post-Kennedy finances:
NYT, June 20 and July 10, 1968. "Lunch
plan at Waverly," June 27, 1968, CF68,
HP. Berman diary, July 25, 1968, Ber-
man files. Andreas to Humphrey, July
28, 1968, CF68, HP. Gene Wyman to
Travis Stewart, July 31, 1968, CF68, HP.
Humphrey to Andreas, Aug. 5, 1968,
CF68, HP. Wyman to Andreas, Aug. 5,
1968, CF68, HP. Andreas to Hum-
phrey, Aug. 7, 1968, CF68, HP. Ber-
man diary, Aug. 15, 1968. Gartner to
Humphrey, June 25, 1968, CF68, HP.
Johnson after RFK death: Tom John-
son to Johnson, June 11, 1968, WHCF
CF Exec PL / HHH, Box 26, JL. Hum-
phrey to Maguire, July 24, 1968, CF68,
HP. Berman diary, July 16 and 17, 1968,
Berman files.
"It's like a football game . . .": *NYT*,
June 13, 1968. Eisele, 338.
"involutions and complexity":

McCarthy interview. Berman diary, June
8, 1968, Berman files. Humphrey memo
for record, June 7, 1968, CF68, HP.
Humphrey longhand notes, McCarthy
visit, June 7, 1968, CF68, HP.
death threats: Berman diary, June 8,
1968, Berman files.

341. Humphrey after RFK death: *Educa-
tion*, 372. Rowe to Humphrey, June 7,
1968, CF68, HP. Humphrey to John-
son, June 7, 1968, WHCF CF Exec PL
HHH, Box 25, JL. Humphrey to Gart-
ner, June 18, 1968, CF68PP, HP. *NYT*,
June 9 and 10, 1968. John Gronouski to
Mondale / Harris, June 10, 1968, CF68,
HP. Freeman to Humphrey, June 10,
1968, CF68, HP. Valenti to Humphrey,
June 10, 1968, CF68, HP. Chester
Cooper longhand memo, June 11, 1968,
Vietnam box, 1965–71, M u / p, HP. Van
Dyk to Humphrey, June 11, 1968, M u /
p, HP. Robert Nathan memo, June 11,
1968, Vietnam box 1965–71, M u / p,
HP. Ida Mae Nowels to Humphrey, June
12 and Humphrey to Ida Mae Nowels,
June 18, 1968, Box 1080, HP. Freeman
to Humphrey, June 12, 1968, CF68. HP.
Dean Acheson to David Ginsburg, June
12, 1968, CF68, HP. Norman Thomas
to Humphrey, June 13, 1968, Box 1081,
HP. Stuart Symington to Humphrey,
June 13, 1968, Vietnam box, 1965–71,
HP. John Stewart to Humphrey, June
13, 1968, M u / p, HP. John Holt to
Humphrey, June 13, 1968, Box 97, MP.
John Roche to Humphrey, June 14, 1968,
WHM u / p, Box 48, HP. Wirtz to
Humphrey, June 17, 1968, M u / p, HP.
John Cowles to Andreas, June 17, 1968,
CF68, HP. Marty Friedman to Hum-
phrey, June 17, 1968, M u / p, HP.
George Reedy memo, June 17, 1968,
CF68 PP, HP. Humphrey to Mondale,
June 18, 1968, CF68 PP HP. Humphrey
to Mrs. George Schaa, June 18, 1968, Box
1080, HP. Joseph Kraft in *WP*, June 18,
1968. Marquis Childs in *WP*, June 19,
1968. Humphrey to Childs, June 19,
1968, M u / p, HP. Humphrey to Joseph
Kraft, June 19, 1968. M u / p, HP. Ber-
man diary, June 19, 1968, Berman files.
Heaney to Freeman, June 7 and 25, 1968,
CF68, PP, HP.
"The President knew it would . . .":
Berman diary, June 6, 1968, Berman files.
"VP to 2nd floor, June 6, 1968, 7:20–
10:45 A.M.," WHDC, JL.
"Did you really mean . . .": Berman
diary, June 7, 1968, Berman files. *NYT*,
June 5–10, 1968. Moyers to Humphrey,

June 6, 1968, CF68 PP, HP. Humphrey to Benton, June 7, 1968, CF68, HP. Rowe to Humphrey, June 7, 1968, CF68, HP.

342. **"ducked and bobbed"**: Humphrey on "Face the Nation," June 30, 1968. Van Dyk to Humphrey, June 11, 1968, M u / p, HP. Acheson to Humphrey, June 12, 1968, CF68, HP. Moyers on Frank Reynolds show, ABC-TV, June 14, 1968, CF68 PP, HP. Strout, June 15, 1968. *New Republic*, June 29, 1968. Reedy to Humphrey, June 17, 1968, CF68, HP. Chalmers Roberts in *WP*, June 19, 1968. Tom Johnson to Johnson, June 19, 1968, WHM u / p, Box 48, HP. Unsigned memo, "The VP's Problem," June 21, 1968, M u / p, HP. Roger Kent to Fred Harris, June 26, 1968, Box 1108, HP.
"Let 'em see you shoot . . .": Frady, 9.
"Whole heaps of folks . . .": Ibid., 7.
"Wallace thinks like I do . . .": Ruth Mehrtens interview for *Time*, July 17, 1968.
"half of my members . . .": Berman diary, Aug. 21, 1968.
"The President didn't run because . . .": Berman diary, June 19, 1968, Berman files.
"Steal" yell in Minnesota: *NYT*, June 23, 1968. David Lebedoff interview, Aug. 27, 1981.

343. **"Steamroller"**: *WP*, June 23, 1968.
"bossed convention": *Newsweek*, Sept. 7, 1968. Mondale to Humphrey, June 29, 1968, CF68, HP. McCandless to Humphrey, July 17, 1968, CF68, HP.
"thin, apathetic, hostile": *WP*, July 29, 1968.
"Without labor in Ohio . . .": Berman diary, July 3, 1968, Berman files. Marty McNamara to Humphrey, July 9, 1968, M u / p, HP. Humphrey to Al Barkan, July 24, 1968, M u / p, HP.
"Honky, go home": *NYT*, July 28, 1968. Los Angeles *Times*, July 28, 1968. Gartner memo, July 28, 1968, SFM 1971–77, HP.
"like a rat running . . .": Hsinhua agency, *NYT*, July 29, 1968, 23.
"to the wall . . .": Berman diary, July 28, 1968, Berman files.
"wash the blood off . . .": *NYT*, July 31, 1968. Berman diary, July 31, 1968, Berman files.
"the joke of an OEO . . .": Ibid., Aug. 3, 1968.
"when you set out to deal . . .": Ibid., July 3, 1968.

344. **"your campaign is badly . . ."**: Sanford to Humphrey, n.d., July 1968, CF68 PP, HP.
"lack of coherence . . .": McCandless interview. Berman diary, July 20, 1968. Berman files.
"campaign coordinator": *NYT*, July 19, 1968. John Hoving letters, Mar 7 and April 11, 1983. Berman diary, July 20, 1968, Berman files. Humphrey to Mondale / Harris et al, July 26, 1968, CF68 PP, HP.
ventriloquist's dummy: *Esquire* cover, Nov. 1966.
staff split: Connell, Rowe, Kampelman, Van Dyk, Rielly, William B. Welsh (Nov. 20, 1980, Aug. 13 and Oct. 15, 1982) interviews. Berman diary, May 3, July 3, 8, 19, 20, 1968, Berman files.
"No intention of breaking . . .": Jim Jones to Johnson, July 18, 1968. WHCF CF, Exec FG 440, Box 549, JL. *WP*, July 18, 1968.
"They sat down one night . . .": Berman diary, Aug. 9, 1968, Berman files.

345. **"In Feb., after Tet . . ."**: Rowan in *WS*, June 18, 1968.
"would emerge on his own . . .": *NYT*, June 17, 1968. *Congressional Quarterly*, June 16 and 18, 1968.
"I may be wrong or stupid but . . .": Tom Johnson to Johnson, June 19, 1968, WHM, u / p, Box 48, HP.
"Trapped": Chester et al., 155.
"It was the father . . .": Berman diary Aug. 9, 1968. Berman files. Willy Brandt letter, Feb. 28, 1983.

346. **"My dad said, if . . ."**: Berman diary, June 25, 1968, Berman files.
"My Childhood": Metromedia TV, July 6, 1964; Humphrey interview with Producer Arthur Barron.
"My Father": *Atlantic Monthly*, Nov. 1966, reprinted *Readers Digest*, Jan. 1967.
"abnegated much of his . . .": Erikson, *Young Man Luther*, 238.
"It's very difficult now . . .": Berman diary, Aug. 9, 1968.
"I didn't ask him to live . . .": *NYT*, June 21, 1968.
"Humphrey Sees Himself . . .": *WP*, June 21, 1968.
"Humphrey's problem, one . . .": Nixon interview with Fentriss, *Time*, July 17, 1968.
"We'll find a way out . . .": Berman diary, June 20, 1968, Berman files.
"I can't be constantly speaking . . .": Ibid., May 31, 1968.

"You can't trust him . . .": Ibid., June 18, 1968. June 17, 1968, 8:45 A.M., WHDC, JL.

347. "a grippy condition": Berman diary, July 8, 1968, Berman files. *NYT*, July 11 and 18, 1968.

"Don't go to California . . .": Berman diary, July 10, 1968, Berman files. July 10, 1968, phone call 11:24 P.M., WHDC, JL.

"The trouble with you, Hubert . . .": Berman diary, July 10, 1968, Berman files.

"The VP fell asleep . . .": Ibid.

"The VP's warmest supporters . . .": Frankel, *NYT*, July 16, 1968.

"Politically painful identification": *NYT*, July 23, 1968.

Hanoi's "irreconcilability": *NYT*, July 24, 1968.

"Post-Vietnam task force": Brzezinski to Humphrey, June 24, 1968, CF68, HP.

"Keep America Hum-Free": *NYT*, July 24, 1968.

"I don't want anything . . .": Berman diary, July 24, 1968, Berman files. *NYT*, July 18, 24, 25, 1968.

348. "We simply can't let this . . .": Ben Read interviews, Sept. 11 and 18, 1981, Nov. 20, 1982, Mar. 15, 1983.

"I am encouraged by . . .": "Vietnam statement," July 25, 1968, CF68, PP, HP. Brzezinski to Rielly, June 20, 1968, Vietnam box 1965–71, M u / p, HP. Humphrey to Brzezinski, June 24, 1968, Vietnam box 1965–71, M u / p, HP. "Building Peace in Southeast Asia," June 25, 1968, Vietnam box, 1965–71, M u / p, HP. Sam Huntington to Rielly et al., June 27, 1968, Vietnam box 1965–71, M u / p, HP. Rielly to Huntington, July 1, 1968, Vietnam box 1965–71, M u / p, HP. Henry Owen and Brzezinski to Humphrey, July 10, 1968, CF68, HP. Huntington to Humphrey, July 14, 1968, CF68, HP. Rielly to Huntington, July 15, Vietnam box 1965–71, M u / p, HP. Bowles to Humphrey, July 21, 1968, M u / p, HP. Brzezinski to Humphrey, July 16, 1968, CF68, HP. Rielly to Humphrey, July 16, 1968, Vietnam box 1965–71, M u / p, HP. Nathan to Harriman, July 16, 1968, M u / p, HP. Nathan to Humphrey, July 16, 1968, M u / p, HP. Humphrey notes, Tom Hughes briefing, July 19, 1968, Vietnam box 1965–71, M u / p, HP. "Vietnam statement" drafts, July 20, 21, 23, 25, 1968, Viet-nam box 1965–71, M u / p, HP. Douglas Bennet drafts, July 21 and 23, 1968, Bennet files.

"I'll have to show it to . . .": Edwin Reuschauer interview, Nov. 17, 1982.

"He was furiously washing . . .": Van Dyk interview, Berman diary, Aug. 5 and Sept. 27, 1968, Berman files. Los Angeles *Times*, July 27, 1968. *WP*, July 29, 1968. "VP and President in Oval Office 8:10–9:21 P.M., July 25, 1968, WHDC, JL.

"savage pressures": *NYT*, July 26, 1968.

349. "revision": Van Dyk interview.

"Would it hurt to wait?": Berman diary, Aug. 2 and 5, 1968, Berman files. Humphrey to Freeman, July 26, 1968, CF68, HP. Humphrey to Clark Kerr, July 27, 1968, Vietnam box 1965–71, M u / p, HP. Ed Firmage to Humphrey July 27, 1968, Vietnam box 1965–71, M u / p, HP. "Vietnam, Toward a Political Settlement and Peace in Southeast Asia," July 28, 30 and Aug. 5, 1968, Vietnam box 1965–71, M u / p, HP. Kampelman to Humphrey, July 29, 1968, Vietnam box 1965–71, M u / p, HP. Richard Hughes to Johnson, July 30, 1968, WHCF CF Exec, FG 440 PL (HH), JL. Huntington to Rielly, July 30, 1968, Vietnam box 1965–71, M u / p, HP. Humphrey to Brzezinski, July 31, 1968, Vietnam box 1965–71, M u / p, HP. *NYT*, Aug. 2, 3, 9, 1968.

"I for one am willing . . .": "Vietnam, Toward a Political Settlement and Peace in Southeast Asia, Draft XI," Aug. 8, 1968, Vietnam box 1965–71, M u / p, HP. *NYT*, Aug. 10, 1968. "VP at ranch, Aug. 9, 1968, 10:30–3 P.M.," WHDC, JL. Doris Kearns interview, Nov. 1, 1982.

"reciprocity . . . restraint . . .": Berman diary, Aug. 12, 1968, Berman files.

"You can get a headline . . .": Ibid., Aug. 18, 1968. "Hubert Humphrey, a Conversation," on Bill Moyers Journal, April 11, 1976. Humphrey interview with Theodore White, n.d., 1969, transcript Box 1, Autobiography files, HP.

"There are situations afoot . . .": Berman diary, Aug. 18, 1968, Berman files. Rielly to Humphrey, July 12, 1968, M u / p, HP.

350. "that they had good communica-tion": Berman diary, Aug. 9, 1968, Berman files.

"had a funny feeling . . .": Ibid.

"You could almost feel . . .": Ibid.

"What would you think if?": Ibid.
"Flabby" frontrunner: Wicker in *NYT*, Aug. 13, 1968. Fred Utavsky to Humphrey, Aug. 10, 1968, Box 1096, HP. Humphrey on "Issues and Answers," Aug. 11, 1968. *WS*, Aug. 11, 1968. Humphrey to O'Brien, Aug. 12, 1968, M u / p, HP. Humphrey to Clark Kerr, Aug. 12, 1968, Vietnam box 1965–71, M u / p, HP. John Bartlow Martin to Humphrey, Aug. 12, 1968, M u / p, HP. McGovern to Humphrey, Aug. 9, 1968, CF68, HP.
"downgrading . . .": Berman diary, Aug. 18, 1968, Berman files.
"Davy Gartner came in . . .": Ibid., Aug. 19, 1968. Johnson phone call to Humphrey, Aug. 18, 1968, 5:15 P.M.. WHDC, JL. *NYT*, Aug. 19 and 20, 1968. Carl Rowan in *WS*, Aug. 21, 1968. *Public Papers of Lyndon B. Johnson, 1968–69*, 896.

351. **Running-mate talk:** *Education*, 490–91. Endicott Peabody letters, Jan. 21 and Mar. 4, 1982. Kampelman interview, *NYT*, Jan. 4, 1971. Jim Jones to Johnson, Aug. 12, 1968, WHCF CF, Exec FG 440, Box 349, JL. *Congressional Quarterly*, July 26, 1968. Berman diary, Aug. 9, 1968, Berman files. Hy Bookbinder to Humphrey, July 24, 1968, M u / p, HP.
Johnson convention plans: Berman diary, July 15, 31 and Aug. 13, 1968, Berman files. Criswell to James Jones, June 18 and 28, 1968, WHCF CF, Exec PL 1 (Conventions), Box 79, JL. Jones to Johnson, July 9, 1968, WHCF, CF, Exec PL-1 (Conventions), Box 79, JL. Bert Bennett to Jim Jones, Aug. 9, 1968, WHCF, CF, Exec PL-1, Box 77, JL. Califano to Johnson, July 11, 1968, WHCF CF, Exec FG 440, Box 349, JL. DeVier Pierson to Johnson, June 21, 1968, WHCF CF, Exec PL-1 (Conventions), JL. Ravnholt to Humphrey, July 11, 1968, Box 1145, HP. Humphrey to Daley, July 19, 1968, CF68, HP. Mitchell to John Bailey, June 18, 1968, Box 97, MP. Mitchell memo for files, July 9, 1968, Box 100, MP. Houston *Chronicle*, July 17, 1968. *NYT*, July 18, 1968.
"wanted the plank to be a Humphrey . . .": Berman diary, Aug. 17, 1968, Berman files.

352. "the narrowness of the gap . . .": David Ginsburg interview.
"there's not ten cents' worth . . .": Chester, Hodgson, and Page, 532.

platform: Willard Wirtz to Humphrey, July 3, 1968, CF68 PP, HP. Mitchell to Boggs, July 5, 1968, Box 97, MP. Jim Jones to Johnson, July 9, 1968, WHCF, CF, Exec PL-1 (Conventions), Box 79, JL. Ravnholt to Humphrey, July 11, 1968, Box 1145, HP. John Stewart to Humphrey, July 20, 1968, Box 1106, HP. Humphrey to Hale Boggs, July 23, 1968, Box 1081, HP. Benton to Humphrey, July 25, 1968, CF68, HP. Charles Murphy, "Statement for Democratic Platform committee," Aug. 2, 1968, Box 65, MP. Ernest Lefever to Humphrey, Aug. 6, 1968, M u / p, HP. Fred Israel to Nathan, Aug. 9, 1968, Box 1106, HP. Fred Dutton to Benton, Aug. 9, 1968, Box 1081, HP. Dutton draft plank, n.d., Aug. 1968, Box 1106, HP. Claiborne Pell draft plank, Aug. 9, 1968, Box 1106, HP. "Our involvement in Vietnam," n.d., Aug. 1968, Box 1106, HP. O'Brien to Humphrey Aug. 10 and Humphrey to O'Brien, Aug. 12, 1968, Box 1106, HP. Humphrey, "Draft A: Vietnam, toward a political settlement and peace in Southeast Asia," Aug. 19, 1968, Box 1106, HP. McGeorge Bundy to Ginsburg, Aug. 15, 1968, CF68, HP. Nathan to Ginsburg, Aug. 15, 1968, Box 1106, HP. Douglas Bennet memo, Aug. 16, 1968, Box 1106, HP. Staff draft resolution on Vietnam, Aug. 17, 1968, Box 1106, HP. Connell to Humphrey, "Required Decisions," Aug. 17, 1968, CF68, HP. Bennet to Welsh, Aug 17, 1968, Box 1106, HP. ADA "Proposal for Democratic Party Platform," n.d., Aug. 1968, Box 1106, HP. Wirtz, "Statement to the Platform committee," Aug. 20, 1968, CF68, HP. Edward Kennedy, speech in Worcester, Mass., Aug. 22, 1968, Box 1106, HP. Murphy to Johnson, Aug. 21, 1968, Box 66, MP. Terence Linklater to Humphrey, Aug. 12, 1968, Box 1081, HP. Rostow to Johnson, Aug. 22, 1968, NSF, Defense, Executive ND, Box 233, JL. Berman diary, Aug. 21, 1968, Berman files. *NYT*, Aug. 23, 1968. Chicago *Tribune*, Aug. 24, 1968. Many other Vietnam plank drafts, n.d., Aug. 1968, Box 1106, HP.
"We can live with it, Hubert": *Education*, 388.
Charles Murphy role: Murphy (Sept. 14, 1981), Ginsburg (Nov. 18, 19, 24, 1982), Welsh interviews. Phone call Murphy to Johnson, Aug. 25, 1968, 2352–0004 A.M. and phone call Johnson

to Murphy, Aug. 26, 1968, 0804–0811
A.M. WHDC, JL.
353. **"The ranch wants to speak . . .":**
Ginsburg interview.
"I can't go further": Berman diary,
Aug. 26, 1968, Berman files.
"Stop the bombing when . . .": *NYT*,
Aug. 27, 1968, 26.
"Stop the bombing of N. Vietnam":
"Vietnam draft," Aug. 26, 1968. CF68,
HP.
"They played with these words . . .":
Berman diary, Aug. 26, 1968, Berman
files. Bill Welsh letter, Jan. 7, 1983. *NYT*,
Aug. 27, 1968, 27.
"upset and angry . . .": *Education*, 389.
"That plank undercuts . . .": Ibid.
Berman diary, Aug. 27, 1968, Berman
files.
354. **"I had become like . . .":** Rielly inter-
view.

31:   CATASTROPHE AT CHICAGO

356. **"come out from under":** Van Dyk,
Rielly interviews.
"I think the policies . . .": *NYT*, Aug.
26, 1968. Berman diary, Aug. 25, 1968,
Berman files.
357. **"Off we go, into battle . . .":** Berman
diary, Aug. 25, 1968, Berman files.
Johnson and convention: Bert Ben-
nett to Jim Jones, Aug. 8, 9, 15, 1968,
WHCF CF PL 1, Box 77, JL. McPherson
to Tom Johnson, Aug. 16, 1968, WHCF
CF, Exec PL / HHH, Box 25, JL. White,
Making of the President 1968, 325–26.
Berman diary, Aug. 13, 21, 1968, Berman files. Jim Jones to Johnson, Aug. 21
and 24, 1968, WHCF CF, Exec FG 440,
Box 349, JL. Manatos to Johnson, Aug.
21, 1968, WHCF CF, Exec PL / HHH,
Box 25, JL. Haywood Smith to Jim
Jones, Aug. 21, 1968, Ibid. Chicago *Sun
Times*, Aug. 24, 1968. *NYT*, Aug. 24,
1968. Phonecalls Johnson to Daley 1603–
1608 and to Criswell 1632–36, Aug. 27,
1968, WHDC, JL. Bruce Solomonson
interview. Eisele, 348.
358. **"Not hawkish, not dovish . . .":**
Berman diary, Aug. 25, 1968, Berman
files. Frankel in *NYT*, Aug. 25, 1968.
Navasky in *NYT*, Aug. 25, 1968. Robert
Squier to O'Brien, Aug. 26, 1968, Box
1113, HP.
Daley-Unruh meeting: Chester,
Hodgson, and Page, 569. Chicago *Daily
News*, Mar. 7, 1969. B. Hersh, 347.

Weaver's warnings: Berman diary,
Aug. 24, 1968, Berman files. Hoover to
Tolson, Aug. 15, 1968, Politics 1976,
HP. DeLoach to Tolson, Aug. 7, 1968,
Politics 1976, HP. Weaver to Hum-
phrey, Aug. 13, 1968, Box 941, HP.
"We want Gene": Berman diary, Aug.
25, 1968, Berman files.
"practically agree . . .": Ibid.
"It won't get us into trouble . . .":
Ibid.
"I've got a lot of friends . . .": Ibid.,
Aug. 26, 1968. Longhand notes, "Hum-
phrey's Doings on August 26," CF6870,
HP.
359. **"have backed us up . . .":** Ibid.
"one man, one vote . . . bossism":
Ramparts, Sept. 1968. *NYT*, Aug. 26,
1968.
"at this Convention": Humphrey to
Shapiro, Aug. 21, 1968, M u / p, HP.
Congressional Quarterly, Aug. 23, 1968.
Eisele, 348.
"Hell, I wish I hadn't . . .": Berman
diary, Aug. 25, 1968, Berman files.
"Get to Daley . . .": Jim Jones to Johnson, Aug. 24, 1968, WHCF CF Exec,
PL, Box 25, JL.
Kennedy "boom": *NYT*, Aug. 25, 26,
27, 1968. Berman diary, Aug. 26 and 27,
1968, Berman file. B. Hersh, 340, 347,
352.
"payoff day": Berman diary, Aug. 26,
1968, Berman files.
"rambles from the ranch": *Education*,
388.
"just waffling all over . . .": Berman
diary, Aug. 26, 1968, Berman files.
"I don't want to hear . . .": Ibid.
Vietnam plank voted: Finney in *NYT*,
Aug. 27 and 28, 1968. Berman diary,
Aug. 27 and 28, 1968, Berman files.
Wicker in *NYT* mag., Aug. 24, 1969.
California caucus debate: Berman
diary, Aug. 27, 1968, Berman files. Jack
Gould in *NYT*, Aug. 28, 1968.
360. **"We've been playing games . . .":**
Berman diary, Aug. 26, 1968, Berman
files.
"as is": *NYT*, Aug. 28, 1968.
"embarrassing to the President":
Berman diary, Aug. 27, 1968, Berman
files. Longhand notes, "Humphrey's
doings on August 27," CF6870, HP.
361. **"If he does come up . . .":** Berman
diary, Aug. 27, 1968, Berman files.
"disclaim the plank": Ibid., Aug. 26,
1968.
"Say in your acceptance speech . . .":

Ibid. Valenti to Humphrey, Aug. 25, 1968, CF68 (including speech drafts), HP. Wechsler in New York *Post*, Aug. 28, 1968.

"perceived as handyman . . .": McClosky, Kirkpatrick, Robert Nathan (Nov. 18, 1980), Kampelman, Welsh interviews. McClosky to Humphrey, Aug. 21, 1968, Box 1075, HP. Carl Kaysen to Nathan, Aug. 21, 1968, Nathan files. William B. Welsh letter, Oct. 22, 1982.

"Mr. President, I want you . . .": McClosky, Nathan interviews.

362. "It would not look like . . .": Ibid.
Hippies, yippies: *NYT*, Aug. 25–30, 1968. *Ramparts*, Sept. 1968. D. Walker, 3.

363. "shoot to kill": Royko, 165.
"Garrison Convention": Krock in *NYT*, Aug. 28, 1968.
"It was the clearing of . . .": D. Walker, 3.

364. "Pigs, pigs": Ibid. *NYT*, Aug. 28–30, 1968. *Ramparts*, Sept. 1968. Lebedoff, *Ward Number Six*, 178.
"What's holding us up . . .": D. Walker, 163. White, *Making of the President 1968*, 344.
"I did not witness . . .": Humphrey interview with Norman Sherman, n.d., probably 1969, Box 2, Autobiography files, HP. Humphrey press statement, Aug. 29, 1968, Box 1113, HP.
"playing up the kooks": Chicago *Daily News*, Aug. 29, 1968.

365. "Gestapo tactics": *NYT*, Aug. 29, 1968.
"The Democrats are finished": White, *Making of the President 1968*, 373.
"I'm not going to worry . . .": Berman diary, Aug. 26, 1968, Berman files.
"I'm going to be president . . .": Eisele, 358. E. Berman, 189.
"I feel like jumping . . .": *Making of the President 1968*, White, 354.

366. "I wish Momma were really here . . .": Ibid. Berman diary, Aug. 30, 1968, Berman files. D. Pleis memo, "What Humphrey did the day he was nominated," Sept. 15, 1968, M u / p, HP.
"I wish my Dad were here": Berman diary, Aug. 30, 1968, Berman files.
"Bless your heart": Ibid.
"It is very disheartening . . .": *NYT*, Aug. 30, 1968. Lord interview. Berman diary, Aug. 30, 1968. Berman files.
"I know I talk too much . . .": White, *Making of the President 1968*, 356.
"OK boys, who's it going . . . ?"

Berman diary, Aug. 29, 1968, Berman files. O'Brien calling list, Aug. 28, 1968, Box 1113, HP. Longhand notes, "Humphrey's doings, Aug. 29, 1968," CF6870, HP.
"Listen, it's going to be Muskie": Berman diary, Aug. 29, 1968, Berman files.

367. "I need Jim Rowe . . .": Ibid. "It's your decision": Humphrey interview, transcript, n.d., Box 2, Autobiography files, HP. Humphrey-Johnson phone calls, 1041 and 1145 A.M. 2:31 and 4:16 P.M. Aug. 29, 1968, WHDC, JL. Richard Hughes (Jan. 3, 1983) interview. Fred Harris letter, Oct. 17, 1983.
"In an equal way, you . . .": Berman diary, Aug. 29, 1968, Berman files.
"Whatever you say, boss": Ibid.
"Well, I've got the best man . . .": Ibid. D. Pleiss memo, "What Humphrey did the day he was nominated," Sept. 15, 1968, Box 1113, HP. Muskie interview, *Fortune*, June 1971.
"Too bad Gene is acting . . .": Berman diary, Aug. 29, 1968, Berman files.

368. "My wattles": Ibid.
speech drafting: Van Dyk to Wirtz / John Stewart, July 8, 1968, CF68, HP. Cousins Aug. 12, McPherson Aug. 8, Moyers Aug. 14, Valenti, Aug. 23, 24, 25, John Stewart Aug. 20, Doug Bennet Aug. 23, Bob Hunter drafts Aug. 23 all in CF68 (including speech drafts), HP. Win Griffith nominating speech draft, Aug. 12, 1968, CF68, HP. Roger Blobaum to Bennet Aug 9, Bob Hunter to Bennet Aug. 16, Philip Zeidman to John Stewart, Aug. 20, Kampelman to John Stewart, Aug 20, 1968—all in Box 1106, HP. Humphrey, "Notes for speech," n.d., Box 1113, HP. Humphrey press release, Aug. 29, 1968, CF68, HP. *NYT*, Aug. 30, 1968.
"We're off": Berman diary, Aug. 29, 1968, Berman files.
"The prayer . . .": Ibid.
"My moment of triumph": *Education*, 394.

369. "I have never had a more difficult . . .": Ibid. John Stewart letter, Nov. 11, 1981.
"my sorrow and my distress . . .": Humphrey acceptance speech, Aug. 29, 1968, Box 1106, HP.
"I knew I was safe . . .": *Education*, 394–95.
"the three basic realities": *NYT*, Aug. 30, 1968.

370. "government in exile": *NYT*, Aug. 30, 1968.
"Goodness me, anybody . . .": Humphrey interview, Roger Mudd, CBS News, Aug. 31, 1968, Wechsler files.
371. "hope of victory far-fetched": Berman diary, Aug. 26, 1968. Berman files.

32:   OUT OF THE GRAND CANYON

372. "overreacted" four times: *NYT*, Sept. 3, 1968. Humphrey to Bishop James Pike, Oct. 1, 1968, Box 1081, HP. Humphrey to Stanley Goodman, Sept. 26, 1968, Box 1081, HP. Averell Harriman to Humphrey, Aug. 31, 1968, CF68, HP.
"My God, the incredible . . .": Humphrey note to Edna Ravnholt, Sept. 13, 1968, Ravnholt files.
Plunge in polls: Humphrey interview transcripts, n.d., probably 1969, Box 2, Autobiography files, HP.
"It's as if we had been pushed . . .": *STPD*, May 25, 1972.
373. "Think about what I should . . .": Humphrey to O'Brien, n.d., CF68PP, HP. Freeman to Humphrey, Aug. 16, 1968, CF68, HP.
"I didn't leave Chicago . . .": Eisele, 366.
"Fred wanted to be VP . . .": Ibid.
"Orville is too much like . . .": Robert Short interview. Oct. 7, 1980.
"just an unbelievable nightmare": Joseph Napolitan interview, Feb. 15, 1983.
Money dries up: Berman diary, Sept. 3, 1968, Berman files. Short interview. Humphrey interview transcripts, Nov. 25–30, probably 1969, Box 2, Autobiography files, HP. Morton Mintz in *WP*, Jan. 18, 1972.
374. "What's wrong . . .": Berman diary, Sept. 3, 1968, Berman files.
"Lyndon who?" Ibid.
"Screw the President:" Ibid., Sept. 1, 1968. Benton to Humphrey, Sept. 3, 1968, CF68, HP.
"Only way to treat a bully": Berman diary, Sept. 3, 1968. Berman files.
"I'll go it alone . . .": Ibid.
"Here's a potential contributor . . .": Humphrey to Andreas, Sept. 6, 1968, CF68, HP.
"Do I really have to go back?": Berman diary, Sept. 3, 1968, Berman files.
375. "I'll take an auto . . .": Ibid., Sept. 4, 1968.

"to work with me closely . . .": Ibid., Sept. 5, 1968.
Borrow $2 million: Short interview. Berman diary, Sept. 3, 1968, Berman files.
"Dump the Hump": *NYT*, Sept. 9 and 10, 1968. *WP*, Sept. 9, 1968. Berman diary, Sept. 10, 21, 23, 24, 1968. Berman files.
"a referendum on human rights": *NYT*, Sept. 10, 1968. Bennet to Humphrey, Dec. 31, 1968, Bennet files. Van Dyk to Humphrey, Sept. 7, 1968, M. u / p, HP.
"so mildly different": *NYT*, Sept. 11, 1968. Berman diary, Sept. 10, 1968, Berman files.
376. "Troops to Come Home": Ibid., Sept. 11, 1968. Houston *Post*, Sept. 11, 1968. *NYT*, Sept. 12, 1968.
"Just made a mistake": Berman diary, Sept. 11, 1968, Berman files.
"When is he going to learn . . .": *WS*, Sept. 29, 1968. George Christian statement, Sept. 12, 1968, M u / p, HP. Humphrey speech at Houston, Sept. 11, 1968, Box 1157, HP. McPherson to Humphrey, Sept. 12, 1968, WHM, u / p, Box 48, HP.
"Nobody can predict . . .": *NYT*, Sept. 11, 1968. *Public Papers of Presidents, Lyndon B. Johnson, 1968–69*, 936.
"The President pulled the rug . . .": Berman diary, Sept. 16 and 20, 1968, Berman files. Rowe to Humphrey and Benton to Humphrey, Sept. 6, 1968, CF68, HP. Mitchell to file, Sept. 4, 1968, Box 100, MP. Mitchell to McGovern, Sept. 5, 1968, Box 97, MP. Humphrey to Jerry Soderberg, Sept. 6, 1968, CF68, HP.
"Themes . . . give the government . . .": Welsh to Humphrey, Sept. 11, 1968, M u / p, HP. "Themes," n.d. and "Draft Statement," n.d., Sept. 1968, unsigned, by Ben Read and Nicholas Katzenbach, Read files. Berman diary, Sept. 18, 1968, Berman files.
"evidence—direct or indirect": "Themes," Read files.
377. "I wish you'd been here . . .": Welsh interview.
"My God, this is what . . .": Ibid.
"sterile" talks: Berman diary, Sept. 13, 1968, Berman files. Welsh to Humphrey, Sept. 13, 1968, Welsh files. Gerald Hursh to Freeman, Sept. 27, 1968, Welsh files. Benton to Humphrey, Sept. 3 and 4, 1968, CF68, HP. Jeno Paulucci

to Humphrey, Sept. 3, 1968, Box 1083, HP. Chicago *Daily News*, Sept. 4, 1968. Moyers to Rowe, Sept. 4, 1968, M u / p, HP. Rielly to Humphrey, Sept. 4, 1968, Box 1158, HP. O'Brien to Kapenstein, Sept. 7, 1968, Box 1146, HP. Andreas to Humphrey, Sept. 7, 1968, CF68, HP. Stan Bregman memo, Sept. 7, 1968, Berman files. Benton to Humphrey, Sept. 8, 1968, CF68, HP. Freeman to Humphrey, Sept. 9, 1968, Box 1148, HP. David Lilienthal to Humphrey, Sept. 9, 1968, Box 1180, HP. Humphrey to Al Spivak, Sept. 9, 1968, M u / p, HP. Sam Lubell in Washington *Daily News*, Sept. 9, 1968, Harriman to Benton Sept. 9, 1968, CF68, HP. Fred Dutton to Joe Napolitan, Sept. 9, 1968, Box 1146, HP. McGovern to Benton, Sept. 10, 1968, CF68, HP. Harriman to Benton, Sept. 10, 1968, CF68, HP. Fulbright to Benton, Sept. 11, 1968, CF68, HP. Brzezinski to Humphrey, Sept. 11, 1968, CF68, HP.
"**Let's face it, Mr. VP**": Berman diary, Sept. 16, 1968, Berman files.
"**At 3 to 1 odds . . .**": Ibid. O'Brien to Freeman, et al., Sept. 12, 1968, Box 1148, HP, Jeno Paulucci to Humphrey, Sept. 12, 1968, Box 1083, HP. Humphrey to Andreas, Sept. 13, 1968, CF68, HP. Frank Karelsen to Humphrey, Sept. 13, 1968, Box 1083, HP. Lyndon Johnson, 555. Humphrey to O'Brien, Sept. 15, 1968, CF68PP, HP. Connell to Humphrey, Sept. 15, 1968, Box 1083, HP. Napolitan to Humphrey, Sept. 14, 1968, M u / p, HP. Van Dyk to Freeman, Sept. 14, 1968, Box 1148, HP. Strout, Sept. 14, 1968. Connell to O'Brien, Sept. 16, 1968, Box 1146, HP. George Carroll to Humphrey, Sept. 16, 1968, CF68PP, HP. Ron Stinnett to Humphrey, Sept. 16, 1968, Box 1083, HP. Charles Murphy to Humphrey, Sept. 17, 1968, Box 65, MP. Johnson message to Texas State Democratic convention, Sept. 17, 1968, WHM u / p, Box 48, HP.

378. "**Most of us are . . .**": *NYT*, Sept. 17 and 20, 1968. Berman diary, Sept. 17 and 19, 1968, Berman files. B. Hersh, 354.
"**I do not think proper . . .**": Humphrey longhand notes, Sept. 18, 1968, WHM u / p, Box 48, HP. Minutes of Cabinet meeting, Sept. 18, 1968, Cabinet Papers, JL.
"**I'm going to seek peace . . .**": *NYT*, Sept. 20 and 21, 1968.

379. "**His stands make Jell-O . . .**": *NYT*, Sept. 21, 1968. Sioux Falls speech, Sept. 19, 1968, MSF, HP. Wechsler in New York *Post*, Sept. 18, 1968. Humphrey to Freeman, Sept. 18, 1968, CF68, HP. John L. Loeb to Humphrey, Sept. 18, 1968, CF68PP, HP. Humphrey to James Loeb, Sept. 18, 1968, Wechsler files. George Reedy to Humphrey, Sept. 18, 1968, WHCF CF, Exec FG 440, Box 349, JL. *Time*, Sept. 18, 1968. Ashman, 156. Witcover, *Resurrection of Richard Nixon*, 197. William S. White in *WP*, Sept. 20, 1968. Connell to Humphrey, "Six Weeks to Go," CF68, HP. Brzezinski to Humphrey, Sept. 21, 1968, CF68, HP. Freeman to O'Brien, Sept. 21, 1968, Box 1146, HP. Gartner to Humphrey, Sept. 21, 1968, "Humphrey's Only Chance," *Economist*, Sept. 21, 1968.
"**so we can get on with . . .**": *NYT*, Sept. 21, 1968. Louisville speech, MSF, HP.
"**Peace . . . every time the VP . . .**": Rowe in "Campaign Policy Committee minutes," Sept. 23, 1968, Box 1146, HP.
"**I didn't say enough about . . .**": Berman diary, Sept. 24, 1968, Berman files. Humphrey interview with Richard Meryman, *Life*, Sept. 27, 1968. Benton to Hedley Donovan, Sept. 26, 1968, CF68, HP.
"**Well, suppose we decide not?**": Berman diary, Sept. 26, 1968. Berman files. Chester, Hodgson, and Page, 644.
"**Okay then let's do it . . .**": Berman diary, Sept. 26, 1968. Berman files.
"**Murderer, racist . . .**": Ibid., Sept. 27, 1968.

380. "**I don't understand it**": Ibid. Gallup, 2162. Ravnholt to Connell, Sept. 23, 1968, CF68, HP. George Reedy to Humphrey, Sept. 23, 1968, CF68 PP, HP. IUE (COPE) *Spotlight*, Sept. 23, 1968. IAM *Machinist*, Sept. 26, 1968. Roger Kent to Humphrey, Sept. 23 and Humphrey to Roger Kent, Sept. 27, 1968, Box 1081, HP. McCarthy to Benton, Sept. 24, 1968, CF68, HP. Benton to Marvin Rosenberg, Sept. 24, 1968, CF68, HP. Humphrey to Freeman, Sept. 24, 1968, CF68, HP. Napolitan to Shelby Storck, Sept. 24, 1968, CF68 PP, HP. Napolitan memo, Sept. 24, 1968, M u / p, HP. Ed Plaut to Humphrey, Sept. 24, 1968, Box 11, KP. Humphrey to Al Spivak, Sept. 24, 1968, M u / p, HP. Humphrey to Napolitan, Sept. 24, 1968, M u / p, HP. Humphrey, "Common-

wealth Club speech," San Francisco, Sept. 26, 1968, Box 1157, HP. Edith Weiss to Humphrey, Sept. 25, 1968, CF68, HP. Benton to Humphrey, Sept. 26, 1968, CF68, HP. Frank Karelsen letter to *NYT*, Sept. 26, 1968, Box 1083, HP. Humphrey to Napolitan, Sept. 26, 1968, CF68, HP. Freeman to Humphrey, Sept. 20 and 27, Box 1158, HP. **"Now just tell me, George . . .":** Berman diary, Sept. 27, 1968, Berman files.
"Mr. VP, I think you still . . .": Ibid.
"I've loused up the situation . . .": Ibid.
"But you were right . . .": Ibid.
"Does it say the basic . . .": Ibid. Welsh letter, Jan. 7, 1983.
"Can Nixon say this will . . .": Berman diary, Sept. 27, 1968, Berman files.
"And they're willing to come out . . .": Ibid.
"Hell no, I'm going to . . .": Ibid.
"just totally shot . . .": Ibid.

381. **"Muriel and I have been talking . . .":** Berman diary, Sept. 28, 1968, Berman files.
"The Ball draft is . . .": Ibid. O'Brien to Humphrey, Sept. 28, 1968, Box 1158, HP. Richard Hughes to Humphrey, Sept. 29, 1968, Welsh files. Prochnau and Larsen, 226.
"There's a man that wants . . .": *NYT*, Sept. 29, 1968. Berman diary, Sept. 28, 1968, Berman files. *Education*, 399. "Notes of Seattle meeting," Oct. 2, 1968, Box 1158, HP. Humphrey interview with Theodore White, n.d., 1969, transcript Box 1, Autobiography files, HP.
"beat and dejected": Berman diary, Sept. 28, 1968, Berman files. Freeman to Humphrey, "Campaign strategy," Sept. 30, 1968, Box 1148 HP. Benton to Humphrey, Sept. 30, 1968, CF68, HP. Richard Crisler to Terry Sanford, Sept. 30, 1968, Box 1083, HP. Sanford to Humphrey, Sept. 30, 1968, CF68, HP.
"I've come to report to you . . .": Van Dyk interview, Van Dyk letter, Mar. 8, 1983. Berman diary, Sept. 29, 1968, Berman files.

382. **"Well I don't want to see . . .":** Van Dyk interview.
"a 50–50 proposition": Berman diary, Sept. 29, 1968, Berman files. Welsh, Ball, Van Dyk, O'Brien, Connell, Rowe, Sherman, Berman interviews.
Utah meetings: Berman diary, Sept. 30, 1968, Berman files.

383. **"something that Harriman can . . .":** Ibid.

384. **"As President, I would . . .":** Humphrey speech, *NYT*, Oct. 1, 1968. *Education*, 402.
"not worth a damn . . .": Berman diary, Sept. 30, 1968, Berman files. Barry Nova interview (Jan. 4, 1983).
Speech drafts: "Draft A: 'Vietnam: Toward a Political Settlement and Peace in Southeast Asia,' " Aug. 14, 1968, CF68, HP. Read-Katzenbach draft, n.d., Sept. 1968, Read files. Ravnholt to Connell, Sept. 23, 1968, CF68 (including speech drafts), HP. Read-Katzenbach-Ball draft, Sept. 27, 1968, Welsh files. Ball redrafts, Sept. 27 and 28, 1968, Welsh files. Ball 2nd redraft, couriered to Paris, Sept. 28, 1968, Welsh files. Welsh memo to Humphrey, n.d., Sept. 1968, Box 1158, HP. Van Dyk draft edited by Humphrey, Sept. 29, 1968; "Vietnam IV," edited by Humphrey, Sept. 29, 1968; longhand speech notes by Humphrey, Sept. 30, 1968; and Salt Lake City speech, Sept. 1968—all in CF68 (including speech drafts), HP. Semifinal draft, "A Message to the American People," Sept. 30, 1968, Welsh files. Humphrey's personal redrafting, n.d., Sept. 1958, Welsh files. Apple in *NYT*, Oct. 1, 1968. Van Dyk letter, March 8, 1983.
"but this is the position . . .": Berman diary, Sept. 30, 1968, Berman files. Robert Squier interviews (Jan. 21 and Feb. 23, 1983). Squier, "Production Manual, Salt Lake City Project," Sept. 30, 1968, Box 1146, HP.
"get him down off the ceiling . . .": Ball interview. Ball, "Deep background briefing," Sept. 30, 1968, Box 1158, HP.
Mr. VP, you have to . . .": Berman diary, Sept. 30, 1968, Berman files.
"Jesus, everybody tells me . . .": Ibid.
"You know, we have other . . .": Ibid. *Education*, 403.

385. **"They wanted to believe . . .":** Ball interview.
"I feel good inside . . .": Eisele, 379.
Speech reaction: Barefoot Sanders to Johnson, Sept. 30, 1968, WHCF CF, Exec FG 440, Box 349, JL. Mary Rather to Johnson, WHCF CF, Exec FG 440, Box 349, JL. Rostow to Johnson, Sept. 30, 1968, WHCF CF, Exec FG 440 Box 349, JL. *WP*, Oct. 1, 1968. AP bulletins, n.d., Oct. 1, 1968, Box 1158, HP. John Bartlow Martin to Humphrey, Oct. 1, 1968, M u / p, HP. Charles Murphy to Johnson, Oct. 1, 1968, WHCF CF

Exec FG 440, Box 349, JL. Apple and Weaver, *NYT*, Oct. 1, 1968. AP bulletin from Paris, Oct. 1, 1968.

33: THE HALLOWEEN PEACE

386. **"He felt good"**: Eisele, 379. Kampelman to Humphrey, Oct. 1, 1968, CF68, HP. O'Brien to McCandless, Oct. 1, 1968, Box 1146, HP. George Papandreou to Walter Heller, Oct. 1, 1968, Box 1149, HP. Heller to Humphrey, Oct. 2, 1968, Box 1081, HP. Ginsburg to Humphrey, Oct. 2, 1968, CF68, HP. Mike Berman to Humphrey, Oct. 4, 1968, CF68, HP. Rowe to Humphrey, Oct. 4, 1968, CF68PP, HP. Benton to Humphrey, Oct. 1, 1968, CF68, HP. Humphrey to O'Brien, Oct. 4, 1968, CF68, HP. McPherson to George Christian, Oct. 4, 1968, WHCF CF, Exec FG 440, Box 349, JL.
"If you mean it . . .": *Education*, 403.
"a political plunger . . .": *NYT*, Oct. 2, 1968. UPI bulletin, Oct. 2, 1968. John Bartlow Martin to Humphrey, Oct. 3, 1968, Box 1148, HP.
"appeals to the same fear . . .": *NYT*, Oct. 2 and 3, 1968. Humphrey-Johnson meeting: Connell to Humphrey, "Agenda," Oct. 4, 1968 M u / p, HP. Jones to Johnson, Oct. 4, 1968, WHD Backup, JL. "VP to Oval Office," Oct. 4, 1968, 7–9:55 P.M , WHDD, JL. Campaign Policy Committee minutes, Oct. 2, 3, 7, 9, 11, 14, 16, 18, 21, 23, 25, 1968, Box 1146, HP. Issues Meeting minutes, Oct. 3, 8, 10, 21, 22, 24, 28, 1968, Box 1146, HP.
387. **"the major issue no doubt"**: Kirkpatrick to Freeman, Oct. 4, 1968, CF68, HP. Mike Berman interview, Oct. 15, 1982.
Task forces: Humphrey's Latin America statement, Oct. 1968, CF6870, HP. Humphrey to Freeman, Sept. 24, 1968, CF68, HP. List of 33 task forces, Nathan to Humphrey, July 25, 1968, CF68, HP. Reports, n.d., Box 1175, HP. Task force platform statements, n.d., Box 1107, HP.
"Humphrey is soft . . .": Kirkpatrick to Freeman, Sept. 27, 1968, Box 1146, HP.
"the objective of this speech is . . .": Freeman in Campaign policy committee minutes, Oct. 11, 1968, Box 1146, HP.
388. **"As president I would stop . . ."**: *NYT*, Oct. 3, 1968. "Nationwide TV speech on Law & Order," Oct. 12, 1968,

MSF, HP. Napolitan to Humphrey, n.d., Oct. 1968, CF68PP, HP. Humphrey to O'Brien, Oct. 7, 1968, CF68PP, HP. Robert Kintner to O'Brien, Oct. 7, 1968, CF68PP, HP. *WP*, Oct. 9, 1968. *Wall Street Journal*, Oct. 9, 1968. Napolitan memo, Oct. 13, 1968, CF68, HP. Napolitan interview in NYT mag., Oct. 13, 1968. Ben Wattenberg to Johnson, Oct. 21 and 23, 1968, WHCF CF, Exec FG 440, Box 349, JL. O'Brien to Robert Kintner, Oct. 17, 1968 and Kintner to O'Brien, Oct. 14, 1968, M u / p, HP. Theodore White in *Columbia Journalism Review*, Winter 1969.
"Our polls showed 30 percent . . .": Al Barkan interview, Feb. 6, 1981. Barkan in Campaign Policy Committee minutes, Sept. 16, 1968, Box 1146, HP. COPE, AFL-CIO, "1968 Elections, Preliminary Report," n.d., 1968, Cope files.
389. **Wallace tide ebbs**: O'Brien to Humphrey, Oct. 5, 1968, CF68PP, HP. I. W. Abel to Steelworker locals, Oct. 21, 1968, Box 1151, HP. Broder, *The Party's Over*, 81.
"bring the boys home": *NYT*, Sept. 10, 1968. Humphrey speech, "Philadelphia Campaign Kickoff Rally," Sept. 9, 1968, MSF, HP.
390. **Private talks in Paris.** William Bundy interview with Paige Mulhollan, May 26, 1969, JL.
391. **Paris progress:** Ibid. Cyrus Vance (May 3, 1983), Katzenbach, Read, Rielly interviews.
392. **"You know that Nixon . . ."**: Eisele, 382. Rowe interview. Rowe to Johnson, Oct. 18, 1968, WHCF CF, Exec PI 1 (Conventions), Box 81, JL.
"See if some momentum . . .": Van Dyk interview. *NYT*, Oct. 18 and 19, 1968. Jim Jones to Johnson, Oct. 19, 1968, WHCF CF, Exec FG 440 Box 349, JL. Loyd Hackler to Jim Jones, Oct. 19, 1968, WHCF CF, Exec FG 440 Box 349, JL.
"Cancel the appointment": Van Dyk interview. *Education*, 404.
"I saw the President . . .": Van Dyk interview. Van Dyk letter, March 18, 1983.
"the expression on the VP's face . . .": James Jones interview. "VP to 2nd floor, Oct. 20, 1968, 9:35–11:45 P.M.," WHDC, JL.
393. **"We were at the point of . . ."**: Read interview. William Bundy interview for JL.

"We've got everything . . .": Vance, Read interviews. Bundy interview for JL.
"My forces can take care . . .": Lyndon Johnson, 520–21.
Hangup in Saigon: Jim Jones to Johnson, Oct. 15, 1968, WHDD Backup, JL. Lyndon Johnson, 523. Bundy interview for JL. Vance, Katzenbach, Read interviews.
China lobby 1948: Solberg, *Riding High*, 156. Ross Y. Koen, *The China Lobby in American Politics*, 22. Stanley Bachrack, *The Committee of One Million*, 55.
394. China Lobby 1968: Bundy, Harriman, and Vance interviews with Paige Mulhollan, JL.
Madam Chennault: Chennault, 170, 188, 190. Thomas Corcoran to Johnson, unsigned, Sept. 6, 1967, CF68PP (Reedy), HP. Walt Rostow letter, Feb. 4, 1983. Lyndon Johnson, 517–18. Safire, 88, 90. Powers, 158, 198. Nixon, 326. Howe and Trott, 52. Tom Ottenad in St. Louis *Post-Dispatch*, Jan. 3, 1969. U.S. Senate Select Intelligence Committee, Hearings "Intelligence Activities," 1975, vol. 6, 164, 194; and "Final Report," 1976, 227. Hersh in *NYT*, June 27, 1973. Seymour Hersh (Sept. 12, 1983), Bui Diem (Dec 14, 1983), and David Corcoran (Dec. 17, 1983) interviews.
"The President will do nothing . . .": Welsh letter, Jan. 7, 1983. Christian to Johnson, Oct. 5, 1968. WHCF CF, Exec FG 440, Box 349, and Christian to Johnson, Oct. 5, 1968, WHCF CF, Exec PL/HHH, Box 25, JL. John Bartlow Martin to Humphrey, Oct. 11, 1968, CF68, HP. Ginsburg to Freeman, Oct. 17, 1968, Box 1148, HP. Nathan to Freeman, Oct. 18, 1968, Box 1148, HP. *NYT*, Oct. 20, 1968. Norris Ellertson to Humphrey, Oct. 8, 1968, Vietnam box 1965–71, Mu/p, HP. President's conference call to candidates, Oct. 16, 1968, 11:41 A.M., WHDC, JL. Presidents meeting with Rowe and Sanford, Oct. 16, 1968, WHDC, JL.
"The longer the present situation . . .": Read interview.
395. FBI wiretap: U.S. Senate Select Intelligence Committee, Hearings "Intelligence Activities," 1975, Vol. 6, 164, 194; and "Final Report," 1976, 227. Hersh in *NYT*, June 27, 1973.
"Implications by some of our folks . . .": Christian, 104. Harry Middleton notes "Meeting in Cabinet room," Oct. 31, 1968, JL.

"he looked around the room . . .": McPherson interview, Sept. 21, 1981.
"Mr. President, I just pray . . .": Lyndon Johnson, 526. Christian, 104.
396. "We have learned a lesson . . .": Charles Bailey in *MT*, Nov. 4, 1968.
"I can't say that . . .": Berman diary, Oct. 31, 1968, Berman files.
"I hope I can keep my VP . . .": Ibid. *Public Papers of Lyndon B. Johnson, 1968–69*, 1099.
397. "No, the President did right . . .": Berman diary, Oct. 31, 1968, Berman files.
"I've been quaking all week . . .": Ibid. Humphrey to O'Brien, Oct. 14, 1968, CF68PP, HP. Rowe to Humphrey, Oct. 14, 1968, CF68PP, HP. Humphrey to Arthur Schlesinger, Oct. 14, 1968, Box 1079, HP. Humphrey to Galbraith, Oct. 19, 1968, CF68PP, HP. Humphrey to Benton, Oct. 19, 1968, CF68, HP. Humphrey to O'Brien, Oct. 21, 1968, Box 1146, HP. Mike Berman to Humphrey, Oct. 21, 1968, CF68, HP. Humphrey to O'Brien, Oct. 21, 1946, CF68PP, HP. Lord to Humphrey, Oct. 22, 1968, Mu/p, HP. *WP*, Oct. 26, 1968. Humphrey to Connell, Oct. 27, 1968, CF68, HP. Mike Berman to Humphrey, Oct. 27, 1968, CF68, HP. Humphrey to James Rosenquist, Oct. 30, 1968, Box 1078, HP. Freeman to Humphrey, Oct. 30, 1968, CF68, HP. McGeorge Bundy to Ginsburg, Nov. 1, 1968, CF68, HP.
"It's just one of those decisions . . .": Berman diary, Oct. 31, 1968, Berman files.
"Forget it, we're going . . .": Ibid., Nov. 1, 1968. John Bartlow Martin to Humphrey, Oct. 3, 1968, Box 1148, HP. Humphrey to O'Brien, Oct. 7, 1968, Box 1145, HP. Humphrey to Terry Sanford, Oct. 7, 1968, CF68PP, HP. O'Brien to Humphrey, Oct. 15 and 19, 1968, CF68PP, HP. Freeman to O'Brien, Oct. 24, 1968, CF68PP, HP. Harris to O'Brien, Oct. 30, 1968, Box 1148, HP.
"Two-three weeks ago . . .": Humphrey speech, Peoria, Nov. 1, 1968, MSF, HP. Polls: Fred Panzer to Johnson, Oct. 1, 3, 7, 10, and 23, 1968, WHCF CF, Exec PL/HHH, Box 25, JL. Connell to Humphrey, Oct. 2, 1968, CF68, HP. "Democratic Poll Memo," Oct. 6, 1968, CF68, HP. Connell memo, Oct. 9, 1968, CF68, HP.
"I want you to tell Hubert . . .":

Rowe interview. Johnson phonecall to Rowe, Peoria, Nov. 1, 1968, 2:30 P.M., WHDD, JL. Van Dyk letter, March 18, 1983.

398. "It's going to be tough . . .": Berman diary, Nov. 1, 1968, Berman files. *NYT*, Nov. 2, 1968.
"falls far short of . . .": *NYT*, Oct. 30, 1968.
"I am a happy man . . .": *NYT*, Oct 31, 1968. Eisele, 387.
"There's going to be a happy time . . .": *NYT*, Nov. 1, 1968.
"It would have been difficult . . .": Howe and Trott, 52. Jim Jones memo to President, "Walt Reports," Nov. 2, 1968, WHDD Backup, JL. Rostow (Nov. 16, 1983), Clark Clifford (Nov. 17, 1983), Bryce Harlow (Nov. 20, 1983), Mr. and Mrs. John Gomien (April 30, 1983), Bundy, Van Dyk, and Sherman interviews. Dean Rusk letter, Sept. 26, 1983. William Bundy letter, Sept. 30, 1983.
"We have no regrets . . .": Humphrey on "Issues and Answers," Nov. 3, 1968.

399. "We exacted ironclad promises . . .": Wright memo, "Texas campaign," n.d., 1968. Mu/p, HP.
"a progressive and compassionate . . .": *Public Papers of Lyndon Johnson, 1968–69*, 1107. *Education*, 405. Rauh in *New Republic*, July 24, 1976.
Year "1968 has been no normal . . .": Humphrey Astrodome speech, Nov. 3, 1968, MSF, HP.

400. Johnson "concerned . . .": Berman diary, Nov. 3, 1968, Berman files.
"no use": Van Dyk interview.
"Well, the old China Lobby . . .": Ibid.
"I'll be damned if . . .": Ibid. Berman diary, Nov. 3, 1968, Berman files.
"As President, I would . . .": Van Dyk interview.
"If the Vietnamese do not come . . .": Ibid. *NYT*, Nov. 4, 1968. Tom Ottenad interview, April 6, 1983. "A conversation with Hubert Humphrey," Bill Moyers Journal, April, 1976.

401. "a doublecrosser . . .": Humphrey tape transcript, n.d., probably Nov. 1969, Box 7, Autobiography files, HP.
"ninety-nine out of 100 men . . .": Van Dyk interview.
"I know of no more essentially . . .": T. H. White, *Making of the President 1968*, 445. Witcover, *Resurrection of Richard Nixon*, 441. Stuart Loory, "Politics of

Make Believe," *PRO*, Nov. 1968.
"No, but our friend in New Mexico . . .": *NYT, June 27, 1973.*

402. "I wish I could vote . . .": *NYT*, Nov. 5, 1968.
"Edgar, we just might do it": E. Berman, 226.
"Democrats have more fun": Chester, Hodgson and Page, 752. *Education*, 405. Napolitan memo, Oct. 19, 1968, CF68, HP.
"I hope I have cleared the way . . .": *NYT*, Nov. 5, 1968.
"taught me the meaning . . .": Squier, Barry Nova, and Napolitan interviews: Berman diary, Nov. 4, 1968, Berman files.

34: DAY OF DEFEAT

403. "I was tired, more tired . . .": *Education*, 6. Humphrey tape transcripts n.d., Box 7, Autobiography files, HP. Berman diary, Nov. 5, 1968, Berman files.
"It was difficult for me . . .": Humphrey tape transcripts, Autobiography files Box 7 HP.

404. "Muriel and I did very little . . .": Ibid.
"boiler room": Berman diary, Nov. 5, 1968, Berman files. John Bartlow Martin to Humphrey, Nov. 4, 1968, CF68, HP.
"The crowd was so enthusiastic . . .": Humphrey tape transcripts, Box 7. Autiography files HP.
"I was quiet . . .": Ibid.

405. "My God we should have . . .": Berman diary, Nov. 5, 1968. Berman files. Hal Greenwood interview. Aug. 25, 1981.
"What Jesse Unruh did . . .": Humphrey tape transcripts, Autobiography files Box 7. HP.
"It looked to me . . .": Ibid.
"tried to give the people . . .": Ibid.
"I knew that the odds . . .": Ibid.
"Edgar, at least we took . . .": Berman diary, Nov. 5, 1968, Berman files.
"I'm going to wake Freddie . . .": Napolitan interview.

406. "I talked to Mr. Nixon . . .": Humphrey tape transcripts, Box 7 Autobiography files, HP.
"It was the most difficult . . .": Ibid.
"It's nice to know": *NYT*, Nov. 6, 1968.
"I shall continue my commitments . . .": *NYT*, Nov. 6, 1968.

"I have a lot of thinking . . .": Berman diary, Nov. 6, 1968 Berman files.
"Well, Mr. Pres., it looks like . . .": Ibid.
"sold down the river . . .": Ibid., Nov. 7, 1968. Humphrey tape transcripts, Box 7, Autobiography files HP.

407. "Jesus, we lost by a little . . .": Berman diary, Nov. 7, 1968. Berman files. Broder, *The Party's Over*, 85. *NYT*, "The Labor Scene," Sept. 3, 1976. Brandon, *Retreat of American Power*, 10. Wicker in *NYT*, June 22, 1975.

"almost by himself . . .": Apple in *NYT*, Nov. 7, 1968. L. O'Brien, 195. Penn Kemble, "Democrats after 1968," *Commentary*, Jan. 1969, 35. Johnson interview with *NYT* Dec. 27, 1969, 1.
"after four years as . . .": Humphrey tape transcripts, Box 7, Autobiography files, HP. Eugenie Anderson to Humphrey, Nov. 13, 1968. CF68 (including speech drafts), HP. Louis Harris speech, Nov. 20, 1968. CF6870, HP. Philip Converse et al., "Continuity and Change in American Politics: Parties and Issues of the 1968 Election," Institute for Social Research. "1968 Election Study," *ISR Newsletter*, Winter 1970. Julie Cahn to Humphrey, Jan. 17, 1969, DNC 1969–73, HP. Geri Joseph report, Nov. 4, 1968, CF68, HP. Connell to Humphrey, Feb. 17, 1969, DNC 1969–73, HP. Kampelman to Humphrey, Mar. 10, 1969, DNC 1969–73, HP.

35: BACK TO MINNESOTA

411. "Well we enjoyed having you . . .": Humphrey to Douglas Humphrey, Jan. 24, Jan. 24, 1969, PFPM, HP. Humphrey to Laurence Rockefeller, April 2, 1969, CF69–77, Box 3, HP.

412. "by just a handful of votes": E. Berman, 232. *NYT*, Dec. 27, 1969, 1. Humphrey to James Loeb, Jan. 5, 1969, Box 11, KP. Jackie Robinson to Humphrey, Jan. 7, 1969, CF68, HP. Humphrey to Inger Stevens, Jan. 24, 1969, PFPA, HP. Roger Kasa interview, Sept. 29, 1980.
"I always told you Nixon . . .": Humphrey to Anton Thompson, PFPA (T), HP.
"Humphrey was lower than . . .": Malkerson interview. Win Griffith in *NYT* mag., Mar. 30, 1969. Edward Elson in U.S. Senate, *Memorial Service*, 78.

413. Norway trip: Humphrey to C. F. Clementsen, April 8, 1969, CF 1969–77, Box 1, HP. Oslo *Morgenposten* (trans.), Jan. 6, 1969. Humphrey interview on Oslo National TV, Jan. 8, 1969. Humphrey to himself, Jan. 16, 1973, PFPA, HP. Humphrey to Anton Thompson, Feb. 8, 1969, CF 1969–77, Box 3, HP. Humphrey to Nixon, Mar. 1, 1969, VIP corr., HP.
"Oh, two or three . . .": Read interview.
"Why are you late?": Ibid.

414. "Muriel and I are going . . .": Humphrey to Eugenie Anderson, May 21, 1969, CF 1969–77, Box 1, HP. *STPPP*, July 27, 1969. *MT*, July 24, 1969.
"You must have your hunting . . .": Read interview.

415. "We feel that this is our event": Ibid. Humphrey report to Nixon, Aug. 29, 1969. VIP corr., HP.
"What do you think about Senator . . ." Read to Humphrey, July 31, 1969, Memos, 1969–71, HP.
"a great deal of thought . . .": *NYT*, July 20, 1969.
"Not what he was . . .": *NYT* mag., Mar. 30, 1969.
"You could see he was struggling . . .": Geri Joseph interview. "Protests Abort Humphrey Speech," University of Mass. *Daily Collegian*, Feb. 25, 1970. "Special Report of Emergency Advisory Committee," University of Mass., May 21, 1970. Humphrey in *The Tech*, April 15, 18, 22, 1969. *Tech Talk*, April 2, 1969.

416. "a fantastic week . . .": *STPPP*, July 27, 1969. *MS*, July 25, 1969. *MT*, July 25, 1969. Humphrey to Kampelman, June 5, 1969, CF69–77, Box 2, HP. Humphrey to Johnson, June 26, 1969, VIP corr., HP. Humphrey to Van Dyk, Nov. 5, 1969, CF 1969–77, Box 3, HP.
"It's a resurrection . . .": E. Berman, 247. Connell to Humphrey, "The New Situation," Aug. 21, 1969, CF6870, HP. Humphrey to Willy Brandt, Oct. 6, 1969, CF69–77, Box 1, HP.
"There's a rumor around . . .": Humphrey to Anton Thompson, Sept. 11, 1969, CF69–77, Box 3, HP.
"I heal rapidly . . .": Humphrey to Eugenie Anderson, Nov. 5, 1969, CF69–77, Box 1, HP. Mike Johnson in *Mac Weekly*, Mar. 19, 1971. *NYT*, Mar. 4, 1969. Humphrey to Anton Thompson, April 7, 1969, PFPA (T), HP. Omaha *World Herald*, Feb. 26, 1970. Humphrey

speech, University of Mass., Feb. 24, 1970, CF70 Box 6, HP. *MT*, June 8, 1970. *WP*, June 14, 1970.
"an agonizing period . . .": Humphrey to Johnson, Sept. 20, 1969, VIP corr., HP. Humphrey to Calvin Didier, Mar. 23 and April 12, 1970, CF70, Box 4, HP.

417. **"The President expressed . . .":** Humphrey memo of conversation, with Nixon/Kissinger, Oct. 11, 1969, VIP corr., HP. Nixon to Humphrey, Sept. 23, 1969, VIP corr., HP.
"I have reason to believe . . .": Humphrey memo of conversation, VIP corr., HP. op cit.
"Wants to get out . . .": *NYT*, Oct. 11, 1968. *WP*, Oct. 11, 1969. Mary McGrory in *WS*, Oct. 11, 1969.
"HHH Praises Nixon": Carroll Kirkpatrick in *WS*, Oct. 11, 1968. Humphrey to Kissinger, Oct. 11, 1968, VIP corr., HP. Nixon to Humphrey, Oct. 14, 1969, VIP corr., HP.
"firm and unequivocal . . .": *NYT*, Feb. 10, 1970. UPI bulletin, "Vietnam withdrawal statement," Feb. 9, 1970. Humphrey to Horace Busby, Jan. 12, 1970, CF70, Box 4, HP. Marquis Childs in *STPPP*, Feb 4, 1970. London *Times*, Mar. 2, 1970.
"the issue that is going . . .": *NYT*, Feb. 10, 1970. Eisele, 427. *STPPP*, Aug. 17, 1970.

418. **"You know he cares":** Humphrey to Jack Chestnut et al., June 19 and 23, July 28, 1970, Box 2, CF70 HP. Chestnut to Andreas, July 1, 1970, Box 6, CF70, HP. Humphrey to D. J. Leary, July 21, 1970, Box 6, CF70, HP. "Humphrey record," Aug. 1970, Box 8, CF70 HP. *MT*, Sept. 20, 1970. Mankato *Free Press*, Oct. 23, 1970. Winona *Daily News*, July 26, 1970. *NYT*, Aug. 4, 1970. Humphrey to Earl Craig, July 24, 1970, Box 6, CF70, HP.
"must let the hardhats . . .": Humphrey speech to ABA, St. Louis, Aug. 11, 1970, Box 6, CF70, HP. Humphrey to Eugenie Anderson, July 3, 1970, Box 6, CF70, HP.
"the culminating irony . . .": *NYT*, Sept. 24, 1970.
"after a lifetime . . .": Humphrey to Eugenie Anderson, Sept. 1, 1970, Box 6, CF70, HP. *New Republic*, Sept. 19, 1970.
"We've got to conserve our . . .": *STPPP*, Oct. 18, 1970.
"a likeable cuss": *MT*, Oct. 24, 1970.

Los Angeles *Times*, Oct. 29, 1970. Clark Mollenhoff, *STPPP*, Oct. 10, 1970. "Humphrey's itinerary," Ann Higgins to D. J. Leary, Oct. 29, 1970, Box 11, CF70, HP. William S. White in *STPPP*, Oct. 20, 1970.

419. **"When I see these little ones . . .":** *STPPP*, Aug. 23, 1970.
"Why, just a change of . . .": Ibid.
"To some politicians . . .": Los Angeles *Times*, Oct. 29, 1970.
"You'll be the belle . . .": Ibid.
"I'd like to walk": Tom Kelm interview.
"The most regressive tax . . .": *MT*, Oct. 23, 1970.
"Pollution is a form of aggression . . .": Humphrey to Ben Wattenberg, Aug. 18, 1970, Box 2, CF70, HP. Humphrey notes for American Inst. of Planners speech, Oct. 7, 1970, Box 2, CF70, HP.

420. **"I would be less than candid . . .":** *NYT*, July 21, 1970. Humphrey to Eugenie Anderson, Nov. 13, 1970, Box 6, CF70, HP.

36: AGAIN, DEFEAT

421. **Harris for DNC:** Humphrey tape transcripts, n.d., Box 8, Autobiography files, HP. Rowe to Humphrey, Nov. 20, 1968, DNC file, HP. O'Brien to Humphrey and Humphrey to O'Brien, Jan. 4, 1969, DNC file, HP. Humphrey to Harris, Jan. 15, 1969, CF68, HP.

422. **"all Democratic voters should . . .":** *Proceedings of the Democratic National Convention*, Chicago, 1968, 248. E. McCarthy, *Year of the People*, 201.
Commission findings: Synopsis of McGovern Commission Required Guidelines," Feb. 1971, DNC file 1969–73, HP. "Preliminary Call for 1972 Delegates to Convention," Feb. 8, 1971, DNC file 1969–73, HP.
"having extricated himself . . .": *WP*, Mar. 4, 1970. Connell memo, Mar. 11, 1970, DNC file, HP. Humphrey to O'Brien, Mar. 26, 1970, DNC file, HP.
McGovern a candidate: McGovern to Humphrey, Jan. 18, 1971, CF71, HP.

423. **"I want to think through . . .":** Humphrey to Eugenie Anderson, Aug. 7, 1969, Box 1, CF69–77, HP.
"I see little reason why . . .": Humphrey press release, Nov. 1970, Box 6, CF70, HP.
Return to Senate: *NYT*, Jan. 21, 1971.

Humphrey to Wm. Proxmire, Feb. 1, 1971, Box 2, Corr. file, Legisl. 1971, HP. Humphrey to Henry Raymont, Feb. 9, 1971, Box 8, AAF73, HP. O'Brien to Humphrey, Feb. 10, 1971, Box 16, Corr. file, Legisl. 1972, HP. Humphrey to Mrs. David Fulton, May 19, 1971, Box 2, Corr. file, Legisl. 1971, HP. *WP*, Mar. 28, 1971. Ken Gray (Nov. 12, 1980), Richard Gilmore (Feb. 4, 1981) interviews.

424. "He's so productive . . .": Gray interview.
"The way they run this . . .": Humphrey to Eugenie Anderson, Nov. 14, 1971, Box 9, CF 1969–77, HP. Gray interview.
"reappearance of the old . . .": Galbraith to Humphrey, Oct. 14, 1971, DNC file, HP.
"You know, Rick . . .": "Notes from Tapes of Foreign Policy discussion," June 21, 1978, 13, Connell files. Heller to Humphrey, Mar. 8, 1971, Box 7, Corr. file, Legisl. 1971, HP.
"Keep me in mind . . .": Humphrey to Javits, Box 2, Corr. files, Legisl. 1971, HP. Humphrey press release, May 23, 1971, Chron. file Feb.-Sept. 1971, HP. Humphrey to Dick Moe, July 16, 1971, Box 16, Corr. file, Legisl. 1971, HP.
"Vietnam on the back burner . . .": Humphrey to Richard Gilmore, Feb. 26, 1971. CF71, HP.
"Economy is the Achilles heel": Humphrey to Chestnut, July 26, 1971, *CFTI*, HP.

425. "presentations": Ibid. Humphrey to Heller, April 27, 1971, Box 3, Corr. files, Legisl. 1971, HP. Heller to Humphrey, May 5, 1971, Box 2, AAF72, HP.
"That's a joke": *NYT*, May 2, 1971.
"When the politicians invite . . .": Ibid.
"winning back the support . . .": *NYT*, Mar. 11, 1971. Humphrey to Palmer Hoyt, Box 16, Corr. files, Legisl. 1971, HP. Jeane Kirkpatrick to Connell, Jan. 21, 1971, CF72, HP. Humphrey on "Meet the Press," Feb. 28, 1971, Box 3, Corr. file, Legisl. 1971, HP. Patrick Buchanan to Nixon, April 19, 1971, CF72, HP. *Congressional Quarterly*, June 18, 1971. Nicholas von Hoffman, "Looking for a President," *Harpers* Sept. 1971. Humphrey to Chestnut, Aug. 28, 1971, CF72, HP. Humphrey to Meany, Sept. 24, 1971, Box 3, Corr. file, Legisl. 1971, HP. George Leader letter for

Humphrey, Sept. 8, 1971, Box 8, CF72, HP. Connell to Humphrey, Oct. 4, 1971, CF72PP, HP.
"Since January I have been on target . . .": Humphrey to Chestnut, July 26, 1971. CF71, HP.
"Sixty-going on '72": Dogole interview, April 14, 1983.
"there was a half billion . . .": *WP*, May 28, 1971. *NYT*, May 14, 1971. Dogole interview.
"I'm not at all sure that . . .": Humphrey to Berman, Mar. 29, 1971, CF72, HP.

426. "He was a swine . . .": Hunter Thompson in *Rolling Stone*, Mar. 1972.
"should be put in a goddam bottle . . .": Ibid. H. S. Thompson, *Great Shark Hunt*, 217.
"return from the graveyard . . .": Hammill in New York *Post*, May 10, 1971. Hammill in New York *Post*, Mar. 23, 1972.
"rather cruel and tough . . .": Humphrey to Charles H. Silver, May 12, 1971, Box 13, AAF71, HP.
"limousine liberal": Gartner to Humphrey, Mar. 22, 1971, Box 1, SFM, 1969–71, HP.
"I know I'll have trouble . . .": Wechsler in New York *Post* June 21, 1972.
"That translates he's abandoned . . .": Ibid.
Pentagon Papers leak: *NYT*, June 13, 1971. *WP*, June 17, 1971.

427. "To tell the truth, I . . .": Baltimore *Sun*, June 26, 1971.
"I was informed about . . .": *STPPP*, June 17, 1971.
"everything that was harmful . . .": *STPPP*, June 22, 1971.
"Humphrey's agony over . . .": *MS*, June 24, 1971.
"I supported the President's . . .": Humphrey to *MS*, July 2, 1971. Humphrey to Joseph Alsop, July 1, 1971, Box 10, Corr. files, Legisl. 1971, HP. Humphrey to Eugenie Anderson, July 26, 1971, Box 9, CF69–77, HP. Humphrey to A. J. Amersaal, Aug. 9, 1971, Box 2, Corr. file Legisl. 1971, HP.
"I know some people won't . . .": *NYT*, June 20, 1971. New York *Post*, June 21, 1971.

428. "With your usual overenthusiasm . . .": Emil Mazey to Humphrey, Aug. 21, 1971, Box 3, Corr. file, Legisl. 1971, HP.

"was only part of what must . . .":
Humphrey to H. B. Hayden, Sept. 7,
1971, Box 3, CF71, Legisl. 1971, HP.
"Nixon is tough . . .": Humphrey to
Eugenie Anderson, Oct. 6, 1971, Box 9,
CF69–72, HP.
"Daddy, as long as I have . . .": *MT*,
Nov. 20, 1971. Humphrey to Kampel-
man, Oct. 31, 1971, CF72, HP. *Time*,
Dec. 6, 1971. *Newsweek*, Dec. 6, 1971.
"ordeal" of primaries: Humphrey to
Eugenie Anderson, Nov. 14, 1971, Box
9, CF69–77, HP.
"whoever gets the nomination . . .":
Eisele, 439.
"I know I'm not the new man . . .":
Humphrey to Eugenie Anderson, Nov.
14, 1971, Box 9, CF69–77, HP.

429. "I think I have a better chance . . .":
Humphrey to Kampelman, Oct. 31,
1971, CF72, HP.
Gallup poll: *NYT*, Dec. 27, 1971.
"We need to get aboard . . .": Hum-
phrey to Chestnut, Nov. 17 and 19, 1971.
CF72, HP.
"I want you as my strong . . .":
Humphrey to Kampelman, Dec. 21,
1971, CF72, HP.
"We cannot wait any longer . . .":
Humphrey to Chestnut, Nov. 10, 1971,
CF72, HP.
"I'm going to take my campaign
. . .": *NYT*, Jan. 11, 1972. Humphrey-
edited Philadelphia speech draft, Jan. 7,
1972, Box 18, KP.
"We the people": *NYT*, Jan. 11, 1972.
"disappointing": Eugene Wyman,
"Memories of the 1972 Campaign Effort,"
n.d., 1972, CF72, HP ("Wyman diary").
Stewart Alsop in *Newsweek*, Jan. 3, 1972.
Dennis Wadley to Humphrey, Jan. 4,
1972, CF72, HP. Humphrey to Howard
K. Smith, Jan. 7, 1972, CF72PP, HP.
Humphrey to Leonard Woodcock, Jan.
10, 1972, Box 2, AAF72, HP.
"or he couldn't have kept . . .": Jack
Chestnut interview, Aug. 24, 1981.

430. "This is it for me": *NYT*, Mar. 12, 1972.
Wyman to Humphrey, Jan. 26, 1972,
CF72PP, HP. Ken Gray to Humphrey,
Jan. 27, 1972, Box 1, AAF72, HP. Connell to Humphrey, Feb. 11, 1972, Box
6, CF72, HP. *New Republic*, Feb. 19,
1972. Mary McGrory in *WS*, Jan. 17,
1972. Ken O'Donnell to Humphrey, Feb.
28, 1972, Box 2, CF72, HP. Humphrey
to Chestnut, Mar. 18, 1972, Box 15,
CF72, HP. Humphrey to Eugenie
Anderson, Mar. 19 and 23, 1972, Box

16, CF69–77, HP. Evans and Novak in
WP, Mar. 23, 1972. Wechsler in New
York *Post*, Mar. 15, 1972.
"Humphrey will stop the flow . . .":
Ken Gray to Martha Nord, Mar. 26,
1972, Box 8, AAF72, HP. Humphrey to
Bower Hawthorne, Mar. 31, 1972, Box
2, AAF72, HP. Humphrey's Florida,
Wisconsin, Pennsylvania, California
campaign schedules 1972, Berman files.
Anthony Lewis to Humphrey, April 12,
1972, Memos file, Memos 1971–75
(Gray, Wallace), HP.
"This isn't the Humphrey . . .":
Hyman Bookbinder to Humphrey, Mar.
20, 1972, Box 1, AAF72, HP.
"things that some of . . .": *NYT*, Mar.
18, 1972. Humphrey remarks in Mil-
waukee, Mar. 20, 1972, *NYT*, editorial,
Mar. 26, 1972.
"error . . . the fine print . . .":
Humphrey to Tom Wicker, Mar. 31,
1972, Box 2, AAF72, HP.
"the trappings of a man . . .": *NYT*
editorial, Mar. 26, 1971. Joseph Kraft in
Chicago *Daily News*, April 14, 1972.
Wechsler to Humphrey, April 14, 1972,
Box 2, AAF72, HP. Victor Navasky in
NYT mag., April 17, 1972. Carl Rowan
to Humphrey, April 19, 1972, Box 1,
SFM 69–71, HP. Humphrey to Carl
Stokes, April 25, 1972, Box 2, AAF72,
HP.

431. "organized rings around . . .":
McGovern interview.
"He starts at 7 . . .": Kilpatrick in *WS*,
April 3, 1972.

432. "I was furious . . .": *STPPP*, July 23,
1972.
"a strong finisher": *NYT*, May 21 and
26, 1972.
"spoilsport": *NYT*, May 23, 1972.
"California is the Superbowl": Humphrey to I. W. Abel, May 16, 1972, Box
16, CF69–77, HP.
"strict instructions not to . . .":
Humphrey to Chestnut, May 12, 1972,
CF72, HP. Humphrey to McGovern Jan.
28 and July 26, 1971, CF72, HP.
"proud to have played . . .": *MS*, May
26, 1972. *NYT*, May 26, 1972. "What do
the McGovern Tax Proposals Really
Mean?" mimeo, n.d., 1972, Berman files.

433. "I'll be damned if . . .": *MS*, May 26,
1972. Humphrey to Dan Spiegel, May
16, 1972, SFM 1971–75, HP. Humphrey to Edmund Brown, June 1, 1972,
CF72PP, HP. Patrick Owens in *Newsday*, June 5, 1972. Peter Jenkins in *NYT*

mag., May 28, 1972. Foley, *The New Senate*, 136.

"the only bright spot . . .": Eugene Wyman diary, CF72, HP.

"We asked for an appointment . . .": Ibid.

"reckless . . .preposterous": *MS*, May 26, 1972.

434. "single most devastating blow . . .": Wicker in *NYT*, June 2, 1972.

"our greatest adventure . . .": UPI Bulletin, Saigon, Oct. 31, 1967.

"destructive" debates: McGovern, *Grassroots*, 184.

"unbelievable!": Wyman diary 33, CF72, HP.

"McGovern Appears Near . . .": Ibid. 34.

"Our campaign slowed to a walk . . .": Ibid.

435. "If we had had our media allocation . . .": Humphrey to Eugenie Anderson, June 9, 1972, CF72, HP. Daniel Spiegel interview, Sept. 21, 1981. David Broder in *WP*, Jan. 18, 1978. Eugenie Anderson to Humphrey, June, 14, 1972, CF72, HP. Humphrey to Chestnut, June 22, 1972, Box 4, CF72, HP. Humphrey to Mike Maloney, June 22, 1972, Box 4, CF72, HP. Humphrey to Dorothy Lyon, June 22, 1972, Box 4, CF72, HP. *NYT*, June 27, 1972. Don Fraser to Humphrey, July 1, 1972, Box 3, AAF72, HP. Tankel, Toll et al. to Democratic Convention Delegates, July 9, 1972, Box 16, CF72, HP. "Minority Report, Credentials Committee, DNC," June 1972, CF72, HP. *Proceedings of the Democratic National Convention*, Miami Beach, 1972, 174, 188, 195. C. W. Harris, Congressional Research Service memo, "Popular Vote, Presidential Primaries 1972," June 30, 1972, Box 2, CF72, HP. Robert Osborn interview, Sept. 29, 1980.

"I just can't take the ridicule . . .": McGovern, *Grassroots*, 222. *WP*, Aug. 4, 1972.

"He was, it is true . . .": Los Angeles *Times*, July 16, 1972.

"was a tremendous goal . . .": *STPPP*, July 23, 1972.

"Somehow a false picture . . ." Roger Kent to Humphrey, July 14, 1972, Box 2, CF72, HP.

436. "Never!": *STPPP*, June 17, 1971.

"It is not easy for me to accept . . .": Humphrey to Roger Kent, July 21, 1972, Box 2, CF72, HP.

"There is a mood . . .": Ibid. Otto von

Habsburg to Humphrey, July 14, 1972, Box 2, CF72, HP. Nixon to Humphrey, July 15, 1972, VIP corr., HP. Fred Manfred in Sioux City *Journal*, July 30, 1972. Humphrey to Mr. and Mrs. John Seabert, Sept. 20, 1972, PFPA, HP. Dean Rusk to Humphrey, Aug. 28, 1972, Box 4, CF72, HP.

37: THE MONEY PROBLEM

437. sold five-cent sandwiches: Robert Harris interview.

furniture sat in van: Humphrey interview with William McGaffin, Chicago *Daily News*, June 13, 1964.

438. loan from Morris Ebin: M. B. Ebin to Milton Kronheim, Nov. 8, 1948, PFPF, HP. Humphrey to Darrell DeVilliers, June 7, 1958, PFPF, HP.

Ewald plot at Waverly for two hundred dollars: DNC release, Oct. 30, 1968. Chicago *Tribune*, Oct. 30, 1968, *NYT*, Oct. 31, 1968. Warranty Deed Record of Sept. 27, 1956, filed June 24, 1958, Wright County, Minn.

Benton and Andreas help at Shattuck: Benton to Andreas, Sept. 22, 1960, Box 16, PFPM, HP.

Johnson ranch plans for Waverly: *NYT*, July 10, 1968. Berman diary, Sept. 1, 1968, Berman files.

Waverly left him "flat": Humphrey to DeVilliers, Sept. 10, 1956, PFPF, HP.

"I had a tough summer until . . .": Humphrey to DeVilliers, June 7, 1958, PFPF, HP.

Speech fees 1969: Box 6, PFPF, HP.

"jail, jail jail": Humphrey to Vi Williams, Mar. 28, 1959, PFPF, HP.

"If anyone asks you . . .": Humphrey to DeVilliers, July 1, 1959, PFPF, HP.

"unbelievable" tax boost: Humphrey to Gates, Feb. 8, 1961, PFPF, HP. *WP*, April 3, 1960. William B. McDonald to Humphrey, Dec. 22, 1960, Box 6, PFPF, HP.

Income tax returns 1942–67 Box 6, PFPF, HP.

should be padded upward: John Hoving interview, March 26, 1983.

Net worth report 1964: Touche, Ross to Humphrey, Sept. 17, 1964. *NYT*, Sept. 22, 1964.

"helter-skelter" list: New York *Journal American*, Oct. 11, 1964.

condominium purchase: Humphrey to DeVilliers, Sept. 22, 1967, PFPF, HP. Humphrey to Lloyd Engelsma, July 11, 1966, Box 6, PFPF, HP.
Blind trust 1965: *NYT*, Mar. 1, 1965.

439. "the one man of wealth who . . .": *Education*, 294.
"when I saw the staggering . . .": Humphrey to DeVilliers, July 2, 1966, PFPF, HP.
DeVilliers "staggered": De Villiers to Humphrey, July 13, 1966, PFPF, HP.
Income 1966: Box 6, PFPF, HP.
Income 1967: Ibid.
"Andreas took advice . . .": Andreas interview. R. Smith.
Andreas into A-D-M: *Fortune*, Oct. 1973, 141.
Net worth report 1968: Humphrey press release, Oct. 9, 1968, Box 1063, HP. MS, June 2, 1969. *MS*, Jan. 1973, Box 1, PFPF, HP.

440. Mutual Income Fund growth: Andreas interview. *Annual Reports*, A-D-M, 1978–83. Standard & Poor, *Corporation Records*, Jan. 1983, 4669–71.
Childrens trusts: Andreas interview.
IRS penalties: *STPPP*, Dec. 22, 1973. Humphrey to Bower Hawthorne, Feb. 8, 1974, Box 6, AAF74, HP. Gartner memo, Mar. 20, 1975, SFM 1971–77 (Gartner), HP. *STPPP*, Mar. 4, 1975, and Oct. 7, 1976.
Campaign contribution 1972: U. S. Senate, Select Committee on Presidential Campaign Activities, *Presidential Campaign Activities of 1972*, Vol. 25, 11719.
Waverly land purchase 1974: *NYT*, Oct. 8, 1976. Jim Herzog in Knoxville *News Sentinel*, July 9, 1978. Warranty deed, Andreas Foundation to Hubert H. Humphrey Trust. Record of Sept. 16, 1974, filed May 8, 1975, Wright county, Minn.
Humphrey never knew: Andreas interview.
"You have enough": Andreas interview. *STPPP*, May 18, 1975. *NYT*, July 26, 1976, and July 11, 1978.
Net worth report 1976: *STPPP*, Oct. 7, 1976. *NYT*, Oct. 8, 1976.
Net worth estimated 1978: *STPPP*, July 11 and 12, 1978. *NYT*, Mar 8 and July 12, 1978. *STPPP*, Oct. 1 and 3, 1981. Andreas letter, Aug. 15, 1983.
"the senator who gets things done . . .": Charles Bailey in *MT*, Feb. 25, 1968.

Waters resignation: Ibid. *NYT*, Feb. 7, 1968, p. 1.

441. "to bring to your attention": *MT*, Feb. 28, 1968. *WP*, Oct. 27, 1969. Mollenhoff, *STPPP*, Oct. 10, 1970.
"our mutual friend": *MT*, Feb. 28, 1968.
"would appreciate your personal . . .": Ibid.
"our team of Napco experts . . .": Ibid.
"Napco "bungle": Ibid. Mollenhoff interview, Sept. 14, 1981.
"boondoggling": *MT*, Feb. 25, 1968. Clark Mollenhoff interview. Cleveland *Plain Dealer*, Mar. 1, 1968.
"start working": *MT*, Feb. 25, 1968.
"advised late of . . .": Ibid.
"certificate of competency": Ibid.

442. Mailster fiasco: Ibid.
Asked by Cowles: Berman diary, April 18, 1968, Berman files.

443. "swingers": Morton Mintz in *WP*, May 13, 1973.
Loeb fined: *STPPP*, May 17, 1973.
Aides and AMPI: Connell to Judge Edward Weinfeld, June 3, 1975, PFPA (C), HP. *STPPP*, June 27, 1974. *WP*, June 27, 1974. Samuel Dash and Fred Thompson, "Report on Humphrey et al. and AMPI," June 24, 1974, SFM, 1971–77 (Gartner), HP. *NYT*, Mar. 15, 1971. *MT*, Mar. 28, 1971.
Chestnut and AMPI: *NYT*, Sept. 1 and Nov. 1, 1973. *STPPP*, Mar. 24 and 27, 1974. "Minority Staff Study," n d. SFM, 1971–77 (Gartner), HP. Gartner to Samuel Dash, May 23, 1974, PFPA (A-E), HP. *WP*, June 27, 1974. *MT*, May 6–9, and June 27, 1975. *MS*, May 6 and June 6, 1975. *STPD*, May 9, 1975. *STPPP*, May 7 and June 27, 1975. Humphrey to Judge Edward Weinfeld, June 16, 1975, PFPA (C), HP. Humphrey statement, May 8, 1975, PFPA (C), HP. Humphrey to David Parr, Dec. 20, 1975, PFPA, HP. F. Thompson, 255. David Dorsen (May 3, 1983), Chestnut and Fred Thompson (May 12, 1983) interviews.

444. Sherman and AMPI: *MT*, Nov. 1970. Gartner memo, July 30, 1974, PFPA (A-E), HP. *NYT*, Aug. 13, 1974. *MT*, Oct. 11, 1974.
Humphrey 1972 campaign contribution report: *NYT*, Mar. 15, 1972. *STPPP*, Mar. 14 and 15, 1972. *STPPP*, June 16, 1973. Humphrey to Sam Ervin, June 27, 1974, PFPA, HP. Ervin to Humphrey, June 28, 1974, PFPA, HP.

Washington *Star-News*, June 28, 1974.
WP. June 27, 1974. *STPPP*, June 28,
1974. "Submission to Watergate Com-
mittee" n.d., June 1974, Misc. Politics,
HP. Humphrey to Dash / Thompson,
July 3, 1974, PFPA (A-E), HP. Staff
memo to Humphrey, July 30, 1974,
PFPM, HP.
Hughes contribution: Jack Anderson
in *WP*, Oct. 13, 1973. Humphrey memo,
n.d., Oct. 1973, PFPA (A-E), HP.
STPPP, Nov. 29 and Dec. 3, 1973, and
Apr. 5, 6, 9, 17, 1974. *NYT*, Sept. 26
and Nov. 29, 1973. Lasky, 372.

445. **Hughes correspondance:** Johnson to
Howard Hughes, May 9, 1968, WHCF
CF 21, JL. Humphrey to Johnson, July
25, 1968, VIP corr. HP.
"I've been embarrassed to tears . . .":
Humphrey to Palmer Hoyt, Aug. 28,
1974, PFPA (A-E), HP. Humphrey to
Robert Pierrot, Aug. 23, 1974, PFPA
(A-E), HP.
"There's no way you can . . .":
STPPP, Apr. 7, 1974.
Watergate findings softened: "Sub-
mission to Watergate Committee," n.d.,
June 1974, Misc. Politics, HP.
"I didn't need it": Humphrey to Hoyt,
Aug. 28, 1974, PFPA (A-E), HP.
"The dairy farmer in politics": *MT*,
April 18, 1975.
I don't want you to bring cash . . .":
Berman diary, April 20, 1968, Berman
files.
"clean up the whole business . . .":
Humphrey to Hoyt, Aug. 28, 1974,
PFPA (A-E), HP.
"Campaign financing is a curse . . .":
NYT, Oct. 13, 1974.

446. **Gulf, Ashland, etc.:** *WP*, June 27, 1974.
Gartner to Jerry McAfee, April 15, 1976,
PFPA (A-E), HP. William E. Jackson to
Gartner, May 4, 1976, SFM, 1971–77
(Gartner), HP. Brooks, *The Games Play-
ers*, 355.
3 M contribution: *MS*, Jan. 22, 1975.
STPPP, Mar. 31, 1976.
Tongsun Park List: *WP*, Oct. 24, 1977.
NYT, Jan. 25, Mar. 10 and 14, 1978. New
York *News*, Mar. 28, 1978. *STPPP*, Jan.
15 and May 19, 1978. U. S. Senate,
Select Committee on Ethics report
"Korean Influence Inquiry," Oct. 10,
1978, 80–87. Daniel Swillinger (May 3,
1983) and George Hritz (June 15, 1983)
interviews.
Presidential "perks": *NYT*, Jan. 6 and
11, 1977.

38:   THE LAST CAMPAIGN

447. **"Many who were on the outside . . .":**
Humphrey to Johnson, July 25, 1972,
VIP corr., HP.
"catastrophic": Connell to Humphrey,
Aug. 17, 1972, CF72 camp. HP.
"You have turned traitor . . .": Ida
Larson to Humphrey, Sept. 25, 1972 and
Humphrey to Ida Larson, Oct. 5, 1972,
Box 6, AAF72, HP.
"Tie yourself to Mondale": Hum-
phrey to Skip Humphrey, Oct. 17, 1972,
Box 21, CF72, HP.

448. **"A leader who struggled to bring
. . .":** *STPPP*, Jan. 23, 1973. Ladybird
Johnson to Humphreys, Feb. 2, 1972,
VIP corr., HP.
"Had we not gone into Vietnam . . .":
Humphrey to W. R. Biggs, Feb. 10,
1973, PFPA (A-E), HP.
Backs Kissinger: *NYT*, July 16, 1975.
Humphrey to Anton Thompson, July 16,
1973, PFPA (T), HP. Humphrey to Mrs.
Lorne Greene, Nov. 5, 1973, PFPA (G),
HP. *STPPP*, Sept. 3, 1973.
Gartner attribution: Gartner inter-
view.

449. **"I didn't like it at all":** Edgar Berman
interview. Dr. W. F. Whitmore to Dr.
Dabney Jarman, Mar. 18, 1974, Berman
files. "Cytology report," by Dr.
Melamed, Memorial hospital, Mar. 13,
1974, Berman files. "Followup and
Progress Report," Dr. W F. Whitmore,
Mar. 13, 1974, Berman files. Humphrey
to Marie-Therese Talbot, April 10, 1974,
PFPA (T), HP. Humphrey to Anton
Thompson, Jan. 30, 1974, PFPA (T),
HP. *NYT*, April 27 and 30, 1974.
"Well, Daddy, that's all I . . .": *MT*,
Jan. 5 and 27, 1974. *NYT*, Jan. 5 and 20,
1974.
"Take me home": Ken Gray interview.
Ursula Culver interview with Naftalin,
Aug. 17, 1978, Naftalin files.
"He got a helluva reaction": Berman
interview, *NYT*, April 15, 1974.
"destroyed by the treatment . . .":
NYT, May 1, 1974.
"better than I have in 5 years": *NYT*,
April 15, 1974. Humphrey to Wendell
Anderson, June 6, 1974, Box 6, AAF73,
HP. Pat O'Connor to Humphrey, July
1, 1975, Box 5, AAF74, HP. "China as
seen by Sen. Humphrey," Jan. 23, 1975,
M u / p, HP. Alf Landon to Humphrey,
Aug. 1, 1974, VIP corr., HP. Hum-
phrey to Eugenie Anderson, Sept. 21,

1974, FFPM, HP. Dr. C. B. Chapman letter, April 15, 1982.

"I must say that I find . . .": *STPPP*, Oct. 22, 1973.

"The nation desperately needs . . .": Humphrey to Geri Joseph, Aug. 5, 1974, Box 6, AAF74, HP.

"I was flaking out . . .": Skip Humphrey interview. Senate report, "U.S. role at World Food Conference, Rome, Nov. 5–16, 1974," M u / p, HP. Clay Holmes to Humphrey, Dec. 5, 1974, Box 6, AAF74, HP. Humphrey to Gartner, Feb. 20, 1974, and Feb. 20, 1975, SFM 1971–6 (Gartner), HP.

450. "C'mon, we're going": Skip Humphrey interview.

"It's hard to sum up . . .": John Stark interview with Connell, n.d., probably 1978, Connell files. *NYT*, April 27, 1975. *CR*, Vol. 121, 8831, May 21, 1975.

451. "We're not a bunch of . . .": *WP*, Nov. 4, 1974.

"Only a government that is big . . .": Humphrey to David Broder, Nov. 25, 1974, Box 6, AAF74, HP.

"I'm kind of a part of history . . .": *STPPP*, May 27, 1974. Humphrey to Anton Thompson, May 21 and July 21, 1975, PFPA (T), HP. Humphrey to Kampelman, July 26, 1975, PFPM, HP. Humphrey to Connell, May 25, 1975, PFPM, HP. St. Cloud *Times*, Aug. 16, 1975. Gartner to Humphrey, Sept. 24, 1975, SFM, 1971–6 (Gartner), HP.

"I am pleased to join . . .": Humphrey to David Roe, Sept. 24, 1974, Box 1, AAF72, HP.

"all those nights in . . .": *NYT*, Nov. 22, 1974. Finley Lewis, 212.

"the 60s are over . . .": John Roche to Humphrey, Feb. 6, 1976, Box 6, AAF76, HP.

"Indeed, yes": Humphrey to Connell, June 4, 1975, PFPM, HP.

"I heard it three times . . .": Connell to Humphrey, May 30, 1975, PFPM, HP.

"I told them that . . .": Humphrey to Connell, June 4, 1975 PFPM, HP.

"Bill, I'm trying to keep in . . .": Humphrey to Connell, July 21, 1975, PFPM, HP.

452. "Yes, I'm worried about this . . .": Humphrey to Marvin Rosenberg, Aug. 29, 1975, PFPM, HP. Peter Hart Assoc., "Survey of Political Climate in Minnesota," Misc / Political: Polls, Lists, Records, 1964–76, HP. Freeman to

Humphrey, Oct. 28, 1975, PFPA, HP. Humphrey to Eugenie Anderson, Nov. 22, 1975, PFPA (A-E), HP. Usula Culver to Humphrey, Nov. 12, 1975, SFM, 1971–5, HP. Henry Brandon in London *Sunday Times*, Dec. 7, 1975. Humphrey to Anton Thompson, Dec. 19, 1975, PFPA (T), HP. Humphrey to Gartner, Nov. 1, Dec. 19 and 24, 1975, SFM 1971–6 (Gartner), HP.

"The idea is getting around . . .": Reston in *NYT*, Oct. 17, 1975.

"The longer I am not . . .": *MT*, Oct. 12, 1975.

"I shall enter no primaries . . .": *NYT*, Nov. 3, 1975.

"I'm not at all sure that's . . .": Humphrey to Eugenie Anderson, Jan. 6, 1976, Box 6, CF76, HP.

"Very active" candidate: *NYT*, Feb. 4, 1976.

"most electable" Democrat: *MS*, Feb. 17, 1976.

"Humphrey's second coming": *PRO*, April 1976.

"We don't need the presidency": *MS*, Feb. 17, 1976. Harry Byrd to Humphrey, Jan. 4, 1976, Box 4, AAF76, HP. McGovern to Humphrey, "A Modest Proposal," n.d., early 1976, Politics 1976, HP. Kampelman to Humphrey, Jan. 28, Mar. 12 and 24, April 19, 1976, PFPA (K), HP. Mary McGrory in *WS*, Mar. 12, 1976. Marianne Means column, Mar. 10 and April 14, 1976, Politics 1976, HP.

"the only way to prevent . . .": Rowe to Humphrey, April 27, 1976, Politics, 1976, HP. Anthony Lewis in *NYT*, Mar. 4, 1976. Clayton Fritchey in *Newsday*, Mar. 15, 1976. *STPPP*, April 1, 1976. Witcover, *Resurrection of Richard Nixon*, 294. Kampelman to Humphrey, April 19 and April 30, 1976. PFPA, HP.

453. "an exceedingly difficult one": *MT*, April 30, 1976.

"They would have torn me apart . . .": Humphrey to Eugenie Anderson, May 22, 1976, PFPA (A-E), HP. *WP*, May 14, 1976.

"I have no organization": *MT*, April 30 and June 13, 1976. Humphrey to Robert Humphrey, May 22, 1976, PF, HP. Gartner to Humphrey, June 13, 1976, SFM 1971–6 (Gartner), HP.

"It's ridiculous . . .": Reston in *NYT*, April 30, 1976. *NYT*, June 18, 1976.

"One night he called me": Berman interview.

"spent two days with him . . .": Ibid.

"He went in as if . . .": Ibid.
"He was up and made the rounds . . .": Ibid.
"As far as we are concerned . . .": *STPPP*, Oct. 2, 1976.

454. "worse than the X-rays . . .": St. Cloud *Times*, Nov. 25, 1976. Dr. W. F. Whitmore to Dr. Edgar Berman, Nov. 9, 1976, Berman files. "Memorial Hospital discharge summary," Nov. 2, 1976, Berman files. "Surgical Pathology report," Dr. M. R. Melamed, Oct. 8, 1976, Berman files. "Followup and Progress Notes," Dr. Alan Yagoda, Feb. 3, 1977, Berman files. "Followup and Progress Notes," Dr. W. F. Whitmore, Mar. 11 and July 21, 1977, Berman files. Mary McGrory in *WS*, Nov. 13, 1976. *NYT*, Jan. 4, 1977.
"The treatments made me feel . . .": Humphrey to Eugenie Anderson, Jan. 23, 1977, PFPA (A-E), HP.
"Told him exactly what it was . . .": Berman interview. "Operative Report," Dr. J. S. Nazarian, Aug. 18, 1977, Berman files. Dr. Vincent de Vita to Humphrey, Sept. 16, 1977, Berman files. Dr. J. S. Nazarian to Dr. Vincent de Vita, Sept. 22, 1977, Berman files. Dr. J. S. Nazarian, "Discharge summary," Oct. 4, 1977, Berman files.
"You Can't Quit": *Reader's Digest*, July 1977. Humphrey to Harriett Humphrey, Feb. 5, 1977, PF, HP. Humphrey to Eppie Lederer, Feb. 11, 1977, PFPA (L), HP. *WP*, Dec. 15, 1976. *STPPP*, Jan. 6, 1977.
"You're always pulling them . . .": Kampelman to Humphrey, July 21, 1977, SFM 1971–76 (Gartner), HP. Humphrey to Carter, Nov. 3, 1976, VIP corr., HP. Carter to Humphrey, Nov. 9, 1976, VIP corr., HP. Humphrey to Carter, Jan. 11, 15, 19, 23, 24, 28, 31 and Feb. 1, 1977, VIP corr., HP. Carter to Humphrey, Jan. 17, 1977, VIP corr., HP.
"Anybody else and you'd say . . .": *Newsweek*, July 25, 1977.
"I don't give a damn if . . .": Eppie Lederer to Humphrey, Mar. 21, 1977. PFPA (L), HP.
Hubert Humphrey Institute: *NYT*, July 29, 1977. *MT*, July 29, 1977. Wendell Anderson interview.

455. "He called me every night . . .": Berman interview.
"Terminal": *NYT*, Aug. 17–20, 1977, Sept. 12 and Oct. 5, 1977. *STPPP*, Oct. 1, 1977.

"a skull on a stick": Cohen, 476
"I may start out a little . . .": Rochester speech, Sept. 20, 1977, MSF, HP. *NYT*, Sept. 20, 1977. Humphrey to Harriett Humphrey, Nov. 22, 1977, PF, HP. Last Senate speech, Oct. 25, 1977. Engelmayer, *Hubert Humphrey*, 335. *WP*, Dec. 5, 1977. *NYT*, Dec. 8, 1977.

456. "And they voted Humphrey . . .": Berman interview.
"Jesus Christ, Lyndon . . .": Ibid.
"a celebration": Bruce Solomonson interview. *STPPP*, Jan. 15–17, 1978.
"He taught us how to . . .": *MS*, Jan. 16, 1978. *NYT*, Jan. 16 and 17, 1978.
Schuller: Humphrey to Schuller, Oct. 1, 1974, PFPA, HP. *NYT*, Jan. 17, 1978. Roy Reed and Max Kampelman, *NYT*, Jan. 15, 1978. Apple in *NYT*, Jan. 16, 1978. Wechsler in New York *Post*, Jan. 17, 1978. *Time*, Jan. 23, 1978. Huron *Daily Plainsman*, Jan. 15, 1978. Watertown *Public Opinion*, Jan. 1978. "Hubert H. Humphrey," funeral program, House of Hope Presbyterian church, St. Paul, Jan. 16, 1978.

39:   THE MAN AND HIS LEGACY

457. Bryan, Norris, LaFollette: Allen Johnson, "William Jennings Bryan," *Dictionary of American Biography*. Richard Lowitt, *Fighting, Liberal, George W. Norris. Lafollette's Autobiography*.

458. "effective man of government": to Haynes Johnson in *WP*, June 23, 1977.
"he can disagree without being disagreeable . . .": McPherson, Cahn, Connell, Freeman interviews.
"as Nelson Polsby said . . .": *Citizens Choice*, 8–9.
"the best of his time": *Memorial Services in Eulogy of HHH*, 1978.
"best speech I ever heard": Baltimore *Sun*, Feb. 20, 1966; Kampelman memo, July 2, 1956, Box 89, HP.

459. last speech the most stirring: Les Malkerson, Naftalin, Heaney, interviews.
"jabber, jabber, jabber": Ruth McPartlin, 1941, Box 1, HP.
his speeches 90 percent of the time: Ken Gray interview.
Shirtsleeve harrangues 1953: Herbert Waters interview.
"Education is essentially . . .": Humphrey to James Benson, April 12,

1962, Personal (A–E), 1919–78, HP. Humphrey to L. P. Devlin, May 28, 1968, Box 1082, HP.
"Enjoying your audience . . .": Humphrey to James Benson, April 12, 1962. Personal (A–E), 1919–78, HP.
"slovenliness of syntax": O'Neill, 385.
"grabbers": Ken Gray interview.
460. "You tossed in a piece . . .": Doug Bennet interview.
"Bennet, the difference . . .": Ibid.
"You just don't capture . . .": Ibid.
"You just don't capture . . .": Ibid.
"You never could get the cadence . . .": Ibid.
You couldn't translate . . .": Ibid.
an old Chautauqua circuit . . .": Robert Squier interview.
perils of accepting invitations: Thomas L. Hughes interview.
461. Four hundred fifty topics, etc.: *CR*, Vol. 95, Index.
"I'm going to learn to do it . . .": Jane Freeman interview.
In 1954 a Senate clerk . . .: Charles Gilbert, "Problems of a Senator."
"I can be a statesman": Ibid.
"I like every subject": *Congressional Quarterly*, Sept. 11, 1964, 2092.
"I'd like to be co-sponsor": Connell interview re Wilderness bill.
"Let's not have one enemy": Andreas interview.
"I knew every senator better . . .": Connell interview.
"Hubert, he's a goddam . . .": Eugene Foley interview.
"Humphrey was the most forceful . . .": Myer Feldman interview with Connell, n.d., 31, Connell files.
462. Peace Corps: "Legislative Record—Bills sponsored and co-sponsored by Hubert Humphrey," n.d., 1965, mimeo, M u / p, HP.
"clip" letters: Ken Gray interview.
widows pension: Berman interview.
Port Savage dredged: Andreas interview.
Freeway re-designed: Douglas Kelm interview.
Legislative list: *Congressional Quarterly* Special Report, Sept. 11, 1964. *Congressional Quarterly* Special Report, Sept. 6, 1968. Guild *Reporter*, Oct. 12, 1968. Albert Saunders, "Highlights of Legislative Record of Hubert Humphrey," 1977, PFPMB, u / p, HP. (This is the most complete list of Humphrey's lawmaking accomplishments. It can also be found in U.S. Senate, *Memorial Services*, 17–25.)
agriculture bills: Compilation by Legislative Reference Service, Jan. 1962, Box 140, HP. James E. Thornton interview, Sept. 21, 1982.
"Let's get Bob Dole . . ." Andreas interview. *CR*, vol. 110, 15442, June 30, 1964.
463. family farm inheritance tax: CR, vol. 122, 25951–6, 25945–6, Aug. 5, 1976. Tax Reform Act of 1976, Publ L. 94–4 55, Title XX, #2003(a), Code section 2032A.
"I learned more about economics . . ." Humphrey interview with Kenneth Harris of London *Observer*, Oct. 19, 1968, CF68, HP.
"to promote the general welfare": Humphrey, "Welfare An Honorable Word in American History," Wheeling *Intelligencer*, Aug. 22, 1949. Humphrey to Lehman, Nov. 2, 1949, Humphrey file, LP. Humphrey speech to Harvard law school forum, Mar. 20, 1950, Box 745, HP.
464 "Hubert, I know you're not . . .": John Hoving interview.
Keep a delegation waiting: Ernest LeFever in Connell "Notes on Foreign Policy Discussion," June 21, 1978, Connell files.
"Give us fifteen minutes": James Rowe interview.
"It was his fatal flaw . . .": John Hoving interview.
Pretty realistic judge: Gilbert, "Problems of a Senator."
465. "My God, Hubert, how can you . . .": Freeman interview.
"If I had to summarize . . .": "Portrait of a President," in *Democratic Fact Book 1968*, M u / p, HP.
"off the track" knowledge: Freeman, Beckington interviews.
"In conversation you would see him . . .": Connell interview.
Wasting hot water at Windsor: Berman interview.
chainstore clothes: Ibid.
Uneasy with Eastern intellectuals: Gilbert, "Problems of a Senator." Carl Auerbach interview with Naftalin, July 13, 1978, Naftalin files.
"He had never been anywhere . . .": Benton interview Columbia University Oral History Project, 1968, 210.
If he had gone to Princeton . . .": Muriel Humphrey interview with Con-

nell, April 30, 1979, p. 97/28, Connell files.

embraced the smallest item: U. S. Senate, *Memorial Services*, Walter T. Ridder, 198–99.

Kennedy "had total staff": Andreas interview

466. **"Jesus, if the guy would only . . .":** Interview for *Time*, Jan. 6, 1949.

Warned to take time to think: Naftalin to Humphrey, Dec. 11, 1947, Box 49, HP. Eugenie Anderson to Humphrey, July 16, 1956, Box 560, HP.

"He could come into a room . . .": Naftalin interview.

"Now we have a little time . . .": Julius Cahn interview.

"If you haven't any tears . . .": Humphrey speech, Rochester, Minn., Sept. 19, 1977, MSF, HP.

to read about himself: Naftalin interview.

As a senator he felt free: "A Conversation with Hubert Humphrey, Bill Moyers Journal, April 11, 1976.

"I'm a man that has matured later . . .": Ibid.

He seemed continuously "on": Martin Agronsky interview.

"I don't have many deep . . .": Bill Moyers Journal, April 11, 1976.

no close friends at all: David Gartner and Norman Sherman interviews.

Kirkpatrick as alter ego: Naftalin, Kampelman, Eugenie Anderson interviews.

Coolness with Freeman 1960: Freeman interview.

467. **"Muriel is my greatest asset":** Humphrey interview with Kenneth Harris, Oct. 19, 1968. CF68, HP.

"Hubert, what are you doing today?": Norman Holmes interview. Feb. 5, 1981.

Sports fan: Van Dyk to Ravnholt, Nov. 20, 1965, PFPMB, HP. Tom Mee letter,

July 16, 1982. Arthur Naftalin, "Naming of the Metrodome," *Greater Minneapolis*, Mar.–April 1982. Ravenholt memo, Oct. 15, 1965. PFPMB, HP. Humphrey to Chestnut, May 22, 1970, SFM 1969–71, HP.

Liked to dance, parties: *WP*, Jan. 20 and 21, 1965. "Hubie the Hoofer," New York *News*, Jan. 26, 1968. Pat Gray (May 14, 1980) and Edna Ravnholt (Sept. 21, 1981) interviews.

Beer by preference: David Gartner interview.

chamois vest in childhood: Humphrey interview with Sherman and others, n.d. Box 2, Autobiography files, HP.

scary stomach upset 1957: Mary Lasker letter, April 25, 1983. Dr. Henry Lax interview, May 14, 1983.

"Microbe phobia": Berman interview.

"chicken blood transfusions": Humphrey notebooks, n.d., PFPA, (P-V), HP.

"proof that God exists . . .": Naftalin interview Humphrey interview with Nannes, "Humphrey of Minnesota." Julian Hartt and Calvin Didier (Aug. 4, 1981) interview.

Perceptive political scientist: Gilbert, "Problems of a Senator".

468. **Handled contradictions well:** Thomas L. Hughes interview.

"a flaw in Humphrey's . . .": McGovern interview.

469. **father's warning against bankers:** Naftalin interview.

"a source of strength": Humphrey speech, Feb. 3, 1965, MSF, HP.

antitrust "modernized": Humphrey speech, May 11, 1965, MSF, HP.

"new" Humphrey: *Fortune*, Aug. 1965, 143.

"We passed it": Connell interview.

"giving him life": Eugene McCarthy interview

Bibliography

MANUSCRIPT COLLECTIONS
The following abbreviations are used in this list: MHS: Minnesota Historical Society; SHSW: State Historical Society of Wisconsin; TPL: Truman Presidential Library.

Americans for Democratic Action Papers, SHSW; Thomas Amlie Papers, SHSW; Eugenie Anderson Papers, MHS; Elmer Benson Papers, MHS; Anita McCormick Blaine Papers, SHSW; Chester Bowles Papers, Yale University Library; Ray P. Chase Papers, MHS; William Connell Papers, MHS; Democratic-Farmer Labor Party Papers, MHS; Democratic National Committee Papers, National Archives, Roosevelt, Truman, Kennedy, and Johnson presidential libraries; Donald M. Fraser Papers, MHS; Orville L. Freeman Papers, MHS; Hubert H. Humphrey Papers, MHS; Lyndon B. Johnson Papers, Johnson Presidential Library; Max Kampelman Papers, MHS; John F. Kennedy Papers, Kennedy Presidential Library; Herbert Lehman Papers, Columbia University Libraries; Walter Lippmann Papers, Yale University Library; James Loeb Papers, SHSW; Eugene McCarthy Papers, MHS; Arthur McGuire Papers, MHS; George MacKinnon Papers, MHS; Minneapolis Central Labor Union Papers, MHS; Minnesota Republican State Central Committee Papers, MHS; G. Theodore Mitau Papers, MHS; Charles S. Murphy Papers, TPL; Philleo Nash Papers, TPL; National Security Council Papers, Johnson Presidential Library; Franklin D. Roosevelt Papers, Roosevelt Presidential Library; Frederick Smedley Papers, Columbia University Libraries; Francis M. Smith Papers, MHS; Norman Thomas Papers, New York Public Library; Harry S. Truman Papers, Truman Presidential Library.

BOOKS, ARTICLES, AND INDIVIDUAL MANUSCRIPTS

Aaron, Benjamin. "Amending the Taft-Hartley Act: A Decade of Frustration." *Industrial and Labor Relations Review* (April 1958).

Abell, Tyler, ed. *Drew Pearson Diaries, 1949–59*. New York: Holt, Rinehart and Winston, 1974.

Acheson, Dean. *Present at the Creation*. New York: W. W. Norton, 1969.

Adamcewicz, Ann. "Hubert H. Humphrey." For Ralph Nader Congress Project, Citizens Look at Congress, August 1972.

Albritton, Robert B. "Social Amelioration through Mass Insurgency." *American Political Science Review* (December 1979).

Alcaly, Roger and David Marmelstein, eds. *The Fiscal Crisis of American Cities*. New York: Vintage Books, 1971.

Alexander, Herbert E. *Financing the 1960 Election*. Princeton: Citizens Research Foundation, 1962.

———. *Money in Politics*. Washington: Public Affairs Press, 1972.

———. *Studies in Money and Politics*. Vols. 3, 6, 17, 19. Princeton: Citizens Research Foundation, 1974.

Alsop, Stewart. "Who Will Be the Democratic Candidate? *Saturday Evening Post* (March 28, 1959).

———. "President Humphrey?" *Saturday Evening Post* (May 8, 1964).

———. "Humphrey, Shadow or Substance?" *Saturday Evening Post* (August 24, 1968).

Amrine, Michael. *This Is Humphrey*. Garden City, N.Y.: Doubleday, 1960.

Anderson, Clinton. *Outsider in the Senate*. New York: World Publ., 1970.

Anderson, Patrick. *All the President's Men*. Garden City, N.Y.: Doubleday, 1968.

Anson, Robert Sam. *McGovern: A Biography*. New York: Holt, Rinehart and Winston, 1972.

Apple, R. W. "Humphrey Remembered." *New York Times* (January 15, 1978).

Asbell, Bernard. *The Senate Nobody Knows*. Garden City, N.Y.: Doubleday, 1978.

Ashford, Nicholas. *Crisis in the Workplace*. Cambridge: MIT Press, 1976.

Ashman, Charles. *Connally*. New York: William Morrow, 1974.

Auerbach, Carl. "Jury Trials and Civil Rights Cases." *New Leader* (April 29, 1957).

Bachrack, Stanley D. *The Committee of One Million: 'China Lobby' Politics, 1953–71*. New York: Columbia University Press, 1976.

Bailey, Charles W. "Never Stop Running: HHH", in Sevareid, Eric, ed. *Candidates 1960*. New York: Basic Books, 1959.

Bain, Richard C. and Judith H. Parris. *Convention Decisions and Voting Records*. Washington: Brookings Institution, 1973.

Baker, Leonard. *The Johnson Eclipse*. New York: Macmillan, 1966.

Baker, Bobby with Larry L. King. *Wheeling and Dealing: Confessions of a Capitol Hill Operator*. New York: W. W. Norton, 1978.

Baker, Russell. "Humphrey, Thunder-Lightning?" *New York Times* magazine (January 11, 1959).

Ball, George. *The Past Has Another Pattern*. New York: W. W. Norton, 1982.

Barbash, Jack. *The Practice of Unionism*. New York: Harper, 1956.

Barnouw, Eric. *The Golden Web: History of Broadcasting in the U.S.*, vol. 2. New York: Oxford University Press, 1968.

Baus, Herbert M. and William B. Ross. *Politics Battle Plan*. New York: Macmillan, 1968.

Berman, Edgar. *Hubert*. New York: G. P. Putnam's, 1979.

Berman, Hyman. "Political Antisemitism in Minnesota During the Great Depression," *Jewish Social Studies* (Summer–Fall 1976).

Berman, Larry. *Planning a Tragedy: The Americanization of the War in Vietnam*. New York: W. W. Norton, 1982.

Berman, William C. *The Politics of Civil Rights in the Truman Administration*. Columbus: Ohio State University Press, 1970.

Bernstein, Barton J., ed. *Politics and Policies of the Truman Administration*. Chicago: Quadrangle, 1970.

Bernstein, Irving. *Turbulent Years: A History of the American Worker*. Boston: Houghton Mifflin, 1970.

———. "George W. Norris." *Labor History* (Winter 1967).

Blair, Clay and Joan. *The Search for JFK*. New York: G. P. Putnam's, 1976.

Blegen, Theodore C. *Minnesota: A History of the State*. Minneapolis: University of Minnesota Press, 1975.

Bolling, Richard. *House Out of Order*. New York: Dutton, 1965.

Bowen, William. "What's New about the New Humphrey." *Fortune* (August 1965).

Bowles, Chester. *Promises to Keep: My Years in Public Life*. New York: Harper, 1971.

Bradlee, Benjamin C. *Conversations with Kennedy*. New York: W. W. Norton, 1975.

Brandon, Henry. *Anatomy of Error: The Inside Story of the Asian War on the Potomac, 1954–69*. Boston: Gambit Press, 1969.

———. *Retreat of American Power*. Garden City, N.Y.: Doubleday, 1973.

Brandt, Willy. *People and Politics: The Years 1960–73*. Boston: Little Brown, 1978.

Brauer, Carl M. *John F. Kennedy and the Second Reconstruction*. New York: Columbia University Press, 1977.

Brennan, Dan. *The President's Right Hand*. A novel. New York: Tower Books, 1967.

Brock, Clifton. *Americans for Democratic Action*. Washington: Public Affairs Press, 1962.

Broder, David. "Triple H Brand of Vice Presidency." *New York Times* magazine (December 6, 1964).

———. "Election of 1968." In Schlesinger, Arthur, ed. *History of American Presidential Elections*. Vol. 4. New York: Chelsea House, 1971.

———. *The Party's Over: The Failure of Politics in America*. New York: Harper, 1972.

Brooks, John. *The Great Leap*. New York: Harper, 1966.

———. *The Games Players*. New York: Times Books, 1980.

Burnham, James. "The Suicidal Mania of American Business." *Partisan Review* (January 1950).

Califano, Joseph A., Jr. *A Presidential Nation*. New York: W. W. Norton, 1975.

Calvert, Greg and Carol Neiman. *A Disrupted History*. New York: Random House, 1971.

Cannon, James P. *History of American Trotskyism*. New York: Pioneer Publ., 1944.

———. *Socialism on Trial*. New York: Pioneer Publ., 1942.

———. *Notebook of an Agitator*. New York: Pioneer Publ., 1958.

Carmichael, Stokely and Charles V. Hamilton. *Black Power. The Politics of Liberation in America*. New York: Random House, 1967.

Caro, Robert A. *The Years of Lyndon Johnson: The Path to Power*. New York: Knopf, 1982.

Cater, Douglass. "What Makes Humphrey Run?" *The Reporter* (March 5, 1959).

———. *The Fourth Branch of Government*. Boston: Houghton Mifflin, 1959.

Chase, Ray P. "Are They Communists or Catspaws?" Pamphlet, c. 1938.

Chennault, Anna. *The Education of Anna*. New York: Times Books, 1980.

Chester, E. W. *Radio, TV and American Politics*. New York: Sheed and Ward, 1969.

Chester, Lewis, Godfrey Hodgson, and Bruce Page. *An American Melodrama: The Presidential Campaign of 1968*. New York: Viking, 1969.

Christian, George. *The President Steps Down*. New York: Macmillan, 1970.

Christlock, Carl H. *The Progressive Era in Minnesota*. St. Paul: Minnesota Historical Society, 1971.

Clark, Joseph S., Jr. *The Senate Establishment*. New York: Hill and Wang, 1963.

———. *Congress: The Sapless Branch*. New York: Harper, 1954.

———. *Congressional Reform*. New York: Crowell, 1965.

Clay, Jim. *Hoffa: An Authorized Biography*. Beaverdam, Va.: Beaverdam Books, 1965.

Clay, Lucius D. *Decision in Germany*. Garden City, N.Y.: Doubleday, 1950.

Clemens, Diane S. *Yalta*. New York: Oxford University Press, 1970.

Cloward, Richard A. and Frances Fox Piven. *Regulating the Poor*. New York: Pantheon, 1971.

———. *The Politics of Turmoil*. New York: Pantheon, 1974.

Cochrane, William. *Farm Prices, Myth and Reality*. Minneapolis: University of Minnesota Press, 1958.

Cohen, Dan. *Undefeated: The Life of Hubert H. Humphrey*. Minneapolis: Lerner Publ., 1978.

C.I.O. *Proceedings of the Eighth Constitutional Convention*. Atlantic City (May 18–22, 1946).

Congressional Quarterly. "Fact Sheet on Vote Comparisons" (August 10, 1956).

————. Special Report: "The Public Record of Lyndon B. Johnson and Hubert H. Humphrey" (September 11, 1964).

————. Special Report: "The Public Records of Hubert H. Humphrey and Sen. Edwin S. Muskie" (September 6, 1968).

————. *Watergate: Chronology of a Crisis.* 2 Vol., 1973–74.

Converse, Philip E. "Continuity and Change in American Political Parties and Issues in the 1968 Election." *American Political Science Review* 63, no. 4 (1969): 1083.

Cooper, Chester. L. *The Lost Crusade: America in Vietnam.* New York: Dodd, Mead, 1970.

Cormier, Frank. *Lyndon B. Johnson: The Way He Was.* Garden City, N.Y.: Doubleday, 1977.

Cormier, Frank and W. J. Eaton. *Reuther.* Englewood Cliffs: Prentice-Hall, 1970.

Crampton, John A. *The National Farmers Union.* Lincoln, Neb.: University of Nebraska Press, 1965.

Dahl, Robert. *Pluralist Democracy in the U.S.* Chicago: Rand McNally, 1967.

Dalfiume, Richard M. *Desegregation of the U.S. Armed Forces.* Columbia, Mo.: University of Missouri Press, 1969.

————. *American Politics Since 1945.* Chicago: Quadrangle, 1969.

David, Paul T., ed. *The Politics of National Party Conventions.* Washington: Brookings Inst., 1960.

Davies, Richard O. *Housing Reform during the Truman Administration.* Columbia, Mo.: University of Missouri Press, 1966.

Davis, James W. *Presidential Primaries: Road to the White House.* New York: Crowell, 1967.

Democratic National Committee. *Democracy at Work: Official Report of the Democratic National Convention Philadelphia, July 12–14, 1948.*

————. *Official Proceedings of the National Convention of 1956.*

————. *Official Proceedings of the Democratic National Convention, Chicago, 1968.*

————. *Official Proceedings of the Democratic National Convention, Miami Beach, 1972.*

Derthick, Martha. *Policymaking for Social Security.* Washington: Brookings Inst., 1979.

Devlin, L. Patrick. "Hubert H. Humphrey: His Speaking Principles and Practice." Dissertation for Ph.D. in Speech. Michigan: Wayne State University, 1966.

————. "Hubert H. Humphrey's 1948 Civil Rights Speech." *Today's Speech.* Vol. 16, no. 3.

————. "Hubert Horatio Humphrey, Man of Words and Deeds." Mimeo (January 1978).

Divine, Robert. *Blowing on the Wind: The Nuclear Test Ban Debate."* New York: Oxford University Press, 1978.

Dobbs, Farrell. *Teamster Rebellion.* New York: Monad Press, 1972.

————. *Teamster Power.* New York: Monad Press, 1973.

————. *Teamster Politics.* New York: Monad Press, 1975.

Donovan, Robert J. *Conflict and Crisis: The Presidency of Harry S Truman, 1945–48.* New York: W. W. Norton, 1977.

————. *Tumultuous Years: The Presidency of Harry S Truman, 1949–53.* New York: W. W. Norton, 1982.

Douglas, Paul. "The Problem of Tax Loopholes." *American Scholar* (Winter 1967–68).

————. *In the Fullness of Time.* New York: Harcourt Brace Jovanovich, 1972.

Draper, Theodore. *The Roots of American Communism.* New York: Viking, 1957.

Drew, Elizabeth. *Senator.* New York: Simon & Schuster, 1979.

————. *Washington Journal.* New York: Random House, 1975.

Dugger, Ronnie. *The Politician: The Life and Times of Lyndon Johnson.* New York: W. W. Norton, 1982.

Dunne, W. F. and M. Childs. *Permanent Counter Revolution: Role of the Trotskyites in the Minneapolis Strike.* New York, n.a., 1934.

Efnor, Claude. "Humphrey's Draft History, World War II." *Northwest Industrial News* (September 1964).

Eisele, Albert. *Almost to the Presidency: A Biography of two American Politicians.* Blue Earth, Minn.: The Piper Co., 1972.

Eisenhower, Dwight D. *Mandate for Change*. Garden City, N.Y.: Doubleday, 1963.
———. *Waging Peace*. Garden City, N.Y.: Doubleday, 1965.
Emerson, B., ed. "Mr. Vice President, are you going to win the election? "Yes, I really believe I am." Humphrey interview, *Saturday Evening Post* (October 19, 1968).
Emerson, Thomas, David Haber, and Norman Dorsen. *Political and Civil Rights in the U.S.* Boston: Little Brown, 1967.
Engelmayer, Sheldon D. and Robert J. Wagman. *Hubert Humphrey: The Man and His Dream*. New York: Methuen, 1978.
Ernst, Harry W. *The Primary That Made a President: West Virginia 1960*. New York: McGraw-Hill, 1962.
Epstein, Lenore et al. "Social Security After Thirty Years." *Social Security Bulletin* (August 1955).
Evans, Rowland and Robert Novak. *LBJ: The Exercise of Power*. New York: New American Library, 1966.
———. *Agony of the G.O.P.* New York: Macmillan, 1965.
Faber, Harold, ed. *Road to the White House*. New York: McGraw-Hill, 1965.
Fairlie, Henry. *The Kennedy Promise: The Politics of Expectation*. Garden City, N.Y.: Doubleday, 1973.
Fentriss, Simmons. "Candidates Up Close." *Time* (October 18, 1968).
Ferman, L. A., ed. "Evaluating the War on Poverty." *Annals of the American Academy of Social and Political Science* (September 1969).
Ferrell, Robert H., ed. *The Eisenhower Diaries*. New York: W. W. Norton, 1981.
Filner, Robert. "Humphrey's Second Coming." *The Progressive* (April 1976).
Fischer, John. "The Lost Liberals." *Harpers* (May 1947).
Fitzgerald, Frances. *Fire in the Lake: The Vietnamese and the Americans in Vietnam*. Boston: Little Brown, 1972.
Foley, Nicholas. *The New Senate*. New Haven: Yale University Press, 1980.
Frady, Marshall. *Wallace*. New York: World Publ. Co., 1968.
Freeland, Richard. *The Truman Doctrine and the Origins of McCarthyism*. New York: Knopf, 1972.
Freidin, Seymour. *A Sense of the Senate*. New York: Dodd Mead, 1972.
Fried, Richard M. *Men against McCarthy*. New York: Columbia University Press, 1976.
Gaddis, John L. *The U.S. and the Origins of the Cold War*. New York: Columbia University Press, 1972.
Gallup, George H. *The Gallup Poll, 1935–71*. 3 vol. New York: Random House, 1972.
Gans, Herbert. *More Equality*. New York: Pantheon, 1973.
Gelb, Leslie. *The Irony of Vietnam*. Washington: Brookings Inst., 1979.
Gieske, Millard L. *Minnesota Farmer-Laborism: The Third-Party Alternative*. Minneapolis: University of Minnesota Press, 1979.
Gilbert, Charles E. "Problems of a Senator: A Study of Legislative Behavior." Dissertation for Ph.D. in Political Science. Illinois: Northwestern Univ. (August 1955).
Gleason, William F. *Daley of Chicago*. New York: Simon and Schuster, 1970.
Goldman, Eric F. *The Crucial Decade and After*. New York: Vintage paperback, 1960.
———. *The Tragedy of Lyndon Johnson*. New York: Knopf, 1969.
Goldstein, Joel K. *The Modern American Vice Presidency*. Princeton: Princeton University Press, 1982.
Goodman, Walter. "1968." *Commentary* (December 1969).
Goodwin, Richard. "The Night McCarthy Turned to Kennedy." *Look* (October 15, 1969).
Gordon, Albert L. *Jews in Transition*. Minneapolis: University of Minnesota Press, 1949.
Gorey, Hays. "I'm a Born Optimist: The Era of Hubert Humphrey." *American Heritage*, (December 1977).
Gorman, J. B. *Kefauver, a Political Biography*. New York: Oxford University Press, 1971.
Gottlieb, Sanford, ed. "The Humphrey-McCarthy Records on Foreign Policy." National Committee for a Sane Nuclear Policy. Pamphlet, 1968.

Goulden, Joseph. *Meany*. New York: Atheneum, 1972

Graff, Henry F. *The Tuesday Cabinet*. Englewood Cliffs, N.J.: Prentice Hall, 1970.

Green, James R. *Grass-Roots Socialism: Radical Movements in the Southwest*. Baton Rouge, La.: Louisiana State University Press, 1975.

Greenfield, Jeff. "What Makes Humphrey Not Run?" *New York Times* magazine (April 4, 1976).

Greenhaw, Wayne. *Watch Out for George Wallace*. Englewood Cliffs, N.J.: Prentice-Hall, 1976.

Griffith, Robert. *The Politics of Fear*. Lexington, Ky.: University of Kentucky Press, 1970.

Griffith, Winthrop. *Humphrey: A Candid Biography*. New York: Morrow, 1965.

———. "He Is Not What He Was." *New York Times* magazine (March 30, 1969).

Gross, Bertram M., ed. *A Great Society*. New York: Basic Books, 1968.

Halberstam, David. *The Unfinished Odyssey*. New York: Random House, 1968.

———. *The Best and the Brightest*. New York: Random House, 1972.

Hall, Perry D., compiler. *The Quotable Humphrey*. Anderson, S.C.: Broke House, 1967.

Hamby, Alonzo L. *Beyond the New Deal*. New York: Columbia University Press, 1974.

———. *The Imperial Years*. New York: Weybright & Talley, 1976.

Hammill, Pete. "Politics Is My Life." *Saturday Evening Post* (October 10, 1964).

Hardin, Charles M. *Politics of Agriculture*. Glencoe, Ill.: Free Press, 1952.

Harding, John. "Community Self-Survey." *Congress Weekly* (March 5, 1948).

Harris, Fred R. *Potomac Fever*. New York: W. W. Norton, 1972.

Harrison, James P. *The Endless War: Fifty Years of Struggle in Vietnam*. New York: Free Press, 1982.

Hartman, Susan. *Truman and the Eightieth Congress*. Columbia, Mo.: University of Missouri Press, 1971.

Hartsough, Mildred. "Transportation as a Facet in the Development of the Twin Cities." *Minnesota History* (September 1926).

———. In Bruce Price, ed. *The Marketing of Farm Products*. Minneapolis: University of Minnesota Press, 1927.

Haveman, Robert H., ed. *A Decade of Federal Anti-Poverty Programs*. New York: Academic Press, 1977.

Haynes, John E. "Liberals, Communists and the Popular Front in Minnesota." The Struggle to Control the Political Directions of the Labor Movement and Organized Liberalism." Dissertation for Ph.D. in Political Science. Minneapolis: University of Minnesota (March 1978).

Heard, Alexander. *The Costs of Democracy*. Chapel Hill, N.C.: University of North Carolina Press, 1960.

Heffner, R. D., ed. "This Process of Growth and Freedom." Humphrey interview, *Saturday Review* (Oct. 12, 1968).

Herring, George C. *America's Longest War: The United States and Vietnam*. New York: Wiley, 1979.

Hersh, Seymour M. *The Price of Power*. New York: Summit Books, 1983.

———. *My Lai Four: A Report on the Massacre and Its Aftermath*. New York: Random House, 1970.

Hicks, John D. *The Populist Revolt*. Minneapolis: University of Minnesota Press, 1931.

——— with Theodore Saloutos. *Twentieth-Century Populism: Agricultural Discontent in the Middle West, 1900–39*. Madison, Wisc.: University of Wisconsin Press, 1951.

Hinderaker, Ivan. "Harold Stassen and the Developments in the Republican Party in Minnesota," Dissertation for Ph.D. in Political Science. Minneapolis: University of Minnesota (June 1949).

Hodgson, Godfrey. *America in our Time*. Garden City, N.Y.: Doubleday, 1976.

Hofstadter, Richard. *Age of Reform*. New York: Vintage paperback, 1955.

———. *Anti-Intellectualism in American Life*. New York: Vintage paperback, 1963.

Howe, Russell W. and Sarah Trott. *The Power Peddlers*. Garden City, N.Y.: Doubleday, 1977.

———. "The Truth at Last—How Nixon Beat Humphrey." *Washington Monthly* no. 12 (1976): 55–62.

Hughes, Emmet J. "Man with One Arrow." *Newsweek* (April 4, 1966).

Hughes, Thomas L. "On the Causes of Our Discontents." *Foreign Affairs* (July 1969).

———. "Liberals, Populists and Foreign Policy." *Foreign Policy* (Fall 1975).

———. "Carter and the Mangement of Contradictions." *Foreign Policy* (Summer 1978).

Humphrey, Hubert H. *Beyond Civil Rights.* New York: Random House, 1964.

———. *The Cause Is Mankind.* New York: Praeger, 1964.

———. *Education of a Public Man.* Garden City, N.Y.: Doubleday, 1976.

———. *Moral Crisis: The Case for Civil Rights.* Minneapolis: Gilbert Publishing Co., 1964.

———. *Political Philosophy of the New Deal.* Baton Rouge, La.: State University Press, 1970.

———. *Tax Loopholes.* Washington: Public Affairs Inst., 1952.

Humphrey, Hubert H., ed. *Integration vs. Segregation.* New York: Crowell, 1964.

Humphrey, Seth K. *Following the Prairie Frontier.* Minneapolis: University of Minnesota Press, 1931.

Huntington, Samuel. "The Bases of Accommodation." *Foreign Affairs* (July 1968).

Hurd, Melba. "Your Voice and Diction." *The Persuader* (November 1941).

Huthmacher, Joseph. *Senator Robert F. Wagner & the Rise of Urban Liberalism.* New York: Atheneum paperback, 1971.

Hyman, Sidney. *Lives of William Benton.* Chicago: University of Chicago Press, 1970.

James, Ralph C. and Estelle D. James. *Hoffa and the Teamsters: A Study of Union Power.* Princeton: Van Nostrand, 1965.

Jarman, Rufus. "The Senate's Gabbiest Freshman," *Saturday Evening Post* (October 1, 1949).

Javits, Jacob. *Order of Battle: A Republican's Call to Reason.* New York: Atheneum, 1964.

Jenkins, Peter. "What This Country Needs Is a Nice Man as President." *New York Times* magazine (May 28, 1972).

Jennett, Richard P. *The Man from Minnesota.* Minneapolis: Joyce Society, 1965.

Jensen, Vernon H. *Heritage of Conflict.* Ithaca, N.Y.: Cornell University Press, 1950.

Johnson, Haynes B. *In the Absence of Power.* New York: Viking, 1980.

Johnson, Lady Bird. *A White House Diary.* New York: Holt, Rinehart and Winston, 1970.

Johnson, Lyndon B. *The Vantage Point.* New York: Holt, Rinehart and Winston, 1971.

Johnson, Sam H. *My Brother Lyndon.* New York: Cowles, 1970.

Johnson, Walter, ed. *Papers of Adlai Stevenson.* 5 vol. Boston: Little Brown, 1972–74.

Kaiser, Robert B. *RFK Must Die!* New York: Dutton, 1970.

Kalb, Bernard and Elie Abel, *The Roots of Involvement.* New York: W. W. Norton, 1971.

Kalb, Marvin and Bernard. *Kissinger.* Boston: Little Brown, 1974.

Kampelman, Max M. "The Communist Party and the CIO." Dissertation for Ph.D. in Political Science. Minneapolis: University of Minnesota, 1952.

———. *The Communist Party and the CIO.* New York: Praeger, 1957.

———. "HHH, Political Scientist," *PS,* the news journal of the ASPA (Spring 1978).

———. "Why They Tried to Get Humphrey to Wear Glasses." *New York Times* (January 18, 1978).

Kearns, Doris. *Lyndon Johnson and the American Dream.* New York: New American Library/Signet paperback, 1977.

Kemble, Penn. "The Democrats After 1968." *Commentary* (January 1969).

Kennedy, John F. *Why England Slept.* New York: Wilfred Funk, 1940.

Koen, Ross Y., *The China Lobby in American Politics.* New York: Harper and Row, 1974.

Kolko, Gabriel. *The Triumph of Conservatism.* New York: Free Press, 1963.

Koskoff, David E. *Joseph P. Kennedy: A Life and Times.* Englewood Cliffs, N.J.: Prentice Hall, 1974.

Kramer, Dale. "The Dunne Brothers of Minneapolis." *Harpers* (March 1942).

———. *The Wild Jackasses.* New York: Hastings House, 1956.

———. "Young Man in a Hurry." *New Republic* (June 16, 1947).

Krock, Arthur. *Memoirs.* New York: Funk & Wagnalls, 1968.

Lader, Lawrence. *Power on the Left: American Radical Movements Since 1946.* New York: W. W. Norton, 1979.

LaFollette, Robert M. *LaFollette's Autobiography.* Madison: University of Wisconsin Press, 1960.

LaFeber, Walter. *America, Russia and the Cold War*. Ithaca, N.Y.: Cornell University Press, 1967.

Larner, Jeremy. *Nobody Knows*. New York: Macmillan, 1968.

Lasch, Christopher. *The Agony of the American Left*. New York: Knopf, 1968.

———. "The Making of the War Class." *Columbia Forum* (Winter 1971).

Lasky, Victor. *It Didn't Start with Watergate*. New York: Dial Press, 1977.

Lass, William E. *Minnesota*. States and the Nation Series. New York: W. W. Norton, 1977.

Latham, Earl. *The Communist Controversy in Washington*. Cambridge: Harvard University Press, 1966.

Lebedoff, David. *The Twenty-First Ballot: A Political Party Struggle in Minnesota*. Minneapolis: University of Minnesota Press, 1969.

———. *Ward Number Six*. New York: Scribner, 1972.

Lee, R. Alton. *Truman and Taft-Hartley*. Lexington, Ky.: University of Kentucky Press, 1966.

LaSueur, Meridel. "Benson of Minnesota." *New Masses* (September 6, 1938).

———. "The Liberal Movement in the North Middle-West," Saturday Lunch Club (Minneapolis) pamphlet, 1951.

Leuchtenburg, William E., ed. *Unfinished Century*. Boston: Little Brown, 1973.

Levy, Guenter. *America in Vietnam*. New York: Oxford University Press, 1978.

Lewis, Finlay. *Mondale: Portrait of an American Politician*. New York: Harper, 1980.

Lewitt, Richard. *Fighting Liberal, George W. Norris*. Urbana, Ill.: University of Illinois Press, 1978.

Lippincott, Benjamin E. *Democracy's Dilemma: The Totalitarian Party in a Free Society*. New York: Ronald Press, 1965.

Loeb, James I. "Confessions of an Egghead." Unpubl. Ms. Loeb Papers, 1952, 1973.

Loory, Stewart. "The Politics of Make-Believe." *The Progressive* (November 1968).

Lowry, W. McNeill. "Education of a Senator." *The Progressive* (May 1951).

Lubell, Samuel. *The Future of American Politics*. New York: Anchor paperback, 1956.

McAuliffe, Mary S. *Crisis on the Left: Cold War Politics and American Liberals, 1947–54*. Amherst, Mass.: University of Massachusetts Press, 1978.

McCarthy, Abigail. *Private Faces, Public Places*. Garden City, N.Y.: Doubleday, 1972.

McCarthy, Eugene. *Year of the People*. Garden City, N.Y.: Doubleday, 1969.

———. *Limits of Power*. New York: Holt, Rinehart and Winston, 1967.

McCarthy, Joe. *The Remarkable Kennedys*. New York: Dial, 1960.

McConnell, Grant. *Decline of Agrarian Democracy*. New York: Atheneum paperback, 1977.

McDermott, William F. "Young Man in Politics, Governor of Minnesota." *Survey Graphic* (July 1940).

MacDonald, Maurice. *Food, Stamps and Income Maintenance*. New York: Academic Press, 1977.

MacDougall, Curtis. *Gideon's Army*. New York: Marzani and Hunsel, 1965.

McGaffin, William. "The Rise of Hubert Humphrey." Chicago *Daily News* (June 13, 1964).

McGovern, George. *Grassroots: The Autobiography of George McGovern*. New York: Random House, 1977.

———. *An American Journey: The Presidential Campaign Speeches of George McGovern*. New York: Random House, 1974.

McLaughlin, Daryl. *The Landrum Griffin Act and Union Democracy*. Ann Arbor, Mich.: University of Michigan Press, 1979.

McMenamin, Michael and Walter McNamara. *Milking the Public*. Chicago: Nelson-Hall, 1980.

McPherson, Harry. *A Political Education*. Boston: Atlantic/Little Brown, 1972.

McWilliams, Carey. "Minneapolis, the Curious Twin." *Common Ground* (Autumn 1946).

———. *A Mask for Privilege*. Boston: Little Brown, 1948.

Mailer, Norman. *Miami and the Siege of Chicago*. New York: World Publ., 1968.

Manfred, Frederick. "Hubert Horatio Humphrey: A memoir." *Minnesota History* (Fall 1979).

Marquart, Frank. *An Auto Workers Journal*. University Park, Pa.: Penn State University Press, 1975.

Martin, John Bartlow. *Adlai Stevenson*. 2 vol. Garden City, N.Y.: Doubleday, 1977.

Martin, Ralph E. and Plaut, Ed. *Front Runner, Dark Horse.* Garden City, N.Y.: Doubleday, 1960.

Martin, Ralph G. *A Man for All People: Hubert H. Humphrey.* New York: Grosset and Dunlap, 1968.

Matusow, Allen. *Farm Politics and Policies in the Truman Years.* Cambridge: Harvard University Press, 1967.

Mayer, George H. *The Political Career of Floyd B. Olson.* Minneapolis: University of Minnesota Press, 1951.

Meryman, Richard. "Hubert Humphrey Talks His Self Portrait." *Life* (September 27, 1968).

Meyers, Constance A. *The Prophet's Army.* Westport, Conn.: Greenwood Press, 1977.

Michener, James A. "HHH: Portrait of a President." *Democratic Fact Book, 1968.* Washington, Democratic National Committee.

Miller, Merle. *Lyndon; an Oral Biography.* New York: G. P. Putnam's, 1980.

Miller, Norman. *The Great Salad Oil Scandal.* New York: Coward-McCann, 1965.

Miller, Seymour M. and Pamela Roby. *The Future of Inequality.* New York: Basic Books, 1970.

Mintz, Morton. "Watergate Reveals Gamey Election Money." Washington *Post* (May 13, 1973).

Mitau, G. Theodore. *Politics in Minnesota.* Minneapolis: University of Minnesota Press, 1970.

———. "The Democratic-Farmer-Labor Party Schism of 1948." *Minnesota History* (Spring 1955).

Moline, Norman T. *Mobility and the Small Town.* Chicago: University of Chicago, Dept. of Geography Research Paper No. 132, n.d.

Morlan, Robert L. *Political Prairie Fire: The Non Partisan League.* Minneapolis: University of Minnesota Press, 1955.

Morison, B. L., "His Honor at 37." *Survey Graphic* (June 1948).

———. "The Amazing Mr. Himphrey." *Survey Graphic* (October 30, 1948).

Morrow, H. Frederick. *Black Man in the White House.* New York: Coward-McCann, 1966.

Moynihan, Daniel Patrick. *Maximum Feasible Misunderstanding: Community Action in the War on Poverty.* New York: Free Press, 1969.

———. "What is Community Action?" *Public Interest* (Fall 1966)

Myrdal, Gunnar. *An American Dilemma.* Rev. ed. New York: Harper, 1962.

Naftalin, Arthur. "Failure of the Farmer-Labor Party to Capture Control of the Minnesota Legislature." *American Political Science Review* 28 (1944): 71.

———. "A History of the Farmer Labor Party in Minnesota." Dissertation for Ph D. in Political Science. Minneapolis: University of Minnesota (February 1948).

———. "Minnesota." In Paul T. David, ed. "The Middle West." *Presidential Nominating Politics in 1952.* Vol. 4. Baltimore: Johns Hopkins Press, 1954.

Nannes, Caspar. "Humphrey of Minnesota." *The Link.* (November 1974).

Navasky, Victor. *Kennedy Justice.* New York: Atheneum, 1971.

———. "Report on the Candidate Named Humphrey." *New York Times* magazine (August 25, 1968).

———. "The Making of a Candidate." *New York Times* magazine (April 17, 1972).

National Commission on Supplies and Shortages. Advisory Committee on National Growth Processes. *Forging America's Future.* Washington: GPO, 1976.

Nevins, Allan. *Herbert Lehman and His Era.* New York: Scribner, 1963.

Newfield, Jack. *Robert F. Kennedy: A Memoir.* New York: Dutton, 1969.

Nichols, Lee. *Breakthrough on the Color Front.* New York: Random House, 1954.

Nixon, Richard M. *Memoirs of Richard Nixon.* New York: Grosset and Dunlap, 1978.

Nordstrand, Marty. *Humphrey.* Washington: Robert B. Luce, 1964.

O'Brien, Gene. "He Comforted the Afflicted and Afflicted the Comfortable." *Hennepin County Review* (January 18, 1978).

O'Brien, Lawrence F. *No Final Victories.* Garden City, N.Y.: Doubleday, 1974.

O'Donnell, Kenneth P. and David F. Powers. *Johnny, We Hardly Knew Ye;* memoirs of John Fitzgerald Kennedy. Boston: Little Brown, 1970.

O'Donovan, Patrick. "How Kefauver Made It In Minnesota," *The Reporter,* April 5, 1956.

O'Neill, William. *Coming Apart: An Informal History of America in the 1960s*. Chicago: Quadrangle, 1971.

Opotowsky, Stan. *The Longs of Louisiana*. New York: Dutton, 1960.

Osborne, John. *White House Watch*. Washington: New Republic Books, 1977.

Page, Joseph A. and Mary-Win O'Brien. *Bitter Wages*. New York: Grossman, 1973.

Pahl, Thomas L. "G-String Conspiracy, Political Reprisal or Armed Revolt? The Minneapolis Trotskyite Trial." *Labor History* (Winter 1967).

Parmet, Herbert. *Jack*. New York: Dial, 1980.

———. *The Presidency of John F. Kennedy*. New York: Dial, 1983.

Patterson, James T. *Mr. Republican*. Boston: Houghton Mifflin, 1972.

Pechter, Marc. *Telling Lives*. Washington: New Republic Books, 1979.

Pentagon Papers: The Defense Dept History of U.S. Decision Making in Vietnam. Sen. Gravel edition. Boston: Beacon Press, 1971.

Plotnick, Robert D. and F. Skidmore. *Progress against Poverty: A Review of the 1964–1974 Decade*. New York: Academic Press, 1975.

Polsby, Nelson. *Citizens Choice: Humphrey or Nixon*. Washington: Public Affairs Press, 1968.

Pomper, Gerald. "The Repeal of Taft-Hartley." *Labor History* (Fall 1961).

———. "The Nomination of Hubert Humphrey for Vice President." *Journal of Politics*. Vol. 23, no. 8.

Porter, Kirk H. and D. B. Johnson. *National Party Platforms, 1840–1968*. Urbana, Ill.: Illinois University Press, 1972.

Powers, Thomas. *The Man Who Kept the Secrets: Richard Helms and the CIA*. New York: Knopf, 1979.

Prochnau, William W. and Richard W. Larsen. *A Certain Democrat: Senator Henry W. Jackson*. Englewood Cliffs, N.J.: Prentice Hall, 1972.

Radosh, Ronald. *American Labor and U.S. Foreign Policy*. New York: Random House, 1969.

Ramparts, editors of. "The Decline and Fall of the Democratic Party." *Ramparts* (September 28, 1968).

Reed, Roy. "Unflagging Despite Setbacks." *New York Times* (January 14, 1978).

Reedy, George. *Lyndon B. Johnson: A Memoir*. Kansas City: Andrews & McMeel, 1982.

———. *The Presidency in Flux*. New York: Columbia University Press, 1973.

———. *Twilight of the Presidency*. New York: World, 1970.

Richan, Willard C. and Allan R. Mendelssohn. *Social Work: The Unloved Profession*. New York: New Viewpoints, 1973.

Richardson, J. "Who is Hubert?" *Esquire* (November 1966).

Ridder, Walter E. "Hustling Hubert Makes His Bid." *Saturday Evening Post* (April 29, 1959).

Ridge, Martin. *Ignatius Donnelly*. Chicago: University of Chicago Press, 1962.

Rinzler, Carol E., ed. *Frankly McCarthy*. Washington: Public Affairs Press, 1969.

Roberts, Chalmers. *First Rough Draft*. New York: Praeger, 1973.

Roberts, Steven B. "The Food Stamp Program, How It Grew." *New York Times* (April 4, 1981).

Robinson, Archie. *George Meany and His Times*. New York: Simon and Schuster, 1981.

Roeser, Thomas. *Ingenious Deceit*. St. Paul: n.a., 1964.

Rogin, Michael P. *The Intellectuals and McCarthy*. Cambridge: MIT Press, 1967.

Rolvaag, O. E., *Giants in the Earth*. New York: Harper, 1927.

Ross, Carl. *The Finnish Factor*. New York Mills, Minn: Parta Printers, 1977.

Ross, Irwin. *The Loneliest Campaign*. New York: New American Library, 1968.

Rostow, Walt W. *The Diffusion of Power*. New York: Macmillan, 1972.

Roszak, Theodore. *The Making of the Counter Culture*. Garden City, N.Y.: Doubleday, 1968.

Rowan, Carl. "Who Gets the Negro Vote." *Look* (November 13, 1956).

Rowen, Hobart. *The Free Enterprisers: Kennedy, Johnson and the Business Establishment*. New York: G. P. Putnam's, 1964.

Royko, Mike. *Boss: Richard J. Daley of Chicago*. New York: Dutton, 1971.

Ruchames, Louis. *Race, Jobs and Politics: The Story of FEPC.* New York: Columbia University Press, 1953.

Ryskind, Allan H. *Hubert.* New Rochelle, N.Y.: Arlington House, 1968.

Safire, William. *Before the Fall: An Inside View of the Pre-Watergate White House.* Garden City, N.Y.: Doubleday, 1975.

Sannes Family Booklet. N.d. c., 1965–66.

Scammon, Richard M., ed. *America at the Polls: A Handbook of American Presidential Election Statistics, 1920–64.* Pittsburgh: University of Pittsburgh Press, 1965.

———. *America Votes 10.* Washington: Government Affairs Institute, 1973.

Schandler, H. Y. *The Unmaking of a President.* Princeton: Princeton University Press, 1977.

Schapsmeier, E. L. and F. H. *Prophet in Politics: Henry A. Wallace and the War Years, 1940–65.* Ames, Iowa: Iowa State University Press, 1970.

Schell, Herbert S. *History of South Dakota.* Lincoln: University of Nebraska Press, 1961.

Schlesinger, Arthur, Jr. *The Age of Roosevelt.* 3 vol. Boston: Houghton Mifflin, 1957–62.

———. *A Thousand Days.* Boston: Houghton Mifflin, 1965.

———. *Robert Kennedy and his Times.* Boston: Houghton Mifflin, 1978.

———. *The Vital Center.* Boston: Houghton Mifflin, 1949.

Seaborg, Glenn T. *Kennedy, Khrushchev and the Test Ban.* Berkeley: University of California Press, 1981.

Searle, R. Newell. *Saving Quetico-Superior.* St. Paul, Minn.: Minnesota Historical Society, 1977.

Sevareid, Eric. *Not So Wild a Dream.* New York: Atheneum paperback, 1978.

———, ed. *Candidates 1960.* New York: Basic Books, 1959.

Shaffer, Samuel. "Humphrey Comes on Strong." *New York Times* magazine (August 25, 1963).

Shannon, David A. *Decline of American Communism.* New York: Harcourt Brace, 1959.

Shannon, William. *The Heir Apparent.* New York: Macmillan, 1967.

———. "In Mid Passage." *The Progressive* (December 1958).

Sherrill, Robert and Harry W. Ernst. *The Drugstore Liberal.* New York: Grossman, 1968.

Shields, James M. *Mr. Progressive: A Biography of Elmer Austin Benson.* Minneapolis: T. S. Dennison Co., 1971.

Shore, William B. "One City's Struggle against Intolerance." *The Progressive* (January 1949).

Sidey, Hugh. "The Horseshedding of Hubert Humphrey." *Life* (August 11, 1972).

Sinnett, Ronald F. and Charles H. Backstrom. *Recount; Minnesota's Close Election.* Washington: National Document Publishers, 1964.

Sitkoff, Harvard. "Harry Truman and the Election of 1948: The Coming of Age of Civil Rights in American Politics." *Journal of Southern History* (November 1971).

Skilling, H. Gordon. *Czechoslovakia's Interrupted Revolution.* Princeton: Princeton University Press, 1976.

Smith, A. R. *Tiger in the Senate: The Biography of Wayne Morse.* Garden City, N.Y.: Doubleday, 1962.

Smith, G. Kerry, ed. *Stress and Campus Response.* San Francisco: Jessen-Bass, 1968.

———. *Twenty Five Years.* San Francisco: Jessen-Bass, 1970.

Smith, Gerald L. K. "Have the Jews Decided to Support Their Billion Dollar Prostitute, Hubert Humphrey?" *The Cross and the Flag* (November 1975).

Smith, Richard N. *Thomas Dewey and His Times.* New York: Simon and Schuster, 1982.

Snider, George R., Jr. "The Kennedy Buildup: A Study of the Role of the Press in Campaign Politics." Honors thesis. Yale University (January 29, 1962).

Solberg, Carl. *Riding High: America in the Cold War.* New York: Mason and Lipscomb, 1973.

Sorensen, Theodore. *Kennedy.* New York: Harper, 1965.

Spangler, Earl. *The Negro in Minnesota.* Minneapolis: T. S. Dennison Co., 1961.

Starobin, Joseph. *American Communism in Crisis.* Cambridge: Harvard University Press, 1972.

Stassen, Harold. *Where I Stand.* Garden City, N.Y.: Doubleday, 1947.

———. *Man Was Meant to Be Free.* Garden City, N.Y.: Doubleday, 1951.

———. "A U. N. Government." *Saturday Evening Post* (May 22, 1943).

Steel, Ronald. *Imperialists and Other Heroes: A Chronicle of the American Empire.* New York: Random House, 1971.

Stewart, John G. "Independence and Control: The Challenge of Senatorial Party Leadership." Chicago: Dissertation for Ph.D. at University of Chicago, 1968.

———. *Our Last Chance: The Democratic Party 1974–76.* New York: Praeger, 1974.

Strout, Richard L. *TRB: Issues and Perspectives on the Presidency.* New York: Macmillan, 1979.

Sundquist, James L. *Politics and Policy.* Washington: Brookings Inst., 1968.

———, ed. *On Fighting Poverty.* New York: Basic Books, 1969.

Thompson, Fred. *At That Point in Time: The Story of the Senate Watergate Committee.* New York: Times Books, 1975.

Thompson, Hunter S. *Fear and Loathing on the Campagin Trail.* San Francisco: Straight Arrow Books, 1973.

———. *The Great Shark Hunt.* New York: Summit Books, 1979.

Toynbee, Polly. "Living through the Boss." *Washington Monthly* 5, no. 4: 1973.

Truman, Harry S. *Memoirs.* 2 vol. Garden City, N.Y.: Doubleday, 1955–56.

Tselos, George D. "The Minneapolis Labor Movement in the 1930s." Dissertation for Ph.D. at University of Minnesota (June 1970).

Tucker, William P. "The Farmers Union Cooperatives." *Sociology and Social Research* (July–August 1947).

Tyler, Gus. "The Case for Hubert Humphrey." *The Progressive* (August 1968).

Tyler, Robert L. "The American Veteran Committee: Out of a Hot War and Into a Cold." *American Quarterly* (Fall 1966).

U. S. Federal Election Committee Reports: *Presidential Filings, 1972* (April 20, 1972); *Presidential Filings 1972* (July 10, 1972); *Presidential Primaries 1972* (September 8, 1972); *Report to Office of Federal Elections* (July 27, 1973); *Humphrey Senatorial Race* Pt. 1 (April 12, 1976); *Committee to Reelect Sen. Humphrey* (October 12, 1976); *Committee to Reelect Sen. Humphrey* (October 22, 1976).

U. S. House, Committee on Budget. "Changing the Pattern of Unemployment" (June 1979); "The Potential of Humphrey Hawkins" (staff report by Jerome Segal. Washington: GPO, 1979).

U. S. House 82nd Congress, 2nd session. Subcommittee of Committee on Government Operations. "Investigation of Racketeering in the Minneapolis Area." *Hearings* (April 9–10, 1954). Washington: GPO, 1954.

U. S. National Commission on the Causes and Prevention of Violence. *To Establish Justice, to Insure Domestic Tranquility.* Washington: GPO, 1969.

U. S. Presidents. *Public Papers of Harry S. Truman* 1952–53. Washington: GPO, 1955; *Public Papers of John F. Kennedy* 1961–63. Washington: GPO, 1963–65; *Public Papers of Lyndon B. Johnson* 1963–65. Washington: GPO, 1964–70.

U. S. Senate, 80th Congress, 1st session. Subcommittee Senate Committee on Labor and Public Welfare. Hearings, *Anti-Discrimination in Employment.* Washington: GPO, 1947.

U. S. Senate, 81st Congress 1st session. Labor and Public Welfare Committee. *Hearings.* Washington: GPO, 1950.

———, 81st Congress, 2nd session Committee on Labor and Public Welfare. *Labor-Management Relations in the Southern Textile Industry. Hearings.* Washington: GPO, 1950–51.

———, 82nd Congress, 2nd session. Heraings before Subcommittee on Labor-Management Problems. On *American Enka Corp.* (June 15–16, 1950). Washington: GPO, 1950.

———, 82nd Congress, 2nd session. Subcommittee of Committee on Labor and General Welfare. *Hearing, Communist Domination of Unions and National Security.* Washington: GPO, 1952.

———, 83rd Congress, 1st session. Subcommittee on Labor-Management Relations. *Public Policy and Communist Domination of Certain Unions.* Washington: GPO, 1953.

———, 84th Congress, 2nd session, Subcommittee on Disarmament. *The Executive Branch and Disarmament Policy.* Washington: GPO, 1956.

————, 85th Congress, 1st session. *Executive Sessions of the Foreign Relations Committee.* Vol. 9. Washington: GPO, 1979.

————, 85th Congress, 2nd session. *Executive Sessions of the Foreign Relations Committee.* Vol. 10. Washington: GPO, 1980.

————, 86th Congress, 1st session. *Executive Sessions of the Foreign Relations Committee.* Vol. 11. Washington: GPO, 1982.

————, 86th Congress, 2nd session. *Executive Sessions of the Foreign Relations Committee.* Vol. 12. Washington: GPO, 1982.

————, 89th Congress, 1st session. Hubert H. Humphrey Report to Committee on Foreign Relations. *The Alliance for Progress.* Washington: GPO, 1963.

————, 93rd Congress, 1st session. Select Committee on Presidential Campaign Activities. *Presidential Campaign Activities of 1972.* 26 vols. Washington: GPO, 1973.

————, 94th Congress, 1st session. Committee on Agriculture. Subcommittee on Foreign Agricultural Policy. Humphrey report: *Hunger and Diplomacy.* U. S. at Food and Agriculture Organization conference. Washington: GPO, 1975.

————, 94th Congress, 1st session. Select Committee on Intelligence. *Hearings: Intelligence Activities.* Vol. 6. Washington: GPO, 1976.

————, 94th Congress, 2nd session. Select Committee on Intelligence. *Intelligence Activities and the Rights of Americans.* Final report. Washington: GPO, 1976.

———— —, 95th Congress, 2nd session. Select Committee on Ethics. *Korean Influence Inquiry.* Washington: GPO, 1978.

————, 95th Congress, 2nd session. *Memorial Services in Eulogy of Hubert H. Humphrey.* Washington: GPO, 1978.

————, 96th Congress, 1st session. Committee on Rules. *Senate Cloture Rules.* Washington: GPO, 1979.

————, 96th Congress, 2nd session. Committee on Rules. *Standing Rules of the Senate.* Washington: GPO, 1980.

Valenti, Jack. *A Very Human President.* New York: W. W. Norton, 1975.

Valenti, Jiri. "Soviet Decision-Making in the Czechoslovakian Crisis of 1968." *Studies in Comparative Communism* (Spring-Summer 1975).

Vernon, Raymond. *Storm over the Multinationals: The Real Issues.* Cambridge: Harvard University Press, 1977.

von Hoffman, Nicholas. "Looking for a President." *Harpers* (September 1971).

Walker, Charles R. "Minneapolis." *Survey Graphic* (October 1936).

————. *American City.* New York: Farrar and Rinehart, 1938.

Walker, Daniel. *Rights in Conflict: Chicago's 7 Brutal Days.* New York: Dutton, 1968.

Wallick, Frank. "I Remember Hubert." *UAW Washington Report* (January 16, 1978).

Walton, Richard J. *Henry Wallace, Harry Truman and the Cold War.* New York: Viking, 1976.

Warren, Frank A., III. *Liberals and Communism: The Red Decade Revisited.* Bloomington, Ind.: Indiana University Press, 1966.

Wechsler, James A. *The Age of Suspicion.* New York: Random House, 1953.

————. *Reflections of a Middle Aged Radical.* New York: Random House, 1960.

Whalen, Richard. *The Founding Father.* New York: New American Library, 1964.

White, Theodore H. *American in Search of Itself.* New York: Harper and Row, 1982.

————. *Breach of Faith: The Fall of Richard Nixon.* New York: Atheneum, 1975.

————. *The Making of the President 1960.* New York: Atheneum, 1961.

————. *The Making of the President 1964.* New York: Atheneum, 1965.

————. *The Making of the President 1968.* New York: Atheneum, 1969.

————. "Summing Up." *New York Times* magazine (April 25, 1982).

White, William S. *Citadel: The Story of the U.S. Senate.* New York: Harper, 1956.

————. *The Professional: Lyndon B. Johnson.* Boston: Houghton Mifflin, 1964.

————. *The Taft Story.* New York: Harper, 1954.

Wilcox, W. W. and W. W. Cochrane. *Economics of American Agriculture*. Englewood Cliffs, N.J.: Prentice-Hall, 1960.

Witcover, Jules. *The Resurrection of Richard Nixon*. New York: Putnam, 1970.

Wofford, Harris. *Of Kennedy and Kings: Making Sense of the Sixties*. New York: Farrar, Straus, and Geroux, 1980.

Youngdale, James. *Populism: A Psychohistorical Perspective*. Port Washington, N.Y.: Kennikat Press, 1975.

NEWSPAPERS AND ADDITIONAL PERIODICAL ARTICLES

(See the note section of this book.)

Author's Note

I want to thank William Forbis for reading the entire manuscript, and Professors Henry Graff and Richard Solberg for scrutinizing various chapter drafts. In my researches I drew upon Humphrey's papers, memoirs (including his own), the recollections of his associates, and newspapers and periodicals of the time. Of Humphrey's associates, some 160 granted interviews; many sent letters and documents. William Connell and Arthur Naftalin generously made available 55 transcripts of interviews conducted for Connell's film biography of Humphrey. I was also able to consult oral history transcripts at various libraries, several of them with Humphrey himself, as well as others already deposited with the Humphrey Papers. Dr. Edgar Berman not only lent his medical files on Humphrey but also made available transcripts of the invaluable day-by-day diary Humphrey instructed him to keep through the 1968 presidential campaign.

I am indebted to the Humphrey Family Advisory Committee for granting permission to research in the voluminous Humphrey Papers at the Minnesota Historical Society in St. Paul. I am grateful to Russell Fridley, director of the MHS, to Dallas Lindgren, presiding archivist, and to Ruth Bauer, Steven Nielsen, Ruby Shields and Katherine Johnson of the MHS Research Center for unfailing help. I wish also to thank Benedict Zobrist and Dennis Pilger of the Truman Library; Harry Middleton, David Humphrey and Nancy Smith of the Johnson Library; William Johnson of the Kennedy Library; Frances Seeben of the Roosevelt Library; and Ed Schamel and Fynnette Eaton of the National Archives. I want to acknowledge the ancestor-hunting prowess of Gary Boyd Roberts of Boston, who established for me that Humphrey of Dakota descended from earliest Puritan forebears and was related to John Adams and a half dozen other presidents.

Index